Cornerstones for Chapter 9

Cornerstones for Chapter 10

Cornerstones for Chapter 11

Cornerstones for Chapter 12

Cornerstones for Chapter 13

Cornerstones for Chapter 14

Cornerstones **Videos**

Each "Cornerstone" in the book is accompanied by a short video clip that students may view online or download onto portable video players. The clips provide clear, step-by-step examples that are consistently presented for today's visual learners. They walk students through each step of every "Cornerstone."

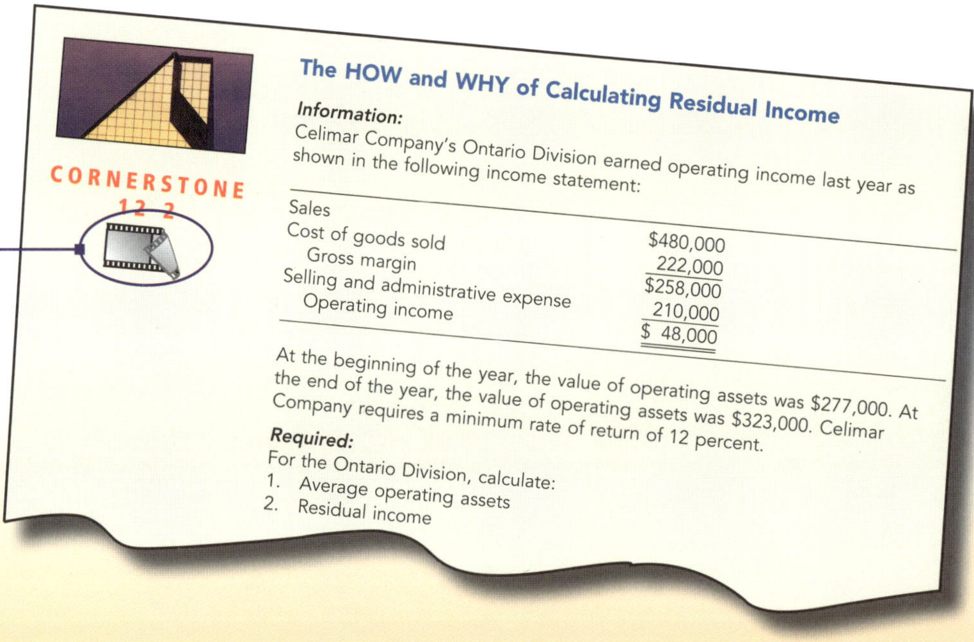

The HOW and WHY of Calculating Residual Income

Information:

Celimar Company's Ontario Division earned operating income last year as shown in the following income statement:

Sales	$480,000
Cost of goods sold	222,000
Gross margin	$258,000
Selling and administrative expense	210,000
Operating income	$ 48,000

At the beginning of the year, the value of operating assets was $277,000. At the end of the year, the value of operating assets was $323,000. Celimar Company requires a minimum rate of return of 12 percent.

Required:

For the Ontario Division, calculate:

1. Average operating assets
2. Residual income

80% of students surveyed wanted access to video presentations to help explain the concepts.

70% of instructors who reviewed these videos indicated they would recommend or require students to use them.

The Cornerstones and the related exercises are effective. They help to guide the student's learning.

—Darlene Lowe, Grant MacEwan University

"The Cornerstones are very clear and well-identified. They bring out the key concepts and principles of each chapter. The Cornerstone examples would remind students about the core principles and techniques required."

—Audra Ong, University of Windsor

"The Cornerstones seem to be very comprehensive. I think students will use them as a quick reference and as a good study tool for exam preparation."

—Robert Biscontri, University of Manitoba

To View these Videos, Visit the *Cornerstones* Website:

www.mowen1ce.nelson.com

FIRST CANADIAN EDITION

CORNERSTONES *of* Managerial Accounting

FIRST CANADIAN EDITION

CORNERSTONES *of* Managerial Accounting

Maryanne M. Mowen
Oklahoma State University

Don R. Hansen
Oklahoma State University

Dan L. Heitger
Miami University

George A. Gekas
Ryerson University

David J. McConomy
Queen's University

NELSON EDUCATION

NELSON EDUCATION

Cornerstones of Managerial Accounting, First Canadian Edition
by Maryanne M. Mowen, Don R. Hansen, Dan L. Heitger, George A. Gekas, and David J. McConomy

Vice President, Editorial Director:
Evelyn Veitch

Vice President, Editorial:
Anne Williams

Senior Acquisitions Editor:
Amie Plourde

Executive Marketing Manager:
David Ward

Technical Reviewer:
Ross Meacher

Developmental Editor:
Jennifer O'Reilly

Photo Researcher/Permissons Coordinator:
Daniela Glass

Senior Content Production Manager:
Imoinda Romain

Production Service:
Cenveo Publisher Services

Copy Editor:
Matthew Kudelka

Proofreader:
Ganesh Ramalingam

Indexer:
Michael Ferreira

Production Coordinator:
Ferial Suleman

Design Director:
Ken Phipps

Managing Designer:
Franca Amore

Cover Concept:
Jennifer Leung

Cover Design:
Johanna Liburd

Cover Image:
Mike Grandmaison/
All Canada Photos

Compositor:
Cenveo Publisher Services

Printer:
RR Donnelley

Printed and bound in the United States of America
2 3 4 14 13 12 11

For more information contact Nelson Education Ltd., 1120 Birchmount Road, Toronto, Ontario, M1K 5G4. Or you can visit our Internet site at http://www.nelson.com

Library and Archives Canada Cataloguing in Publication

Cornerstones of managerial accounting / Maryanne M. Mowen . . . [et al.]. — 1st Canadian ed.

Includes index.
ISBN 978-0-17-650361-1

1. Managerial accounting—Textbooks. I. Mowen, Maryanne M.

HF5657.4.C66 2011 658.15'11 C2011-902178-1

ISBN-13: 978-0-17-650361-1
ISBN-10: 0-17-650361-7

"This book is dedicated to our students—past, present, and future—
who are at the heart of our passion for teaching."

Maryanne Mowen, Don Hansen, and Dan Heitger

"To my past, present, and future students. Also, to my sons Andrew and Michael,
the special people in my life who keep me going and make everything possible."

George Gekas

"This book is dedicated to my wife, Candace, without whose support
and encouragement I would never have succeeded."

David McConomy

Brief Contents

Contents

PREFACE

Managerial accounting builds on financial accounting concepts, so this text is designed to follow a financial accounting course. As opposed to financial accounting, whose objective is the construction and reporting of financial statements, managerial accounting challenges students to interrelate and interconnect managerial accounting topics whose ultimate purpose is better decision making. One of our goals is to better present the linkages among certain managerial accounting concepts that form the body of managerial accounting knowledge.

Beginning in 2006, South-Western began researching how accounting students read and use their textbooks. Hundreds of students from a variety of institutions were surveyed to better understand how they study and prepare for accounting class. Students were asked:

How do you read introductory accounting textbooks?
What do you consider most important in introductory accounting textbooks?

Based on these survey responses, several conclusions were reached:

- The primary driver of success in accounting is homework.
- Students believe a textbook helps them succeed, but they are using books differently than the previous generation.
- Students use books as a source of examples and descriptions to help them complete homework. They may skim the text before or after class, but very few read the text from beginning to end.

As a result of this research, the *Cornerstones* approach was created to provide students with greater efficiency and more relevance, promising better results. Cornerstones provides students with the confidence to be more independent, allowing instructors more time to teach additional concepts.

Cornerstones of Managerial Accounting, First Canadian Edition, introduces students to key managerial accounting concepts and principles ("Cornerstones"). The unique framework uses Cornerstones boxes in each chapter to demonstrate fundamental calculations. There is a Cornerstone for every major calculation in the book. Cornerstone examples are clear, consistently formatted, and step-by-step to help students understand key concepts and complete homework. Each Cornerstone has four parts: Information, Required, Solution, and Why.

The ***Information*** portion of each Cornerstone provides the necessary data to arrive at a solution.

The ***Required*** section provides students with each step that must be completed.

The ***Solution*** shows the calculations for each of the required steps in the problem. Students can use these solutions as a model to help them complete similar problems in the homework.

The ***Why*** section of each Cornerstone encourages students to think about the business decisions surrounding each technique.

The HOW and WHY of Preparing a Production Budget

CORNERSTONE 9-2

Information:
Budgeted units to be sold for each quarter: 1,000, 1,200, 1,500, and 2,000. Assume that company policy requires 20 percent of the next quarter's sales in ending inventory and that beginning inventory of t-shirts for the first quarter of the year was 180. Assume also that sales for the first quarter of 2011 are estimated at 1,000 units.

Required:
1. Calculate the desired ending inventory in units for each quarter of the year. What is the ending inventory in units for the year?
2. Prepare a production budget for each quarter and for the year.

Solution:
1. Ending inventory, quarter 1 = 0.20 × 1,200 units = 240
   Ending inventory, quarter 2 = 0.20 × 1,500 units = 300
   Ending inventory, quarter 3 = 0.20 × 2,000 units = 400
   Ending inventory, quarter 4 = 0.20 × 1,000 units = 200
   Ending inventory for the year = Ending inventory for quarter 4 = 200 units

2.

Moose Patties Inc.
Production Budget
For the Year Ended December 31, 2010

	Quarter				
	1	2	3	4	Year
Sales in units	1,000	1,200	1,500	2,000	5,700
Desired ending inventory*	240	300	400	200	200
Total needs	1,240	1,500	1,900	2,200	5,900
Less: Beginning inventory**	(180)	(240)	(300)	(400)	(180)
Units to be produced	1,060	1,260	1,600	1,800	5,720

*Ending inventory for quarter each is calculated in part 1.
**Recall that the beginning inventory for one quarter is equal to the ending inventory of the preceding quarter.

WHY:
Because the production budget allows us to translate the requirements of the sales budget into the actual units that need to be produced to meet the needs of the company's operations, including inventory levels as set by corporate policy.

As they work through the calculations, students are encouraged to think about the pros and cons of each method.

End-of-chapter Cornerstone Exercises are linked to one or more specific *Cornerstones* features, providing a valuable reference as students complete homework on their own.

Cornerstone Exercise 9-22 PREPARING A PRODUCTION BUDGET

OBJECTIVE 2
CORNERSTONE 9-2

Sherwood Inc. makes pet crates. In the first four months of the coming year, Sherwood expects the following unit sales:

January	30,000
February	29,000
March	31,000
April	34,000

Sherwood's policy is to have 15 percent of next month's sales in ending inventory. On January 1, it is expected that there will be 4,200 crates on hand.

Required:

Prepare a production budget for the first quarter of the year. Show the number of crates that should be produced each month as well as for the quarter in total.

The in-chapter Cornerstones boxes and the exercises are closely linked, fostering independent learning.

Each Cornerstone in the book is accompanied by a short video podcast that students may view online or download to a portable video player. The podcasts provide clear, step-by-step examples designed for today's visual learners. They walk students through each step of each Cornerstone.

To view these videos, visit the *Cornerstones of Managerial Accounting* website at: http://www.mowen1ce.nelson.com.

"I like the direct ability to transfer and hence reproduce the successful mastery of a concept ... [which] reinforces the material. It is simple, straightforward, and identifiable to and by the student. It would work well in a distance course too."

—Elliott Currie, University of Guelph

Managers of all organizations, whether in manufacturing, wholesale, service, e-commerce, not-for-profit, or government, must make decisions in an increasingly complex and changing environment. Now more than ever, managers must have a firm grasp of managerial accounting concepts to understand how their decisions affect costs, profits, and entire business operations. We believe this text provides a solid learning platform on which students can build their business decisions.

Features of the First Canadian Edition

- The First Canadian Edition has been divided into four parts: Planning, Costing, Control, and Short- and Long-Term Decision Making. Each part opens with a section detailing the interrelationship between the chapters within the part.
- Integrative Exercises are comprehensive exercises that bring together concepts from multiple chapters to offer an additional challenge to students and more variety when assigning homework. They occur after Chapters 4, 10, and 14.
- Each Cornerstone box includes a Why section that provides a clear context for applying key equations.
- Every chapter has one or two CMA Exam Questions (provided by CMA Canada) as part of the end-of-chapter exercises.
- Each chapter opens with an up-to-date, real-life vignette that looks at how businesses apply managerial accounting concepts every day. Each vignette is accompanied by an online video.
- Where appropriate, selected *Cornerstones* podcasts have been revised to reflect Canadian accounting practices.
- To foster in-class discussion, the answers to the Q&A boxes have been moved off the page into a separate section at the back of the book.

INSTRUCTOR'S RESOURCES

NETA **The Nelson Education Teaching Advantage (NETA)** program is designed to deliver research-based resources that promote student engagement and higher-order thinking so as to enable the success of Canadian students and educators.

Testing Advantage Resources Nelson Education Ltd. understands that the highest quality multiple-choice Test Bank provides the means to measure ***higher-level thinking*** skills as well as recall. In response to instructor concerns, and recognizing the importance of multiple-choice testing in today's classroom, we have created the assessment component of the Nelson Education Teaching Advantage (NETA) program to ensure the value of our Test Banks.

The assessment component of our NETA program was created in partnership with David DiBattista, a 3M National Teaching Fellow, professor of psychology at Brock University, and researcher in the area of multiple-choice testing. All Test Bank authors have received training by Professor DiBattista in constructing effective multiple-choice questions and creating questions that assess higher-level thinking. Professor DiBattista has also reviewed selected chapters of the *Cornerstones of Managerial Accounting* Test Bank to ensure that these best practices have been followed.

All NETA Test Banks are accompanied by David DiBattista's guide for instructors, *Multiple Choice Tests: Getting Beyond Remembering*. This guide has been designed to help you use Nelson Test Banks to achieve the desired outcomes in your course. Select the "NETA Assessment" button on the Instructor's Resource CD for a digital copy of this valuable resource, as well as the *Cornerstones of Managerial Accounting* Test Bank and computerized Test Bank (see "Instructor's Resource CD" below for more information).

neta
engagement | assessment | success
NELSON EDUCATION TEACHING ADVANTAGE

Instructor's Resource CD Key instructor ancillaries are provided on the Instructor's Resource CD (ISBN 0-17-661688-8), offering instructors the ultimate tool for customizing lectures and presentations. The IRCD includes the following:

- *Instructor's Manual.* The Instructor's Manual for *Cornerstones of Managerial Accounting* includes suggested in-class assignments, discussion questions, lesson plans, a video integration guide, and more.
- *NETA Test Bank and ExamView® Computerized Test Bank.* Test Bank files are provided in rich text format for easy editing and printing with all common word-processing formats. All Test Bank questions are also provided in the ExamView® computerized version. This easy-to-use software is compatible with Microsoft Windows and Mac. Create tests by selecting questions from the question bank, modifying these questions as desired, and adding new questions you write yourself. You can administer quizzes online and export tests to WebCT, Blackboard, and other formats. A copy of *Multiple Choice Tests: Getting Beyond Remembering* accompanies the testing materials for *Cornerstones of Managerial Accounting*. The Test Bank for the First Canadian Edition was prepared by Linda Lindsay of the University of Lethbridge.
- *Microsoft® PowerPoint®.* Key concepts from *Cornerstones of Managerial Accounting* are presented in PowerPoint format, with generous use of figures, photographs, and short tables from the text. The PowerPoint slides for the First Canadian Edition were prepared by Howard Leaman of the University of Guelph—Humber.
- *Solutions Manual.* This manual, prepared by the authors of the text, has been independently checked for accuracy by Ross Meacher, C.A. It contains complete solutions to each question, exercise, problem, and case in the text. Also included are separate files for the *Solution Transparency Masters.*
- *Spreadsheet Solutions.* The complete solutions to the Excel-based Spreadsheet Exercises are provided.

Chapter Video Clips Available on DVD (ISBN 0-17-662882-7) and online at http://www.mowen1ce.nelson.com, these videos are designed to enrich and support chapter concepts. Each of the 14 video segments presents real business issues faced by a variety of service and manufacturing organizations. The video cases have been chosen to accompany the chapter openers in the textbook, and challenge your students to study business issues and develop solutions to business problems.

STUDENT RESOURCES

Companion Website Visit **http://www.mowen1ce.nelson.com** for additional resources, including spreadsheet templates, self-testing review quizzes, glossary terms, and the *Cornerstones* video podcasts. The website resources were adapted by Thomas Manning of the University of Guelph.

Aplia Founded in 2000 by economist and Stanford professor Paul Romer, Aplia is an educational technology company dedicated to improving learning by increasing student effort and engagement. Currently, Aplia products have been used by more than 650,000 students at over 750 institutions.

aplia™ Engage. Prepare. Educate.

For students, Aplia offers a way to stay on top of coursework with regularly scheduled homework assignments. Interactive tools and additional content are provided to further increase engagement and understanding.

For professors, Aplia offers high-quality, auto-graded assignments, which ensure that students put forth effort on a regular basis throughout the term. These assignments have been developed for a range of textbooks and are easily customized for individual teaching schedules. The Aplia course for the First Canadian Edition was prepared by Anthony Chan of Ryerson University.

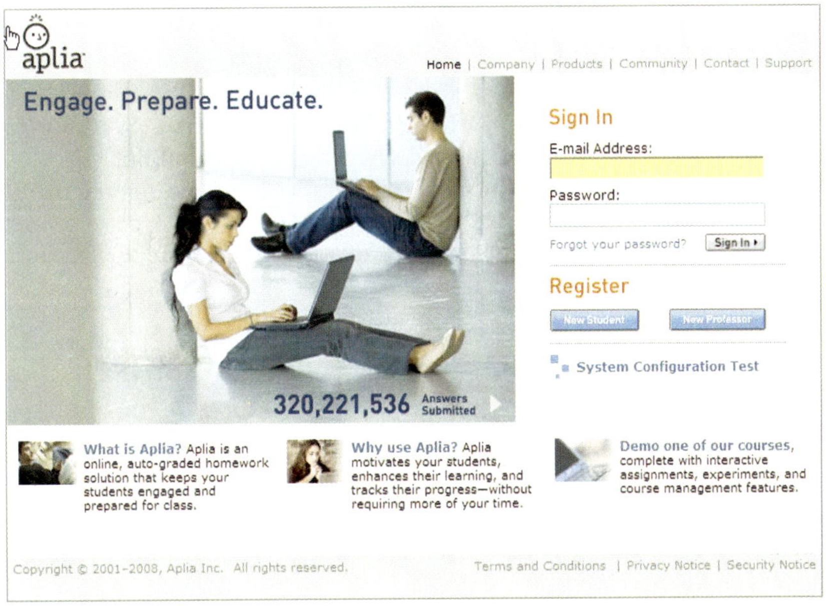

ACKNOWLEDGMENTS

We have received assistance from many people who have contributed to this book.

We are grateful for the assistance and support provided by Ryerson University and the Queen's University School of Business.

Our appreciation is also extended to the Canadian Institute of Chartered Accountants (CICA), the Institute of Chartered Accountants of Ontario (ICAO), the Society of Management Accountants of Canada (SMAC), and the Certified General Accountants' Association of Canada (CGAC), and to the other sources as indicated for their generous permission to use or adapt problems from their publications.

We would like to thank the reviewers of this text for their insights and suggestions. The following people helped shape the First Canadian Edition:

Ibrahim Aly, Concordia University
Robert Biscontri, University of Manitoba
Shannon Butler, University of Western Ontario
Elliott Currie, University of Guelph
Ian Feltmate, Acadia University
Mark Gandey, Bishop's University
Wallace Lockhart, University of Regina
Darlene Lowe, Grant MacEwan University
Audra Ong, University of Windsor
Andrews Oppong, Dalhousie University
Pattie Proulx, Carleton University
John Siambolopoulos, University of Western Ontario (King's College)
Lawrence Tenenbaum, McGill University

This book was adapted from the U.S. 3rd edition by Mowen, Hansen, and Heitger. We appreciate the U.S. authors' willingness to share their work with us. This book has certainly benefited from their experience and contribution.

Many people at Nelson Education also earn our deepest thanks for their thoughtful contributions. Special thanks go to Jenny O'Reilly, our developmental editor.

Finally, special recognition is due to our families for understanding the demands of our work and supporting our efforts.

George Gekas
David J. McConomy
July 2011

About the **Authors**

George Gekas is an Associate Professor of Management Accounting at the Ted Rogers School of Business Management at Ryerson University in Toronto. Prior to his appointment to Ryerson, he taught for more than 25 years at several universities in Canada, the United States, and Europe. His academic career includes appointments with the University College of Cape Breton, Algoma University College, Ryerson University, the University of Maryland, the American College of Greece (Deree), and the University of Western Ontario.

Dr. Gekas received his first honours B.A. degree from the Athens University of Economics in Greece. He then earned a Master of Economics from Lakehead University, honours Bachelor of Commerce and MBA degrees from the University of Windsor, and a Ph.D. from Hull University in England. In addition, he is a Certified Management Accountant (CMA), awarded the prestigious FCMA designation, and is actively involved in the Society of Management Accountants of Ontario, for which he has held a number of positions. Currently he is Chair of its Complaints Committee. Recently, he was appointed CMA in residence at the Ted Rogers School of Business Management, the first such appointment in Canada.

Dr. Gekas has published a number of articles on a wide variety of business topics, as well as teaching aids and manuals. His expertise covers the financial management spectrum, with a focus on strategic management, operational efficiency, accountability, and corporate performance.

As a university educator and educational administrator, Dr. Gekas has been involved in a variety of capacities in a number of post-secondary educational projects and is fully immersed in the issues facing Canadian post-secondary institutions and universities. He also has a strong interest in community and social development.

David J. McConomy is an Assistant Professor at the Queen's University School of Business. He graduated with an MBA from Queen's University with a major in Finance and Accounting in 1969 after receiving a BA (Econ) from Loyola College (now part of Concordia University) in Montreal. Since qualifying as a chartered accountant with Arthur Andersen & Co. in Toronto, his 30-year career in business has focused on the finance and accounting requirements of small to medium-sized companies.

He has gained considerable experience assisting young companies, mainly in the technology field, in strategic planning and corporate finance. As Chief Financial Officer of Systemhouse Ltd. (which was later sold to MCI and subsequently to EDS), he was instrumental in taking that company public. During his tenure with Systemhouse, revenues rose from $16.5 million to in excess of $100 million.

With Antares Electronics Inc., he raised $20 million (through venture capital investments, sale-and-leaseback transactions, and the restructuring of bank lines of credit) to enable the company to become one of *Profit* magazine's fastest growing companies, as revenues increased over a three-year period from $36 million to

$100 million. Later, he helped CommetiX Computer Systems Inc. to become a public company and to raise funds from a variety of sources to fund its growth.

Since joining the faculty of the Queen's School of Business in 2001, he has won numerous Faculty Teaching Awards. He prides himself in engaging with students both within the classroom and outside of it.

Mr. McConomy has taught accounting, financial management, and business strategy (at the undergraduate and MBA levels) on both a full-time and part-time basis at Queen's University, the University of Ottawa, and internationally with the Academy of Economic Studies in Bucharest, Romania, and in Beijing, China.

Maryanne M. Mowen is Associate Professor of Accounting at Oklahoma State University. She received her Ph.D. from Arizona State University. She brings an interdisciplinary perspective to teaching and writing in cost and management accounting, with degrees in history and economics. She also teaches classes in ethics and the impact of the Sarbanes-Oxley Act on accountants. Her scholarly research is in the areas of management accounting, behavioural decision theory, and compliance with the Sarbanes-Oxley Act. She has published articles in journals such as *Decision Science, Journal of Economics and Psychology*, and *Journal of Management Accounting Research.* Dr. Mowen has served as a consultant to mid-sized and Fortune 100 companies, and works with corporate controllers on management accounting issues. Outside the classroom, she enjoys hiking, traveling, reading mysteries, and working crossword puzzles.

Don R. Hansen is the Head of the School of Accounting and Kerr McGee Chair at Oklahoma State University. He received his Ph.D. from the University of Arizona in 1977. He has an undergraduate degree in mathematics from Brigham Young University. His research interests include activity-based costing and mathematical modelling. He has published articles in both accounting and engineering journals, including *Accounting Review, Journal of Management Accounting Research, Accounting Horizons*, and *Accounting Organizations and Society.* He has served on the editorial board of *Accounting Review.* His outside interests include family, church activities, reading, movies, watching sports, and studying Spanish.

Dan L. Heitger is Associate Professor of Accounting and Co-Director of the Center for Business Excellence at Miami University. He received his Ph.D. from Michigan State University and his undergraduate degree in accounting from Indiana University. He actively works with executives and students of all levels in developing and teaching courses in managerial and cost accounting, risk management, and business reporting. He co-founded an organization that provides executive education for large international organizations. His interactions with business professionals, through executive education and the Center, allow him to bring a current and real-world perspective to his writing. His published research focuses on managerial accounting and risk management issues and has appeared in *Harvard Business Review, Behavioral Research in Accounting, Issues in Accounting, Journal of Accountancy*, and *Management Accounting Quarterly.* His outside interests include hiking with his family in the National Park system.

PLANNING

Part 1

A company must put a plan in place in order to determine what it expects to accomplish over some future period of time. Planning is the act of determining what the alternatives are and developing a complete understanding of what must be done to take advantage of the alternatives that are available. Planning consists of developing a detailed set of tasks that need to be accomplished if the company is going to succeed. The end result of the planning process is a set of budgets that outline, in detail, what the company expects of each division, department, and employee.

Senior management must have a vision of where they want to take the company, and they must be able to detail this vision in a set of working documents, or budgets, that will outline the exact steps that are necessary and expected of every part of the organization. One can think of a budget as a road map that outlines all of the steps that are required to accomplish the objective. Budgets will be in a significant amount of detail in order to convey to every part of the business what is expected of the individuals involved and how each division, department, and employee will interact with other parts of the business if it is to succeed.

Without a plan, a company will have no means of determining whether it is progressing toward its ultimate objectives. In many instances, the simple act of planning will enable a company to evaluate its strengths and weaknesses so that it will be able to tailor the plan to the capabilities available to it. A good planning process will consist of asking the "tough questions" about the possibilities that can be accomplished and challenging each person within the organization to perform at the very highest level.

In many companies, the planning process enables senior management to communicate their wishes and desires to every level of the organization. Planning is as important to not-for-profit organizations as it is to profit-making corporations. Every organization has limited resources available to it to accomplish its objectives. Planning enables managers to deploy these limited resources in the most effective manner.

Chapter 1

Introduction to Managerial Accounting

TRACY WHITESIDE/SHUTTERSTOCK

After studying Chapter 1, you should be able to:

1. Explain the meaning of managerial accounting.
2. Explain the differences between managerial accounting and financial accounting.
3. Identify and explain the current focus of managerial accounting.
4. Describe the role of managerial accountants in an organization.
5. Explain the importance of ethical behaviour for managers and managerial accountants.
6. Identify three accounting designations available in Canada.

Experience Managerial Decisions

with BuyCostumes.com

The greatest benefit of managerial accounting is also its biggest challenge—to provide managers with information that improves decisions and creates organizational value. This information helps inform managers about the impact of various strategic and operational decisions on key nonfinancial performance measures and their eventual impact on the organization's financial performance. The information is challenging to prepare and analyze because it requires an understanding of all value chain components that affect the organization, including research and development, production, marketing, distribution, and customer service.

Since its inception in 1999, **BuyCostumes.com** has blended the right managerial accounting information and an innovative business model to provide costumes to customers in over 50 countries. Using the Internet and marketing creativity, BuyCostumes.com serves a market of 150 million U.S. consumers that spend $3.6 million on costumes each year! According to CEO Jalem Getz, BuyCostumes.com measures key performance indicators to guide its decision making. For example, managerial accountants analyze measures of customer satisfaction, average time between order placement and costume arrival for each shipping method, and the profitability of individual customer types. As customer trends change, competitors emerge, and technological advances occur, BuyCostumes.com's managerial accounting information adapts to provide crucial insight into the company's performance and how its strategy should evolve to remain the world's largest Internet costume retailer.

In writing this textbook, we wanted to show our readers the importance and relevance of managerial accounting to decision making. Therefore, each chapter begins with a quick look (e.g., Experience Managerial Decisions with BuyCostumes.com) at how different companies—ones that you likely recognize—use the managerial accounting topics studied in that particular chapter. Also, we teamed up with Kicker, a real company, and interviewed its top management extensively for stories about their firm and its use of accounting information. You will see boxes in each chapter called "Here's The Real Kicker," detailing how the company has used managerial accounting information in its operations. In addition, each chapter includes an exercise or problem based on actual Kicker experience. Without further ado, let's get better acquainted with Kicker.

buycostumes.com©
the web's most popular costume store!

Here's The Real Kicker

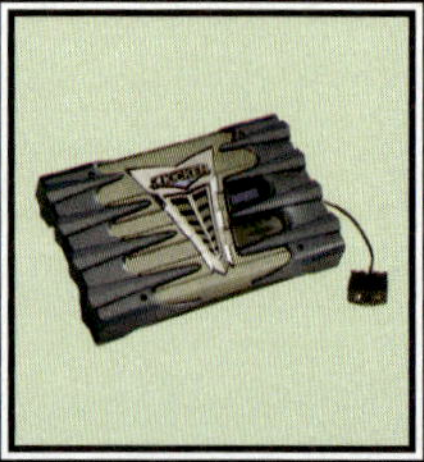

GEM-SEN AND LIVIN' LOUD KICKER

Gem-Sen's roots are in the world of consumer electronics. It started back in 1884 and today is considered a pioneer in distributing and marketing high-end automotive sound systems, with offices in Toronto, Ontario, and Coral Springs, Florida.

Gem-Sen is well known not only for its distribution of some of the finest brands in specialty electronics, but also as a dynamic marketing force. Gem-Sen prides itself in complementing these great brands with a distribution program that includes product training and street-level marketing.

Over the past decade, Gem-Sen has successfully penetrated the licensed merchandise product arena with some of the world's top brands. It has also entered the exciting world of home entertainment by distributing respected lines such as JL Audio, Lovan Furniture, Kicker Headphones, and Pure Acoustics. Gem-Sen is also a stocking distributor for Sony, Maxell, Caselogic, TDK, Energizer Batteries, and Livin' Loud Kicker.

Twenty-five years ago, car stereos were tinny, underpowered affairs. They could power a radio or an 8-track tape deck. But the in-home listening experience coveted by audio buffs eluded the automobile market. In 1980, Stillwater Designs virtually invented the high-performance car audio enclosure market when company founder and president Steve Irby developed the Original Kicker®. It was the first full-range speaker enclosure designed specifically for automotive use.

Kicker, a subdivision of Stillwater Designs, began in 1973 as a two-person operation, custom designing and building professional sound and musical instrument speaker systems for churches, auditoriums, and entertainers. Building upon the success of the Original Kicker, the company concentrated on the car audio market, applying the same research and design skills that made its first product so successful to the development of a complete line of high-performance components for car audio. What was once a company with two employees in a single-car garage is now a corporation with more than 200 employees.

The Kicker brand includes many high-performance car stereo products, including subwoofers, midrange and midbass drivers, tweeters, crossovers, matched component systems, speakers, and power amplifiers. Kicker is proud to have won the prestigious AudioVideo International Auto Sound Grand Prix Award, sponsored annually by *AudioVideo International* magazine. Winners are selected by retailers based on fidelity of sound reproduction, design engineering, reliability, craftsmanship, product integrity, and cost/performance ratio. In 2003, seven Kicker products earned Grand Prix awards.

While Stillwater Designs originally handled research and design (R&D), manufacturing, and sales, it now concentrates primarily on R&D and sales. The bulk of manufacturing has been outsourced (performed by outside firms on a contract basis), though the company still builds some product and plans to build even more as it moves into its new facility for factory-installed audio systems. Engineering and audio research is Kicker president and chief executive officer Steve Irby's first love, and he still heads its design team. The day-to-day involvement of top management, coupled with an energetic workforce of talented individuals in all areas of the company's operations and an innate ability to create truly musical components, has been the reason for the company's remarkable success.

KICKER®

OBJECTIVE 1
Explain the meaning of managerial accounting.

What Is Managerial Accounting?

What do we mean by managerial accounting? Quite simply, **managerial accounting** is the provision of accounting information for a company's internal users. It is the firm's internal accounting system and is designed to support the information needs of managers. Unlike financial accounting, managerial accounting is not bound by any formal criteria such as generally accepted accounting principles (GAAP) or International Financial Reporting Standards (IFRS). Managerial accounting has three broad objectives:

1. To provide information for planning the organization's actions.
2. To provide information for controlling the organization's actions.
3. To provide information for making effective decisions.

Using recent examples from many companies in both the for-profit and not-for-profit sectors, this textbook explains how all manufacturing (e.g., aircraft producer—**Boeing Corporation**), merchandising (e.g., clothing retailer—**The Bay**), and service (e.g., public accounting firm—**KPMG**) organizations use managerial accounting information and concepts. For instance, hospital administrators, presidents of corporations, dentists, educational administrators, and city managers all can improve their managerial skills by being well grounded in the basic concepts and use of managerial accounting information for planning, controlling, and decision making. It should be noted that many companies (over 2,500 large multinationals in total) increasingly are deciding to publicly release large quantities of managerial accounting information, typically given only to internal users, through optional reports known as corporate sustainability reports (e.g., **Tim Hortons**, **McDonald's**), social responsibility reports (e.g., **IBM**, **Canada Post**), or citizenship reports (e.g., **General Electric**). The release of these reports—typically referred to as CSR reports—often occurs because firms want to manage their reputation by preparing and releasing such information themselves, rather than having Internet bloggers, newspapers, and 24-hour cable news networks publish their own estimates of such information. Some leading companies (e.g., **PepsiCo**) have even moved so far as to combine their CSR report with their annual report, the result being a single, integrated report containing both traditional financial accounting information and managerial accounting information. Clearly the demand for managerial accounting information continues to grow.

Information Needs for Planning, Control, and Decision Making

Managerial accounting information is needed by a number of individuals. In particular, managers and empowered workers need comprehensive, up-to-date information for the following activities: (1) planning, (2) controlling, and (3) decision making. Exhibit 1-1 shows how these activities relate to one another.

The detailed formulation of action to achieve a particular end is the management activity called **planning**. Planning requires setting objectives and identifying methods to achieve those objectives. For example, a firm may set the objective of increasing its short-term and long-term profitability by improving the overall quality of its products. **DaimlerChrysler** drastically improved the quality and profitability of its **Chrysler** automobile division during the beginning of the 21st century to the point where its quality surpassed that of **Mercedes-Benz** (also owned by DaimlerChrysler).[1] By improving product quality, firms like DaimlerChrysler should be able to reduce scrap and rework, decrease the number of customer complaints and warranty work, reduce the resources currently assigned to inspection, and so on, thus increasing profitability. To realize these benefits, management must develop some specific methods that, when implemented, will lead to the achievement of the desired objective. A plant manager, for example, may start a supplier evaluation program to identify and select suppliers that are willing and able to supply defect-free parts. Empowered workers may be able to identify production causes of defects and to develop new methods for producing products that will reduce scrap and rework and the need for inspection. The new methods should be clearly specified and detailed.

Planning is only half the battle. Once a plan is created, it must be implemented and its implementation monitored by managers and workers to ensure that it is being carried out as intended. The managerial activity of monitoring a plan's implementation

Exhibit 1-1

Uses of Managerial Accounting Information

[1] Sarah A. Webster and Joe Guy Collier, "Fixing a Car Company: Zetsche on Mercedes: 'A Lot of Work Is Ahead,'" *Detroit Free Press.* Taken from http://forums.mbworld.org/forums/showthread.php?t=121650 on April 8, 2008.

and taking corrective action as needed is referred to as **controlling**. Control is usually achieved by comparing actual performance with expected performance. This information can be used to evaluate or to correct the steps being taken to implement a plan. Based on the feedback, a manager (or worker) may decide to let the plan continue as is, take corrective action of some type to put the actions back in harmony with the original plan, or do some midstream replanning.

The managerial accounting information used for planning and control purposes can be either financial or nonfinancial in nature. For example, by redesigning operations, a firm can reduce production time, the number of hours needed for an assembly, downtime, and energy consumed, while increasing output per hour. All of these relate to nonfinancial performance. Yet they have a positive impact on financial metrics.

The process of choosing among competing alternatives is called **decision making**. This managerial function is intertwined with planning and control in that a manager cannot successfully plan or control the organization's actions without making decisions regarding competing alternatives. For instance, **BMW** plans to offer a car that runs on gasoline and hydrogen. Decisions can be improved if information about the alternatives (e.g., pertaining to gasoline vs. hydrogen vs. hybrid combinations of these two automobile fuel options) is gathered and made available to managers. One of the major roles of the managerial accounting information system is to supply information that facilitates decision making. For example, Kicker's vice president of sales and marketing wondered whether or not to hold tent sales in certain cities. He had information on sales and the related expenses of holding each tent sale. This information, along with his knowledge of competitive conditions and customers' needs, will improve his ability to select appropriate cities for the tent sales.

OBJECTIVE 2

Explain the differences between managerial accounting and financial accounting.

Accounting Info Systems
Financial Accounting ← → Managerial Accounting

Comparison of Managerial and Financial Accounting

There are two basic kinds of accounting information systems: managerial accounting and financial accounting. **Financial accounting** is primarily concerned with producing information (financial statements) for *external* users, including investors, creditors, customers, suppliers, government agencies (Canadian Food Inspection Agency, etc.), and labour unions. This information has historical orientation and is used for such things as investment decisions, stewardship evaluation, monitoring activity, and regulatory measures. Financial statements must conform to certain rules and conventions that are defined by various agencies, such as the Ontario Securities Commission (OSC), and the IFRS. These rules pertain to issues such as the recognition of revenues; timing of expenses; and recording of assets, liabilities, and shareholders' equity.

The managerial accounting system produces information for *internal* users, such as managers, executives, and workers. Thus, managerial accounting could be properly called *internal accounting*, and financial accounting could be called *external accounting*. Specifically, managerial accounting identifies, collects, measures, classifies, and reports financial and nonfinancial information that is useful to internal users in planning, controlling, and decision making.

When comparing managerial accounting to financial accounting, several differences can be identified. Some of the more important differences follow and are summarized in Exhibit 1-2.

- *Targeted users.* As mentioned, managerial accounting focuses on providing information for internal users, while financial accounting focuses on providing information for external users.
- *Restrictions on inputs and processes.* Managerial accounting is not subject to the requirements of generally accepted accounting principles. The inputs and processes of financial accounting are well defined and, in fact, restricted. Only certain kinds of economic events qualify as inputs, and processes must follow generally accepted methods. Unlike financial accounting, managerial accounting has no official body that prescribes the format, content, and rules for selecting inputs and processes and

Exhibit 1-2

Comparison of Managerial and Financial Accounting

Managerial Accounting	Financial Accounting
1. Internally focused.	1. Externally focused.
2. No mandatory rules.	2. Must follow externally imposed rules.
3. Financial and nonfinancial information; subjective information possible.	3. Objective financial information.
4. Emphasis on the future.	4. Historical orientation.
5. Internal information and decision making based on decisions, departments, products, and jobs.	5. Information about the firm as a whole.
6. Broad, multidisciplinary.	6. More self-contained.

preparing financial reports. Also, whereas financial accounting information is historical (i.e., looking through the rearview mirror), managerial accounting information is forward-looking (i.e., looking through the front windshield). Managers are free to choose whatever information they want—provided it can be justified on a cost–benefit basis.

- *Type of information.* The restrictions imposed by financial accounting tend to produce objective and verifiable financial information. For managerial accounting, information may be financial or nonfinancial and may be much more subjective in nature.
- *Time orientation.* Financial accounting has a historical orientation. It records and reports events that have already happened. Although managerial accounting also records and reports events that have already occurred, it strongly emphasizes providing information about future events. Management, for example, may want to know what it will cost to produce a product next year. Knowing this information helps in planning material purchases and making pricing decisions, among other things. This future orientation is needed to support the managerial functions of planning and decision making.
- *Degree of aggregation.* Managerial accounting provides measures and internal reports used to evaluate the performance of entities, product lines, departments, and managers. Essentially, detailed information is needed and provided. Financial accounting, on the other hand, focuses on overall firm performance, providing a more aggregated viewpoint.
- *Breadth.* Managerial accounting is much broader than financial accounting. It includes aspects of managerial economics, industrial engineering, and management science as well as numerous other areas.

aggregation = collected.

Breadth = wide Range.

The accounting system should be designed to provide both financial and managerial accounting information. The key point here is flexibility—the system should be able to supply different information for different purposes.

Current Focus of Managerial Accounting

OBJECTIVE 3
Identify and explain the current focus of managerial accounting.

The business environment in which companies operate has changed dramatically over the past several decades. For instance, advances in technology, the Internet, the opening of markets around the world, increased competitive pressures, and increased complexity of strategy (e.g., alliances between Tim Hortons and **Wendy's**) and operations all have combined to produce a global business environment. Effective managerial accounting systems also have changed in order to provide information that helps improve companies' planning, control, and decision-making activities. Several important uses of managerial accounting resulting from these advances include new methods of estimating product and service cost and profitability, understanding customer orientation, evaluating the business from a cross-functional perspective, and providing information useful in improving total quality.

New Methods of Costing Products and Services

Today's companies need focused, accurate information on the cost of the products and services they produce. Years ago, a company might have produced a few products that were roughly similar to one another. Only the cost of materials and labour might have differed from one product to another. Figuring out the cost of each unit was relatively easy. Now, however, with the increase in technology and automation, it is more difficult to generate the costing information needed by management to make a wide variety of decisions. As Peter Drucker, internationally respected management guru, points out:

> *Traditional cost accounting in manufacturing does not record the cost of nonproducing such as the cost of faulty quality, or of a machine being out of order, or of needed parts not being on hand. Yet these unrecorded and uncontrolled costs in some plants run as high as the costs that traditional accounting does record. By contrast, a new method of cost accounting developed in the last 10 years—called "activity-based" accounting—records all costs. And it relates them, as traditional accounting cannot, to value-added.*[2]

Activity-based costing (ABC) is a more detailed approach to determining the cost of goods and services. ABC improves costing accuracy by emphasizing the cost of the many activities or tasks that must be done to produce a product or offer a service. **United Parcel Service Inc. (UPS)** used ABC to discover and manage the cost of the activities involved with shipping packages by truck, as opposed to by plane, in order to beat **FedEx** at its overnight delivery business in quick mid-distance (up to 500 miles) overnight deliveries.[3] Process-value analysis focuses on the way in which companies create value for customers. The objective is to find ways to perform necessary activities more efficiently and to eliminate those that do not create customer value.

Customer Orientation

Customer value is a key focus because firms can establish a competitive advantage by creating better customer value for the same or lower cost than competitors or creating equivalent value for lower cost than that of competitors. Customer value is the difference between what a customer receives and what the customer gives up when buying a product or service. When we talk about customer value, we consider the complete range of tangible and intangible benefits that a customer receives from a purchased product. Customers receive basic and special product features, service, quality, instructions for use, reputation, brand name, and other important factors. On the other hand, customers give up the cost of purchasing the product, the time and effort spent acquiring and learning to use the product, and the costs of using, maintaining, and disposing of it.

Strategic Positioning Effective cost information can help the company identify strategies that increase customer value and, in so doing, create a sustainable competitive advantage.[4] Generally, firms choose one of two general strategies: (1) cost leadership and (2) superior products through differentiation (highest performance quality, most desired product features, best customer service, etc.). The objective of the cost leadership strategy is to provide the same or better value to customers at a *lower* cost than competitors. A differentiation strategy, on the other hand, strives to increase customer value by providing something to customers not provided by competitors. For example, **Best Buy**'s Geek Squad of computer technicians creates a competitive advantage for Best Buy by providing 24-hour in-home technical assistance for

[2] Peter F. Drucker, "We Need to Measure, Not Count," *The Wall Street Journal* (April 13, 1993): A14.

[3] Charles Haddad and Jack Ewing, "Ground Wars: UPS's Rapid Ascent Leaves FedEx Scrambling," *Business Week* (May 21, 2001): 64–68.

[4] C. Rutledge and R. Williams, "A Seat at the Table," *OutlookJournal* (June 2004). Taken from http://www.accenture.com/xd/xd.asp?it=enweb&xd=ideas%5Coutlook%5C2_2004%5Cm on October 6, 2005.

its customers. Accurate cost information is important to see whether or not the additional service provided by the Geek Squad adds more to revenue than it does to cost.

Product Life Cycles A new product progresses through a series of stages: conception, introduction into the market, growth, maturity, and, finally, decline and eventual withdrawal from the market. This sequence is known as the product life cycle, and it is associated with different marketing strategies and product mixes that require different planning and control decisions.

Product life cycles range from a few months for trendy goods to many years for appliances and automobiles. Similarly, each stage of the product life cycle may be long or short depending on the product. For example, technology-based products usually have a long development stage and a relatively short market life. Other products, such as airplanes, have market lives many times longer than the development stage. To effectively plan and control the production of goods or services, management accountants must consider the product's life cycle. The key element for planning and control purposes is that managers identify and track revenues and costs over the product's entire life cycle.

The Value Chain Successful pursuit of cost leadership and/or differentiation strategies requires an understanding of a firm's value chain. The **value chain** refers to the set of business functions that add value to an organization's products or services. For the company to succeed, all stages of the various functions, such as R&D, product design, production, marketing, distribution, and customer service, need to add value to the final product.

The value chain is a systematic approach to examining the development of a firm's competitive advantage. It was created by M.E. Porter in his book *Competitive Advantage* (1980). When value is built into each stage of a product or service, this increases the total value delivered by the organization.

Clearly, not all functions are equally important to the success of a company. That said, no matter what product or service an organization produces, it must try to create goods and services that are valued by its customers. According to Porter, *value chain primary activities* include the following:

- *Inbound logistics*—raw materials and goods are received from the company's suppliers.
- *Operations*—goods are manufactured or assembled. This includes "individual" operations, such as room service (for a hotel chain).
- *Outbound logistics*—sending finished goods to wholesalers, retailers, or the final consumer.
- *Marketing and sales*—developing a marketing communications and promotions mix to meet the needs of targeted customers.
- *Service*—providing customers with installation, after-sales service, complaint handling, and so on.

Also, the value chain includes a number of *support activities*:

- *Procurement*—securing the lowest prices for inputs of the highest quality, and deciding which components or operations will be provided in-house and which will be outsourced.
- *Technology development*—innovating to reduce costs. This includes sustaining competitive advantage through lean manufacturing, customer relationship management, Internet marketing activities, and so on.
- *Human resources management*—effectively managing recruitment, selection, training, development, and remuneration of employees, who are a vital resource.
- *Developing infrastructure*—which includes strategic planning in terms of structuring the firm's reporting, planning, control, management information systems, and so on.

Management accountants play a key role in delivering all value chain functions. They provide estimated revenue and cost data for each stage of a product's life. This

Exhibit 1-3

The Value Chain

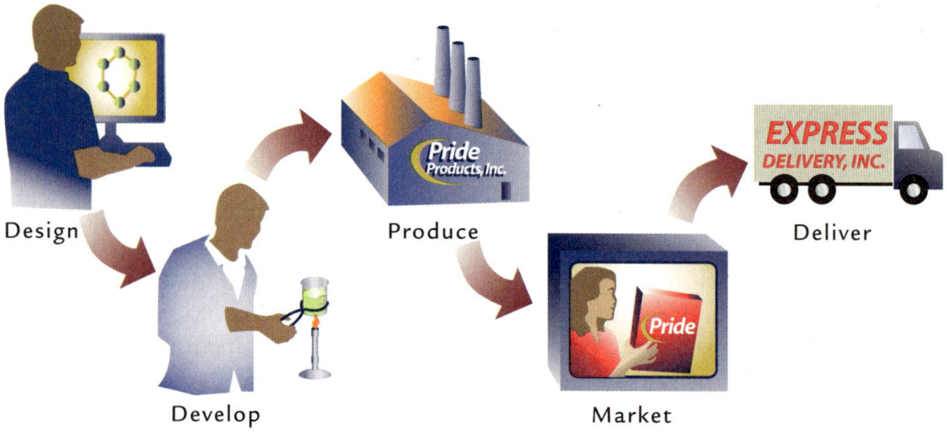

includes devising methods for reducing costs and production time, and making marketing decisions that have a significant impact on sales. Management accountants decide whether a company sells its products directly to a chain of retail stores or indirectly through a wholesaler, and at what price. They also decide which transportation system should be used (e.g., air cargo, trucks, or trains), and which warranty, if any, will be offered on products.

Exhibit 1-3 illustrates the value chain. A managerial accounting system should track information about a wide variety of activities that span the value chain. For example, prior to issuing final approval for its most recent version of the iPhone, **Apple** spent considerable effort researching the cost of developing and manufacturing the iPhone, as well as the amount of money potential customers would be willing to spend to purchase it. Also, customer value can be increased by improving the speed of delivery and response. FedEx exploited this part of the value chain and successfully developed a service that was not being offered by any postal service in the world. Today, many customers believe that delivery delayed is delivery denied, which indicates that a good managerial accounting system ought to develop and measure indicators of customer satisfaction.

Assume a company with two departments: Assembly and Finishing. The value- and non-value-added activities may be classified as shown in Exhibit 1-4.

It is important to note that companies have internal customers as well. For example, the procurement process acquires and delivers parts and materials to producing departments. Providing high-quality parts on a timely basis to managers of producing departments is just as vital for procurement as it is for the company as a whole to provide high-quality goods to external customers. The emphasis on managing the internal value chain and servicing internal customers has revealed the importance of a cross-functional perspective.

Cross-Functional Perspective

In managing the value chain, a managerial accountant must understand and measure many functions of the business. Contemporary approaches to costing may include initial design and engineering costs, as well as manufacturing costs, and the costs of distribution, sales, and service. An individual well-schooled in the various definitions of cost, who understands the shifting definitions of cost from the short-run to the long-run, can be invaluable in determining what information is relevant in decision making. For example, strategic decisions may require a cost definition that assigns the costs of all value chain activities. In a long-run decision environment, in order to perform customer profitability analyses that identify their most, and least, profitable

Exhibit 1-4

Value and Non-Value-Added Activities

Operations	Average time (days)
1. Assembling department	
Receiving	4
Quality control	2
Storage	20–30
Move to production	1
Waiting for use	6
Setup of machinery	1
Assembly Process	**6**
Move to inspection	1
Move to finishing	1
Total time in Assembling:	42–52 days
2. Finishing department	
Receiving	1
Move to production	1
Waiting for use	10–24
Setup of machinery	1
Finishing Process	**4**
Inspection	1
Packaging Process	**1**
Move to dockside	1
Storage	3
Ship to customer	2–8
Total time in Finishing:	25–45 days
Total processing time:	67–97 days
Total non-value-added time:	56–86 days
Assembling value-added time:	**6 days**
Finishing value-added time:	**5 days**
Total value-added time:	**11 days**

customers, an industry may spend many millions of dollars. However, a short-run decision to determine the profitability of a special order (e.g., **Canadian Tire Corporation**'s order for extra tires) may require only the incremental costs of the special order in a single functional area.

Why try to relate managerial accounting to marketing, management, engineering, finance, and other business functions? When a value chain approach is taken and customer value is emphasized, we see that these disciplines are interrelated; a decision affecting one affects the others. For example, salespeople may offer deep discounts at the end of the year to meet their sales targets. Customers, of course, buy more product. The company's factories may have to work double shifts, with a great deal of overtime pay, to meet this sudden increase in demand. A cross-functional perspective allows us to see the big picture—to see that the increased revenue came at the expense of much higher product costs. This broader vision allows managers to increase quality, reduce the time required to service customers (both internal and external), and improve efficiency.

Total Quality Management

Continuous improvement is the continual search for ways to increase the overall efficiency and productivity of activities by reducing waste, increasing quality, and managing costs. Managerial accounting information about the costs of products, customers, processes, and other objects of management interest can be the basis for identifying problems and alternative solutions.

Continuous improvement is fundamental for establishing excellence. Providing products with little waste and ensuring that they perform according to specifications are the twin objectives of world-class firms. A philosophy of **total quality management**, in which manufacturers strive to create an environment that will enable workers to manufacture perfect (zero-defect) products, has replaced the "acceptable quality" attitudes of the past. This emphasis on quality has also created a demand for a managerial accounting system that provides financial and nonfinancial information about quality, including quality cost measurement and reporting for both manufacturing and service industries. For example, in response to increasing customer complaints regarding its laptop computer repair process, **Toshiba** formed an alliance with UPS in which UPS picks up the broken laptop, fixes it, and returns the repaired laptop to the customer. In order for this alliance to work effectively, both Toshiba and UPS require relevant managerial accounting information regarding the cost of existing poor quality and efforts to improve future quality.[5]

Many companies, such as DaimlerChrysler, increasingly are using techniques such as Six Sigma and Design for Six Sigma (DFSS), together with various types of cost information, to achieve improved quality performance. Specifically, Chrysler's goal is "to meet customer requirements and improve vehicle and system reliability while reducing development costs and cultivating innovation."[6] On a related note, many companies attempt to increase organizational value by eliminating wasteful activities that exist throughout the value chain. In eliminating such waste, companies usually find that their accounting must also change. This change in accounting, referred to as **lean accounting**, organizes costs according to the value chain and collects both financial and nonfinancial information. The objective is to provide information to managers that supports their waste reduction efforts and to provide financial statements that better reflect overall performance, using both financial and nonfinancial information.

Finally, one of the more recent tasks of managerial accountants is to help carry out the company's enterprise risk management (ERM) approach. ERM is a formal way for managerial accountants to identify and respond to the most important threats and business opportunities facing the organization. ERM is becoming increasingly important for long-term success. For example, it is well recognized that **Wal-Mart**'s expert crisis management processes and teams repeatedly responded to the aftermath of Hurricane Katrina throughout Louisiana and Mississippi better and faster than did either local or federal government agencies. The results of many public accounting firm surveys highlight the growing importance that organizations place on conducting effective risk management practices.[7]

Time as a Competitive Element

Time is a crucial element in all phases of the value chain. World-class firms reduce time to market by compressing design, implementation, and production cycles. These firms deliver products or services quickly by eliminating non-value-added time, which is time of no value to the customer (e.g., the time a product spends on the loading dock). Interestingly, decreasing non-value-added time appears to go hand in hand with increasing quality.[8]

What about the relationship between time and product life cycles? The rate of technological innovation has increased for many industries, and the life of a particular product can be quite short. Managers must be able to respond quickly and decisively to changing market conditions. Information to allow them to accomplish this must be available. For example, **Hewlett-Packard** has found that it is better to be 50 percent over budget in new product development than to be six months late. This

[5] T. Friedman, "*The World Is Flat: A Brief History of the Twenty-First Century*," Farrar, Straus and Giroux: New York, New York, 2005.

[6] Kevin Kelly, "Chrysler Continues Quality Push," WardsAuto.Com. Taken from http://wardsauto.com/microsites/newsarticle.asp on September 30, 2005.

[7] *Enterprise Risk Management: Tools and Techniques for Effective Implementation.* Institute of Management Accountants, Montvale, New Jersey, 2007: 1–31.

[8] An excellent analysis of time as a competitive element is contained in A. Faye Borthick and Harold P. Roth, "Accounting for Time: Reengineering Business Processes to Improve Responsiveness," *Journal of Cost Management* (Fall 1993): 4–14.

correlation between cost and time is the kind of information that should be available from a managerial accounting information system.

Efficiency

While quality and time are important, improving these dimensions without corresponding improvements in profit performance may be futile, if not fatal. Improving efficiency is also a vital concern. Both financial and nonfinancial measures of efficiency are needed. Cost is a critical measure of efficiency. Trends in costs over time and measures of productivity changes can provide important measures of the efficacy of continuous improvement decisions. For these efficiency measures to be of value, costs must be properly defined, measured, and assigned; furthermore, production of output must be related to the inputs required, and the overall financial effect of productivity changes should be calculated.

futile - pointless

The Role of the Managerial Accountant

OBJECTIVE 4
Describe the role of managerial accountants in an organization.

Today's business press writes about world-class firms. These are firms at the cutting edge of customer support. They know their market and their product. They strive to continually improve product design, manufacture, and delivery. These companies can compete with the best of the best in a global environment. Managerial accountants must support management in all phases of business decision making. As specialists in accounting, they must be intelligent, well prepared, up-to-date with new developments, and familiar with the customs and practices of all countries in which their firms operate. They are expected to be knowledgeable about the legal environment of business and, in particular, about the Sarbanes-Oxley Act of 2002.

Structure of the Company

The role of managerial accountants in an organization is one of support. They assist those individuals who are responsible for carrying out an organization's basic objectives. Positions that have direct responsibility for the basic objectives of an organization are referred to as **line positions**. Positions that are supportive in nature and have only indirect responsibility for an organization's basic objectives are called **staff positions**.

line positions = Direct Responsibility
Staff positions - Indirect Responsibilty

For example, assume that the basic mission of an organization is to produce and sell laser printers. The vice presidents of manufacturing and marketing, the factory manager, and the assemblers are all line positions. The vice presidents of finance and human resources, the cost accountant, and the purchasing manager are all staff positions.

Kicker's organization chart is shown in Exhibit 1-5. Because one of the basic objectives of the organization is to design, produce, and sell audio equipment, the president, general manager, and vice presidents for sales and marketing and operations hold line positions. Although managerial accountants, such as controllers and cost accounting managers, may wield considerable influence in the organization, they have no authority over the managers in the production area. The managers in line positions are the ones who set policy and make the decisions that impact the company. However, by supplying and interpreting accounting information, managerial accountants can have significant input into policies and decisions.

The **controller**, or chief accounting officer, for Kicker is located in the administration department. She supervises all accounting functions and reports directly to the general manager and chief operating officer (COO).

Because of the critical role that managerial accounting plays in the operation of an organization, the controller is often viewed as a member of the top management team and is encouraged to participate in planning, controlling, and decision-making activities. As the chief accounting officer, the controller has responsibility for both internal and external accounting requirements. In larger firms, this charge may include direct responsibility for internal auditing, cost accounting, financial accounting

Exhibit 1-5

Kicker Inc. Organizational Chart

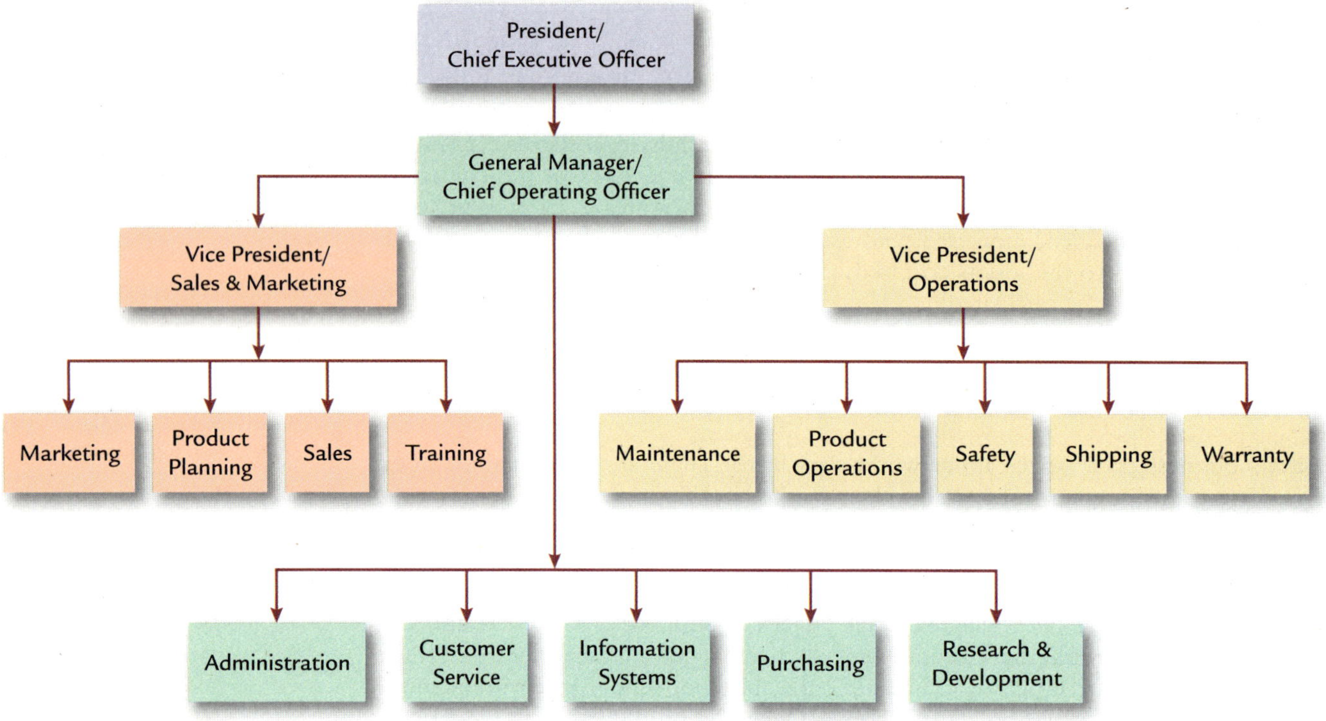

KICKER®

(including government reports and financial statements), systems accounting (including analysis, design, and internal controls), and taxes. The duties and organization of the controller's office vary from firm to firm. For example, in some firms, the internal audit department may report directly to the financial vice president; similarly, the systems department may report directly to the financial vice president or some other vice president.

In larger companies, the controller is separate from the treasury department. The **treasurer** is responsible for the finance function. Specifically, the treasurer raises capital and manages cash and investments. The treasurer may also be in charge of credit and collection and insurance.

Sarbanes-Oxley Act of 2002

In June 2002, the United States Congress passed the **Sarbanes-Oxley Act (SOX)**. This legislation was passed in response to the collapse of **Enron** and the revelations of securities fraud and accounting misconduct associated with companies such as **WorldCom**, **Adelphia**, and **HealthSouth**. The Sarbanes-Oxley Act (SOX) established stronger government control and regulation of public companies in the United States. SOX applies to **publicly traded companies**, which issue shares traded on U.S. stock exchanges. Major sections of SOX relate to (among others) enhanced auditor independence, tightened regulation of corporate governance, control over management, and management/auditor assessment of the firm's internal controls. SOX also led to increased attention to corporate ethics, which is discussed in the next section.

Importantly, private companies (such as Kicker), not-for-profit entities, and governmental agencies or entities are not covered by SOX. However, these entities have been affected by SOX through their dealings with constituents and their boards of directors. In particular, the intense scrutiny of internal control under SOX is a feature that many would like to see applied to not-for-profit entities. Internal control is a process put into place by management and the board of directors to ensure that objectives are achieved in the areas of effectiveness and efficiency of operations, reliability of financial reporting, and compliance with applicable laws and regulations.[9] All entities should achieve their legitimate objectives, and good internal control can help ensure that. Managerial accountants, through the offices of internal auditing or the chief financial officer (CFO), are the people in the organization who are expected to help their organizations comply with SOX.

Managerial Accounting, Ethical Conduct, and Social Responsibility

OBJECTIVE 5
Explain the importance of ethical behaviour for managers and managerial accountants.

profits be attained through legal and ethical means.

Virtually all managerial accounting practices were developed to assist managers in maximizing profits. Traditionally, actions regarding the economic performance of the firm have been the overriding concern. Yet managers and managerial accountants should not become so focused on profits that they develop a belief that the only goal of a business is maximizing its net worth. The objective of profit maximization should be constrained by the requirement that profits be achieved through legal and ethical means. While this has always been an implicit assumption of managerial accounting, the assumption should be made explicit. To help achieve this objective, many of the problems in this text require explicit consideration of ethical issues.

Ethical Behaviour

Ethical behaviour involves choosing actions that are right, proper, and just. Behaviour can be right or wrong; it can be proper or improper; and the decisions we make can be fair or unfair. Though people often differ in their views of the meaning of the ethical terms cited, there seems to be a common principle underlying all ethical systems. This principle is expressed by the belief that each member of a group bears some responsibility for the well-being of other members. Willingness to sacrifice one's self-interest for the well-being of the group is the heart of ethical action.

This notion of sacrifice produces some core values—values that describe what is meant by right and wrong in more concrete terms. James W. Brackner, writing for the "Ethics Column" in *Management Accounting*, made the following observation:

> *For moral or ethical education to have meaning, there must be agreement on the values that are considered "right." Ten of these values are identified and described by Michael Josephson in "Teaching Ethical Decision Making and Principled Reasoning." The study of history, philosophy, and religion reveals a strong consensus as to certain universal and timeless values essential to the ethical life.*
>
> *These 10 core values yield a series of principles that delineate right and wrong in general terms. Therefore, they provide a guide to behavior.*[10]

The 10 core values referred to in the quotation include the following:

1. Honesty
2. Integrity
3. Promise keeping
4. Fidelity = faithfulness = loyalty
5. Fairness
6. Caring for others
7. Respect for others
8. Responsible citizenship
9. Pursuit of excellence
10. Accountability = Responsibility

[9] Definition taken from COSO Internal Control Integrated Framework, http://www.coso.org/publications/executive_summary_integrated_framework.htm.

[10] James W. Brackner, "Consensus Values Should Be Taught," *Management Accounting* (August 1992): 19. For a more complete discussion of the 10 core values, see also Michael Josephson, *Teaching Ethical Decision Making and Principled Reasoning, Ethics Easier Said Than Done* (The Josephson Institute, Winter Los Angeles, CA: 1988): 29–30.

Many of the well-known accounting scandals, such as those involving Adelphia, WorldCom, HealthSouth, and **Parmalat**, provide evidence of the pressures faced by top managers and accountants to produce large net income numbers, especially in the short term. Unfortunately, such individuals often give into these pressures when faced with questionable revenue- and cost-related judgments. For example, the scandal at WorldCom was committed because the CEO, Bernie Ebbers, coerced several of the top accountants at WorldCom to wrongfully record journal entries in the company's books that capitalized millions of dollars in costs as assets (i.e., on the balance sheet) rather than as expenses (i.e., on the income statement) that would have dramatically lowered current period net income. Eventually, WorldCom was forced to pay hundreds of millions of dollars to the U.S. government and to shareholders for its illegal and unethical actions. In addition, several of the top executives were sentenced to extensive prison time for their actions. The recent subprime mortgage crisis also highlights the importance of ethical considerations as some banks tried to increase their profits either by lending individuals more money than they could reasonably afford or using terms that were intentionally less clear, or transparent, than many outsiders thought they should be.[11]

As some of these examples point out, though it may seem contradictory, sacrificing self-interest for the collective good might not only be right and bring a sense of individual worth but might also make good business sense. Companies with a strong code of ethics can create strong customer and employee loyalty. While liars and cheats may win on occasion, their victories often are short-lived. Companies in business for the long term find that it pays to treat all of their constituents with honesty and loyalty.

Company Codes of Ethical Conduct

To promote ethical behaviour by managers and employees, organizations commonly establish standards of conduct referred to as Company Codes of Conduct. One needs only to hear the name "Enron" to be reminded of the importance of ethical conduct. A quick review of various corporate codes of conduct shows some common ground. For example, **Adobe**'s code of conduct is guided by a set of core values around conducting business in an ethical and socially responsible manner. This includes sound corporate governance, a focus on employee success, caring for the environment, conscientious supply chain management, and active participation in the global community. Boeing's Code of Conduct states that it will "conduct its business fairly, impartially, in an ethical and proper manner, and in full compliance with all applicable laws and regulations." All employees must sign the code, and the company "requires that they understand the code, and ask questions, seek guidance, report suspected violations, and express concerns regarding compliance with this policy and the related procedures."[12]

In 2009, **Loblaws Companies** outlined its approach to social responsibility and expressed its achievements and core values in a Corporate Social Responsibility Report (CSR). That document linked the company to five core values:

- Respecting the environment
- Sourcing with integrity
- Making a positive difference in the community
- Reflecting the nation's diversity
- Being a great place to work

Reflecting those values, in 2009, Loblaws implemented the following:

- *Plastic bag diversion:* It applied a national 5-cent charge for every plastic bag provided at checkout. This led to more than 1.3 billion plastic bags being diverted from Canadian landfills by the end of 2009.

[11] Jane Sasseen, "FBI Widens Net Around Subprime Industry: With 14 Companies Under Investigation, the Bureau's Scope is the Entire Securitization Process," *Business Week Online* (January 30, 2008). Taken from http://www.businessweek.com/bwdaily/dnflash/content/jan2008/db20080129_728982.htm?chan=search on February 12, 2008.

[12] Taken from Adobe website www.adobe.com/corporateresponsibility

- *Improved fuel efficiency:* In its efforts to reduce its carbon footprint, it achieved a 2 percent improvement in transport fleet fuel efficiency per kilometre.
- *Sourcing with integrity:* The company committed itself to sustainably sourcing 100 percent of all seafood sold in its stores by year end 2013.

In addition, Loblaws did the following:

- Reduced its national refrigerant leak rate by 5 percent as a result of 56 corporate banner stores having alternative refrigeration systems that significantly reduced refrigerant requirements.
- Established a target to reduce nonrecyclable packaging on private label brands by 50 percent by 2013. Once this is achieved, the company's packaging will be 79 percent recyclable.
- Installed a wind turbine at the Atlantic Superstore in Porters Lake, Nova Scotia.
- Granted $8.9 million to more than 1,500 families across Canada through the President's Choice Children's Charity.
- Announced corporate donations of more than $24 million to help support local charities, programs, and organizations across Canada.
- Grew sales of Canadian produce by 16 percent during its Grown Close to Home campaign.
- Reduced sodium content in more than 50 private label products.
- Increased the number of female store managers by 53.7 per cent (since 2008).*

Important parts of corporate codes of conduct are integrity, performance of duties, and compliance with the rule of law. They also uniformly prohibit the acceptance of kickbacks and improper gifts, insider trading, and misappropriation of corporate information and assets.

Standards of Ethical Conduct for Managerial Accountants

Organizations commonly establish standards of conduct for their managers and employees. Professional associations also establish ethical standards. All three Canadian accounting bodies: Canadian Institute of Chartered Accountants (CICA), **Certified Management Accountants (CMA)**, and **Certified General Accountants (CGA)**—have established ethical standards for accountants. Professional accountants are bound by these codes of conduct, which stress the importance of competence, confidentiality, integrity, and credibility or objectivity.

To illustrate an application of the code, suppose a manager's bonus is linked to reported profits, with the bonus increasing as profits increase. Thus, the manager has an incentive to find ways to increase profits, including unethical approaches. For example, a manager could increase profits by delaying promotions of deserving employees or by using cheaper parts to produce a product. In either case, if the motive is simply to increase the bonus, the behaviour could be labelled as unethical. Neither action is in the best interest of the company or its employees. Yet where should the blame be assigned? After all, the reward system strongly encourages the manager to increase profits. Is the reward system at fault, or is the manager who chooses to increase profits at fault? Or both?

In reality, both the manager and reward system are probably at fault. It is important to design evaluation and reward systems so that incentives to pursue undesirable behaviour are minimized. Yet designing a perfect reward system is not a realistic expectation. Managers also have an obligation to avoid abusing the system. Basically, the prospect of an increased bonus (e.g., a favour) should not influence a manager to engage in unethical actions.

Can ethics be taught? Philosophers and ethicists from Socrates to those studying business ethics today agree that ethics can be taught and, even more important, learned. Students know that they have been taught in the ways of ethical conduct from preschool on. When they encounter new situations, ethical behaviour must be defined and reinforced. When you came to university, you were no doubt advised of the importance of doing your own work (not cheating) and of properly citing sources used in your papers and presentations. Clearly, individual rules were not intrinsically a part of you—they were taught. Similarly, accountants and businesspeople must be advised of the finer points of business ethics and of the behaviour appropriate to the job. For example, the head chef of a restaurant may be given some choice steaks as a gift for doing business with a meat supplier. Is this OK? The novice may think that it is—but this is wrong! It is the acceptance of a gift meant to render the chef less objective in his or her choice of supplier. The chef could be fired for such behaviour. In fact, many corporate codes of conduct explicitly outlaw such behaviour.

Perhaps the biggest challenge with ethical dilemmas is that when they arise, employees frequently do not realize (1) that such a dilemma has arisen or (2) the "correct" action that should be taken to rectify the dilemma. Therefore, rather than attempt to study numerous ethical issues in one place, each chapter of this text includes an ethical dilemma or situation designed to increase student awareness of the types of conduct considered unethical in business.

OBJECTIVE 6
Identify three accounting designations available in Canada.

Accounting Designations and Career Opportunities

As with the legal and medical professions, the accounting profession relies on certification to help promote ethical behaviour, as well as to provide evidence that the holder has achieved a minimum level of professional competence.

Accounting embraces all management functions, including purchasing, manufacturing, wholesaling, retailing, and a variety of marketing and transportation activities. It deals with all facets of an organization and provides an excellent opportunity for gaining a broad range of knowledge. Thus, accountants acquire many necessary general management skills. This is why today, probably more than ever before, more CEOs come from the ranks of accounting than from any other area, such as marketing, production, or engineering. Because some of you may want to pursue a career in accounting, you would find it helpful to know your career options in accounting.

Canada has three major professional accounting designations and self-regulating organizations:

Society of Management Accountants of Canada—CMA CANADA

This society confers the CMA (Certified Management Accountant), an internationally recognized designation. CMAs are strategic and financial management professionals who combine accounting expertise with professional management skills to provide leadership, innovation, and an integrating perspective to organizational decision making. CMAs use their management skills to lead an organization's growth and their accounting skills to track its progress. They add value to a business by developing total business solutions, identifying new market opportunities, and protecting/maximizing shareholder value.

Canadian Institute of Chartered Accountants (CICA)

The CICA confers the **Chartered Accountant (CA)** designation. The CA education program focuses on external financial reports and, in particular, the auditing functions. The CA is one of Canada's most valued designations and is recognized internationally. It prepares leaders in senior financial, tax, advisory, and assurance roles. Chartered Accountants are valued for their integrity and expertise as practitioners of public accounting.

Exhibit 1-6

CMA Code of Professional Ethics

All Members, Students and Firms will adhere to the following Code of Professional Ethics of CMA Ontario:

A Member, Student or Firm will act at all times with:

(a) responsibility for and fidelity to public needs;
(b) fairness and loyalty to such Member's, Student's or Firm's associates, clients and employers; and
(c) competence through devotion to high ideals of personal honour and professional integrity.

A Member, Student or Firm will:

(a) maintain at all times independence of thought and action;
(b) not express an opinion on financial reports or statements without first assessing her or his relationship with her or his client to determine whether such Member, Student or Firm might expect her or his opinion to be considered independent, objective and unbiased by one who has knowledge of all the facts; and
(c) when preparing financial reports or statements or expressing an opinion on financial reports or statements, disclose all material facts known to such Member, Student or Firm in order not to make such financial reports or statements misleading, acquire sufficient information to warrant an expression of opinion and report all material misstatements or departures from generally accepted accounting principles.

A Member, Student or Firm will:

(a) not disclose or use any confidential information concerning the affairs of such Member's, Student's or Firm's employer or client unless acting in the course of his or her duties or except when such information is required to be disclosed in the course of any defence of himself or herself or any associate or employee in any lawsuit or other legal proceeding or against alleged professional misconduct by order of lawful authority of the Board or any Committee of CMA Ontario in the proper exercise of their duties but only to the extent necessary for such purpose;
(b) inform his or her employer or client of any business connections or interests of which such Member's, Student's or Firm's employer or client would reasonably expect to be informed;
(c) not, in the course of exercising his or her duties on behalf of such Member's, Student's or Firm's employer or client, hold, receive, bargain for or acquire any fee, remuneration or benefit without such employer's or client's knowledge and consent; and
(d) take all reasonable steps, in arranging any engagement as a consultant, to establish a clear understanding of the scope and objectives of the work before it is commenced and will furnish the client with an estimate of cost, preferably before the engagement is commenced, but in any event as soon as possible thereafter.

A Member, Student or Firm will:

(a) conduct himself or herself toward Members, Students and Firms with courtesy and good faith;
(b) not commit an act discreditable to the profession;
(c) not engage in or counsel any business or occupation which, in the opinion of CMA Ontario, is incompatible with the professional ethics of a management accountant;
(d) not accept any engagement to review the work of a Member, Student or Firm for the same employer except with the knowledge of that Member, Student or Firm, or except where the connection of that Member, Student or Firm with the work has been terminated, unless the Member, Student or Firm reviews the work of others as a normal part of his or her responsibilities;
(e) not attempt to gain an advantage over Members, Students and Firms by paying or accepting a commission in securing management accounting or public accounting work;
(f) uphold the principle of adequate compensation for management accounting and public accounting work; and
(g) not act maliciously or in any other way which may adversely reflect on the public or professional reputation or business of a Member, Student or Firm.

A Member, Student or Firm will:

(a) at all times maintain the standards of competence expressed by the Board from time to time;
(b) disseminate the knowledge upon which the profession of management accounting is based to others within the profession and generally promote the advancement of the profession;
(c) undertake only such work as he or she is competent to perform by virtue of his or her training and experience and will, where it would be in the best interests of an employer or client, engage, or advise the employer or client to engage, other specialists;
(d) expose before the proper tribunals of CMA Ontario any incompetent, unethical, illegal or unfair conduct or practice of a Member, Student or Firm which involves the reputation, dignity or honour of CMA Ontario; and
(e) endeavour to ensure that a professional partnership or company, with which such Member, Student or Firm is associated as a partner, principal, director, officer, associate or employee, abides by the Code of Professional Ethics and the Rules of Professional Conduct established by CMA Ontario.*

Certified General Accountants Association of Canada (CGAAC)

The CGAAC confers the CGA (Certified General Accountant) designation. The CGA program provides a broad-based education in accounting and financial management. The CGAAC ensures that its members merit the confidence and trust of all who rely on their professional knowledge, skills, judgment, and integrity. It does so by regulating qualification, performance, and discipline standards. Competence and currency are cornerstones of a CGA's skill set.

Education in Canada is a provincial or territorial jurisdiction. Therefore, accounting students wishing to pursue one of the accounting designations need to register with the appropriate provincial or territorial organization. In Ontario. for example, the provincial professional accounting associations are the ICAO (the Institute of Chartered Accountants of Ontario), CGA Ontario, and CMA Ontario. Students who qualify for admission and who pass a national examination are awarded a professional accounting designation from the corresponding accounting organization.

For further information, visit the websites of the three Accounting Organizations: www.cma-canada.org; www.cica.ca; and www.cga-canada.org.

Management Accounting for Service and Not-for-Profit Organizations

Management accounting was primarily developed for manufacturing firms. However, management accounting concepts have evolved over the years and today apply to all types of organizations, including service and not-for-profit organizations.

Service organizations, such as hotels, real estate agencies, insurance companies, law firms, consultants of all kinds, libraries, government agencies, schools, and hospitals, do not make or sell tangible goods but instead provide services. Unlike products, services cannot be stored and can differ from one establishment to another or from one service provider to another. The services they provide are sometimes difficult to define. For example, schools offer a service but the output of education is not easy to measure. The same can be said for hospitals, where patient care and health are also difficult to quantify and measure.

Western economies, including Canada's, have moved from manufacturing-based economies to service- and knowledge-based economies. Innovation- and technology-based industries are also service-based. Increasingly more people work for the service industries than for manufacturing industries. For example, in terms of the number of employees, the travel industry—clearly a service industry—is larger than the North American automotive industry (i.e., **GM**, Chrysler, and **Ford**), which has recently been reduced to a much smaller entity than it once was.

Management accounting applies also to not-for-profit organizations. Much like for-profit firms, not-for-profit organizations need to prepare budgets and performance evaluations, assess the efficiency and effectiveness of various programs and services, raise funds, and invest wisely.

Contemporary not-for-profit leaders and managers, though they may have noble social objectives that go beyond the maximization of profit, still have to develop at least basic skills in management accounting. Expecting someone else to manage finances and do the "number crunching" is clearly asking for trouble. Basic skills in management accounting should be developed according to appropriate plans and controls in order to ensure the integrity of procedures and processes. Managers should learn how to generate financial reports, analyze data, and really understand the organization's financial condition. Management accounting shows the "reality" of the situation at hand; as such, it is one of the most important tasks for those who manage healthy not-for-profit organizations.

In all organizations, managers and administrators are better equipped to deal with work issues when they understand management accounting concepts.

Summary of Learning Objectives

LO1. Explain the meaning of managerial accounting.

- Managerial accounting information is used to identify problems, solve problems, and evaluate performance.
- Managerial accounting information helps managers in planning, controlling, and decision making.
- Planning is the detailed formulation of action to achieve a particular end.
- Controlling is the monitoring of a plan's implementation.
- Decision making is choosing among competing alternatives.

LO2. Explain the differences between managerial accounting and financial accounting.

- Managerial accounting is
  - Intended for internal users
  - Not subject to rules for external financial reporting (e.g., GAAP and IFRS regulations)
  - Subjective
  - Able to use both financial and nonfinancial measures of performance
  - Able to give a broader, interdisciplinary perspective
- Financial accounting is
  - Directed toward external users
  - Subject to externally imposed rules (e.g., GAAP and IFRS regulations)
  - Able to provide audited, objective financial information

LO3. Identify and explain the current focus of managerial accounting.

- It supports management focus on customer value, total quality management, and time-based competition.
- Information about value chain activities and customer sacrifice (such as post-purchase costs) is collected and made available.
- Activity-based management is a major innovative response to the demand for more accurate and relevant managerial accounting information.
- The nature of managerial accounting information system may depend on strategic position of the firm:
  - Cost leadership strategy
  - Product differentiation strategy
  - Lean accounting

LO4. Describe the role of managerial accountants in an organization.

- They are responsible for identifying, collecting, measuring, analyzing, preparing, interpreting, and communicating information.
- They must be sensitive to the information needs of managers.
- They serve as staff members of the organization and are part of the management team.

LO5. Explain the importance of ethical behaviour for managers and managerial accountants.

- A strong ethical sense is needed to resist efforts to change economic information that may present an untrue picture of firm performance.
- Many firms have a written code of ethics or code of conduct.
- The CMA has a code of ethics for managerial accountants.

LO6. Identify three accounting designations available in Canada.

- Certified Management Accountant (CMA)
- Chartered Accountant (CA)
- Certified General Accountant (CGA)

Key Terms

Discussion Questions

1. What is managerial accounting?
2. What are the three broad objectives of managerial accounting?
3. Who are the users of managerial accounting information?
4. Should a managerial accounting system provide both financial and nonfinancial information? Explain.
5. What is meant by controlling?
6. Describe the connection between planning, feedback, and controlling.
7. How do managerial accounting and financial accounting differ?
8. Explain the role of financial reporting in the development of managerial accounting. Why has this changed in recent years?
9. Explain the meaning of customer value. How is focusing on customer value changing managerial accounting?
10. Explain why today's managerial accountant must have a cross-functional perspective.
11. Briefly explain the practice of enterprise risk management and the role that can be played by managerial accountants in enterprise risk management.
12. What is the value chain? Why is it important?
13. What is the difference between a staff position and a line position?
14. The controller should be a member of the top management staff. Do you agree or disagree? Explain.
15. What is ethical behaviour? Is it possible to teach ethical behaviour in a managerial accounting course?
16. Briefly describe some of the common themes or pressures faced by executives who commit corporate fraud.
17. Identify the three forms of accounting designation. Which designation do you believe is best? Why?

Multiple-Choice Exercises

1-1 The provision of accounting information for internal users is known as

a. managerial accounting.
b. accounting.
c. financial accounting.
d. information provision.
e. accounting for planning and control.

1-2 The users of managerial accounting information include

a. for-profit companies.
b. not-for-profit organizations.

c. city governments.
d. educational institutions.
e. all of the above.

1-3 Setting objectives and identifying methods to achieve those objectives is called

a. controlling.
b. decision making.
c. planning.
d. performance evaluation.
e. none of the above.

1-4 The process of choosing among competing alternatives is called

a. controlling.
b. decision making.
c. planning.
d. performance evaluation.
e. none of the above.

1-5 Which of the following is a characteristic of managerial accounting?

a. There is an internal focus.
b. Subjective information may be used.
c. There is an emphasis on the future.
d. It is broad-based and multidisciplinary.
e. All of the above.

1-6 Which of the following is a characteristic of financial accounting?

a. There is an internal focus.
b. Subjective information may be used.
c. There is a historical orientation.
d. It is broad-based and multidisciplinary.
e. None of the above.

1-7 In terms of strategic positioning, which two general strategies may be chosen by a company?

a. activity-based costing and value chain emphasis
b. revenue production and cost enhancement
c. cost leadership and product differentiation
d. increasing customer value and decreasing supplier orientation
e. product differentiation and cost enhancement

1-8 Managerial accountants in an organization are typically

a. line positions.
b. marketing positions.
c. staff positions.
d. production positions.
e. selling positions.

1-9 The chief accounting officer for a firm is the

a. chief executive officer.
b. chief operating officer.
c. vice president of sales.
d. production head.
e. controller.

1-10 Which of the following is typically found in a corporation's code of ethics?

a. respect for others
b. integrity
c. honesty
d. competence
e. all of the above

Exercises

OBJECTIVE 1

Exercise 1-11 THE MANAGERIAL PROCESS

Each of the following scenarios requires the use of accounting information to carry out one or more of the three managerial objectives: planning, control (including performance evaluation), or decision making.

a. **Laboratory Manager:** A medical laboratory approached me recently and offered us its entire range of blood tests. It provided a price list revealing the amount it is willing to pay for each test. In many cases, the prices are below what we normally charge. I need to know the costs of the individual tests to assess the feasibility of accepting its offer and perhaps suggest some price adjustments on some of the tests.

b. **Operating Manager:** This report indicates that we have 30 percent more defects than originally targeted. An investigation into the cause has revealed the problem. We were using a lower-quality material than expected, and the waste has been higher than normal. By switching to the quality level originally specified, we can reduce the defects to the planned level.

c. **Divisional Manager:** Our market share has increased because of higher-quality products. Current projections indicate that we should sell 25 percent more units than last year. I want a projection of the effect that this increase in sales will have on profits. I also want to know our expected cash receipts and cash expenditures on a month-by-month basis. I have a feeling that some short-term borrowing may be necessary.

d. **Plant Manager:** Foreign competitors are producing goods with lower costs and delivering them more rapidly than we can to customers in our markets. We need to decrease the cycle time and increase the efficiency of our manufacturing process. There are two proposals that should help us accomplish these goals, both of which involve investing in computer-aided manufacturing. I need to know the future cash flows associated with each system and the effect each system has on unit costs and cycle time.

e. **Manager:** At the last board meeting, we established an objective of earning a 25 percent return on sales. I need to know how many units of our product we need to sell to meet this objective. Once I have the estimated sales in units, we need to outline a promotional campaign that will take us where we want to be. However, in order to compute the targeted sales in units, I need to know the expected unit price and a lot of cost information.

f. **Manager:** Perhaps the Hippocrates Medical Clinic should not offer a full range of medical services. Some services seem to be having a difficult time showing any kind of profit. I am particularly concerned about the mental health service. It has not shown a profit since the clinic opened. I want to know what costs can be avoided if I drop the service. I also want some assessment of the impact on the other services we offer. Some of our patients may choose this clinic because we offer a full range of services.

Required:

Select the managerial accounting objective(s) that are applicable for each scenario: planning, controlling, or decision making.

OBJECTIVE 2

Exercise 1-12 DIFFERENCES BETWEEN MANAGERIAL ACCOUNTING AND FINANCIAL ACCOUNTING

Jenna Suarez, the controller for Arben Company, has faced the following situations in the past two weeks:

a. Ben Heald, head of production, wondered whether it would be more cost effective to buy parts partially assembled or to buy individual parts and assemble them at the Arben factory.
b. The president of Arben reminded Jenna that the shareholders' meeting was coming up, and he needed her to prepare a PowerPoint® presentation showing the income statement and balance sheet information for last year.
c. Ellen Johnson, vice president of sales, has decided to expand the sales offices for next year. She sent Jenna the information on next year's rent and depreciation information for budgeting purposes.
d. Jenna's assistant, Mike, received the information from Ellen on depreciation and added it to depreciation expenses and accumulated depreciation on office equipment.
e. Jenna compared the budgeted spending on materials used in production with the actual spending on materials used in production. Materials spending was significantly higher than expected. She set up a meeting to discuss this outcome with Ben Heald so that he could explain it.

Required:

Determine whether each request is relatively more *managerial accounting oriented* or *financial accounting oriented*.

Exercise 1-13 CUSTOMER VALUE, STRATEGIC POSITIONING

OBJECTIVE 3

Adriana Alvarado has decided to purchase a personal computer. She has narrowed the choices to two: Drantex and Confiar. Both brands have the same processing speed, 6.4 gigabytes of hard-disk capacity, two USB ports, a DVD drive, and each comes with the same basic software support package. Both come from mail-order companies with good reputations. The selling price for each is identical. After some review, Adriana discovers that the cost of operating and maintaining Drantex over a three-year period is estimated to be $300. For Confiar, the operating and maintenance cost is $600. The sales agent for Drantex emphasized the lower operating and maintenance costs. The agent for Confiar, however, emphasized the service reputation of the product and the faster delivery time (Confiar can be purchased and delivered one week sooner than Drantex). Based on all the information, Adriana has decided to buy Confiar.

Required:

1. What is the total product purchased by Adriana?
2. How does the strategic positioning differ for the two companies?
3. When asked why she decided to buy Confiar, Adriana responded, "I think that Confiar offers more value than Drantex." What are the possible sources of this greater value? What implications does this have for the managerial accounting information system?
4. Suppose that Adriana's decision was prompted mostly by the desire to receive the computer quickly. Informed that it was losing sales because of the longer time to produce and deliver its products, the management of the company producing Drantex decided to improve delivery performance by improving its internal processes. These improvements decreased the number of defective units and the time required to produce its product. Consequently, delivery time and costs both decreased, and the company was able to lower its prices on Drantex. Explain how these actions translate into strengthening the competitive position of the Drantex PC relative to the Confiar PC. Also discuss the implications for the managerial accounting information system.

Exercise 1-14 LINE VERSUS STAFF

OBJECTIVE 4

The following describes the job responsibilities of two employees of Barney Manufacturing.

Joan Dennison, Cost Accounting Manager. Joan is responsible for measuring and collecting costs associated with the manufacture of the garden hose product line. She is also responsible for preparing periodic reports that compare the actual costs with planned costs. These reports are provided to the production line managers and the plant manager. Joan helps to explain and interpret the reports.

Steven Swasey, Production Manager. Steven is responsible for the manufacture of the high-quality garden hose. He supervises the line workers, helps to develop the production schedule, and is responsible for seeing that production quotas are met. He is also held accountable for controlling manufacturing costs.

Required:

Identify Joan and Steven as line or staff and explain your reasons.

OBJECTIVE 5

Exercise 1-15 ETHICAL BEHAVIOUR

Consider the following true scenario between Dave, a printer, and Steve, an assistant in the local university's athletic department.

Steve: Dave, our department needs to have 10,000 posters printed for the basketball team for next year. Here's the mock-up, and we'll need them in a month. How much will you charge?

Dave: Well, given the costs I have for ink and paper, I can come in at around $5,000.

Steve: Great, here's what I want you to do. Print me up an invoice for $7,500. That's our budget. Then, when they pay you, you give me a cheque for $2,500. I'll make sure that you get the job.

Required:

Is this ethical? What should Dave do?

OBJECTIVE 5

Exercise 1-16 ETHICAL BEHAVIOUR

Manager: If I can reduce my costs by $40,000 during this last quarter, my division will show a profit that is 10 percent above the planned level, and I will receive a $10,000 bonus. However, given the projections for the fourth quarter, it does not look promising. I really need that $10,000. I know of one way that I can qualify. All I have to do is lay off my three most expensive salespeople. After all, most of the orders are in for the fourth quarter, and I can always hire new sales personnel at the beginning of the next year.

Required:

What is the right choice for the manager to make? Why did the ethical dilemma arise? Is there any way to redesign the accounting reporting system to discourage the type of behaviour that the manager is contemplating?

OBJECTIVE 5

Exercise 1-17 ETHICAL ISSUES

The following statements have appeared in newspaper editorials:

1. Business students come from all segments of society. If they have not been taught ethics by their families and by their elementary and secondary schools, a business school can have little effect.
2. Sacrificing self-interest for the collective good won't happen unless a majority of people also accept this premise.
3. Competent executives manage people and resources for the good of society. Monetary benefits and titles are simply the by-products of doing a good job.
4. Unethical firms and individuals, like high rollers in Las Vegas, are eventually wiped out financially.

Required:

Assess and comment on each of the statements.

Exercise 1-18 ETHICAL ISSUES

OBJECTIVE 5

The Bedron Company is a closely held investment service group that has been quite successful over the past five years, consistently providing most members of the top management group with 50 percent bonuses. In addition, both the chief financial officer and the chief executive officer have received 100 percent bonuses. Bedron expects this trend to continue.

Recently, Bedron's top management group, which holds 35 percent of the outstanding shares of common stock, has learned that a major corporation is interested in acquiring Bedron. The other corporation's initial offer is attractive and is several dollars per share higher than Bedron's current share price. One member of management told a group of employees under him about the potential offer. He suggested that they might want to purchase more Bedron stock at the current price in anticipation of the takeover offer.

Required:

Do you think that the employees should take the action suggested by their boss? Suppose the action is prohibited by Bedron's code of ethics. Now suppose that it is not prohibited by Bedron's code of ethics. Is the action acceptable in that case?

Exercise 1-19 COMPANY CODES OF CONDUCT

OBJECTIVE 5

Using the Internet, locate the code of conduct for three different companies. Briefly describe each code of conduct. How are they similar? How are they different?

CMA Problem*

CMA Problem 1-1 COST CLASSIFICATION AND BEHAVIOUR—MCQ

1. Consider a single hard copy of this textbook as a cost object. What would be the best two labels to classify the relation between this cost object and the following two costs of producing the cost object respectively: (1) the paper; and (2) the one-time fees paid to the authors (i.e., not royalties)?
   a. (1) direct cost (2) variable cost
   b. (1) variable cost (2) unavoidable cost
   c. (1) fixed cost (2) variable cost
   d. (1) direct cost (2) fixed cost
   e. (1) avoidable cost (2) variable cost
2. Given a cost has already been identified as a variable cost, which of the following additional descriptions of the cost is incompatible with that identification?
   a. The cost, in total, does not change with changes in the volume of the cost driver.
   b. The cost can be traced directly to the cost object.
   c. The cost, in total, does change with changes in the volume of the cost driver.
   d. The cost cannot be traced directly to the cost object.
   e. The cost is not a prime cost.
3. The total direct labour cost of producing 100 units of Product X is $50. The direct material cost of producing the 100 units is perfectly variable and the cost driver is the number of units produced. The cost of the direct material traced to each unit is $1.25. Indirect costs are completely fixed at $75 for the production of the 100 units. What are the total conversion costs for the 100 units of Product X?
   a. $275
   b. $250
   c. $200
   d. $175
   e. $125

Chapter 2

Basic Managerial Accounting Concepts

After studying Chapter 2, you should be able to:

1. Explain the meaning of cost and how costs are assigned to products and services.
2. Define the various costs of manufacturing products and providing services as well as the costs of selling and administration.
3. Prepare income statements for manufacturing and service organizations.

HANS NELEMAN/THE IMAGE BANK/GETTY

Experience Managerial Decisions

Canada's Worst Cell Phone Bill

If you are reading this, the chances are that you own a cell phone. About 75 percent of Canadians—some 25 million people—have a cell phone. Worldwide there are some 5 billion cell phones. This makes the cell phone industry one of the most profitable in the world.

The first mobile phone was produced by **Motorola** in 1973. It took about 10 years for the first cell phone (the Motorola Dyna TAC) to become commercially available. In the 1990s, commercially viable cellular networks mushroomed and cell usage took off, penetrating not only developed nations' markets but also the developing economies.

The modern cell phone is not just a phone. It is also a watch, a camera, a calculator, a calendar, and an alarm clock. Modern mobile phones also support many other services such as e-mail, Internet access, and gaming. Bluetooth and infrared technology offer more advanced computing ability through so-called "smart phones."

"Canada's Worst Cell Bill" (CBC *Marketplace* video) offers insight into the exorbitant and questionable billing practices of many cell service providers—practices that will make you reconsider the details of your own cell plan.

How Does Your Plan Work?

- If it is a pay-as-you-go plan, do you have to add more money so that the unused minutes you have paid for do not expire?
- If you are using your cell phone abroad, what are the roaming charges?
- If you have signed a contract, are you sure you know what you have signed up for? And what are your cancellation fees?
- Are incoming calls and texting really free?
- Overall, why do cell phone customers seem to be so confused about the myriad charges they face?

What Is the *Real* Cost of a Cell Phone?

- How much does it cost you? And how little does it cost the phone company?
- Is your cell company charging too much?
- What is the true cost of the service your cell company is providing?
- What drives the costs of cell usage?
- If the cost to you is 15 cents per minute and the cost to the company is only one-third of a cent, is the markup of 4,400 percent justified?

These and many such questions are dealt with throughout this text. Through your managerial accounting studies, you will soon become a cost expert and be able to answer these questions yourself.

Here's The Real Kicker

Kicker collects and analyzes many types of costs. In the manufacturing area, the company keeps track of direct materials, direct labour, and overhead. These costs, of course, make up the cost of goods sold that goes on Kicker's monthly income statement. Nonmanufacturing costs include the costs of selling and administration. However, this information is decomposed into a series of accounts that helps Kicker's management in budgeting and decision making.

The sales function, for example, is broken down into three areas: selling, customer service, and marketing. Selling works directly with dealers and outside sales representatives. Customer service handles calls from dealers and decides whether or not a problem is covered under warranty. Marketing is responsible for advertising, promotions, and tent shows. One of the largest marketing events is Kicker's annual Big Air Bash, an extravaganza of music, food, cars, and extreme sports demonstrations. Held in conjunction with the Specialty Equipment Market Association (SEMA) show, the Big Air Bash is held outside of the Hard Rock Hotel and Casino in Las Vegas. The expenses associated with the show include the modification of show cars in Kicker's in-house garage. Kicker mechanics customized cars to make room for speakers and heavy-duty amps. With a souped-up engine, new fibreglass exterior, and trick paint, the cars are ready for show. Other "veteran" show cars and pickup trucks are refreshed with additional trick paint, larger tires, and Kicker's newest amps and speakers. You can feel the music from outside the truck.

Tent shows are smaller-scale affairs often held several times a year throughout North America. Kicker brings its semitrailer full of products and sound equipment as well as a couple of show trucks. Then, a large tent is set up to sell Kicker merchandise, explain products, and sell the previous year's models at greatly reduced prices. Fun and relaxed, the tent shows appeal to Kicker's customer base and provide a chance to look at the new models. The cost of each tent show is carefully tracked and compared with that show's revenue. Sites that don't provide sales revenue greater than cost are not booked for the coming year.

Like many of today's companies, Kicker tracks costs carefully for use in decision making. The general cost categories discussed in this chapter help the company organize cost information and relate it to decision making.

KICKER®

OBJECTIVE 1

Explain the meaning of cost and how costs are assigned to products and services.

The Meaning and Uses of Cost

One of the most important tasks of managerial accounting is to determine the cost of products, services, customers, and other items of interest to managers. Therefore, we need to understand the meaning of cost and the ways in which costs can be used to make decisions, both for small entrepreneurial businesses and for large international businesses. For example, consider a small gourmet restaurant and its owner Courtney, who also is the head chef. In addition to understanding the complexities of gourmet food preparation, Courtney needs to understand the breakdown of the restaurant's costs into various categories in order to make effective operating decisions. Cost categories of particular interest include direct costs (food and beverages) and indirect costs (laundry of linens). On a larger scale, local banks operating in university communities often look at the cost of providing basic chequing account services to students. These accounts typically lose money—that is, the accounts cost more to service than they yield in fees and interest revenue. However, the bank finds that students already banking with them are more likely to take out student loans through the bank, and these loans are very profitable. As a result, the bank may actually decide to expand its offerings to students when the related loan business is considered. Now, let's define "cost" and more fully describe its managerial importance.

Cost

Cost is the amount of cash or cash equivalent sacrificed for goods and/or services that are expected to bring a current or future benefit to the organization. If a furniture manufacturer buys lumber for $10,000, then the cost of that lumber is $10,000 cash. Sometimes, one asset is traded for another asset. Then the cost of the new asset is measured by the value of the asset given up (the cash equivalent). If the same manufacturer trades office equipment valued at $8,000 for a forklift, then the cost of the forklift is the $8,000 value of the office equipment traded for it. Cost is a dollar measure of the resources used to achieve a given benefit. Managers strive to minimize the cost of achieving benefits. Reducing the cost required to achieve a given benefit means that a firm is becoming more efficient.

Costs are incurred to produce future benefits. In a profit-making firm, those benefits usually mean revenues. As costs are used up in the production of revenues, they are said to expire. Expired costs are called **expenses**. On the income statement, expenses are deducted from revenues to determine income (also called *profit*). For a company to remain in business, revenues must be larger than expenses. In addition, the income earned must be large enough to satisfy the owners of the firm.

We can look more closely at the relationship between cost and revenue by focusing on the units sold. The revenue per unit is called **price**. In our everyday conversation, we have a tendency to use cost and price as synonyms, because the price of an item (e.g., a cell phone) is the cost to us. However, accounting courses take the viewpoint of the owner of the company. In that case, cost and price are *not* the same. Instead, for the company, *revenue* and *price* are the same. Price must be greater than cost in order for the firm to earn income. Hence, managers need to know cost and trends in cost. For example, the price a consumer pays for a fleece jacket from **Roots** might be $200, while the total cost that the company incurs to design, manufacture, deliver, and service that jacket is much lower than the $200 price it charges consumers.

Accumulating and Assigning Costs

Accumulating costs is the way that costs are measured and recorded. The accounting system typically does this job quite well. When a telephone bill comes into the company, the bookkeeper records an addition to the telephone expense account and an addition to the liability account, Accounts Payable. In this way, the cost is *accumulated*. It would be easy to tell, at the end of the year, the total spending on telephone expense. Accumulating costs tells the company what was spent. However, that usually is not enough information. The company also wants to know *why* the money was spent. In other words, it wants to know how costs were assigned to cost objects.

Assigning costs is the way that a cost is linked to some cost object. A cost object is something for which a company wants to know the cost. For example, of the total telephone expense, how much was for the sales department, and how much was for manufacturing? *Assigning* costs tells the company why the money was spent. In this case, cost assignment tells whether the money spent on telephone expense was to support the manufacturing or the selling of the product. As we will discuss in later chapters, cost assignment typically is more difficult than cost accumulation.

Cost Objects

Managerial accounting systems are structured to measure and assign costs to entities called *cost objects*. A **cost object** is any item such as a product, customer, department, project, geographic region, plant, and so on, for which costs are measured and assigned. For example, if the **Royal Bank of Canada** wants to determine the cost of a platinum credit card, then the cost object is the platinum credit card. All costs related to the platinum card are added in, such as the cost of mailings to potential customers, the cost of telephone lines dedicated to the card, the portion of the computer department that processes platinum card transactions and bills, and so on. In a more personal example, suppose that you are considering taking a course during the summer session. Taking the course is the cost object, and the cost would include tuition, books, fees, transportation, and (possibly) housing. Notice that you could also include the forgone earnings from a summer job (assuming that you cannot work while taking summer classes), which would be an opportunity cost. (The concept of opportunity cost will be discussed more fully later in this chapter.)

We will discuss various methods of assigning costs to cost objects in the succeeding chapters.

Assigning Costs to Cost Objects

Costs can be assigned to cost objects in a number of ways. Relatively speaking, some methods are more accurate, and others are simpler. The choice of a method depends on a number of factors, such as the need for accuracy. The notion of accuracy is a relative concept and has to do with the reasonableness and logic of the cost assignment methods used. The objective is to measure and assign costs as well as possible, given management objectives. For example, suppose you and three of your friends go out to dinner at a local pizza parlor. When the bill comes, everything has been added together for a total of $36. How much is your share? One easy way to find your share is to divide the bill evenly among you and your friends. In that case, you each owe $9 ($36/4). But suppose that one of you had a small salad and drink (totalling $5), while another had a specialty pizza, appetizer, and beer (totalling $15). Clearly, it is possible to identify what each person had and assign costs that way. The second method is more accurate, but also more work. Which method you choose will depend on how important it is to you to assign the specific meal costs to each individual. It is the same way in accounting. There are a number of ways to assign costs to cost objects. Some methods are quick and easy but may be inaccurate. Other methods are much more accurate, but involve much more work (in business, more work equals more expense).

Cost Classification

A cost is a payment of cash or the commitment to pay cash in the future for the purpose of generating revenues. For example, cash or a note payable signed to purchase supplies is the cost of supplies. In managerial accounting, costs are classified according to the decision-making needs of management.

Different costs are used for different purposes. Cost definitions can vary according to the objective being served. Thus costs can be classified into groups using a variety of criteria. The classification of costs helps make sense of the great variety of costs, which facilitates decision making.

The following cost groups and terms are introduced and defined later in this chapter:

- Direct costs (material and labour)
- Indirect costs (material and labour)
- Prime costs
- Conversion costs
- Product costs
- Period costs
- Variable costs (step costs and not)
- Fixed costs (committed and discretionary)
- Mixed costs
- Selling costs
- Administrative costs

It should be emphasized that there is only one pool of costs. Then, using different criteria, we can "break out" the pool into various categories. So the pool of costs can be classified as—for example—"Direct or Indirect Costs," "Prime or Conversion Costs," "Product or Period Costs," "Selling or Administrative Costs," or "Variable, Fixed, or Mixed Costs."

To facilitate control, selling and administrative expenses may be reported by level of responsibility. For example, selling expenses may be reported in terms of products, salespersons, departments, divisions, or territories. Likewise, administrative expenses may be reported in terms of areas such as human resources, computer services, legal, accounting, or finance.

Step costs are costs that vary at quantity intervals. For example, if a hotel housekeeper is expected to clean 10 rooms per shift, the cost of hiring an additional housekeeper changes with every 11th, 21st, and 31st room that is occupied. The cost remains the same, however, for any occupancy rate between zero and 10, 11 and 20, 21 and 30 rooms, and so on.

Committed fixed costs cannot be avoided. For example, an executive's salary and the amount of amortization represent committed fixed costs. *Discretionary* fixed costs can be modified. For example, research and development costs and advertising costs can be curtailed under budgetary constraints.

Tracing Direct Costs **Direct costs** are those costs that can be easily and accurately traced to a cost object. When we say that a cost is easy to trace, we often mean that the relationship between the cost and the object can be physically observed and is easy to track. The more costs that can be traced to the object, the more accurate are the cost assignments. For example, suppose that chef Courtney, from our earlier discussion, wants to know the cost of emphasizing fresh, in-season fruits and vegetables in her entrées. The purchase cost of the fruits and vegetables would be relatively easy to determine. Some costs, however, are hard to trace.

Indirect costs are costs that cannot be easily and accurately traced to a cost object. For example, Courtney incurs additional costs in scouting the outlying farms and farmers' markets (as opposed to simply ordering fruits and vegetables from a distributor). She must use her own time and automobile to make the trips. Farmers' markets may not deliver, so Courtney must arrange for a coworker with a van to pick up the produce. By definition, fruits and vegetables that are currently in season will be out of season (i.e., unavailable) in a few weeks. This seasonality means that Courtney must spend more time revising menus and developing new recipes that can be adapted to restaurant conditions. In addition, waste and spoilage may increase until Courtney and the kitchen staff learn just how much to order. These costs are difficult to assign to the meals prepared and sold. Therefore, they are indirect costs. Exhibit 2-1 shows direct and indirect costs being assigned to cost objects. Exhibit 2-2 provides another schematic for classifying costs.

Assigning Indirect Costs Even though indirect costs cannot be traced to cost objects, it is still important to assign them. This assignment usually is accomplished by using allocation.

Allocation means that an indirect cost is assigned to a cost object by using a reasonable and convenient method. Since no clearly observable causal relationship exists, allocating indirect costs is based on convenience or some assumed causal linkage. For

Exhibit 2-1

Object Costing

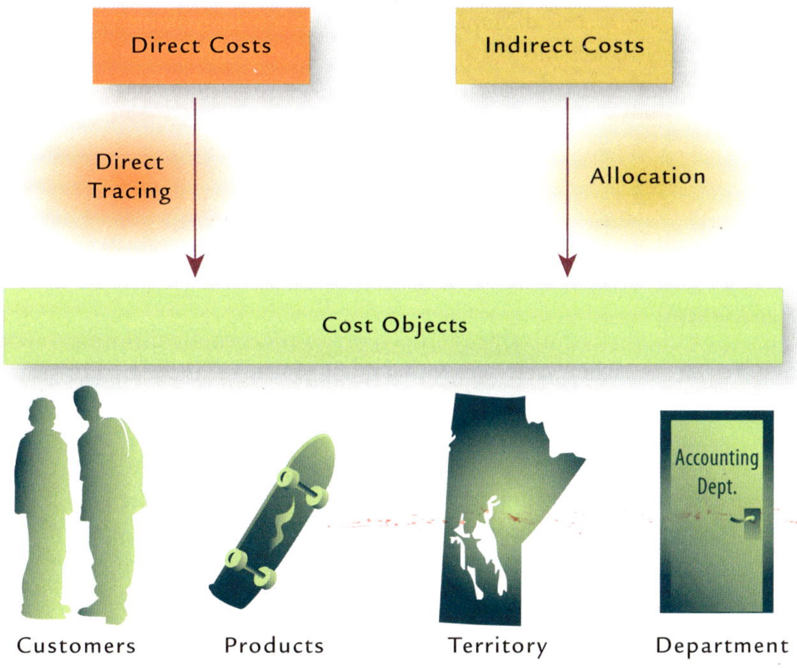

Exhibit 2-2

Cost Classification

Cost Classification	Types of Costs
A. In relation to cost object	Direct (easily traceable) Indirect (nontraceable needs to be allocated)
B. In relation to changes of activity	Fixed (total remains constant in the relevant range) Variable (total varies according to the level of activity) Mixed (part variable, part fixed) Step (it increases at certain activity levels)
C. In relation to the classification in the financial statements	Product (inventorial) Prime Conversion Period (expensed)

example, consider the cost of heating and lighting a plant in which five products are manufactured. Suppose that this utility cost is to be assigned to these five products. It is difficult to see any causal relationship between utility costs and each unit of product manufactured. Therefore, a convenient way to allocate this cost is to assign it in proportion to the direct labour hours used by each product. This method is relatively easy and accomplishes the purpose of ensuring that all costs are assigned to units produced. Allocating indirect costs is important for a variety of reasons. For example, allocating indirect costs to products is needed to determine the value of inventory and of cost of goods sold. Perhaps more important, as companies become more complex in the number and types of products and services they offer to customers, the need to understand, allocate, and effectively control indirect costs becomes increasingly important. In addition, indirect costs represent an increasingly large percentage of total costs for many companies.

Direct and indirect costs occur in service businesses as well. For example, a bank's cost of printing and mailing monthly statements to chequing account holders is a direct cost of the product—chequing accounts. However, the cost of office furniture in the bank is an indirect cost for the chequing accounts.

Other Categories of Cost

In addition to being categorized as either direct or indirect, costs are often analyzed with respect to their behaviour patterns, or the way in which a cost changes when the level of the output changes.

A **variable cost** is one that increases in total as output increases and decreases in total as output decreases. For example, the denim used in making jeans is a variable cost. As the company makes more jeans, it needs more denim.

A **fixed cost** is a cost that does not increase in total as output increases and does not decrease in total as output decreases. For example, the cost of property taxes on the factory building stays the same no matter how many pairs of jeans the company makes. How can that be, since property taxes can and do change? While the cost changes, it is not because output changes. Rather, it changes because the city or county government decides to raise taxes. Variable and fixed costs are covered more extensively in Chapter 3.

Most costs are neither fixed nor variable; they are *mixed*, having both variable and fixed components.

Mixed costs = Variable + Fixed costs

An **opportunity cost** is the benefit given up or sacrificed when one alternative is chosen over another. For example, an opportunity cost of being in accounting class may be the wages you would have earned during that time if you were working rather than going to school. Opportunity cost differs from accounting cost in that the opportunity cost is never included in the accounting records, because it is the cost of something that did not occur. Opportunity costs are important to decision making, as we will see more clearly in Chapter 9.

We will discuss various methods of assigning costs to cost objects in the succeeding chapters.

CONCEPT Q&A

Make a list of the costs you are incurring for your classes this term. Which costs are direct costs for your university course(s)? Which costs are indirect? Now, from your list of total costs, which ones are direct costs of this course? Which are indirect?

Answers on pages 711 to 715.

Product and Service Costs

OBJECTIVE 2

Define the various costs of manufacturing products and providing services as well as the costs of selling and administration.

Output represents one of the most important cost objects. There are two types of output: products and services.

Products are goods produced by converting raw materials through the use of labour and indirect manufacturing resources, such as the manufacturing plant, land, and machinery. Televisions, hamburgers, automobiles, computers, clothes, and furniture are examples of products.

Services are tasks or activities performed for a customer or an activity performed by a customer using an organization's products or facilities. Insurance coverage, medical care, dental care, funeral care, and accounting are examples of service activities performed for customers. Car rental, video rental, and skiing are examples of services where the customer uses an organization's products or facilities.

Organizations that produce products are called **manufacturing organizations**. Organizations that provide services are called **service organizations**. Managers of both types of organizations need to know how much individual products or services cost. Accurate cost information is vital for profitability analysis and strategic decisions concerning product design, pricing, and product mix. Incidentally, retail organizations, such as **La Senza**, buy finished products from other organizations, such as manufacturers, and then sell them to customers. The accounting for inventory and cost of goods sold for retail organizations, often referred to as merchandisers, is much simpler than for manufacturing organizations and is usually covered extensively in introductory financial accounting courses. Therefore, the focus here is on manufacturing and service organizations.

Services differ from products in many ways. First, a service is intangible. The buyers of services cannot see, feel, hear, or taste a service before it is bought. Second, services are perishable; they cannot be stored for future use by a consumer but must be consumed when performed. Inventory valuation, so important for products, is not an issue for services. In other words, because service organizations do not produce and sell products as part of their regular operations, they have no inventory asset on the balance sheet. Third, providers of services and buyers of services must usually be in direct contact for an exchange to take place. For example, an eye examination requires both the patient and the optometrist to be present. However, producers of products need not have direct contact with the buyers of their goods. Thus, buyers of automobiles never need to have contact with the engineers and assembly line workers that produced their automobiles. The overall way in which a company costs services in terms of classifying related costs as either direct or indirect is very similar to the way in which it costs products. The main difference in costing is that products have inventories, and services do not.

ETHICS Tracking costs can also act as an early warning system for unauthorized activity and possible ethical problems. For example, **Metropolitan Life Insurance Company** was dismayed to learn that some of its agents were selling policies as retirement plans. This practice is illegal, and it cost the company more than $20 million in fines as well as $50 million in refunds to policyholders.[1] More accurate and comprehensive data tracking regarding sales, individual agents, types of policies, and policyholders could have alerted Metropolitan Life to a potential problem. Thus, we can see that tracking costs can serve many different and important purposes.◆

Product Costs

Managerial accountants must decide what types of managerial accounting information to provide to managers, how to measure such information, and when and to whom to communicate the information. For example, when making most strategic and operating decisions, managers typically rely on managerial accounting information that is prepared in whatever manner the managerial accountant believes provides the

[1] Roush, Chris, "Fields of Green—and Disaster Areas," *Business Week* (January 9, 1995): 94.

best analysis for the decision at hand. Therefore, the majority of the managerial accounting issues explained in this book do not reference a formal set of external rules, but instead consider the context of the given decision (relevant vs. irrelevant cost information for make-or-buy decisions, full cost vs. functional cost information for pricing decisions, etc.).

However, there is one major exception. Managerial accountants must follow specific external reporting rules (i.e., generally accepted accounting principles) when their companies provide outside parties with cost information about the amount of ending inventory on the balance sheet and the cost of goods sold on the income statement. In order to calculate these two amounts, managerial accountants must subdivide costs into functional categories: production and period (i.e., nonproduction). The following section describes the process for categorizing costs as either product or period in nature.

Product (manufacturing) costs are those costs, both direct and indirect, of producing a product in a manufacturing firm or of acquiring a product in a merchandising firm and preparing it for sale. Therefore, only costs in the *production* section of the value chain are included in product costs. A key feature of product costs is that they are inventoried. Product costs initially are added to an inventory account and remain in inventory until they are sold, at which time they are transferred to cost of goods sold (COGS). Product costs can be further classified as direct materials, direct labour, and manufacturing overhead, which are the three cost elements that can be assigned to products for external financial reporting (e.g., inventories or COGS). Exhibit 2-3 shows how direct materials, direct labour, and overhead become product costs.

Direct Materials

Direct materials are those materials that are a part of the final product and can be directly traced to the goods being produced. The cost of these materials can be directly charged to products because physical observation can be used to measure the quantity used by each product. Materials that become part of a

Exhibit 2-3

Product Costs Include Direct Materials, Direct Labour, and Overhead

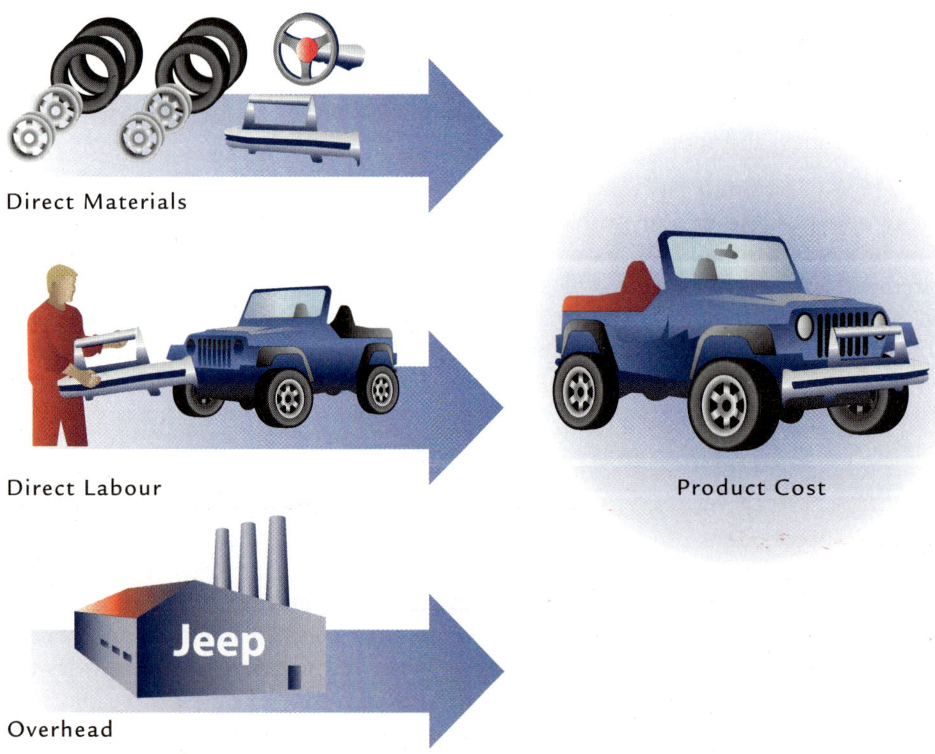

product usually are classified as direct materials. For example, tires on a new **Porsche** automobile, alcohol in an **Estée Lauder** cologne, and denim in a pair of **Diesel** jeans are all part of direct materials for manufacturers of these products.

A closely related term is raw materials. Often, the inventory of materials is called the *raw materials account.* Materials in the raw materials account do not become *direct materials* until they are withdrawn from inventory for use in production. The raw materials inventory account can include indirect materials as well as direct materials. Indirect materials are used in the production process but the amount used by each unit cannot be easily determined and, as a result, these costs are treated as indirect costs (as discussed later).

Direct Labour

Direct labour is the labour that can be directly traced to the goods being produced. Physical observation can be used to measure the amount of labour used to produce a product. Those employees who convert direct materials into a product are classified as direct labour. For example, workers on an assembly line at **Dell Computers** are classified as direct labour.

Just as there were indirect materials in a company, there may also be indirect labour. This labour is not direct labour since these workers do not actually make the product. However, their contribution is necessary to production. An example of indirect labour in a production setting is the maintenance crew that performs regularly scheduled preventative maintenance every week at **Abitibi Consolidated Inc.** in Thunder Bay, Ontario. Indirect labour is included in overhead and, therefore, is an indirect cost rather than a direct cost.

Manufacturing Overhead

All product costs other than direct materials and direct labour are put into a category called **manufacturing overhead**. In a manufacturing firm, manufacturing overhead also is known as *factory burden* or *indirect* manufacturing costs. Costs are included as manufacturing overhead if they cannot be traced to the cost object of interest (e.g., unit of product). The manufacturing overhead cost category contains a wide variety of items. Examples of manufacturing overhead costs include depreciation on plant buildings and equipment, janitorial and maintenance labour, plant supervision, materials handling, power for plant utilities, and plant property taxes. The important thing to remember is that all costs in the factory are classified as direct materials, direct labour, or manufacturing overhead. No product cost can be omitted from classification, no matter how far removed you might think it is from the actual production of a product. Earlier we mentioned that indirect materials and indirect labour are included in overhead. In manufacturing, the glue used in furniture or toys is an example, as is the cost of oil to grease cookie sheets for producing cookies.

CONCEPT Q&A

Focus on any object in the room. What do you think the direct materials for that object might include? What kind of direct labour might have worked on that object? Finally, what types of overhead costs might have been incurred by the company that produced it?

Answers on pages 711 to 715.

Total Product Cost

The total product cost equals the sum of direct materials, direct labour, and manufacturing overhead. The unit product cost equals total product cost divided by the number of units produced. Cornerstone 2-1 shows how to calculate total product cost and per unit product cost.

Product costs include direct materials, direct labour, and manufacturing overhead. Once the product is finished, no more costs attach to it. That is, any costs associated with storing, selling, and delivering the product are not product costs, but instead are period costs.

Prime and Conversion Costs

Product costs of direct materials, direct labour, and manufacturing overhead are sometimes grouped into prime cost and conversion cost. **Prime cost** is the sum of direct materials cost and direct labour cost. **Conversion cost** is the sum of direct labour cost and manufacturing overhead cost. For a manufacturing firm, conversion cost can be interpreted as the cost of

CORNERSTONE 2-1

The HOW and WHY of Calculating Product Cost in Total and Per Unit

Information:

BlueDenim Company makes blue jeans. Last week, direct materials (denim, thread, zippers, and rivets) costing $48,000 were put into production. Direct labour of $30,000 (50 workers × 40 hours × $15 per hour) was incurred. Overhead equalled $72,000. By the end of the week, the company had manufactured 30,000 pairs of jeans.

Required:

Calculate the total product cost for last week. Calculate the cost of one pair of jeans that was produced last week.

Solution:

Direct materials	$ 48,000
Direct labour	30,000
Overhead	72,000
Total product cost	$150,000

Per-unit product cost = $150,000/30,000 = $5

Therefore, one pair of jeans costs $5 to produce.

WHY:

1. To price products right.
2. To price finished goods and WIP ending inventories right.
3. To determine product profitability correctly.

ANALYTICAL Q&A

A company produced and sold 1,000 units last month. Direct materials totalled $4,000, direct labour totalled $5,000, and overhead amounted to $10,000. (1) What is total prime cost for last month? (2) What is conversion cost per unit?

Answers on pages 711 to 715.

converting raw materials into a final product. Cornerstone 2-2 shows how to calculate prime cost and conversion cost for a manufactured product.

Period Costs

The costs of production are assets that are carried in inventories until the goods are sold. There are other costs of running a company, referred to as *period costs*, that are not carried in inventory.

Period costs are all costs that are not product costs (i.e., all areas of the value chain except for production). The cost of office supplies, research and development activities, the CEO's salary, and advertising are examples of period costs. For example, a 30-second advertisement during highly watched shows such as the Super Bowl costs $1 million or so. The Super Bowl's ratings are high, with many millions of people watching; even so, there are some who question the wisdom of spending such high sums of money for 30 seconds of advertising exposure. Managerial accountants help executives at companies like **Apple Computer** determine whether such costly advertising campaigns generate enough additional sales revenue over the long run to make them profitable.

Period costs cannot be assigned to products or appear as part of the reported values of inventories on the balance sheet. Instead, period costs typically are expensed in the period in which they are incurred. However, if a period cost is expected to provide an economic benefit (i.e., revenues) beyond the next year, then it is recorded as an asset (i.e., capitalized) and allocated to expense through depreciation throughout its useful life. The cost associated with the purchase of a delivery truck is an example

The HOW and WHY of Calculating Prime Cost and Conversion Cost in Total and Per Unit

CORNERSTONE 2-2

Information:

BlueDenim Company makes blue jeans. Last week, direct materials (denim, thread, zippers, and rivets) costing $48,000 were put into production. Direct labour of $30,000 (50 workers × 40 hours × $15 per hour) was incurred. Overhead equalled $72,000. By the end of the week, the company had manufactured 30,000 pairs of jeans.

Required:

Calculate the total prime cost for last week. Calculate the per-unit prime cost. Calculate the total conversion cost for last week. Calculate the per-unit conversion cost.

Solution:

Direct materials	$48,000
Direct labour	30,000
Total prime cost	$78,000

Per-unit prime cost = $78,000/30,000 = $2.60

Direct labour	$ 30,000
Overhead	72,000
Total conversion cost	$102,000

Per-unit conversion cost = $102,000/30,000 = $3.40

Note: Remember that prime cost and conversion cost do NOT equal total product cost. This is because direct labour is part of BOTH prime cost and conversion cost.

WHY:

To be able to determine accurately the expenses for each accounting period and therefore the profits. Also, to be able to capitalize expenditures for assets and depreciate (amortize) them accordingly.

of a period cost that would be capitalized when incurred and then recognized as an expense over the useful life of the truck. Exhibit 2-4 depicts the distinction between product and period costs and how each type of cost eventually becomes an expense on the income statement. As shown in the exhibit, product costs, which are capitalized as an inventory asset, are expensed on the income statement as cost of goods sold to match against the revenues generated from the sale of the inventory. However, capitalized period costs are depreciated to expense on the income statement over the asset's useful life to match against the revenues generated by the asset over its useful life.

In a manufacturing organization, the level of period costs can be significant (often greater than 25 percent of sales revenue), and controlling them may bring greater cost savings than the same effort exercised in controlling production costs. For example, in 2007, **Nike**'s period expenses were 35 percent of its revenue ($5,669,000,000/ $16,325,900,000)! For service organizations, the relative importance of selling and administrative costs depends on the nature of the service produced. Physicians and dentists, for example, do relatively little marketing and thus have very low selling costs. On the other hand, a grocery chain may incur substantial marketing costs. Period costs often are divided into selling costs and administrative costs.

Exhibit 2-4

The Impact of Product vs. Period Costs on the Financial Statements

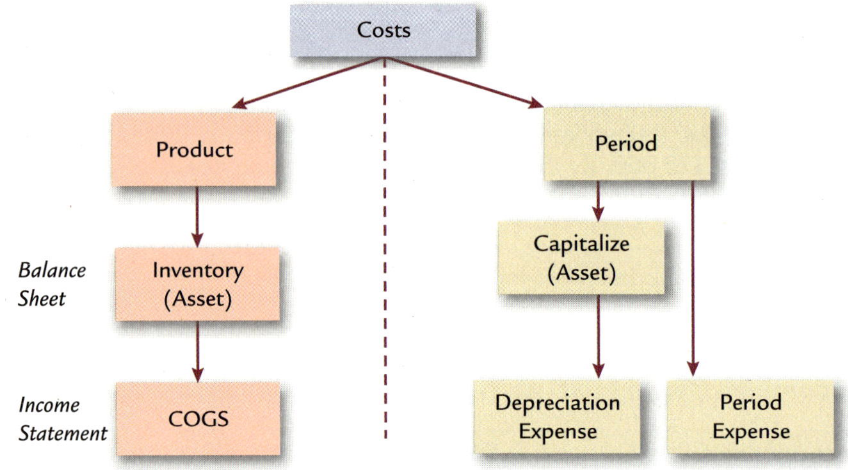

Selling Costs Those costs necessary to market, distribute, and service a product or service are **selling costs**. They are often referred to as *order-getting* and *order-filling* costs. Examples of selling costs include salaries and commissions of sales personnel, advertising, warehousing, shipping, and customer service. The first two items are examples of order-getting costs; the last three are order-filling costs.

Administrative Costs All costs associated with research, development, and general administration of the organization that cannot reasonably be assigned to either selling or production are **administrative costs**. General administration has the responsibility of ensuring that the various activities of the organization are properly integrated so that the overall mission of the firm is realized. The president of the firm, for example, is concerned with the efficiency of selling, production, and research and development activities. Proper integration of these activities is essential to maximizing the overall profits of a firm. Examples of general administrative costs are executive salaries, legal fees, printing the annual report, and general accounting. Research and development costs are the costs associated with designing and developing new products and must be expensed in the period incurred.

As with product costs, it is often helpful to distinguish between direct period costs and indirect period costs. Service companies also make this important distinction. For example, a surgical centre would show that surgical gauze and anesthesia are direct costs used for an operation because it could be determined how much gauze or anesthesia was used for each procedure or patient. Other examples of direct costs in service industries include the chef in a restaurant, a surgical nurse attending an open heart operation, and a pilot for **WestJet**.

Alternatively, though shampoo and hair spray are used in a beauty shop, the exact amount used in each individual's hair cut is not easily determinable. As a result, the costs associated with shampoo and hair spray would be considered indirect, or overhead, costs and allocated, rather than traced, to individual hair cuts. Examples of indirect labour costs in a service setting include the surgical assistants in a hospital who clean up the operating room after surgery, dispose of certain used materials, and sterilize the reusable instruments. Indirect labour is included in overhead. The rental of a Santa suit for the annual company Christmas party would be an example of an indirect cost that would be expensed in the period incurred. Though these costs do not affect the calculation of inventories or COGS (i.e., because they are service companies), their correct classification nonetheless affects numerous decisions and planning and control activities for managers, as we will discuss in detail in future chapters.

Preparing Financial Statements for Manufacturing Operations

OBJECTIVE 3
Prepare income statements for manufacturing and service organizations.

The earlier definitions of product, selling, and administrative costs provide a good conceptual overview of these important costs. However, the actual calculation of these costs in practice is a bit more complicated. Let's take a closer look at just how costs are calculated for purposes of preparing the external financial statements, focusing first on manufacturing firms.

Financial Statements for Manufacturing Operations

The operations of a business can be classified as one of the following:

- service
- merchandising
- manufacturing

The accounting for service and merchandising businesses is described and illustrated in basically all financial accounting courses. This text focuses mainly on manufacturing businesses. However, most of the managerial accounting concepts discussed in this text also apply to service and merchandising businesses.

The cost of a manufactured product includes the cost of materials used in making the product. It also includes the cost of converting those materials into a finished product. Thus, the cost of a finished product includes the following:

- Direct materials cost
- Direct labour cost
- Factory overhead cost

Direct Materials Cost

Manufactured products begin with raw materials, which are converted into finished products. The cost of any material that is an integral part of the finished product is classified as a **direct materials cost**. Direct materials costs include, for example, the cost of the electronic components in a television, and the tires on an automobile. To be classified as a direct materials cost, the material must:

(a) be easily traceable and recognizable, as well as integral to the finished product, *and*
(b) reflect a significant portion of the total cost of the product.

Insignificant costs such as the glue used to produce a TV or the lubricants used to make automobile tires shine might be classified as factory overhead costs.

Direct Labour Cost

Most manufacturing products use employee labour to convert materials into finished products. The wages of employees who are integral to the finished product are classified as a **direct labour cost**. For example, machine operators' wages for assembling a TV are direct labour costs, and so are mechanics' wages for manufacturing an automobile. As with direct materials cost, a direct labour cost must:

(a) be easily traceable to production, as well as an integral part to the finished product; *and*
(b) reflect a significant portion of the total cost of the product.

The wages of the cleaning staff who clean the car or TV factory are not a direct labour cost, nor are those of the security staff who guard the factory at night. This is because cleaning and security costs are not an integral part of, or a significant cost of, each TV or car. Instead, such costs are classified as a factory overhead cost.

Factory Overhead Cost (Manufacturing Overhead)

Costs other than direct materials cost and direct labour cost that are incurred in the manufacturing process are combined and classified as **factory overhead cost**. All factory overhead costs are indirect costs of the product. Factory overhead costs may include the following:

- Heat and light for the factory
- Power to run the machines
- Salaries for factory supervisors
- Factory caretaking wages
- Equipment repair and maintenance
- Property taxes on factory buildings and land
- Insurance on factory buildings
- Amortization of factory plant and equipment

Factory overhead cost also includes costs for materials that do not enter directly into the finished product. Examples include lubricants, glue, buffing compounds, and machine coolants.

When you total direct material, direct labour, and factory overhead, you arrive at **manufacturing costs**.

The retained earnings and cash flow statements for a manufacturing business are similar to those illustrated in financial accounting courses for service and merchandising businesses. However, the balance sheet and income statement for a manufacturing business are more complex.

Balance Sheet for a Manufacturing Business

A manufacturing business reports three types of inventory on its balance sheet. **Materials inventory** consists of the costs of the direct and indirect materials that have not entered the manufacturing process. **Work in process inventory (WIP)** consists of the direct materials, direct labour, and factory overhead costs for products that have entered the manufacturing process but are not yet completed. WIP inventory includes all products still being made, regardless of the level of completion (i.e., they could be 10, 20, 30, or 90 percent complete). **Finished goods inventory** consists of completed (or finished) products that have not been sold. Exhibit 2-5 below illustrates how inventories are reported on the balance sheets of a merchandising and a manufacturing business respectively.

Income Statement for a Manufacturing Business

The income statements for merchandising and manufacturing businesses differ mainly in how they report the cost of goods purchased and the cost of goods manufactured during the period. These differences are shown in Exhibit 2-6.

A merchandising business purchases merchandise ready for resale to customers. The total cost of the *finished goods available for sale* during the period is determined by adding beginning finished goods inventory to net purchases. The *cost of finished goods sold* is determined by subtracting ending finished goods inventory from cost of merchandise available for sale.

A manufacturer makes the products it sells, using direct materials, direct labour, and factory overhead. The total cost of making products that are available for sale during the period is called the **cost of goods manufactured**.

Exhibit 2-5

Balance Sheet Reporting of Inventories

Merchandising Business		**Manufacturing Business**	
Current assets:		Current assets:	
Cash	$ 100,000	Cash	$ 100,000
Accounts receivable	300,000	Accounts receivable	300,000
Finished Goods Inventory	**150,000**	**Finished Goods Inventory**	**150,000**
Supplies	50,000	**WIP Inventory**	**20,000**
Total current assets	$ 600,000	**Raw Material Inventory**	**80,000**
		Supplies	50,000
		Total current assets	$ 700,000

Exhibit 2-6

Income Statements: Merchandising and Manufacturing

Merchandising Business		**Manufacturing Business**	
Sales	$1,000,000	Sales	$1,000,000
Beginning **finished goods** inventory	$ 100,000	Beginning **finished goods** inventory	$ 100,000
Plus **net purchases**	800,000	Plus **cost of goods manufactured**	800,000
Cost of finished goods available for sale	$ 900,000	Cost of finished goods available for sale	$ 900,000
Less ending finished goods inventory	150,000	Less ending finished goods inventory	150,000
Cost of merchandise sold	$ 750,000	Cost of merchandise sold	$ 750,000
Gross profit	$ 250,000	Gross profit	$ 250,000

To determine the *cost of goods sold*, and thus to prepare the income statement, first the cost of goods manufactured needs to be calculated. The cost of goods manufactured is often determined by preparing a *statement of cost of goods manufactured*. A model of such a statement is shown below.

Statement of Cost of Goods Manufactured

Direct materials:	
Direct materials beginning inventory	$XXX
Plus purchases of direct materials	XXX
Cost of materials available for use	$XXX
Less direct materials ending inventory	XXX
Cost of direct materials used	$XXX
Plus direct labour	XXX
Plus factory overhead	XXX
Total manufacturing costs incurred	$XXX
Plus work-in-process beginning inventory	XXX
Less work-in-process ending inventory	XXX
Cost of goods manufactured	$XXX

The statement of cost of goods manufactured is prepared using these three steps:

Step 1. Determine the *cost of direct materials used.*

Materials inventory, January 1, 2012	$ 65,000
Plus materials purchased	100,000
Cost of materials available for use	$ 165,000
Less materials inventory, December 31, 2012	45,000
Cost of direct materials used	$ 120,000

Step 2. Determine the *total manufacturing costs incurred.*

Cost of direct materials used in production (Step 1)	$120,000
All direct labour	210,000
All factory overhead	70,000
Total manufacturing costs incurred	$400,000

The total manufacturing costs incurred in 2012 of $400,000 are determined by adding the direct materials used in production (Step 1), the direct labour cost, and the factory overhead costs.

Step 3. Determine the *cost of goods manufactured.*

Total manufacturing costs incurred (Step 2)	$ 400,000
Work-in-process inventory, January 1, 2012	$ 50,000
Total manufacturing costs	$ 450,000
Less work-in-process inventory, December 31, 2012	$ 80,000
Cost of goods manufactured	$ 380,000

The cost of goods manufactured of $380,000 is determined by adding to the manufacturing costs the WIP beginning inventory and subtracting the WIP ending inventory. Thus the statement of cost of goods manufactured is shaped as follows:

Statement of Costs of Goods Manufactured
For the Year Ended December 31, 2012

Materials inventory, January 1, 2012	$ 65,000
Plus materials purchased	100,000
Cost of materials available for use	$ 165,000
Less materials inventory, December 31, 2012	45,000
Cost of direct materials used	$ 120,000
Plus direct labour	210,000
Plus factory overhead	70,000
Total current manufacturing costs incurred	$ 400,000
Plus work-in-process inventory, January 1, 2012	$ 50,000
Total manufacturing costs	$ 450,000
Less work-in-process inventory, December 31, 2012	$ 80,000
Cost of goods manufactured	$ 380,000

Income Statement
For the Year Ended December 31, 2012

Sales	$700,000
Cost of goods sold:	
Finished goods inventory, January 1, 2012	$100,000
Cost of goods manufactured	380,000
Cost of finished goods available for sale	480,000
Less finished goods inventory, December 31, 2012	80,000
Cost of goods sold	$400,000
Gross profit	300,000
Operating expenses:	
Selling expenses	120,000
Administrative expenses	90,000
Total operating expenses	$210,000
Net income	$ 90,000

The *cost of finished goods available for sale* is determined by adding the beginning finished goods inventory to the cost of goods manufactured during the period. The **cost of goods sold** is determined by subtracting the ending finished goods inventory from the cost of finished goods available for sale.

Cost of Goods Manufactured: A Second Look

The *cost of goods manufactured* represents the total product cost of goods *completed* during the current period and transferred to finished goods inventory. The only costs assigned to goods completed are the manufacturing costs of direct materials, direct labour, and manufacturing overhead. So, why don't we just add together the current period's costs of direct materials, direct labour, and manufacturing overhead to arrive at cost of goods sold? The reason is inventories of materials and work in process. For instance, some of the materials purchased in the current period likely were used in production (i.e., transferred from materials inventory to work-in-process inventory during the period). However, other materials likely were not used in production, and thus remain in materials inventory at period end. Also, some of the units that were worked on (and thus allocated labour and manufacturing overhead costs) in the current period likely were completed during the period (i.e., transferred from work-in-process inventory to finished goods inventory during the period). However, other units worked on during the period likely were not completed during the period, and thus remain in work-in-process inventory at period end. In calculating cost of goods

The HOW and WHY of Calculating the Direct Materials Used in Production

CORNERSTONE 2-3

Information:

BlueDenim Company makes blue jeans. On May 1, BlueDenim had $68,000 of materials in inventory. During the month of May, the company purchased $210,000 of materials. On May 31, materials inventory equalled $22,000.

Required:

Calculate the direct materials used in production for the month of May.

Solution:

Materials inventory, May 1	$ 68,000
Purchases	210,000
Materials inventory, May 31	(22,000)
Direct materials used in production	$256,000

WHY:

Because manufacturing costs include direct materials used in the production, and if we were to omit direct materials, the manufacturing costs would be understated. Also, this calculation of DM used allows us to determine the ending materials inventories. (BI of Raw Material plus DM purchased less DM used equals EI of Raw Materials.)

sold, we need to distinguish between the total manufacturing cost for the current period and the manufacturing costs associated with the units that were completed during the current period (i.e., cost of goods manufactured).

Let's take a look at direct materials. Suppose a company had no materials on hand at the beginning of the month, then bought $15,000 of direct materials during the month and used all of them in production. The entire $15,000 would be properly called *direct materials.* Usually, though, the company has some materials on hand at the beginning of the month. These materials are the beginning inventory of materials. Let's say that this beginning inventory of materials cost $2,500. Then during the month, the company would have a total of $17,500 of materials that could be used in production ($2,500 from beginning inventory and $15,000 purchased during the month). Typically, the company would not use the entire amount of materials on hand in production. Perhaps they use only $12,000 of materials. Then, the cost of direct materials used in production this month is $12,000 and the remaining $5,500 of materials is the ending inventory of materials. This reasoning can be easily expressed in a formula.

$$\text{Beginning inventory of materials} + \text{Purchases} - \text{Direct materials used in production} = \text{Ending inventory of materials}$$

While this computation is logical and simple, it does not express the result for which we usually are looking. We are usually trying to figure out the amount of direct materials used in production—not the amount of ending inventory. Cornerstone 2-3 shows how to compute the amount of direct materials used in production.

Once the direct materials are calculated, the direct labour and manufacturing overhead *for the time period* can be added to get the total manufacturing cost for the period. Now we need to consider the second type of inventory—work in process.

Work in process, often abbreviated as WIP, is the cost of the partially completed goods that are still on the factory floor at the end of a time period. These are units that have been started but are not finished. They have value, but not as much as they

CORNERSTONE 2-4

The HOW and WHY of Calculating Cost of Goods Manufactured (COGM)

Information:

Recall that BlueDenim Company makes blue jeans. During the month of May, the company purchased $210,000 of materials. On May 31, materials inventory equalled $22,000. During the month of May, BlueDenim Company incurred direct labour cost of $135,000 and manufacturing overhead of $150,000. Inventory information is as follows:

	May 1	May 31
Materials	$68,000	$22,000
Work in process	50,000	16,000

Required:

Calculate the cost of goods manufactured for the month of May. Calculate the cost of one pair of jeans assuming that 115,000 pairs of jeans were completed during May.

Solution:

Direct materials*	$256,000
Direct labour	135,000
Manufacturing overhead	150,000
Total manufacturing cost for May	$541,000
WIP, May 1	50,000
WIP, May 31	(16,000)
Cost of goods manufactured	$575,000

* Direct materials = $68,000 + $210,000 − $22,000 = $256,000
This amount was calculated in Cornerstone 2-3.
Per-unit cost of goods manufactured = $575,000/115,000 units = $5

WHY:

Because this calculation allows the determination of what it costs (direct material, direct labour, and overhead) to manufacture completed units of a product in the current period. The costs of incomplete units (WIPEI) are passed on to the next accounting period. This accounting treatment is in compliance with the requirement to report only current costs in the current period.

will when they are completed. Just as there are beginning and ending inventories of materials, there are beginning and ending inventories of WIP. We must adjust the total manufacturing cost for the time period for the inventories of WIP. When that is done, we will have the total cost of the goods that were completed and transferred from work-in-process inventory to finished goods inventory during the time period. Cornerstone 2-4 shows how to calculate the cost of goods manufactured for a particular time period.

Cost of Goods Sold

To meet external reporting requirements, costs must be classified into three categories: production, selling, and administration. Remember that product costs are initially put into inventory. They become expenses only when the products are sold, which matches the expenses of manufacturing the product to the sales revenue generated by the product at the time it is sold. Therefore, the expense of manufacturing is not the cost of goods manufactured; instead it is the cost of the goods that are sold.

The HOW and WHY of Calculating Cost of Goods Sold (COGS)

CORNERSTONE 2-5

Information:
Recall that BlueDenim Company makes blue jeans. During the month of May, 115,000 pairs of jeans were completed at a cost of goods manufactured of $575,000. Suppose that on May 1, BlueDenim had 10,000 units in the finished goods inventory costing $50,000 and on May 31, the company had 26,000 units in the finished goods inventory costing $130,000.

Required:
Prepare a cost of goods sold statement for the month of May. Calculate the number of pairs of jeans that were sold during May.

Solution:

BlueDenim Company
Cost of Goods Sold Statement
For the Month of May

Cost of goods manufactured	$ 575,000
Finished goods inventory, May 1	50,000
Finished good inventory, May 31	(130,000)
Cost of goods sold	$ 495,000
Number of units sold:	
Finished goods inventory, May 1	10,000
Units finished during May	115,000
Finished goods inventory, May 31	(26,000)
Units sold during May	99,000

WHY:
Because we need to know the cost of what was sold to determine accurately the profit for the accounting period by subtracting it from revenue.

Cost of goods sold represents the cost of goods that were sold during the period and, therefore, transferred from finished goods inventory on the balance sheet to cost of goods sold on the income statement (i.e., as an inventory expense). Cornerstone 2-5 shows how to calculate the cost of goods sold.

The ending inventories of materials, WIP, and finished goods are important because they are assets and appear on the balance sheet (as current assets). The cost of goods sold is an expense that appears on the income statement. Selling and administrative costs are period costs and also appear on the income statement as an expense. Collectively, Cornerstones 2-3, 2-4, and 2-5 depict the flow of costs through the three inventories (materials, work in process, and finished goods) and finally into cost of goods sold.

Income Statement: Manufacturing Firm

The income statement for a manufacturing firm is displayed in Cornerstone 2-6. This income statement follows the traditional format taught in an introductory financial accounting course. Notice that the income statement covers a certain period of time (i.e., the month of May in Cornerstone 2-6). However, the time period may vary. The key point is that all sales revenue and expenses attached to that period of time appear on the income statement.

Look at the income statement in Cornerstone 2-6. First, the heading tells us what type of statement it is, for what firm, and for what period of time. Then, the

CORNERSTONE 2-6

The HOW and WHY of Preparing an Income Statement for a Manufacturing Firm

Information:
Recall that BlueDenim Company sold 99,000 pairs of jeans during the month of May at a total cost of $495,000. Each pair sold at a price of $8. BlueDenim also incurred two types of selling costs: commissions equal to 10 percent of the sales price, and other selling expenses of $120,000. Administrative expense totalled $85,000.

Required:
Prepare an income statement for BlueDenim for the month of May.

Solution:

BlueDenim Company
Income Statement
For the Month of May

Sales revenue (99,000 × $8)		$792,000
Cost of goods sold		495,000
Gross margin		$297,000
Less:		
Selling expense		
Commissions (0.10 × $792,000)	$ 79,200	
Fixed selling expense	120,000	199,200
Administrative expense		85,000
Operating income		$ 12,800

WHY:
Because it is mandatory for reporting purposes (to the Canada Revenue Agency). Also, because it is fundamental in determining the firm's profitability and therefore its income tax liability.

income statement itself always begins with "sales revenue" (or "sales" or "revenue"). The sales revenue is the price multiplied by the units sold. After the sales revenue is determined, the firm must calculate expenses for the period.

Notice that the expenses are separated into three categories: production (cost of goods sold), selling, and administrative. The first type of expense is the cost of producing the units sold, or the cost of goods sold. This amount was computed and explained in Cornerstone 2-5. Remember that the cost of goods sold is the cost of producing the units that were sold during the time period. It includes direct materials, direct labour, and manufacturing overhead. It does *not* include any selling or administrative expenses. In the case of a retail (i.e., a merchandising) firm, the cost of goods sold represents the total cost of the goods sold when they were purchased from an outside supplier. Therefore, the cost of goods sold for a retailer equals the purchase costs adjusted for the beginning and ending balances in its single inventory account. A merchandising firm, such as **Old Navy**, has only one inventory account because it does not transform the purchased good into a different form by adding materials, labour, and overhead, as does a manufacturing firm.

Gross margin is the difference between sales revenue and cost of goods sold. It shows how much the firm is making over and above the cost of the units sold. Gross margin does *not* equal operating income or profit. Selling and administrative expenses have not yet been subtracted. However, gross margin does provide useful information. If gross margin is positive, the firm at least charges prices that cover the product cost. In addition, the firm can calculate its gross margin percentage (gross

The HOW and WHY of Calculating the Percentage of Sales Revenue for Each Line on the Income Statement

CORNERSTONE 2-7

Information:
Recall that BlueDenim Company's income statement for the month of May was shown in Cornerstone 2-6.

Required:
Calculate the percentage of sales revenue represented by each line of the income statement.

Solution:

BlueDenim Company
Income Statement
For the Month of May

			Percent*
Sales revenue (99,000 × $8)		$792,000	100.0
Cost of goods sold		495,000	62.5
Gross margin		$297,000	37.5
Less:			
Selling expense			
Commissions (0.10 × $792,000)	$ 79,200		
Fixed selling expense	120,000	199,200	25.2
Administrative expense		85,000	10.7
Operating income		$ 12,800	1.6

* Steps in calculating the percentages:

1. Sales revenue percent = $792,000/$792,000 = 1.00 or 100% (sales revenue is always 100% of itself)
2. Cost of goods sold percent = $495,000/$792,000 = 0.625 or 62.5%
3. Gross margin percent = $297,000/$792,000 = 0.375 or 37.5%
4. Selling expense percent = $199,200/$792,000 = 0.252 or 25.2% (this has been rounded)
5. Administrative expense percent = $85,000/$792,000 = 0.107 or 10.7% (this has been rounded)
6. Operating income expense percent = $12,800/$792,000 = 0.016 or 1.6% (this has been rounded)

WHY:
Because the absolute amounts do not always tell the entire story. The percentage of sales revenue allows for comparisons across the board, no matter how big or small the absolute amounts.

margin/sales revenue), as shown in Cornerstone 2-7, and compare it with the average gross margin percentage for the industry to see if its experience is in the ballpark with other firms in the industry. Gross margin percentage varies significantly by industry. Grocery stores such as **Sobeys** traditionally have low profit margins. They earn only a few pennies per food item (e.g., a bag of sugar). Luxury stores such as jewellery stores enjoy a high profit margin of 300 percent and over. The overall profitability of low-margin companies is driven by high turnover, that is, high sales (a grocery store sells many bags of sugar). The overall profitability of a jewellery store is driven by the high profit margin since a jewellery store sells fewer pieces of jewellery than a grocery store sells grocery items.

Finally, selling expense and administrative expense for the period are subtracted from gross margin to arrive at operating income. Operating income is the key figure from the income statement; it is profit, and shows how much the owners are actually earning from the company. Again, calculating the percentage of operating income (i.e., operating income/sales revenue) and comparing it to the average for the industry gives the owners valuable information about relative profitability.

CORNERSTONE 2-8

The HOW and WHY of Preparing an Income Statement for a Service Organization

Information:

Komala Information Systems designs and installs human resources software for small companies. Last month, Komala had software licensing costs of $5,000, service technicians costs of $35,000, and research and development costs of $55,000. Selling expenses were $5,000, and administrative expenses equalled $7,000. Sales totalled $130,000.

Required:

Prepare an income statement for Komala Information Systems for the past month.

Solution:

Komala Information Systems
Income Statement
For the Past Month

Sales revenues:		$130,000
Less operating expenses:		
Software licensing	$ 5,000	
Service technicians	35,000	
Research and development	55,000	
Selling expenses	5,000	
Administrative expenses	7,000	107,000
Operating income		$ 23,000

WHY:

Because it is mandatory for reporting purposes (CRA). Also, because it is fundamental in determining the firm's profitability and therefore its income tax liability.

The income statement can be analyzed further by calculating the percentage of sales revenue represented by each line of the statement, as was done in Cornerstone 2-7. How can management use this information? The first thing that jumps out is that operating income is less than 2 percent of sales revenue. That's a very small percentage. Unless this is common for the blue jeans manufacturing business, BlueDenim's management should work hard to increase the percentage. Selling expense is a whopping 25.2 percent of sales! Do commissions really need to be that high? Or is the price too low (compared to competitors' prices)? Can cost of goods sold be reduced? Is 62.5 percent reasonable? These are questions that are suggested by Cornerstone 2-7, but not answered. Answering the questions is the job of management.

ANALYTICAL Q&A

Your friend, Ted, mentioned that **Zellers** department store marks up sweaters by 100 percent. "Wow," said Ted, "So a sweater that costs them $25 is sold for $50—they're making $25 in profit (operating income)!"Is Ted correct? Refer to the income statement from Cornerstone 2-7. What line would include the $50 price of the sweater? What line would include the $25 original cost (to the store) of the sweater? What line would include the $25 that is over and above the cost?

Answers on pages 711 to 715.

Income Statement: Service Firm

In a service organization, there is no product to purchase (e.g., a merchandiser like **RONA**) or to manufacture (e.g., **Toshiba**), and, therefore, there are no beginning or ending inventories. As a result, there is no cost of goods sold or gross margin on the income statement. Instead, the cost of providing services appears along with the other operating expenses of the company. For example, **Southwest Airlines**' 2007 income statement begins with total operating revenues of $9,861,000,000 and subtracts total operating expenses of $9,070,000,000 to arrive at an operating income of $791,000,000. An income statement for a service firm is shown in Cornerstone 2-8.

Summary of Learning Objectives

LO1. Explain the meaning of cost and how costs are assigned to products and services.

- Cost is the cash or cash-equivalent value sacrificed for goods and services that are expected to bring a current or future benefit to the organization.
- Managers use cost information to determine the cost of objects such as products, projects, plants, and customers.
- Direct costs are traced to cost objects based on cause-and-effect relationships.
- Indirect (i.e., overhead) costs are allocated to cost objects based on assumed relationships and convenience.

LO2. Define the various costs of manufacturing products and providing services as well as the costs of selling and administration.

- Products are goods that either are purchased or produced by converting raw materials through the use of labour and indirect manufacturing resources, such as plants, land, and machinery. Services are tasks performed for a customer or activities performed by a customer using an organization's products or facilities.
- Product costs are those costs, both direct and indirect, of acquiring a product in a merchandising business and preparing it for sale or of producing a product in a manufacturing business. Product costs are classified as inventory on the balance sheet and then expensed as cost of goods sold on the income statement when the inventory is sold.
- Selling costs are the costs of marketing and distributing goods and services and administrative costs are the costs of organizing and running a company.
- Both selling and administrative costs are period costs.

LO3. Prepare income statements for manufacturing and service organizations.

- The cost of goods manufactured (COGM) represents the total product cost of goods *completed* during the period and transferred to finished goods inventory. The cost of goods sold (COGS) represents the cost of goods that were sold during the period and, therefore, transferred from finished goods inventory to cost of goods sold. For a retailer, there is no COGM, and COGS equals the beginning inventory plus net purchases minus ending inventory.
- For manufacturing and merchandising firms, cost of goods sold is subtracted from sales revenue to arrive at gross margin. In addition, for manufacturing firms, cost of goods manufactured must first be calculated before calculating cost of goods sold.
- Service firms do not calculate gross margin because they do not purchase or produce inventory for sale and, as a result, do not have a cost of goods sold (i.e., inventory expense).
- All firms next subtract selling and administrative expense to arrive at net income.

Summary of Important Equations

1. Total product cost = Direct materials + Direct labour + Manufacturing overhead
2. $\text{Unit product cost} = \dfrac{\text{Total product cost}}{\text{number of units}}$
3. Prime cost = Direct materials + Direct labour
4. Conversion cost = Direct labour + Manufacturing overhead
5. Direct materials used in production = Beginning inventory of materials + Purchases − Ending inventory of materials

6. Cost of goods manufactured = Direct materials used in production + Direct labour used in production + Manufacturing overhead costs used in production + Beginning WIP inventory − Ending WIP inventory
7. Cost of goods sold = Beginning finished goods inventory + Cost of goods manufactured − Ending finished goods inventory

CORNERSTONES FOR CHAPTER 2

CORNERSTONE 2-1 The HOW and WHY of calculating product cost in total and per unit, page 38

CORNERSTONE 2-2 The HOW and WHY of calculating prime cost and conversion cost in total and per unit, page 39

CORNERSTONE 2-3 The HOW and WHY of calculating the direct materials used in production, page 45

CORNERSTONE 2-4 The HOW and WHY of calculating cost of goods manufactured (COGM), page 46

CORNERSTONE 2-5 The HOW and WHY of calculating cost of goods sold (COGS), page 47

CORNERSTONE 2-6 The HOW and WHY of preparing an income statement for a manufacturing firm, page 48

CORNERSTONE 2-7 The HOW and WHY of calculating the percentage of sales revenue for each line on the income statement, page 49

CORNERSTONE 2-8 The HOW and WHY of preparing an income statement for a service organization, page 50

Key Terms

Accumulating costs, 31
Administrative costs, 40
Allocation, 33
Assigning costs, 31
Conversion cost, 37
Cost, 30
Cost object, 31
Cost of goods manufactured, 42
Cost of goods sold, 44
Direct costs, 33
Direct labour, 37
Direct labour cost, 41
Direct materials, 36
Direct materials cost, 41
Expenses, 31
Factory overhead cost, 41
Finished goods inventory, 42
Fixed cost, 34
Gross margin, 48
Indirect costs, 33
Manufacturing costs, 42
Manufacturing organizations, 35
Manufacturing overhead, 37
Materials inventory, 42
Opportunity cost, 34
Period costs, 38
Price, 31
Prime cost, 37
Product (manufacturing) costs, 36
Products, 35
Selling costs, 40
Service organizations, 35
Services, 35
Variable cost, 34
Work in process inventory (WIP), 42

Review Problem

Product Costs, Cost of Goods Manufactured Statement, and the Income Statement

Brody Company makes industrial cleaning solvents. Various chemicals, detergent, and water are mixed together and then bottled in 10-gallon drums. Brody provided the following information for last year:

Raw materials purchases	$250,000
Direct labour	140,000
Depreciation on factory equipment	45,000
Depreciation on factory building	30,000
Depreciation on headquarters building	50,000
Factory insurance	15,000
Property taxes:	
Factory	20,000
Headquarters	18,000
Utilities for factory	34,000
Utilities for sales office	1,800
Administrative salaries	150,000
Indirect labour salaries	156,000
Sales office salaries	90,000
Beginning balance, Raw Materials	124,000
Beginning balance, WIP	124,000
Beginning balance, Finished Goods	84,000
Ending balance, Raw Materials	102,000
Ending balance, WIP	130,000
Ending balance, Finished Goods	82,000

Last year, Brody completed 100,000 units. Sales revenue equalled $1,200,000, and Brody paid a sales commission of 5 percent of sales.

Required:

1. Calculate the direct materials used in production for last year.
2. Calculate total prime cost.
3. Calculate total conversion cost.
4. Prepare a cost of goods manufactured statement for last year. Calculate the unit product cost.
5. Prepare a cost of goods sold statement for last year.
6. Prepare an income statement for last year. Show the percentage of sales that each line item represents.

Solution:

1. Direct materials = $124,000 + $250,000 – $102,000 = $272,000
2. Prime cost = $272,000 + $140,000 = $412,000
3. First, calculate total overhead cost:

Depreciation on factory equipment	$ 45,000
Depreciation on factory building	30,000
Factory insurance	15,000
Factory property taxes	20,000
Factory utilities	34,000
Indirect labour salaries	156,000
Total overhead	$300,000

Conversion cost = $140,000 + $300,000 = $440,000

4.

Direct materials	$272,000
Direct labour	140,000
Overhead	300,000
Total manufacturing cost	$712,000
+ Beginning WIP	124,000
− Ending WIP	130,000
Cost of goods manufactured	$706,000

$$\text{Unit product cost} = \frac{\$706,000}{100,000 \text{ units}} = \$7.06$$

5.

Cost of goods manufactured	$706,000
+ Beginning inventory, Finished goods	84,000
− Ending inventory, Finished goods	82,000
Cost of goods sold	$708,000

6. First, compute selling expense and administrative expense:

Utilities, sales office	$ 1,800
Sales office salaries	90,000
Sales commissions ($1,200,000 × 0.05)	60,000
Selling expense	$151,800
Depreciation on headquarters building	$ 50,000
Property taxes, headquarters	18,000
Administrative salaries	150,000
Administrative expense	$218,000

Brody Company
Income Statement
For Last Year

		Percent
Sales	$1,200,000	100.00
Cost of goods sold	708,000	59.00
Gross margin	$ 492,000	41.00
Less:		
Selling expense	151,800	12.65
Administrative expense	218,000	18.17
Operating income	$ 122,200	10.18

Discussion Questions

1. What is a cost object? Give some examples.
2. What is the difference between accumulating cost and assigning cost?
3. What is a direct cost? An indirect cost? Can the same cost be direct for one purpose and indirect for another? Give an example.
4. What is the cost of goods manufactured?
5. Define *prime cost* and *conversion cost*. Why can't prime cost be added to conversion cost to get total product cost?
6. What is the difference between a product and a service? Give an example of each.
7. Explain the difference between cost and expense.
8. How does a period cost differ from a product cost?
9. What is allocation?
10. Define *manufacturing overhead*.
11. Explain the difference between direct materials purchases in a month and direct materials for the month.

12. Why do firms like to calculate a percentage column on the income statement (in which each line item is expressed as a percentage of sales)?
13. What is the difference between the income statement for a manufacturing firm and the income statement for a service firm?
14. Define *selling cost*. Give five examples of selling cost.
15. What is the difference between cost of goods manufactured and cost of goods sold?

Multiple-Choice Exercises

2-1 Accumulating costs means that

a. costs must be summed and entered on the income statement.
b. each cost must be linked to some cost object.
c. costs must be measured and tracked.
d. costs must be allocated to units of production.
e. costs have expired and must be transferred from the balance sheet to the income statement.

2-2 Product (or manufacturing) costs consist of

a. direct materials, direct labour, and selling costs.
b. direct materials, direct labour, overhead, and operating expense.
c. prime costs and conversion costs.
d. prime costs and overhead.
e. selling and administrative costs.

Last year, Wachman produced and sold 1,000 units at a price of $75 each. Total selling and administrative expense was $30,000.

2-3 Wachman Company produces a product with the following per-unit costs:

Direct materials	$15
Direct labour	6
Manufacturing overhead	10

Conversion cost per unit was

a. $15.
b. $21.
c. $31.
d. $16.
e. none of the above.

2-4 Refer to the Wachman Company information in Multiple-Choice Exercise 2-3. Total gross margin for last year was

a. $75,000.
b. $44,000.
c. $61,000.
d. $9,000.
e. $31,000.

2-5 The accountant in a factory that produces biscuits for fast-food restaurants wants to assign costs to boxes of biscuits. Which of the following costs can be traced directly to boxes of biscuits?

a. the cost of flour and baking soda
b. the wages of the mixing labour
c. the cost of the boxes
d. the cost of packing labour
e. all of the above

2-6 Which of the following is an indirect cost?

a. the cost of denim in a jeans factory
b. the cost of mixing labour in a factory that makes over-the-counter pain relievers
c. the cost of restriping the parking lot at a perfume factory
d. the cost of bottles in a shampoo factory
e. all of the above

2-7 Bobby Dee's is an owner-operated company that details (thoroughly cleans—inside and out) automobiles. Bobby Dee's is which of the following?

a. retailer
b. wholesaler
c. manufacturing firm
d. service firm
e. none of the above

2-8 Kellogg's makes a variety of breakfast cereals. Kellogg's is which of the following?

a. retailer
b. wholesaler
c. manufacturing firm
d. service firm
e. none of the above

2-9 Target is which of the following?

a. retailer
b. wholesaler
c. manufacturing firm
d. service firm
e. none of the above

2-10 Stone Inc. is a company that purchases goods (e.g., chess sets, pottery) from overseas and resells them to gift shops in Canada. Stone Inc. is which of the following?

a. retailer
b. wholesaler
c. manufacturing firm
d. service firm
e. none of the above

2-11 JackMan Company produces diecast metal bulldozers for toy shops. JackMan estimated the following average costs per bulldozer:

Direct materials	$8.65
Direct labour	1.10
Manufacturing overhead	0.95

Prime cost per unit is

a. $8.65.
b. $1.10.
c. $0.95.
d. $2.05.
e. $9.75.

2-12 Which of the following is a period expense?

a. factory insurance
b. CEO salary
c. direct labour
d. factory maintenance
e. all of the above

2-13 Last year, Barnard Company incurred the following costs:

Direct materials	$ 50,000
Direct labour	20,000
Manufacturing overhead	130,000
Selling expense	40,000
Administrative expense	36,000

Barnard produced and sold 10,000 units at a price of $31 each.
Prime cost per unit is

a. $7.00.
b. $20.00.
c. $15.00.
d. $5.00.
e. $27.60.

2-14 Refer to the Barnard Company information in Multiple-Choice Exercise 2-13. Conversion cost per unit is

a. $7.00.
b. $20.00.
c. $15.00.
d. $5.00.
e. $27.60.

2-15 Refer to the Barnard Company information in Multiple-Choice Exercise 2-13. The cost of goods sold per unit is

a. $7.00.
b. $20.00.
c. $15.00.
d. $5.00.
e. $27.60.

2-16 Refer to the Barnard Company information in Multiple-Choice Exercise 2-13. The gross margin per unit is

a. $24.00.
b. $11.00.
c. $16.00.
d. $26.00.
e. $3.40.

2-17 Refer to the Barnard Company information in Multiple-Choice Exercise 2-13. The total period expense is

a. $276,000.
b. $200,000.
c. $76,000.
d. $40,000.
e. $36,000.

2-18 Refer to the Barnard Company information in Multiple-Choice Exercise 2-13. Operating income is

a. $34,000.
b. $110,000.
c. $234,000.
d. $270,000.
e. $74,000.

Cornerstone Exercises

OBJECTIVE 2
CORNERSTONE 2-1

Cornerstone Exercise 2-19 TOTAL PRODUCT COST AND PER-UNIT PRODUCT COST

Slapshot Company makes ice hockey sticks. Last week, direct materials (wood, paint, Kevlar, and resin) costing $24,000 were put into production. Direct labour of $40,000 (20 workers × 100 hours × $20 per hour) was incurred. Manufacturing overhead equalled $56,000. By the end of the week, the company had manufactured 4,000 hockey sticks.

Required:

Calculate the total product cost for last week. Also calculate the per-unit cost of one hockey stick that was produced last week.

OBJECTIVE 2
CORNERSTONE 2-2

Cornerstone Exercise 2-20 PRIME COST AND CONVERSION COST

Slapshot Company makes ice hockey sticks. Last week, direct materials (wood, paint, Kevlar, and resin) costing $24,000 were put into production. Direct labour of $40,000 (20 workers × 100 hours × $20 per hour) was incurred. Manufacturing overhead equalled $56,000. By the end of the week, the company had manufactured 4,000 hockey sticks.

Required:

Calculate the total prime cost for last week. Calculate the per-unit prime cost. Also calculate the total conversion cost for last week. Calculate the per-unit conversion cost.

OBJECTIVE 3
CORNERSTONE 2-3

Cornerstone Exercise 2-21 DIRECT MATERIALS USED IN PRODUCTION

Slapshot Company makes ice hockey sticks. On June 1, Slapshot had $42,000 of materials in inventory. During the month of June, the company purchased $180,000 of materials. On June 30, materials inventory equalled $51,000.

Required:

Calculate the direct materials used in production for the month of June.

OBJECTIVE 3
CORNERSTONE 2-4

Cornerstone Exercise 2-22 COST OF GOODS MANUFACTURED

Slapshot Company makes ice hockey sticks. During the month of June, the company purchased $180,000 of materials. Also during the month of June, Slapshot Company incurred direct labour cost of $165,000 and manufacturing overhead of $215,000. Inventory information is as follows:

	June 1	June 30
Materials	$42,000	$51,000
Work in process	60,000	71,000

Required:

Calculate the cost of goods manufactured for the month of June. Calculate the cost of one hockey stick assuming that 18,000 sticks were completed during June.

OBJECTIVE 3
CORNERSTONE 2-5

Cornerstone Exercise 2-23 COST OF GOODS SOLD

Slapshot Company makes ice hockey sticks. During the month of June, 18,000 sticks were completed at a cost of goods manufactured of $540,000. Suppose that on June 1, Slapshot had 5,000 units in finished goods inventory costing $160,000 and on June 30, 7,000 units in finished goods inventory costing $215,000.

Required:

Prepare a cost of goods sold statement for the month of June. Calculate the number of sticks that were sold during June.

OBJECTIVE 3
CORNERSTONE 2-6

Cornerstone Exercise 2-24 MANUFACTURING FIRM INCOME STATEMENT

Slapshot Company makes ice hockey sticks and sold 16,000 sticks during the month of June at a total cost of $485,000. Each stick sold at a price of $90. Slapshot also incurred two types of selling costs: commissions equal to 15 percent of the sales price, and other selling expense of $200,000. Administrative expense totalled $115,000.

Required:

Prepare an income statement for Slapshot for the month of June.

Cornerstone Exercise 2-25 INCOME STATEMENT PERCENTAGES

OBJECTIVE 3
CORNERSTONE 2-7

Slapshot Company makes ice hockey sticks and sold 16,000 sticks during the month of June at a total cost of $485,000. Each stick sold at a price of $90. Slapshot also incurred two types of selling costs: commissions equal to 15 percent of the sales price, and other selling expense of $200,000. Administrative expense totalled $115,000.

Required:

Prepare an income statement for Slapshot for the month of June and calculate the percentage of sales revenue represented by each line of the income statement. Round answers to one decimal place.

Cornerstone Exercise 2-26 SERVICE ORGANIZATION INCOME STATEMENT

OBJECTIVE 3
CORNERSTONE 2-8

Allstar Exposure designs and sells advertising services to small, relatively unknown companies. Last month, Allstar had sales commissions costs of $50,000, technology costs of $75,000, and research and development costs of $200,000. Selling expenses were $10,000, and administrative expenses equalled $35,000. Sales totalled $410,000.

Required:

Prepare an income statement for Allstar for the past month.

Exercises

Exercise 2-27 COST ASSIGNMENT

OBJECTIVE 1

The sales staff of Central Media (a locally owned radio and cable television station) consists of two salespeople, Derek and Lawanna. During March, the following salaries and commissions were paid:

	Derek	Lawanna
Salary	$25,000	$30,000
Commissions	6,000	1,500

Derek spends 100 percent of his time selling advertising. Lawanna spends two-thirds of her time selling advertising and the remaining one-third on administrative work. Commissions are paid only on sales.

Required:

1. Accumulate these costs by account by filling in the following table:

Cost	Salaries	Commissions
Derek		
Lawanna		
Total		

2. Assign the costs of salaries and commissions to selling expense and administrative expense by filling in the following table:

Cost	Selling Costs	Administrative Costs
Derek's salary		
Lawanna's salary		
Derek's commissions		
Lawanna's commissions		
Total		

OBJECTIVE 1

Exercise 2-28 PRODUCTS VERSUS SERVICES, COST ASSIGNMENT

Holmes Company produces wooden playhouses. When a customer orders a playhouse, it is delivered in pieces with detailed instructions on how to put it together. Some customers prefer that Holmes puts the playhouse together, and they purchase the playhouse plus the installation package. Holmes then pulls two workers off the production line and sends them to construct the playhouse on site.

Required:

1. What two products does Holmes sell? Classify each one as a product or a service.
2. Do you think Holmes assigns costs individually to each product or service? Why or why not?
3. Describe the opportunity cost of the installation process.

OBJECTIVE 1

Exercise 2-29 ASSIGNING COSTS TO A COST OBJECT, DIRECT AND INDIRECT COSTS

Hummer Company uses manufacturing cells to produce its products (a *cell* is a manufacturing unit dedicated to the production of subassemblies or products). One manufacturing cell produces small motors for lawn mowers. Suppose that the motor manufacturing cell is the cost object. Assume that all or a portion of the following costs must be assigned to the cell.

a. Salary of cell supervisor
b. Power to heat and cool the plant in which the cell is located
c. Materials used to produce the motors
d. Maintenance for the cell's equipment (provided by the maintenance department)
e. Labour used to produce motors
f. Cafeteria that services the plant's employees
g. Depreciation on the plant
h. Depreciation on equipment used to produce the motors
i. Ordering costs for materials used in production
j. Engineering support (provided by the engineering department)
k. Cost of maintaining the plant and grounds
l. Cost of the plant's personnel office
m. Property tax on the plant and land

Required:

Classify each of the costs as a direct cost or an indirect cost to the motor manufacturing cell.

OBJECTIVE 2

Exercise 2-30 TOTAL AND UNIT PRODUCT COST

Martinez Manufacturing Inc. showed the following costs for last month:

Direct materials	$7,000
Direct labour	3,000
Manufacturing overhead	2,000
Selling expense	8,000

Last month, 6,000 units were produced and sold.

Required:

1. Classify each of the costs as product cost or period cost.
2. What is total product cost for last month?
3. What is the unit product cost for last month?

Exercise 2-31 COST CLASSIFICATION

OBJECTIVE ➤ 2

Alpha Company incurred the following costs last year:

Direct materials	$216,000
Factory rent	24,000
Direct labour	120,000
Factory utilities	6,300
Supervision in the factory	50,000
Indirect labour in the factory	30,000
Depreciation on factory equipment	9,000
Sales commissions	27,000
Sales salaries	65,000
Advertising	37,000
Depreciation on the headquarters building	10,000
Salary of the corporate receptionist	30,000
Other administrative costs	175,000
Salary of the factory receptionist	28,000

Required:

1. Classify each of the costs using the following table format. Be sure to total the amounts in each column.
   Example: Direct materials, $216,000.

	Product Cost			Period Cost	
Costs	Direct Materials	Direct Labour	Manufact. Overhead	Selling Expense	Administrative Expense
Direct materials	$216,000				

2. What was the total product cost for last year?
3. What was the total period cost for last year?
4. If 30,000 units were produced last year, what was the unit product cost?

Exercise 2-32 CLASSIFYING COST OF PRODUCTION

OBJECTIVE ➤ 2

A factory manufactures jelly. The jars of jelly are packed six to a box, and the boxes are sold to grocery stores. The following types of cost were incurred:

Jars
Sugar
Fruit
Pectin (thickener used in jams and jellies)
Boxes
Depreciation on the factory building
Cooking equipment operators' wages
Filling equipment operators' wages
Packers' wages
Janitors' wages
Receptionist's wages
Telephone
Utilities
Rental of Santa Claus suit (for the annual Christmas party for factory children)
Supervisory labour salaries
Insurance on factory building
Depreciation on factory equipment
Oil to lubricate filling equipment

Required:

Classify each of the costs as direct materials, direct labour, or overhead by using the following table. The row for "Jars" is filled in as an example.

Costs	Direct Materials	Direct Labour	Manufact. Overhead
Jars	X		

OBJECTIVE 2

Exercise 2-33 PRODUCT COST IN TOTAL AND PER UNIT

Fos Company manufactures digital cameras. In January, Fos produced 6,400 cameras with the following costs:

Direct materials	$400,000
Direct labour	80,000
Manufacturing overhead	320,000

There were no beginning or ending inventories of WIP.

Required:

1. What was total product cost in January?
2. What was product cost per unit in January?

OBJECTIVE 2

Exercise 2-34 PRIME COST AND CONVERSION COST

Refer to the data provided in **Exercise 2-33.**

Required:

1. What was the total prime cost in January?
2. What was the prime cost per unit in January?
3. What was the total conversion cost in January?
4. What was the conversion cost per unit in January?

OBJECTIVE 3

Exercise 2-35 DIRECT MATERIALS USED

Hannah Banana Bakers makes chocolate chip cookies for cafe restaurants. In June, Hannah Banana purchased $15,500 of materials. On June 1, the materials inventory was $3,700. On June 30, $1,600 of materials remained in materials inventory.

Required:

What is the cost of the direct materials used in production during June?

OBJECTIVE 3

Exercise 2-36 COST OF GOODS SOLD

Allyson Ashley makes jet skis. During the year, Allyson manufactured 54,000 jet skis. Finished goods inventory had the following units:

January 1	2,100
December 31	2,750

Required:

1. How many jet skis did Allyson sell during the year?
2. If each jet ski had a product cost of $1,125, what was the cost of goods sold last year?

OBJECTIVE 3

Exercise 2-37 DIRECT MATERIALS USED, COST OF GOODS MANUFACTURED

In March, AEK Company purchased materials costing $14,000 and incurred direct labour cost of $20,000. Overhead totalled $36,000 for the month. Information on inventories was as follows:

	March 1	March 31
Materials	$8,600	$2,300
Work in process	1,700	9,000
Finished goods	7,000	6,500

Required:

1. What was the cost of direct materials for March?
2. What was the total manufacturing cost in March?
3. What was the cost of goods manufactured for March?

Exercise 2-38 COST OF GOODS SOLD

OBJECTIVE 3

Refer to the data provided in **Exercise 2-37.**

Required:

What was the cost of goods sold for March?

Exercise 2-39 COST OF GOODS SOLD, SALES REVENUE, INCOME STATEMENT

OBJECTIVE 3

Jasper Company provided the following information for last year:

Sales in units	300,000
Selling price	$9
Direct materials	$150,000
Direct labour	$325,000
Manufacturing overhead	$215,000
Selling expense	$437,000
Administrative expense	$854,000

Last year, beginning and ending inventories of work in process and finished goods equalled zero.

Required:

Calculate the cost of goods sold for last year.

Exercise 2-40 INCOME STATEMENT

OBJECTIVE 3

Refer to the data provided in **Exercise 2-39.**

Required:

1. Calculate the sales revenue for last year.
2. Prepare an income statement for Jasper Company for last year.

Exercise 2-41 INCOME STATEMENT

OBJECTIVE 3

Refer to the data provided in **Exercise 2-39.**

Required:

Prepare an income statement for Jasper Company for last year. Calculate the percentage of sales for each line item on the income statement. Round percentages to the nearest tenth of a percent.

Problems

Problem 2-42 MANUFACTURING, COST CLASSIFICATION, INCOME STATEMENT SERVICE FIRM PRODUCT COSTS AND SELLING AND ADMINISTRATIVE COSTS, INCOME STATEMENT

OBJECTIVE 2 3

P=3.50
Dec sold =10,000

Pop's Drive-Thru Burger Heaven produces and sells hamburgers. Each burger is wrapped and put in a "burger bag," which also includes a serving of fries and a soft drink. The price for the burger bag is $3.50. During December, 10,000 burger bags were sold. The restaurant employs students part-time to cook and fill orders. There is one supervisor (the owner, Napioler Purba). Pop's maintains a pool of part-time employees so that the number of employees scheduled can be adjusted to the changes in demand. Demand varies on a weekly as well as a monthly basis.

A janitor is hired to clean the building early each morning. Cleaning supplies are used by the janitor, as well as the staff, to wipe counters, wash cooking equipment, and so on. The building is leased from a local real estate company; it has no seating capacity. All orders are filled on a drive-thru basis.

The supervisor schedules work, opens the building, counts the cash, advertises, and is responsible for hiring and firing. The following costs were incurred during December:

Hamburger meat	$4,500
Buns, lettuce, pickles, and onions	800
Frozen potato strips	1,250
Wrappers, bags, and condiment packages	600
Other ingredients	660
Part-time employees' wages	7,250
Napioler Purba's salary	3,000
Utilities	1,500
Rent	1,800
Depreciation, cooking equipment, and fixtures	600
Advertising	500
Janitor's wages	520
Janitorial supplies	150
Accounting fees	1,500
Taxes	4,250

Pop's accountant, Elena DeMarco, does the bookkeeping, handles payroll, and files all necessary taxes. She noted that there were no beginning or ending inventories of materials. To simplify accounting for costs, Elena assumed that all part-time employees are production employees and that Napioler Purba's salary is selling and administrative expense. She further assumed that all rent and depreciation expense are part of product cost. Finally, she decided to put all taxes into one category, taxes, and to treat them as administrative expense.

Required:

1. Classify each of the costs for Pop's December operations using the table format given below. Be sure to total the amounts in each column.
   Example: Hamburger meat, $4,500.

Cost	Direct Materials	Direct Labour	Manufact. Overhead	Selling and Administrative
Hamburger meat	$4,500			
Total				

2. Prepare an income statement for the month of December.
3. Elena made some simplifying assumptions. Were those reasonable? Suppose a good case could be made that the portion of the employees' time spent selling the burger bags was really a part of sales. In that case, would it be better to divide their time between production and selling? Should Napioler Purba's time be divided between marketing and administrative duties? What difference (if any) would that make on the income statement?

OBJECTIVE 1

Problem 2-43 COST ASSIGNMENT, DIRECT COSTS

Harry Tonini, owner of an inkjet printer, has agreed to allow Mary and Katerina, two friends who are pursuing master's degrees, to print several papers for their graduate courses. However, he has imposed two conditions. First, they must supply their own paper. Second, they must pay Harry a fair amount for the usage of the ink cartridge. Harry's printer takes two types of cartridges, a black one and a colour one that contains the inks necessary to print in colour. Black replacement cartridges cost $25.50 each and print approximately 850 pages. The colour replacement cartridges cost $31 and print approximately 310 colour pages. One ream of paper costs $2.50 and contains

500 sheets. Mary's printing requirements are for 500 pages, while Katerina's are for 1,000 pages.

Required:

1. Assuming that both women write papers using text only (i.e., black ink), what is the total amount owed to Harry by Mary? By Katerina?
2. What is the total cost of printing (ink and paper) for Mary? For Katerina?
3. Now suppose that Katerina illustrates her writing with many large colourful pie charts and pictures and that about 20 percent of her total printing is primarily colour. Mary uses no colour illustrations. What is the total amount owed to Harry by Katerina? What is the total cost of printing (ink and paper) for Katerina?

Problem 2-44 COST OF DIRECT MATERIALS, COST OF GOODS MANUFACTURED, COST OF GOODS SOLD

OBJECTIVE 3

Bisby Company manufactures fishing rods. At the beginning of July, the following information was supplied by its accountant:

Raw materials inventory	$40,000
Work-in-process inventory	21,000
Finished goods inventory	23,200

During July, the direct labour cost was $43,500, raw materials purchases were $64,000, and the total overhead cost was $108,750. The inventories at the end of July were:

Raw materials inventory	$19,800
Work-in-process inventory	32,500
Finished goods inventory	22,100

Required:

1. What is the cost of the direct materials used in production during July?
2. What is the cost of goods manufactured for July?
3. What is the cost of goods sold for July?

Problem 2-45 PREPARATION OF INCOME STATEMENT: MANUFACTURING FIRM

OBJECTIVE 3

Laworld Inc. manufactures small camping tents. Last year, 200,000 tents were made and sold for $60 each. Each tent includes the following costs:

Direct materials	$18
Direct labour	12
Manufacturing overhead	16

The only selling expenses were a commission of $2 per unit sold and advertising totalling $100,000. Administrative expenses, all fixed, equalled $300,000. There were no beginning or ending finished goods inventories. There were no beginning or ending work-in-process inventories.

Required:

1. Calculate the product cost for one tent. Calculate the total product cost for last year.
2. Prepare an income statement for external users. Did you need to prepare a supporting statement of cost of goods manufactured? Explain.
3. Suppose 200,000 tents were produced (and 200,000 sold) but that the company had a beginning finished goods inventory of 10,000 tents produced in the prior year at $40 per unit. The company follows a first-in, first-out policy for its inventory (meaning that the units produced first are sold first for purposes of cost flow). What effect does this have on the income statement? Show the new statement.

OBJECTIVE 3

Problem 2-46 COST OF GOODS MANUFACTURED, COST OF GOODS SOLD

Hayward Company, a manufacturing firm, has supplied the following information from its accounting records for the month of May:

Direct labour cost	$10,500
Purchases of raw materials	15,000
Supplies used	675
Factory insurance	350
Commissions paid	2,500
Factory supervision	2,225
Advertising	800
Material handling	3,750
Materials inventory, May 1	3,475
Work-in-process inventory, May 1	12,500
Finished goods inventory, May 1	6,685
Materials inventory, May 31	9,500
Work-in-process inventory, May 31	14,250
Finished goods inventory, May 31	4,250

Required:

1. Prepare a statement of cost of goods manufactured.
2. Prepare a statement of cost of goods sold.

OBJECTIVE 1 2

Problem 2-47 COST IDENTIFICATION

Following is a list of cost items described in the chapter as well as a list of brief descriptive settings for each item.

Cost terms:

a. Opportunity cost
b. Period cost
c. Product cost
d. Direct labour cost
e. Selling cost
f. Conversion cost
g. Prime cost
h. Direct materials cost
i. Manufacturing overhead cost
j. Administrative cost

Settings:

1. Marcus Burbosa, manager of Timmins Optical, estimated that the cost of plastic, wages of the technician producing the lenses, and overhead totalled $30 per pair of single-vision lenses.
2. Linda was having a hard time deciding whether to return to school. She was concerned about the salary she would have to give up for the next four years.
3. Randy Harris is the finished goods warehouse manager for a medium-sized manufacturing firm. He is paid a salary of $90,000 per year. As he studied the financial statements prepared by the local chartered accounting firm, he wondered how his salary was treated.
4. Jamie Young is in charge of the legal department at company headquarters. Her salary is $95,000 per year. She reports to the chief executive officer.
5. All factory costs that are not classified as direct materials or direct labour.
6. The new product required machining, assembly, and painting. The design engineer asked the accounting department to estimate the labour cost of each of the three operations. The engineer supplied the estimated labour hours for each operation.
7. After obtaining the estimate of direct labour cost, the design engineer estimated the cost of the materials that would be used for the new product.
8. The design engineer totalled the costs of materials and direct labour for the new product.

9. The design engineer also estimated the cost of converting the raw materials into its final form.
10. The auditor for a soft drink bottling plant pointed out that the depreciation on the delivery trucks had been incorrectly assigned to product cost (through overhead). Accordingly, the depreciation charge was reallocated on the income statement.

Required:

Match the items with the settings. More than one cost classification may be associated with each setting; however, select the setting that seems to fit the item best. When you are done, each cost term will be used just once.

Problem 2-48 INCOME STATEMENT, COST OF SERVICES PROVIDED, SERVICE ATTRIBUTES

OBJECTIVE 2 3

Berry Company is an architectural firm located in Toronto, Ontario. The company works with small and medium-size construction businesses to prepare building plans according to client contract. Berry employs 10 professionals and 5 staff. The following data are provided for last year:

Number of designs completed and sold	700
Beginning inventory of direct materials	$20,000
Beginning inventory of designs in process	$60,000
Ending inventory of direct materials	$0
Ending inventory of designs in process	$100,000
Purchases, direct materials	$40,000
Direct labour	$800,000
Manufacturing overhead	$100,000
Administrative expense	$150,000
Selling expense	$60,000

Required:

1. Calculate the cost of services sold.
2. Assume that the average fee for a design is $2,100. Prepare an income statement for Berry Company.
3. Refer to the cost of services sold (calculated in Requirement 1). What is the dominant cost? Will this always be true of service organizations? If not, provide an example of an exception.
4. Why does Berry Company show zero inventory of finished plans? What change(s) in the company could result in a positive finished goods inventory?

Problem 2-49 COST OF GOODS MANUFACTURED, INCOME STATEMENT

OBJECTIVE 3

W. W. Phillips Company produced 4,000 leather recliners during the year. These recliners sell for $400 each. Phillips had 500 recliners in finished goods inventory at the beginning of the year. At the end of the year, there were 700 recliners in finished goods inventory. Phillips' accounting records provide the following information:

Purchases of raw materials	$320,000
Beginning materials inventory	46,800
Ending materials inventory	66,800
Direct labour	200,000
Indirect labour	40,000
Rent, factory building	42,000
Depreciation, factory equipment	60,000
Utilities, factory	11,900
Salary, sales supervisor	90,000
Commissions, salespersons	180,000
General administration	300,000
Beginning work-in-process inventory	13,040
Ending work-in-process inventory	14,940
Beginning finished goods inventory	80,000
Ending finished goods inventory	114,100

Here's The Real Kicker

Kicker uses information on cost behaviour to guide new programs. For example, the variable cost of manufacturing speakers led Kicker to work with its manufacturers to both increase quality and decrease cost. Fixed costs at the Stillwater location also received attention. A few years ago Safety Director Terry Williams faced a problem with worker safety. Cost information based on a number of indicators revealed the problem:

- The cost of workmen's compensation insurance was high.
- The workmen's compensation experience rating was high.
- The number of injuries was up.
- The number of injuries requiring time off was up.
- The number of back injuries (the most serious type) was up.
- The average cost per injury was up.

Terry looked for the root cause of the problem and discovered that improper lifting led to the more serious back injuries. He instituted a comprehensive safety program emphasizing 20 minutes of stretching exercises each day (five minutes before work, five minutes after each break, and five minutes after lunch).

Was the program a success? At first, the workers resisted the stretching, so Terry got them weight belts. The workers hated them. They went back to stretching. But this time, any worker who refused to stretch had to wear the weight belt for 30 days. This was a highly visible sign of failure to adhere to the program. In addition, Kicker's president was a big proponent of the safety program. He explained the impact of the increased insurance premiums and lost work time on the Kicker profit-sharing program. The profit-sharing program is an important extra for Kicker employees; each employee makes it his or her job to contribute to the bottom line whenever possible.

Over several months, workers bought into the program. The indicators decreased dramatically. The cost of workmen's compensation insurance decreased by nearly 50 percent, the average cost per injury is less than 5 percent of the presafety program cost, and there is no lost work time.

KICKER®

Chapter 2 discussed various types of costs and took a close look at manufacturing and service costs. However, the primary concern of the chapter was organizing costs into production, selling, and administrative costs. Related schedules of the cost of goods manufactured, cost of goods sold, and income statements were built. Now it is time to focus on cost behaviour—the way costs change as the related activity changes.

Cost behaviour represents the foundation on which managerial accounting is built, much like the critical role played by the theoretical pyramid in financial accounting. Financial accounting contains critical assumptions (e.g., the economic entity assumption) and principles (e.g., matching principle), in order to help financial accountants properly record transactions and prepare financial statements. In much the same way, managers must properly understand cost behaviour in order to make wise decisions. For example, a **Grant Thornton** survey of 300 U.S. business leaders and senior executives reported that 79 percent of CEOs focus on understanding and managing costs in an attempt to increase company value.[1] This textbook provides numerous examples of how understanding cost behaviour improves managerial decision making.

Costs can be variable, fixed, or mixed. Knowing how costs change as output changes is essential to planning, controlling, and decision making. For example, suppose that BlueDenim Company expects demand for its jeans product to increase by 10 percent next year. How will that affect the total costs budgeted for the factory? Clearly, BlueDenim will need 10 percent more raw materials (denim, thread, zippers, and so on). In addition, it will need more cutting and sewing labour because someone will need to make the additional jeans, so these costs are variable in nature. But the factory building will probably not need to be expanded. Neither will the factory need an additional receptionist or plant manager. So those costs are fixed in nature. As long as BlueDenim's accountant understands the behaviour of the fixed and variable costs, it will be possible to develop a fairly accurate budget for the next year.

Budgeting, deciding to keep or drop a product line, and evaluating the performance of segments all benefit from knowledge of cost behaviour (e.g., in 2008, **GM** decided to focus on its four core brands—Chevrolet, Buick, GMC, and Cadillac—and to close its doors to the Hummer, Pontiac, and Saturn brands). In fact, failure to know and understand cost behaviour can lead to poor—even disastrous—decisions. This

[1] *Grant Thornton LLP Survey of U.S. Business Leaders*, 12th Edition, 2006.

chapter discusses cost behaviour in depth so that a proper foundation is laid for its use in studying other cost management topics.

Basics of Cost Behaviour

OBJECTIVE 1
Explain the meaning of cost behaviour, and define and describe fixed and variable costs.

Cost behaviour is the general term for describing whether a cost changes when the level of output changes. A cost that does not change in total as output changes is a *fixed cost*. A *variable cost*, on the other hand, increases in total with an increase in output and decreases in total with a decrease in output. Let's first review the basics of cost and output measures. Then we will look at fixed and variable costs.

Measures of Output and the Relevant Range

In order to determine the behaviour of a cost, we need to have a good grasp of the cost under consideration and a measure of the output associated with the activity. The terms *fixed cost* and *variable cost* do not exist in a vacuum; they only have meaning when related to some output measure. In other words, a cost is fixed or variable with respect to some output measure or driver. In order to understand the behaviour of costs, we must first determine the underlying business activity and ask ourselves "What causes the cost of this particular activity to go up (or down)?" A **cost driver** is a causal measurement that causes costs to change. Identifying and managing cost drivers helps managers better predict and control costs.

Let's look at some examples. Suppose that BlueDenim Company wants to classify its product costs as either variable or fixed with respect to the number of jeans produced. In this case, the number of jeans produced is the driver. Clearly, the use of raw materials (denim, thread, zippers, and buttons) varies with the number of jeans produced. So, we could say that materials costs are variable with respect to the number of units produced. How about electricity to run the sewing machines? That, too, is variable with respect to the number of jeans produced because the more jeans that are produced, the more sewing machine time is needed, and the more electricity it takes. Finally, what about the cost of supervision for the sewing department? Whether the company produces many pairs of jeans or fewer pairs of jeans, the cost of supervision is unchanged. So, we would say that supervision is fixed with respect to the number of jeans produced within the relevant range.

The **relevant range** is the range of output over which the assumed cost relationship is valid for the normal operations of a firm. The relevant range limits the cost relationship to the range of operations that the firm normally expects to occur. Let's consider BlueDenim's cost relationships more carefully. We said that the salary of the supervisor is strictly fixed. But is that true? If the company produced just a few pairs of jeans a year, it would not even need a supervisor. Surely the owner could handle that task (and probably a good number of other tasks as well). On the other hand, suppose that BlueDenim increased its current production by two or three times, perhaps by adding a second and third shift. One supervisor could not possibly handle all three shifts. So, when we talk about supervision cost, we are implicitly talking about it for the range of production that normally occurs. We now take a closer look at fixed, variable, and mixed costs. In each case, the cost is related to only one driver and is defined within the relevant range.

Fixed Costs

Fixed costs are costs that *in total* are constant within the relevant range as the level of output increases or decreases. For example, a fleet of airplanes represents a fixed cost to an airline because, within the relevant range, the cost does not change as the number of flights or the number of passengers changes. Similarly, the rental cost of warehouse space by a wholesaler is fixed for the term of the lease. If the wholesaler's sales go up or down, the cost of the leased warehouse stays the same.

To illustrate fixed cost behaviour, consider a factory operated by SyBan, a company that produces unlabelled personal computers. The assembly department of the factory assembles components into completed personal computers. Assume that SyBan wants to look at the cost relationship between supervision cost and the number of computers processed. The assembly department can process up to 50,000 computers per year. The assemblers (direct labour) are supervised by a production line manager who is paid $32,000 per year. The company was established five years ago. Currently, the factory produces 40,000 to 50,000 computers per year. Production has never fallen below 20,000 computers in a year. The cost of supervision for several levels of production is as follows:

SyBan
Cost of Supervision

Number of Computers Produced	Total Cost of Supervision	Unit Cost
20,000	$32,000	$1.60
30,000	32,000	1.07
40,000	32,000	0.80
50,000	32,000	0.64

The cost relationship considered is between supervision cost and the number of computers processed. The number of computers processed is called the *output measure*, or *driver.* Since the firm has been processing between 20,000 and 50,000 computers per year, the relevant range is 20,000 to 50,000. Notice that the *total* cost of supervision remains constant within this range as more computers are processed. SyBan pays $32,000 for supervision regardless of whether it processes 20,000, 40,000, or 50,000 computers.

Pay particular attention to the words *in total* in the definition of fixed costs. While the total cost of supervision remains unchanged as more computers are processed, the unit cost does change as the level of output changes. As the example in the table shows, within the relevant range, the unit cost of supervision decreases from $1.60 to $0.64. Because of the behaviour of per-unit fixed costs, it is easy to get the impression that the fixed costs themselves are affected by changes in the level of output. But that is not true. Instead, higher output means that the fixed costs can be spread over more units and are thus smaller per unit. Unit fixed costs can often be misleading and may lead to poor decisions. It is often safer to work with total fixed costs.

Let's take a look at the graph of fixed costs given in Exhibit 3-1. We see that for the relevant range, fixed cost behaviour is described by a horizontal line. Notice that at 40,000 computers processed, supervision cost is $32,000; at 50,000 computers processed, supervision is also $32,000. This line visually demonstrates that cost remains unchanged as the level of the activity driver varies. For the relevant range, total fixed costs are simply an amount. For the company, supervision cost amounted to $32,000 for any level of output between 20,000 and 50,000 computers processed. Thus, supervision is a fixed cost and can be expressed as:

$$\text{Supervision cost} = \$32{,}000$$

Strictly speaking, this equation assumes that the fixed costs are $32,000 for all levels (as if the line extends to the vertical axis as indicated by the dashed portion in Exhibit 3-1). Though this assumption is not true, it is harmless if the operating decisions are confined to the relevant range.

Can fixed costs change? Of course, but this possibility does not make them variable. They are fixed at a new higher (or lower) rate. Going back to SyBan, suppose that the company gives a raise to the assembly department supervisor. Instead of being paid $32,000 per year, the salary is $34,000 per year. The cost of supervision within the relevant range is $34,000 per year. However, supervision cost is still *fixed* with respect to the number of computers produced.

By their nature, fixed costs are difficult to change quickly—that is why they are considered fixed. Two types of fixed costs are commonly recognized: discretionary fixed costs and committed fixed costs.

ANALYTICAL Q&A

In Exhibit 3-1, the fixed cost of supervision is drawn at $32,000. If the supervisor's salary is raised to $34,000 per year, can you draw in the new fixed cost line on Exhibit 3-1?

Answers on pages 711 to 715.

Exhibit 3-1

Fixed Cost of Supervision

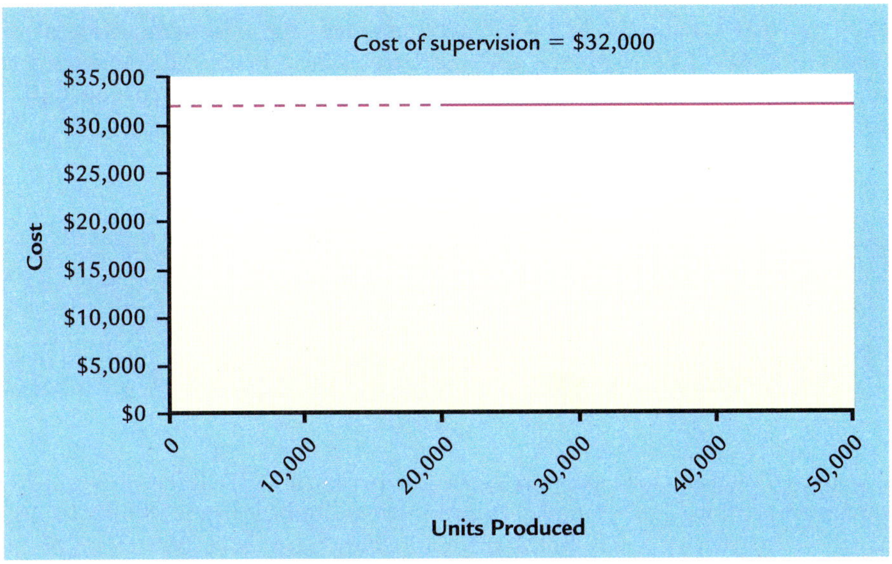

Two type of Fixed costs
(1) Discretionary fixed costs
(2) Commited Fixed costs

Discretionary fixed costs are fixed costs that can be changed or avoided relatively easily at management discretion. For example, advertising is a discretionary fixed cost. Advertising cost depends on the decision by management to purchase print, radio, or video advertising. This cost might depend on the size of the ad or the number of times it runs, but it does *not* depend on the number of units produced and sold. Management can easily decide to increase or decrease dollars spent on advertising.

Two days prior to the beginning of the 2006–07 season, the **National Football League (NFL)** was forced to make a decision involving discretionary costs. Specifically, the league realized that **Wilson Sporting Goods** had already manufactured 500,000 footballs (of the 900,000 total footballs that would be needed for the entire season) with the signature of the outgoing NFL commissioner—Paul Tagliabue—instead of the incoming commissioner—Roger Goodell. The decision facing the NFL was whether to play the entire season or approximately only half the season with the incoming commissioner's signature on the balls. If the 500,000 existing balls were given away to high schools (as the NFL eventually decided to do), then the $250,000 additional cost to produce another 500,000 balls with the new signature represents a discretionary cost to the league because it could be changed (i.e., avoided) relatively easily.[2] The $250,000 is a discretionary cost that is entirely fixed as the NFL will need to purchase the additional footballs regardless of the number of games played (the driver for football cost).

Committed fixed costs, on the other hand, are fixed costs that cannot be easily changed. Often, committed fixed costs are those that involve a long-term contract (e.g., leasing of machinery or warehouse space) or the purchase of property, plant, and equipment. For example, a construction company may lease heavy-duty earth-moving equipment for a period of three years. The lease cost is a committed fixed cost.

CONCEPT Q&A

Consider the cost of a wedding reception. What costs are fixed? What costs are variable? What output measure did you use in classifying the costs as fixed or variable?

Answers on pages 711 to 715.

Variable Costs

Variable costs are defined as costs that in total vary in direct proportion to changes in output within the relevant range. The costs of producing and assembling the propeller on each boat manufactured by **Evinrude** (of **Bombardier Recreational Products**) represent variable costs for a manufacturer. In a dentist's office,

[2] T. Lowry, "Two-Minute Warning," *Business Week* (September 4, 2006): 12.

certain supplies, such as dental floss, X-ray film, and disposable bibs, vary with the number of patients seen. The cost of fruits such as blueberries and strawberries that **Yogen Früz** uses to top its frozen yogurt, varies with the number of clients served.

To illustrate, let's expand the SyBan example to include the cost of the DVD-ROM drive that is inserted in each computer. Here the cost is the cost of direct materials—the DVD-ROM drive—and the output measure is the number of computers processed. Each computer requires one DVD-ROM drive costing $40. The cost of DVD-ROM drives for various levels of production is as follows:

SyBan
Cost of DVD-ROM Drives

Number of Computers Produced	Total Cost of DVD-ROM Drives ($)	Unit Cost ($)
20,000	800,000	40
30,000	1,200,000	40
40,000	1,600,000	40
50,000	2,000,000	40

As more computers are produced, the total cost of DVD-ROM drives increases in direct proportion. For example, as production doubles from 20,000 to 40,000 units, the *total* cost of DVD-ROM drives doubles from $800,000 to $1,600,000. Notice also that the unit cost of direct materials is constant.

Variable costs can also be represented by a linear equation. Here, total variable costs depend on the level of output. This relationship can be described by the following equation:

Total variable costs = Variable rate × Amount of output

The relationship that describes the cost of disk drives is:

Total variable cost = $40 × Number of computers

Exhibit 3-2 shows graphically that variable cost behaviour is represented by a straight line extending out from the origin. Notice that at zero units processed, total variable cost is zero. However, as units produced increase, the total variable cost also increases. It can be seen that total cost increases in direct proportion to increases in the number of computers processed; the rate of increase is measured by the slope of the line. At 50,000 computers processed, the total cost of disk drives is $2,000,000 (or $40 × 50,000 computers processed); at 30,000 computers processed, the total cost would be $1,200,000. Exhibit 3-2 illustrates variable cost behaviour for the DVD-ROM drives. Exhibit 3-3 contrasts variable cost behaviour with fixed cost behaviour.

Exhibit 3-2

SyBan Computers Variable Cost of DVD-ROM Drives

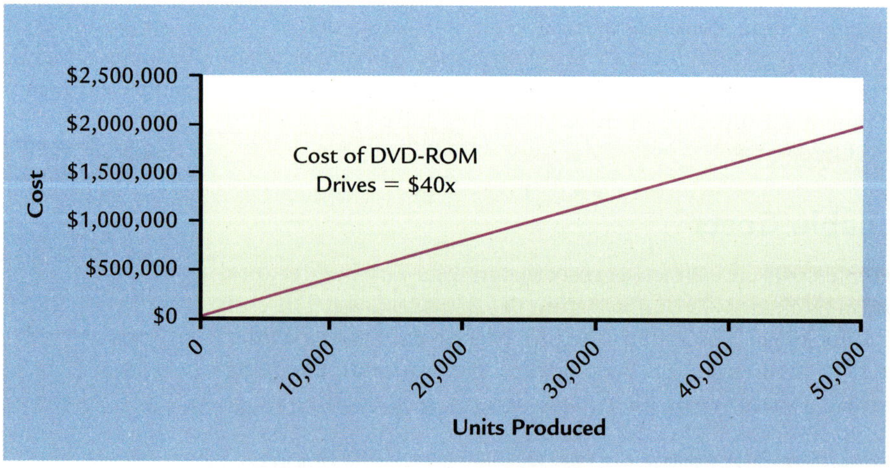

Exhibit 3-3

Variable–Fixed cost

	Total Cost	Unit Cost
Variable Cost	Varies in direct proportion to changes in activity	Is fixed throughout the relevant range
Fixed Cost	Remains fixed throughout the relevant range	Varies inversely with changes in activity throughout the relevant range

Are Real-World Cost Relationships Linear?

The graphs of fixed and variable costs that were just reviewed show cost relationships that are straight lines. Is this reasonable? Are real-world cost relationships linear?

In the SyBan example, the DVD-ROM drives cost $40 each—no matter how many were purchased. However, if only a few drives were bought, surely the per-unit cost would be higher—perhaps more than double. So, there are economies of scale in producing larger quantities of output. For example, at extremely low levels of output workers often use more materials per unit or require more time per unit than they do at higher levels of output. Then, as the level of output increases, economies of scale arise as workers experience a learning curve and figure out how to use materials and time more efficiently such that the variable cost per unit decreases as more and more output is produced. Therefore, when economies of scale are present, the true total cost function is increasing at a decreasing rate, as shown in Exhibit 3-4. Some managers refer to this type of cost behaviour as **semi-variable**.

When unit costs change in this way, how do we choose the correct variable rate? Fortunately, the relevant range can help us out. Recall that *relevant range* is defined as the range of activity for which the assumed cost relationships are valid. Exhibit 3-4 shows us how the relevant range can be used to see how well a straight line approximates variable cost. Note that for units of output below 20,000 on the x-axis, the approximation appears to break down. Therefore, managers must be extremely careful

Exhibit 3-4

Nonlinearity of Variable Costs

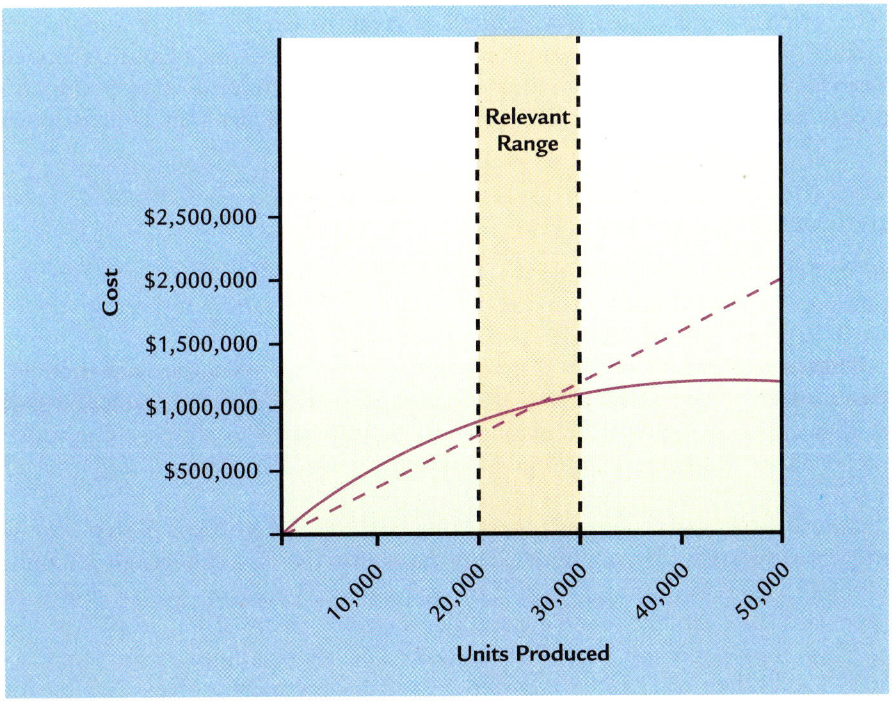

in applying cost behaviour assumptions to decision making whenever the output level falls outside of the company's relevant range of operations.

OBJECTIVE 2
Define and describe mixed and step costs.

Mixed Costs and Step Costs

While strictly fixed and variable costs are easy to handle, many costs do not fall into those categories. Often, costs are a combination of fixed and variable costs (mixed costs) or have an increased fixed component at specified intervals (step costs).

Mixed Costs

Mixed costs are costs that have both a fixed and a variable component. For example, sales representatives are often paid a salary plus a commission on sales. Suppose that SyBan has 10 sales representatives, each earning a salary of $30,000 per year plus a commission of $25 per computer sold. The activity is selling, and the output measure is units sold. If 50,000 computers are sold, then the total cost associated with the sales representatives is $1,550,000—the sum of the fixed salary cost of $300,000 (10 × $30,000) and the variable cost of $1,250,000 ($25 × 50,000).

The formula for a mixed cost is as follows:

Total cost = Total fixed cost + Total variable cost

For SyBan, the cost of the sales representatives is represented by the following equation:

Total cost = $300,000 + ($25 × Number of computers sold)

The following table shows the selling cost for different levels of sales activity:

SyBan Computers Inc.

Fixed Cost of Selling ($)	Variable Cost of Selling ($)	Total Cost ($)	Computers Sold	Selling Cost per Unit ($)
300,000	500,000	800,000	20,000	40.00
300,000	750,000	1,050,000	30,000	35.00
300,000	1,000,000	1,300,000	40,000	32.50
300,000	1,250,000	1,550,000	50,000	31.00

The graph for our mixed-cost example is given in Exhibit 3-5 (assuming a relevant range of 0 to 50,000 units). Mixed costs are represented by a line that intercepts the vertical axis (at $300,000 for this example). The y-intercept corresponds to the fixed cost, and the slope of the line gives the variable cost per unit of activity driver (slope is $25 for this example).

Step Cost Behaviour

So far in our discussion of cost behaviour, we have assumed that the cost function is continuous. In reality, some cost functions may be discontinuous; these costs are known as *step costs* (or semi-fixed).

A **step cost** displays a constant level of cost for a range of output and then jumps to a higher level of cost at some point, where it remains for a similar range of output. Items that display a step cost behaviour must be purchased in chunks. The width of the step defines the range of output for which a particular amount of the resource applies.

Exhibits 3-6A and B illustrate step costs. Exhibit 3-6A shows a step cost with relatively narrow steps. These narrow steps mean that the cost changes in response to fairly small changes in output. Often, if the steps are very narrow, we can approximate the step cost as a strictly variable cost. For example, Copy-2-Go, a photocopying shop, buys copy paper by the 20-ream box. The shop typically uses three boxes per day. The cost of copy paper is a step cost with very narrow steps. Exhibit 3-6B,

Exhibit 3-5

Mixed Cost Behaviour

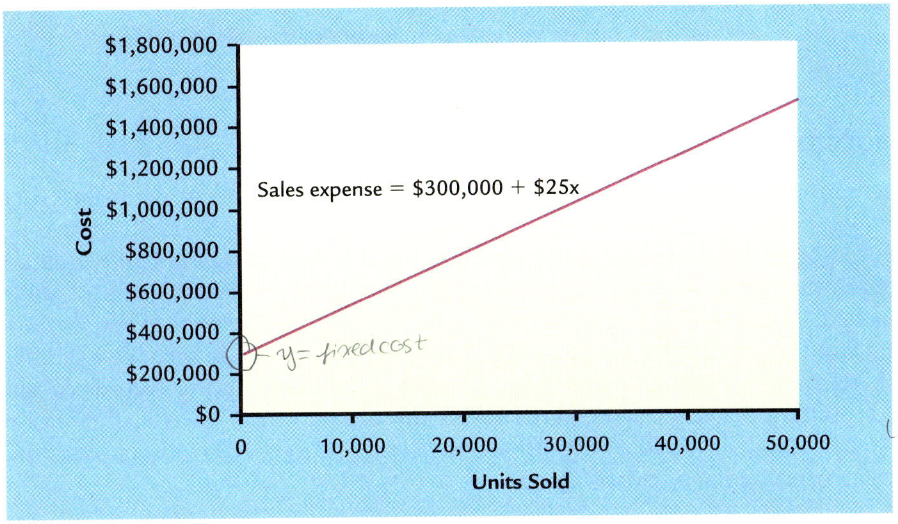

Exhibit 3-6A

A Step Cost with Narrow Steps

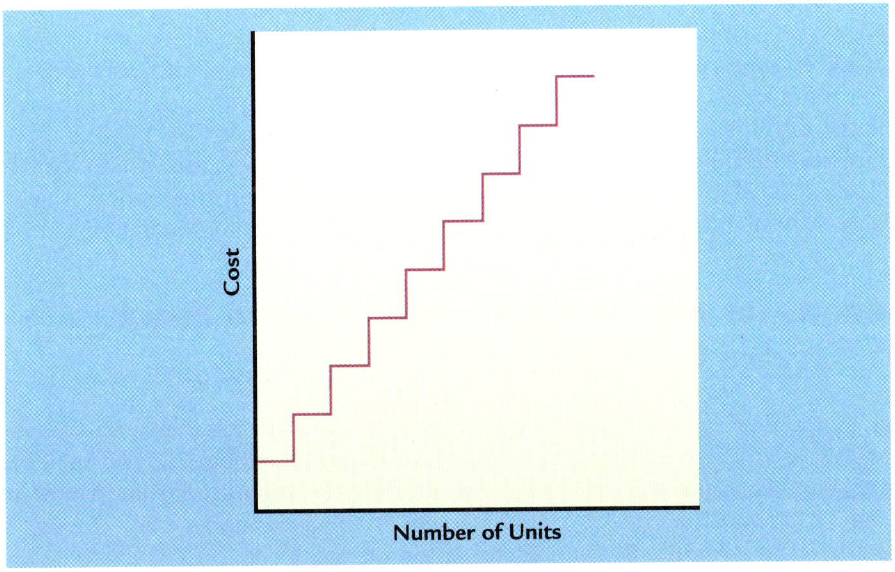

Exhibit 3-6B

B Step Cost with Wide Steps

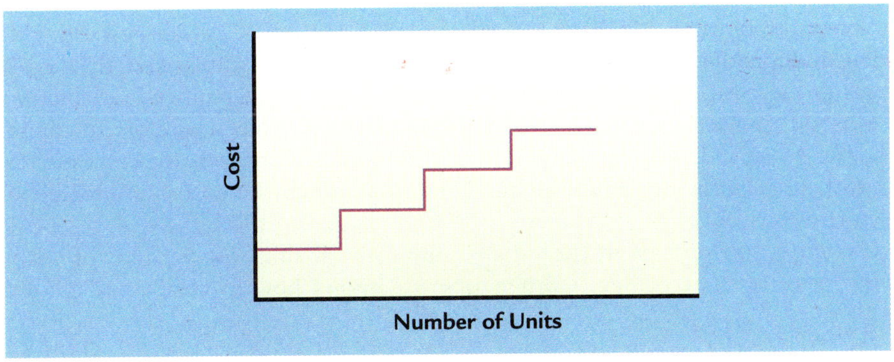

however, shows a step cost with relatively wide steps. An example of this type of cost is a factory that leases production machinery. Suppose that each machine can produce 1,000 units per month. If production ranges from 0 to 1,000 units, only one machine is needed. However, if production increases to amounts between 1,001 and 2,000 units, a second machine must be leased. Many so-called fixed costs may be, in reality, step costs.

Accounting Records and Mixed Costs

Sometimes it is easy to identify the variable and fixed components of a mixed cost, as in the example given earlier for SyBan's sales representatives. Many times, however, the only information available is the total cost and a measure of output. For example, the accounting system will usually record both the total cost of maintenance and the number of maintenance hours provided during a given period of time. How much of the total maintenance cost represents a fixed cost and how much represents a variable cost is not revealed by the accounting records. (In fact, the accounting records may not even reveal the breakdown of costs in the sales representative example.) Often, the total cost is simply recorded with no attempt to segregate the fixed and variable costs.

Need for Cost Separation into Fixed and Variable Costs

Accounting records typically show only the total cost. Therefore, it is necessary to separate the total cost into its fixed and variable components. Only through a formal effort to separate costs can all costs be classified into the appropriate cost behaviour categories.

If mixed costs are a very small percentage of total costs, formal cost separation may be more trouble than it's worth. In this case, mixed costs could be assigned to either the fixed or variable cost category without much concern for the classification error or its effect on decision making. Alternatively, the total mixed cost could be arbitrarily divided between the two cost categories. However, this option is seldom available. Mixed costs for many firms are large enough to call for separation.

OBJECTIVE 3
Separate mixed costs into their fixed and variable components using the high-low method, the scattergraph method, and the method of least squares.

Methods for Separating Mixed Costs into Fixed and Variable Components

Three methods of separating a mixed cost into its fixed and variable components are commonly used: the high-low method, the scattergraph method, and the method of least squares. Each method requires the simplifying assumption of a linear cost relationship. Therefore, before we examine each of these methods more closely, let's review the expression of cost as an equation for a straight line.

$$\text{Total cost} = \text{Fixed cost} + (\text{Variable rate} \times \text{Output})$$

The **dependent variable** is a variable whose value depends on the value of another variable. In the previous equation, total cost is the dependent variable; it is the cost we are trying to predict.

The **independent variable** is a variable that measures output and that explains changes in the cost or other dependent variable. A good independent variable is one that causes or is closely associated with the dependent variable. Therefore, many managers refer to an independent variable as a cost driver. The **intercept** corresponds to fixed cost. Graphically, the intercept is the point at which the cost line intercepts the cost (vertical) axis.

The **slope** corresponds to the variable rate (the variable cost per unit of output); it is the slope of the cost line. Cornerstone 3-1 shows how to create and use a cost formula.

independent variable = cost driver
intercept = fixed cost
variable rate = slope.

The HOW and WHY of Creating and Using a Cost Formula

CORNERSTONE 3-1

Information:
The art and graphics department of Wolftown College decided to equip each faculty office with an inkjet colour printer (computers were already in place). Sufficient colour printers had monthly depreciation of $250.
The department purchased paper in boxes of 10,000 sheets (20 reams of 500 sheets each) for $35 per box. Ink cartridges cost $30 and will print, on average, 300 pages.

Required:
1. Create a formula for the monthly cost of inkjet printing in the art and graphics department.
2. If the department expects to print 4,400 pages next month, what is the expected fixed cost? Total variable cost? Total printing cost?

Solution:
1. The cost formula takes the following form:

   Total cost = Fixed cost + (Variable rate × Number of pages)

   The monthly fixed cost is $250 (the cost of printer depreciation), as it does not vary according to the number of pages printed. The variable costs are paper and ink, as both vary with the number of pages printed.

   Cost of paper per page is $35/10,000 = $0.0035
   Cost of ink per page is $30/300 = $0.10

   Variable rate per page is $0.0035 + $0.10 = $0.1035

   The cost formula is:

   Total cost of printing = $250 + ($0.1035 × Number of pages)

2. Expected fixed cost for next month is $250.

   Expected variable cost for next month is $0.1035 × 4,400 pages = $455.40
   Expected total printing cost for next month is $250 + $455.40 = $705.40

WHY:
Because it is beneficial to identify the variable and fixed-cost components separately.

Since the accounting records reveal only total cost and output, those values must be used to estimate the fixed cost and variable rate. Three methods can be used to estimate these two items: the high-low method, the scattergraph method, and the method of least squares (i.e., regression).

The following example with the same data will be used with each method so that comparisons among them can be made. The example focuses on materials handling cost for LaBico Company, a manufacturer of household cleaning products. Materials handling involves moving materials from one area of the factory, say the raw materials storeroom, to another area, such as workstation 6. Large, complex organizations have found that the cost of moving materials can be quite large. Understanding the behaviour of this cost is an important part of deciding how to reduce the cost.

LaBico's controller has accumulated data for the materials handling activity. The plant manager believes that the number of material moves is a good activity driver for the activity. Assume that the accounting records of LaBico disclose the following materials handling costs and number of material moves for the past 9 months:

Month	Materials Handling Cost ($)	Number of Moves
January	2,000	**100**
February	3,090	125
March	2,780	175
April	1,990	200
May	7,500	**500**
June	5,300	300
July	3,800	250
August	6,300	400
September	5,600	475

The High-Low Method

From basic geometry, we know that two points are needed to determine a line. Once we know the two points on a line, then its equation can be determined. Recall that the fixed cost is the *intercept* of the total cost line and that the variable rate is the *slope* of the line. Given two points, the slope and the intercept can be determined. The **high-low method** is a method of separating mixed costs into fixed and variable components by using just the high and low data points. Four steps must be taken in the high-low method.

ANALYTICAL Q&A

When working high-low problems, it helps to circle the high and low points so that you don't become confused. Right now, go to the data given for materials handling cost and number of moves, and circle the high point and the low point.

Answers on pages 711 to 715.

Step 1: Find the high point and the low point for a given data set. The *high point* is defined as the point with the *highest activity* or *output level*. The *low point* is defined as the point with the *lowest activity* or *output level*. It is important to note that the high and low points are identified by looking at the activity levels and not the costs. In some cases the highest (or lowest) activity level might also be associated with the highest (or lowest) cost, whereas in other cases it is not. Therefore, the managerial accountant must be careful to use the activity level in identifying the high and low data points for the analysis, regardless of whether or not the high (or low) activity level is associated with the high (or low) cost. In the data for materials handling cost, the high output occurred in May, with 500 material moves and total cost of $7,500. The low output was in January with 100 material moves and total cost of $2,000.

Step 2: Using the high and low points, calculate the variable rate. To perform this calculation, we recognize that the variable rate, or slope, is the change in the total cost divided by the change in output.

$$\text{Variable rate} = \frac{\text{High point cost} - \text{Low point cost}}{\text{High point output} - \text{Low point output}}$$

Using the high and low points for our example, the variable rate would be as follows:

$$\text{Variable rate} = \frac{(\$7{,}500 - \$2{,}000)}{(500 - 100)} = \frac{\$5{,}500}{400} = \$13.75$$

Step 3: Calculate the fixed cost using the variable rate (from step 2) using either the high or low point.

$$\text{Fixed cost} = \text{Total cost at high point} - (\text{Variable rate} \times \text{Output at high point})$$

OR

$$\text{Fixed cost} = \text{Total cost at low point} - (\text{Variable rate} \times \text{Output at low point})$$

Let's use the high point to calculate fixed cost.

$$\text{Fixed cost} = \$7{,}500 - (\$13.75 \times 500) = \$625$$

Step 4: Form the cost formula for materials handling based on the high-low method.

$$\text{Total cost} = \$625 + (\$13.75 \times \text{Number of moves})$$

Cornerstone 3-2 shows how to use the high-low method to construct a cost formula. Once we have the cost formula, we can use it in budgeting and in performance control. For example, suppose that the number of moves for November is expected to be 350. Budgeted materials handling cost would be $5,437.50, or $625 + ($13.75 × 350). Alternatively, suppose that the controller wondered whether or not October's materials handling cost of $6,240 was reasonably close to what would have been predicted. Our cost formula would predict October's cost of $6,469 (rounded). (This amount is found by multiplying $13.75 times the 425 actual moves and then adding fixed cost of $625.) The actual cost is just $229 different from the predicted cost and probably would be judged to be reasonably close to the budgeted cost. Cornerstone 3-3 shows how to use the high-low method to calculate predicted total variable cost and total cost for budgeted output.

Let's look at one last point. Notice that monthly data were used to find the high and low points and to calculate the fixed cost and variable rate. This means that the cost formula is the fixed cost *for the month*. Suppose, however, that the company wants to use that formula to predict cost for a different period of time, say a year. In that case, the variable cost rate is just multiplied by the budgeted amount of the independent variable for the year. The intercept, or fixed cost, must be adjusted. To convert monthly fixed cost to yearly fixed cost, simply multiply the monthly fixed cost by 12 (because there are 12 months in a year). If weekly data were used to calculate the fixed and variable costs, one would multiply the weekly fixed cost by 52 to convert it to yearly fixed cost, and so on. Cornerstone 3-3 shows how to use the high-low method to calculate predicted total variable cost and total cost for budgeted output in which the time period differs from the data period.

ANALYTICAL Q&A

Right now, calculate the fixed cost by using the *low* point and the variable rate calculated in step 2. (You will get the same fixed cost, $625.)

Answers on pages 711 to 715.

The high-low method has several important advantages.

One advantage is its objectivity. That is, any two people using the high-low method on a particular data set will arrive at the same answer.

Also, the high-low method allows a manager to get a quick fix on a cost relationship by using only two data points. For example, a manager may have only two months of data. Sometimes this will be enough to get a crude approximation of the cost relationship.

In addition, the high-low method is simple, inexpensive, and easily communicated to other individuals, even those who are not comfortable with numerical analyses. For these reasons, managerial accountants often use the high-low method.

However, the high-low method also has several disadvantages that lead some managers to believe that it is not as good as the other methods at separating mixed costs into fixed and variable components. Why? First, the high and low points often can be what are known as outliers. They may represent atypical cost-activity relationships. For instance, if in the LaBico example the high output had been 1,000 moves (rather than 500) due to some extremely unusual business activity during a given month, then this high point likely would have fallen outside of the company's relevant range of operations and, therefore, represented an outlier. In the case of outliers, the cost formula computed using these two points will not represent what usually takes place. The scattergraph method can help a manager avoid this trap by selecting two points that appear to be representative of the general cost-activity pattern. Second, even if the high and low points are not outliers, other pairs of points may be more representative. To stress the likelihood of this possibility, a high-low analysis of 50 weeks of data would ignore 96 percent (i.e., 48 out of the 50 weeks) of the data! Again, the scattergraph method allows the choice of more representative points.

Scattergraph Method

The **scattergraph method** is a way to see the cost relationship by plotting the data points on a graph. The first step in applying the scattergraph method is to plot the data

CORNERSTONE 3-2

The HOW and WHY of Using the High-Low Method

Information:

BlueDenim Company makes blue jeans. The company controller wants to calculate the fixed and variable costs associated with electricity used in the factory. Data for the past eight months were collected:

Month	Electricity Cost ($)	Machine Hours
January	3,255	460
February	3,485	500
March	4,100	600
April	3,300	470
May	3,312	470
June	2,575	350
July	3,910	570
August	4,200	590

Required:

Using the high-low method, calculate the fixed cost of electricity, calculate the variable rate per machine hour, and construct the cost formula for total electricity cost.

Solution:

Step 1—Find the high and low points: The high number of machine hours is in March, and the low number of machine hours is in June. (*Hint:* Did you notice that the high cost of $4,200 was for August? Yet August is not the high point because its number of machine hours is not the highest activity level. Remember, the high point is associated with the highest activity level; the low point is associated with the lowest activity level.)

Step 2—Calculate the variable rate:

Variable rate = (High cost − Low cost)/(High machine hours − Low machine hours)
= ($4,100 − $2,575) / (600 − 350) = $1,525/250
= $6.10 per machine hour

Step 3—Calculate the fixed cost:

Fixed cost = Total cost − (Variable rate × Machine hours)

Let's choose the high point with cost of $4,100 and machine hours of 600.

Fixed cost = $4,100 − ($6.10 × 600) = $4,100 − $3,660 = $440

(*Hint:* Check your work by computing fixed cost using the low point.)

Step 4—Construct a cost formula: If the variable rate is $6.10 per machine hour and fixed cost is $440 per month, then the formula for monthly electricity cost is:

Total electricity cost = $440 + ($6.10 × Machine hours)

WHY:

Because it is a simple, frequently used method to separate mixed costs into variable and fixed components.

points so that the relationship between materials handling costs and activity output can be seen. This plot is referred to as a scattergraph and is shown in Exhibit 3-7A. The vertical axis is total cost (materials handling cost), and the horizontal axis is the driver

The HOW and WHY of Using the High-Low Method to Calculate Predicted Total Variable Cost and Total Cost for Budgeted Output

CORNERSTONE 3-3

Information:
Recall that BlueDenim Company constructed the following formula for monthly electricity cost. (Refer to Cornerstone 3-2 to see how the fixed cost per month and the variable rate were computed.)

Total electricity cost = $440 + ($6.10 × Machine hours)

Required:
Assume that 550 machine hours are budgeted for the month of September. Use the previous cost formula for the following calculations:

1. Calculate total variable electricity cost for September.
2. Calculate total electricity cost for September.

Solution:

1. Total variable electricity cost = Variable rate × Machine hours
 = $6.10 × 550
 = $3,355
2. Total electricity cost = Fixed cost + (Variable rate × Machine hours)
 = $440 + ($6.10 × 550)
 = $440 + $3,355
 = $3,795

Required:
Assume that 6,500 machine hours are budgeted for the coming year. Use the previous cost formula to make the following calculations:

1. Calculate total variable electricity cost for the year.
2. Calculate total fixed electricity cost for the year.
3. Calculate total electricity cost for the coming year.

Solution:

1. Total variable electricity cost = Variable rate × Machine hours
 = $6.10 × 6,500
 = $39,650
2. There's a trick here; the cost formula is for the month, but we are being asked to budget electricity for the year. Thus we will need to multiply the fixed cost for the month by 12 (the number of months in a year).

 Total fixed electricity cost = Fixed cost × 12 months in a year
 = $440 × 12
 = $5,280
3. Total electricity cost = 12($440) + ($6.10 × 6,500)
 = $5,280 + $39,650
 = $44,930

WHY:
Because the H-L method lends itself not only to assisting with separating mixed costs but also to using the cost formula as a prediction model for future variable and total costs.

or output measure (number of moves). Looking at Exhibit 3-7A, we see that the relationship between materials handling costs and number of moves is reasonably linear; cost goes up as the number of moves goes up, and vice versa.

Now let's examine Exhibit 3-7B to see if the line determined by the high and low points is representative of the overall relationship. Notice that three points lie above the high-low line and five lie below it. This realization does not give us confidence in the high-low results for fixed and variable costs. In particular, we might wonder if the variable cost (slope) is somewhat higher than it should be and the fixed cost is somewhat lower than it should be.

Exhibit 3-7A

LaBico's Materials Handling Cost Scattergraph Showing Data Points

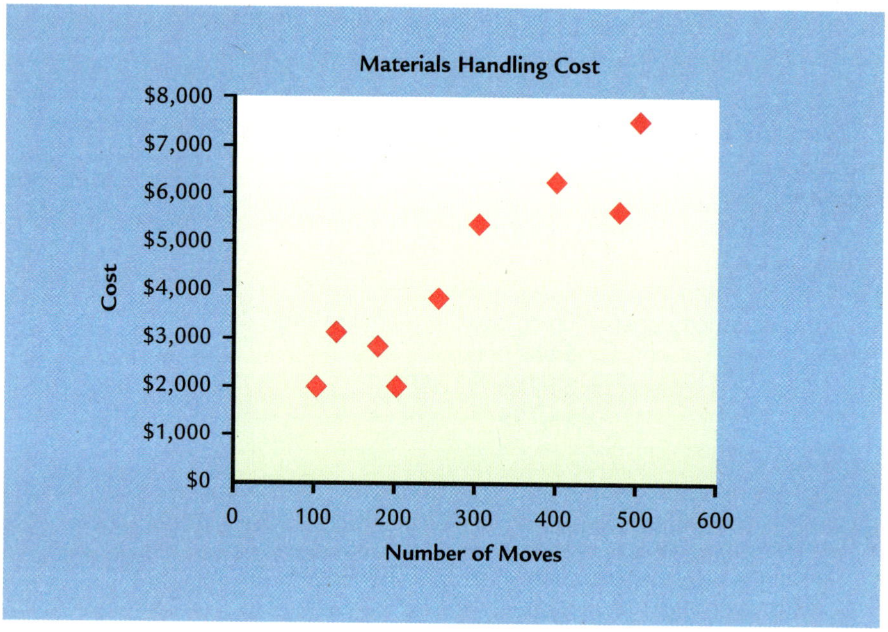

Exhibit 3-7B

Scattergraph with the High-Low Cost Line

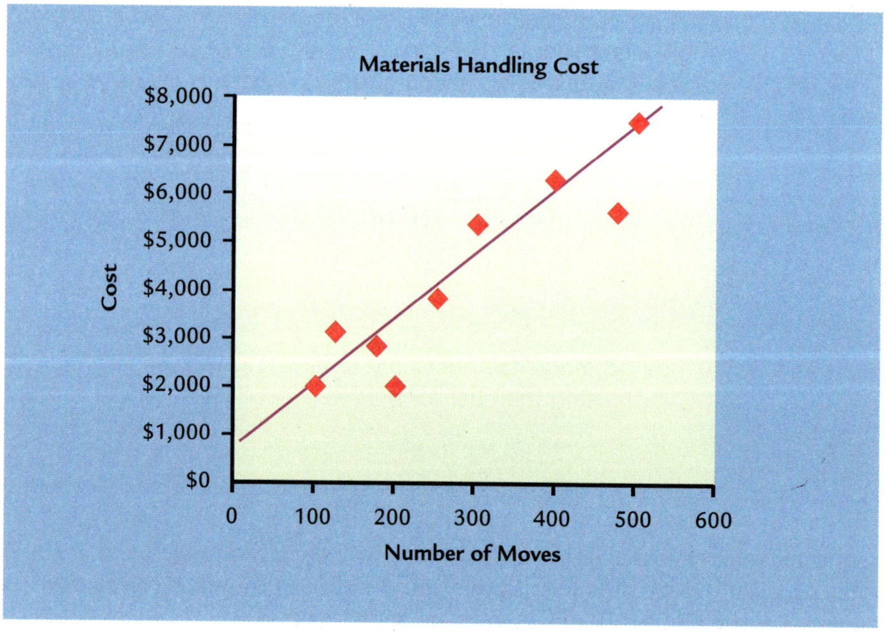

Thus, one purpose of a scattergraph is to see whether or not a straight line reasonably describes the cost relationship. Additionally, inspecting the scattergraph may reveal one or more points that do not seem to fit the general pattern of behaviour. Upon investigation, it may be discovered that these points (the outliers) were due to some irregular occurrences that are not expected to happen again. This knowledge might justify their elimination and perhaps lead to a better estimate of the underlying cost function.

We can use the scattergraph to visually fit a line to the data points on the graph. Of course, the manager or cost analyst will choose the line that appears to fit the points the best, and perhaps that choice will take into account past experience with the behaviour of the cost item. Experience may provide a good intuitive sense of how materials handling costs behave; the scattergraph then becomes a useful tool to quantify this intuition. Fitting a line to the points in this way is how the scattergraph method works. Keep in mind that the scattergraph and other statistical aids are tools that can help managers improve their judgment. Using the tools does not restrict the manager from using judgment to alter any of the estimates produced by formal methods.

Examine Exhibit 3-7A carefully. Based only on the information contained in the graph, how would you fit a line to the points in it? Of course, an infinite number of lines might go through the data, but let's choose one that goes through the point for January (100, \$2,000) and intersects the y-axis at \$800. This gives us the straight line shown in Exhibit 3-7C. The fixed cost, of course, is \$800, the intercept. We can use the high-low method to determine the variable rate.

First, remember that our two points are (100, \$2,000) and (0, \$800). Next, use these two points to compute the variable rate (the slope):

$$\text{Variable rate} = \frac{\text{High point cost} - \text{Low point cost}}{\text{High point number of moves} - \text{Low point number of moves}}$$

$$= (\$2{,}000 - \$800)/(100 - 0)$$
$$= \$1{,}200/100$$
$$= \$12$$

Thus the variable rate is \$12 per material move.

Exhibit 3-7C

Scattergraph with the Cost Line Fitted by Visual Inspection

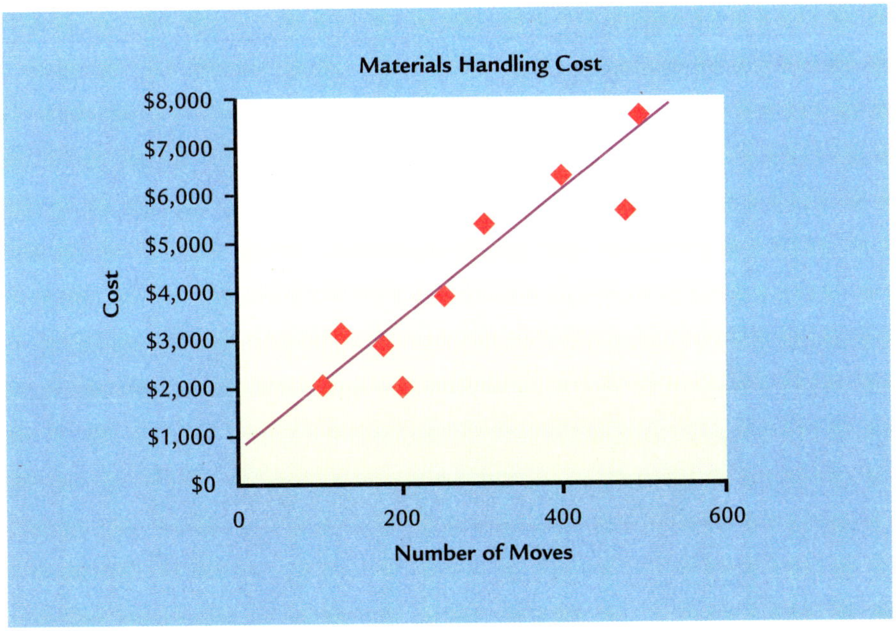

Fob 2 557 PM

The fixed cost and variable rate for materials handling cost have now been identified. The cost formula for the materials handling activity can be expressed as:

$$\text{Total cost} = \$800 + \$12 \times \text{Number of moves}$$

Using this formula, the total cost of materials handling for between 100 and 500 moves can be predicted and then broken down into fixed and variable components. For example, assume that 350 moves are planned for November. Using the cost formula, the predicted cost is $5,000 [$800 + ($12 × 350)]. Of this total cost, $800 is fixed, and $4,200 is variable.

A significant advantage of the scattergraph method is that it allows a cost analyst to inspect the data visually. Exhibits 3-8A, B, and C illustrate cost behaviour situations that are not appropriate for the simple application of the high-low method. Exhibit 3-8A shows a nonlinear relationship between cost and output. An example of this type of relationship is a volume discount given on direct materials or evidence of learning by workers (e.g., as more hours are worked, the total cost increases at a decreasing rate due to the increased efficiency of the workers). Exhibit 3-8B shows an upward shift in cost if more than X_1 units are made—perhaps because an additional supervisor must be hired or a second shift run. Exhibit 3-8C shows outliers that do not represent the overall cost relationship.

CONCEPT Q&A

Draw a straight line through the high and low points on each graph in Exhibit 3-8. Can you see that these lines, the high-low lines, could give misleading information on fixed and variable costs?

Answers on pages 711 to 715.

The cost formula for materials handling was obtained by fitting a line to two points [(0, $800) and (100, $2,000)] in Exhibit 3-7C. Judgment was used to select the line. Whereas one person may decide that the best-fitting line is the one passing through those points, others, using their own judgment, may decide that the best line passes through other pairs of points.

The scattergraph method suffers from the lack of any objective criterion for choosing the best-fitting line. The quality of the cost formula depends on the quality of the subjective judgment of the analyst. The high-low method removes the subjectivity in the choice of the line. Regardless of who uses the method, the same line will result.

Looking again at Exhibits 3-7B and 3-7C, we can compare the results of the scattergraph method with those of the high-low method. There is a difference between the fixed cost components and the variable rates. The predicted materials handling cost for 350 moves is $5,000 according to the scattergraph method and $5,438 according to the high-low method. Which is correct? Since the two methods can produce significantly different cost formulas, the question of which method is the best naturally arises. Ideally, a method that is objective and, at the same time, produces the best-fitting line is needed. Let's take a look at the method of least squares.

Exhibit 3-8A

Scattergraphs with Nonlinear Cost

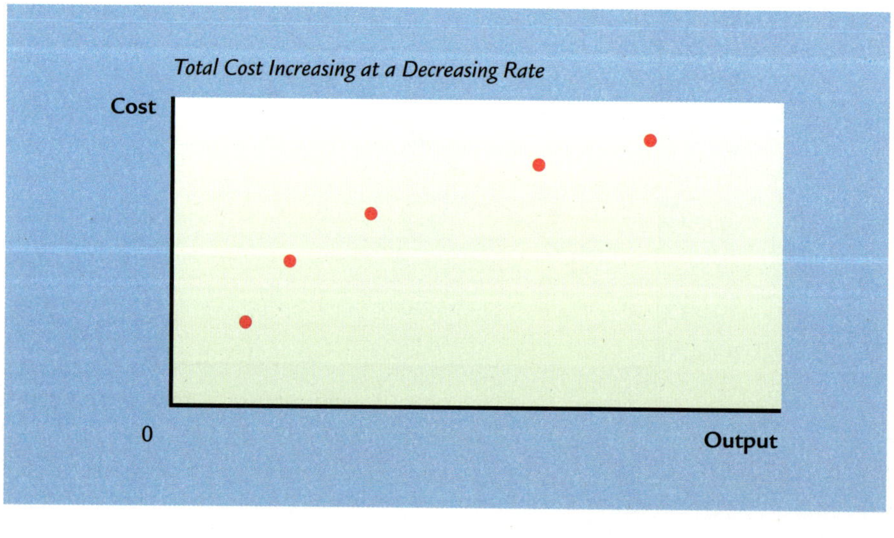

Exhibit 3-8B

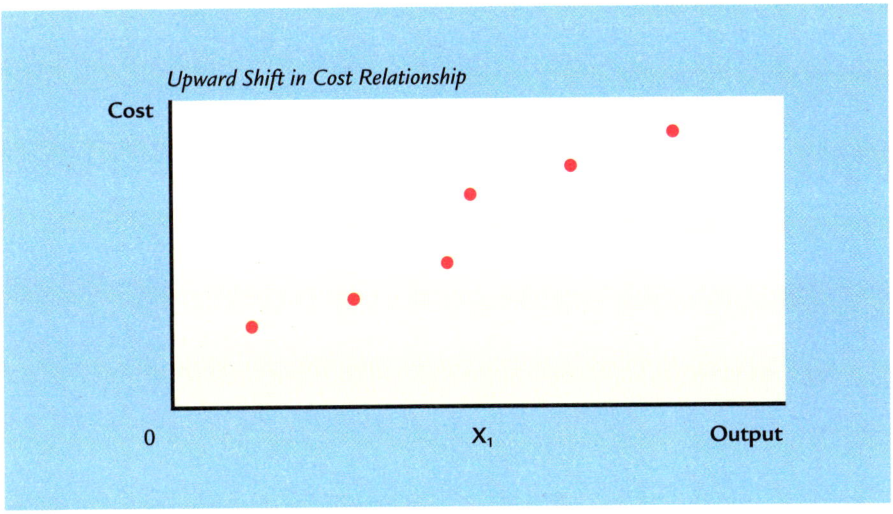

Exhibit 3-8C

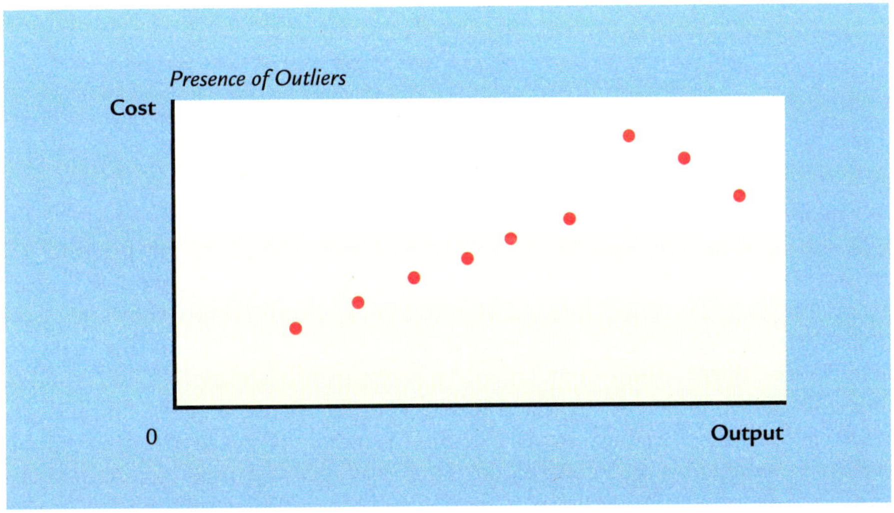

The Method of Least Squares

The **method of least squares (regression)** is a statistical way to find the *best-fitting* line through a set of data points. One advantage of the method of least squares is that for a given set of data, it will always produce the same cost formula. Basically, the best-fitting line is the one in which the data points are closer to the line than to any other line. What do we mean by closest? Let's take a look at Exhibit 3-9. Notice that there are a series of data points and a line—we'll assume that it is the regression line calculated by the method of least squares. The data points do not all lie directly on the line; this is typical. However, the regression line better describes the pattern of the data than other possible lines. This best description results because the squared deviations between the regression line and each data point are, in total, smaller than the sum of the squared deviations of the data points and any other line. The least squares statistical formulas can find the one line with the smallest sum of squared deviations. In other words, this method identifies the regression line that minimizes the cost prediction errors or differences between predicted costs (i.e., on the regression line) and actual costs (i.e., the actual data points). Given that the method of least squares generates the smallest possible cost prediction errors, many managers refer to it as the most accurate method.

Exhibit 3-9

Line Deviations

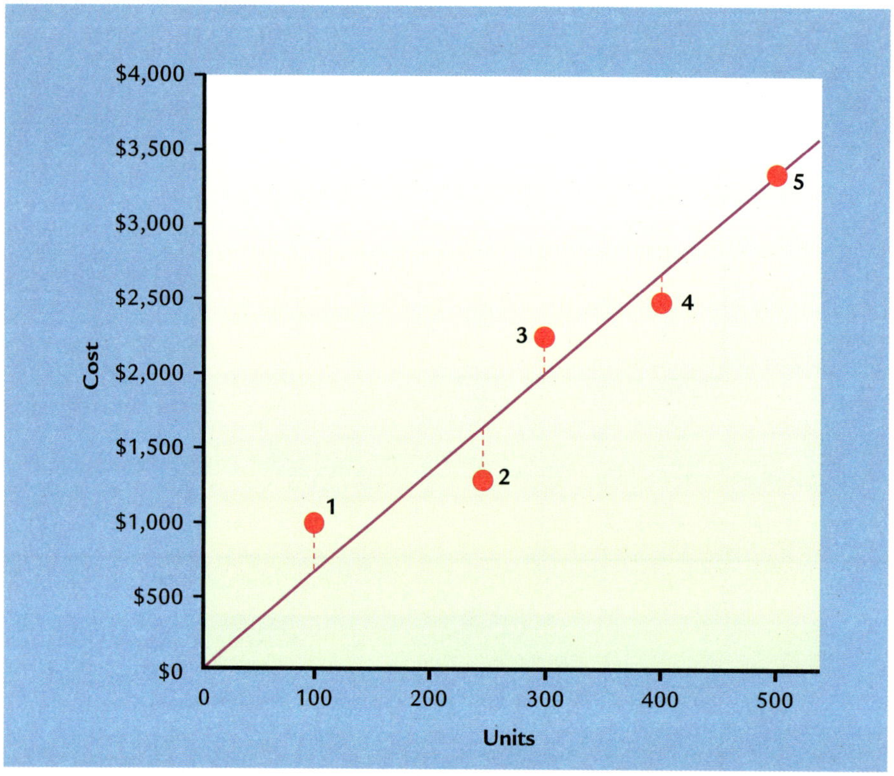

Formerly, the method of least squares had to be calculated by hand. It was a complicated and lengthy process. Today, spreadsheet programs for personal computers have regression packages. It is easy to use them to input data and to let the programs calculate the fixed cost and variable rate. Exhibit 3-10 shows a printout from a Microsoft Excel® spreadsheet regression that was run on the data from LaBico. Notice that the intercept term is the fixed cost, which is $789 (rounded). The variable rate is shown as "X Variable 1"; in other words, it is the first independent variable. So, the variable rate is $12.38 (rounded). We can use the output of regression in budgeting and control the same way that we used the results of the high-low and scattergraph methods.

Exhibit 3-10

A Portion of the Summary Output from Excel for LaBico

	A	B
1	**Coefficients:**	
2	**Intercept**	**788.7806**
3	**X Variable 1**	**12.38058**

Sheet1 / Sheet2 / Sheet3

The HOW and WHY of Using the Regression Method to Calculate Fixed Cost and the Variable Rate and to Construct a Cost Formula and to Determine Budgeted Cost

CORNERSTONE 3-4

Information:
BlueDenim Company makes blue jeans. The company controller wants to calculate the fixed and variable costs associated with electricity used in the factory. Data for the past eight months are collected:

Month	Electricity Cost ($)	Machine Hours
January	3,255	460
February	3,485	500
March	4,100	600
April	3,300	470
May	3,312	470
June	2,575	350
July	3,910	570
August	4,200	590

Coefficients shown by a regression program are:

Intercept	321
X Variable 1	6.38

Required:
Use the results of regression to perform the following.

1. Calculate the fixed cost of electricity and the variable rate per machine hour.
2. Construct the cost formula for total electricity cost.
3. Calculate the budgeted cost for next month, assuming that 550 machine hours are budgeted.

Solution:

1. The fixed cost and the variable rate are given directly by regression.

   Fixed cost = $321
   Variable rate = $6.38

2. The cost formula is:

   Total electricity cost = $321 + ($6.38 × Machine hours)

3. Budgeted electricity cost = $321 + ($6.38 × 550) = $3,830

WHY:
Because the regression method is using an objective statistical formula that provides the best or most accurate cost estimates and that generates the smallest possible cost prediction errors.

Suppose that LaBico expects the number of moves for November to be 350. Budgeted materials handling cost would be $5,122, or $789 + ($12.38 × 350). Alternatively, suppose the controller wondered whether or not October's materials handling cost of $6,240 was reasonably close to what would have been predicted. Our cost formula would predict October cost of $6,051 (rounded). (This amount is found by multiplying $12.38 times the 425 actual moves and then adding the fixed cost of $789.) The actual cost is just $189 different from the predicted cost and probably would be judged to be reasonably close to the budgeted cost. Cornerstone 3-4 shows how to use results of regression to construct a cost formula.

Managerial Judgment

Managerial judgment is critically important in determining cost behaviour and is by far the most widely used method in practice. Many managers simply use their experience and past observation of cost relationships to determine fixed and variable costs. This method, however, may take a number of forms. Some managers simply assign some costs to the fixed category and others to the variable category. They ignore the possibility of mixed costs. Thus, a chemical firm may regard materials and utilities as strictly variable, with respect to kilograms of chemical produced, and all other costs as fixed. Even labour, the textbook example of a strictly variable cost, may be fixed for this firm. The appeal of this method is simplicity. Before opting for this method, management would do well to make sure that each cost is predominantly fixed or variable and that the decisions being made are not highly sensitive to errors in classifying costs as fixed or variable.

To illustrate the use of judgment in assessing cost behaviour, consider **Elgin Sweeper Company**, a leading manufacturer of motorized street sweepers. Using production volume as the measure of activity output, Elgin revised its chart of accounts to organize costs into fixed and variable components. Elgin's accountants used their knowledge of the company to assign expenses to either a fixed or variable category, using a decision rule that categorized an expense as fixed if it were fixed at least 75 percent of the time and as variable if it were variable at least 75 percent of the time.[3]

Management may instead identify mixed costs and divide these costs into fixed and variable components by deciding what the fixed and variable parts are; that is, they may use experience to say that a certain amount of a cost is fixed and that the rest therefore must be variable. Suppose that a small business had a photocopier with a fixed cost of $3,000 per year. The variable component could be computed by using one or more cost/volume data points. This approach has the advantage of accounting for mixed costs but is subject to a similar type of error as the strict fixed/variable dichotomy. That is, management may be wrong in its assessment.

CONCEPT Q&A

Suppose that you own a small business with a photocopier that a neighbouring business owner asks to use occasionally. What is the average cost of copying one page? What cost items would you include? Now consider Kinko's: What cost items do you think it would include?

Answers on pages 711 to 715.

Finally, management may use experience and judgment to refine statistical estimation results. Perhaps the experienced manager might "eyeball" the data and throw out several points as being highly unusual or revise the results of estimation to take account of projected changes in cost structure or technology. For example, **Tecnol Medical Products Inc.** radically changed its method of manufacturing medical face masks. Traditionally, face-mask production was labour intensive, requiring hand stitching. Tecnol developed its own highly automated equipment and became the industry's low cost supplier—besting both **Johnson & Johnson** and **3M**. Tecnol's rapid expansion into new product lines and European markets means that historical data on costs and revenues are for the most part irrelevant. Tecnol's management must look forward, not back, to predict the impact of changes on profit.[4] Statistical techniques are highly accurate in depicting the past, but they cannot foresee the future, which of course is what management really wants.

The advantage of using managerial judgment to separate fixed and variable costs is its simplicity. In situations in which the manager has a deep understanding of the firm and its cost patterns, this method can give good results. However, if the manager does not have good judgment, errors will occur. Therefore, it is important to consider the experience of the manager, the potential for error, and the effect that error could have on related decisions.

ETHICS There are ethical implications to the use of managerial judgment. Managers use their knowledge of fixed and variable costs to make important decisions, such as whether to switch suppliers, expand or contract production, or lay off

[3] John P. Callan, Wesley N. Tredup, and Randy S. Wissinger, "Elgin Sweeper Company's Journey Toward Cost Management," *Management Accounting* (July 1991): 24–27.

[4] Stephanie Anderson Forest, "Who's Afraid of J&J and 3M," *Business Week* (December 5, 1994): 66, 68.

workers. These decisions affect the lives of workers, suppliers, and customers. The ethical manager will make sure that he or she has the best information possible when making these decisions. In addition, the manager will not let personal factors affect the use of cost information. For example, suppose that the purchasing department manager has a good friend who wants to supply some materials for production. The price of the materials is slightly lower than that of the current supplier; however, the friend's company will not ensure 100 percent quality control—and that will lead to additional costs for rework and warranty repair. The ethical manager will include these additional costs along with the purchase price to calculate the full cost of purchasing from the friend's company.◆

Summary of Learning Objectives

LO1. Explain the meaning of cost behaviour, and define and describe fixed and variable costs.

- Cost behaviour is the way a cost changes in relation to changes in activity output.
- Time horizon is important because costs can change from fixed to variable depending on whether the decision takes place over the short run or the long run.
- Variable costs change *in total* as the driver, or output measure, changes. Usually, we assume that variable costs increase in direct proportion to increases in activity output.
- Fixed costs do not change *in total* as activity output changes.

LO2. Define and describe mixed and step costs.

- Mixed costs have both a variable and a fixed component.
- Step costs remain at a constant level of cost for a range of output and then jump to a higher level of cost at some point, where it remains for a similar range of output.
- Cost objects that display a step cost behaviour must be purchased in chunks.
- The width of the step defines the range of output for which a particular amount of the resource applies.

LO3. Separate mixed costs into their fixed and variable components using the high-low method, the scattergraph method, and the method of least squares.

- In the high-low method, only two data points are used—the high point and the low point with respect to activity level. These two points then are used to compute the intercept and the slope of the line on which they lie.
- The high-low method is objective and easy, but a nonrepresentative high or low point will lead to an incorrectly estimated cost relationship.
- The scattergraph method involves inspecting a graph showing total mixed cost at various output levels and selecting two points that seem to best represent the relationship between cost and output, and drawing a straight line. The intercept gives an estimate of the fixed cost component and the slope an estimate of the variable cost per unit of activity.
- The scattergraph method is a good way to identify nonlinearity, the presence of outliers, and the presence of a shift in the cost relationship. Its disadvantage is that it is subjective.
- The method of least squares uses all of the data points (except outliers) on the scattergraph and produces a line that best fits all of the points.
- The method of least squares offers ways to assess the reliability of cost equations.
- Managers use their experience and knowledge of cost and activity-level relationships to identify outliers, understand structural shifts, and adjust parameters due to anticipated changing conditions.

Summary of Important Equations

1. Cost formula: Total cost = Total fixed cost + (variable rate × units of output)
2. Total variable cost = Variable rate × Units of output

CORNERSTONES FOR CHAPTER 3

CORNERSTONE 3-1 The HOW and WHY of creating and using a cost formula, page 85

CORNERSTONE 3-2 The HOW and WHY of using the high-low method, page 88

CORNERSTONE 3-3 The HOW and WHY of using the high-low method to calculate predicted total variable cost and total cost for budgeted output, page 89

CORNERSTONE 3-4 The HOW and WHY of using the regression method to calculate fixed cost and the variable rate and to construct a cost formula and to determine budgeted cost, page 95

Key Terms

Committed fixed costs, 79
Cost behaviour, 77
Cost driver, 77
Dependent variable, 84
Discretionary fixed costs, 79
Fixed costs, 77
High-low method, 86
Independent variable, 84
Intercept, 84
Method of least squares (regression), 93
Mixed costs, 82
Relevant range, 77
Scattergraph method, 87
Semi-variable, 81
Slope, 84
Step cost, 82
Variable costs, 79

OBJECTIVE 4
Use a personal computer spreadsheet program to perform the method of least squares.

Appendix: Using the Regression Programs

Computing the regression formula manually is tedious, even with only a few data points. As the number of data points increases, manual computation becomes impractical. Fortunately, spreadsheet packages such as Microsoft Excel have regression routines that will perform the computations. All you need to do is input the data. The spreadsheet regression program supplies more than the estimates of the coefficients. It also provides information that can be used to see how reliable the cost equation is—a feature that is not available for the scattergraph and high-low methods.

The first step in using the computer to calculate regression coefficients is to enter the data. Exhibit 3-11 shows the computer screen that you would see if you entered the LaBico data on moves into a spreadsheet. It is a good idea to label your variables as is done in the exhibit. That is, the months are labelled, as are column B for moving costs and column C for number of moves. The next step is to run the regression. In Excel, the regression routine is located under the tools menu (located toward the top right of the screen). When you pull down the tools menu, you will see other menu possibilities. Choose add in, and then add the data analysis tools. When the data analysis tools have been added, data analysis will appear at the bottom of the tools menu; click on data analysis and then on regression.

Exhibit 3-11

Spreadsheet Data for LaBico

	A	B	C	D	E	F	G	H
1	Month	Cost	# Moves					
2	January	$2,000	100					
3	February	3,090	125					
4	March	2,780	175					
5	April	1,990	200					
6	May	7,500	500					
7	June	5,300	300					
8	July	3,800	250					
9	August	6,300	400					
10	September	5,600	475					
11								
12								
13								
14								

Sheet1 / Sheet2 / Sheet3

When the regression screen pops up, you can tell the program where the dependent and independent variables are located. Simply place the cursor at the beginning of the independent rectangle and then (again using the cursor) block the values under the independent variable column—in this case, cells c2 through c10. Then, move the cursor to the beginning of the dependent rectangle, and block the values in cells b2 through b10. Finally, you need to tell the computer where to place the output. Block a nice-size rectangle, say cells a13 through f 20, and click on OK. In less than the blink of an eye, the regression output is complete. The regression output is shown in Exhibit 3-12.

Now, let's take a look at the output in Exhibit 3-12. First, let's locate the fixed cost and variable rate coefficients. At the bottom of the exhibit, the intercept and X Variable 1 are shown, and the next column gives their coefficients. Rounding, the fixed cost is 789 and the variable rate is 12.38. Now we can construct the cost formula for materials handling cost. It is:

$$\text{Materials handling cost} = \$789 + (\$12.38 \times \text{Number of moves})$$

We can use this formula to predict the materials handling cost for future months as we did with the formulas for the high-low and scattergraph methods.

Since the regression cost formula is the best-fitting line, it should produce better predictions of materials handling costs. For 350 moves, the total materials handling cost predicted by the least squares line is $5,122 [$789 + ($12.38 × 350)], with a

Exhibit 3-12

Regression Output for LaBico

	A	B	C	D	E	F	G	H
1	SUMMARY OUTPUT							
2								
3	*Regression Statistics*							
4	Multiple R	0.92436						
5	R Square	0.854442						
6	Standard Error	810.1969						
7	Observations	9						
8								
9								
10		*Coefficients*						
11	Intercept	788.7806						
12	X Variable 1	12.38058						
13								
14								
15								

Sheet1 / Sheet2 / Sheet3

fixed component of $789 plus a variable component of $4,333. Using this prediction as a standard, the scattergraph line most closely approximates the least squares line.

While the computer output in Exhibit 3-12 can give us the fixed and variable cost coefficients, its major usefulness lies in its ability to provide information about reliability of the estimated cost formula. This is a feature not provided by either the scattergraph or high-low methods.

Goodness of Fit

Regression routines provide information on goodness of fit. Goodness of fit tells us how well the independent variable predicts the dependent variable. This information can be used to assess reliability of the estimated cost formula, a feature not provided by either the scattergraph or high-low methods. The printout in Exhibit 3-12 provides a wealth of statistical information. However, we will look at just one more feature—the coefficient of determination, or R^2. (The remaining information is discussed in statistics classes and higher-level accounting classes.)

The LaBico example suggests that the number of moves can explain changes in materials handling costs. The scattergraph shown in Exhibit 3-7A confirms this belief because it reveals that materials handling costs and activity output (as measured by number of moves) seem to move together. It is quite likely that a significant percentage of the total variability in cost is explained by our output variable. We can determine statistically just how much variability is explained by looking at the coefficient of determination. The percentage of variability in the dependent variable explained by an independent variable (in this case, a measure of activity output) is called the **coefficient of determination (R^2)**. The higher the percentage of cost variability explained, the better job the independent variable does of explaining the dependent variable. Since R^2 is the percentage of variability explained, it always has a value between 0 and 1.00. In the printout in Exhibit 3-12, the coefficient of determination is labelled R Square (R^2). The value given is 0.85 (rounded), which means that 85 percent of the variability in the materials handling cost is explained by the number of moves. How good is this result? There is no cutoff point for a good versus bad coefficient of determination. Clearly, the closer R^2 is to 1.00, the better. Is 85 percent good enough? How about 73 percent? Or even 46 percent? The answer is that it depends. If your cost equation yields a coefficient of determination of 75 percent, you know that your independent variable explains three-fourths of the variability in cost. You also know that some other factor or combination of factors explains the remaining one-fourth. Depending on your tolerance for error, you may want to improve the equation by trying different independent variables (e.g., materials handling hours worked rather than number of moves) or by trying multiple regression. (Multiple regression uses two or more independent variables. This topic is saved for later courses.)

We note from the computer output in Exhibit 3-12 that the R^2 for materials handling cost is 0.85. In other words, material moves explain about 85 percent of the variability in the materials handling cost. This is not bad. However, something else explains the remaining 15 percent. LaBico's controller may want to keep this in mind when using the regression results.

Appendix: Summary of Learning Objectives

LO4. Use a personal computer spreadsheet program to perform the method of least squares.

Key Term for Appendix

Coefficient of determination (R^2), 100

Review Problem

Kim Wilson, controller for Max Enterprises, has decided to estimate the fixed and variable components associated with the company's shipping activity. She has collected the following data for the past six months:

Packages Shipped	Total Shipping Costs ($)
10	800
20	1,100
15	900
12	900
18	1,050
25	1,250

Required:

1. Estimate the fixed and variable components for the shipping costs using the high-low method. Using the cost formula, predict the total cost of shipping if 14 packages are shipped.
2. Estimate the fixed and variable components using the method of least squares. Using the cost formula, predict the total cost of shipping if 14 packages are shipped.
3. (Appendix) For the method of least squares, explain what the coefficient of determination tells us.

Solution:

1. The estimate of fixed and variable costs using the high-low method is as follows:

$$\begin{aligned}\text{Variable rate} &= (\$1{,}250 - \$800)/(25 - 10)\\ &= \$450/15\\ &= \$30 \text{ per package}\end{aligned}$$

$$\text{Fixed amount} = \$1{,}250 - \$30(25) = \$500$$

$$\begin{aligned}\text{Total cost} &= \$500 + \$30X\\ &= \$500 + \$30(14)\\ &= \$920\end{aligned}$$

2. The output of a spreadsheet regression routine is as follows:
Regression output:

Constant	509.911894273125
Std Err of Y Est	32.1965672507378
R Squared	0.969285364659814
No. of Observations	6
Degrees of Freedom	4
X Coefficient(s)	29.4052863436125
Std Err of Coef	2.61723229918858

Y = $509.91 + $29.41(14) = $921.65

3. The coefficient of determination (R^2) tells us that about 96.9 percent of total shipping cost is explained by the number of packages shipped.

Discussion Questions

1. Why is knowledge of cost behaviour important for managerial decision making? Give an example to illustrate your answer.
2. What is a driver? Give an example of a cost and its corresponding output measure or driver.

3. Suppose a company finds that shipping cost is $3,560 each month plus $6.70 per package shipped. What is the cost formula for monthly shipping cost? Identify the independent variable, the dependent variable, the fixed cost per month, and the variable rate.
4. Some firms assign mixed costs to either the fixed or variable cost categories without using any formal methodology to separate them. Explain how this practice can be defended.
5. Explain the difference between committed and discretionary fixed costs. Give examples of each.
6. Explain why the concept of relevant range is important when dealing with step costs.
7. Why do mixed costs pose a problem when it comes to classifying costs into fixed and variable categories?
8. Describe the cost formula for a strictly fixed cost such as depreciation of $15,000 per year.
9. Describe the cost formula for a strictly variable cost such as electrical power cost of $1.15 per machine hour (i.e., every hour the machinery is run, electrical power cost goes up by $1.15).
10. What is the scattergraph method, and why is it used? Why is a scattergraph a good first step in separating mixed costs into their fixed and variable components?
11. Describe how the scattergraph method breaks out the fixed and variable costs from a mixed cost. Now describe how the high-low method works. How do the two methods differ?
12. What are the advantages of the scattergraph method over the high-low method? The high-low method over the scattergraph method?
13. Describe the method of least squares. Why is this method better than either the high-low method or the scattergraph method?
14. What is meant by the best-fitting line?
15. Explain the meaning of the coefficient of determination.

Multiple-Choice Exercises

3-1 A factor that causes or leads to a change in a cost or activity is a(n)

a. driver.
b. intercept.
c. slope.
d. variable term.
e. cost object.

3-2 Which of the following would probably be a variable cost in a soda bottling plant?

a. direct labour
b. bottles
c. carbonated water
d. power to run the bottling machine
e. all of the above

3-3 Which of the following would probably be a fixed cost in an automobile insurance company?

a. application forms
b. time spent by adjusters to evaluate accidents
c. the salary of customer service representatives
d. all of the above

3-4 The following cost formula was developed by using monthly data for a hospital.

$$\text{Total cost} = \$51{,}400 + (\$125 \times \text{Number of patient days})$$

The term $51,400

a. is the variable rate.
b. is the intercept.
c. is the dependent variable.
d. is the independent variable.
e. cannot be determined from the above formula.

3-5 The following cost formula was developed using monthly data for a hospital.

$$\text{Total cost} = \$51{,}400 + (\$125 \times \text{Number of patient days})$$

The term $125

a. is the variable rate.
b. is the intercept.
c. is the dependent variable.
d. is the independent variable.
e. cannot be determined from the above formula.

3-6 The following cost formula was developed using monthly data for a hospital.

$$\text{Total cost} = \$51{,}400 + (\$125 \times \text{Number of patient days})$$

The term "Number of patient days"

a. is the variable rate.
b. is the intercept.
c. is the dependent variable.
d. is the independent variable.
e. cannot be determined from the above formula.

3-7 The following cost formula was developed using monthly data for a hospital.

$$\text{Total cost} = \$51{,}400 + (\$125 \times \text{Number of patient days})$$

The term "Total cost"

a. is the variable rate.
b. is the intercept.
c. is the dependent variable.
d. is the independent variable.
e. cannot be determined from the above formula.

3-8 The following cost formula for total purchasing cost in a factory was developed using monthly data.

$$\text{Purchasing cost} = \$123{,}800 + (\$15 \times \text{Number of purchase orders})$$

Next month, 2,000 purchase orders are predicted. The total cost predicted for the purchasing department next month

a. is $2,000.
b. is $153,800.
c. is $30,000.
d. is $123,800.
e. cannot be determined from the above formula.

3-9 An advantage of the high-low method is that it

a. is objective.
b. is subjective.
c. is the most accurate method.
d. removes outliers.
e. is descriptive of nonlinear data.

3-10 The following six months of data were collected on maintenance cost and the number of machine hours in a factory:

Month	Maintenance Cost ($)	Machine Hours
January	16,900	5,600
February	13,900	4,500
March	10,900	3,800
April	11,450	3,700
May	13,050	4,215
June	16,990	4,980

Select the independent and dependent variables.

	Independent Variable	Dependent Variable
a.	Maintenance cost	Machine hours
b.	Machine hours	Maintenance cost
c.	Maintenance cost	Month
d.	Machine hours	Month
e.	Month	Maintenance cost

3-11 The following six months of data were collected on maintenance cost and the number of machine hours in a factory:

Month	Maintenance Cost ($)	Machine Hours
January	16,900	5,600
February	13,900	4,500
March	10,900	3,800
April	11,450	3,700
May	13,050	4,215
June	16,990	4,980

Select the correct set of high and low months.

	High	Low
a.	January	April
b.	January	March
c.	June	March
d.	June	April

3-12 An advantage of the scattergraph method is that it

a. is objective.
b. is easier to use than the high-low method.
c. is the most accurate method.
d. removes outliers.
e. is descriptive of nonlinear data.

3-13 The cost formula for monthly supervisory cost in a factory is

$$\text{Total cost} = \$4,500$$

This cost

a. is strictly variable.
b. is strictly fixed.
c. is a mixed cost.
d. is a step cost.
e. cannot be determined from this information.

3-14 (Appendix) In the method of least squares, the coefficient that tells the percentage of variation in the dependent variable that is explained by the independent variable is

a. the intercept term.
b. the x-coefficient.
c. the coefficient of correlation.
d. the coefficient of determination.
e. none of the above.

Cornerstone Exercises

Cornerstone Exercise 3-15 CREATING AND USING A COST FORMULA

OBJECTIVE 3
CORNERSTONE 3-1

Big Thumbs Company manufactures portable flash drives for computers. Big Thumbs incurs monthly depreciation costs of $15,000 on its plant equipment and monthly advertising costs of $3,000 to place advertisements in magazines. Also, each drive requires materials and manufacturing overhead resources. On average, the company uses 280,000 grams of materials to manufacture 5,000 flash drives per month. Each gram of material costs $0.10. In addition, manufacturing overhead resources are driven by machine hours. On average, the company incurs $22,500 of manufacturing overhead resources to produce 5,000 flash drives per month.

Required:

1. Create a formula for the monthly cost of flash drives for Big Thumbs.
2. If the department expects to manufacture 6,000 flash drives next month, what is the expected fixed cost (assume that 6,000 units is within the company's current relevant range)? Total variable cost? Total manufacturing cost (i.e., both fixed and variable)?

Cornerstone Exercise 3-16 USING HIGH-LOW TO CALCULATE FIXED COST, CALCULATE THE VARIABLE RATE, AND CONSTRUCT A COST FUNCTION

OBJECTIVE 3
CORNERSTONE 3-2

Pizza Vesuvio makes specialty pizzas. Vesuvio's controller wants to calculate the fixed and variable costs associated with labour used in the restaurant. Data for the past eight months were collected:

Month	Labour Cost ($)	Employee Hours
January	7,000	360
February	8,140	550
March	9,010	585
April	9,787	610
May	8,490	480
June	2,450	350
July	9,490	570
August	7,531	310

Required:

Using the high-low method, calculate the fixed cost of labour, calculate the variable rate per employee hour, and construct the cost formula for total labour cost.

OBJECTIVE 3
CORNERSTONE 3-3

Cornerstone Exercise 3-17 USING HIGH-LOW TO CALCULATE PREDICTED TOTAL VARIABLE COST AND TOTAL COST FOR BUDGETED OUTPUT

Refer to the Pizza Vesuvio company information in **Cornerstone Exercise 3-16.** Assume that Pizza Vesuvio used this information to construct the following formula for monthly labour cost.

Total labour cost = \$5,200 + (\$7.52 × Employee hours)

Required:

Assume that 675 employee hours are budgeted for the month of September. Use the total labour cost formula for the following calculations:

1. Total variable labour cost for September.
2. Total labour cost for September.

OBJECTIVE 3
CORNERSTONE 3-4

Cornerstone Exercise 3-18 USING HIGH-LOW TO CALCULATE PREDICTED TOTAL VARIABLE COST AND TOTAL COST FOR A TIME PERIOD THAT DIFFERS FROM THE DATA PERIOD

Refer to the Pizza Vesuvio company information in **Cornerstone Exercise 3-16.** Assume that Pizza Vesuvio used this information to construct the following formula for monthly labour cost.

Total labour cost = \$5,200 + (\$7.52 × Employee hours)

Required:

Assume that 4,000 employee hours are budgeted for the coming year. Use the total labour cost formula to make the following calculations:

1. Total variable labour cost for the year.
2. Total fixed labour cost for the year.
3. Total labour cost for the coming year.

OBJECTIVE 3
CORNERSTONE 3-5

Cornerstone Exercise 3-19 USING REGRESSION TO CALCULATE FIXED COST, CALCULATE THE VARIABLE RATE, CONSTRUCT A COST FORMULA, AND DETERMINE BUDGETED COST

Refer to the Pizza Vesuvio company information in **Cornerstone Exercise 3-16.** Coefficients shown by a regression program for this data are:

Intercept	1,145
X Variable	13.82

Required:

Use the results of regression to do the following:

1. Calculate the fixed cost of labour and the variable rate per employee hour.
2. Construct the cost formula for total labour cost.
3. Calculate the budgeted cost for next month, assuming that 675 employee hours are budgeted. Round answers to the nearest dollar.

Exercises

OBJECTIVE 1

Exercise 3-20 VARIABLE AND FIXED COSTS

What follows are a number of resources that are used by a manufacturer of futons. Assume that the output measure or cost driver is the number of futons produced. All direct labour is paid on an hourly basis, and hours worked can be easily changed by management. All other factory workers are salaried.

a. Power to operate a drill (to drill holes in the wooden frames of the futons)
b. Cloth to cover the futon mattress
c. Salary of the factory receptionist
d. Cost of food and decorations for the annual Canada Day party for all factory employees
e. Fuel for a forklift used to move materials in a factory
f. Depreciation on the factory
g. Depreciation on a forklift used to move partially completed goods
h. Wages paid to workers who assemble the futon frame
i. Wages paid to workers who maintain the factory equipment
j. Cloth rags used to wipe the excess stain off the wooden frames

Required:

Classify the resource costs as variable or fixed.

Exercise 3-21 COST BEHAVIOUR, CLASSIFICATION

OBJECTIVE 1

Luccheti Concrete Company owns enough ready-mix trucks to deliver up to 100,000 cubic metres of concrete per year (considering each truck's capacity, weather, and distance to each job). Total truck depreciation is $200,000 per year. Raw materials (cement, gravel, and so on) cost about $25 per cubic metres of cement.

Required:

1. Prepare a graph for truck depreciation. Use the vertical axis for cost and the horizontal axis for cubic metres of cement.
2. Prepare a graph for raw materials. Use the vertical axis for cost and the horizontal axis for cubic metres of cement.
3. Assume that the normal operating range for the company is 90,000 to 96,000 cubic metres per year. Classify truck depreciation and raw materials as variable or fixed costs.

Exercise 3-22 CLASSIFYING COSTS AS FIXED OR VARIABLE IN A SERVICE ORGANIZATION

OBJECTIVE 1

Orangeville Community Hospital has five laboratory technicians who are responsible for doing a series of standard blood tests. Each technician is paid a salary of $30,000. The lab facility represents a recent addition to the hospital and cost $300,000. It is expected to last 20 years. Equipment used for the testing cost $10,000 and has a life expectancy of five years. In addition to the salaries, facility, and equipment, Alva expects to spend $200,000 for chemicals, forms, power, and other supplies. This $200,000 is enough for 200,000 blood tests.

Required:

Assuming that the driver (measure of output) for each type of cost is the number of blood tests run, classify the costs by completing the following table. Put a check mark in the appropriate box for variable cost, discretionary fixed cost, or committed fixed cost.

Cost Category	Variable Cost	Discretionary Fixed Cost	Committed Fixed Cost
Technician salaries			
Laboratory facility			
Laboratory equipment			
Chemicals and other supplies			

Exercise 3-23 COST BEHAVIOUR

OBJECTIVE 1

Alisha Incorporated manufactures medical stints for use in heart bypass surgery. Based on past experience, Alisha has found that its total maintenance costs can be represented by the following formula: Maintenance cost = $310,000 + $18.50X, where X = Number of heart stints. Last year, Alisha produced 150,000 stints. Actual maintenance costs for the year were as expected. Round all answers to two decimal places.

Required:

1. What is the total maintenance cost incurred by Alisha last year?
2. What is the total fixed maintenance cost incurred by Alisha last year?
3. What is the total variable maintenance cost incurred by Alisha last year?
4. What is the maintenance cost per unit produced?
5. What is the fixed maintenance cost per unit?
6. What is the variable maintenance cost per unit?

OBJECTIVE 1

Exercise 3-24 COST BEHAVIOUR

Refer to the Alisha Incorporated information in **Exercise 3-23**. However, now assume that Alisha produced 80,000 stints (rather than 150,000). Round all answers to two decimal places.

Required:

1. What is the total maintenance cost incurred by Alisha last year?
2. What is the total fixed maintenance cost incurred by Alisha last year?
3. What is the total variable maintenance cost incurred by Alisha last year?
4. What is the maintenance cost per unit produced?
5. What is the fixed maintenance cost per unit?
6. What is the variable maintenance cost per unit?

OBJECTIVE 2

Exercise 3-25 STEP COSTS, RELEVANT RANGE

OK Inc. produces large industrial machinery. OK has a machining department and a group of direct labourers called machinists. Each machinist is paid $50,000 and can machine up to 500 units per year. OK also hires supervisors to develop machine specification plans and to oversee production within the machining department. Given the planning and supervisory work, a supervisor can oversee, at most, three machinists. OK's accounting and production history shows the following relationships between number of units produced and the costs of materials handling and supervision (measured on an annual basis):

Units Produced	Direct Labour ($)	Supervision ($)
0–500	36,000	40,000
501–1,000	72,000	40,000
1,001–1,500	108,000	40,000
1,501–2,000	144,000	80,000
2,001–2,500	180,000	80,000
2,501–3,000	216,000	80,000
3,001–3,500	252,000	120,000
3,501–4,000	288,000	120,000

Required:

1. Prepare a graph that illustrates the relationship between direct labour cost and number of units produced in the machining department. (Let cost be the vertical axis and number of units produced the horizontal axis.) Would you classify this cost as a strictly variable cost, a fixed cost, or a step cost?
2. Prepare a graph that illustrates the relationship between the cost of supervision and the number of units produced. (Let cost be the vertical axis and number of units produced the horizontal axis.) Would you classify this cost as a strictly variable cost, a fixed cost, or a step cost?
3. Suppose that the normal range of activity is between 1,400 and 1,500 units and that the exact number of machinists are currently hired to support this level of activity. Further suppose that production for the next year is expected to increase by an additional 500 units. By how much will the cost of direct labour increase? Cost of supervision?

OBJECTIVE 2

Exercise 3-26 MIXED COSTS

Ivan Dimitrov owns an art gallery. He accepts paintings and sculptures on consignment and then receives 20 percent of the price of each piece as his fee. Space is limited, and there are costs involved, so Ivan is careful about accepting artists. When he does accept one, he arranges for an opening show (usually for three hours on a weekend night) and sends out invitations to his customer list. At the opening, he serves wine, soft drinks, and appetizers to create a comfortable environment for prospective customers to view the new works and to chat with the artist. On average, each opening costs $500. Ivan has given as many as 20 opening shows in a year. The total cost of running the gallery, including rent, furniture and fixtures, utilities, and a part-time assistant, amounts to $80,000 per year.

Required:

1. Prepare a graph that illustrates the relationship between the cost of giving opening shows and the number of opening shows given. (Let opening show cost be the vertical axis and number of opening shows given the horizontal axis.) Would you classify this cost as a strictly variable cost, a fixed cost, or a mixed cost?
2. Prepare a graph that illustrates the relationship between the cost of running the gallery and the number of opening shows given. (Let gallery cost be the vertical axis and number of opening shows given the horizontal axis.) Would you classify this cost as a strictly variable cost, a fixed cost, or a mixed cost?
3. Prepare a graph that illustrates the relationship between Ivan's total costs (the sum of the costs of giving opening shows and running the gallery) and the number of opening shows given. (Let total cost be the vertical axis and number of opening shows given the horizontal axis.) Would you classify this cost as a strictly variable cost, a fixed cost, or a mixed cost?

Exercise 3-27 MIXED COSTS AND COST FORMULA

OBJECTIVE 3

Refer to the Ivan Dimitrov art gallery information in **Exercise 3-26**.

Required:

1. Assume that the cost driver is number of opening shows. Develop the cost formula for the gallery's costs for a year.
2. Using the formula developed in Requirement 1, what is the total cost for Ivan in a year with 12 opening shows? With 14 opening shows?

Exercise 3-28 HIGH-LOW METHOD

OBJECTIVE 3

Luisa Crimini has been operating a beauty shop in a university town for the past 10 years. Recently, Luisa rented space next to her shop and opened a tanning salon. She anticipated that the costs for the tanning service would primarily be fixed but found that tanning salon costs increased with the number of appointments. Costs for this service over the past eight months are as follows:

Month	Tanning Appointments	Total Cost ($)
January	700	1,758
February	2,000	2,140
March	3,100	2,790
April	2,500	2,400
May	1,500	1,800
June	2,300	2,275
July	2,150	2,200
August	3,000	2,640

Required:

1. Which month represents the high point? The low point?
2. Using the high-low method, compute the variable rate for tanning. Compute the fixed cost per month.
3. Using your answers to Requirement 2, write the cost formula for tanning services.
4. Calculate the total predicted cost of tanning services for September for 2,500 appointments using the formula found in Requirement 3. Of that total cost, how much is the total fixed cost for September? How much is the total predicted variable cost for September?

OBJECTIVE 3

Exercise 3-29 SCATTERGRAPH METHOD

Refer to the Luisa Crimini company information in **Exercise 3-28.**

Required:

Prepare a scattergraph based on Luisa's data. Use cost for the vertical axis and number of tanning appointments for the horizontal. Based on an examination of the scattergraph, does there appear to be a linear relationship between the cost of tanning services and the number of appointments?

OBJECTIVE 3

Exercise 3-30 METHOD OF LEAST SQUARES

Refer to the Luisa Crimini company information in **Exercise 3-28.**

Required:

1. Compute the cost formula for tanning services using the results from the method of least squares.
2. Using the formula computed in Requirement 1, what is the predicted cost of tanning services for September for 2,500 appointments?

OBJECTIVE 3

Exercise 3-31 HIGH-LOW METHOD, COST FORMULAS

During the past year, the high and low use of three different resources for Fly High Airlines occurred in July and April. The resources are airplane depreciation, fuel, and airplane maintenance. The number of airplane flight hours is the driver. The total costs of the three resources and the related number of airplane flight hours are as follows:

Resource	Airplane Flight Hours	Total Cost ($)
Airplane depreciation:		
High	44,000	18,000,000
Low	28,000	18,000,000
Fuel:		
High	44,000	445,896,000
Low	28,000	283,752,000
Airplane maintenance:		
High	44,000	15,792,000
Low	28,000	11,504,000

Required:

Use the high-low method to answer the following questions.

1. What is the variable rate for airplane depreciation? The fixed cost?
2. What is the cost formula for airplane depreciation?
3. What is the variable rate for fuel? The fixed cost?
4. What is the cost formula for fuel?
5. What is the variable rate for airplane maintenance? The fixed cost?
6. What is the cost formula for airplane maintenance?
7. Using the three cost formulas that you developed, predict the cost of each resource in a month with 36,000 airplane flight hours.

OBJECTIVE 3

Exercise 3-32 CHANGING THE COST FORMULA FOR A MONTH TO THE COST FORMULA FOR A YEAR

Refer to the Fly High Airlines company information in **Exercise 3-31.**

Required:

1. Develop annual cost formulas for airplane depreciation, fuel, and airplane maintenance.
2. Using the three annual cost formulas that you developed, predict the cost of each resource in a year with 480,000 airline flight hours.

Exercise 3-33 METHOD OF LEAST SQUARES, DEVELOPING AND USING THE COST FORMULA

OBJECTIVE 3

The method of least squares was used to develop a cost equation to predict the cost of receiving. Ninety-six data points from monthly data were used for the regression. The following computer output was received:

Intercept	23,100
Slope	316

The driver used was number of parts inspected.

Required:

1. What is the cost formula?
2. Using the cost formula from Requirement 1, identify each of the following: independent variable, dependent variable, variable rate, and fixed cost per month.
3. Using the cost formula, predict the cost of parts inspection for a month in which 2,500 parts are inspected.

Exercise 3-34 METHOD OF LEAST SQUARES, BUDGETED TIME PERIOD IS DIFFERENT FROM TIME PERIOD USED TO GENERATE RESULTS

OBJECTIVE 3

Refer to the company information in **Exercise 3-33.**

Required:

1. What is the cost formula for a year?
2. Using the cost formula from Requirement 1, predict the cost of parts inspection for a year in which 29,000 parts are inspected.

Exercise 3-35 IDENTIFYING THE PARTS OF THE COST FORMULA; CALCULATING MONTHLY, QUARTERLY, AND YEARLY COSTS USING A COST FORMULA BASED ON MONTHLY DATA

OBJECTIVE 3

Gordon Company's controller, Eric Junior, estimated the following formula, based on monthly data, for overhead cost:

$$\text{Overhead cost} = \$109{,}743 + (\$80.75 \times \text{Direct labour hours})$$

Required:

1. Link each term in column A to the corresponding term in column B.

Column A	Column B
Overhead cost	Variable rate (slope)
$109,743	Independent variable
$80.75	Fixed cost (intercept)
Direct labour hours	Dependent variable

2. If next month's budgeted direct labour hours equal 5,000, what is the budgeted overhead cost?
3. If next quarter's budgeted direct labour hours equal 18,000, what is the budgeted overhead cost?
4. If next year's budgeted direct labour hours equal 58,000, what is the budgeted overhead cost?

Exercise 3-36 (APPENDIX) METHOD OF LEAST SQUARES USING COMPUTER SPREADSHEET PROGRAM

OBJECTIVE 4

The controller for Beckham Company believes that the number of direct labour hours is associated with overhead cost. He collected the following data on the number of direct labour hours and associated factory overhead cost for the months of January through August.

Month	Number of Direct Labour Hours	Overhead Cost ($)
January	689	5,550
February	700	5,590
March	720	5,650
April	690	5,570
May	680	5,570
June	590	5,410
July	750	5,720
August	675	5,608

Required:

1. Using a computer spreadsheet program such as Excel, run a regression on these data. Print out your results.
2. Using your results from Requirement 1, write the cost formula for overhead cost. (You may round the fixed cost to the nearest dollar and the variable rate to the nearest cent.)
3. What is R^2 based on your results? Do you think that the number of direct labour hours is a good predictor of factory overhead cost?
4. Assuming that expected September direct labour hours are 700, what is expected factory overhead cost using the cost formula in Requirement 2?

OBJECTIVE 4

Exercise 3-37 (APPENDIX) METHOD OF LEAST SQUARES USING COMPUTER SPREADSHEET PROGRAM

Susan Lewis, owner of a florist shop, is interested in predicting the cost of delivering floral arrangements. She collected monthly data on the number of deliveries and the total monthly delivery cost (depreciation on the van, wages of the driver, and fuel) for the past year.

Month	Number of Deliveries	Delivery Cost ($)
January	100	1,200
February	550	1,800
March	85	1,100
April	115	1,050
May	160	1,190
June	590	1,980
July	500	1,800
August	520	1,700
September	100	1,100
October	200	1,275
November	260	1,400
December	450	2,200

Required:

1. Using a computer spreadsheet program such as Excel, run a regression on these data. Print out your results.
2. Using your results from Requirement 1, write the cost formula for delivery cost. (You may round the fixed cost to the nearest dollar and the variable rate to the nearest cent.)
3. What is R^2 based on your results? Do you think that the number of direct labour hours is a good predictor of delivery cost?
4. Using the cost formula in Requirement 2, what would predicted delivery cost be for a month with 300 deliveries?

Problems

Problem 3-38 IDENTIFYING FIXED, VARIABLE, MIXED, AND STEP COSTS

OBJECTIVE 1 2

Consider each of the following independent situations:

a. A computer service agreement in which a company pays $150 per month and $15 per hour of technical time.
b. Fuel cost of the company's fleet of motor vehicles.
c. The cost of beer for a bar.
d. The cost of computer printers and copiers in your university.
e. Rent for a dental office.
f. The salary of a receptionist in a law firm.
g. The wages of counter help in a fast-food restaurant.
h. The salaries of dental hygienists in a three-dentist office. One hygienist can take care of 120 cleanings per month.
i. Electricity cost, which includes a $15 per month billing charge and an additional amount depending on the number of kilowatt-hours used.

Required:

1. For each situation, describe the cost as one of the following: fixed cost, variable cost, mixed cost, or step cost. (*Hint:* First, consider what the driver or output measure is. If additional assumptions are necessary to support your cost type decision, be sure to write them down.)

   Example: Raw materials used in production—Variable cost

2. Change your assumption(s) for each situation so that the cost type changes to a different cost type. List the new cost type and the changed assumption(s) that gave rise to it.

   Example: Raw materials used in production. Changed assumption—the materials are difficult to obtain, and a year's worth must be contracted for in advance. Now, this is a fixed cost. (This is the case with diamond sales by DeBeers Inc. to its sightholders. See the following website for information: http://www.keyguide.net/sightholders.)

Problem 3-39 IDENTIFYING USE OF THE HIGH-LOW, SCATTERGRAPH, AND LEAST SQUARES METHODS

OBJECTIVE 3

Consider each of the following independent situations:

a. Shaniqua Metahi just started her new job as controller for St. Matthias General Hospital. She wants to get a feel for the cost behaviour of various departments of the hospital. Shaniqua first looks at the radiology department. She has annual data on total cost and the number of procedures that have been run for the past 15 years. However, she knows that the department upgraded its equipment substantially two years ago and is doing a wider variety of tests. So, Shaniqua decides to use data for just the past two years.
b. Francis Hidalgo is a summer intern in the accounting department of a manufacturing firm. His boss assigned him a special project to determine the cost of manufacturing a special order. Francis needs information on variable and fixed overhead, so he gathers monthly data on overhead cost and machine hours for the past 60 months and enters them into his personal computer. A few keystrokes later, he has information on fixed and variable overhead costs.
c. Ron Wickstead sighed and studied his computer printout again. The results made no sense to him. He seemed to recall that sometimes it helped to visualize the cost relationships. He reached for some graph paper and a pencil.
d. Bajwa Mohammad had hoped that she could find information on the actual cost of promoting new products. Unfortunately, she had spent the weekend going through the files and was only able to find data on the total cost of the sales department by month for the past three years. She was also able to figure out the number of new

product launches by month for the same time period. Now, she had just 15 minutes before a staff meeting in which she needed to give the vice president of sales an expected cost of the average new product launch. A light bulb went off in her head, and she reached for paper, pencil, and a calculator.

Required:

Determine which of the following cost separation methods is being used: the high-low method, the scattergraph method, or the method of least squares.

OBJECTIVE 1

Problem 3-40 IDENTIFYING VARIABLE COSTS, COMMITTED FIXED COSTS, AND DISCRETIONARY FIXED COSTS

Required:

Classify each of the following costs for a jeans manufacturing company as a variable cost, committed fixed cost, or discretionary fixed cost.

a. The cost of buttons.
b. The cost to lease warehouse space for completed jeans. The lease contract runs for two years at $5,000 per year.
c. The salary of a summer intern.
d. The cost of landscaping and mowing the grass. The contract with a local mowing company runs from month to month.
e. Advertising in a national magazine for teenage girls.
f. Electricity to run the sewing machines.
g. Oil and spare needles for the sewing machines.
h. Quality training for employees—typically given for four hours at a time, every six months.
i. Food and beverages for the company Canada Day picnic.
j. Natural gas to heat the factory during the winter.

OBJECTIVE 3

Problem 3-41 SCATTERGRAPH, HIGH-LOW METHOD, AND PREDICTING COST FOR A DIFFERENT TIME PERIOD FROM THE ONE USED TO DEVELOP A COST FORMULA

Farnsworth Company has gathered data on its overhead activities and associated costs for the past 10 months. Tracy Heppler, a member of the controller's department, has convinced management that overhead costs can be better estimated and controlled if the fixed and variable components of each overhead activity are known. One such activity is receiving raw materials (unloading incoming goods, counting goods, and inspecting goods), which she believes is driven by the number of receiving orders. Ten months of data have been gathered for the receiving activity and are as follows:

Month	Receiving Orders	Receiving Cost ($)
1	1,000	18,000
2	700	15,000
3	1,500	28,000
4	1,200	17,000
5	1,300	25,000
6	1,100	21,000
7	1,600	29,000
8	1,400	24,000
9	1,700	27,000
10	900	16,000

Required:

1. Prepare a scattergraph based on the 10 months of data. Does the relationship appear to be linear?
2. Using the high-low method, prepare a cost formula for the receiving activity. Using this formula, what is the predicted cost of receiving for a month in which 1,450 receiving orders are processed?

3. Prepare a cost formula for the receiving activity for a quarter. Based on this formula, what is the predicted cost of receiving for a quarter in which 4,650 receiving orders are anticipated? Prepare a cost formula for the receiving activity for a year. Based on this formula, what is the predicted cost of receiving for a year in which 18,000 receiving orders are anticipated?

Problem 3-42 METHOD OF LEAST SQUARES, PREDICTING COST FOR DIFFERENT TIME PERIODS FROM THE ONE USED TO DEVELOP A COST FORMULA

OBJECTIVE 3

Refer to the Farnsworth Company information in **Problem 3-41**. However, now assume that Tracy has used the method of least squares on the receiving data and has gotten the following results:

Intercept	3,212
Slope	15.15

Required:

1. Using the results from the method of least squares, prepare a cost formula for the receiving activity.
2. Using the formula from Requirement 1, what is the predicted cost of receiving for a month in which 1,450 receiving orders are processed? (Round your answer to the nearest dollar.)
3. Prepare a cost formula for the receiving activity for a quarter. Based on this formula, what is the predicted cost of receiving for a quarter in which 4,650 receiving orders are anticipated? Prepare a cost formula for the receiving activity for a year. Based on this formula, what is the predicted cost of receiving for a year in which 18,000 receiving orders are anticipated?

Problem 3-43 COST BEHAVIOUR, HIGH-LOW METHOD, PRICING DECISION

OBJECTIVE 1 2 3

Fonseca, Ruiz, and Dunn is a large, local accounting firm located in downtown Toronto. Carlos Ruiz, one of the firm's founders, appreciates the success his firm has enjoyed and wants to give something back to his community. He believes that an inexpensive accounting services clinic could provide basic accounting services for small businesses located in a working-class neighbourhood. He wants to price the services at cost.

Since the clinic is brand new, it has no experience to go on. Carlos decided to operate the clinic for two months before determining how much to charge per hour on an ongoing basis. As a temporary measure, the clinic adopted an hourly charge of $25, half the amount charged by Fonseca, Ruiz, and Dunn for professional services.

The accounting services clinic opened on January 1. During January, the clinic had 120 hours of professional service. During February, the activity was 150 hours. Costs for these two levels of activity usage are as follows:

	120 Professional Hours ($)	150 Professional Hours ($)
Salaries:		
Senior accountant	2,500	2,500
Office assistant	1,200	1,200
Internet and software subscriptions	700	850
Consulting by senior partner	1,200	1,500
Depreciation (equipment)	2,400	2,400
Supplies	905	1,100
Administration	500	500
Rent (offices)	2,000	2,000
Utilities	332	365

Required:

1. Classify each cost as fixed, variable, or mixed, using hours of professional service as the activity driver.

Here's The Real Kicker

Kicker separates cost into fixed and variable components by using judgment. Because the bulk of manufacturing is outsourced, the cost of a set of speakers starts with the purchase price from the manufacturer. This cost is strictly variable in nature. Additional variable costs include duty (ranging from 9 to 30 percent—electronics are at the high end) and freight, as all units are shipped to Stillwater, Oklahoma, for distribution to customers. In-house labour may be needed at Kicker's Stillwater facilities, and that cost has both fixed (salaried workers) and variable (temporary workers) components.

The entire salaried staff in Stillwater, research and development, depreciation on property, plant and equipment, utilities, and so on, are all fixed.

These fixed and variable costs are used in cost-volume-profit analysis (performed monthly) and in management decision making. For example, the monthly cost-volume-profit figures can be used to monitor the effect of changing volume on profit and spotlight increases in fixed and variable costs. If costs are going up, management finds out about the problem early and can make adjustments.

KICKER®

OBJECTIVE 1

Determine the break-even point in number of units and in total sales dollars.

Break-Even Point in Units and in Sales Dollars

Cost-volume-profit (CVP) analysis estimates how changes in costs (both variable and fixed), sales volume, and price affect a company's profit. CVP is a powerful tool for planning and decision making. In fact, CVP is one of the most versatile and widely applicable tools used by managerial accountants to help managers make better decisions.

The **break-even point** is the point where total revenue equals total cost (i.e., the point of zero profit). New start-up companies typically experience losses (negative operating income) initially and view their first break-even period as a significant milestone. For example, online retail pioneer **Amazon.com** was founded in 1994 but did not break even for the first time until the fourth quarter of 2001! Also, managers become very interested in CVP analysis during times of economic trouble. For example, to the dismay of many of its shareholders, **Sirius Satellite Radio** signed shock-jock Howard Stern to a five-year, $500 million employment contract for joining the young company. As a result of Stern's monstrous contract cost, some analysts estimated that Sirius would need an additional 2.4 million subscribers (i.e., customers) to reach break even. Therefore, CVP analysis helps managers pinpoint problems and find solutions.

CVP analysis can address many other issues as well, such as the number of units that must be sold to break even, the impact of a given reduction in fixed costs on the break-even point, and the impact of an increase in price on profit. Additionally, CVP analysis allows managers to do sensitivity analysis by examining the impact of various price or cost levels on profit.

Since CVP analysis shows how revenues, expenses, and profits behave as volume changes, it is natural to begin by finding the firm's break-even point in units sold.

Using Operating Income in Cost-Volume-Profit Analysis

Remember from Chapter 2 that operating income is total revenue minus total expense. For the income statement, expenses were classified according to function, that is, the manufacturing (or service provision) function, the selling function, and the administrative function. For CVP analysis, however, it is much more useful to organize costs into fixed and variable components. The focus is on the firm as a whole. Therefore, the costs refer to all costs of the company—production, selling, and administration. So variable costs are all costs that increase as more units are sold, including direct materials, direct labour, variable overhead, and variable selling and administrative costs. Similarly, fixed costs include fixed overhead and fixed selling and administrative expenses. The income statement format that is based on the separation of costs into fixed and variable components is called the **contribution margin income statement**.

Exhibit 4-1

Contribution Margin Income Statement

Sales	(50,000 units × $20)	$1,000,0000
Variable costs	(50,000 units × $8)	400,000
Contribution margin	(50,000 units × $12)	600,000
Fixed costs		500,000
Income from operations		100,000

Contribution Margin

Contribution margin is defined as the excess of sales over variable costs:

Contribution margin = Sales − Variable costs

Contribution margin refers to the amount left after the variable costs are covered to contribute toward the fixed costs. Once the fixed costs are covered, any remaining additional contribution margin increases income from operations.

Contribution margin is especially useful because it provides insight into the profit potential of a company. To illustrate, assume the following data for GGW Co.:

Sales:	50,000 units
Sales price per unit:	$ 20 per unit
Variable cost per unit	$ 8 per unit
Fixed costs:	$500,000

Exhibit 4-1 illustrates an income statement for GGW Co. prepared in a contribution margin format.

Contribution Margin Ratio

The contribution margin can also be expressed as a percentage. The **contribution margin ratio** indicates the percentage of each sales dollar available to cover fixed costs and to provide income from operations. The contribution margin ratio is computed as follows:

Contribution margin ratio = Contribution margin/Sales

The contribution margin ratio in the case of GGW is:

$600,000/$1,000,000 = 60%

The contribution margin ratio is most useful when the increase or decrease in sales volume is measured in sales dollars. In this case, the change in sales dollars multiplied by the contribution margin ratio equals the change in income from operations, as shown below.

$$\text{Change in income from operations} = \text{Change in sales dollars} \times \text{Contribution margin ratio}$$

To illustrate, if GGW adds $100,000 in sales orders, its income from operations will increase by:

$100,000 × 60% = $60,000

That is, income from operations will increase from $100,000 to $160,000 when sales increase from $1,000,000 to $1,100,000.

Variable costs as a percentage of sales are equal to 100 percent minus the contribution margin ratio. Thus, the variable costs for GGW are 40 percent (100% – 60%) of sales, or, in absolute numbers, $440,000 ($1,100,000 – $660,000). The total contribution margin, $440,000, can also be computed directly by multiplying the total sales by the contribution margin ratio ($1,100,000 × 40% = $440,000).

The contribution margin ratio is also useful in developing business strategies. For example, assume that a company has a high contribution margin ratio and is producing below 100 percent of capacity. In this case, a large increase in income from operations can be expected from an increase in sales volume. Therefore, the company might consider implementing a special sales campaign to increase sales. In contrast, a company with a small contribution margin ratio will probably want to give more attention to reducing costs before attempting to promote sales.

Unit Contribution Margin

The unit contribution margin is also useful for analyzing the profit potential of proposed decisions. The **unit contribution margin** is computed as follows:

Unit contribution margin = Sales price per unit − Variable cost per unit

To illustrate, if GGW's unit selling price is $20 and its variable cost per unit is $8, the unit contribution margin is $12, as shown below:

Sales price per unit − Variable cost per unit = $20 − $8
= $12

The unit contribution margin is most useful when the increase or decrease in sales volume is measured in sales units (quantities). In this case, the change in sales volume (units) multiplied by the unit contribution margin equals the change in income from operations, as shown below:

Change in income from operations = Change in sales units × Unit contribution margin

To illustrate, assume that GGW's sales could be increased by 15,000 units, from 50,000 to 65,000. GGW income from operations would increase by $180,000, as shown below.

Change in sales units × Unit contribution margin
= Change in income from operations
15,000 × $12 = $180,000

Let's use Whittier Company, a manufacturer of mulching lawn mowers, for an example. Whittier's controller has budgeted the following production costs for the coming year:

Direct materials per mower	$ 180
Direct labour per mower	100
Variable factory overhead per mower	25
Total fixed factory overhead	15,000

Whittier also has $30,000 in fixed selling and administrative expense, as well as a $20 sales commission on each mower sold. In the coming year, Whittier Company plans to produce and sell 1,000 mowers at a price of $400 each.

The total variable cost per mower includes direct materials, direct labour, variable overhead per unit, and the sales commission. Thus, variable cost per unit is $325 ($180 + $100 + $25 + $20). The total fixed expense includes fixed factory overhead and fixed selling and administrative expense; the total fixed expense is $45,000 ($15,000 + $30,000). Notice that both the variable cost per mower and the total fixed expense include all types of cost—both product and selling cost across the value chain.

The contribution margin income statement for Whittier Company for the coming year is shown in Cornerstone 4-1.

The HOW and WHY of Preparing a Contribution Margin Income Statement

CORNERSTONE 4-1

Information:
Whittier Company plans to sell 1,000 mowers at $400 each in the coming year. Product costs include:

Direct materials per mower	$ 180
Direct labour per mower	100
Variable factory overhead per mower	25
Total fixed factory overhead	15,000

Variable selling expense is a commission of $20 per mower; fixed selling and administrative expense totals $30,000.

Sales = 400,000
VC = 325,000
Cm 75,000
FC (45000)
OI 30,000

Required:
1. Calculate the total variable cost per unit.
2. Calculate the total fixed expense for the year.
3. Prepare a contribution margin income statement for Whittier Company for the coming year.

Solution:
1. Variable cost per unit

$$= \text{Direct materials} + \text{Direct labour} + \begin{array}{c}\text{Variable factory}\\ \text{overhead}\end{array} + \begin{array}{c}\text{Variable}\\ \text{selling expense}\end{array}$$
$$= \$180 + \$100 + \$25 + \$20$$
$$= \$325$$

2. Total fixed expense = Fixed factory overhead + Fixed selling and administrative expense
$$= \$15,000 + \$30,000 = \$45,000$$

3.

Whittier Company
Contribution Margin Income Statement
For the Coming Year

	Total	**Per Unit**
Sales ($400 × 1,000 mowers)	$400,000	$400
Total variable expense ($325 × 1,000)	325,000	325
Total contribution margin	$ 75,000	$ 75
Total fixed expense	45,000	
Operating income	$ 30,000	

Sales = 400,000
VE = (325000)
Cm 75,000
FE (45,000)
OI = 30,000

WHY:
Because such a statement provides some unique advantages over the conventional income statement, one of which is to facilitate the cost-volume-profit analysis.

Notice that the contribution margin income statement in Cornerstone 4-1 shows a total contribution margin of $75,000. The per-unit contribution margin is $75 ($400 − $325). That is, every mower sold contributes $75 toward fixed expense and operating income.

What does Whittier's contribution margin income statement show? First, of course, we notice that Whittier will more than break even at sales of 1,000 mowers.

In fact, it expects an operating income of $30,000. Clearly, Whittier would just break even if total contribution margin equalled the total fixed cost. Let's see how to calculate the break-even point.

Break-Even Point in Units

If the contribution margin income statement is recast as an equation, it becomes more useful for solving CVP problems. The operating income equation is:

$$\text{Operating income} = \text{Sales} - \text{Total variable expenses} - \text{Total fixed expenses}$$

Notice that all we have done is remove the total contribution margin line from Exhibit 4-1, since it is identical to sales minus total variable expense. This equation is the basis of all our coming work on CVP. We can think of it as the basic CVP equation.

We can expand the operating income equation by expressing sales revenues and variable expenses in terms of unit dollar amounts and the number of units sold. Specifically, sales revenue is equal to the unit selling price times the number of units sold, and total variable costs are equal to the unit variable cost times the number of units sold. With these expressions, the operating income equation becomes:

$$\text{Operating income} = (\text{Price} \times \text{Number of units sold}) - (\text{Variable cost per unit} \times \text{Number of units sold}) - \text{Total fixed cost}$$

At the break-even point, of course, operating income equals $0. Let's see how we can use the operating income equation to find the break-even point in units for Whittier Company. Recall that Whittier Company sells mowers at $400 each, and variable cost per mower is $325. Total fixed cost equals $45,000.

$$(\$400 \times \text{Break-even units}) - (\$325 \times \text{Break-even units}) - \$45{,}000 = \$0$$

$$(\$75 \times \text{Break-even units}) - \$45{,}000 = \$0$$

$$\text{Break-even units} = \frac{\$45{,}000}{\$75}$$

$$\text{Break-even units} = 600$$

It is easy to see that a contribution margin income statement for Whittier Company, with sales of 600 mowers, does result in zero operating income.

Sales ($400 × 600 mowers)	$240,000
Total variable expense ($325 × 600)	195,000
Total contribution margin	$ 45,000
Total fixed expense	45,000
Operating income	$ 0

When Whittier breaks even, total contribution margin equals total fixed cost. Exhibit 4-2 illustrates this important observation.

The operating income equation can be rearranged as follows to show the number of units at break even:

$$\text{Break-even units} = \frac{\text{Total fixed cost}}{\text{Price} - \text{Variable cost per unit}}$$

In other words, the break-even units are equal to the fixed cost divided by the contribution margin per unit. So, if a company sells enough units for the contribution margin to just cover fixed costs, it will earn zero operating income. In other words, it will break even. It is quicker to solve break-even problems using this break-even version of the operating income equation than it is using the original operating income equation. Cornerstone 4-2 shows how to use the break-even units equation to solve for the break-even point for Whittier Company.

Exhibit 4-2

Contribution Margin and Fixed Cost at Break Even for Whittier Company

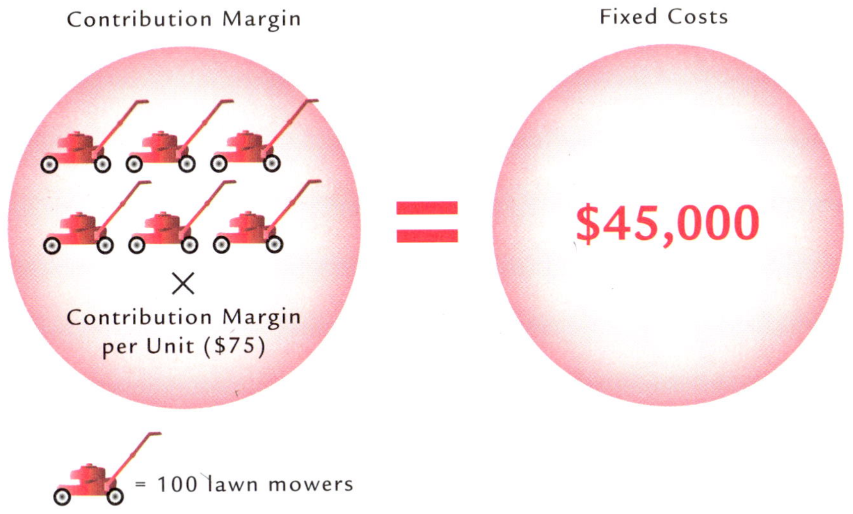

Break-Even Point in Sales Dollars

In some cases when using CVP analysis, managers may prefer to use sales revenue as the measure of sales activity instead of units sold. A units sold measure can be converted to a sales revenue measure by multiplying the unit selling price by the units sold. For example, the break-even point for Whittier Company is 600 mulching mowers. Since the selling price for each lawn mower is \$400, the break-even volume in sales revenue is \$240,000 (\$400 × 600).

Any answer expressed in units sold can be easily converted to one expressed in sales revenues, but the answer can be computed more directly by developing a separate formula for the sales revenue case. In this case, the important variable is sales dollars, so both the revenue and the variable costs must be expressed in dollars instead of units. Since sales revenue is always expressed in dollars, measuring that variable is no problem. Let's look more closely at variable costs and see how they can be expressed in terms of sales dollars.

To calculate the break-even point in sales dollars, total variable costs are defined as a percentage of sales rather than as an amount per unit sold. For example, suppose that a company sells a product for \$10 per unit and incurs a variable cost of \$6 per unit. Of course, the remainder is contribution margin of \$4 (\$10 – \$6). If 10 units are sold, total variable costs are \$60 (\$6 × 10 units). Alternatively, since each unit sold earns \$10 of revenue and has \$6 of variable cost, one could say that 60 percent of each dollar of revenue earned is attributable to variable cost (\$6/\$10). Thus, sales revenues of \$100 would result in total variable costs of \$60 (0.60 × \$100).

This 60 percent is the variable cost ratio. The **variable cost ratio** is the proportion of each sales dollar that must be used to cover variable costs. The variable cost ratio can be computed using either total data or unit data. The percentage of sales dollars remaining after variable costs are covered is the contribution margin ratio.

The *contribution margin ratio* is the proportion of each sales dollar available to cover fixed costs and provide for profit. In this example, if the variable cost ratio is 60 percent of sales, then the contribution margin ratio must be the remaining 40 percent of sales. It makes sense that the complement of the variable cost ratio is the contribution margin ratio. After all, total variable costs and total contribution margin sum to sales revenue.

Just as the variable cost ratio can be computed using total or unit figures, the contribution margin ratio, 40 percent in our example, can also be computed in these two ways. That is, one can divide the total contribution margin by total sales (\$40/\$100), or one can use the unit contribution margin divided by price (\$4/\$10). Naturally, if the variable cost ratio is known, it can be subtracted from 1 to yield the contribution

CORNERSTONE 4-2

The HOW and WHY of Solving for the Break-Even Point in Units

Information:

Whittier Company plans to sell 1,000 mowers at $400 each in the coming year. Product costs include:

Direct materials per mower	$ 180
Direct labour per mower	100
Variable factory overhead per mower	25
Total fixed factory overhead	15,000

Variable selling expense is a commission of $20 per mower; fixed selling and administrative expense totals $30,000.

Required:

1. Calculate the total variable cost per unit.
2. Calculate the total fixed expense for the year.
3. Calculate the number of mowers that Whittier Company must sell to break even.
4. Check your answer by preparing a contribution margin income statement based on the break-even point.

Solution:

1. Variable cost per unit = Direct materials + Direct labour + Variable factory overhead + Variable selling expense
   = $180 + $100 + $25 + $20 = $325
2. Total fixed expense = Fixed factory overhead + Fixed selling and administrative expense
   = $15,000 + $30,000 = $45,000
3. $$\text{Break-even number of mowers} = \frac{\text{Total fixed expense}}{(\text{Price} - \text{Variable cost})}$$
   $$= \frac{\$45,000}{(\$400 - \$325)} = 600$$
4. Contribution margin income statement based on 600 mowers.

Sales ($400 × 600 mowers)	$240,000
Total variable expense ($325 × 600)	195,000
Total contribution margin	$ 45,000
Total fixed expense	45,000
Operating income	$ 0

Indeed, selling 600 units does yield a zero profit.

WHY:

Because a firm needs to know how many units need to be sold to break even.

margin ratio (1 − 0.60 = 0.40). Cornerstone 4-3 shows how the income statement can be expanded to yield the variable cost ratio and the contribution margin ratio.

Notice in Cornerstone 4-3, Requirement 3, that sales revenue, variable costs, and contribution margin have been expressed as a percent of sales. The variable cost ratio is 0.8125 ($325,000/$400,000); the contribution margin ratio is 0.1875 (computed either as 1 − 0.8125, or $75,000/$400,000).

The HOW and WHY of Calculating the Variable Cost Ratio and the Contribution Margin Ratio

CORNERSTONE 4-3

Information:

Whittier Company plans to sell 1,000 mowers at $400 each in the coming year. Variable cost per unit is $325. Total fixed cost is $45,000.

Required:

1. Calculate the variable cost ratio.
2. Calculate the contribution margin ratio using unit figures.
3. Prepare a contribution margin income statement based on the budgeted figures for next year. In a column next to the income statement, show the percentages based on sales for sales, total variable costs, and total contribution margin.

Solution:

1. $$\text{Variable cost ratio} = \frac{\text{Variable cost per unit}}{\text{Price}} = \frac{\$325}{\$400} = 0.8125\text{, or } 81.25\%$$

2. $$\text{Contribution margin per unit} = \text{Price} - \text{Variable cost per unit} = \$400 - \$325 = \$75$$

$$\text{Contribution margin ratio} = \frac{\text{Contribution margin per unit}}{\text{Price}} = \frac{\$75}{\$400} = 0.1875\text{, or } 18.75\%$$

3. Contribution margin income statement based on budgeted figures:

		Percent of Sales
Sales ($400 × 1,000 mowers)	$400,000	100.00
Total variable expense (0.8125 × $400,000)	325,000	81.25
Total contribution margin	$ 75,000	18.75
Total fixed expense	45,000	
Operating income	$ 30,000	

WHY:

Because it is useful to express the variable cost and contribution margin per unit, not only in absolute dollars but also as a percentage of price.

How do fixed costs relate to the variable cost ratio and contribution margin ratio? Since the total contribution margin is the revenue remaining after total variable costs are covered, it must be the revenue available to cover fixed costs and contribute to profit. How does the relationship of fixed cost to contribution margin affect operating income? There are three possibilities: Fixed cost can equal contribution margin; fixed cost can be less than contribution margin; or fixed cost can be greater than contribution margin. *If fixed cost equals contribution margin, then operating income is $0 (the company is at break even).* If fixed cost is less than contribution margin, the company earns a positive operating income. Finally, if fixed cost is greater than contribution margin, then the company faces an operating loss.

CONCEPT Q&A

1. If the contribution margin ratio is 30 percent, what is the variable cost ratio?
2. If the variable cost ratio is 77 percent, what is the contribution margin ratio?
3. Explain why the contribution margin ratio and the variable cost ratio always total 100 percent.

Answers on pages 711 to 715.

Now, let's turn to the equation for calculating the break-even point in sales dollars. One way of calculating break-even sales revenue is to multiply the break-even units by the price. However, often the company is a multiple-product firm, and it can be difficult to figure the break-even point for each product sold. The operating income equation can be used to solve for break-even sales for Whittier as follows:

$$\text{Operating income} = \text{Sales} - \text{Total variable expenses} - \text{Total fixed expenses}$$

$$\begin{aligned}
\$0 &= \text{Break-even sales} \\
&\quad - (0.8125 \times \text{Break-even sales}) - \$45{,}000 \\
\$0 &= \text{Break-even sales } (1.00 - 0.8125) - \$45{,}000 \\
\text{Break-even sales} &= \frac{\$45{,}000}{(1.00 - 0.8125)} \\
\text{Break-even sales} &= \$240{,}000
\end{aligned}$$

So, Whittier Company has sales of $240,000 at the break-even point.

Just as it was quicker to use an equation to calculate the break-even units directly, it is helpful to have an equation to calculate the break-even sales dollars. This equation is:

$$\text{Break-even sales} = \frac{\text{Total fixed expenses}}{\text{Contribution margin ratio}}$$

Cornerstone 4-4 shows how to obtain the break-even point in sales dollars for Whittier Company.

Equation Formula Approach to Break-Even Analysis

The formula approach to break-even analysis uses an algebraic equation to calculate the BEP. The equation represents the variable costing income statement and shows the relationships among revenue, fixed cost, variable cost, volume, and profit. The income statement equation is: Sales = VC + FC + Pr

$$\begin{aligned}
\text{BE:}\quad (P \times Q) &= Q \times VCU + FC + O \\
P \times Q - Q \times VCU &= FC \\
Q(P - VCU) &= FC \\
QCM &= FC \\
Q &= FC/CM
\end{aligned}$$

where

$$\begin{aligned}
P &= \text{Selling price per unit} \\
Q &= \text{quantity (volume or number of units)} \\
P(Q) &= \text{total revenue} \\
VCU &= \text{variable cost per unit} \\
VC(Q) &= \text{total variable cost} \\
FC &= \text{total fixed cost}
\end{aligned}$$

Thus, break-even volume equals total fixed cost divided by contribution margin per unit.

Because this equation is simply a formulaic representation of an income statement, profit can be set equal to zero to solve for the break-even point. At the point where profit equals $0, total revenues are equal to total costs, and break-even point (BEP) in units can be found by solving the equation.

The BEP provides a starting point for planning future operations. Managers want to earn operating profit rather than simply cover costs. Substituting an amount other than zero for the profit (Pr) term in the break-even formula converts break-even analysis to cost-volume-profit analysis.

The HOW and WHY of Solving for the Break-Even Point in Sales Dollars

CORNERSTONE 4-4

Information:
Whittier Company plans to sell 1,000 mowers at $400 each in the coming year. Total variable expense per unit is $325. Total fixed expense is $45,000.

Required:
1. Calculate the contribution margin ratio.
2. Calculate the sales revenue that Whittier Company must make to break even by using the break-even point in sales equation.
3. Check your answer by preparing a contribution margin income statement based on the break-even point in sales dollars.

Solution:
1. Contribution margin per unit = Price − Variable expense per unit
$$= \$400 - \$325 = \$75$$

$$\text{Contribution margin ratio} = \frac{\text{Contribution margin per unit}}{\text{Price}}$$
$$= \frac{\$75}{\$400} = 0.1875, \text{ or } 18.75\%$$

[*Hint:* The contribution margin ratio comes out cleanly to four decimal places. Don't round it, and your break-even point in sales dollars will yield an operating income of $0 (rather than being a few dollars off due to rounding).]

Notice that the variable cost ratio equals 0.8125, or the difference between 1.0000 and the contribution margin ratio.

2. Calculate the break-even point in sales dollars:

$$\text{Break-even sales dollars} = \frac{\text{Total fixed expense}}{\text{Contribution margin ratio}}$$
$$= \frac{\$45,000}{0.1875} = \$240,000$$

3. Contribution margin income statement based on sales of $240,000:

Sales	$240,000
Total variable expense (0.8125 × $240,000)	195,000
Total contribution margin	$ 45,000
Total fixed expense	45,000
Operating income	$ 0

Indeed, sales equal to $240,000 does yield a zero profit.

WHY:
Because a firm needs to know how much sales (revenue) it needs to break even.

Units to Be Sold to Achieve a Target Income

OBJECTIVE 2
Determine the number of units that must be sold, and the amount of revenue required, to earn a targeted profit.

While the break-even point is useful information and an important benchmark for relatively young companies, most companies would like to earn operating income greater than $0. CVP analysis gives us a way to determine how many units must be sold, or how much sales revenue must be generated, to earn a particular target income. Let's look first at the number of units that must be sold to earn a targeted operating income.

Remember that at the break-even point, operating income is $0. How can the equations used in our earlier break-even analyses be adjusted to find the number of units that must be sold to earn a target income? The answer is that we add the target income amount to the fixed costs. Let's try it two different ways—with the operating income equation and with the basic break-even equation.

Remember that the equation for the operating income is:

$$\text{Operating income} = (\text{Price} \times \text{Units sold}) - (\text{Unit variable cost} \times \text{Units sold}) - \text{Fixed cost}$$

To solve for positive operating income, replace the operating income term with the target income. Recall that Whittier Company sells mowers at $400 each, incurs variable cost per unit of $325, and has total fixed expense of $45,000. Suppose that Whittier wants to make a target operating income of $37,500. The number of units that must be sold to achieve that target income is calculated as follows:

$$\$37{,}500 = (\$400 \times \text{Number of units}) - (\$325 \times \text{Number of units}) - \$45{,}000$$

$$\text{Number of units} = \frac{(\$37{,}500 + \$45{,}000)}{(\$400 - \$325)} = 1{,}100$$

Does the sale of 1,100 units really result in operating income of $37,500? The contribution margin income statement provides a good check.

Sales ($400 × 1,100)	$440,000
Total variable expense ($325 × 1,100)	357,500
Total contribution margin	$ 82,500
Total fixed expense	45,000
Operating income	$ 37,500

Indeed, selling 1,100 units does yield operating income of $37,500.

The operating income equation can be used to find the number of units to sell to earn a targeted income. However, it is quicker to adjust the break-even units equation by adding target income to the fixed cost. This adjustment results in the following equation:

$$\text{Number of units to earn target income} = \frac{\text{Fixed cost} + \text{Target income}}{\text{Price} - \text{Variable cost per unit}}$$

This equation was used when calculating the 1,100 units needed to earn operating income of $37,500. Cornerstone 4-5 shows how Whittier Company can use this approach.

Another way to check the number of units to be sold to yield a target operating income is to use the break-even point. As shown in Cornerstone 4-5, Whittier must sell 1,100 lawn mowers, or 500 more than the break-even volume of 600 units, to earn a profit of $37,500. The contribution margin per lawn mower is $75. Multiplying $75 by the 500 lawn mowers above break even produces the operating income of $37,500 ($75 × 500). This outcome demonstrates that contribution margin per unit for each unit above break even is equivalent to operating income per unit. Since the break-even point had already been computed, the number of lawn mowers to be sold to yield a $37,500 operating income could have been calculated by dividing the unit contribution margin into the target income and adding the resulting amount to the break-even volume.

In general, assuming that fixed costs remain the same, the impact on a firm's income resulting from a change in the number of units sold can be assessed by multiplying the unit contribution margin by the change in units sold. For example, if 1,400 lawn mowers instead of 1,100 are sold, how much more operating income will be earned? The change in units sold is an increase of 300 lawn mowers, and the unit

The HOW and WHY of Solving for the Number of Units to Be Sold to Earn a Target Operating Income

CORNERSTONE 4-5

Information:

Whittier Company sells mulching mowers at $400 each. Variable cost per unit is $325, and total fixed costs are $45,000.

Required:

1. Calculate the number of units that Whittier Company must sell to earn operating income of $37,500.
2. Check your answer by preparing a contribution margin income statement based on the number of units calculated.

Solution:

1. $$\text{Number of units} = \frac{(\text{Target income} + \text{Total fixed expense})}{(\text{Price} - \text{Variable cost per unit})}$$
$$= \frac{(\$45{,}000 + \$37{,}500)}{(\$400 - \$325)} = 1{,}100$$

2. Contribution margin income statement based on sales of 1,100 units:

Sales ($400 × 1,100)	$440,000
Total variable expense ($325 × 1,100)	357,500
Total contribution margin	$ 82,500
Total fixed expense	45,000
Operating income	$ 37,500

Indeed, selling 1,100 units does yield operating income of $37,500.

WHY:

Because firms need not only to break even but also to generate a target profit. Finding how many units need to be sold to achieve this target profit is crucial for the success of the firm.

contribution margin is $75. Thus, operating income will increase by $22,500 ($75 × 300) over the $37,500 initially calculated, and total operating income will be $60,000.

Sales Revenue to Achieve a Target Income

Consider the following question: How much sales revenue must Whittier generate to earn an operating income of $37,500? This question is similar to the one we asked earlier in terms of units but phrases the question directly in terms of sales revenue. To answer the question, add the targeted operating income of $37,500 to the $45,000 of fixed cost and divide by the contribution margin ratio. Then, the equation is the following:

$$\text{Sales dollars to earn target income} = \frac{\text{Fixed cost} + \text{Target income}}{\text{Contribution margin ratio}}$$

Cornerstone 4-6 shows how to calculate the sales revenue needed to earn a target operating income of $37,500.

Whittier must earn revenues equal to $440,000 to achieve a profit target of $37,500. Since break-even sales equals $240,000, additional sales of $200,000 ($440,000 – $240,000) must be earned above break even. Notice that multiplying the contribution

CONCEPT Q&A

Lorna makes and sells decorative candles through gift shops. She knows she must sell 200 candles a month to break even. Every candle has a contribution margin of $1.50. So far this month, Lorna has sold 320 candles. How much has Lorna earned so far this month in operating income? If she sells 10 more candles, by how much will income increase?

Answers on pages 711 to 715.

CORNERSTONE 4-6

The HOW and WHY of Solving for the Sales Needed to Earn a Target Operating Income

Information:

Whittier Company sells mulching mowers at $400 each. Variable cost per unit is $325, and total fixed costs are $45,000.

Required:

1. Calculate the contribution margin ratio.
2. Calculate the sales that Whittier Company must make to earn an operating income of $37,500.
3. Check your answer by preparing a contribution margin income statement based on the sales dollars calculated.

Solution:

1. $\text{Contribution margin ratio} = \frac{(\$400 - \$325)}{\$400} = 0.1875$

2. $\text{Sales dollars} = \frac{(\text{Target income} + \text{Total fixed expense})}{\text{Contribution margin ratio}}$

   $= \frac{(\$45{,}000 + \$37{,}500)}{0.1875} = \$440{,}000$

3. Contribution margin income statement based on sales revenue of $440,000:

Sales	$440,000
Total variable expense (0.8125 × $440,000)	357,500
Total contribution margin	$ 82,500
Total fixed expense	45,000
Operating income	$ 37,500

Indeed, sales revenue of $440,000 does yield operating income of $37,500.

WHY:

Because firms need to know what volume of sales is necessary to achieve a target profit.

margin ratio by revenues above break even yields the profit of $37,500 (0.1875 × $200,000). Above break even, the contribution margin ratio is a profit ratio; therefore, it represents the proportion of each sales dollar attributable to profit. For Whittier Company, every sales dollar earned above break even increases profits by $0.1875.

In general, assuming that fixed costs remain unchanged, the contribution margin ratio can be used to find the profit impact of a change in sales revenue. To obtain the total change in profits from a change in revenues, multiply the contribution margin ratio times the change in sales. For example, if sales revenues are $400,000 instead of $440,000, how will the expected profits be affected? A decrease in sales revenues of $40,000 will cause a decrease in profits of $7,500 (0.1875 × $40,000).

Income Taxes Impact on Break-Even Analysis

Thus far we have (as so many people would like to) ignored income taxes. However, in most countries, private enterprises are subject to income taxes. What is the impact of income taxes on break-even analysis? And how will changes in the structure of variable costs and fixed costs affect net income?

The only change in the general break-even equation approach we have used all along would be on the right-hand side of the following equation:

$$\text{Target sales} - \text{Variable expenses} - \text{Fixed expenses} = \text{Target income after-tax}/(1 - \text{tax rate})$$

That is, the target income (earnings) before taxes (EBT) is divided by (1 – tax rate) to obtain the target earnings after taxes (EAT). As a shortcut to computing the effects of changes in sales volume on after-tax income, we use the following formula:

$$BE = [FC + NI/(1 - T)]/CM$$

To illustrate, assume the following data:

Fixed costs	$800,000
Target profit	$600,000
Unit selling price	$ 90
Unit variable cost	$ 50
Unit contribution margin	$ 40
Tax rate	40%

$$\begin{aligned} BE &= [\$800{,}000 + \$600{,}000/(1 - 0.40)]/\$40 \\ &= \$800{,}000 + \$1{,}000{,}000/\$40 \\ &= \$1{,}800{,}000/\$40 \\ &= 45{,}000 \text{ units} \end{aligned}$$

Thus, instead of 20,000 units being necessary to break even ($800,000/$40 = 20,000), 45,000 units are needed to generate EAT of $600,000. A total of 22,500 extra units need to be sold to generate a target profit of $600,000 after paying for the income taxes.

Note that each unit beyond the break-even point adds to after-tax net profit at the unit contribution margin multiplied by (1 – income tax rate). Also, the break-even point itself does not change no matter what the income tax rate is. Why? Because there is no income tax at a level of zero profits.

The Profit-Volume Graph

OBJECTIVE 3
Prepare a profit-volume graph and a cost-volume-profit graph, and explain the meaning of each.

It may be helpful in understanding CVP relationships to see them portrayed visually. A graphical representation can help managers see the difference between variable cost and revenue. It may also help them understand quickly what impact an increase or decrease in sales will have on the break-even point. Two basic graphs are the profit-volume graph and the cost-volume-profit graph.

A **profit-volume graph** visually portrays the relationship between profits (operating income) and units sold. The profit-volume graph is the graph of the operating income equation [Operating income = (Price × Units) – (Unit variable cost × Units) – Total fixed cost]. In this graph, operating income is the dependent variable, and units is the independent variable. Usually, values of the independent variable are measured along the horizontal axis, and values of the dependent variable are measured along the vertical axis.

To make this discussion more concrete, a simple set of data will be used. Assume that Tyson Company produces a single product with the following cost and price data:

Total fixed costs	$100
Variable costs per unit	5
Selling price per unit	10

Exhibit 4-3

Profit-Volume Graph

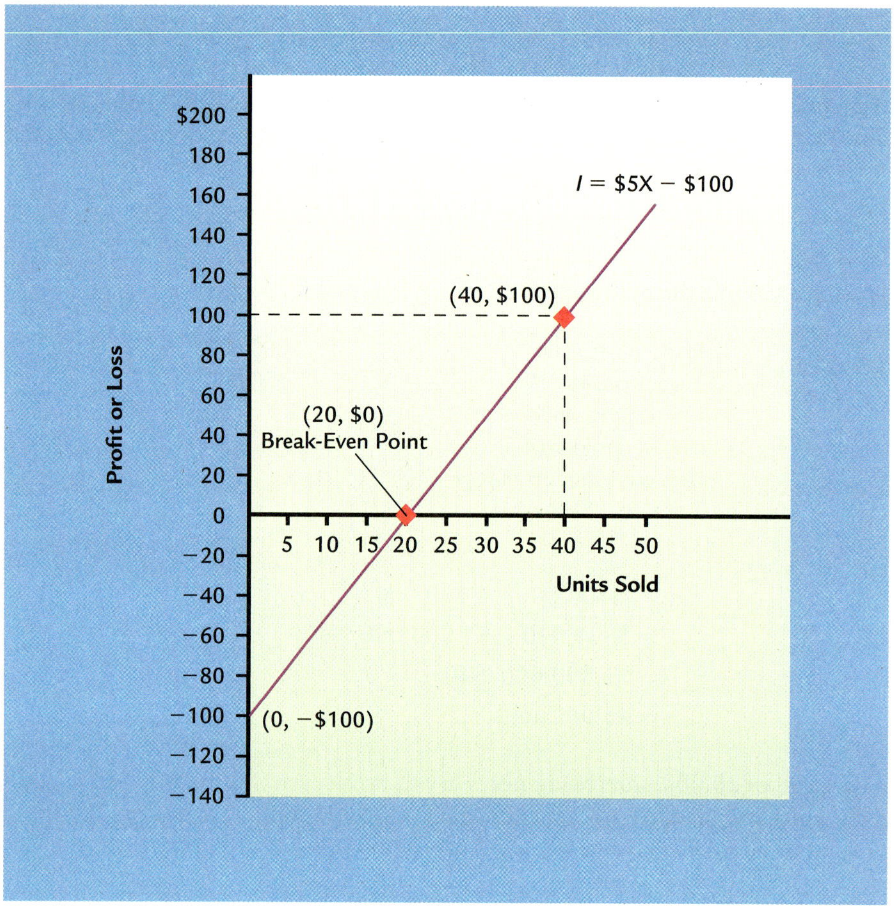

Using these data, operating income can be expressed as:

Operating income = ($10 × Units) − ($5 × Units) − $100
= ($5 × Units) − $100

This relationship can be graphed by plotting units along the horizontal axis and operating income (or loss) along the vertical axis. Two points are needed to graph a linear equation. While any two points will do, the two points often chosen are those that correspond to zero units sold and zero profits. When units sold are 0, Tyson experiences an operating loss of $100 (or an operating income of −$100). The point corresponding to zero sales volume, therefore, is (0, −$100). When no sales take place, the company suffers a loss equal to its total fixed costs. When operating income is $0, the units sold are equal to 20. The point corresponding to zero profits (break even) is (20, $0). These two points, plotted in Exhibit 4-3, define the profit-volume graph.

The graph in Exhibit 4-3 can be used to assess Tyson's profit (or loss) at any level of sales activity. For example, the profit associated with the sale of 40 units can be read from the graph by (1) drawing a vertical line from the horizontal axis to the profit line and (2) drawing a horizontal line from the profit line to the vertical axis. As illustrated in Exhibit 4-3, the profit associated with sales of 40 units is $100. The profit-volume graph, while easy to interpret, fails to reveal how costs change as sales volume changes. An alternative approach to graphing can provide this detail.

The Cost-Volume-Profit Graph

The **cost-volume-profit graph** depicts the relationships among cost, volume, and profits (operating income) by plotting the total revenue line and the total cost line

Exhibit 4-4

Cost-Volume-Profit Graph

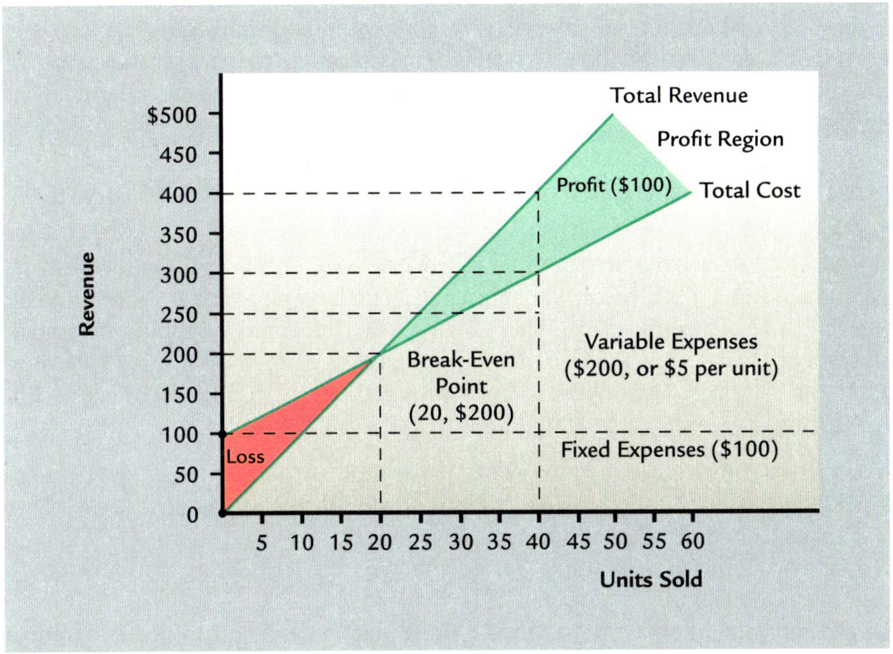

on a graph. To obtain the more detailed relationships, it is necessary to graph two separate lines: the total revenue line and the total cost line. These two lines are represented by the following two equations:

$$\text{Revenue} = \text{Price} \times \text{Units}$$

$$\text{Total cost} = (\text{Unit variable cost} \times \text{Units}) + \text{Fixed cost}$$

Using the Tyson Company example, the revenue and cost equations are:

$$\text{Revenue} = \$10 \times \text{Units}$$
$$\text{Total cost} = (\$5 \times \text{Units}) + \$100$$

To portray both equations in the same graph, the vertical axis is measured in dollars, and the horizontal axis is measured in units sold.

Again, two points are needed to graph each equation. For the revenue equation, setting number of units equal to 0 results in revenue of $0; setting number of units equal to 20 results in revenue of $200. Therefore, the two points for the revenue equation are (0, $0) and (20, $200). For the cost equation, units sold of 0 and units sold of 20 produce the points (0, $100) and (20, $200). The graph of each equation appears in Exhibit 4-4.

Notice that the total revenue line begins at the origin and rises with a slope equal to the selling price per unit (a slope of 10). The total cost line intercepts the vertical axis at a point equal to total fixed costs and rises with a slope equal to the variable cost per unit (a slope of 5). When the total revenue line lies below the total cost line, a loss region is defined. Similarly, when the total revenue line lies above the total cost line, a profit region is defined. The point where the total revenue line and the total cost line intersect is the break-even point. To break even, Tyson Company must sell 20 units and, thus, receive $200 in total revenues.

Now, let's compare the information available from the CVP graph with that available from the profit-volume graph. To do so, consider the sale of 40 units. Recall that the profit-volume graph revealed that 40 units produced profits of $100. Examine

Exhibit 4-4 again. The CVP graph also shows profits of $100, but it reveals more as well. The CVP graph discloses that total revenues of $400 and total costs of $300 are associated with the sale of 40 units. Furthermore, the total costs can be broken down into fixed costs of $100 and variable costs of $200. The CVP graph provides revenue and cost information not provided by the profit-volume graph. Unlike the profit-volume graph, some computation is needed to determine the profit associated with a given sales volume. Nonetheless, because of the greater information content, managers are likely to find the CVP graph a more useful tool.

Underlying Assumptions of Cost-Volume-Profit Analysis

Underlying Assumptions of CVP Analysis CVP analysis focuses on relationships among selling price, variable costs, fixed costs, volume, and profits. This model is a useful planning tool that can provide information about the impact on profits when changes are made in the cost structure or in the sales level. Several important but necessary assumptions are made in the CVP model. To begin with, the following assumptions can be stated about CVP analysis:

- It is a short run decision making tool.
- It is based on historical costs and prices that are subject to change.
- It is better suited for single, not multiple products.
- Productivity, efficiency, technology, and market conditions are constant (i.e., that costs do not change).
- An accurate way has been devised to separate cost in variable and fixed components.
- Total fixed costs are constant within the relevant range. This assumption, in part, indicates that no capacity additions will be made during the period being considered.
- There is linearity between costs and revenue.
- Prices and costs are known with certainty.
- Sales mix is constant.
- Sales and production are equal; thus, there is no material fluctuation in inventory levels. This assumption is necessary because fixed cost can be allocated to inventory at a different rate each year. Because CVP and variable costing both focus on cost behaviour, they are distinctly compatible with each other.

Linear Cost and Revenue Functions CVP assumes that cost and revenue functions are linear; that is, they are straight lines. But, as was discussed in Chapter 3 on cost behaviour, these functions are often not linear. They may be curved or step functions. Fortunately, it is not necessary to consider all possible ranges of production and sales for a firm. Remember that CVP analysis is a short-run decision-making tool. (We know that it is short run in orientation because some costs are fixed.) It is only necessary for us to determine the current operating range, or relevant range, for which the linear cost and revenue relationships are valid. Once a relevant range has been identified, then the cost and price relationships are assumed to be known and constant.

Prices and Costs Known with Certainty In actuality, firms seldom know prices, variable costs, and fixed costs with certainty. A change in one variable usually affects the value of others. Often, there is a probability distribution to consider. Furthermore, there are formal ways of explicitly building uncertainty into the CVP model. These issues are explored in the section on incorporating risk and uncertainty into CVP analysis.

Constant Sales Mix In single-product analysis, the sales mix is obviously constant—the one product accounts for 100 percent of sales. Multiple-product break-even analysis requires a constant sales mix. However, it is virtually impossible to predict with certainty the sales mix. Typically, this constraint is handled in practice through sensitivity analysis. By using the capabilities of spreadsheet analysis, the sensitivity of variables to a variety of sales mixes can be readily assessed.

Summary of Effects of Changes on Break-Even Point

The break-even point in sales changes in the same direction as changes in the variable cost per unit and fixed costs. In contrast, the break-even point in sales changes in the *opposite* direction as changes in the unit selling price. These changes on the break-even point in sales are summarized below.

Type of Change	Direction of change	Effect of Change on BE Sales
Fixed cost	Increase	Increase
	Decrease	Decrease
Unit variable cost	Increase	Increase
	Decrease	Decrease
Unit selling price	Increase	Decrease
	Decrease	Increase

Multiple-Product Analysis

OBJECTIVE 4
Apply cost-volume-profit analysis in a multiple-product setting.

Cost-volume-profit analysis is fairly simple in the single-product setting. However, most firms produce and sell a number of products or services. Even though CVP analysis becomes more complex with multiple products, the operation is reasonably straightforward. Let's see how we can adapt the formulas used in a single-product setting to a multiple-product setting by expanding the Whittier Company example.

Whittier Company has decided to offer two models of lawn mowers: a mulching mower that sells for $400 and a riding mower that sells for $800. The marketing department is convinced that 1,200 mulching mowers and 800 riding mowers can be sold during the coming year. The controller has prepared the following projected income statement based on the sales forecast:

	Mulching Mower	Riding Mower	Total
Sales	$480,000	$640,000	$1,120,000
Less: Variable expenses	390,000	480,000	870,000
Contribution margin	$ 90,000	$160,000	$ 250,000
Less: Direct fixed expenses	30,000	40,000	70,000
Product margin	$ 60,000	$120,000	$ 180,000
Less: Common fixed expenses			26,250
Operating income			$ 153,750

Note that the controller has separated *direct fixed expenses* from *common fixed expenses*. The **direct fixed expenses** are those fixed costs that can be traced to each segment and would be avoided if the segment did not exist. The **common fixed expenses** are the fixed costs that are not traceable to the segments and would remain even if one of the segments was eliminated.

Break-Even Point in Units

The owner of Whittier is somewhat apprehensive about adding a new product line and wants to know how many of each model must be sold to break even. If you were given the responsibility of answering this question, how would you respond? One possible response is to use the equation developed earlier in which fixed costs were divided by the contribution margin. This equation presents a problem, however; it was developed for single-product analysis. For two products, there are two prices and two variable costs per unit. The variable cost per unit is derived from the income statement. For the mulching mower, total variable costs are $390,000 based

CONCEPT Q&A

Suppose that the revenue line in Exhibit 4-4 had a steeper slope due to a higher price. What would that imply for the break-even point? For the amount of operating income (profit) for units sold above break even? Now suppose that the revenue line remains unchanged, but that variable cost per unit increases. How would this increase affect the total cost line? What would this increase imply for the break-even point? For the amount of operating income (profit) for units sold above break even?

Answers on pages 711 to 715.

on sales of 1,200 units, yielding a per-unit variable cost of $325 ($390,000/1,200). For the riding mower, total variable costs are $480,000 based on sales of 800 units, yielding a per-unit variable cost of $600 ($480,000/800). Then, the mulching mower has a contribution margin per unit of $75 ($400 − $325); the riding mower has a contribution margin per unit of $200 ($800 − $600).

One possible solution is to apply the analysis separately to each product line. It is possible to obtain individual break-even points when income is defined as product margin. Break even for the mulching mower is as follows:

$$\text{Mulching mower break-even units} = \frac{\text{Fixed cost}}{(\text{Price} - \text{Unit variable cost})} = \frac{\$30{,}000}{\$75} = 400 \text{ units}$$

Break even for the riding mower can be computed as well:

$$\text{Riding mower break-even units} = \frac{\text{Fixed cost}}{(\text{Price} - \text{Unit variable cost})} = \frac{\$40{,}000}{\$200} = 200 \text{ units}$$

Thus, 400 mulching mowers and 200 riding mowers must be sold to achieve a break-even product margin. But a break-even product margin covers only direct fixed costs; the common fixed costs remain to be covered. Selling these numbers of lawn mowers would result in a loss equal to the common fixed costs. This level of sales is not the break-even point for the firm as a whole; somehow the common fixed costs must be factored into the analysis.

Allocating the common fixed costs to each product line before computing a break-even point may resolve this difficulty. The problem with this approach is that allocation of the common fixed costs is arbitrary. Thus, no meaningful break-even volume is readily apparent.

Another possible solution is to convert the multiple-product problem into a single-product problem. If this can be done, then all of the single-product CVP methodology can be applied directly. The key to this conversion is to identify the expected sales mix, in units, of the products being marketed. **Sales mix** is the relative combination of products being sold by a firm.

Determining the Sales Mix

The sales mix is measured in units sold. For example, if Whittier plans on selling 1,200 mulching mowers and 800 riding mowers, then the sales mix in units is 1,200:800. Usually, the sales mix is reduced to the smallest possible whole numbers. Thus, the relative mix, 1,200:800, can be reduced to 12:8, and further reduced to 3:2. That is, Whittier expects that for every three mulching mowers sold, two riding mowers will be sold.

An endless number of different sales mixes can be used to define the break-even volume in a multiple-product setting. For example, a sales mix of 2:1 will define a break-even point of 550 mulching mowers and 275 riding mowers. The total contribution margin produced by this mix is $96,250 [($75 × 550) + ($200 × 275)]. Similarly, if 350 mulching mowers and 350 riding mowers are sold (corresponding to a 1:1 sales mix), then the total contribution margin is also $96,250 [($75 × 350) + ($200 × 350)]. Since total fixed costs are $96,250, both sales mixes define break-even points. Fortunately, every sales mix need not be considered. Can Whittier really expect a sales mix of 2:1 or 1:1? For every two mulching mowers sold, does Whittier expect to sell a riding mower? Or, for every mulching mower, can Whittier really sell one riding mower?

According to Whittier's marketing study, a sales mix of 3:2 can be expected. This is the ratio that should be used; all others can be ignored. The sales mix that is expected to prevail should be used for CVP analysis.

The HOW and WHY of Calculating the Break-Even Units for a Multiple-Product Firm

CORNERSTONE 4-7

Information:

Recall that Whittier Company sells two products: mulching mowers priced at $400 and riding mowers priced at $800. The variable costs per unit are $325 per mulching mower and $600 per riding mower. Total fixed expense is $96,250. Whittier's expected sales mix is three mulching mowers to two riding mowers.

Required:

1. Form a package of mulching and riding mowers based on the sales mix, and calculate the package contribution margin.
2. Calculate the break-even point in units for mulching mowers and for riding mowers.
3. Check your answers by preparing a contribution margin income statement.

Solution:

1. Each package consists of three mulching mowers and two riding mowers:

Product	Price	Unit Variable Cost	Unit Contribution Margin	Sales Mix	Package Contribution Margin
Mulching	$400	$325	$ 75	3	$225
Riding	800	600	200	2	400
Package total					$625

The three mulching mowers in the package yield $225 (3 × $75) in contribution margin. The two riding mowers in the package yield $400 (2 × $200) in contribution margin. Thus, a package of five mowers (three mulching and two riding) has a total contribution margin of $625.

2. $$\text{Break-even packages} = \frac{\text{Fixed cost}}{\text{Package contribution margin}} = \frac{\$96{,}250}{\$625} = 154 \text{ packages}$$

   Mulching mower break-even units = 154 × 3 = 462
   Riding mower break-even units = 154 × 2 = 308

3. Income statement—break-even solution:

	Mulching Mower	Riding Mower	Total
Sales	$184,800	$246,400	$431,200
Less: Variable expenses	150,150	184,800	334,950
Contribution margin	$ 34,650	$ 61,600	$ 96,250
Less: Total fixed expenses			96,250
Operating income			$ 0

WHY:

Because, as in the case of a single-product firm, a multiple-product firm needs to know how many units of each product in the product mix are necessary to be sold to break even.

Sales Mix and Cost-Volume-Profit Analysis Defining a particular sales mix allows the conversion of a multiple-product problem into a single-product CVP format. Since Whittier expects to sell three mulching mowers for every two riding mowers, it can define the single product it sells as a package containing three mulching mowers and two riding mowers. By defining the product as a package, the multiple-product problem is converted into a single-product one. To use the approach of break-even point in units, the package selling price and the variable cost per package must be known. To compute these package values, the sales mix, individual product prices, and individual variable costs are needed. Cornerstone 4-7 shows how the overall break-even point for each product can be determined.

The complexity of the approach of break-even point in units increases dramatically as the number of products increases. Imagine performing this analysis for a firm with several hundred products. This observation seems more overwhelming than it actually is. Computers can easily handle a problem with so much data. Furthermore, many firms simplify the problem by analyzing product groups rather than individual products. Another way to handle the increased complexity is to switch from the units sold to the sales revenue approach. This approach can accomplish a multiple-product CVP analysis using only the summary data found in an organization's income statement. The computational requirements are much simpler.

Break-Even Point in Sales Dollars

To illustrate the break-even point in sales dollars, the same examples will be used. However, the only information needed is the projected income statement for Whittier Company as a whole.

Sales	$1,120,000
Less: Variable costs	870,000
Contribution margin	$ 250,000
Less: Fixed costs	96,250
Operating income	$ 153,750

Notice that this income statement corresponds to the total column of the more detailed income statement examined previously. The projected income statement rests on the assumption that 1,200 mulching mowers and 800 riding mowers will be sold (a 3:2 sales mix). The break-even point in sales revenue also rests on the expected sales mix. (As with the units sold approach, different sales mixes will produce different results.)

With the income statement, the usual CVP questions can be addressed. For example, how much sales revenue must be earned to break even? Cornerstone 4-8 shows how to calculate the break-even point in sales dollars for a multiple-product firm.

The break-even point in sales dollars implicitly uses the assumed sales mix but avoids the requirement of building a package contribution margin. No knowledge of individual product data is needed. The computational effort is similar to that used in the single-product setting. Moreover, the answer is still expressed in sales revenue. Unlike the break-even point in units, the answer to CVP questions using sales dollars is still expressed in a single summary measure. The sales revenue approach, however, does sacrifice information concerning individual product performance.

CONCEPT Q&A

Suppose a men's clothing store sells two brands of suits: designer suits with a contribution margin of $600 each and regular suits with a contribution margin of $500 each. At break even, the store must sell a total of 100 suits a month. Last month, the store sold 100 suits in total but incurred an operating loss. There was no change in fixed cost, variable cost, or price. What happened?

Answers on pages 711 to 715.

OBJECTIVE 5
Explain the impact of risk, uncertainty, and changing variables on cost-volume-profit analysis.

Cost-Volume-Profit Analysis and Risk and Uncertainty

Because firms operate in a dynamic world, they must be aware of changes in prices, variable costs, and fixed costs. They must also account for the effect of risk and uncertainty. The break-even point can be affected by changes in price, unit

The HOW and WHY of Calculating the Break-Even Sales Dollars for a Multiple-Product Firm

CORNERSTONE 4-8

Information:

Recall that Whittier Company sells two products that are expected to produce total revenue next year of $1,120,000 and total variable costs of $870,000. Total fixed costs are expected to equal $96,250.

Required:

1. Calculate the break-even point in sales dollars for Whittier Company.
2. Check your answer by preparing a contribution margin income statement.

Solution:

1. The contribution margin ratio

$$= \frac{\$250{,}000}{\$1{,}120{,}000} = 0.22$$

$$\text{Break-even sales} = \frac{\text{Fixed cost}}{\text{Contribution margin ratio}} = \frac{\$96{,}250}{0.22} = \$437{,}500$$

[*Note:* Total break-even sales differ slightly between Cornerstones 4-7 and 4-8 ($431,200 vs. $437,500) due to the rounding of the contribution margin ratio to only two decimal places (0.22).]

2. Income statement—break-even solution:

Sales	$437,500
Less: Variable costs (0.78 × $437,500)	341,250
Contribution margin	$ 96,250
Less: Fixed costs	96,250
Operating income	$ 0

WHY:

Because, as in the case of a single-product firm, management needs to know the sales volume of each product in the sales mix necessary to break even.

contribution margin, and fixed cost. Managers can use CVP analysis to handle risk and uncertainty.

For example, France-based **Airbus** reported in 2006 its first ever loss, which resulted from a decreased sales volume and major costly production delays involving a redesign of its "extra wide-body" passenger jet to compete with **Boeing**'s 787 Dreamliner. In response to this loss, Airbus used CVP analysis to estimate how a $2.6 billion reduction in its annual variable and fixed costs, as well as various reductions in its $144 million unit jet price, would affect its annual profit.[1]

For a given sales mix, CVP analysis can be used as if the firm were selling a single product. However, when the prices of individual products change, the sales mix can be affected because consumers may buy relatively more or less of the product. Keep in mind that a new sales mix will affect the units of each product that need to be sold in order to achieve a desired profit target. If the sales mix for the coming period is uncertain, it may be necessary to look at several different mixes. In this way, a manager gains insight into the possible outcomes facing the firm.

[1] "Planemaker Airbus to report its first annual loss," *USA Today* (January 18, 2007): 3B.

Exhibit 4-5

Summary of the Effects of Alternative 1

	Before the Increased Advertising	With the Increased Advertising
Units sold	1,600	1,725
Unit contribution margin	× $75	× $75
Total contribution margin	$120,000	$129,375
Less: Fixed expenses	45,000	53,000
Operating income	$ 75,000	$ 76,375

	Difference in Profit
Change in sales volume	125
Unit contribution margin	× $75
Change in contribution margin	$ 9,375
Less: Change in fixed expenses	8,000
Increase in operating income	$ 1,375

Exhibit 4-6

Summary of the Effects of Alternative 2

	Before the Proposed Price Decrease	With the Proposed Price Decrease
Units sold	1,600	1,900
Unit contribution margin	× $75	× $50
Total contribution margin	$120,000	$95,000
Less: Fixed expenses	45,000	45,000
Operating income	$ 75,000	$50,000

	Difference in Profit
Change in contribution margin ($95,000 – $120,000)	$(25,000)
Less: Change in fixed expenses	—
Decrease in operating income	$(25,000)

Exhibit 4-7

Summary of the Effects of Alternative 3

	Before the Proposed Price Decrease and Advertising Increase	With the Proposed Price Decrease and Advertising Increase
Units sold	1,600	2,600
Unit contribution margin	× $75	× $50
Total contribution margin	$120,000	$130,000
Less: Fixed expenses	45,000	53,000
Operating income	$ 75,000	$ 77,000

	Difference in Profit
Change in contribution margin ($130,000 – $120,000)	$10,000
Less: Change in fixed expenses ($53,000 – $45,000)	8,000
Increase in operating income	$ 2,000

Suppose that Whittier Company recently conducted a market study of the mulching lawn mower that revealed three different alternatives:

1. *Alternative 1:* If advertising expenditures increase by \$8,000, then sales will increase from 1,600 units to 1,725 units.
2. *Alternative 2:* A price decrease from \$400 to \$375 per lawn mower will increase sales from 1,600 units to 1,900 units.
3. *Alternative 3:* Decreasing price to \$375 *and* increasing advertising expenditures by \$8,000 will increase sales from 1,600 units to 2,600 units.

Should Whittier maintain its current price and advertising policies, or should it select one of the three alternatives described by the marketing study?

The first alternative, increasing advertising costs by \$8,000 with a resulting sales increase of 125 units, is summarized in Exhibit 4-5. This alternative can be analyzed by using the contribution margin per unit of \$75. Since units sold increase by 125, the increase in total contribution margin is \$9,375 (\$75 × 125 units). However, since fixed costs increase by \$8,000, profits only increase by \$1,375 (\$9,375 − \$8,000). Notice that we need to look only at the incremental increase in total contribution margin and fixed expenses to compute the increase in total operating income.

For the second alternative, the price is dropped to \$375 (from \$400), and the units sold increase to 1,900 (from 1,600). The effects of this alternative are summarized in Exhibit 4-6. Here, fixed expenses do not change, so only the change in total contribution margin is relevant. For the current price of \$400, the contribution margin per unit is \$75 (\$400 − \$325), and the total contribution margin is \$120,000 (\$75 × 1,600). For the new price, the contribution margin drops to \$50 per unit (\$375 − \$325). If 1,900 units are sold at the new price, then the new total contribution margin is \$95,000 (\$50 × 1,900). Dropping the price results in a profit decline of \$25,000 (\$120,000 − \$95,000).

The third alternative calls for a decrease in the unit selling price and an increase in advertising costs. Like the first alternative, the profit impact can be assessed by looking at the incremental effects on contribution margin and fixed expenses. The incremental profit change can be found by (1) computing the incremental change in total contribution margin, (2) computing the incremental change in fixed expenses, and (3) adding the two results. As shown in Exhibit 4-7, the current total contribution margin (for 1,600 units sold) is \$120,000. Since the new unit contribution margin is \$50, the new total contribution margin is \$130,000 (\$50 × 2,600 units). Thus, the incremental increase in total contribution margin is \$10,000 (\$130,000 − \$120,000). However, to achieve this incremental increase in contribution margin, an incremental increase of \$8,000 in fixed costs is needed. The net effect is an incremental increase in operating income of \$2,000.

Of the three alternatives identified by the marketing study, the third alternative promises the most benefit. It increases total operating income by \$2,000. The first alternative increases operating income by only \$1,375, and the second *decreases* operating income by \$25,000.

These examples are all based on a units sold approach. However, we could just as easily have applied a sales revenue approach. The answers would be the same.

Introducing Risk and Uncertainty

An important assumption of CVP analysis is that prices and costs are known with certainty. This assumption is seldom accurate. Risk and uncertainty are a part of business decision making and must be dealt with somehow. Formally, risk differs from uncertainty in that under risk, the probability distributions of the variables are known; under uncertainty, they are not known. For purposes of CVP analysis, however, the terms will be used interchangeably.

How do managers deal with risk and uncertainty? There are a variety of methods. First, of course, is that management must realize the uncertain nature of future prices, costs, and quantities. Next, managers move from consideration of a break-even point to what might be called a "break-even band." In other words, given the uncertain nature of the data, perhaps a firm might break even when 1,800 to 2,000 units are sold instead of at the point estimate of 1,900 units. Furthermore, managers may engage in sensitivity or what-if analysis. In this instance, a computer spreadsheet is helpful, as managers set up the break-even (or targeted profit) relationships and then check to see the impact that varying costs and prices have on quantity sold. Two concepts useful to management are margin of safety and operating leverage. Both of these concepts may be considered measures of risk. Each requires knowledge of fixed and variable costs.

Margin of Safety When making decisions about business opportunities and changes in sales mix, managers often consider the **margin of safety (MS)**, which is the excess of budgeted or actual sales over break-even sales. The margin of safety indicates the possible decrease in sales that may occur before an operating loss results. Thus, if the margin of safety is low, even a small decline in sales revenue may result in an operating loss. The margin of safety may be expressed in the following ways:

- Dollars of sales
- Units of sales
- Percent of current sales

The following formulas are applicable:

Margin of safety in units: Actual sales in units – Break-even sales in units
Margin of safety in dollars: Actual sales in \$ – Break-even sales in \$
Margin of safety% : Margin of safety in units/Actual unit sales
or Margin of safety in \$/Actual sales in \$

An MS calculation allows management to determine how close to a "danger level" the company is operating and, as such, provides an indication of risk. The lower the MS, the more carefully management must watch sales and control costs so that it will not generate a net loss. At low margins of safety, managers are less likely to take advantage of opportunities that, if incorrectly analyzed or forecasted, could send the company into a loss position. To illustrate, assume the following data:

Sales	\$500,000
Sales at the break-even point	\$400,000
Unit selling price	\$ 25

The MS in dollars of sales is \$100,000 (\$500,000 –\$400,000). The MS in units is 4,000 units (\$100,000/\$25). The MS expressed as a percentage of current sales is 20 percent, as computed below:

$$\begin{aligned} MS &= (\text{sales} - \text{sales at BEP})/\text{Sales} \\ &= (\$500{,}000 - \$400{,}000)/\$500{,}000 \\ &= 20\% \end{aligned}$$

Therefore, the current sales may decline \$100,000, 4,000 units, or 20 percent before an operating loss occurs.

Exhibit 4-8 shows the calculation of the margin of safety and the margin of safety ratio. Cornerstone 4-9 shows the expected margin of safety for Whittier Company.

The margin of safety can be viewed as a crude measure of risk. There are always events, unknown when plans are made, that can lower sales below the original expected level. In the event that sales take a downward turn, the risk of suffering losses is less if a firm's expected margin of safety is large than if the margin of safety is small. Managers who face a low margin of safety may wish to consider actions to increase sales or decrease costs. These steps will increase the margin of safety and lower the risk of incurring losses.

The HOW and WHY of Computing the Margin of Safety

CORNERSTONE 4-9

Information:
Recall that Whittier Company plans to sell 1,000 mowers at $400 each in the coming year. Whittier has variable costs of $325 and fixed costs of $45,000. Break-even units were previously calculated as 600.

Required:
1. Calculate the margin of safety for Whittier Company in terms of the number of units.
2. Calculate the margin of safety for Whittier Company in terms of sales revenue.

Solution:
1. Margin of safety in units = 1,000 − 600 = 400
2. Margin of safety in sales revenue = $400(1,000) − $400(600) = $160,000

WHY:
Because a firm needs to estimate the risk of suffering losses. If the margin of safety is small, a small decline in sales may eliminate the projected profit.

Operating Leverage In physics, a lever is a simple machine used to multiply force. Basically, the lever multiplies the effort applied to create more work. The larger the load moved by a given amount of effort, the greater is the mechanical advantage. In financial terms, operating leverage is concerned with the relative mix of fixed costs and variable costs in an organization. It is sometimes possible to trade off fixed costs for variable costs. As variable costs decrease, the unit contribution margin increases, making the contribution of each unit sold that much greater. In such a case, fluctuations in sales have an increased effect on profitability. Thus, firms that have realized lower variable costs by increasing the proportion of fixed costs will benefit with greater increases in profits as sales increase than will firms with a lower proportion of fixed costs. Fixed costs are being used as leverage to increase profits. Unfortunately, it is also true that firms with a higher operating leverage will experience greater reductions in profits as sales decrease. **Operating leverage** is the use of fixed costs to extract higher percentage changes in profits as sales activity changes.

CONCEPT Q&A

Two companies have identical sales revenue of $15 million. Is it true that both have the same operating income and the same margin of safety? Is it possible that one company has a higher margin of safety?

Answers on pages 711 to 715.

Exhibit 4-8

The Margin of Safety

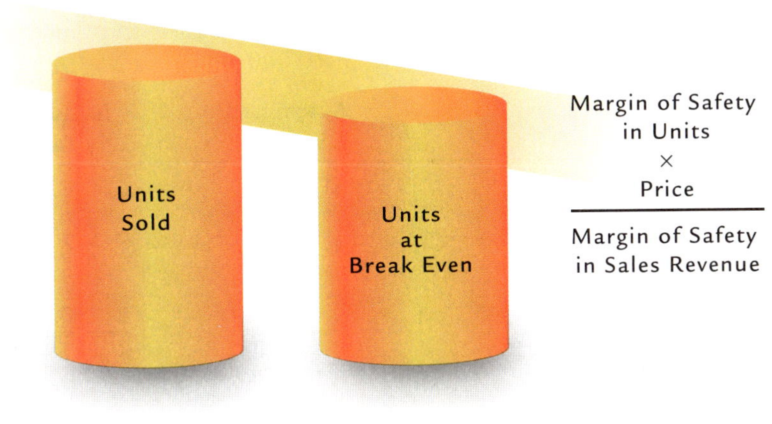

CORNERSTONE 4-10

The HOW and WHY of Computing the DOL

Information:

Recall that Whittier Company plans to sell 1,000 mowers at $400 each in the coming year. Whittier has variable costs of $325 and fixed costs of $45,000. Operating income at that level of sales was previously computed as $30,000.

Required:

Calculate the degree of operating leverage for Whittier Company.

Solution:

$$\text{Degree of operating leverage} = \frac{\text{Total contribution margin}}{\text{Operating income}}$$

$$= \frac{(\$400 - \$325)(1{,}000\text{ units})}{\$30{,}000}$$

$$= 2.5$$

WHY:

Because by calculating the DOL we can predict what will be the affect on operating income given a change in sales or the risk involved by fluctuating sales levels as a result of the cost structure (portion of fixed versus variable costs).

The **degree of operating leverage (DOL)** can be measured for a given level of sales by taking the ratio of contribution margin to operating income, as follows:

$$\text{Degree of operating leverage} = \frac{\text{Contribution margin}}{\text{Operating income}}$$

If fixed costs are used to lower variable costs such that contribution margin increases and operating income decreases, then the degree of operating leverage increases—signalling an increase in risk. Cornerstone 4-10 shows how to compute the degree of operating leverage for Whittier Company.

The greater the degree of operating leverage, the more that changes in sales will affect operating income. Because of this phenomenon, the mix of costs that an organization chooses can have a considerable influence on its operating risk and profit level. A company's mix of fixed costs relative to variable costs is referred to as its **cost structure**. Often, a company changes its cost structure by taking on more of one type of cost in exchange for reducing its amount of the other type of cost. For example, as Canadian companies try to compete more effectively with foreign competitors' significantly lower hourly labour costs (i.e., a variable cost), many are altering their cost structures by taking on more plant machine automation (i.e., a fixed cost) in exchange for using less labour.

To illustrate the impact of these concepts on management decision making, consider a firm that is planning to add a new product line. In adding the line, the firm can choose to rely heavily on automation or on labour. If the firm chooses to emphasize automation rather than labour, fixed costs will be higher, and unit variable costs will be lower. Relevant data for a sales level of 10,000 units follow:

	Automated System	Manual System
Sales	$1,000,000	$1,000,000
Less: Variable costs	500,000	800,000
Contribution margin	$ 500,000	$ 200,000
Less: Fixed costs	**375,000**	**100,000**
Operating income	$ 125,000	$ 100,000
Unit selling price	$ 100	$ 100
Unit variable cost	50	80
Unit contribution margin	50	20

The HOW and WHY of Computing the Impact of Increased Sales on Operating Income Using the DOL

CORNERSTONE 4-11

Information:

Recall that Whittier Company had expected to sell 1,000 mowers and earn operating income equal to $30,000 next year. Whittier's degree of operating leverage is equal to 2.5. The company plans to increase sales by 20 percent next year.

Required:

1. Calculate the percent change in operating income expected by Whittier Company for next year using the degree of operating leverage.
2. Calculate the operating income expected by Whittier Company next year using the percent change in operating income calculated in Requirement 1.

Solution:

1. Percent change in operating income = DOL × % change in sales
   = 2.5 × 20% = 50%
2. Expected operating income = $30,000 + (0.5 × $30,000) = $45,000

WHY:

Because the DOL can be used directly to calculate the changes in operating income by simply multiplying DOL by the percentage change in sales without constructing a full income statement.

Just by computing the new income statements, one may safely say that the automated system has a higher operating leverage simply because the fixed costs are higher than the fixed costs for the manual system.

The degree of operating leverage for the automated system is 4.0 ($500,000/$125,000). The degree of operating leverage for the manual system is 2.0 ($200,000/$100,000). What happens to profit in each system if sales increase by 40 percent? We can generate the following income statements to see the following:

	Automated System	Manual System
Sales	$1,400,000	$1,400,000
Less: Variable costs	700,000	1,120,000
Contribution margin	$ 700,000	$ 280,000
Less: Fixed costs	375,000	100,000
Operating income	$ 325,000	$ 180,000

Profits for the automated system would increase by $200,000 ($325,000 − $125,000) for a 160 percent increase. In the manual system, profits increase by only $80,000 ($180,000 − $100,000) for an 80 percent increase. The automated system has a greater percentage increase because it has a higher degree of operating leverage.

The degree of operating leverage can be used directly to calculate the change in operating income that would result from a given percentage change in sales.

Percentage change in operating income = DOL × Percent change in sales

Since sales are predicted to increase by 40 percent, and the DOL for the automated system is 4.0, operating income increases by 160 percent. Since operating income based on the original sales level is $125,000, the operating income based on the increased sales level would be $325,000 [$125,000 + ($125,000 × 1.6)]. Similarly, for the manual system, increased sales of 40 percent and DOL of 2.0 imply increased operating income of 80 percent. Therefore, operating income based on the increased sales level would be $180,000 [$100,000 + ($100,000 × 0.8)]. Cornerstone 4-11 illustrates the impact of increased sales on operating income using the degree of operating leverage.

In choosing between the two systems, the effect of operating leverage is a valuable piece of information. Higher operating leverage multiplies the impact of increased sales on income. However, the effect is a two-edged sword. As sales decrease, the automated system will also show much higher percentage decreases. Moreover, the increased operating leverage is available under the automated system because of the presence of increased fixed costs. The break-even point for the automated system is 7,500 units ($375,000/$50), whereas the break-even point for the manual system is 5,000 units ($100,000/$20). Thus, the automated system has greater operating risk. The increased risk, of course, provides a potentially higher profit level as long as units sold exceed 9,167. Why 9,167? Because that is the quantity for which the operating income for the automated system equals the operating income for the manual system.

The quantity at which two systems produce the same operating income is referred to as the **indifference point**. This number of units is computed by setting the operating income equations of the two systems equal and solving for number of units:

$$\$50\ (\text{Units}) - \$375{,}000 = \$20\ (\text{Units}) - \$100{,}000$$
$$\text{Units} = 9{,}167$$

In choosing between the automated and manual systems, the manager must consider the likelihood that sales will exceed 9,167 units. If after careful study there is a strong belief that sales will easily exceed this level, then the choice is obviously the automated system. On the other hand, if sales are unlikely to exceed 9,167 units, then the manual system is preferable. Exhibit 4-9 summarizes the relative differences between the manual and automated systems in terms of some of the CVP concepts.

Sensitivity Analysis and Cost-Volume-Profit

The widespread use of personal computers and spreadsheets has placed sensitivity analysis within reach of most managers. An important tool, **sensitivity analysis** is a "what-if" technique that examines the impact of changes in underlying assumptions on an answer. It is relatively simple to input data on prices, variable costs, fixed costs, and sales mix and to set up formulas to calculate break-even points and expected profits. Then, the data can be varied as desired to see how changes impact the expected profit.

In the example on operating leverage, a company analyzed the impact on profit of using an automated versus a manual system. The computations were essentially done by hand, and too much variation is cumbersome. Using the power of a computer, it would be an easy matter to change the sales price in $1 increments between $75 and $125, with related assumptions about quantity sold. At the same time, variable and fixed costs could be adjusted. For example, suppose that the automated system has fixed costs of $375,000 but that those costs could easily double in the first year and come back down in the second and third years as bugs are worked out of the system and workers learn to use it. Again, the spreadsheet can effortlessly handle the many computations.

A spreadsheet, while wonderful for cranking out numerical answers, cannot do the most difficult job in CVP analysis. That job is determining the data to be entered in the first place. The managerial accountant must be aware of the cost and price distributions of the firm as well as of the impact of changing economic conditions on

Exhibit 4-9

Differences between a Manual and an Automated System

	Manual System	Automated System
Price	Same	Same
Variable cost	Relatively higher	Relatively lower
Fixed cost	Relatively lower	Relatively higher
Contribution margin	Relatively lower	Relatively higher
Break-even point	Relatively lower	Relatively higher
Margin of safety	Relatively higher	Relatively lower
Degree of operating leverage	Relatively lower	Relatively higher
Down-side risk	Relatively lower	Relatively higher
Up-side potential	Relatively lower	Relatively higher

these variables. The fact that variables are seldom known with certainty is no excuse for ignoring the impact of uncertainty on CVP analysis. Fortunately, sensitivity analysis can also give managers a feel for the degree to which a poorly forecast variable will affect an answer. That is also an advantage.

ETHICS It is important to note that the CVP results are only one input into business decisions. There are many other factors that may bear on decisions to choose one type of process over another, for example, or whether or not to delete certain costs. Businesses and non-profit entities often face trade-offs involving safety. Ethical concerns also have an important place in CVP analysis. One possibility is that cost of potential problems can be estimated and included in the CVP results. Often, however, the costs and probabilities are not known with sufficient certainty. In that case, these factors are included in the ultimate decision-making process. Chapter 12, on short-run decision making, covers this topic in more detail.◆

Summary of Learning Objectives

LO1. Determine the break-even point in number of units and in total sales dollars.

- At break even, total costs (variable and fixed) equal total sales revenue.
- Break-even units equal total fixed costs divided by the contribution margin (price minus variable cost per unit).
- Break-even revenue equals total fixed costs divided by the contribution margin ratio.

LO2. Determine the number of units that must be sold, and the amount of revenue required, to earn a targeted profit.

- To earn a target (desired) profit, total costs (variable and fixed) plus the amount of target profit must equal total sales revenue.
- Units to earn target profit equal total fixed costs plus target profit divided by the contribution margin.
- Sales revenue to earn target profit equals total fixed costs plus target profit divided by the contribution margin ratio.

LO3. Prepare a profit-volume graph and a cost-volume-profit graph, and explain the meaning of each.

- CVP assumes linear revenue and cost functions, no finished goods ending inventories, constant sales mix, and that selling prices and fixed and variable costs are known with certainty.
- Profit-volume graphs plot the relationship between profit (operating income) and units sold. Break-even units are shown where the profit line crosses the horizontal axis.
- CVP graphs plot a line for total costs and a line for total sales revenue. The intersection of these two lines is the break-even point in units.

LO4. Apply cost-volume-profit analysis in a multiple-product setting.

- Multiple-product analysis requires the expected sales mix.
- Break-even units for each product will change as the sales mix changes.
- Increased sales of high contribution margin products decrease the break-even point.
- Increased sales of low contribution margin products increase the break-even point.

LO5. Explain the impact of risk, uncertainty, and changing variables on cost-volume-profit analysis.

- Uncertainty regarding costs, prices, and sales mix affect the break-even point.
- Sensitivity analysis allows managers to vary costs, prices, and sales mix to show various possible break-even points.
- Margin of safety shows how far the company's actual sales and/or units are above or below the break-even point.
- Operating leverage is the use of fixed costs to increase the percentage changes in profits as sales activity changes.

Summary of Important Equations

1. $\text{Sales revenue} = \text{Price} \times \text{Units sold}$
2. $\text{Operating income} = (\text{Price} \times \text{Units sold}) - (\text{Unit variable cost} \times \text{Units sold}) - \text{Fixed cost}$
3. $\text{Break-even point in units} = \dfrac{\text{Fixed cost}}{(\text{Price} - \text{Unit variable cost})}$
4. $\text{Contribution margin ratio} = \dfrac{\text{Total contribution margin}}{\text{Sales}}$ or $= \dfrac{(\text{Price} - \text{Unit variable cost})}{\text{Price}}$
5. $\text{Variable cost ratio} = \dfrac{\text{Total variable cost}}{\text{Sales}}$ or $= \dfrac{\text{Unit variable cost}}{\text{Price}}$
6. $\text{Break-even point in sales dollars} = \dfrac{\text{Fixed cost}}{\text{Contribution margin ratio}}$ or $= \dfrac{\text{Fixed cost}}{(1 - \text{Variable cost ratio})}$
7. $\text{Margin of safety} = \text{Sales} - \text{Break-even sales}$
8. $\text{Degree of operating leverage} = \dfrac{\text{Total contribution margin}}{\text{Operating income}}$
9. $\text{Percentage change in profits} = \text{Degree of operating leverage} \times \text{Percent change in sales}$

CORNERSTONES FOR CHAPTER 4

Key Terms

Break-even point, 124
Common fixed expenses, 141
Contribution margin, 125
Contribution margin income statement, 124
Contribution margin ratio, 125
Cost structure, 150
Cost-volume-profit graph, 138
Degree of operating leverage (DOL), 150
Direct fixed expenses, 141
Indifference point, 152
Margin of safety (MS), 148
Operating leverage, 149
Profit-volume graph, 137
Sales mix, 142
Sensitivity analysis, 152
Unit contribution margin, 126
Variable cost ratio, 129

Review Problem

I. Single Product Cost-Volume-Profit Analysis

Cutlass Company's projected profit for the coming year is as follows:

	Total	Per Unit
Sales	$200,000	$20
Less: Variable expenses	120,000	12
Contribution margin	$ 80,000	$ 8
Less: Fixed expenses	64,000	
Operating income	$ 16,000	

Required:

1. Compute the variable cost ratio and the contribution margin ratio
2. Compute the break-even point in units.
3. Compute the break-even point in sales dollars.
4. How many units must be sold to earn a profit of $30,000?
5. Using the contribution margin ratio, compute the additional profit that Cutlass would earn if sales were $25,000 more than expected.
6. For the projected level of sales, compute the margin of safety in units and in sales dollars.
7. Calculate the degree of operating leverage. Now suppose that Cutlass revises the forecast to show a 30 percent increase in sales over the original forecast. What is the percent change in operating income expected for the revised forecast? What is the total operating income expected by Cutlass after revising the sales forecast?

Solution:

1. $$\text{Variable cost ratio} = \frac{\text{Total variable cost}}{\text{Sales}} = \frac{\$120{,}000}{\$200{,}000} = 0.60\text{, or } 60\%$$

$$\text{Contribution margin ratio} = \frac{\text{Contribution margin}}{\text{Sales}} = \frac{\$80{,}000}{\$200{,}000} = 0.40\text{, or } 40\%$$

2. The break-even point is computed as follows:

$$\text{Units} = \frac{\text{Fixed cost}}{(\text{Price} - \text{Unit variable cost})}$$
$$= \frac{\$64{,}000}{(\$20 - \$12)}$$
$$= \frac{\$64{,}000}{\$8} = 8{,}000 \text{ units}$$

3. The break-even point in sales dollars is computed as follows:

$$\text{Break-even sales dollars} = \frac{\text{Fixed cost}}{\text{Contribution margin ratio}}$$
$$= \frac{\$64{,}000}{0.40}$$
$$= \$160{,}000$$

4. The number of units that must be sold to earn a profit of $30,000 is calculated as follows:

$$\text{Units} = \frac{(\$64{,}000 + \$30{,}000)}{\$8}$$
$$= \frac{\$94{,}000}{\$8}$$
$$= 11{,}750 \text{ units}$$

5. The additional contribution margin on additional sales of $25,000 would be 0.40 × $25,000 = $10,000.

6. Margin of safety in units = Projected units − Break-even units
= 10,000 − 8,000 = 2,000 units

Margin of safety in sales dollars = $200,000 − $160,000, or $40,000 in sales revenues

7. $$\text{Degree of operating leverage} = \frac{\text{Contribution margin}}{\text{Operating income}}$$
$$= \frac{\$80{,}000}{\$16{,}000} = 5.0$$

Percent change in operating income = Degree of operating leverage × % Change in sales
= 5.0 × 30%
= 150%

Expected operating income = $16,000 + (1.5 × $16,000)
= $40,000

II. Multiple-Product Cost-Volume-Profit Analysis

Alpha Company produces and sells two products: Alpha-Basic and Alpha-Deluxe. In the coming year, Alpha expects to sell 3,000 units of Alpha-Basic and 1,500 units of Alpha-Deluxe. Information on the two products is as follows:

	Alpha-Basic	Alpha-Deluxe
Price	$120	$200
Variable cost per unit	40	80

Total fixed costs are $140,000.

Required:

1. What is the sales mix of Alpha-Basic to Alpha-Deluxe?
2. Compute the break-even quantity of each product.

Solution:

1. The sales mix of Alpha-Basic to Alpha-Deluxe is 3,000:1,500 or 2:1.
2. Each package consists of two Alpha-Basic and one Alpha-Deluxe:

Product	Price	Unit Variable Cost	Unit Contribution Margin	Sales Mix	Package Unit Contribution Margin
Alpha-Basic	$120	$40	$ 80	2	$160
Alpha-Deluxe	200	80	120	1	120
Package total					$280

$$\text{Break-even packages} = \frac{\text{Total fixed cost}}{\text{Package contribution margin}}$$

$$= \frac{\$140{,}000}{\$280}$$

$$= 500 \text{ packages}$$

Alpha-Basic break-even units = $500 \times 2 = 1{,}000$
Alpha-Deluxe break-even units = $500 \times 1 = 500$

Discussion Questions

1. Explain how CVP analysis can be used for managerial planning.
2. Describe the difference between the units sold approach to CVP analysis and the sales revenue approach.
3. Define the term *break-even point.*
4. Explain why contribution margin per unit becomes profit per unit above the break-even point.
5. What is the variable cost ratio? The contribution margin ratio? How are the two ratios related?
6. Suppose a firm with a contribution margin ratio of 0.3 increased its advertising expenses by $10,000 and found that sales increased by $30,000. Was it a good decision to increase advertising expenses? Suppose that the contribution margin ratio is now 0.4. Would it be a good decision to increase advertising expenses?
7. Define the term *sales mix,* and give an example to support your definition.
8. Explain how CVP analysis developed for single products can be used in a multiple-product setting.
9. Since break-even analysis focuses on making zero profit, it is of no value in determining the units a firm must sell to earn a targeted profit. Do you agree or disagree with this statement? Why?
10. How does targeted profit enter into the break-even units equation?
11. Explain how a change in sales mix can change a company's break-even point.
12. Define the term *margin of safety.* Explain how it can be used as a crude measure of operating risk.
13. Explain what is meant by the term *operating leverage.* What impact does increased leverage have on risk?
14. How can sensitivity analysis be used in conjunction with CVP analysis?
15. Why is a declining margin of safety over a period of time an issue of concern to managers?

Multiple-Choice Exercises

4-1 If the variable cost per unit goes up,

	Contribution margin	Break-even point
a.	increases	increases.
b.	increases	decreases.

c.	decreases	decreases.
d.	decreases	increases.
e.	decreases	remains unchanged.

4-2 The amount of revenue required to earn a targeted profit is equal to

a. fixed cost divided by contribution margin.
b. fixed cost divided by contribution margin ratio.
c. fixed cost plus targeted profit divided by contribution margin ratio.
d. targeted profit divided by contribution margin ratio.
e. targeted profit divided by variable cost ratio.

4-3 Break-even revenue for the multiple-product firm can

a. be calculated by dividing total fixed cost by the overall contribution margin ratio.
b. be calculated by dividing segment fixed cost by the overall contribution margin ratio.
c. be calculated by dividing total fixed cost by the package contribution margin.
d. be calculated by multiplying total fixed cost by the contribution margin ratio.
e. not be calculated; break-even revenue can only be computed for a single-product firm.

4-4 In the cost-volume-profit graph,

a. the break-even point is found where the total revenue curve crosses the x-axis.
b. the area of profit is to the left of the break-even point.
c. the area of loss cannot be determined.
d. both the total revenue curve and the total cost curve appear.
e. neither the total revenue curve nor the total cost curve appear.

4-5 An important assumption of cost-volume-profit analysis is that

a. both costs and revenues are linear functions.
b. all cost and revenue relationships are analyzed within the relevant range.
c. there is no change in inventories.
d. sales mix remains constant.
e. all of the above are assumptions of cost-volume-profit analysis.

4-6 The use of fixed costs to extract higher percentage changes in profits as sales activity changes involves

a. margin of safety.
b. operating leverage.
c. degree of operating leverage.
d. sensitivity analysis.
e. variable cost reduction.

4-7 If the margin of safety is 0, then

a. the company is operating at a loss.
b. the company is precisely breaking even.
c. the company is earning a small profit.
d. the margin of safety cannot be less than or equal to 0; it must be positive.
e. none of the above is true.

4-8 The contribution margin is the

a. amount by which sales exceed fixed costs.
b. difference between sales and total expenses.
c. difference between sales and operating income.
d. difference between sales and total variable expense.
e. difference between variable expense and fixed expense.

Use the following information for 4-9 and 4-10.
Corleone Company produces a single product with a price of $15, variable costs per unit of $12, and fixed costs of $9,000.

4-9 Corleone's break-even point in units

a. is 600.
b. is 750.
c. is 9,000.
d. is 3,000.
e. cannot be determined from the information given.

4-10 The variable cost ratio and the contribution margin ratio for Corleone are

	Variable cost ratio	Contribution margin ratio
a.	80%	80%.
b.	20%	80%.
c.	20%	20%.
d.	80%	20%.

e. The contribution margin ratio cannot be determined from the information given.

4-11 If a company's fixed costs rise by $10,000, which of the following will be true?

a. The break-even point will decrease.
b. The variable cost ratio will increase.
c. The break-even point will be unchanged.
d. The variable cost ratio will decrease.
e. The contribution margin ratio will be unchanged.

4-12 Solemon Company has fixed costs of $15,000, variable cost per unit of $5, and a price of $8. If Solemon wants to earn a targeted profit of $3,600, how many units must be sold?

a. 6,200
b. 5,000
c. 1,200
d. 3,720
e. 1,875

Cornerstone Exercises

Cornerstone Exercise 4-13 VARIABLE COST, FIXED COST, CONTRIBUTION MARGIN INCOME STATEMENT

OBJECTIVE 1
CORNERSTONE 4-1

Head-First Company plans to sell 5,000 bicycle helmets at $70 each in the coming year. Product costs include:

Direct materials per helmet	$ 30
Direct labour per helmet	5
Variable overhead per helmet	12
Total fixed factory overhead	14,000

Variable selling expense is a commission of $2 per helmet; fixed selling and administrative expense totals $15,400.

Required:

1. Calculate the total variable cost per unit.

2. Calculate the total fixed expense for the year.
3. Prepare a contribution margin income statement for Head-First Company for the coming year.

OBJECTIVE 1
CORNERSTONE 4-2

Cornerstone Exercise 4-14 BREAK-EVEN POINT IN UNITS

Head-First Company plans to sell 5,000 bicycle helmets at $70 each in the coming year. Unit variable cost is $49 (includes direct materials, direct labour, variable overhead, and variable selling expense). Total fixed cost equals $29,400 (includes fixed factory overhead and fixed selling and administrative expense).

Required:

1. Calculate the break-even number of helmets.
2. Check your answer by preparing a contribution margin income statement based on the break-even units.

OBJECTIVE 1
CORNERSTONE 4-3

Cornerstone Exercise 4-15 VARIABLE COST RATIO, CONTRIBUTION MARGIN RATIO

Head-First Company plans to sell 5,000 bicycle helmets at $70 each in the coming year. Unit variable cost is $49 (includes direct materials, direct labour, variable overhead, and variable selling expense). Fixed factory overhead is $14,000 and fixed selling and administrative expense is $15,400.

Required:

1. Calculate the variable cost ratio.
2. Calculate the contribution margin ratio.
3. Prepare a contribution margin income statement based on the budgeted figures for next year. In a column next to the income statement, show the percentages based on sales for sales, total variable costs, and total contribution margin.

OBJECTIVE 1
CORNERSTONE 4-4

Cornerstone Exercise 4-16 BREAK-EVEN POINT IN SALES DOLLARS

Head-First Company plans to sell 5,000 bicycle helmets at $70 each in the coming year. Variable cost is 70 percent of the sales price; contribution margin is 30 percent of sales price. Total fixed cost equals $29,400 (includes fixed factory overhead and fixed selling and administrative expense).

Required:

1. Calculate the sales revenue that Head-First must make to break even by using the break-even point in sales equation.
2. Check your answer by preparing a contribution margin income statement based on the break-even point in sales dollars.

OBJECTIVE 2
CORNERSTONE 4-5

Cornerstone Exercise 4-17 UNITS TO EARN TARGET INCOME

Head-First Company plans to sell 5,000 bicycle helmets at $70 each in the coming year. Unit variable cost is $49 (includes direct materials, direct labour, variable overhead, and variable selling expense). Total fixed cost equals $29,400 (includes fixed factory overhead and fixed selling and administrative expense).

Required:

1. Calculate the number of helmets Head-First must sell to earn operating income of $81,900.
2. Check your answer by preparing a contribution margin income statement based on the number of units calculated.

OBJECTIVE 2
CORNERSTONE 4-6

Cornerstone Exercise 4-18 SALES NEEDED TO EARN TARGET INCOME

Head-First Company plans to sell 5,000 bicycle helmets at $70 each in the coming year. Variable cost is 70 percent of the sales price; contribution margin is 30 percent of sales price. Total fixed cost equals $29,400 (includes fixed factory overhead and fixed selling and administrative expense).

Required:

1. Calculate the sales revenue that Head-First must make to earn operating income of $81,900.
2. Check your answer by preparing a contribution margin income statement based on the sales dollars calculated in Requirement 1.

Cornerstone Exercise 4-19 BREAK-EVEN POINT IN UNITS FOR A MULTIPLE-PRODUCT FIRM

OBJECTIVE 4
CORNERSTONE 4-7

Suppose that Head-First Company now sells both bicycle helmets and motorcycle helmets. The bicycle helmets are priced at $70 and have variable costs of $49 each. The motorcycle helmets are priced at $220 and have variable costs of $143 each. Total fixed costs for Head-First as a whole equals $54,600 (includes all fixed factory overhead and fixed selling and administrative expense). Next year, Head-First expects to sell 5,000 bicycle helmets and 1,000 motorcycle helmets.

Required:

1. Form a package of bicycle and motorcycle helmets based on the sales mix expected for the coming year.
2. Calculate the break-even point in units for bicycle helmets and for motorcycle helmets.
3. Check your answer by preparing a contribution margin income statement.

Cornerstone Exercise 4-20 BREAK-EVEN SALES DOLLARS FOR A MULTIPLE-PRODUCT FIRM

OBJECTIVE 4
CORNERSTONE 4-8

Head-First Company now sells both bicycle helmets and motorcycle helmets. Next year, Head-First expects to produce total revenue of $570,000 and total variable costs of $388,000. Total fixed costs are expected to be $54,600.

Required:

1. Calculate the break-even point in sales dollars for Head-First. (Round the contribution margin ratio to four significant digits.)
2. Check your answer by preparing a contribution margin income statement.

Cornerstone Exercise 4-21 MARGIN OF SAFETY

OBJECTIVE 5
CORNERSTONE 4-9

Head-First Company plans to sell 5,000 bicycle helmets at $70 each in the coming year. Unit variable cost is $49 (includes direct materials, direct labour, variable overhead, and variable selling expense). Total fixed cost equals $29,400 (includes fixed factory overhead and fixed selling and administrative expense). Break-even units equal 1,400.

Required:

1. Calculate the margin of safety in terms of the number of units.
2. Calculate the margin of safety in terms of sales revenue.

Cornerstone Exercise 4-22 DEGREE OF OPERATING LEVERAGE

OBJECTIVE 5
CORNERSTONE 4-10

Head-First Company plans to sell 5,000 bicycle helmets at $70 each in the coming year. Unit variable cost is $49 (includes direct materials, direct labour, variable overhead, and variable selling expense). Total fixed cost equals $29,400 (includes fixed factory overhead and fixed selling and administrative expense). Operating income at 5,000 units sold is $75,600.

Required:

Calculate the degree of operating leverage. (Round your answer to the nearest tenth.)

Cornerstone Exercise 4-23 IMPACT OF INCREASED SALES ON OPERATING INCOME USING THE DEGREE OF OPERATING LEVERAGE

OBJECTIVE 5
CORNERSTONE 4-11

Head-First Company had planned to sell 5,000 bicycle helmets at $70 each in the coming year. Unit variable cost is $49 (includes direct materials, direct labour, variable overhead, and variable selling expense). Total fixed cost equals $29,400 (includes fixed factory overhead and fixed selling and administrative expense). Operating income at 5,000 units sold is $75,600. The degree of operating leverage is 1.4. Now Head-First expects to increase sales by 15 percent next year.

Required:

1. Calculate the percent change in operating income expected.
2. Calculate the operating income expected next year using the percent change in operating income calculated in Requirement 1.

Exercises

OBJECTIVE 1

Exercise 4-24 BASIC BREAK-EVEN CALCULATIONS

Suppose that Adams Company sells a product for $16. Unit costs are as follows:

Direct materials	$3.90
Direct labour	1.40
Variable overhead	2.10
Variable selling and administrative expense	1.60

Total fixed overhead is $52,000 per year, and total fixed selling and administrative expense is $37,950.

Required:

1. Calculate the variable cost per unit and the contribution margin per unit.
2. Calculate the contribution margin ratio and the variable cost ratio.
3. Calculate the break-even units.
4. Prepare a contribution margin income statement at the break-even number of units.

OBJECTIVE 1

Exercise 4-25 CONTRIBUTION MARGIN, CONTRIBUTION MARGIN RATIO, BREAK-EVEN POINT IN UNITS, BREAK-EVEN SALES REVENUE

Next year, Jefferson Company expects to sell 140,000 units at $7.60 each. Variable costs are 60 percent of sales price. Fixed costs total $349,600.

Required:

1. Calculate the contribution margin per unit.
2. Calculate the break-even point in units.
3. Calculate the break-even sales revenue.
4. Prepare an income statement for Jefferson at break even.

OBJECTIVE 1

Exercise 4-26 CONTRIBUTION MARGIN RATIO, VARIABLE COST RATIO, BREAK-EVEN SALES REVENUE

The controller of Dynamic Company prepared the following projected income statement:

Sales	$90,000
Less: Variable costs	72,000
Contribution margin	$18,000
Less: Fixed costs	6,900
Operating income	$11,100

Required:

1. Calculate the contribution margin ratio.
2. Calculate the variable cost ratio.
3. Calculate the break-even sales revenue for Dynamic.

Exercise 4-27 INCOME STATEMENT, BREAK-EVEN UNITS, UNITS TO EARN TARGET INCOME

OBJECTIVE 2

Cameo Company sold 27,000 units last year at $14 each. Variable cost was $9.50, and fixed costs were $126,000.

Required:

1. Prepare an income statement for Cameo Company for last year.
2. Calculate the break-even point in units.
3. Calculate the units that Cameo must sell to earn operating income of $9,900 next year.

Exercise 4-28 UNITS SOLD TO BREAK EVEN, UNIT VARIABLE COST, UNIT MANUFACTURING COST, UNITS TO EARN TARGET INCOME

OBJECTIVE 1

Prachi Company produces and sells disposable foil baking pans to retailers for $2.45 per pan. The variable costs per pan are as follows:

Direct materials	$0.27
Direct labour	0.58
Variable overhead	0.63
Variable selling	0.17

Fixed manufacturing costs total $131,650 per year. Administrative costs (all fixed) total $18,350.

Required:

1. Compute the number of pans that must be sold for Prachi to break even.
2. What is the unit variable cost? What is the unit variable manufacturing cost? Which is used in cost-volume-profit analysis and why?
3. How many pans must be sold for Prachi to earn operating income of $12,600?
4. How much sales revenue must Prachi have to earn operating income of $12,600?

Exercise 4-29 MARGIN OF SAFETY

OBJECTIVE 5

Chase Company produces and sells strings of colourful indoor/outdoor lights for holiday display to retailers for $6.28 per string. The variable costs per string are as follows:

Direct materials	$1.27
Direct labour	1.58
Variable overhead	0.63
Variable selling	0.17

Fixed manufacturing costs total $231,650 per year. Administrative costs (all fixed) total $315,390. Chase expects to sell 380,000 strings of light next year.

Required:

1. Calculate the break-even point in units.
2. Calculate the margin of safety in units.
3. Calculate the margin of safety in dollars.

Exercise 4-30 CONTRIBUTION MARGIN, UNIT AMOUNTS, BREAK-EVEN UNITS

OBJECTIVE 1

Information on four independent companies follows. Calculate the correct amount for each question mark. (Round your answers to two significant digits.)

	A	B	C	D
Sales	$15,000	$?	$?	$10,600
Total variable costs	5,000	11,700	9,750	?
Total contribution margin	$10,000	$ 3,900	$?	$?
Total fixed costs	?	4,000	?	4,452
Operating income (loss)	$ 500	$?	$ 364	$ 848

(Continued)

Required:

1. Compute the contribution margin per unit, and calculate the break-even point in units (round to the nearest unit). Calculate the contribution margin ratio and the break-even sales revenue.
2. The divisional manager has decided to increase the advertising budget by $100,000. This will increase sales revenues by $1 million. By how much will operating income increase or decrease as a result of this action?
3. Suppose sales revenues exceed the estimated amount on the income statement by $315,000. Without preparing a new income statement, by how much are profits underestimated?
4. Compute the margin of safety based on the original income statement.
5. Compute the degree of operating leverage based on the original income statement. If sales revenues are 20 percent greater than expected, what is the percentage increase in operating income? Round operating leverage to two decimal places.

OBJECTIVE 2 4

Problem 4-43 MULTIPLE-PRODUCT ANALYSIS, CHANGES IN SALES MIX, SALES TO EARN TARGET OPERATING INCOME

Gosnell Company produces two products: squares and circles. The projected income for the coming year, segmented by product line, follows:

	Squares	Circles	Total
Sales	$300,000	$2,500,000	$2,800,000
Less: Variable expenses	100,000	500,000	600,000
Contribution margin	$200,000	$2,000,000	$2,200,000
Less: Direct fixed expenses	28,000	1,500,000	1,528,000
Product margin	$172,000	$ 500,000	$ 672,000
Less: Common fixed expenses			100,000
Operating income			$ 572,000

The selling prices are $30 for squares and $50 for circles.

Required:

1. Compute the number of units of each product that must be sold for Gosnell Company to break even.
2. Assume that the marketing manager changes the sales mix of the two products so that the ratio is three squares to five circles. Repeat Requirement 1.
3. Refer to the original data. Suppose that Gosnell can increase the sales of squares with increased advertising. The extra advertising would cost an additional $245,000, and some of the potential purchasers of circles would switch to squares. In total, sales of squares would increase by 25,000 units, and sales of circles would decrease by 5,000 units. Would Gosnell be better off with this strategy?

OBJECTIVE 1 2 3 5

Problem 4-44 COST-VOLUME-PROFIT EQUATION, BASIC CONCEPTS, SOLVING FOR UNKNOWNS

Nutri-Tress Company produces combination shampoos and conditioners in individual-use bottles for hotels. Each bottle sells for $0.36. The variable costs for each bottle (materials, labour, and overhead) total $0.27. The total fixed costs are $58,500. During the most recent year, 830,000 bottles were sold.

Required:

1. What is the break-even point in units for Nutri-Tress? What is the margin of safety in units for the most recent year?
2. Prepare an income statement for Nutri-Tress's most recent year.
3. How many units must be sold for Nutri-Tress to earn a profit of $36,000?
4. What is the level of sales dollars needed for Nutri-Tress to earn operating income of 20 percent of sales?

Problem 4-45 CONTRIBUTION MARGIN RATIO, BREAK-EVEN SALES, OPERATING LEVERAGE

OBJECTIVE 1 5

Arta Company produces plastic mailboxes. The projected income statement for the coming year follows:

Sales	$560,400
Less: Variable costs	257,784
Contribution margin	$302,616
Less: Fixed costs	150,000
Operating income	$152,616

Required:

1. Compute the contribution margin ratio for the mailboxes.
2. How much revenue must Arta earn in order to break even?
3. What is the effect on the contribution margin ratio if the unit selling price and unit variable cost each increase by 10 percent?
4. Suppose that management has decided to give a 3 percent commission on all sales. The projected income statement does not reflect this commission. Recompute the contribution margin ratio, assuming that the commission will be paid. What effect does this have on the break-even point?
5. If the commission is paid as described in Requirement 4, management expects sales revenues to increase by $80,000. How will this affect operating leverage? Is it a sound decision to implement the commission? Support your answer with appropriate computations.

Problem 4-46 MULTIPLE PRODUCTS, BREAK-EVEN ANALYSIS, OPERATING LEVERAGE

OBJECTIVE 4 5

Carlyle Lighting Products produces two different types of lamps: a floor lamp and a desk lamp. Floor lamps sell for $30, and desk lamps sell for $20. The projected income statement for the coming year follows:

Sales	$600,000
Less: Variable costs	400,000
Contribution margin	$200,000
Less: Fixed costs	150,000
Operating income	$ 50,000

The owner of Carlyle estimates that 60 percent of the sales revenues will be produced by floor lamps and the remaining 40 percent by desk lamps. Floor lamps are also responsible for 60 percent of the variable expenses. Of the fixed expenses, one-third are common to both products, and one-half are directly traceable to the floor lamp product line.

Required:

1. Compute the sales revenue that must be earned for Carlyle to break even.
2. Compute the number of floor lamps and desk lamps that must be sold for Carlyle to break even.
3. Compute the degree of operating leverage for Carlyle Lighting Products. Now assume that the actual revenues will be 40 percent higher than the projected revenues. By what percentage will profits increase with this change in sales volume?

Problem 4-47 MULTIPLE-PRODUCT BREAK EVEN

OBJECTIVE 1 4

Polaris Inc. manufactures two types of metal stampings for the automobile industry: door handles and trim kits. Fixed costs equal $146,000. Each door handle sells for $12 and has variable costs of $9; each trim kit sells for $8 and has variable costs of $5.

Required:

1. What are the contribution margin per unit and the contribution margin ratio for door handles and for trim kits?
2. If Polaris sells 20,000 door handles and 40,000 trim kits, what is the operating income?
3. How many door handles and how many trim kits must be sold for Polaris to break even?
4. Assume that Polaris has the opportunity to rearrange its plant to produce only trim kits. If this is done, fixed costs will decrease by $35,000, and 70,000 trim kits can be produced and sold. Is this a good idea? Explain.

OBJECTIVE 1 5

Problem 4-48 COST-VOLUME-PROFIT, MARGIN OF SAFETY

Victoria Company produces a single product. Last year's income statement is as follows:

Sales (29,000 units)	$1,218,000
Less: Variable costs	812,000
Contribution margin	$ 406,000
Less: Fixed costs	300,000
Operating income	$ 106,000

Required:

1. Compute the break-even point in units and sales dollars.
2. What was the margin of safety for Victoria Company last year?
3. Suppose that Victoria Company is considering an investment in new technology that will increase fixed costs by $250,000 per year but will lower variable costs to 45 percent of sales. Units sold will remain unchanged. Prepare a budgeted income statement assuming that Victoria makes this investment. What is the new break-even point in units and sales dollars, assuming that the investment is made?

OBJECTIVE 1 5

Problem 4-49 COST-VOLUME-PROFIT, MARGIN OF SAFETY

Isaac Company had revenues of $930,000 last year with total variable costs of $353,400 and fixed costs of $310,000.

Required:

1. What is the variable cost ratio for Isaac? What is the contribution margin ratio?
2. What is the break-even point in sales revenue?
3. What was the margin of safety for Isaac last year?
4. Isaac is considering starting a multimedia advertising campaign that is supposed to increase sales by $7,500 per year. The campaign will cost $5,000. Is the advertising campaign a good idea? Explain.

OBJECTIVE 1

Problem 4-50 USING THE BREAK-EVEN EQUATIONS TO SOLVE FOR PRICE AND VARIABLE COST PER UNIT

Solve the following independent problems.

Required:

1. Sarah Company's break-even point is 1,500 units. Variable cost per unit is $300; total fixed costs are $120,000 per year. What price does Sarah charge?
2. Jesper Company charges a price of $3.50; total fixed costs are $160,000 per year, and the break-even point is 128,000 units. What is the variable cost per unit?

OBJECTIVE 1 2 5

Problem 4-51 CONTRIBUTION MARGIN, COST-VOLUME-PROFIT, MARGIN OF SAFETY

Candyland Inc. produces a particularly rich praline fudge. Each 300-gram box sells for $5.60. Variable unit costs are as follows:

Pecans	$0.70
Sugar	0.35
Butter	1.85
Other ingredients	0.34
Box, packing material	0.76
Selling commission	0.20

Fixed overhead cost is $32,300 per year. Fixed selling and administrative costs are $12,500 per year. Candyland sold 35,000 boxes last year.

Required:

1. What is the contribution margin per unit for a box of praline fudge? What is the contribution margin ratio?
2. How many boxes must be sold to break even? What is the break-even sales revenue?
3. What was Candyland's operating income last year?
4. What was the margin of safety?
5. Suppose that Candyland Inc. raises the price to $6.20 per box but anticipates a sales drop to 31,500 boxes. What will be the new break-even point in units? Should Candyland raise the price? Explain.

Problem 4-52 BREAK-EVEN SALES, OPERATING LEVERAGE, CHANGE IN INCOME

OBJECTIVE 1 5

Income statements for two different companies in the same industry are as follows:

	Company A	Company B
Sales	$500,000	$500,000
Less: Variable costs	400,000	200,000
Contribution margin	$100,000	$300,000
Less: Fixed costs	50,000	250,000
Operating income	$ 50,000	$ 50,000

Required:

1. Compute the degree of operating leverage for each company.
2. Compute the break-even point for each company. Explain why the break-even point for Company B is higher.
3. Suppose that both companies experience a 50 percent increase in revenues. Compute the percentage change in profits for each company. Explain why the percentage increase in Company B's profits is so much larger than that of Company A.

Problem 4-53 CONTRIBUTION MARGIN, BREAK-EVEN SALES, MARGIN OF SAFETY

OBJECTIVE 1 5

Suppose that Kicker had the following sales and cost experience (in thousands of dollars) for May of the current year and for May of the prior year:

	May, Current Year	May, Prior Year
Total sales	$ 43,560	$ 41,700
Less:		
Purchase price paid	(17,000)	(16,000)
Additional labour and supplies	(1,400)	(1,200)
Commissions	(1,250)	(1,100)
Contribution margin	$ 23,910	$ 23,400
Less:		
Fixed warehouse cost	(680)	(500)
Fixed administrative cost	(4,300)	(4,300)
Fixed selling cost	(5,600)	(5,000)
Research and development	(9,750)	(4,000)
Operating income	$ 3,580	$ 9,600

In August of the prior year, Kicker started an intensive quality program designed to enable it to build original equipment manufacture (OEM) speaker systems for a major automobile company. The program was housed in research and development. In the beginning of the current year, Kicker's accounting department exercised tighter control over sales commissions, ensuring that no dubious (e.g., double) payments were made. The increased sales in the current year required additional warehouse space that Kicker rented in town.

Required:

1. Calculate the contribution margin ratio for May of both years.
2. Calculate the break-even point in sales dollars for both years.
3. Calculate the margin of safety in sales dollars for both years.
4. Analyze the differences shown by your calculations in Requirements 1, 2, and 3.

Cases

OBJECTIVE 1 4

Case 4-54 COST-VOLUME-PROFIT WITH MULTIPLE PRODUCTS, SALES MIX CHANGES, CHANGES IN FIXED AND VARIABLE COSTS

Artistic Woodcrafting Inc. began several years ago as a one-person cabinet-making operation. Employees were added as the business expanded. Last year, sales volume totalled $850,000. Volume for the first five months of the current year totalled $600,000, and sales were expected to be $1.6 million for the entire year. Unfortunately, the cabinet business in the region where Artistic Woodcrafting is located is highly competitive. More than 200 cabinet shops are all competing for the same business.

Artistic currently offers two different quality grades of cabinets: Grade I and Grade II, with Grade I being the higher quality. The average unit selling prices, unit variable costs, and direct fixed costs are as follows:

	Unit Price	Unit Variable Cost	Direct Fixed Cost
Grade I	$3,400	$2,686	$95,000
Grade II	1,600	1,328	95,000

Common fixed costs (fixed costs not traceable to either cabinet) are $35,000. Currently, for every three Grade I cabinets sold, seven Grade II cabinets are sold.

Required:

1. Calculate the number of Grade I and Grade II cabinets that are expected to be sold during the current year.
2. Calculate the number of Grade I and Grade II cabinets that must be sold for the company to break even.
3. Artistic Woodcrafting can buy computer-controlled machines that will make doors, drawers, and frames. If the machines are purchased, the variable costs for each type of cabinet will decrease by 9 percent, but common fixed costs will increase by $44,000. Compute the effect on operating income, and also calculate the new break-even point. Assume the machines are purchased at the beginning of the sixth month. Fixed costs for the company are incurred uniformly throughout the year.
4. Refer to the original data. Artistic Woodcrafting is considering adding a retail outlet. This will increase common fixed costs by $70,000 per year. As a result of adding the retail outlet, the additional publicity and emphasis on quality will allow the firm to change the sales mix to 1:1. The retail outlet is also expected to increase sales by 30 percent. Assume that the outlet is opened at the beginning of the sixth month. Calculate the effect on the company's expected profits for the current year, and calculate the new break-even point. Assume that fixed costs are incurred uniformly throughout the year.

Case 4-55 ETHICS AND A COST-VOLUME-PROFIT APPLICATION

OBJECTIVE 1

Danna Lumus, the marketing manager for a division that produces a variety of paper products, is considering the divisional manager's request for a sales forecast for a new line of paper napkins. The divisional manager has been gathering data so that he can choose between two different production processes. The first process would have a variable cost of $10 per case produced and fixed costs of $100,000. The second process would have a variable cost of $6 per case and fixed costs of $200,000. The selling price would be $30 per case. Danna had just completed a marketing analysis that projects annual sales of 30,000 cases.

Danna is reluctant to report the 30,000 forecast to the divisional manager. She knows that the first process would be labour intensive, whereas the second would be largely automated with little labour and no requirement for an additional production supervisor. If the first process is chosen, Hussan Khalil, a good friend, will be appointed as the line supervisor. If the second process is chosen, Jerry and an entire line of labourers will be laid off. After some consideration, Danna revises the projected sales downward to 22,000 cases.

She believes that the revision downward is justified. Since it will lead the divisional manager to choose the manual system, it shows a sensitivity to the needs of current employees—a sensitivity that she is afraid her divisional manager does not possess. He is too focused on quantitative factors in his decision making and usually ignores the qualitative aspects.

Required:

1. Compute the break-even point for each process.
2. Compute the sales volume for which the two processes are equally profitable. Identify the range of sales for which the manual process is more profitable than the automated process. Identify the range of sales for which the automated process is more profitable than the manual process. Why does the divisional manager want the sales forecast?
3. Discuss Danna's decision to alter the sales forecast. Do you agree with it? Is she acting ethically? Is her decision justified since it helps a number of employees retain their employment? Should the impact on employees be factored into decisions? In fact, is it unethical not to consider the impact of decisions on employees?

CMA Problem*

CMA Problem 4-1 COST-VOLUME-PROFIT ANALYSIS—ATTICA CANDY COMPANY

Attica Candy Company is a wholesale distributor of candy. The company services grocery, convenience, and drug stores in a large metropolitan area. Attica has achieved small but steady growth in sales over the past few years, while candy prices have been increasing. The company is formulating its plans for the coming fiscal year. Following is the data used to project the current year's after-tax net income of $110,400.

Average selling price	$ 4.00	per box
Average variable costs:		
Cost of candy	$ 2.00	per box
Selling expenses	0.40	per box
	$ 2.40	per box
Annual fixed costs:		
Selling	$ 160,000	
Administrative	280,000	
	$ 440,000	
Expected annual sales volume (390,000 boxes)	$ 1,560,000	
Tax rate	40%	

Manufacturers of candy have announced they will increase prices of their products an average of 15 percent in the coming year due to increases in raw materials (sugar, cocoa, peanuts, etc.) and labour costs. Attica Candy Company expects all other costs will remain at the same rates or levels as the current year.

Required:

a. How was the $110,400 net income figure calculated?
b. What is Attica Candy Company's break even in boxes of candy for the current year?
c. What selling price per box must Attica Candy Company charge to cover the 15 percent increase in the cost of candy and still maintain the current contribution margin ratio?
d. What volume of sales in dollars must Attica Candy Company achieve in the coming year to maintain the same net income after taxes as projected for the current year if the selling price of candy remains at $4 per box and the cost of candy increases 15 percent?
e. How many units would have to be sold next year to generate a net income equal to 10 percent of revenue?

Integrative Exercise 1

Cost Behaviour and Cost-Volume-Profit Analysis for Many Glacier Hotel

Chapters	Objectives	Cornerstones
2	2-2	3-2
3	3-3	4-2
4	4-1	4-5
	4-2	4-7
	4-4	4-9
	4-5	

The purpose of this integrated exercise is to demonstrate the interrelationship between cost estimation techniques and subsequent uses of cost information. In particular, this exercise illustrates how the variable and fixed cost information estimated from a high-low analysis can be used in a single- and multiple-product CVP analysis.

Using the High-Low Method to Estimate Variable and Fixed Costs

Located on Swiftcurrent Lake in Glacier National Park, Many Glacier Hotel was built in 1915 by the Great Northern Railway. In an effort to supplement its lodging revenue, the hotel decided in 1998 to begin manufacturing and selling small wooden canoes decorated with symbols hand painted by Native people living near the park. Due to the great success of the canoes, the hotel began manufacturing and selling paddles as well in 2001. Many hotel guests purchase a canoe and paddles for use in self-guided tours of Swiftcurrent Lake. Because production of the two products began in different years, the canoes and paddles are produced in separate production facilities and employ different labourers. Each canoe sells for $500, and each paddle sells for $50. A 2001 fire destroyed the hotel's accounting records. However, a new system put into place before the 2002 season provides the following aggregated data for the hotel's canoe and paddle manufacturing and marketing activities:

Manufacturing Data:

Year	Number of Canoes Manufactured	Total Canoe Manufacturing Costs	Year	Number of Paddles Manufactured	Total Paddle Manufacturing Costs
2007	250	106,000	2007	900	38,500
2006	275	115,000	2006	1,200	49,000
2005	240	108,000	2005	1,000	42,000
2004	310	122,000	2004	1,100	45,500
2003	350	130,000	2003	1,400	56,000
2002	400	140,000	2002	1,700	66,500

Marketing Data:

Year	Number of Canoes Sold	Total Canoe Marketing Costs	Year	Number of Paddles Sold	Total Paddle Marketing Costs
2007	250	45,000	2007	900	7,500
2006	275	47,500	2006	1,200	9,000
2005	240	44,000	2005	1,000	8,000
2004	310	51,000	2004	1,100	8,500
2003	350	55,000	2003	1,400	10,000
2002	400	60,000	2002	1,700	11,500

Required:

1. High-Low Cost Estimation Method
   a. Use the high-low method to estimate the per-unit variable costs and total fixed costs for the *canoe* product line.
   b. Use the high-low method to estimate the per-unit variable costs and total fixed costs for the *paddle* product line.
2. Cost-Volume-Profit Analysis, Single-Product Setting

   Use CVP analysis to calculate the break-even point in units for:
   a. The *canoe* product line *only* (i.e., single-product setting)
   b. The *paddle* product line *only* (i.e., single-product setting)
3. Cost-Volume-Profit Analysis, Multiple-Product Setting

   The hotel's accounting system data show an average sales mix of approximately 300 canoes and 1,200 paddles each season. Significantly more paddles are sold relative to canoes because some inexperienced canoe guests accidentally break one or more paddles, while other guests purchase additional paddles as presents for friends and relatives. In addition, for this multiple-product CVP analysis, assume the existence of an additional $30,000 of common fixed costs for a customer service hotline used for both canoe and paddle customers. Use CVP analysis to calculate the break-even point in units for both the canoe and paddle product lines combined (i.e., the multiple-product setting).
4. Cost Classification
   a. Classify the manufacturing costs, marketing costs, and customer service hotline costs either as production expenses or period expenses.
   b. For the period expenses, further classify them into either selling expenses or general and administrative expenses.
5. Sensitivity Cost-Volume-Profit Analysis and Production Versus Period Expenses, Multiple-Product Setting

   If both the variable and fixed *production* expenses (refer to your answer to part 1) associated with the *canoe* product line increased by 5% (beyond the estimate from the high-low analysis), how many canoes and paddles would need to be sold in order to earn a target income of $96,000? Assume the same sales mix and additional fixed costs as in part 3.
6. Margin of Safety

   Calculate the hotel's margin of safety (both in units and in sales dollars) for Many Glacier Hotel, assuming it sells 700 canoes and 2,500 paddles next year.

COSTING

Part 2

Costing is the process of assigning costs incurred by a company to the end object. The end object could be the product being produced or a division, department, or activity that the company engages in. While it may seem simple to assign costs, there are many complications that prevent us from simply taking the total cost and determining the total number of units produced or services rendered. The purpose of analyzing costs in detail is to ensure that costs are being allocated properly to the product, service, or component of the company. This is particularly important as companies must operate their businesses in the most efficient manner possible.

Cost is often the first element of the analysis on which companies base their pricing decisions or decisions to continue producing products—or, indeed, to remain in business at all. Some elements of cost are relatively simple and straightforward; with other elements, it is far more difficult to determine how they should be accounted for. In any operation there will be a variety of different types of costs, and each must be understood in order to determine the best way to handle it.

There are no "rules" in managerial accounting that must be followed, as there are in financial accounting. In the following chapters, we focus on developing "tools" and "techniques" to apply in the analytical process. A company must decide for itself which of these approaches will be used and how the information will be interpreted. In the end analysis, we use different costs for different purposes. When analyzing costs, it is important to define as specifically as possible the costs the analysis is referring to. The term "cost" must be qualified before we know how the information can be used.

In all instances, the analysis of "cost" will provide managers with information to help them make the best possible decisions in order to improve the company's operations. The result, it is hoped, will be more profit as a result of fully understanding the information available in the accounting system. If we do not understand our costs, we cannot properly manage our business. In this instance, "information" is indeed "power."

Chapter 5

Job-Order Costing

After studying Chapter 5, you should be able to:

1. Describe the differences between job-order costing and process costing, and identify the types of firms that would use each method.
2. Compute the predetermined overhead rate, and use the rate to assign overhead to units or services produced.
3. Identify and set up the source documents used in job-order costing.
4. Describe the cost flows associated with job-order costing.
5. (Appendix 5A) Prepare the journal entries associated with job-order costing.
6. (Appendix 5B) Allocate support department costs to producing departments.

VEER ROYALTY FREE

Experience Managerial Decisions
with Creating Dinners

Businesses that produce and sell fresh, fully cooked entrées have proliferated in recent years to help families and individuals, especially busy dual-income families, with meal preparation. **Creating Dinners** of Dartmouth, Nova Scotia, is operated by husband-and-wife team Greg and Paula Dunn. Greg is the chef and Paula oversees the operations. Creating Dinners prepares meals that are healthy and convenient for the family. Customers pay to have Creating Dinners do all the shopping and cooking for them. So one can say that Creating Dinners is in the business of creating time for families and individuals. The stress and the time costs of menu planning, shopping, chopping, cooking, and cleaning up are passed on to the business.

Creating Dinners runs a modern preparation facility designed to help customers make nutritious and delicious ready-to-cook meals that can be customized to the family's tastes. Customers view online monthly menus, choose the dates and times that are convenient for them, and place their orders on the Creating Dinners online secured website.

How do Greg and Paula decide what price to charge for each meal? That is the purpose of job-order costing. Overpricing the meals would drive customers away from Creating Dinners to the nearest competition. Underpricing would erode profit margins and risk business failure. In fact, Greg and Paula are already losing money. They have invested some $30,000 of their own money in the business in addition to some government funding and have already exhausted their line of credit.

Something needs to be done. Each meal is priced at $4 so that a family of four can eat for under $20. Do they need more promotion to bring extra customers to the store? Greg has been promoting the business by becoming a celebrity chef with a cooking column in the local paper. His wife, who has a job at a local university, besides being an MBA student and a mother, is thinking of leaving her job to dedicate herself full-time to the business. They are also thinking of starting a franchise operation. But would that be wise before the business turns a profit?

What is the real cost of doing business? What is the cost of material, labour, and overhead going into each meal cooked? A streamlining of meal costs certainly would improve things, but how will the cost of each meal ordered be calculated?

Here's The Real Kicker

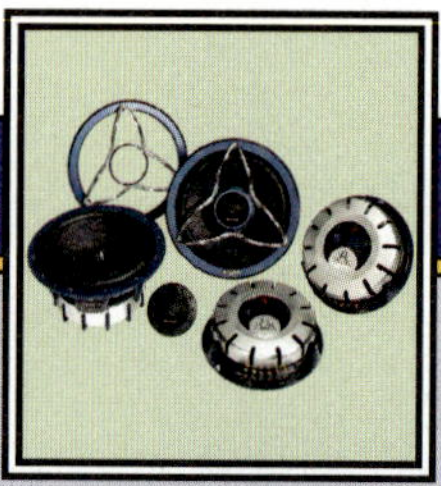

In the 1970s, Kicker began operations in Steve Irby's garage. Steve was an engineering student at Oklahoma State University and also a keyboard player with a local band. The band needed speakers but couldn't afford new ones. Steve and his father built wooden boxes and fitted them with second-hand components. Word spread, and other bands asked for speakers. Steve partnered with a friend to fill the orders. Then, a friend who worked in the oil fields asked if Steve could rig up speakers for his pickup truck. Long days bouncing over rough fields went more smoothly with music, but the built-in audio systems at the time were awful. Steve designed and built a speaker to fit behind the driver's seat, and Kicker was born.

At first, each job was made to order to fit a particular truck or car. The price Steve charged depended heavily on the cost of the job. Since each job was different, the various costs had to be computed individually. Clearly, the costs of wood, fabric, glue, and components were traceable to each job. Steve could also trace labour time. But the other costs of design time, use of power tools, and space were lumped together to create an overhead rate. To the extent that the price of a job was greater than its costs, Steve earned a profit.

KICKER®

OBJECTIVE 1
Describe the differences between job-order costing and process costing, and identify the types of firms that would use each method.

Characteristics of the Job-Order Environment

Companies can be divided into two major types, depending on whether or not their products/services are unique. Firms producing unique products or services require a job-order accounting system. A tailor making bespoke suits, a construction company that remodels homes, a service station that fixes your car, and a lawyer who handles your real estate transaction are examples that fall into this category. On the other hand, those firms producing similar products or services can use a process-costing accounting system. **BP**, one of the world's largest oil producers, falls into this latter category as its barrels of oil are indistinguishable from one another. The characteristics of a company's actual production process give rise to whether it needs a job-order or a process-costing accounting system.

Process Production and Costing

Firms in process industries mass-produce large quantities of similar or homogeneous products. Examples of process manufacturers include food, cement, petroleum, and chemical firms. One litre of paint is the same as another litre; one bottle of aspirin is the same as another bottle. The important point is that the cost of one unit of a product is identical to the cost of another. Service firms can also use a process-costing approach. For example, cheque-clearing departments of banks incur a uniform cost to clear a cheque, no matter the size of the cheque or the name of the payee.

Process firms accumulate production costs by process or by department for a given period of time. The output for the process for that period of time is measured. Unit costs are computed by dividing the process costs for the given period by the output of the period. This approach to cost accumulation is known as a **process-costing system** and is examined in detail in Chapter 6. A comparison of job-order costing and process costing is given in Exhibit 5-1.

Exhibit 5-1

Comparison of Job-Order and Process Costing

Job-Order Costing	Process Costing
1. Wide variety of distinct products	1. Homogeneous products
2. Costs accumulated by job	2. Costs accumulated by process or department
3. Unit cost computed by dividing total job costs by units produced on that job	3. Unit cost computed by dividing process costs of the period by the units produced in the period

Job-Order Production and Costing

Firms operating in job-order industries produce a wide variety of services or products that are quite distinct from one another. Customized or built-to-order products fit into this category, as do services that vary from customer to customer.

A **job**, then, is one distinct unit or set of units. For example, it may be a remodelling job for a specific family, or a set of 12 tables for the children's reading room of the local library. Common job-order processes include printing, construction, furniture making, medical and dental services, automobile repair, and beautician services. Often a job is associated with a particular customer order. The key feature of job-order costing is that the cost of one job differs from that of another and must be kept track of separately.

Where costs are assigned and accumulated by job, the approach is called a **job-order costing system**. In a job-order firm, collecting costs by job provides vital information for management. For example, prices frequently are based on costs in a job-order environment.

The variety of product-costing definitions discussed in Chapter 2 applies to both job-order and process costing. We will use them here to illustrate job-order costing procedures. Production costs consist of direct materials, direct labour, and overhead. Direct materials and direct labour are typically fairly easy to trace to individual jobs. In fact, this tracing will be considered later in this chapter in the section on source documents. It is overhead that presents the problem. By definition, overhead is all production costs other than direct materials and direct labour. Some of these might be easily traced to jobs, but most cannot. The solution is to apply overhead to production. The next section examines in detail the way overhead is treated.

Normal Costing and Overhead Application

OBJECTIVE 2
Compute the predetermined overhead rate, and use the rate to assign overhead to units or services produced.

Unit costs are very important because managers need accurate cost information on materials, labour, and overhead when making decisions. For example, **Bechtel Construction**, whose projects include the Channel Tunnel connecting England and France, typically bills its clients at set points throughout construction. As a result, it is important that the unit cost be generated in a timely fashion. Job-order costing using a normal cost system will give the company the unit cost information it needs.

Actual Costing versus Normal Costing

Two ways are commonly used to measure the costs associated with production: actual costing and normal costing.

Actual costing requires the firm to use the actual cost of all direct materials, direct labour, and overhead used in production to determine unit cost. While intuitively reasonable, this method has drawbacks.

Normal costing requires the firm to assign actual costs of direct materials and direct labour to units produced and to apply overhead to units based on a predetermined estimate. Normal costing is more widely used in practice.

Actual Costing

In an **actual cost system**, only *actual* costs of direct materials, direct labour, and overhead are used to determine unit cost. Strict actual cost systems are rarely used because they cannot provide accurate unit cost information on a timely basis. Per-unit computation of the direct materials and direct labour costs is not the problem. The main problem with using actual costing is overhead. Overhead items do not have the direct relationship that direct materials and direct labour do. For example, how much of a security guard's salary should be assigned to a unit of product or service? Even if the firm averages overhead cost by totalling manufacturing overhead costs for a given period and then divides this total by the number of units produced, distorted costs can occur. The

CONCEPT Q&A

Give an example of a business in your community that would use job-order costing, and tell why it would be appropriate. Give an example of a business in your community that would use process costing and tell why it would be appropriate.

Answers on pages 711 to 715.

Exhibit 5-2

Costing Systems and Inventory Valuation

Cost Accumulation System	Actual	Normal	Standard
Job Order	Actual direct material Actual direct labour Actual overhead	Actual direct material Actual direct labour Overhead applied using predetermined rate (predetermined rate times actual input)	Standard direct material Standard direct labour Overhead applied using predetermined rate (predetermined rate times standard input)

distortion can be traced to uneven incurrence of overhead costs and uneven production from period to period.

The first problem is that many overhead costs are not incurred uniformly throughout the year. For example, actual repair cost occurs whenever a machine breakdown occurs. This timing can make overhead costs in the month of a machine breakdown higher than in other months. The second problem, nonuniform production levels, can mean that low production in one month would give rise to high unit overhead costs, and high production in another month would give rise to low unit overhead costs. Yet the production process and total overhead costs may remain unchanged. Clearly, one solution would be to wait until the end of the year to total the actual overhead costs and divide by the total actual production.

Unfortunately, waiting until the end of the year to compute a unit overhead cost is unacceptable. A company needs unit cost information throughout the year. This information is needed on a timely basis both for interim financial statements and to help managers make decisions such as pricing. Most decisions requiring unit cost information simply cannot wait until the end of the year. Managers must react to day-to-day conditions in the marketplace in order to maintain a sound competitive position.

Normal Costing Normal costing solves the problems associated with actual costing. A **normal cost system** determines unit cost by adding actual direct materials, actual direct labour, and estimated overhead. Overhead can be estimated by approximating the year's actual overhead at the *beginning* of the year and then using a predetermined rate throughout the year to obtain the needed unit cost information. Virtually all firms use normal costing. Exhibit 5-2 shows how actual, normal, and standard costing systems price inventories.

Importance of Unit Costs to Manufacturing Firms

Unit cost is a critical piece of information for a manufacturer. Unit costs are essential for valuing inventory, determining income, and making a number of important decisions.

Disclosing the cost of inventories and determining income are financial reporting requirements that a firm faces at the end of each period. In order to report the cost of its inventories, a firm must know the number of units on hand and the unit cost. The cost of goods sold (COGS), used to determine income, also requires knowledge of the units sold and their unit cost.

It should be pointed out that full cost information is useful as an input for a number of important internal decisions as well as for financial reporting. In the long run, for any product to be viable, its price must cover its full cost. Decisions to introduce a new product, to continue a current product, and to analyze long-run prices are examples of important internal decisions that rely on full unit cost information.

CONCEPT Q&A

The TV reality series *Trading Spaces* involves two pairs of homeowners who, with the guidance of an interior designer and the help of a professional carpenter, redo one room in each other's house. Each pair has 48 hours and $1,000 to accomplish the renovation. At the end of each show, the host and interior designer total up the "costs" of the redecoration project. Typically, the cost comes in at pennies under $1,000. What costs are included in the $1,000? What costs are not? Does each redecoration really cost under $1,000? (*Hint:* Think about direct materials, direct labour, and overhead in your answer.)

Answers on pages 711 to 715.

Importance of Unit Costs to Service Firms

Like manufacturing firms, service and not-for-profit firms require unit cost information. Conceptually, the way companies accumulate and assign costs is the same whether or not the firm is a manufacturer. The service firm must first identify the service "unit" being provided. A hospital would accumulate costs by patient, patient day, and type of procedure (e.g., X-ray, complete blood count test). A governmental agency must also identify the service provided. For example, city government might provide household trash collection and calculate the cost by truck run or number of houses served.

Service firms use cost data in much the same way that manufacturing firms do. They use costs to determine profitability, the feasibility of introducing new services, and so on. However, because service firms do not produce physical products, they do not need to value work-in-process and finished goods inventories. Of course, they may have supplies, and the inventory of supplies is simply valued at historical cost.

Not-for-profit firms must track costs to be sure that they provide their services in a cost-efficient way. Governmental agencies have a fiduciary responsibility to taxpayers to use funds wisely. Fiduciary responsibility requires accurate accounting for costs. Without such responsibility, questionable results can occur.

A cost accounting system measures and assigns costs so that the unit cost of a product or service can be determined. Unit cost is a critical piece of information for both manufacturing and service firms. Bidding is a common requirement in the markets for specialized products and services (e.g., such as bids for special tools, audits, legal services, and medical tests and procedures). For example, it would be virtually impossible for **Ernst & Young** to submit a meaningful bid to one of its large audit clients without knowing the unit costs of the products or services to be produced. Because unit cost information is so vital, its accuracy is essential.

Normal Costing and Estimating Overhead

In normal costing, overhead must be estimated and applied to production. The basics of overhead application can be described in three steps. The first step is to calculate the predetermined overhead rate. The second step is to apply overhead to production throughout the year. The third step is to reconcile the difference between the total actual overhead incurred during the year and the total overhead applied to production.

Step One: Calculating the Predetermined Overhead Rate

The **predetermined overhead rate** is calculated at the beginning of the year by dividing the total estimated annual overhead by the total estimated level of associated activity or cost driver. Estimated overhead is simply the firm's best estimate of the amount of overhead (utilities, indirect labour, depreciation, etc.) to be incurred in the coming year. The estimate is often based on last year's figures and is adjusted for anticipated changes in the coming year.

The associated activity level depends on which activity is best associated with overhead. Often, the activity chosen is the number of direct labour hours or the direct labour cost. This makes sense when much of overhead cost is associated with direct labour (e.g., fringe benefits, worker safety training programs, the cost of running the personnel department). The number of machine hours could be a good choice for a company with automated production. Then, much of the overhead cost might consist of equipment maintenance, depreciation on machinery, electricity to run the machinery, and so on. The estimated activity level is simply the number of direct labour hours, or machine hours, expected for that activity in the coming year.

The predetermined overhead rate is calculated using the following formula:

$$\text{Overhead rate} = \frac{\text{Estimated annual overhead}}{\text{Estimated annual activity level}}$$

CORNERSTONE 5-1

The HOW and WHY of Calculating the Predetermined Overhead Rate and Applying Overhead to Production

Information:

At the beginning of the year, Argus Company estimated the following costs:

Overhead	$360,000
Direct labour cost	720,000

Argus uses normal costing and applies overhead on the basis of direct labour cost. (Direct labour cost is equal to total direct labour hours worked multiplied by the wage rate.) For the month of February, direct labour cost was $56,000.

Required:

1. Calculate the predetermined overhead rate for the year.
2. Calculate the overhead applied to production in February.

Solution:

1. Predetermined overhead rate $= \dfrac{\$360{,}000}{\$720{,}000}$

   $= 0.50$, or 50 percent of direct labour cost
2. Overhead applied to February production $= 0.50 \times \$56{,}000 = \$28{,}000$

WHY:

Because a predetermined overhead rate is needed in advance or at the beginning of a new accounting period. The actual rate is determined at the year end.

Notice that the predetermined overhead rate includes estimated amounts in *both* the numerator and the denominator. This estimation is necessary because the predetermined overhead rate is calculated in advance, usually at the beginning of the year. It is impossible to use actual overhead or actual activity level for the year because at that time, the company does not know what the actual levels will be. Therefore, only estimated or budgeted amounts are used in calculating the predetermined overhead rate.

Step Two: Applying Overhead to Production Once the overhead rate has been computed, the company can begin to apply overhead to production. **Applied overhead** is found by multiplying the predetermined overhead rate by the actual use of the associated activity for the period. Suppose that a company has an overhead rate of $5 per machine hour. In the first week of January, the company used 9,000 hours of machine time. The overhead applied to the week's production is $45,000 ($5 × 9,000). The total cost of product for that first week is the actual direct materials and direct labour, plus the applied overhead. The concept is the same for any time period. So, if the company runs its machines for 50,000 hours in the month of January, applied overhead for January would be $250,000 ($5 × 50,000). Cornerstone 5-1 shows how to calculate the predetermined overhead rate and how to use that rate to apply overhead to production.

Step Three: Reconciling Applied Overhead with Actual Overhead or Allocating Applied Overhead to WIP and Finished Goods Ending Inventories Recall that two types of overhead must be taken into consideration. One is actual overhead, and those costs are tracked throughout the year in the overhead account. The second type is applied overhead. Overhead applied to production is computed throughout the year and is added to actual direct materials and actual direct labour to get total product cost. At the end of the year, however, it is time to reconcile any difference between actual and applied overhead and to correct the cost of goods sold account to reflect actual overhead spending.

Suppose that Proto Company had actual overhead of $400,000 for the year but had applied $390,000 to production. Notice that the amount of overhead applied to production ($390,000) differs from the actual overhead ($400,000). Since the predetermined overhead rate is based on estimated data, applied overhead will rarely equal actual overhead. Since only $390,000 was applied in our example, the firm has *underapplied* overhead by $10,000. If applied overhead had been $410,000, then too much overhead would have been applied to production. The firm would have *overapplied* overhead by $10,000. The difference between actual overhead and applied overhead represents overapplied or underapplied overhead. If actual overhead is greater than applied overhead, then the variance is called **underapplied overhead**. If actual overhead is less than applied overhead, then the variance is called **overapplied overhead**. If overhead has been underapplied, then product cost has been understated; in this case, the cost appears lower than it really is. Conversely, if overhead has been overapplied, then product cost has been overstated; in this case, the cost appears higher than it really is. Exhibit 5-3 illustrates the concepts of over- and underapplied overhead.

These overhead variances occur because it is impossible to perfectly estimate future overhead costs and production activity. The presence of overhead variances is virtually inevitable. A problem arises if the overhead variances are not corrected. At year-end, costs reported on the financial statements must be actual, not estimated, amounts. Thus, something must be done with the overhead variance. Most often, the entire overhead variance is assigned to Cost of Goods Sold. This practice is justified on the basis of materiality, the same principle used to justify expensing the entire cost of a stapler in the period acquired rather than depreciating its cost over the life of the stapler. Since the overhead variance is usually relatively small, the method of disposition is not a critical matter. All production costs should appear in cost of goods sold eventually. Thus, the undervalued overhead is added to Cost of Goods Sold, and the overapplied overhead is subtracted from Cost of Goods Sold. For example, assume that Proto Company has an ending balance in its Cost of Goods Sold account equal to $607,000. The underapplied overhead variance of $10,000 would be added to produce a new adjusted balance of $617,000. (Since applied overhead was $390,000, and actual overhead was $400,000, production costs were *understated* by $10,000. Cost of Goods Sold must be increased to correct the problem.) If the variance had been overapplied, it would have been subtracted from Cost of Goods Sold to produce a new balance of $597,000. Cornerstone 5-2 shows how to reconcile actual overhead with applied overhead for the Argus Company example.

Exhibit 5-3

Actual and Applied Overhead

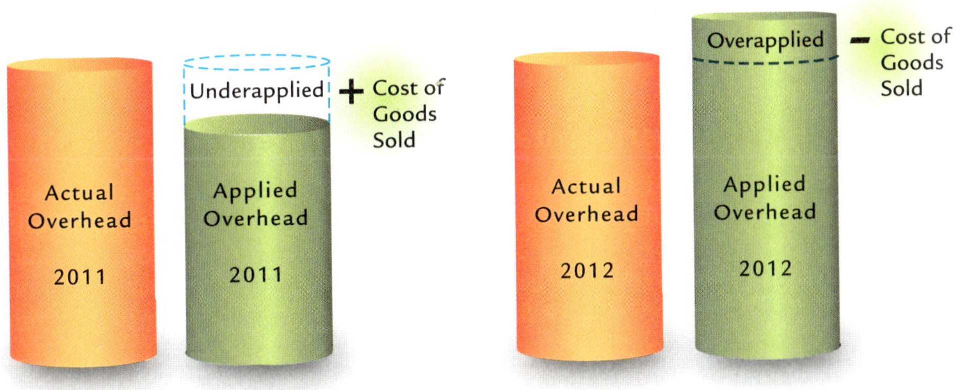

CORNERSTONE 5-2

The HOW and WHY of Reconciling Actual Overhead with Applied Overhead

Information:

At the beginning of the year, Argus Company estimated the following:

Overhead	$360,000
Direct labour cost	720,000

By the end of the year, actual data are:

Overhead	$375,400
Direct labour cost	750,000

Argus uses normal costing and applies overhead on the basis of direct labour cost. At the end of the year, Cost of Goods Sold (before adjusting for any overhead variance) is $632,000.

Required:

1. Calculate the overhead variance for the year.
2. Dispose of the overhead variance by adjusting Cost of Goods Sold.

Solution:

1. Predetermined overhead rate $= \frac{\$360{,}000}{\$720{,}000} = 0.50$ of direct labour cost

   Overhead applied for the year $= 0.50 \times \$750{,}000 = \$375{,}000$

Actual overhead	$375,400
Applied overhead	375,000
Overhead variance—underapplied	$ 400

2.

Unadjusted COGS	$632,000
Add: Overhead variance—underapplied	400
Adjusted COGS	$632,400

WHY:

Because there is a need to determine the WIP and finished goods ending inventories and correct the cost of goods sold to reflect the actual cost (not the overapplied or underapplied overhead).

If the overhead variance is material, or large, another approach would be taken. That approach, allocating the variance among the ending balances of Work in Process, Finished Goods, and Cost of Goods Sold accounts, is discussed in more detail in more advanced managerial accounting courses.

Plantwide and Departmental Overhead Rates

The description of overhead application so far has emphasized the plantwide overhead rate. A **plantwide overhead rate** is a single overhead rate calculated by using all estimated overhead for a factory divided by the estimated activity level across the entire factory. However, some companies believe that multiple overhead rates give more accurate costing information. Service firms, or service departments of manufacturing firms, can also use separate overhead rates to charge out their services.

A **departmental overhead rate** is simply estimated overhead for a department divided by the estimated activity level for that same department. The steps involved in

The HOW and WHY of Calculating Predetermined Departmental Overhead Rates and Appling Overhead to Production

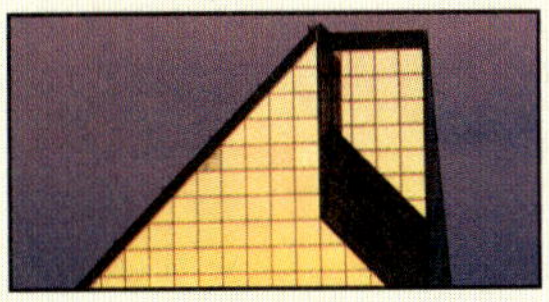

CORNERSTONE 5-3

Information:

At the beginning of the year, Sorrel Company estimated the following:

	Machining Department	Assembly Department	Total
Overhead	$240,000	$360,000	$600,000
Direct labour hours	135,000	240,000	375,000
Machine hours	200,000	—	200,000

Sorrel uses departmental overhead rates. In the machining department, overhead is applied on the basis of machine hours. In the assembly department, overhead is applied on the basis of direct labour hours. Actual data for the month of June are as follows:

	Machining Department	Assembly Department	Total
Overhead	$22,500	$30,750	$53,250
Direct labour hours	11,000	20,000	31,000
Machine hours	17,000	—	17,000

Required:

1. Calculate the predetermined overhead rates for the machining and assembly departments.
2. Calculate the overhead applied to production in each department for the month of June.
3. By how much has each department's overhead been overapplied? Underapplied?

Solution:

1. Machining department overhead rate $= \dfrac{\$240,000}{200,000}$

   $= \$1.20$ per machine hour

   Assembly department overhead rate $= \dfrac{\$360,000}{240,000}$

   $= \$1.50$ per direct labour hour

2. Overhead applied to machining in June $= \$1.20 \times 17,000 = \$20,400$
   Overhead applied to assembly in June $= \$1.50 \times 20,000 = \$30,000$

	Machining Department	Assembly Department
Actual overhead	$22,500	$30,750
Applied overhead	20,400	30,000
Underapplied overhead	$ 2,100	$ 750

WHY:

Because, as in the case of a plantwide predetermined overhead rate, a departmental overhead rate is needed at the beginning of the year to apply overhead. The actual overhead and overhead rate are known only at the year end.

calculating and applying overhead are the same as those involved for one plantwide overhead rate. The company has as many overhead rates as it has departments. Cornerstone 5-3 shows how to calculate and apply departmental overhead rates.

CORNERSTONE 5-4

The HOW and WHY of Calculating Plantwide Overhead Rate and Appling Overhead to Production

Information:

At the beginning of the year, Sorrel Company estimated the following:

	Machining Department	Assembly Department	Total
Overhead	$240,000	$360,000	$600,000
Direct labour hours	135,000	240,000	375,000
Machine hours	200,000	—	200,000

Sorrel has decided to use a plantwide overhead rate based on direct labour hours. Actual data for the month of June are as follows:

	Machining Department	Assembly Department	Total
Overhead	$22,500	$30,750	$53,250
Direct labour hours	11,000	20,000	31,000
Machine hours	17,000	—	17,000

Required:

1. Calculate the predetermined plantwide overhead rate.
2. Calculate the overhead applied to production for the month of June.
3. Calculate the overhead variance for the month of June.

Solution:

1. Predetermined plantwide overhead rate $= \dfrac{\$600,000}{375,000}$

   $= \$1.60$ per direct labour hour

2. Overhead applied in June $= \$1.60 \times 31,000 = \$49,600$
3. Overhead variance = Actual overhead − Applied overhead

   $= \$53,250 - \$49,600$

   $= \$3,650$ underapplied

WHY:

Because at the beginning of the accounting period, we need to have an estimate to calculate how much overhead to add to the actual material and labour costs.

It is important to realize that departmental overhead rates simply carve total overhead into two or more parts. The departments can be added back to get plantwide overhead. Cornerstone 5-4 shows how this is done.

Considerable emphasis has been placed on describing how overhead costs are treated because this is the key to normal costing. Now it is time to see how normal costing is used to develop unit costs in the job-order costing system.

Unit Costs in the Job-Order System

In a job-order environment, predetermined overhead rates are always used because the completion of a job rarely coincides with the completion of a fiscal year. Therefore, in the remainder of this chapter, normal costing is used.

The unit cost of a job is the total cost of the job (materials used on the job, labour worked on the job, and applied overhead) divided by the number of units in the job.

Although the concept is simple, the practical reality of the computation can be somewhat more complex because of the recordkeeping involved. Let's look at a simple example.

Suppose that Stan Johnson forms a new company, Johnson Leathergoods, which specializes in the production of custom leather products. Stan believes that there is a market for one-of-a-kind leather purses, briefcases, and backpacks. In January, its first month of operation, he obtains two orders: the first is for 20 leather backpacks for a local sporting goods store; the second is for 10 distinctively tooled briefcases for the coaches of a local university. Stan agrees to provide these orders at a price of cost plus 50 percent. The first order, the backpacks, will require direct materials (leather, thread, buckles), direct labour (cutting, sewing, assembling), and overhead. Assume that overhead is applied using direct labour hours. Suppose that the materials cost $1,000 and the direct labour costs $1,080 (120 hours at $9 per hour). If the predetermined overhead rate is $2 per direct labour hour, then the overhead applied to this job is $240 (120 hours at $2 per hour). The total cost of the backpacks is $2,320, and the unit cost is $116, computed as follows:

Direct materials	$1,000
Direct labour	1,080
Overhead	240
Total cost	$2,320
÷ Number of units	÷ 20
Unit cost	$ 116

Since cost is so closely linked to price in this case, it is easy to see that Stan will charge the sporting goods store $3,480 (cost of $2,320 plus 50 percent of $2,320), or $174 per backpack.

This is a simplified example of how Stan will arrive at the total cost of a single job. But how does he know that actual materials will cost $1,000 or that actual direct labour for this particular job will come to $1,080? In order to determine those figures, Stan will need to keep track of costs using a variety of source documents. These documents are described in the next section.

The Conversion Process

All organizations convert inputs (material, labour, and overhead) into outputs. In general, product costs are incurred in the production (conversion) area and period costs are incurred in all nonproduction areas. Exhibit 5-4 compares the conversion activities of different types of organizations.

The major distinction of retail firms relative to service and manufacturing firms is that retailers have a much lower degree of conversion than the other two types of firms.

Exhibit 5-4

Degrees of Conversion in Firms

Low Degree of Conversion
The degree of conversion is limited to adding convenience in terms of where and when and in what quantities (packages).

Examples: gas stations, travel agencies, hair salons, department stores.

Moderate Degree of Conversion
The degree of conversion is small, usually just before delivery, such as when installing, packaging, washing, and labelling.

Examples: oil change stores, florists, butcher shops, car washes.

High Degree of Conversion
The degree of conversion is high as the input is transformed greatly.

Examples: construction companies, manufacturing companies, restaurants, mining companies.

Note: Firms engaging in only low or moderate degrees of conversion ordinarily have only one inventory account (merchandise inventory).

For example, when employees of a retail store open shipping containers, hang clothing on racks, and tag merchandise with sales tickets, a labour cost for conversion is incurred. However, retail clothing stores do not attach the stock workers' wages to inventory; such labour costs are treated as period costs and are expensed when incurred. The clerical cost savings from expensing outweigh the value of any slightly improved information that might result from assigning such costs to products or services.

Note that many service companies engage in a high degree of conversion. Firms of professionals (such as accountants, architects, lawyers, engineers, and surveyors) convert labour and other resource inputs (material and overhead) into completed services (audit reports, blueprints, legal papers, and property, mechanical assessment, survey reports).

In high-conversion firms, the informational benefit gained from accumulating the material, labour, and overhead costs incurred to produce output significantly exceed clerical accumulation costs. For instance, when constructing a house, certain types of costs are quite significant. The clerical cost of accumulating direct labour costs is a fraction of the direct labour costs.

In the past, direct material and direct labour cost represented the largest percentage of production costs. In the current automated production environment, direct labour cost has become a very low percentage of product cost; thus, "prime cost" has lost much of its significance.

Firms engaging in a high degree of conversion normally have three inventory accounts: (1) Raw Material Inventory, (2) Work in Process Inventory, and (3) Finished Goods Inventory. Service firms have an inventory account for the supplies used in the conversion process and could have a Work in Process Inventory account, but these firms do not normally have a Finished Goods Inventory account because services typically cannot be warehoused.

OBJECTIVE 3
Identify and set up the source documents used in job-order costing.

Keeping Track of Job Costs with Source Documents

Accounting for job-order production begins by preparing the source documents that are used to keep track of the costs of jobs. In a job-order firm, where price is so often based on cost, it is critically important to keep careful track of the costs of a job. Ethical issues arise when a firm adds costs from one job to the job-order sheet of another job. The first job is undercosted and underpriced while the second job is overcosted and overpriced. Customers rely on the professionalism and honesty of the job-order firm in recordkeeping.

Job-Order Cost Sheet

Every time a new job is started, a job-order cost sheet is prepared. The earlier computation for Stan's backpack job, which lists the total cost of materials, labour, and overhead for a single job, is the simplest example of a job-order cost sheet.

The **job-order cost sheet** is prepared for every job; it is subsidiary to the Work in Process account and is the primary document for accumulating all costs related to a particular job. Exhibit 5-5 illustrates a simple job-order cost sheet.

The job-order cost sheet contains all information pertinent to a job. For a simple job, the job-order cost sheet is quite brief, containing only the job description (backpacks) and cost of materials, labour, and overhead added during the month.

Johnson Leathergoods had only two jobs in January; these could be easily identified by calling them "Backpacks" and "Briefcases." Some companies may find that the customer's name is sufficient to identify a job. For example, a construction company may identify its custom houses as the "Kumar Residence" or the "Malkovich Residence."

As more and more jobs are produced, a company will usually find it most convenient to number them. For example, it may number them as Job 13, Job 22, or Job 44. Perhaps the

CONCEPT Q&A

Job-order cost sheets are subsidiary to the Work in Process account. Can you think of other accounts that have subsidiary accounts? (*Hint:* Consider Accounts Receivable or Accounts Payable. What might their respective subsidiary accounts be?)

Answers on pages 711 to 715.

Exhibit 5-5

Job-Order Cost Sheet

Johnson Leathergoods
Job-Order Cost Sheet

Job Name: Backpacks Date Started: Jan. 3, 20XX Date Completed: Jan. 29, 20XX

Direct materials	$1,000
Direct labour	1,080
Applied overhead	240
Total cost	$2,320
÷ Number of units	÷ 20
Unit cost	$ 116

job number starts with the year so that the first job of 2011 is 2011-1, the second is 2011-2, and so on. The key point is that each job is unique and must have a uniquely identifiable name. This name, or job-order number, heads the job-order cost sheet.

Work in process consists of all incomplete work. In a job-order system, this will be all of the unfinished jobs. The balance in Work in Process at the end of the month will be the total of all the job-order cost sheets for the incomplete jobs.

A job-order costing system must have the ability to identify the quantity of direct materials, direct labour, and overhead consumed by each job. In other words, documentation and procedures are needed to associate the manufacturing inputs used by a job with the job itself. This need is satisfied through the use of materials requisitions for direct materials, time tickets for direct labour, and source documents for other activity drivers that might be used in applying overhead.

Materials Requisitions

The cost of direct materials is assigned to a job by the use of a source document known as a **materials requisition form**, which is illustrated in Exhibit 5-6. Notice that the form asks for the type, quantity, and unit price of the direct materials issued and, most important, the number of the job. Using this form, the cost accounting department can enter the cost of direct materials onto the correct job-order cost sheet.

If the accounting system is automated, this posting may entail directly entering the data at a computer terminal, using the materials requisition forms as source documents. A program enters the cost of direct materials into the record for each job. In addition to providing essential information for assigning direct materials costs to jobs,

Exhibit 5-6

Materials Requisition Form

Materials Requisition Number: 012

Date: January 11, 20XX
Department: Assembly
Job: Briefcases

Description	Quantity	Cost/Unit	Total Cost
Buckles	10	$3	$30

Authorized Signature Doug Lawson

the materials requisition form may also include other data items, such as a requisition number, a date, and a signature. These items are useful for maintaining proper control over a firm's inventory of direct materials. The signature, for example, transfers responsibility for the materials from the storage area to the person receiving the materials, usually a production supervisor.

No attempt is made to trace the cost of other materials, such as supplies, lubricants, and the like, to a particular job. You will recall that these indirect materials are assigned to jobs through the predetermined overhead rate.

Time Tickets

Time tickets are used only for direct labourers. Since indirect labour is common to all jobs, these costs belong to overhead and are allocated using one or more predetermined overhead rates.

CONCEPT Q&A

Suppose that Johnson Leathergoods created an automated tooling department and decides to track the number of machine hours used on each job. Design a source document for this purpose.

Answers on pages 711 to 715.

Direct labour must be associated with each particular job. The means by which direct labour costs are assigned to individual jobs is the source document known as a time ticket (Exhibit 5-7). Each day, the employee fills out a time ticket that identifies his or her name, wage rate, and the hours worked on each job. These time tickets are collected and transferred to the cost accounting department, where the information is used to post the cost of direct labour to individual jobs. Again, in an automated system, posting involves entering the data into the computer.

Source Documents for Other Activity

The company may use an overhead application base other than direct labour hours. In that case, other source documents may be required. For example, machine hours may be used to apply overhead. Then, a new document must be developed. A source document that will track the machine hours used by each job can be modelled on job time tickets.

All completed job-order cost sheets of a firm can serve as a subsidiary ledger for the finished goods inventory. Then, the Work in Process account consists of all of the job-order cost sheets for the unfinished jobs. The Finished Goods Inventory account consists of all the job-order cost sheets for jobs that are complete but not yet sold. As finished goods are sold and shipped, the cost records will be pulled (or deleted) from the finished goods inventory file. These records then form the basis for

Exhibit 5-7

Time Ticket

Job Time Ticket #: 008

Employee Name: Bruce Wilson
Date: January 12, 20XX

Start Time	Stop Time	Total Time	Hourly Rate	Amount	Job Number
8:00	10:00	2	$9	$18	Backpacks
10:00	11:00	1	9	9	Briefcases
11:00	12:00	1	9	9	Backpacks
1:00	5:00	4	9	36	Backpacks

Approved by: *Doug Lawson*
(Department Supervisor)

calculating a period's cost of goods sold. We will examine the flow of costs through these accounts next.

Cost Flow

OBJECTIVE 4
Describe the cost flows associated with job-order costing.

Cost flow describes the way costs are accounted for from the point at which they are incurred to the point at which they are recognized as an expense on the income statement. The principal interest in a job-order costing system is the flow of manufacturing costs. Accordingly, we begin with a description of exactly how the three manufacturing cost elements—direct materials, direct labour, and overhead—flow through Work in Process, into Finished Foods, and, finally, into Cost of Goods Sold. Exhibit 5-8 illustrates the cost flow from purchasing materials to selling the final product. The simplified job-shop environment provided by Johnson Leathergoods will continue to serve as an example. To start the business, Stan leased a small building and bought the necessary production equipment. Recall that he obtained two orders for January: one for 20 backpacks for a local sporting goods store and a second for 10 briefcases for the coaches of a local university. Both orders will be sold for manufacturing costs plus 50 percent. Stan expects to average two orders per month for the first year of operation.

Stan created two job-order cost sheets, one for each order. The first job-order cost sheet is for the backpacks; the second is for the briefcases.

Accounting for Materials

Since the company is just starting business, it has no beginning inventories. To produce the backpacks and briefcases in January and to have a supply of materials on hand at the beginning of February, Stan purchases, on account, $2,500 of raw materials (leather, webbing for backpack straps, heavy-duty thread, buckles). Physically, the materials are put in a materials storeroom. In the accounting records, the Raw Materials and the Accounts Payable accounts are each increased by $2,500. Raw Materials is an inventory

Exhibit 5-8

Cost Flow under Job-Order Costing

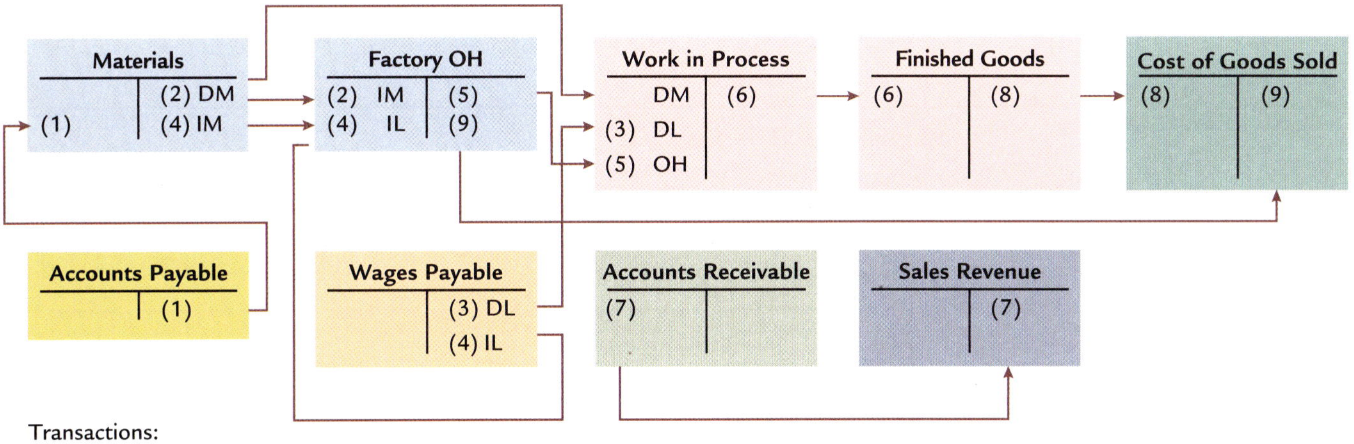

Transactions:
(1) Materials purchased.
(2) Materials requisitioned to jobs.
(3) Direct Labour used in production of jobs.
(4) Factory OH incurred in production of jobs.
(5) Factory OH applied to jobs by the predetermined OH rate.
(6) Job completed.
(7) Units of the completed job that were sold.
(8) Cost of the units sold.
(9) Close underapplied factory OH to cost of goods sold.

account (it appears on the balance sheet under current assets). It also is the controlling account for all raw materials. Any purchase increases the Raw Materials account.

When the production supervisor needs materials for a job, materials are removed from the storeroom. The cost of the materials is removed from the Raw Materials account and added to the Work in Process account. Of course, in a job-order environment, the materials moved from the storeroom to work stations on the factory floor must be "tagged" with the appropriate job name. Suppose that Stan needs $1,000 of materials for the backpacks and $500 for the briefcases. Then, the job-order cost sheet for the backpacks would show $1,000 for direct materials, and the job-order cost sheet for the briefcases would show $500 for direct materials. Exhibit 5-9 summarizes the raw materials cost flow into these two jobs.

The Raw Materials account increased by $2,500 due to purchases and decreased by $1,500 as materials were withdrawn for use in production. So, what is the balance in the Raw Materials account after these two transactions? It is $1,000. This is calculated by taking the beginning balance in the Raw Materials account of $0, adding $2,500 of purchases, and subtracting $1,500 of materials used in production.

Accounting for Direct Labour Cost

Since two jobs were in progress during January, Stan must determine not only the total number of direct labour hours worked but also the time worked on each job. The backpacks required 120 hours at an average wage rate of $9 per hour, for a total direct labour cost of $1,080. For the briefcases, the total was $450, based on 50 hours at an average hourly wage of $9. These amounts are posted to each job's cost sheet. The summary of the labour cost flows is given in Exhibit 5-10. Notice that the direct labour costs assigned to the two jobs exactly equal the total labour costs assigned to Work in Process. Remember that the labour cost flows reflect only direct labour cost. Indirect labour is assigned as part of overhead.

More accounts are involved in this transaction than meet the eye in Exhibit 5-10. Accounting for labour cost is a complex process because the company must keep track of Canada Pension Plan, Employment Insurance, income taxes, vacation time, and so on. We will concentrate on the concept that direct labour adds to the cost of the product or service and not on the details of the various labour-related accounts.

Accounting for Applied Overhead

The use of normal costing means that actual overhead costs are not assigned directly to jobs. Overhead is applied to each job by using a predetermined rate. Actual

Exhibit 5-9

Summary of Materials Cost Flows

Microsoft Excel - Summary of Materials Cost Flows.xls

	A	B	C	D	E	F	G	H
1	Raw Materials Account							
2	Beginning balance		$ 0					
3	Add: Purchases		2,500					
4	Less: Direct materials charged to jobs		1,500					
5	Ending balance		$1,000					
6								
7			Work-in-Process Account					
8	Job: Backpacks				Job: Briefcases			
9	Direct materials		$1,000		Direct materials		$500	
10	Direct labour				Direct labour			
11	Applied overhead				Applied overhead			
12	Total cost				Total cost			
13	Number of units		÷ 20		Number of units		÷ 10	
14	Unit cost				Unit cost			
15								

Sheet1 / Sheet2 / Sheet3

Exhibit 5-10

Summary of Direct Labour Cost Flows

Microsoft Excel - Summary of Direct Labour Cost Flows.xls

	A	B	C	D	E	F	G
1	Wages Payable Account						
2	Direct labour hours for backpacks		120				
3	Direct labour hours for briefcases		50				
4	Total direct labour hours		170				
5	Wage rate		× $9				
6	Total direct labour		$1,530				
7							
8			Work-in-Process Account				
9	Job: Backpacks				Job: Briefcases		
10	Direct materials		$1,000		Direct materials		$500
11	Direct labour		1,080		Direct labour		450
12	Applied overhead				Applied overhead		
13	Total cost				Total cost		
14	Number of units		÷ 20		Number of units		÷ 10
15	Unit cost				Unit cost		
16							

overhead costs incurred must be accounted for as well, but on an overall (not a job-specific) basis.

Overhead costs can be assigned using a single plantwide overhead rate or departmental rates. Typically, direct labour hours is the measure used to calculate a plantwide overhead rate, and departmental rates are based on drivers such as direct labour hours, machine hours, or direct materials dollars. The use of a plantwide rate has the virtue of being simple and reduces data collection requirements. To illustrate these two features, assume that total estimated overhead cost for Johnson Leathergoods is \$9,600, and the estimated direct labour hours total 4,800 hours. Accordingly, the predetermined overhead rate is:

$$\text{Overhead rate} = \frac{\$9{,}600}{4{,}800} = \$2 \text{ per direct labour hour}$$

For the backpacks, with a total of 120 hours worked, the amount of applied overhead cost posted to the job-order cost sheet is \$240 (\$2 × 120). For the briefcases, the applied overhead cost is \$100 (\$2 × 50). Note also that assigning overhead to jobs only requires a rate and the direct labour hours used by the job. Since direct labour hours are already being collected to assign direct labour costs to jobs, overhead assignment will not demand any additional data collection.

Accounting for Actual Overhead Costs

Overhead has been applied to the jobs, but what about the actual overhead incurred? To illustrate how actual overhead costs are recorded, assume that Johnson Leathergoods incurred the following indirect costs for January:

Lease payment	\$200
Utilities	50
Equipment depreciation	100
Indirect labour	65
Total overhead costs	\$415

It is important to understand that the actual overhead costs never enter the Work in Process account. The usual procedure is to record actual overhead to the Overhead Control account. Then, at the end of a period (typically a year), actual overhead is reconciled with applied overhead, and, if the variance is immaterial, it is closed to Cost of Goods Sold.

Exhibit 5-11

Accounting for Cost of Goods Sold

In a job-order firm, units can be produced for a particular customer, or they can be produced with the expectation of selling the units later. If a job is produced especially for a customer (as with the backpacks) and then shipped to the customer, then the cost of the finished job becomes the cost of goods sold. When the backpacks are finished, Cost of Goods Sold increases by $2,320, while Work in Process decreases by the same amount (the job is no longer incomplete, so its costs cannot stay in Work in Process). Then, the sale is recognized by increasing both Sales Revenue and Accounts Receivable by $3,480 (cost plus 50 percent of cost, or $2,320 + $1,160).

A schedule of cost of goods sold usually is prepared at the end of each reporting period (e.g., monthly and quarterly). Exhibit 5-14 presents such a schedule for Johnson Leathergoods for January. Typically, the overhead variance is not material and, therefore, is closed to the Cost of Goods Sold account.

The cost of goods sold before an adjustment for an overhead variance is called **normal cost of goods sold**.

After the adjustment for the period's overhead variance takes place, the result is called the **adjusted cost of goods sold**. It is this latter figure that appears as an expense on the income statement.

However, closing the overhead variance to the cost of goods sold account is not done until the end of the year. Variances are expected each month because of nonuniform production and nonuniform actual overhead costs. As the year unfolds, these monthly variances should, by and large, offset each other so that the year-end variance is small. Nonetheless, to illustrate how the year-end overhead variance would be treated, we will close out the overhead variance experienced by Johnson Leathergoods in January.

Notice that there are two cost of goods sold figures in Exhibit 5-14. The first is normal cost of goods sold and is equal to actual direct materials, actual direct labour, and applied overhead for the jobs that were sold. The second figure is adjusted cost of goods sold. The adjusted cost of goods sold is equal to normal cost of goods sold plus or minus the overhead variance. In this case, overhead has been underapplied (actual overhead of $415 is $75 higher than the applied overhead of $340), so this amount is added to normal cost of goods sold. If the overhead variance shows overapplied overhead, then that amount will be subtracted from normal cost of goods sold.

Suppose that the backpacks had not been ordered by a customer but had been produced with the expectation that they could be sold through a subsequent marketing effort. Then, all 20 units might not be sold at the same time. Assume that on January 31, there were 15 backpacks sold. In this case, the cost of goods sold figure is the unit cost times the number of units sold ($116 × 15, or $1,740). The unit cost figure is found on the cost sheet in Exhibit 5-12.

Sometimes it is simpler to use a briefer version of the job-order cost sheet in order to calculate ending Work in Process, Finished Goods, and Cost of Good Sold. (This is particularly true when working homework and test questions.) Cornerstone 5-5 shows how to set up such a version to calculate account balances.

Exhibit 5-14

Statement of Cost of Goods Sold

Statement of Cost of Goods Sold	
Beginning finished goods inventory	$ 0
Cost of goods manufactured	2,320
Goods available for sale	$2,320
Less: Ending finished goods inventory	0
Normal cost of goods sold	$2,320
Add: Underapplied overhead	75
Adjusted cost of goods sold	$2,395

The HOW and WHY of Preparing Brief Job-Order Cost Sheets

CORNERSTONE 5-5

Information:

At the beginning of June, Galway Company had two jobs in process, Job 78 and Job 79, with the following accumulated cost information:

	Job 78	Job 79
Direct materials	$1,000	$ 800
Direct labour	600	1,000
Applied overhead	750	1,250
Balance, June 1	$2,350	$3,050

During June, two more jobs (80 and 81) were started. The following direct materials and direct labour costs were added to the four jobs during the month of June:

	Job 78	Job 79	Job 80	Job 81
Direct materials	$500	$1,110	$ 900	$100
Direct labour	400	1,400	2,000	320

At the end of June, Jobs 78, 79, and 80 were completed. Only Job 79 was sold. On June 1, the balance in Finished Goods was zero.

Required:

1. Calculate the overhead rate based on direct labour cost.
2. Prepare a brief job-order cost sheet for the four jobs. Show the balance as of June 1 as well as direct materials and direct labour added in June. Apply overhead to the four jobs for the month of June, and show the ending balances.
3. Calculate the ending balances of Work in Process and Finished Goods as of June 30.
4. Calculate Cost of Goods Sold for June.

Solution:

1. Ordinarily, the predetermined overhead rate is calculated using estimated overhead and, in this case, estimated direct labour cost. Those figures were not given. However, it is possible to work backward from the applied overhead by the beginning of June for Jobs 78 and 79.

   Applied overhead = Predetermined overhead rate × Actual activity level

   For Job 78,

$$\$750 = \text{Predetermined overhead rate} \times \$600$$

$$\text{Predetermined overhead rate} = \frac{\$750}{\$600}$$

$$= 1.25\text{, or 125 percent of direct labour cost}$$

   (The predetermined overhead rate using Job 79 is identical.)

2.

	Job 78	Job 79	Job 80	Job 81
Beginning balance, June 1	$2,350	$ 3,050	$ 0	$ 0
Direct materials	500	1,110	900	100
Direct labour	400	1,400	2,000	320
Applied overhead	500*	1,750*	2,500*	400*
Total, June 30	$3,750	$ 7,310	$ 5,400	$ 820

* $500 = $400 × 1.25; $1,750 = $1,400 × 1.25; $2,500 = $2,000 × 1.25; $400 = $320 × 1.25

CORNERSTONE 5-5 (continued)

3. By the end of June, Jobs 78, 79, and 80 have been transferred out of Work in Process. Therefore, the ending balance in Work in Process consists only of Job 81.

Work in process, June 30	$820

While three jobs (78, 79, and 80) were transferred out of Work in Process and into Finished Goods during June, only two jobs remain (Jobs 78 and 80).

Finished goods, June 1	$ 0
Job 78	3,750
Job 80	5,400
Finished goods, June 30	$9,150

4. One job, Job 79, was sold during June.

Cost of Goods Sold	$7,310

WHY:
Because we need to determine the ending inventories of WIP and Finished Goods as well as Cost of Goods Sold.

Accounting for Nonmanufacturing Costs

Manufacturing costs, however, are not the only costs experienced by a firm. Nonmanufacturing costs are also incurred. Recall that costs associated with selling and general administrative activities are period costs. Selling and administrative costs are never assigned to the product; they are not part of the manufacturing cost flows.

To illustrate how these costs are accounted for, assume Johnson Leathergoods had the following additional transactions in January:

Advertising circulars	$ 75
Sales commission	125
Office salaries	500
Depreciation, office equipment	50

The first two transactions fall in the category of selling expense and the last two into the category of administrative expense. So, the selling expense account would increase by $200 ($75 + $125), and the administrative expense account would increase by $550 ($500 + $50).

Controlling accounts accumulate all of the selling and administrative expenses for a period. At the end of the period, all of these costs flow to the period's income statement. An income statement for Johnson Leathergoods is shown in Exhibit 5-15.

With the preparation of the income statement, the flow of costs through the manufacturing, selling, and administrative expense accounts is complete. A more detailed look at the actual accounting for these cost flows is undertaken in Appendix 5A to this chapter.

Job Order Costing for Service Firms

A job order costing system may be used for service firms as well. Architects, accountants, lawyers, tutors, physicians, and advertising agencies provide services to individual clients, students, or patients. In such cases, the client, student, or patient can be viewed as a job for which costs are accumulated and reported.

Exhibit 5-15

Income Statement

Johnson Leathergoods Income Statement For the Month Ended January 31, 20XX		
Sales		$3,480
Less: Cost of goods sold		2,395
Gross margin		$1,085
Less selling and administrative expenses:		
Selling expenses	$200	
Administrative expenses	550	750
Net operating income		$ 335

The primary product costs for a service business are direct labour and overhead. Any materials or supplies used in rendering services are normally insignificant. For that reason, materials and supply costs are included in the overhead cost. As in a manufacturing business, direct labour and overhead costs of rendering services to a client are accumulated in a Work in Process account. Each job/client has its own job cost sheet and Work in Process account.

When a job is completed and the client is billed, the costs are transferred to a Cost of Services account. Such an account is similar to the Cost of Goods Sold account for a merchandising or manufacturing business.

A Finished Goods account is not necessary. This is because the revenues for the services are recorded only after the services are provided.

In practice, other considerations unique to service businesses may need to be considered. For example, a service business may bill clients on a weekly or monthly basis rather than when a job is completed. In such cases, a portion of the costs related to each billing will be transferred from the Work in Process account to the Cost of Services account. A service business may also bill clients for services in advance; these would be accounted for as deferred revenue until the services are completed.

The cost flow for a service business using job order costing is shown in Exhibit 5-16 below.

Exhibit 5-16

Cost Flow for a Service Firm

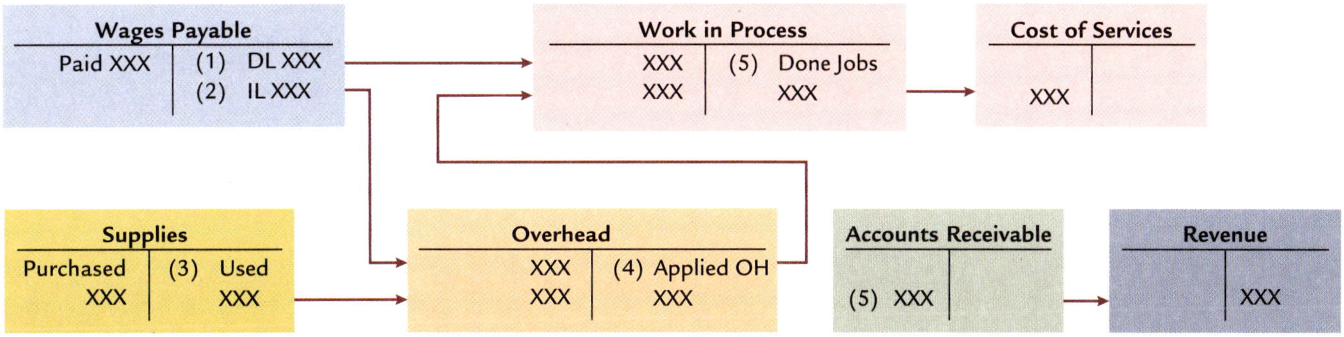

Transactions:
(1) Direct labour used in service jobs.
(2) Indirect labour (OH) incurred in providing service.
(3) Supplies used in providing service.
(4) OH applied to service jobs using the predetermined OH rate.
(5) Service job was completed.

Exhibit 5-17

Typical Cost Flow Journal Entries

(1) *To record cost of raw material purchased on account*

Raw Material Inventory	280,000	Accounts Payable	280,000

(2) *To record raw material transferred to production*

Work in Process Inventory	284,000	Raw Material Inventory	284,000

(3) *To accrue factory wages for direct labour*

Work in Process Inventory	530,000	Salaries and Wages Payable	530,000

(4) *To record supplies used*

Variable Overhead Control	115,200	Supplies Inventory	115,200

(5) *To record payments, and cost of fixed costs*

Fixed Overhead Control	98,880	Sundry Accounts Payable	39,000
		Accumulated Depreciation—Factory Equipment	56,880
		Prepaid Insurance	3,000

(6) *To record the assignment of actual overhead costs to WIP Inventory*

Work in Process Inventory	214,080	Variable Overhead Control	115,200
		Fixed Overhead Control	98,880

(7) *To record the transfer of work completed during the period*

Finished Goods Inventory	1,028,080	Work in Process Inventory	1,028,080

(8) *To record sales price of goods sold on account during the period*

Accounts Receivable	1,460,000	Sales	1,460,000

(9) *To record cost price of goods sold during the period*

Cost of Goods Sold	1,028,080	Finished Goods Inventory	1,028,080

Summary of Learning Objectives

LO1. Describe the differences between job-order costing and process costing, and identify the types of firms that would use each method.

- Job-order firms collect costs by job.
- Job-order firms produce heterogeneous products/services—each unit or batch has a different total cost.
- Job-order firms include construction, custom cabinetry, dentistry, medical services, and automotive repair.
- Process firms produce homogeneous products.

- In process firms, the cost of one batch or unit is the same as another batch or unit.
- Process firms include paint manufacturing, cheque clearing, and toy manufacturing.

LO2. Compute the predetermined overhead rate, and use the rate to assign overhead to units or services produced.

- Predetermined overhead is total budgeted overhead divided by total budgeted activity level.
- Overhead is applied by multiplying the rate by the actual activity usage.
- Applied overhead is added to total actual direct materials and direct labour cost, which is divided by number of units to yield unit cost.

LO3. Identify and set up the source documents used in job-order costing.

- Job-order cost sheets summarize all costs associated with a job.
- Materials requisition forms are used to request direct materials for a job.
- Time tickets show the number of labour hours worked on a job.

LO4. Describe the cost flows associated with job-order costing.

- The job-order cost sheet is subsidiary to the Work in Process account.
- The balance in Work in Process consists of the balances of all incomplete jobs.
- The cost of a finished job is transferred out of Work in Process and into Finished Goods.
- The cost of jobs sold is transferred out of Finished Goods and into Cost of Goods Sold.

Summary of Important Equations

1. $\text{Predetermined overhead rate} = \dfrac{\text{Estimated annual overhead}}{\text{Estimated annual activity level}}$
2. Applied overhead = Predetermined overhead rate × Actual activity usage
3. Overhead variance = Applied overhead − Actual overhead
4. Adjusted COGS = Unadjusted COGS ± Overhead variance

   (*Note*: Applied overhead > Actual overhead *means* Overapplied overhead
   Applied overhead < Actual overhead *means* Underapplied overhead)
5. $\text{Departmental overhead rate} = \dfrac{\text{Estimated departmental overhead}}{\text{Estimated departmental activity level}}$
6. Total product cost = Total direct materials + Total direct labour + Applied overhead
7. $\text{Unit product cost} = \dfrac{\text{Total product cost}}{\text{Number of units}}$

CORNERSTONES FOR CHAPTER 5

CORNERSTONE 5-1 The HOW and WHY of calculating the predetermined overhead rate and applying overhead to production, page 186

CORNERSTONE 5-2 The HOW and WHY of reconciling actual overhead with applied overhead, page 188

CORNERSTONE 5-3 The HOW and WHY of calculating predetermined departmental overhead rates and applying overhead to production, page 189

CORNERSTONE 5-4 The HOW and WHY of calculating plantwide overhead rate and applying overhead to production, page 190

CORNERSTONE 5-5 The HOW and WHY of preparing brief job-order cost sheets, page 201

Key Terms

Actual cost system, 183
Actual costing, 183
Adjusted cost of goods sold, 200
Applied overhead, 186
Cost flow, 195
Departmental overhead rate, 188
Job, 183
Job-order cost sheet, 192
Job-order costing system, 183
Materials requisition form, 193
Normal cost of goods sold, 200
Normal cost system, 184
Normal costing, 183
Overapplied overhead, 187
Plantwide overhead rate, 188
Predetermined overhead rate, 185
Process-costing system, 182
Time tickets, 194
Underapplied overhead, 187

OBJECTIVE 5
Prepare the journal entries associated with job-order costing.

Appendix 5A: Journal Entries Associated with Job-Order Costing

The transactions that flow through the accounts in job-order costing are entered into the accounting system by making journal entries and posting them to the accounts.

Let's summarize the various transactions that occurred during the month of January for Johnson Leathergoods.

1. Purchased raw materials costing $2,500 on account.
2. Requisitioned materials costing $1,500 for use in production.
3. Recognized direct labour costing $1,530 (that is, it was not paid in cash but was shown as a liability in the Wages Payable account).
4. Applied overhead to production at the rate of $2 per direct labour hour. A total of 170 direct labour hours were worked.
5. Incurred actual overhead costs of $415.
6. Completed the backpack job and transferred it to Finished Goods.
7. Sold the backpack job at cost plus 50 percent.
8. Closed underapplied overhead to Cost of Goods Sold.

The journal entries for each of the above transactions are as follows:

1.	Raw Materials	2,500	
	Accounts Payable		2,500
2.	Work in Process	1,500	
	Raw Materials		1,500
3.	Work in Process	1,530	
	Wages Payable		1,530
4.	Work in Process	340	
	Overhead Control		340
5.	Overhead Control	415	
	Lease Payable		200
	Utilities Payable		50
	Accumulated Depreciation		100
	Wages Payable		65
6.	Finished Goods	2,320	
	Work in Process		2,320
7.	Cost of Goods Sold	2,320	
	Finished Goods		2,320
	Accounts Receivable	3,480	
	Sales Revenue		3,480
8.	Cost of Goods Sold	75	
	Overhead Control		75

Journal entry 1 shows that the purchase of materials increases the raw materials account as well as the Accounts Payable account. In other words, the company has increased both assets (materials on hand) and liabilities (through Accounts Payable).

Entry 2 shows the transfer from the materials storeroom to the factory floor. In other words, the materials are no longer awaiting requisition; they are being used. Therefore, the Work in Process account goes up, but the Raw Materials account goes down.

Entry 3 recognizes the contribution of direct labour. The amount of direct labour wages is added to Work in Process and also is added to the liability account, Wages Payable.

Entry 4 recognizes the application of overhead to the jobs. Since 170 hours of direct labour were worked, and the overhead rate is $2 per direct labour hour, then $340 has been applied to overhead. Notice that this overhead application increases the Work in Process account and shows as a credit to Overhead Control.

Entry 5 shows that the actual overhead incurred is debited to Overhead Control. The credit is to the various payable accounts and Accumulated Depreciation.

Exhibit 5-18

Posting of Journal Entries to the Accounts

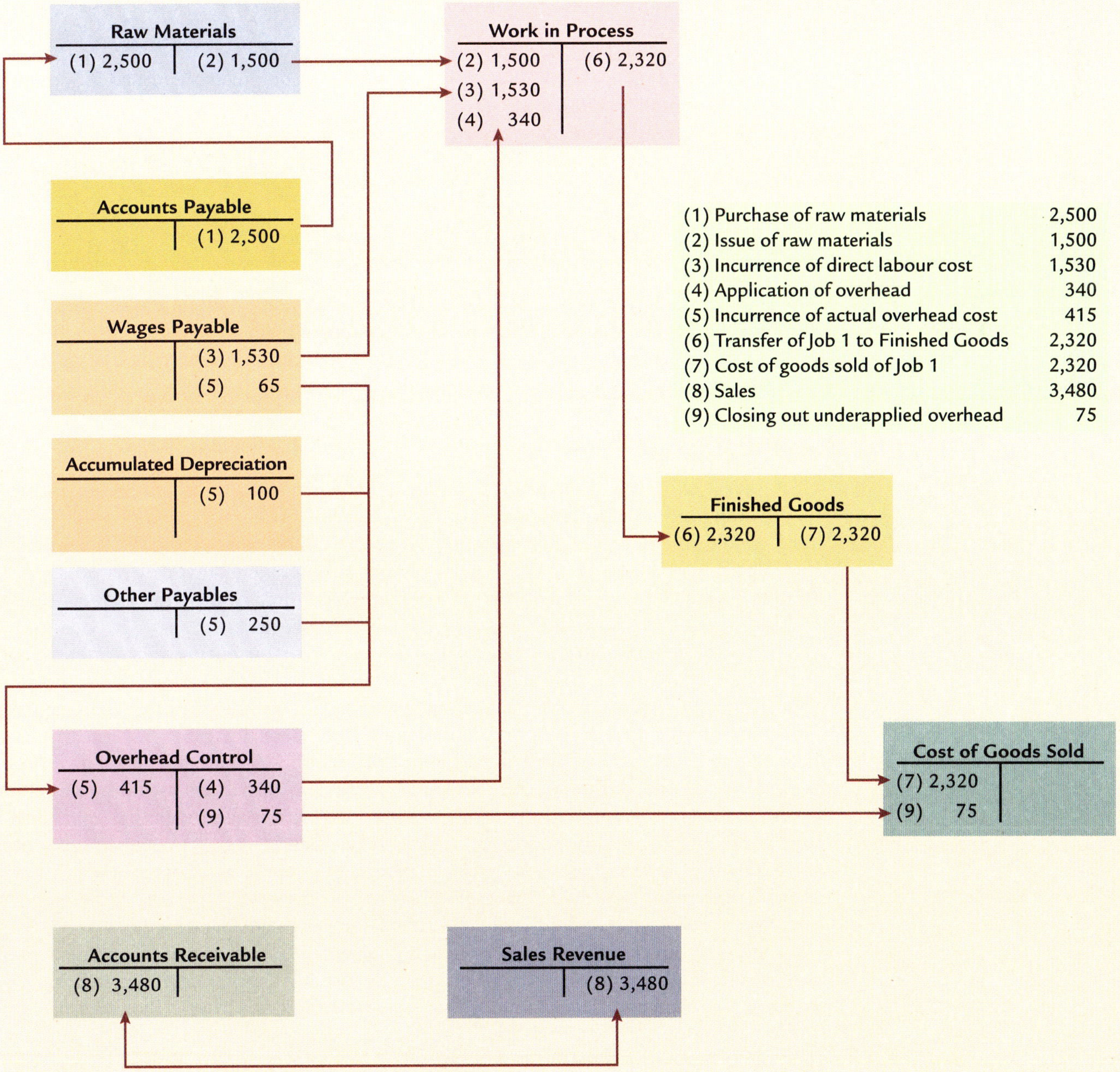

Entry 6 shows the transfer of the backpack job from Work in Process to Finished Goods. We find the appropriate cost by referring to the job-order cost sheet in Exhibit 5-12.

Entry 7 consists of two journal entries. First, we recognize the cost of the backpack job by debiting Cost of Goods Sold for the cost and crediting Finished Goods. This entry mirrors the physical movement of the backpacks out of the warehouse and to the customer. Second, the sales price is shown. It is very important to separate the cost of the job from the sale. This always requires two entries.

Finally, in entry 8, we check the Overhead Control account. It has a debit balance of $75, indicating that the overhead variance is $75 underapplied. To bring the balance to zero, then, Overhead Control must be credited $75, and Cost of Goods Sold must be debited $75.

Exhibit 5-18 summarizes these journal entries and posts them to the appropriate accounts.

Appendix 5A: Summary of Learning Objectives

LO5. Prepare the journal entries associated with job-order costing.

- Direct materials and direct labour are charged to Work in Process.
- Applied overhead costs are charged to Work in Process. Actual overhead costs are charged to Overhead Control.
- When units are completed, their total cost is debited to Finished Goods and credited to Work in Process.
- When units are sold, their total cost is debited to Cost of Goods Sold and credited to Finished Goods.

OBJECTIVE 6
Allocate support department costs to producing departments.

Appendix 5B: Support Department Cost Allocation

The costs of resources shared by two or more services or products are referred to as **common costs**. For example, the cost of a maintenance department is shared by producing departments that use these services. How to assign these shared costs to individual producing departments is the focus of this appendix.

Types of Departments

Nearly every company or factory has producing departments and support departments.

Producing departments are directly responsible for creating the products or services sold to customers. For example, a public accounting firm might have producing departments devoted to auditing, tax, and management advisory services. In a factory, producing departments are those that work directly on the products being manufactured, such as the grinding and assembly departments.

Support departments provide essential services for producing departments, but they do not actually make the product or service being sold. Examples include the maintenance, grounds, engineering, housekeeping, personnel, and photocopying departments.

Once producing and support departments have been identified, overhead costs that belong exclusively to each department are identified—these are direct overhead costs. For example, a factory cafeteria would have direct costs such as food, salaries of cooks and servers, depreciation on dishwashers and stoves, and supplies (e.g., dishwasher detergent, napkins, plastic forks). Direct overhead costs of a producing department would include supplies, supervisory salaries, and depreciation on equipment used in that department. Overhead that cannot easily be assigned to a producing or support department is assigned to a catchall department such as "general factory."

Once the direct overhead costs of each department are determined, the next step is to assign the support department costs to producing departments. These costs are assigned to producing departments by using **causal factors** (drivers) that measure the consumption of the services. Each producing department's share of the support department costs is added to that department's direct overhead cost. This total

Exhibit 5-19

Steps for Determining Product Costs by Using Predetermined Departmental Overhead Rates

1. Departmentalize the firm.
2. Classify each department as a support department or a producing department.
3. Trace all overhead costs in the firm to a support department or producing department.
4. Assign support department costs to the producing departments using drivers that measure the consumption of support department services.
5. Calculate predetermined overhead rates for producing departments.
6. Assign overhead costs to the units of individual products using the predetermined overhead rates.

estimated overhead is then divided by a unit-level driver to obtain a predetermined overhead rate for each producing department. Overhead rates are calculated only for producing departments because products only pass through producing departments. Exhibit 5-19 summarizes the steps involved. Steps 1 through 4 are explained in this appendix; steps 5 and 6 are explained in Cornerstone 5-3 of this chapter.

ETHICS Deliberations about discontinuing a support department need to be kept confidential. Ethical professional practice requires this and more. For example, it may be tempting to use confidential information about the discontinuance of a support department to provide an unfair advantage to a friend or relative who may be the owner of an outside service firm that essentially would be replacing the support department.◆

Clearly, then, there are good reasons for allocating support department costs. The validity of these reasons, however, depends on the accuracy and fairness of the cost assignments made.

Methods of Support Department Cost Allocation

A plantwide overhead rate adds together all of the direct overhead costs of the producing departments and all costs of any support departments to calculate a single plantwide overhead rate and assign overhead to units produced. However, many firms find that a single overhead rate does not adequately assign costs to various products. In that case, departmental overhead rates may be used. Then it is necessary to allocate support department costs to the producing departments in order to calculate departmental overhead rates.

The three methods of assigning costs of multiple support departments to producing departments are the *direct method*, the *sequential method*, and the *reciprocal method*. The direct method ignores interactions and assigns support department costs directly to producing departments. Ignoring these interactions and allocating service costs directly to producing departments may produce unfair and inaccurate cost assignments. For example, the power department, although a support department, may use 30 percent of the services of the maintenance department. By not assigning some maintenance costs to the power department, its costs are understated. As a result, a producing department that is a heavy user of power and an average or below-average user of maintenance may then receive, under the direct method, a cost allocation that is understated. The sequential method considers some of the interaction effects, and the reciprocal method fully considers all interactions. In determining which support department cost allocation method to use, companies must determine the extent of support department interaction and weigh the individual costs and benefits of each method. In the next three sections, the direct, sequential, and reciprocal methods are discussed.

CONCEPT Q&A

What is the major disadvantage of the direct method?

Answers on pages 711 to 715.

Exhibit 5-20

Illustration of the Direct Method

Suppose there are two support departments, Power and Maintenance, and two producing departments, Grinding and Assembly, each with a "bucket" of directly traceable overhead cost.
Objective: Distribute all maintenance and power costs to Grinding and Assembly using the direct method.

Direct method—Allocate maintenance and power costs only to Grinding and Assembly.

After allocation—Zero cost in Maintenance and Power; all overhead cost is in Grinding and Assembly.

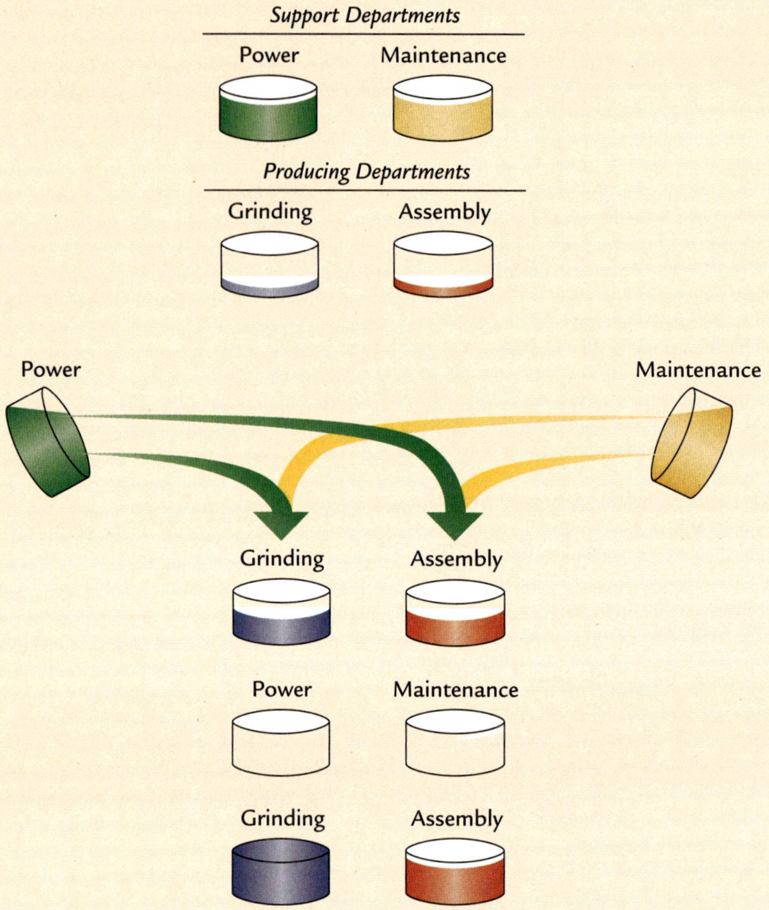

Direct Method The **direct method** ignores support department interactions and assigns support department costs *only* to the producing departments. The direct method is the simplest and most straightforward way to assign support department costs.

Exhibit 5-20 illustrates the way support department costs are allocated to producing deparments using the direct method. We see that by using the direct method, support department cost is assigned to producing departments only. No cost from one support department is given to another support department. Thus, no support department interaction is recognized. Cornerstone 5-6 shows how the direct method is used to assign the costs of two support departments to two producing departments. Notice that the interactions of the service departments are ignored and do not enter the calculations for assigning costs to producing departments.

Sequential Method of Allocation The **sequential (or step) method** of allocation recognizes that interactions among support departments occur. However, the sequential method does not fully account for support department interaction. Cost allocations are performed in a step-down fashion, following a predetermined ranking procedure. Usually, the sequence is defined by ranking the support departments in order of the amount of service rendered, from the greatest to the least, where degree of service is measured by the direct costs of each support department.

Exhibit 5-21 provides a visual portrayal of the sequential method. First, the support departments are ranked, usually in accordance with direct costs; here, the power department is first, then the maintenance department. Next, power costs are allocated

The HOW and WHY of Assigning Support Department Costs by Using the Direct Method

CORNERSTONE 5-6

Information:
Departmental data:

	Support Departments		Producing Departments	
	Power	Maintenance	Grinding	Assembly
Direct overhead costs*	$250,000	$160,000	$100,000	$ 60,000
Expected activity:				
Kilowatt-hours	—	200,000	600,000	200,000
Maintenance hours	1,000	—	4,500	4,500

* Overhead costs that are directly traceable to the department.

Required:
Using the direct method, assign the support department costs to the producing departments.

Solution:
Calculate usage or allocation ratios:

	Grinding	Assembly
Power: 600,000/(600,000 + 200,000)	0.75	—
200,000/(600,000 + 200,000)	—	0.25
Maintenance: 4,500/(4,500 + 4,500)	0.50	—
4,500/(4,500 + 4,500)	—	0.50

	Support Departments		Producing Departments	
	Power	Maintenance	Grinding	Assembly
Direct costs	$ 250,000	$ 160,000	$100,000	$ 60,000
Power[a]	(250,000)	—	187,500	62,500
Maintenance[b]		(160,000)	80,000	80,000
Total	$ 0	$ 0	$367,500	$202,500

[a] Using the allocation ratios for Power: 0.75 × $250,000; 0.25 × $250,000.
[b] Using the allocation ratios for Maintenance: 0.50 × $160,000; 0.50 × $160,000.

WHY:
Because support department costs (cost centres) need to be absorbed by the producing departments (profit centers).

to the maintenance department and the two producing departments. Finally, the costs of the maintenance department are allocated only to producing departments.

The costs of the support department rendering the greatest service are assigned to all support departments below it in the sequence and to all producing departments. The costs of the support department next in sequence are similarly allocated and so on. *In the sequential method, once a support department's costs are allocated, it never receives a subsequent allocation from another support department.* In other words, costs of a support department are never allocated to support departments above it

CONCEPT Q&A

Why is the sequential method considered to be more accurate than the direct method?

Answers on pages 711 to 715.

Exhibit 5-21

Illustration of the Sequential Method

Suppose there are two support departments, Power and Maintenance, and two producing departments, Grinding and Assembly, each with a "bucket" of directly traceable overhead cost.

Objective: Distribute all maintenance and power costs to Grinding and Assembly using the sequential method.

Step 1: Rank service departments—#1 Power, #2 Maintenance.

Step 2: Distribute power costs to Maintenance, Grinding, and Assembly.

Then, distribute maintenance to Grinding and Assembly.

After allocation—Zero cost in Maintenance and Power; all overhead cost is in Grinding and Assembly.

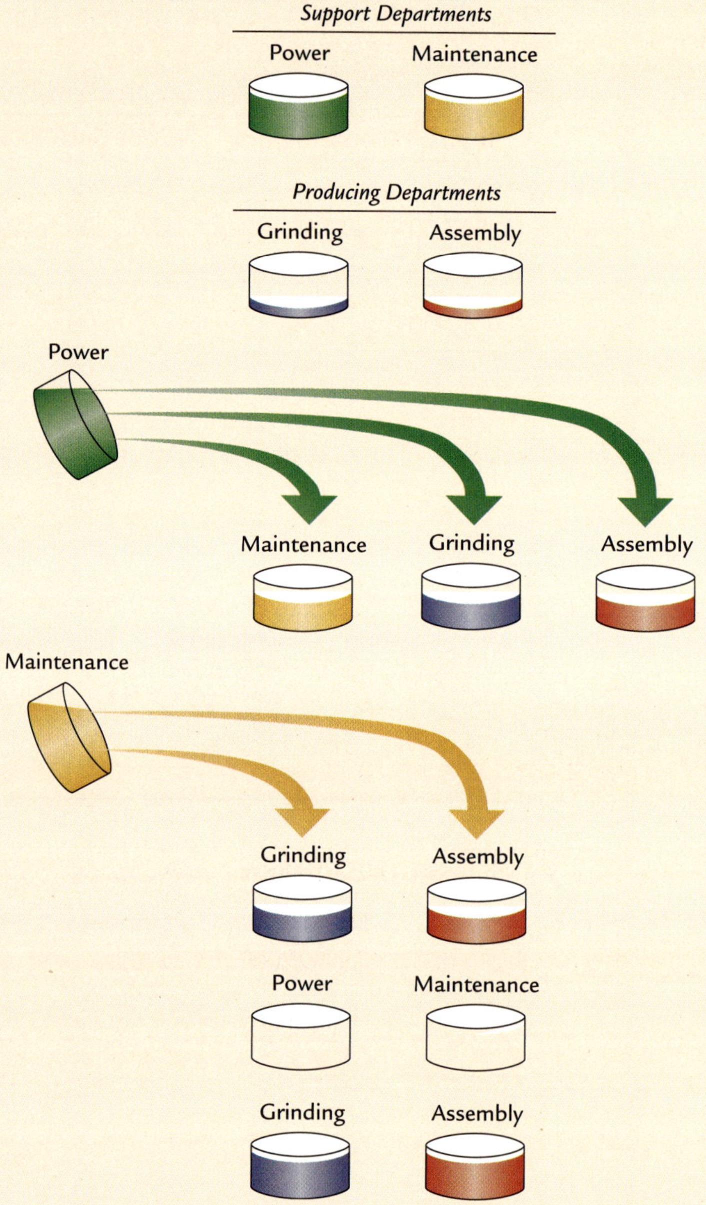

in the sequence. *Also, note that the costs allocated from a support department are its direct costs plus any costs it receives in allocations from other support departments.*

Cornerstone 5-7 shows how to assign support department cost to producing departments by using the sequential method. The power department will be allocated first since its direct cost is higher, followed by the maintenance department. Note that the allocation ratios for the maintenance department ignore the usage by the power department because Power is above Maintenance in the allocation sequence. Unlike the direct method, the sequential method recognizes some interactions among the support departments. The reciprocal method corrects this deficiency.

Reciprocal Method of Allocation The **reciprocal method** of allocation recognizes all interactions among support departments (See Cornerstone 5-8). Under the reciprocal method, one support department's use by another figures in determining the

The HOW and WHY of Assigning Support Department Costs by Using the Sequential Method

CORNERSTONE 5-7

Information:

Departmental data:

	Support Departments		Producing Departments	
	Power	**Maintenance**	**Grinding**	**Assembly**
Direct overhead costs*	$250,000	$160,000	$100,000	$ 60,000
Expected activity:				
Kilowatt-hours	—	200,000	600,000	200,000
Maintenance hours	1,000	—	4,500	4,500

* Overhead costs that are directly traceable to the department.

Required:

Using the sequential method, assign the support department costs to the producing departments.

Solution:

Calculate usage ratios:

	Maintenance	Grinding	Assembly
Power: 200,000/(200,000 + 600,000 + 200,000)	0.20	—	—
600,000/(200,000 + 600,000 + 200,000)	—	0.60	—
200,000/(200,000 + 600,000 + 200,000)	—	—	0.20
Maintenance: 4,500/(4,500 + 4,500)	—	0.50	—
4,500/(4,500 + 4,500)	—	—	0.50

	Support Departments		Producing Departments	
	Power	**Maintenance**	**Grinding**	**Assembly**
Direct costs	$ 250,000	$ 160,000	$100,000	$ 60,000
Power[a]	(250,000)	50,000	150,000	50,000
Maintenance[b]	—	(210,000)	105,000	105,000
	$ 0	$ 0	$355,000	$215,000

[a] Using the usage ratios for Power: 0.20 × $250,000; 0.60 × $250,000; 0.20 × $250,000.
[b] Using the usage ratios for Maintenance: 0.50 × $210,000; 0.50 × $210,000.

WHY:

Because support departments are cost centres and they do not generate revenue, their costs must be allocated to revenue centres such as the production departments. Thus the production departments carry their own costs plus those of the support departments.

total cost of each support department, where the total cost reflects interactions among the support departments. Then, the new total of support department costs is allocated to the producing departments. This method fully accounts for support department interaction by using a system of simultaneous linear equations. The reciprocal method is not widely used due to its complexity.

Another factor in allocating support department cost is the rapid change in technology. Many firms currently find that support department cost allocation is useful for them. However, the move toward activity-based costing and just-in-time manufacturing can virtually eliminate the need for support department cost allocation.

CORNERSTONE 5-8

The HOW and WHY of Assigning Support Department Costs Using the Reciprocal Method

Information:

Corfu Company has two departments: Human Resources (HR) and Custodial Services (CS). It also has two producing departments: Domestic Sales and Exports.

The costs of the HR department are allocated on the basis of the number of employees. The costs of CS are allocated on the basis of square footage. Corfu Company used the reciprocal method to allocate support department costs.

	Support Departments		Producing Departments	
	HR	Custodial	Domestic sales	Export sales
Direct overhead costs	$150,000	$360,000	$125,000	$80,000
Number of employees	–	60	45	80
Square footage	1,500	–	6,000	14,000

Required:

1. Develop a simultaneous equations system of total costs for the support departments. Solve for the total reciprocal costs of each support department (round reciprocated costs to the nearest dollar using four digits in the allocation ratios).
2. Using the reciprocal method, allocate the costs of HR and CS to the producing departments (round to the nearest dollar).
3. What if the allocation ratios were rounded into six rather than four digits? How would that affect any rounding error in the allocation of costs?

Solution:

1. Proportion of employees in Custodial Services = 60/(60 + 45 + 80)
   = 0.3243

   Proportion of Square Footage in Human Resources
   = 1,500/(1,500 + 6,000 + 14,000) = 0.0698

   Let *HR* = Human Resources and CS = Custodial Services

   $HR = \$150{,}000 + 0.0698CS$
   $CS = \$360{,}000 + 0.3243HR$

Solving for Human Resources:

$$\begin{aligned} HR &= \$150{,}000 + 0.0698CS \\ &= \$150{,}000 + 0.0698(\$360{,}000 + 0.3243HR) \\ &= \$150{,}000 + \$25{,}128 + 0.0226HR \\ 0.9774HR &= \$175{,}128 \\ HR &= \$179{,}177 \end{aligned}$$

Solving for Custodial Services:

$$\begin{aligned} CS &= \$360{,}000 + 0.3243HR \\ &= \$360{,}000 + 0.3243(\$179{,}177) \\ &= \$418{,}107 \end{aligned}$$

2. Allocation ratios:

   Proportion of employees in Custodial Services = 60/(60 + 45 + 80) = 0.3243
   Proportion of employees in Domestic sales = 45/(60 + 45 + 80) = 0.2432
   Proportion of employees in Export sales = 80/(60 + 45 + 80) = 0.4324

CORNERSTONE 5-8 *(continued)*

Proportion of sq. ft. in Domestic sales = 6,000/(1,500 + 6,000 + 14,000)
= 0.2791

Proportion of sq. ft. in Export sales = 14,000/(1,500 + 6,000 + 14,000)
= 0.6512

Proportion of sq. ft. in Human Resources = 1,500/(1,500 + 6,000 + 14,000)
= 0.0698

	Proportion of Driver Used by			
	Human Resources	Custodial Services	Domestic Sales	Export Sales
Human Resources	—	0.3243	0.2432	0.4324
Custodial Services	0.0698	—	0.2791	0.6512

	Support Departments		Producing Departments	
	Human	Custodial	Domestic	Exports
Direct costs	$ 150,000	$ 360,000	$125,000	$ 80,000
Allocate:				
Human Resources[1]	(179,177)	58,107	43,576	77,476
Custodial Services[2]	29,184	(418,107)	116,694	272,271
Total after allocation	$ 7*	$ 0	$285,270	$429,747

[1] Custodial Services = 0.3243 × $179,177 = $58,107; Domestic = 0.2432 × $179,177 = $43,576; Exports = 0.4324 × $179,177 = $77,476

[2] Human Resources = 0.0698 × $418,107 = $29,184; Domestic = 0.2791 × $418,107 = $116,694; Exports = 0.6512 × $418,107 = $272,271

* Difference due to rounding.

3. Rounding the allocation ratios to six significant digits would produce a more precise allocation of costs and would reduce rounding error. We can see that there is a $7 rounding error in Human Resources in Requirement 2. This is due to the rounding of the allocation ratios.

WHY:
Using the reciprocal method to allocate support department costs ensures that the amount of support department costs allocated to each of the producing departments most accurately reflects the true costs incurred by each producing department. It is preferable to the sequential method if there is a major difference in allocated costs between the two methods.

Appendix 5B: Summary of Learning Objectives

LO6. Allocate support department costs to producing departments.

- Producing departments actually make the products or services. Support departments provide service to the producing departments.
- When departmental overhead rates are used, the costs of support departments must be allocated to the producing departments.
- Three methods of support department cost allocation are direct method, sequential method, and reciprocal method.

CORNERSTONES FOR APPENDIX 5B

Key Terms for Appendix 5B

Causal factors, 208
Common costs, 208
Direct method, 210
Producing departments, 208
Reciprocal method, 212
Sequential (or step) method, 210
Support departments, 208

Review Problems

I. Job Cost Using Plantwide and Departmental Overhead Rates

Lindberg Company uses a normal job-order costing system. There are two departments, Assembly and Finishing, through which most jobs pass. Selected budgeted and actual data for the past year follow:

	Assembly	Finishing
Budgeted overhead	$330,000	$1,000,000
Actual overhead	110,000	520,000
Expected activity (direct labour hours)	150,000	25,000
Expected machine hours	25,000	125,000

During the year, several jobs were completed. Data pertaining to one such job, Job 330, follow:

Direct materials	$730,000
Direct labour cost:	
Assembly (5,000 hours @ $12 per hr.)	$60,000
Finishing (400 hours @ $12 per hr.)	$4,800
Machine hours used:	
Assembly	100
Finishing	1,200
Units produced	10,000

Lindberg Company uses a plantwide predetermined overhead rate based on direct labour hours (DLH) to assign overhead to jobs.

Required:

1. Compute the predetermined overhead rate.
2. Using the predetermined rate, compute the per-unit manufacturing cost for Job 330. (Round the unit cost to the nearest cent.)
3. Recalculate the unit manufacturing cost for Job 330 using departmental overhead rates. Use direct labour hours for Assembly and machine hours for Finishing.

Solution:

1. Predetermined overhead rate = $1,330,000/175,000 = $7.60 per DLH. Add the budgeted overhead for the two departments, and divide by the total expected direct labour hours (DLH = 150,000 + 25,000).
2.

Direct materials	$730,000
Direct labour ($12 × 5,400)	64,800
Overhead ($7.60 × 5,400 DLH)	41,040
Total manufacturing costs	$835,840
Unit cost ($835,840/10,000)	$ 83.58

3. $$\text{Predetermined rate for Assembly} = \frac{\$330{,}000}{150{,}000} = \$2.20 \text{ per DLH.}$$

$$\text{Predetermined rate for Finishing} = \frac{\$1{,}000{,}000}{125{,}000} = \$8 \text{ per machine hour}$$

Direct materials	$730,000
Direct labour	64,800
Overhead:	
Assembly ($2.20 × 5,000)	11,000
Finishing ($8 × 1,200)	9,600
Total manufacturing costs	$815,400
Unit cost ($815,400/10,000)	$ 81.54

II. Calculation of Work in Process and Cost of Goods Sold with Multiple Jobs

Olympia Kitchen and Bath (OKB) Company designs and installs upscale kitchens and bathrooms. On May 1, there were three jobs in process, Jobs 77, 78, and 79. During May, two more jobs were started, Jobs 80 and 81. By May 31, Jobs 77, 78, and 80 were completed. The following data were gathered:

	Job 77	Job 78	Job 79	Job 80	Job 81
May 1 balance	$875	$1,140	$410	$ 0	$ 0
Direct materials	690	320	500	3,500	2,750
Direct labour	450	420	80	1,800	1,300

Overhead is applied at the rate of 150 percent of direct labour cost. Jobs are sold at cost plus 30 percent. Operating expenses for May totalled $2,700.

Required:

1. Prepare job-order cost sheets for each job as of May 31.
2. Calculate the ending balance in Work in Process (as of May 31) and Cost of Goods Sold for May.
3. Construct an income statement for OKB Company for the month of May.

Solution:

1.

	Job 77	Job 78	Job 79	Job 80	Job 81
May 1 balance	$ 875	$1,140	$ 410	$ 0	$ 0
Direct materials	690	320	500	3,500	2,750
Direct labour	450	420	80	1,800	1,300
Applied overhead	675	630	120	2,700	1,950
Totals	$2,690	$2,510	$1,110	$8,000	$6,000

2. Ending balance in Work in Process = Job 79 + Job 81
= $1,110 + $6,000
= $7,110

Cost of Goods Sold for May = Job 77 + Job 78 + Job 80
= $2,690 + $2,510 + $8,000
= $13,200

3.

OKB Company
Income Statement
For the Month Ended May 31, 20XX

Sales*	$17,160
Cost of goods sold	13,200
Gross margin	$ 3,960
Less: Operating expenses	2,700
Operating income	$ 1,260

* Sales = $13,200 + 0.30($13,200) = $17,160

III. Allocation: Direct and Sequential Methods

Barok Manufacturing produces machine parts on a job-order basis. Most business is obtained through bidding. Most firms competing with Barok bid full cost plus a 20 percent markup. Recently, with the expectation of gaining more sales, Barok reduced its markup from 25 percent to 20 percent. The company operates two service departments and two producing departments. The budgeted costs and the normal activity levels for each department are given below.

	Service Departments		Producing Departments	
	A	B	C	D
Direct overhead costs	$100,000	$200,000	$100,000	$50,000
Number of employees	8	7	30	30
Maintenance hours	2,000	200	6,400	1,600
Machine hours	—	—	10,000	1,000
Labour hours	—	—	1,000	10,000

The direct costs of Department A are allocated on the basis of employees; those of Department B are allocated on the basis of maintenance hours. Departmental overhead rates are used to assign costs to products. Department C uses machine hours, and Department D uses labour hours.

The firm is preparing to bid on a job (Job K) that requires three machine hours per unit produced in Department C and no time in Department D. The expected prime costs per unit are $67.

Required:

1. Allocate the service costs to the producing departments by using the direct method.
2. What will the bid be for Job K if the direct method of allocation is used?
3. Allocate the service costs to the producing departments by using the sequential method.
4. What will the bid be for Job K if the sequential method is used?

Solution:

1.

	Service Departments		Producing Departments	
	A	B	C	D
Direct overhead costs	$ 100,000	$ 200,000	$100,000	$ 50,000
Department A[a]	(100,000)	—	50,000	50,000
Department B[b]	—	(200,000)	160,000	40,000
Total	$ 0	$ 0	$310,000	$140,000

[a] Department A costs are allocated on the basis of the number of employees in the producing departments, Departments C and D. The percentage of Department A cost allocated to Department C = 30/(30 + 30) = 0.50. Cost of Department A allocated to Department C = 0.50 × $100,000 = $50,000. The percentage of Department A cost allocated to Department D = 30/(30 + 30) = 0.50. Cost of Department A allocated to Department D = 0.50 × $100,000 = $50,000.

[b] Department B costs are allocated on the basis of maintenance hours used in the producing departments, Departments C and D. The percentage of Department B cost allocated to Department C = 6,400/(6,400 + 1,600) = 0.80. Cost of Department B allocated to Department C = 0.80 × $200,000 = $160,000. The percentage of Department B cost allocated to Department D = 1,600/(6,400 + 1,600) = 0.20. Cost of Department B allocated to Department D = 0.20 × $200,000 = $40,000.

2. Department C: Overhead rate = $310,000/10,000 = $31 per machine hour. Product cost and bid price:

Prime cost	$ 67
Overhead (3 × $31)	93
Total unit cost	$160

Bid price = $160 × 1.2 = $192

3.

	Service Departments		Producing Departments	
	A	B	C	D
Direct overhead costs	$ 100,000	$ 200,000	$100,000	$ 50,000
Department B[a]	40,000	(200,000)	128,000	32,000
Department A[b]	(140,000)	—	70,000	70,000
Total	$ 0	$ 0	$298,000	$152,000

[a] Department B ranks first because its direct costs are higher than those of Department A. Department B costs are allocated on the basis of maintenance hours used in Department A, and producing Departments C and D. Percent of Department B cost allocated to Department A is 0.20 [2,000/(2,000 + 6,400 + 1,600)]; cost of Department B allocated to Department A = 0.20 × $200,000 = $40,000. The percentage of Department B cost allocated to Department C = 6,400/(2,000 + 6,400 + 1,600) = 0.64. Cost of Department B allocated to Department C = 0.64 × $200,000 = $128,000. The percentage of Department B cost allocated to Department D = 1,600/(2,000 + 6,400 + 1,600) = 0.16. Cost of Department B allocated to Department D = 0.16 × $200,000 = $32,000.

[b] Department A costs are allocated on the basis of number of employees in the producing departments, Departments C and D. The percentage of Department A cost allocated to Department C = 30/(30 + 30) = 0.50. Cost of Department A allocated to Department C = 0.50 × $140,000 = $70,000. The percentage of Department A cost allocated to Department D = 30/(30 + 30) = 0.50. Cost of Department A allocated to Department D = 0.50 × $140,000 = $70,000. (*Note:* Department A cost is no longer $100,000. It is $140,000 due to the $40,000 that was allocated from Department B.)

4. Department C: Overhead rate = $298,000/10,000 = $29.80 per machine hour.
Product cost and bid price:

Prime cost	$ 67.00
Overhead (3 × $29.80)	89.40
Total unit cost	$156.40

Bid price = $156.40 × 1.2 = $187.68

Discussion Questions

1. What are job-order costing and process costing? What types of firms use job-order costing? Process costing?
2. Give some examples of service firms that might use job-order costing, and explain why it is used in those firms.
3. What is normal costing? How does it differ from actual costing?
4. Why are actual overhead rates seldom used in practice?
5. Explain how overhead is assigned to production when a predetermined overhead rate is used.
6. What is underapplied overhead? When Cost of Goods Sold is adjusted for underapplied overhead, will the cost increase or decrease? Why?
7. What is overapplied overhead? When Cost of Goods Sold is adjusted for overapplied overhead, will the cost increase or decrease? Why?
8. Suppose that you and a friend decide to set up a lawn mowing service next summer. Describe the source documents that you would need to account for your activities.
9. Why might a company decide to use departmental overhead rates instead of a plantwide overhead rate?
10. What is the role of materials requisition forms in a job-order costing system? Time tickets? Predetermined overhead rates?
11. Carver Company uses a plantwide overhead rate based on direct labour cost. Suppose that during the year, Carver raises its wage rate for direct labour. How would that affect overhead applied? The total cost of jobs?
12. What is an overhead variance? How is it accounted for typically?
13. Is the cost of a job related to the price charged? Explain.
14. If a company decides to increase advertising expense by $25,000, how will that affect the predetermined overhead rate? Eventual cost of goods sold?
15. How can a departmental overhead system be converted to a plantwide overhead system?
16. (Appendix 5B) Describe the difference between producing and support departments.
17. (Appendix 5B) Assume that a company has decided not to allocate any support department costs to producing departments. Describe the likely behaviour of the

managers of the producing departments. Would this be good or bad? Explain why allocation would correct this type of behaviour.

18. (Appendix 5B) Why is it important to identify and use causal factors to allocate support department costs?
19. (Appendix 5B) Identify some possible causal factors for the following support departments:
    a. Cafeteria
    b. Custodial services
    c. Laundry
    d. Receiving, shipping, and storage
    e. Maintenance
    f. Personnel
    g. Accounting
20. (Appendix 5B) Explain the difference between the direct method and the sequential method.

Multiple-Choice Exercises

5-1 Which of the following statements is true?

a. Job-order costing is used only in manufacturing firms.
b. The job cost sheet is subsidiary to the Work in Process account.
c. Job-order costing is simpler to use than process costing because the recordkeeping requirements are less.
d. Process costing is used only for services.
e. All of the above are true.

5-2 The ending balance of which of the following accounts is calculated by summing the totals of the open (unfinished) job-order cost sheets?

a. Raw Materials
b. Work in Process
c. Finished Goods
d. Cost of Goods Sold
e. Overhead Control

5-3 In a normal costing system, the cost of a job includes

a. actual direct materials, actual direct labour, and actual overhead.
b. estimated direct materials, estimated direct labour, and estimated overhead.
c. actual direct materials, actual direct labour, actual overhead, and actual selling cost.
d. actual direct materials, actual direct labour, and estimated (applied) overhead.
e. none of the above. Job-order costing requires the use of actual, not normal, costing.

5-4 The predetermined overhead rate is

a. calculated at the end of each month.
b. calculated at the end of the year.
c. equal to actual overhead divided by actual activity level for a period.
d. equal to estimated overhead divided by actual activity level for a period.
e. calculated at the beginning of the year.

5-5 The predetermined overhead rate equals

a. actual overhead divided by actual activity level for a period.
b. estimated overhead divided by estimated activity level for a period.
c. actual overhead minus estimated overhead.
d. actual overhead multiplied by actual activity level for a period.
e. one-twelfth of estimated overhead.

5-6 Applied overhead is

a. an important part of normal costing.
b. never used in normal costing.
c. an important part of actual costing.
d. the predetermined overhead rate multiplied by estimated activity level.
e. the predetermined overhead rate multiplied by estimated activity level for the month.

5-7 The overhead variance is overapplied if

a. actual overhead is less than applied overhead.
b. actual overhead is more than applied overhead.
c. applied overhead is less than actual overhead.
d. estimated overhead is less than applied overhead.
e. estimated overhead is more than applied overhead.

5-8 Which of the following is typically a job-order costing firm?

a. paint manufacturer
b. pharmaceutical manufacturer
c. large regional medical centre
d. cement manufacturer
e. cleaning products manufacturer

5-9 Which of the following is typically a process-costing firm?

a. paint manufacturer
b. custom cabinetmaker
c. large regional medical centre
d. law office
e. custom framing shop

5-10 When materials are requisitioned for use in production in a job-order costing firm, the cost of materials is added to the

a. Raw Materials account.
b. Work in Process account.
c. Finished Goods account.
d. Accounts Payable account.
e. Cost of Goods Sold account.

5-11 When a job is completed, the total cost of the job is

a. subtracted from the Raw Materials account.
b. subtracted from the Work in Process account.
c. subtracted from the Finished Goods account.
d. added to the Accounts Payable account.
e. subtracted from the Cost of Goods Sold account.

5-12 The costs of a job are accounted for on the

a. materials requisition sheet.
b. time ticket.
c. requisition for overhead application.
d. job-order cost sheet.
e. sales invoice.

5-13 Wilson Company has a predetermined overhead rate of $5 per direct labour hour. The job-order cost sheet for Job 145 shows 1,000 direct labour hours costing $10,000 and materials requisitions totalling $7,500. Job 145 had 500 units completed and transferred to Finished Goods. What is the cost per unit for Job 145?

a. $35
b. $135
c. $30
d. $45
e. $22,500

5-14 (Appendix 5A) When a job costing $2,000 is finished but not sold, the following journal entry is made:

a.	Cost of Goods Sold	2,000	
	Finished Goods		2,000
b.	Finished Goods	2,000	
	Cost of Goods Sold		2,000
c.	Finished Goods	2,000	
	Work in Process		2,000
d.	Work in Process	2,000	
	Finished Goods		2,000
e.	Cost of Goods Sold	2,000	
	Sales		2,000

5-15 (Appendix 5B) Those departments responsible for creating products or services that are sold to customers are referred to as

a. profit making departments.
b. support departments.
c. cost centres.
d. production departments.
e. none of the above.

5-16 (Appendix 5B) Those departments that provide essential services to producing departments are referred to as

a. revenue generating departments.
b. support departments.
c. profit centres.
d. production departments.
e. none of the above.

5-17 (Appendix 5B) An example of a producing department is

a. a materials storeroom.
b. the maintenance department.
c. engineering design.
d. assembly.
e. all of the above.

5-18 (Appendix 5B) An example of a support department is

a. data processing.
b. personnel.
c. a materials storeroom.
d. payroll.
e. all of the above.

5-19 (Appendix 5B) The method that assigns support department costs only to producing departments in proportion to each department's usage of the service is known as

a. the sequential method.
b. the proportional method.
c. the reciprocal method.
d. the direct method.
e. none of the above.

5-20 (Appendix 5B) The method that assigns support department costs by giving partial recognition to support department interactions is known as

a. the sequential method.
b. the proportional method.
c. the reciprocal method.
d. the direct method.
e. none of the above.

5-21 (Appendix 5B) The method that assigns support department costs by giving full recognition to support department interactions is known as

a. the sequential method.
b. the proportional method.
c. the reciprocal method.
d. the direct method.
e. none of the above.

Cornerstone Exercises

Cornerstone Exercise 5-22 PREDETERMINED OVERHEAD RATE, OVERHEAD APPLICATION

OBJECTIVE 2
CORNERSTONE 5-1

At the beginning of the year, Kreskin Company estimated the following costs:

Overhead	$450,000
Direct labour cost	600,000

Kreskin uses normal costing and applies overhead on the basis of direct labour cost. (Direct labour cost is equal to total direct labour hours worked multiplied by the wage rate.) For the month of December, direct labour cost was $38,900.

Required:

1. Calculate the predetermined overhead rate for the year.
2. Calculate the overhead applied to production in December.

Cornerstone Exercise 5-23 OVERHEAD VARIANCE (OVER- OR UNDERAPPLIED), CLOSING TO COST OF GOODS SOLD

OBJECTIVE 2
CORNERSTONE 5-2

At the end of the year, Kreskin Company provided the following actual information:

Overhead	$456,500
Direct labour cost	607,200

Kreskin uses normal costing and applies overhead at the rate of 75 percent of direct labour cost. At the end of the year, Cost of Goods Sold (before adjusting for any overhead variance) was $890,000.

Required:

1. Calculate the overhead variance for the year.
2. Dispose of the overhead variance by adjusting Cost of Goods Sold.

Cornerstone Exercise 5-24 PREDETERMINED DEPARTMENTAL OVERHEAD RATES, APPLYING OVERHEAD TO PRODUCTION

OBJECTIVE 2
CORNERSTONE 5-3

At the beginning of the year, Badger Company estimated the following:

	Cutting Department	Sewing Department	Total
Overhead	$378,000	$450,000	$828,000
Direct labour hours	131,200	200,000	331,200
Machine hours	210,000	—	210,000

Badger uses departmental overhead rates. In the cutting department, overhead is applied on the basis of machine hours. In the sewing department, overhead is applied on the basis of direct labour hours. Actual data for the month of June are as follows:

	Cutting Department	Sewing Department	Total
Overhead	$32,612	$35,750	$68,362
Direct labour hours	11,800	16,000	27,800
Machine hours	17,840	—	17,840

Required:

1. Calculate the predetermined overhead rates for the cutting and sewing departments.
2. Calculate the overhead applied to production in each department for the month of June.
3. By how much has each department's overhead been overapplied? Underapplied?

OBJECTIVE 2
CORNERSTONE 5-4

Cornerstone Exercise 5-25 CONVERT DEPARTMENTAL DATA TO PLANTWIDE DATA, PLANTWIDE OVERHEAD RATE, APPLY OVERHEAD TO PRODUCTION

At the beginning of the year, Badger Company estimated the following:

	Cutting Department	Sewing Department	Total
Overhead	$378,000	$450,000	$828,000
Direct labour hours	131,200	200,000	331,200
Machine hours	210,000	—	210,000

Badger has decided to use a plantwide overhead rate based on direct labour hours. Actual data for the month of June are as follows:

	Cutting Department	Sewing Department	Total
Overhead	$32,612	$35,750	$68,362
Direct labour hours	11,800	16,000	27,800
Machine hours	17,840	—	17,840

Required:

1. Calculate the predetermined plantwide overhead rate.
2. Calculate the overhead applied to production for the month of June.
3. Calculate the overhead variance for the month of June.

OBJECTIVE 3
CORNERSTONE 5-5

Cornerstone Exercise 5-26 PREPARE JOB-ORDER COST SHEETS, PREDETERMINED OVERHEAD RATE, ENDING BALANCE OF WIP, FINISHED GOODS, AND COGS

At the beginning of June, Donewell Company had two jobs in process, Job 44 and Job 45, with the following accumulated cost information:

	Job 44	Job 45
Direct materials	$4,600	$1,175
Direct labour	1,200	1,000
Applied overhead	750	625
Balance, June 1	$6,550	$2,800

During June, two more jobs (46 and 47) were started. The following direct materials and direct labour costs were added to the four jobs during the month of June:

	Job 44	Job 45	Job 46	Job 47
Direct materials	$1,500	$6,100	$ 800	$700
Direct labour	1,000	2,400	2,000	600

At the end of June, Jobs 44, 45, and 47 were completed. Only Job 45 was sold. On June 1, the balance in Finished Goods was zero.

Required:

1. Calculate the overhead rate based on direct labour cost.
2. Prepare a brief job-order cost sheet for the four jobs. Show the balance as of June 1 as well as direct materials and direct labour added in June. Apply overhead to the four jobs for the month of June, and show the ending balances.
3. Calculate the ending balances of Work in Process and Finished Goods as of June 30.
4. Calculate the Cost of Goods Sold for June.

Exercises

Exercise 5-27 JOB-ORDER COSTING VERSUS PROCESS COSTING

OBJECTIVE 1

a. Paint manufacturing
b. Auto manufacturing
c. Toy manufacturing
d. Custom cabinet making
e. Airplane manufacturing (e.g., 767s)
f. Personal computer assembly
g. Furniture making
h. Custom furniture making
i. Dental services
j. Hospital services
k. Paper manufacturing
l. Auto repair
m. Architectural services
n. Landscape design services
o. Light bulb manufacturing

Required:

Identify each of these preceding types of businesses as either job-order or process costing.

Exercise 5-28 JOB-ORDER COSTING VERSUS PROCESS COSTING

OBJECTIVE 1

a. Auto manufacturing
b. Dental services
c. Auto repair
d. Costume making

Required:

For each of the given types of industries, give an example of a firm that would use job-order costing. Then, give an example of a firm that would use process costing.

Exercise 5-29 CALCULATING THE PREDETERMINED OVERHEAD RATE, APPLYING OVERHEAD TO PRODUCTION

OBJECTIVE 2

At the beginning of the year, Natrina Company estimated the following:

Overhead	$570,000
Direct labour hours	95,000

Natrina uses normal costing and applies overhead on the basis of direct labour hours. For the month of March, direct labour hours were 7,400.

Required:

1. Calculate the predetermined overhead rate for Natrina.
2. Calculate the overhead applied to production in March.

OBJECTIVE ➤ 2

Exercise 5-30 CALCULATING THE PREDETERMINED OVERHEAD RATE, APPLYING OVERHEAD TO PRODUCTION, RECONCILING OVERHEAD AT THE END OF THE YEAR, ADJUSTING COST OF GOODS SOLD FOR UNDER- AND OVERAPPLIED OVERHEAD

At the beginning of the year, Olivar Company estimated the following:

Overhead	$216,000
Direct labour hours	80,000

Olivar uses normal costing and applies overhead on the basis of direct labour hours. For the month of January, direct labour hours were 7,950. By the end of the year, Olivar showed the following actual amounts:

Overhead	$226,000
Direct labour hours	82,600

Assume that unadjusted Cost of Goods Sold for Olivar was $235,670.

Required:

1. Calculate the predetermined overhead rate for Olivar.
2. Calculate the overhead applied to production in January.
3. Calculate the total applied overhead for the year. Was overhead over- or underapplied? By how much?
4. Calculate adjusted Cost of Goods Sold after adjusting for the overhead variance.

OBJECTIVE ➤ 2

Exercise 5-31 CALCULATING DEPARTMENTAL OVERHEAD RATES AND APPLYING OVERHEAD TO PRODUCTION

At the beginning of the year, Videosym Company estimated the following:

	Assembly Department	Testing Department	Total
Overhead	$620,000	$180,000	$800,000
Direct labour hours	155,000	20,000	175,000
Machine hours	80,000	120,000	200,000

Videosym uses departmental overhead rates. In the assembly department, overhead is applied on the basis of direct labour hours. In the testing department, overhead is applied on the basis of machine hours. Actual data for the month of March are as follows:

	Assembly Department	Testing Department	Total
Overhead	$53,000	$15,500	$68,500
Direct labour hours	13,000	1,680	14,680
Machine hours	6,800	13,050	19,850

Required:

1. Calculate the predetermined overhead rates for the assembly and testing departments.
2. Calculate the overhead applied to production in each department for the month of March.
3. By how much has each department's overhead been overapplied? Underapplied?

OBJECTIVE ➤ 3

Exercise 5-32 JOB-ORDER COST SHEET

On June 1, Job 24 had a beginning balance of $330. During June, direct materials of $475 and direct labour of $280 were added to the job. Overhead is applied to production at the rate of 75 percent of direct labour cost.

Required:

1. Set up a simple job-order cost sheet for Job 24. What is the total cost of Job 24?
2. If Job 24 consisted of five units, what is the unit cost?

Exercise 5-33 SOURCE DOCUMENTS

OBJECTIVE 3

For each of the following independent situations, give the source document that would be referred to for the necessary information.

Required:

1. Direct materials costing $460 are requisitioned for use on a job.
2. Greiner's Garage uses a job-order costing system. Overhead is applied to jobs based on direct labour hours. Which source document gives the number of direct labour hours worked on Job 2011-276?
3. Pasilla Investigative Services bills clients on a monthly basis for costs to date. Job 3-48 involved an investigator following the client's business partner for a week by automobile. Mileage is billed at number of miles times $0.75.
4. The foreman on the Jackson job wonders what the actual direct materials cost was for that job.

Exercise 5-34 APPLYING OVERHEAD TO JOBS, COSTING JOBS

OBJECTIVE 4

Herron Company designs and builds retaining walls for individual customers. On August 1, there were two jobs in process: Job 730 with a beginning balance of $10,400, and Job 731 with a beginning balance of $8,600. Herron applies overhead at the rate of $11 per direct labour hour. Direct labour wages average $10 per hour.

Data on August costs for all jobs are as follows:

	Job 730	Job 731	Job 732	Job 733
Direct materials	$1,200	$8,000	$2,100	$3,000
Direct labour cost	1,800	4,000	200	800

During August, Jobs 732 and 733 were started. Job 730 was completed on August 17, and the client was billed at cost plus 40 percent. All other jobs remained in process.

Required:

1. Calculate the number of direct labour hours that were worked on each job in August.
2. Calculate the overhead applied to each job during the month of August.
3. Prepare job-order cost sheets for each job as of the end of August.
4. Calculate the balance in Work in Process on August 31.
5. What is the price of Job 730?

Exercise 5-35 APPLYING OVERHEAD TO JOBS, COSTING JOBS

OBJECTIVE 4

Perrine Company builds internal conveyor equipment to client specifications. On October 1, Job 877 was in process with a cost of $20,520 to date.

During October, Jobs 878, 879, and 880 were started. Data on costs added during October for all jobs are as follows:

	Job 877	Job 878	Job 879	Job 880
Direct materials	$13,960	$ 7,000	$ 350	$4,800
Direct labour	13,800	10,000	1,500	4,000

Overhead is applied to production at the rate of 85 percent of direct labour cost. Job 878 was completed on October 28, and the client was billed at cost plus 50 percent. All other jobs remained in process.

Required:

1. Prepare a brief job-order cost sheet showing the October 1 balances of all four jobs, plus the direct materials and direct labour costs during October. (There is no need to calculate applied overhead at this point or to total the costs.)
2. Calculate the overhead applied during October.
3. Calculate the balance in Work in Process on October 31.
4. What is the price of Job 878?

OBJECTIVE 4

Exercise 5-36 BALANCE OF WORK IN PROCESS AND FINISHED GOODS, COST OF GOODS SOLD

Velos Company uses job-order costing. At the end of the month, the following information was gathered:

Job #	Total Cost	Complete?	Sold?
301	$ 610	Yes	No
302	1,300	Yes	Yes
303	460	No	No
304	2,670	Yes	No
305	3,800	Yes	No
306	230	No	No
307	300	Yes	Yes
308	650	No	No
309	1,035	No	No
310	217	No	No

The beginning balance of Finished Goods was zero.

Required:

1. Calculate the balance in Work in Process at the end of the month.
2. Calculate the balance in Finished Goods at the end of the month.
3. Calculate Cost of Goods Sold for the month.

OBJECTIVE 4

Exercise 5-37 JOB-ORDER COST SHEETS, BALANCE IN WORK IN PROCESS AND FINISHED GOODS

Berne Company, a job-order costing firm, worked on three jobs in July. Data are as follows:

	Job 73	Job 74	Job 75
Balance, July 1	$8,450	$0	$0
Direct materials	$7,450	$12,300	$16,150
Direct labour	$12,000	$10,500	$23,000
Machine hours	400	350	1,000

Overhead is applied to jobs at the rate of $20 per machine hour. By July 31, Jobs 73 and 75 were completed. Jobs 70 and 73 were sold. Job 74 remained in process. On July 1, the balance in Finished Goods was $49,000 (consisting of Job 70 for $19,000 and Job 72 for $30,000).

Berne prices its jobs at cost plus 30 percent. During July, variable marketing expenses were 10 percent of sales, and fixed marketing expenses were $2,000; administrative expenses were $4,800.

Required:

1. Prepare job-order cost sheets for all jobs in process during July, showing all costs through July 31.
2. Calculate the balance in Work in Process on July 31.
3. Calculate the balance in Finished Goods on July 31.
4. Calculate Cost of Goods Sold for July.
5. Prepare an income statement for Berne Company for the month of July.

OBJECTIVE 4

Exercise 5-38 COST FLOWS

Consider the following independent jobs. Overhead is applied in Department 1 at the rate of $6 per direct labour hour. Overhead is applied in Department 2 at the rate of $8 per machine hour. Direct labour wages average $10 per hour in each department.

	Job 213	Job 214	Job 217	Job 225
Total sales revenue	$?	$4,375	$5,600	$1,150
Price per unit	$12	$?	$14	$5
Materials used in production	$365	$?	$488	$207
Department 1, direct labour cost	$?	$700	$2,000	$230
Department 1, machine hours	15	35	50	12
Department 2, direct labour cost	$50	$100	$?	$0
Department 2, machine hours	25	50	?	?
Department 1, overhead applied	$90	$?	$1,200	$138
Department 2, overhead applied	$?	$400	$160	$0
Total manufacturing cost	$855	$3,073	$?	$575
Number of units	?	350	400	?
Unit cost	$8.55	$?	$9.87	$?

Required:

Fill in the missing data for each job.

Exercise 5-39 JOB COST FLOWS

OBJECTIVE 4

Ionia Company uses a normal job-order costing system. The company has two departments through which most jobs pass. Overhead is applied using a plantwide overhead rate of $12 per direct labour hour. During the year, several jobs were completed. Data pertaining to one such job, Job 9-601, follow:

Direct materials	$18,000
Direct labour cost:	
Department A (6,000 hours @ $6)	$36,000
Department B (1,000 hours @ $6)	$6,000
Machine hours used:	
Department A	100
Department B	1,200
Units produced	10,000

Required:

1. Compute the total cost of Job 9-601.
2. Compute the per-unit manufacturing cost for Job 9-601.

For Requirements 3 and 4, assume that Ionia uses departmental overhead rates. In Department A, overhead is applied at the rate of $3 per direct labour hour. In Department B, overhead is applied at the rate of $7 per machine hour.

3. Compute the total cost of Job 9-601.
4. Compute the per-unit manufacturing cost for Job 9-601.

Exercise 5-40 CALCULATION OF WORK IN PROCESS AND COST OF GOODS SOLD WITH MULTIPLE JOBS

OBJECTIVE 4

Greenthumb Landscape Design designs landscape plans and plants the material for clients. On April 1, there were three jobs in process, Jobs 68, 69, and 70. During April, two more jobs were started, Jobs 71 and 72. By April 30, Jobs 69, 70, and 72 were completed and sold. The following data were gathered:

	Job 68	Job 69	Job 70	Job 71	Job 72
Balance, April 1	$540	$1,230	$990	—	—
Direct materials	700	560	75	$3,500	$2,750
Direct labour	500	600	90	2,500	2,000

Overhead is applied at the rate of 120 percent of direct labour cost. Jobs are sold at cost plus 40 percent. Selling and administrative expenses for April totalled $3,670.

Required:

1. Prepare job-order cost sheets for each job as of April 30.
2. Calculate the ending balance in Work in Process (as of April 30) and Cost of Goods Sold for April.
3. Construct an income statement for Greenthumb Landscape Design for the month of April.

OBJECTIVE 5

Exercise 5-41 (APPENDIX 5A) JOURNAL ENTRIES

Garrity Inc. uses a job-order costing system. During the month of May, the following transactions occurred:

a. Purchased materials on account for $27,800.
b. Requisitioned materials totalling $21,000 for use in production. Of the total, $9,300 was for Job 58, $6,900 for Job 59, and the remainder for Job 60.
c. Incurred direct labour for the month of $27,000, with an average wage of $15 per hour. Job 58 used 800 hours; Job 59, 600 hours; and Job 60, 400 hours.
d. Incurred and paid actual overhead of $15,500 (credit Various Payables).
e. Charged overhead to production at the rate of $7.50 per direct labour hour.
f. Completed and transferred Jobs 58 and 59 to Finished Goods.
g. Sold Job 57 (see beginning balance of Finished Goods) and Job 58 to their respective clients on account for a price of cost plus 40 percent.

Beginning balances as of May 1 were:

Materials	$ 5,170
Work in Process	0
Finished Goods (Job 58)	31,400

Required:

1. Prepare the journal entries for transactions (a) through (g).
2. Prepare brief job-order cost sheets for Jobs 58, 59, and 60.
3. Calculate the ending balance of Raw Materials.
4. Calculate the ending balance of Work in Process.
5. Calculate the ending balance of Finished Goods.

OBJECTIVE 6

Exercise 5-42 (APPENDIX 5B) DIRECT METHOD OF SUPPORT DEPARTMENT COST ALLOCATION

Dexter Company is divided into two operating divisions: Battery and Small Motors. The company allocates power and human resources costs to each operating division using the direct method. Power costs are allocated on the basis of the number of machine hours and human resources costs on the basis of the number of employees. Support department cost allocations using the direct method are based on the following data:

	Support Departments		Operating Divisions	
	Power	Human Resources	Battery	Small Motors
Overhead costs	$100,000	$205,000	$180,000	$93,500
Machine hours	2,000	2,000	5,000	3,000
Number of employees	20	30	20	60
Direct labour hours			15,000	80,000

Required:

1. Calculate the allocation ratios for Power and Human Resources. (Carry these calculations out to three significant digits.)
2. Allocate the support service costs to the producing departments.
3. Assume departmental overhead rates are based on direct labour hours. Calculate the overhead rate for the Battery Division and for the Small Motors Division. (Round overhead rates to the nearest cent.)

Exercise 5-43 (APPENDIX 5B) SEQUENTIAL METHOD OF SUPPORT DEPARTMENT COST ALLOCATION

OBJECTIVE 6

Refer to **Exercise 5-42** for data. Now assume that Dexter Company uses the sequential method to allocate support department costs to the producing departments. Human Resources is allocated first in the sequential method for Dexter.

Required:

1. Calculate the allocation ratios for Power and Human Resources. (Carry these calculations out to three significant digits.)
2. Allocate the support service costs to the producing departments.
3. Assume departmental overhead rates are based on direct labour hours. Calculate the overhead rate for the Battery Division and for the Small Motors Division. (Round overhead rates to the nearest cent.)

Problems

Problem 5-44 OVERHEAD APPLICATION AND JOB-ORDER COSTING

OBJECTIVE 2 4

Julian Company is a job-order costing firm that uses a plantwide overhead rate based on direct labour hours. Estimated information for the year is as follows:

Overhead	$665,000
Direct labour hours	100,000

Julian worked on five jobs in July. Data are as follows:

	Job 210	Job 211	Job 212	Job 213	Job 214
Balance, July 1	$32,780	$51,770	$29,600	$0	$0
Direct materials	$25,500	$39,800	$24,450	$13,600	$18,420
Direct labour cost	$60,000	$28,500	$41,500	$23,000	$21,300
Direct labour hours	4,000	1,900	2,700	1,500	1,400

By July 31, Jobs 210 and 212 were completed and sold. The remaining jobs were in process.

Required:

1. Calculate the plantwide overhead rate for Julian Company.
2. Prepare job-order cost sheets for each job showing all costs through July 31.
3. Calculate the balance in Work in Process on July 31.
4. Calculate Cost of Goods Sold for July.

Problem 5-45 JOB COST, SOURCE DOCUMENTS

OBJECTIVE 1 3

Zeta Detective Agency performs investigative work for a variety of clients. Recently, Alban Insurance Company asked Zeta to investigate a series of suspicious claims for whiplash. In each case, the claimant was driving on a freeway and was suddenly rear-ended by an Alban-insured client. The claimants were all driving old, uninsured automobiles. The Alban clients reported that the claimants suddenly changed lanes in front of them, and the accidents were unavoidable. Alban suspected that these "accidents" were the result of insurance fraud. Basically, the claimants cruised the expressways in virtually worthless cars, attempting to cut in front of expensive late-model cars that would surely be insured. Alban believed that the injuries were faked.

Inspector Clouseau spent 37 hours shadowing the claimants and taking pictures as necessary. His surveillance methods located the office of a doctor used by all claimants. He also took pictures of claimants performing tasks that they had sworn were now impossible to perform due to whiplash injuries. Hercule Poirot spent 48 hours using the Internet to research court records in adjoining provinces to locate the names of the claimants and their doctor. He found a pattern of similar insurance claims for each of the claimants.

Zeta Detective Agency bills clients for detective time at $120 per hour. Transportation is charged at $0.50 per kilometre. The agency logged in 510 kilometres on the Alban job. The film and developing amounted to $120.

Required:

1. Prepare a job-order cost sheet for the Alban job.
2. Why is overhead not specified in the charges? How does Zeta charge clients for the use of overhead (e.g., the ongoing costs of their office—supplies, paper for notes and reports, telephone, utilities)?
3. The kilometres are tallied from a source document. Design a source document for this use, and make up data for it that would total the 510 kilometres driven on the Alban job.

OBJECTIVE 4

Problem 5-46 CALCULATING ENDING WORK IN PROCESS, INCOME STATEMENT

Akra Prosthetics Company produces artificial limbs for individuals. Each prosthetic is unique. On January 1, three jobs, identified by the name of the person being fitted with the prosthetic, were in process with the following costs:

	Asher	Ayce	Wollner
Direct materials	$100	$ 340	$ 780
Direct labour	350	700	1,050
Applied overhead	280	560	840
Total	$730	$1,600	$2,670

During the month of January, two more jobs were started, Johns and Burton. Materials and labour costs incurred by each job in January are as follows:

	Materials	Direct Labour
Asher	$ 600	$ 300
Ayce	550	200
Wollner	860	250
Johns	1,310	1,650
Burton	260	180

Wollner and Johns's prosthetics were completed and sold by January 31.

Required:

1. If overhead is applied on the basis of direct labour dollars, what is the overhead rate?
2. Prepare simple job-order cost sheets for each of the five jobs in process during January.
3. What is the ending balance of Work in Process on January 31? What is the Cost of Goods Sold in January?
4. Suppose that Akra Prosthetics Company prices its jobs at cost plus 20 percent. In addition, during January, marketing and administrative costs of $850 were incurred. Prepare an income statement for the month of January.

OBJECTIVE 2

Problem 5-47 OVERHEAD APPLIED TO JOBS, DEPARTMENTAL OVERHEAD RATES

Watson Products Inc. uses a normal job-order costing system. Currently, a plantwide overhead rate based on machine hours is used. Marlon Burke, the plant manager, has heard that departmental overhead rates can offer significantly better cost assignments than a plantwide rate can offer. Watson has the following data for its two departments for the coming year:

	Department A	Department B
Overhead costs (expected)	$50,000	$22,000
Normal activity (machine hours)	20,000	16,000

Required:

1. Compute a predetermined overhead rate for the plant as a whole based on machine hours.
2. Compute predetermined overhead rates for each department using machine hours. (Carry your calculations out to three decimal places.)
3. Job 73 used 20 machine hours from Department A and 50 machine hours from Department B. Job 74 used 50 machine hours from Department A and 20 machine hours from Department B. Compute the overhead cost assigned to each job using the plantwide rate computed in Requirement 1. Repeat the computation using the departmental rates found in Requirement 2. Which of the two approaches gives the fairer assignment? Why?
4. Repeat Requirement 3, assuming the expected overhead cost for Department B is $40,000 (not $22,000). For this company, would you recommend departmental rates over a plantwide rate?

Problem 5-48 OVERHEAD RATES, UNIT COSTS

OBJECTIVE 2

Xanning Company manufactures specialty tools to customer order. There are three producing departments. Departmental information on budgeted overhead and various activity measures for the coming year is as follows:

	Welding	Assembly	Finishing
Estimated overhead	$200,000	$22,000	$250,000
Direct labour hours	4,500	10,000	6,000
Direct labour cost	$90,000	$150,000	$120,000
Machine hours	5,000	1,000	2,000

Currently, overhead is applied on the basis of machine hours using a plantwide rate. However, Janine, the controller, has been wondering whether it might be worthwhile to use departmental overhead rates. She has analyzed the overhead costs and drivers for the various departments and decided that Welding and Finishing should base their overhead rates on machine hours and that Assembly should base its overhead rate on direct labour hours.

Janine has been asked to prepare bids for two jobs with the following information:

	Job 1	Job 2
Direct materials	$4,500	$8,600
Direct labour cost	$1,000	$2,000
Direct labour hours:		
Welding	10	20
Assembly	60	20
Finishing	30	80
Number of machine hours:		
Welding	50	30
Assembly	40	5
Finishing	110	165

The typical bid price includes a 30 percent markup over full manufacturing cost.

Required:

1. Calculate a plantwide rate for Xanning Company based on machine hours. What is the bid price of each job using this rate?
2. Calculate departmental overhead rates for the producing departments. What is the bid price of each job using these rates? (Round all answers to the nearest dollar.)

Problem 5-49 CALCULATE JOB COST AND USE IT TO CALCULATE PRICE

OBJECTIVE 2 4

Suppose that back in the 1970s, Steve was asked to build speakers for two friends. The first friend, Jan, needed a speaker for her band. The second friend, Ed, needed a speaker built into the back of his hatchback automobile. Steve figured the following costs for each:

	Jan's Job	Ed's Job
Materials	$50	$75
Labour hours	10	20

Steve knew that Jan's job would be easier, since he had experience in building the type of speaker she needed. Her job would not require any special equipment or specialized fitting. Ed's job, on the other hand, required specialized design and precise fitting. Steve thought he might need to build a mock-up of the speaker first, to fit it into the space. In addition, he might have to add to his tool collection to complete the job. Normally, Steve figured a wage rate of $6 per hour and charged 20 percent of labour and materials as an overhead rate.

Required:

1. Prepare job-order cost sheets for the two jobs, showing total cost.
2. Which cost do you think is more likely to be accurate? How might Steve build in some of the uncertainty of Ed's job into a budgeted cost?

OBJECTIVE 4 5

Problem 5-50 (APPENDIX 5A) UNIT COST, ENDING WORK IN PROCESS, JOURNAL ENTRIES

During August, Pamell Inc. worked on two jobs. Data relating to these two jobs follow:

	Job 64	Job 65
Units in each order	50	100
Units sold	50	—
Materials requisitioned	$1,240	$985
Direct labour hours	410	583
Direct labour cost	$6,150	$8,745

Overhead is assigned on the basis of direct labour hours at a rate of $12. During August, Job 64 was completed and transferred to Finished Goods. Job 65 was the only unfinished job at the end of the month.

Required:

1. Calculate the per-unit cost of Job 64.
2. Compute the ending balance in the Work in Process account.
3. Prepare the journal entries reflecting the completion and sale on account of Job 64. The selling price is 160 percent of cost.

OBJECTIVE 4 5

Problem 5-51 (APPENDIX 5A) JOURNAL ENTRIES, JOB COSTS

The following transactions occurred during the month of April for Olakala Company:

a. Purchased materials costing $3,000 on account.
b. Requisitioned materials totalling $1,700 for use in production, $500 for Job 443 and the remainder for Job 444.
c. Recorded 50 hours of direct labour on Job 443 and 100 hours on Job 444 for the month. Direct labourers are paid at the rate of $8 per hour.
d. Applied overhead using a plantwide rate of $7.50 per direct labour hour.
e. Incurred and paid in cash actual overhead for the month of $1,230.
f. Completed and transferred Job 443 to Finished Goods.
g. Sold on account Job 442, which had been completed and transferred to Finished Goods in March, for cost ($2,000) plus 25 percent.

Required:

1. Prepare journal entries for transactions (a) through (e).
2. Prepare job-order cost sheets for Jobs 443 and 444. Prepare journal entries for transactions (f) and (g).

3. Prepare a statement of cost of goods manufactured for April. Assume that the beginning balance in the Raw Materials account was $1,400 and that the beginning balance in the Work in Process account was zero.

Problem 5-52 (APPENDIX 5A) PREDETERMINED OVERHEAD RATES, VARIANCES, COST FLOWS

OBJECTIVE 2 4 5

Playmore Costume Company, located in Toronto, sews costumes for plays and musicals. Playmore considers itself primarily a service firm, as it never produces costumes without a pre-existing order and only purchases materials to the specifications of the particular job. Any finished goods ending inventory is temporary and is zeroed out as soon as the show producer pays for the order. Overhead is applied on the basis of direct labour cost. During the first quarter of the year, the following activity took place in each of the accounts listed:

Work in Process

Bal.	17,000	Complete	245,000
DL	80,000		
OH	140,000		
DM	40,000		
Bal.	32,000		

Finished Goods

Bal.	40,000	Sold	210,000
Complete	245,000		
Bal.	75,000		

Overhead

	138,500		140,000
		Bal.	1,500

Cost of Goods Sold

210,000	

Job 32 was the only job in process at the end of the first quarter. A total of 1,000 direct labour hours at $10 per hour were charged to Job 32.

Required:

1. Assuming that overhead is applied on the basis of direct labour cost, what was the overhead rate used during the first quarter of the year?
2. What was the applied overhead for the first quarter? The actual overhead? The under- or overapplied overhead?
3. What was the cost of the goods manufactured for the quarter?
4. Assume that the overhead variance is closed to the Cost of Goods Sold account. Prepare the journal entry to close out the Overhead Control account. What is the adjusted balance in Cost of Goods Sold?
5. For Job 32, identify the costs incurred for direct materials, direct labour, and overhead.

Problem 5-53 (APPENDIX 5A) OVERHEAD APPLICATION, JOURNAL ENTRIES, JOB COST

OBJECTIVE 2 4 5

At the beginning of the year, Pexto Company budgeted overhead of $180,000 as well as 15,000 direct labour hours. During the year, Job K456 was completed with the following information: direct materials cost, $2,340; direct labour cost, $3,600. The average wage for Pexto Company employees is $10 per hour.

By the end of the year, 15,400 direct labour hours had actually been worked, and Pexto Company incurred the following actual overhead costs for the year:

Equipment lease	$ 5,000
Depreciation on building	20,000
Indirect labour	100,000
Utilities	15,000
Other overhead	45,000

Required:

1. Calculate the overhead rate for the year.
2. Calculate the total cost of Job K456.

3. Prepare the journal entries to record actual overhead and to apply overhead to production for the year.
4. Is overhead overapplied or underapplied? By how much?
5. Assuming that the normal cost of goods sold for the year is $700,000, what is the adjusted cost of goods sold?

OBJECTIVE 1 4 5

Problem 5-54 (APPENDIX 5A) JOURNAL ENTRIES, T-ACCOUNTS

Lowder Inc. builds custom conveyor systems for warehouses and distribution centres. During the month of July, the following occurred:

a. Purchased materials on account for $42,630.
b. Requisitioned materials totalling $27,000 for use in production: $12,500 for Job 703 and the remainder for Job 704.
c. Recorded direct labour payroll for the month of $26,320 with an average wage of $14 per hour. Job 703 required 780 direct labour hours; Job 704 required 1,100 direct labour hours.
d. Incurred and paid actual overhead of $19,950.
e. Charged overhead to production at the rate of $10 per direct labour hour.
f. Completed Job 703 and transferred it to finished goods.
g. Kept Job 704, which was started during July, in process at the end of the month.
h. Sold Job 700, which had been completed in May, on account for cost plus 30 percent.

Beginning balances as of July 1 were:

Raw Materials	$ 6,070
Work in Process (for Job 703)	10,000
Finished Goods (for Job 700)	6,240

Required:

1. Prepare the journal entries for events (a) through (e).
2. Prepare simple job-order cost sheets for Jobs 703 and 704.
3. Prepare the journal entries for events (f) and (h).
4. Calculate the ending balances of the following:
   a. Raw Materials
   b. Work in Process
   c. Finished Goods

OBJECTIVE 6

Problem 5-55 (APPENDIX 5B) SUPPORT DEPARTMENT COST ALLOCATION

MedServices Inc. is divided into two operating departments: Laboratory and Tissue Pathology. The company allocates delivery and accounting costs to each operating department. Delivery costs include the costs of a fleet of vans and drivers that drive throughout the province each day to clinics and doctors' offices to pick up samples and deliver them to the centrally located laboratory and tissue pathology offices. Delivery costs are allocated on the basis of the number of samples. Accounting costs are allocated on the basis of the number of transactions processed. No effort is made to separate fixed and variable costs; however, only budgeted costs are allocated. Allocations for the coming year are based on the following data:

	Support Departments		Producing Departments	
	Delivery	Accounting	Laboratory	Pathology
Overhead costs	$240,000	$270,000	$345,000	$456,000
Number of samples	—	—	70,200	46,800
Transactions processed	2,000	200	24,700	13,300

Required:

1. Assign the support department costs by using the direct method.
2. Assign the support department costs by using the sequential method.

Problem 5-56 (APPENDIX 5B) SUPPORT DEPARTMENT COST ALLOCATION: COMPARISON OF METHODS OF ALLOCATION

OBJECTIVE 6

Bender Automotive Works Inc. manufactures a variety of front-end assemblies for automobiles. A front-end assembly is the unified front of an automobile that includes the headlamps, fender, and surrounding metal/plastic. Bender has two producing departments: Drilling and Assembly. Usually, the front-end assemblies are ordered in batches of 100.

Two support departments provide support for Bender's operating units: Maintenance and Power. Budgeted data for the coming quarter follow. The company does not separate fixed and variable costs.

	Support Departments		Producing Departments	
	Maintenance	Power	Drilling	Assembly
Overhead costs	$320,000	$400,000	$163,000	$ 90,000
Machine hours	—	22,500	30,000	7,500
Kilowatt-hours	40,000	—	36,000	324,000
Direct labour hours	—	—	5,000	40,000

The predetermined overhead rate for Drilling is computed on the basis of machine hours; direct labour hours are used for Assembly.

Recently, a truck manufacturer requested a bid on a three-year contract that would supply front-end assemblies to a nearby factory. The prime costs for a batch of 100 front-end assemblies are $1,817. It takes two machine hours to produce a batch in the drilling department and 50 direct labour hours to assemble the 100 front-end assemblies in the assembly department.

Bender's policy is to bid full manufacturing cost, plus 15 percent.

Required:

1. Prepare bids for Bender Automotive Works by using each of the following allocation methods:
   a. Direct method.
   b. Sequential method.
2. Which method most accurately reflects the cost of producing the front-end assemblies? Why?

Cases

Case 5-57 OVERHEAD ASSIGNMENT: ACTUAL AND NORMAL ACTIVITY COMPARED

OBJECTIVE 1 2

Reynolds Printing Company specializes in wedding announcements. Reynolds uses an actual job-order costing system. An actual overhead rate is calculated at the end of each month using actual direct labour hours and overhead for the month. Once the actual cost of a job is determined, the customer is billed at actual cost plus 50 percent.

During April, Mrs. Lucky, a good friend of owner Jane Reynolds, ordered three sets of wedding announcements to be delivered May 10, June 10, and July 10, respectively. Reynolds scheduled production for each order on May 7, June 7, and July 7, respectively. The orders were assigned job numbers 115, 116, and 117, respectively.

Reynolds assured Mrs. Lucky that she would attend each of her daughters' weddings. Out of sympathy and friendship, she also offered a lower price. Instead of cost plus 50 percent, she gave her a special price of cost plus 25 percent. Additionally, she agreed to wait until the final wedding to bill for the three jobs.

On August 15, Reynolds asked her accountant to bring her the completed job-order cost sheets for Jobs 115, 116, and 117. She also gave instructions to lower the price as had been agreed upon. The cost sheets revealed the following information:

	Job 115	Job 116	Job 117
Cost of direct materials	$250.00	$250.00	$250.00
Cost of direct labour (5 hours)	25.00	25.00	25.00
Cost of overhead	200.00	400.00	400.00
Total cost	$475.00	$675.00	$675.00
Total price	$593.75	$843.75	$843.75
Number of announcements	500	500	500

Reynolds could not understand why the overhead costs assigned to Jobs 116 and 117 were so much higher than those for Job 115. She asked for an overhead cost summary sheet for the months of May, June, and July, which showed that actual overhead costs were $20,000 each month. She also discovered that direct labour hours worked on all jobs were 500 hours in May and 250 hours each in June and July.

Required:

1. How do you think Mrs. Lucky will feel when she receives the bill for the three sets of wedding announcements?
2. Explain how the overhead costs were assigned to each job.
3. Assume that Reynolds's average activity is 500 hours per month and that the company usually experiences overhead costs of $240,000 each year. Can you recommend a better way to assign overhead costs to jobs? Recompute the cost of each job and its price given your method of overhead cost assignment. Which method do you think is best? Why?

OBJECTIVE 2 5

Case 5-58 ASSIGNING OVERHEAD TO JOBS—ETHICAL ISSUES

Miroslav Klose, CMA and controller of the Parts Division of Matthaus Inc., was meeting with Franz Beckenbauer, manager of the division. The topic of discussion was the assignment of overhead costs to jobs and their impact on the division's pricing decisions. Their conversation was as follows:

Miroslav: Franz, as you know, about 25 percent of our business is based on government contracts, with the other 75 percent based on jobs from private sources won through bidding. During the past several years, our private business has declined. We have been losing more bids than usual. After some careful investigation, I have concluded that we are overpricing some jobs because of improper assignment of overhead costs. Some jobs are also being underpriced. Unfortunately, the jobs being overpriced are coming from our higher-volume, labour-intensive products; thus, we are losing business.

Franz: I think I understand. Jobs associated with our high-volume products are being assigned more overhead than they should be receiving. Then, when we add our standard 40 percent markup, we end up with a higher price than our competitors, who assign costs more accurately.

Miroslav: Exactly. We have two producing departments, one labour-intensive and the other machine-intensive. The labour-intensive department generates much less overhead than the machine-intensive department. Furthermore, virtually all of our high-volume jobs are labour-intensive. We have been using a plantwide rate based on direct labour hours to assign overhead to all jobs. As a result, the high-volume, labour-intensive jobs receive a greater share of the machine-intensive department's overhead than they deserve. This problem can be greatly alleviated by switching to departmental overhead rates. For example, an average high-volume job would be assigned $100,000 of overhead using a plantwide rate and only $70,000 using departmental rates. The change would lower our bidding price on high-volume jobs by an average of $42,000 per job. By increasing the accuracy of our product costing, we can make better pricing decisions and win back much of our private-sector business.

Franz: Sounds good. When can you implement the change in overhead rates?

Miroslav: It won't take long. I can have the new system working within four to six weeks—certainly by the start of the new fiscal year.

Franz: Hold it. I just thought of a possible complication. As I recall, most of our government contract work is done in the labour-intensive department. This new overhead assignment scheme will push down the cost on the government jobs, and we will lose revenues. They pay us full cost plus our standard markup. This business is not threatened by our current costing procedures, but we can't switch our rates for only the private business. Government auditors would question the lack of consistency in our costing procedures.

Miroslav: You do have a point. I thought of this issue also. According to my estimates, we will gain more revenues from the private sector than we will lose from our government contracts. Besides, the costs of our government jobs are distorted; in effect, we are overcharging the government.

Franz: They don't know that and never will unless we switch our overhead assignment procedures. I think I have the solution. Officially, let's keep our plantwide overhead rate. All of the official records will reflect this overhead costing approach for both our private and government business. Unofficially, I want you to develop a separate set of books that can be used to generate the information we need to prepare competitive bids for our private-sector business.

Required:

1. Do you believe that the solution proposed by Franz is ethical? Explain.
2. Suppose that Miroslav decides that Franz's solution is not right and objects strongly. Further suppose that, despite Miroslav's objections, Franz insists strongly on implementing the action. What should Miroslav do?

CMA Problems*

CMA Problem 5-1 JOB ORDER COSTING—THEBES INCORPORATED

Thebes Inc. is a manufacturer of furnishings for infants and children. The company uses a normal job order costing system. Thebes's WIP inventory at April 30, 2012, consisted of the following jobs:

Job Number	Items	Units	Accumulated Cost
CBS102	Cribs	20,000	$ 900,000
PLP086	Playpens	15,000	420,000
DRS114	Dressers	25,000	250,000
			$1,570,000

The company's finished goods inventory, using the FIFO method, consisted of five items:

Item	Quantity and Unit Cost	Accumulated Cost
Cribs	7,500 units @ $64 each	$ 480,000
Strollers	13,000 units @ $23 each	299,000
Carriages	11,200 units @ $102 each	1,142,400
Dressers	21,000 units @ $55 each	1,155,000
Playpens	19,400 units @ $35 each	679,000
		$3,755,400

Thebes applies factory overhead on the basis of direct labour hours. The company's factory overhead budget for the fiscal year ending May 31, 2012, totalled $4,500,000

*© 2010 CMA Ontario. Reproduced with Permission.

and the company plans to expend 600,000 direct labour hours during this period. Through the first 11 months of the year, a total of 555,000 direct labour hours were worked and total factory overhead amounted to $4,273,500.

At the end of April, the balance in Thebes's raw materials inventory account, which includes both raw materials and purchased parts, was $668,000. Additions to and requisitions from raw materials inventory during the month of May included:

	Raw Materials	Purchased Parts
Additions	$242,000	$396,000
Requisitions:		
Job CBS102	51,000	104,000
Job PLP086	3,000	10,800
Job DRS114	124,000	87,000
Job STR077 (10,000 strollers)	2,000	81,000
Job CRG098 (5,000 carriages)	65,000	187,000

During the month of May, Thebes's factory payroll consisted of the following:

Account	Hours	Cost
CBS102	12,000	$122,400
PLP086	4,400	43,200
DRS114	19,500	200,500
STR077	3,500	30,000
CRG098	14,000	138,000
Indirect	3,000	29,400
Supervision		57,600
		$621,100

The following jobs were completed and the unit sales for the month of May:

Job number	Items	Quantity
CBS102	Cribs	20,000
PLP086	Playpens	15,000
STR077	Strollers	10,000
CRG098	Carriages	5,000

Items	Quantity Shipped
Cribs	17,500
Playpens	21,000
Strollers	14,000
Dressers	18,000
Carriages	6,000

Required:

1. Describe when it is appropriate for a company to use a job order cost system.
2. Calculate the dollar balance in Thebes's WIP inventory account as of May 31, 2012
3. Calculate the dollar amount related to the playpens in Thebes's finished goods inventory as of May 31, 2012.
4. Explain the proper accounting treatment for over- or underapplied overhead balances when using a job-order cost system.

CMA Problem 5-2 (APPENDIX 5B) DEPARTMENTAL COSTING AND COST ALLOCATION—CORINTH LTD.

Corinth Ltd. consists of four departments: personnel and purchasing, which are service departments; and machining and painting, which are production departments. Budgeted data for the year consisted of the following:

Chapter 6

Process Costing

After studying Chapter 6, you should be able to:

1. Describe the basic characteristics and cost flows associated with process manufacturing.
2. Define *equivalent units* and explain their role in process costing. Explain the differences between the weighted average method and the FIFO method of accounting for process costs.
3. Prepare a departmental production report using the weighted average method.
4. Explain how nonuniform inputs and multiple processing departments affect process costing.
5. (Appendix) Prepare a departmental production report using the FIFO method.

MERTEN MERTEN/PHOTOLIBRARY

Experience Managerial Decisions
with BP

The only consideration that most people give to gasoline is the price charged at the local pump. However, **BP**, one of the largest energy companies in the world, has been thinking about this issue and a lot more for quite a long time. BP was founded in 1901 after William D'Arcy obtained permission from the Shah of Persia to dig for oil in what is now the Iranian desert. BP drastically expanded its reach as it built a new refinery in Australia in 1924 and then established new exploration and excavation sites in places such as Canada, South America, Africa, and Europe, in addition to its Middle Eastern sites. As of the early 21st century, BP had active excavation and production occurring in 22 countries. BP runs its processes nonstop—24 hours a day, 365 days a year—to produce to full capacity, which represents 2.6 million barrels of oil each day or approximately 30 barrels every second! Producing that much of anything is a bit mind-boggling, which hints at the importance of BP's effective process-costing system in determining the costs associated with its numerous products, which include gasoline, heating fuel, greases, and asphalt.

In order to determine costs for a particular process, BP needs to know the total costs of production and the total number of units processed in a specified period of time. The costs include raw crude oil, which varies widely from sweet West Texas crude to heavier Canadian crude, plus labour and management overhead. Other costs include catalysts, which enhance the reactivity to make a molecule actually turn into something else, and chemicals, which become part of the final product. BP goes to a lot of trouble to combine its process-costing system outputs, current market prices, and a linear programming model in order to calculate the most profitable mix of products to produce from a given mix of raw crude materials. Determining the costs associated with running a refinery with a continuous production process is complex. However, by calculating process costs and carefully setting production levels and product mixes, BP is able to manage this complex process at its facilities around the globe, thereby providing continued big profits for use in future energy discovery and distribution efforts (and, unfortunately, to pay for the cost of the Gulf of Mexico oil spill in 2010).

Here's The Real Kicker

Stillwater Designs builds a limited number of items on site. The manufacturing activities include designing and building prototypes and rebuilding of warranty returns (only of certain models such as the square L7s). Rebuilding of warranty returns follows a process manufacturing structure. All units are alike and go through the same steps. First, the woofers are removed from the cabinet, and the cabinet is stripped and cleaned. The speaker is torn down to its structures with all chemicals and glues removed. The speaker is passed through a demagnetizing process so that all metal pieces and shavings can be removed. The speaker is rebuilt using a recone kit to replace damaged and defective parts. Once the cabinets and speakers are ready, they are assembled, tested, and boxed. Assembly involves placing the speakers in the enclosures (cabinets) and connecting the wire harnesses. There are two tests: the in-phase test and the air-leak test. The in-phase test is to make sure that the power is hooked up correctly. Overall checking for air leaks is the final test. The product must be properly sealed because an air leak can damage the woofer.

Notice that the rebuilding and assembly processes are sequential. When finished, the rebuilt speakers and cabinets are transferred from the rebuilding process to the assembly process. Also, note that the cost of the final product is the cost of the materials transferred in from the rebuilding process, plus the cost of the other components and materials added, plus the assembly conversion cost. For example, at the end of the assembly process, the assembled product is packaged for delivery. In this simple process application, it is easy to see that some materials are added at the beginning of the assembly process (the cabinet and components) and some at the end of the process (packaging). The Kicker example also makes it possible to catch a glimpse of how process costing handles multiple departments.

KICKER®

OBJECTIVE 1

Describe the basic characteristics and cost flows associated with process manufacturing.

Characteristics of Process Manufacturing

A company's production process helps to determine the best way of accounting for its costs. Let's assume that a large number of similar products pass through an identical set of processes. Since each product within a product line passing through these processes would receive similar "doses" of materials, labour, and manufacturing overhead, the company's accountant would see no need to accumulate costs by batches (a job-order costing system). Instead, the accountant should recommend accumulating costs by process.

Process costing works well whenever relatively homogeneous products pass through a series of processes and they receive similar amounts of manufacturing costs. Large manufacturing plants, such as for chemicals, tires, and food, use process costing. For example, Americans purchase about 100 million bags of chocolate chips every year, many of which are made by **Nestle**. Nestle accounts for the costs of its vast chocolate chip production by using a process-costing system.

Let's consider the process-costing environment of **Healthblend Nutritional Supplements**, in Markham, Ontario, which manufactures various products including minerals, herbs, and vitamins. Healthblend uses three processes, each centred in a producing department: picking, encapsulation, and bottling. In the picking department, direct labour selects the appropriate herbs, vitamins, minerals, and inert materials (typically some binder such as cornstarch) for the product to be manufactured. Then, the materials are measured and combined in a mixer to blend them thoroughly. When the mix is complete, the resulting mixture is sent to the encapsulation department. In encapsulating, the vitamin, mineral, or herb blend is loaded into a machine that fills one-half of a gelatin capsule. The filled half is matched to another half of the capsule, and a safety seal is applied. This process is entirely mechanized. Manufacturing overhead in this department consists of depreciation on machinery, maintenance of machinery, supervision, fringe benefits, lights, and power. The final department is the bottling department. Filled capsules are transferred to this department, loaded into a hopper, and automatically counted into bottles. Filled bottles are mechanically capped, and direct labour then manually packs the correct number of bottles into boxes to ship to retail outlets.

Types of Processes

Production at Healthblend Nutritional Supplements is an example of sequential processing. **Sequential processing** requires that units pass through one process before they can be worked on in later processes. Exhibit 6-1 shows the sequential pattern of the manufacture of Healthblend's minerals, herbs, and vitamins.

Exhibit 6-1

Sequential Processing Illustrated

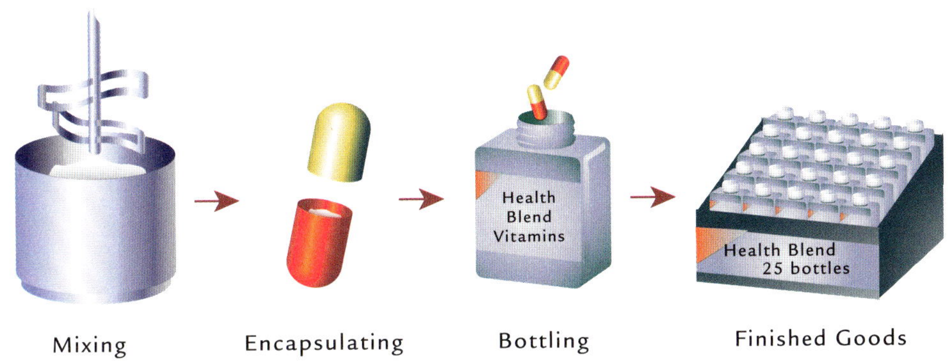

To summarize, in a process firm, units typically pass through a series of manufacturing or producing departments; in each department or process is an operation that brings a product one step closer to completion. As well, in each department, materials, labour, and manufacturing overhead may be needed. Upon completion of a particular process, the partially completed goods are transferred to the next department. After passing through the final department, the goods are completed and transferred to the warehouse.

Parallel processing is another processing pattern that requires two or more sequential processes to produce a finished good. Partially completed units (e.g., two subcomponents) can be worked on simultaneously in different processes and then brought together in a final process for completion. Consider, for example, the manufacture of hard disc drives for personal computers. In one series of processes, write heads and cartridge disc drives are produced, assembled, and tested. In a second series of processes, printed circuit boards are produced and tested. These two major subcomponents then come together for assembly in the final process. Exhibit 6-2 portrays this type of process pattern. Notice that processes 1 and 2 can occur independently of (or parallel to) processes 3 and 4.

Other forms of parallel processes also exist. However, regardless of which processing pattern exists within a firm, all units produced share a common property. Since units are homogeneous and subjected to the same operations for a given process, each unit produced in a period should receive the same unit cost. Understanding how unit costs are computed requires an understanding of the manufacturing cost flows that take place in a process-costing firm.

How Costs Flow through the Accounts in Process Costing

The manufacturing cost flows for a process-costing system are generally the same as those for a job-order system. As raw materials are purchased, the cost of these materials flows into a Raw Materials Inventory account. Similarly, raw materials, direct labour, and applied

Exhibit 6-2

Parallel Processing Illustrated

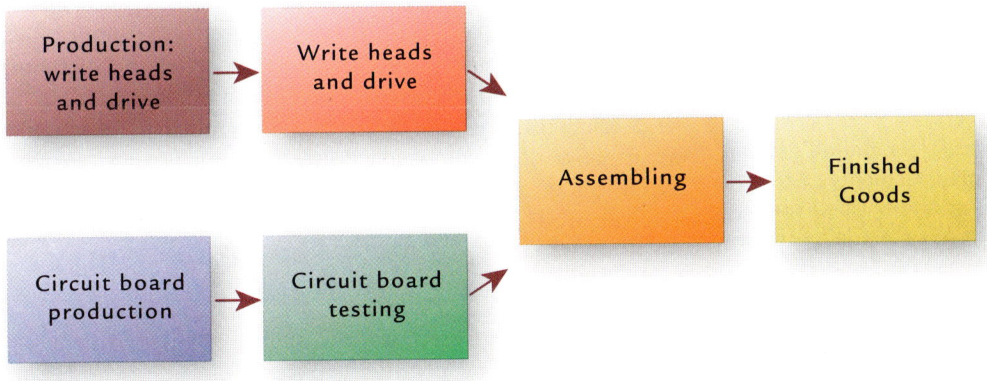

Exhibit 6-3

Flow of Manufacturing Costs through the Accounts of a Process-Costing Firm

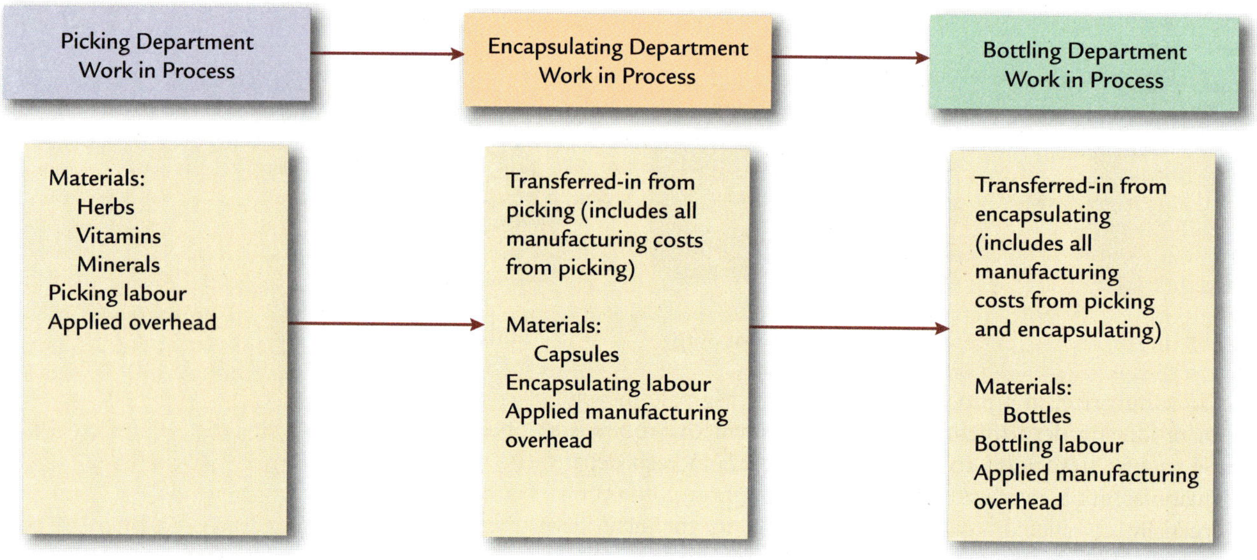

manufacturing overhead costs flow into a Work in Process (WIP) account. When goods are completed, the cost of the completed goods is transferred from WIP to the Finished Goods account. Finally, as goods are sold, the cost of the finished goods is transferred to the Cost of Goods Sold account. The journal entries generally parallel those described in a job-order costing system.

Although job-order and process cost flows are generally similar, some differences exist. In process costing, each producing department has its own WIP account. As goods are completed in one department, they are transferred to the next department. Exhibit 6-3 illustrates this process for Healthblend. Notice that a product (let's say multivitamins) starts out in the picking department, where the proper amounts of vitamin, mineral, and inert materials are mixed. Picking direct labour and applied manufacturing overhead are recognized and added to the picking WIP account. When the mixture is properly blended, it is transferred to the encapsulating department, where capsules are filled. The filled capsules are transferred out to the bottling department. In bottling, the capsules are bottled and the bottles are packaged. The important point is that as the product is transferred from one department to another, so are all of the costs attached to that product. By the end of the process, all manufacturing costs end up in the final department (here, bottling) with the final product. Let's attach some costs to the various departments and follow them through the accounts. Cornerstone 6-1 shows how cost flows are computed when there are no WIP inventories.

Cornerstone 6-1 shows that when the multivitamin mixture is transferred from the picking department to the encapsulating department, it takes $2,200 of cost along with it. **Transferred-in costs** are costs transferred from a prior process to a subsequent process. From the viewpoint of the subsequent process, transferred-in costs are a type of raw material cost. The same relationship exists between the encapsulating and bottling departments. The completed bottles of multivitamins are transferred to the finished goods warehouse at a total cost of $5,460.

CONCEPT Q&A

Will process costing be the same for sequential and parallel processing systems?

Answers on pages 711 to 715.

ANALYTICAL Q&A

Encapsulating transferred $5,000 of partially completed goods to Bottling. Bottling added $3,000 of manufacturing cost and then transferred the completed goods to the finished goods warehouse. What two journal entries would be made for these transactions?

Answers on pages 711 to 715.

Accumulating Costs in the Production Report

In process costing, costs are accumulated by department for a period of time. The **production report** is the document that

The HOW and WHY of Calculating Cost Flows without Work in Process

CORNERSTONE 6-1

Information:

Suppose that Healthblend decides to produce 2,000 bottles of multivitamins with the following costs:

	Picking Department	Encapsulating Department	Bottling Department
Direct materials	$1,700	$1,000	$800
Direct labour	50	60	300
Applied manufacturing overhead	450	500	600

Required:

1. Calculate the costs transferred out of each department.
2. Prepare journal entries that reflect these cost transfers.

Solution:

1.

	Picking Department	Encapsulating Department	Bottling Department
Direct materials	$1,700	$1,000	$ 800
Direct labour	50	60	300
Applied manufacturing overhead	450	500	600
Costs added	$2,200	$1,560	$1,700
Costs transferred in	0	2,200	3,760
Costs transferred out	$2,200	$3,760	$5,460

2. Journal entries:

Work in Process (Encapsulating)	2,200	
Work in Process (Picking)		2,200
Work in Process (Bottling)	3,760	
Work in Process (Encapsulating)		3,760
Finished Goods	5,460	
Work in Process (Bottling)		5,460

WHY:

The purpose of cost accounting is to assign the costs of manufacturing products to the proper inventory accounts. Therefore, understanding how the costs flow through the system is essential to assigning such costs. Starting with the simple case allows us to focus on the critical elements without undue complications.

summarizes the manufacturing activity that takes place in a process department for a given period of time. A production report contains information on costs transferred in from prior departments as well as costs added in the department such as direct materials, direct labour, and manufacturing overhead; it is subsidiary to the WIP account, just as the job-order cost sheet is subsidiary to the WIP account in a job-order costing system.

A production report provides information about the physical units processed in a department and also about the manufacturing costs associated with them. Thus, a production report is divided into a unit information section and a cost information section. The unit information section has two major subdivisions: (1) units to account for and (2) units accounted for. Similarly, the cost information section has two major subdivisions: (1) costs to account for and (2) costs accounted for. A production report traces the flow of units through a department, identifies the costs charged to the department, shows the computation of unit costs, and reveals the disposition of the department's costs for the reporting period.

Service and Manufacturing Firms

Any product or service that is basically homogeneous and repetitively produced can take advantage of a process-costing approach. Let's look at three possibilities: services, manufacturing firms with a just-in-time (JIT) orientation, and traditional manufacturing firms.

Cheque processing in a bank, teeth cleaning by a hygienist, air travel between Calgary and Vancouver, sorting mail by postal code, and laundering and pressing shirts are examples of homogeneous services that are repetitively produced. Although services cannot be stored, it is possible for firms engaged in service production to have WIP inventories. For example, a batch of tax returns can be partially completed at the end of a period. However, many services are provided so quickly that there are no WIP inventories. Teeth cleaning, funerals, surgical operations, sonograms, and carpet cleaning are a few examples where WIP inventories virtually would be nonexistent. Therefore, process costing for services is relatively simple. The total costs for the period are divided by the number of services provided to compute unit cost.

Manufacturing firms may also operate without significant WIP inventories. Specifically, firms that have adopted a JIT approach to manufacturing view the carrying of unnecessary inventories as wasteful. These firms try to reduce WIP inventories to very low levels. Furthermore, JIT firms usually structure their manufacturing so that process costing can be used to determine product costs.

In many JIT firms, work cells are created that produce a product or subassembly from start to finish. Costs are collected by cell for a period of time, and output for the cell is measured for the same period. Unit costs are computed by dividing the costs of the period by output of the period. There is no ambiguity concerning what costs belong to the period and how output is measured. One of the objectives of JIT manufacturing is simplification. Keep this in mind as you study the process-costing requirements of manufacturing firms that carry WIP inventories. The difference between the two settings is impressive and illustrates one of the significant benefits of JIT.

Finally, traditional manufacturing firms may have significant beginning and ending WIP inventories. It is the presence of these inventories that leads to much of the complication surrounding process costing. These complications are due to several factors such as the presence of beginning and ending WIP inventories and different approaches to the treatment of beginning inventory cost. These complicating factors are discussed in the following sections.

OBJECTIVE 2
Define *equivalent units* and explain their role in process costing. Explain the differences between the weighted average method and the FIFO method of accounting for process costs.

The Impact of Work-in-Process Inventories on Process Costing

The computation of unit cost for the work performed during a period is a key part of the production report. This unit cost is needed both to compute the cost of goods transferred out of a department and to value ending work-in-process (EWIP) inventory. Conceptually, calculating the unit cost is easy—just divide total cost by the number of units produced. However, the presence of WIP inventories causes two problems. First, defining the units produced can be difficult, given that some units produced during a period are complete, while those in ending WIP are not. This is handled through the concept of equivalent units of production. Second, how should the costs and work of beginning work-in-process (BWIP) inventory be treated? Should they be counted with the current period work and costs or treated separately? Two methods have been developed to solve this problem: the weighted average method and the FIFO method.

Equivalent Units of Production

By definition, EWIP is not complete. Thus, a unit completed and transferred out during the period is not identical (or equivalent) to one in EWIP inventory, and the cost attached to the two units should not be the same. In computing the unit cost, the output of the period must be defined. A major problem of process costing is making this definition.

To illustrate the output problem of process costing, assume that Department A had the following data for October:

Units in BWIP	—
Units completed	1,000
Units in EWIP (25 percent complete)	600
Total manufacturing costs	$11,500

ANALYTICAL Q&A

In March, a company completed 8,000 tonnes of aluminum ingots and had 2,500 tonnes of ingots in EWIP, 60 percent complete. Calculate the equivalent units for March.

Answers on pages 711 to 715.

What is the output in October for this department? 1,000? 1,600? If the answer is 1,000 units, the effort expended on the units in EWIP is ignored. Furthermore, the manufacturing costs incurred in October belong both to the units completed and to the partially completed units in EWIP. On the other hand, if the answer is 1,600 units, the fact that the 600 units in EWIP are only partially completed is ignored. Somehow, output must be measured so that it reflects the effort expended on both completed and partially completed units.

The solution is to calculate equivalent units of output. **Equivalent units of output** are the complete units that could have been produced given the total amount of manufacturing effort expended for the period under consideration. Determining equivalent units of output for transferred-out units is easy; a unit would not be transferred out unless it were complete. Thus, every transferred-out unit is one equivalent unit. Units remaining in EWIP inventory, however, are not complete. Thus, someone in production must "eyeball" EWIP to estimate its degree of completion. Estimating the degree of completion is an act that requires judgment and, at the same time, ethical behaviour. For example, overestimating the degree of completion will increase the equivalent units of output and decrease per-unit costs. This outcome, in turn, would cause an increase in both net income (cost of goods sold will be less) and in assets (WIP cost will increase). Deliberately overestimating the degree of completion would clearly be in violation of ethical professional practice. Cornerstone 6-2 illustrates how to calculate equivalent units of production, with the assumption that the degree of completion has been fairly assessed and stated.

Knowing the output for a period and the manufacturing costs for the department for that period, a unit cost can be calculated. The unit cost can then be used to determine the cost of units transferred out and the cost of the units in EWIP. Cornerstone 6-3 shows how the calculations are done when there is no BWIP. The unit cost of $10 is used to assign a cost of $10,000 ($10 × 1,000) to the 1,000 units transferred out and a cost of $1,500 ($10 × 150) to the 600 units in EWIP. Notice that the cost of the EWIP is obtained by multiplying the unit cost by the equivalent units, not the actual number of partially completed units.

Two Methods of Treating Beginning Work-in-Process Inventory

The calculations illustrated by Cornerstones 6-2 and 6-3 become more complicated when there are BWIP inventories. The work already done on these partially completed units represents prior-period work, and the costs assigned to them are prior-period costs. In computing a current-period unit cost for a department, two approaches have evolved for dealing with the prior-period output and prior-period costs found in BWIP: the weighted average method and the FIFO method.

The **weighted average costing method** combines beginning inventory costs and work done with current-period costs and work to calculate this period's unit cost. In essence, the costs and work carried over from the prior period are counted as if they belong to the current period. Thus, beginning inventory work and costs are pooled with current work and costs, and an average unit cost is computed and applied to both units transferred out and units remaining in ending inventory.

ANALYTICAL Q&A

During March, a moulding process transferred out 9,000 equivalent units to the grinding department and had 1,250 equivalent units in EWIP. The cost per equivalent unit for March was $8.00. Calculate the cost of goods transferred out and the cost of the EWIP.

Answers on pages 711 to 715.

CORNERSTONE 6-2

The HOW and WHY of Calculating Equivalent Units of Production: No Beginning Work in Process

Concept:

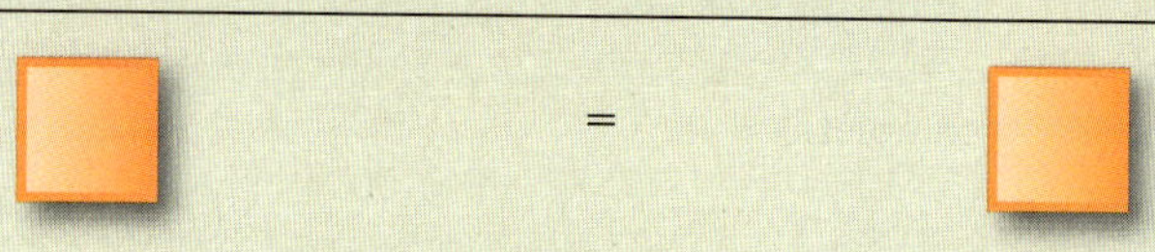

100 units completed = 100 equivalent units

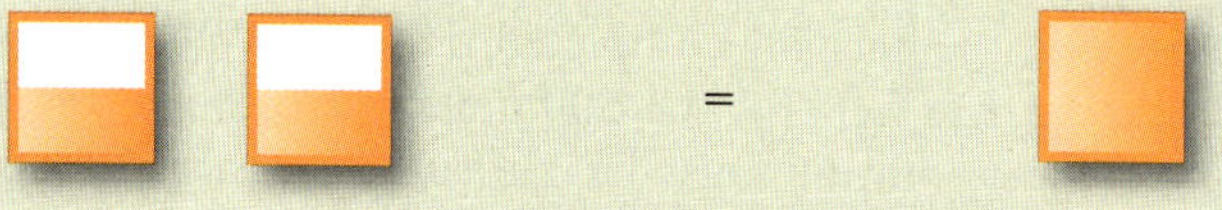

200 units, 50 percent complete = 100 equivalent units

Information:

October data: 1,000 units completed; 600 units, 25 percent complete

Required:

Calculate the equivalent units for October.

Solution:

1,000 units completed = 1,000 equivalent units

600 units × 0.25	=	150 equivalent units
October output	=	1,150 equivalent units

WHY:

Using equivalent units is the method whereby we can appropriately allocate costs among fully completed units and partially completed units in a fair manner. Since partially completed units should only attract the amount of costs in proportion to their stage of completion, this is an essential step in determining cost allocation.

The **FIFO costing method**, on the other hand, separates work and costs of the equivalent units in beginning inventory from work and costs of the equivalent units produced during the current period. Only current work and costs are used to calculate this period's unit cost. It is assumed that units from beginning inventory are completed first and transferred out. The costs of these units include the costs of the work done in the prior period as well as the current-period costs necessary to complete the units. Units

The HOW and WHY of Measuring Output and Assigning Costs: No Beginning Work in Process

CORNERSTONE 6-3

Information:
Manufacturing costs of the period, \$11,500; units transferred out, 1,000; units in EWIP, 600 (25 percent complete).

Required:
1. Calculate the unit cost.
2. Calculate the cost of goods transferred out and the cost of EWIP.

Solution:
1. Equivalent units:

Units completed	1,000
Units in EWIP × 25 percent (600 × 0.25)	150
Equivalent units	1,150

2. Cost assignment:

$$\text{Cost per equivalent unit} = \frac{\$11{,}500}{1{,}150} = \$10$$

Cost of goods transferred out = \$10 per unit × 1,000 equivalent units = \$10,000
Cost of EWIP = \$10 per unit × 150 equivalent units = \$1,500

WHY:
Knowing the costs and the equivalent units will permit the assigning of costs to the units in an appropriate and fair manner. Starting with no beginning inventory simplifies the process and allows us to focus on the critical elements of cost assignment.

started in the current period are divided into two categories: units started and completed and units started but not finished (EWIP). Units in both of these categories are valued using the current period's cost per equivalent unit.

If product costs do not change from period to period, or if there is no BWIP inventory, the FIFO and weighted average methods yield the same results. The weighted average method is discussed in more detail in the next section. Further discussion of the FIFO method is found in the chapter appendix.

Weighted Average Costing

OBJECTIVE 3
Prepare a departmental production report using the weighted average method.

The weighted average costing method treats beginning inventory costs and the accompanying equivalent output as if they belong to the current period. This is done for costs by adding the manufacturing costs in BWIP to the manufacturing costs incurred during the current period. The total cost is treated as if it were the current period's total manufacturing cost. Similarly, beginning inventory output and current period output are merged in the calculation of equivalent units. Under the weighted average method, equivalent units of output are computed by adding units completed to equivalent units in EWIP. Notice that the equivalent units in BWIP are included in the computation. Consequently, these units are counted as part of the current period's equivalent units of output.

CONCEPT Q&A

What is the key difference between FIFO and the weighted average costing methods?

Answers on pages 711 to 715.

Overview of the Weighted Average Method

The essential conceptual and computational features of the weighted average method are illustrated by Cornerstone 6-4. The example uses production data for Healthblend's picking department for July. The objective is to calculate a unit cost for

July and to use this unit cost to value goods transferred out and EWIP. Unit cost is simply costs of the period divided by output of the period. Thus, output needs to be calculated and costs defined for July to value goods transferred out and EWIP.

Cornerstone 6-4 illustrates that costs from BWIP are pooled with costs added to production during July. These total pooled costs ($13,650) are averaged and assigned to units transferred out and to units in EWIP. On the output side, it is necessary to concentrate on the degree of completion of all units at the end of the period. There is no need to be concerned with the percentage of completion of BWIP inventory. The only issue is whether these units are complete or not by the end of July. Thus, equivalent units are computed by pooling manufacturing efforts from June and July.

CORNERSTONE 6-4

The HOW and WHY of Measuring Output and Assigning Costs: Weighted Average Method

Information:

Production:	
Units in process, July 1, 75 percent complete	20,000 litres
Units completed and transferred out	50,000 litres
Units in process, July 31, 25 percent complete	10,000 litres
Costs:	
Work in process, July 1	$3,525
Costs added during July	10,125

Required:

1. Calculate an output measure for July.
2. Assign costs to units transferred out and EWIP using the weighted average method.

Solution:

1. Equivalent units:

Key:  = 10,000 units completed  = 10,000 units, 25% complete

Output for July:
60,000 total units ⟶ Become 52,500 equivalent units

Units completed:
BWIP:

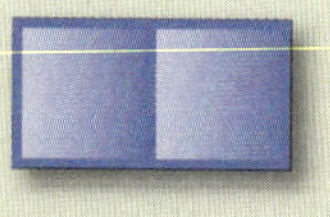 = 20,000

Units Started and Completed:

 = 30,000 50,000

\+ EWIP, 25% complete:

 = 2,500

52,500

CORNERSTONE 6-4 *(continued)*

2. Cost assignment:

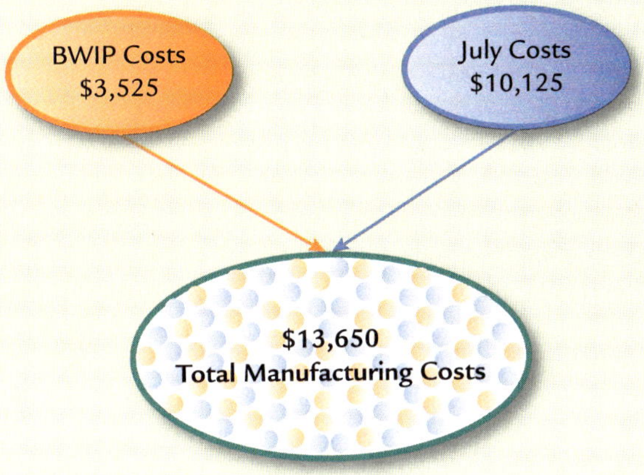

Cost/unit = $13,650/52,500 = $0.26

Transferred out ($0.26 × 50,000)	$13,000
EWIP ($0.26 × 2,500)	650
Total cost assigned	$13,650

WHY:
The valuation of beginning inventory introduces a new complication as there are several methods of valuing inventory. If the weighted average method is used, each unit processed during the period will be valued using the same costs. In order to do the calculations, the cost of beginning work-in-process inventory is added to the current period costs; the total costs are then assigned to the output for the period, both the fully completed units and the partially completed units at the end of the period.

Five Steps in Preparing a Production Report

The elements of Cornerstone 6-4 are used to prepare a production report. Recall that the production report summarizes cost and manufacturing activity for a producing department for a given period of time. The production report is subsidiary to the WIP account for a department. The following five steps describe the general pattern of a process-costing production report:

1. Physical flow analysis.
2. Calculation of equivalent units.
3. Computation of unit cost.
4. Valuation of inventories (goods transferred out and EWIP).
5. Cost reconciliation.

These five steps provide structure to the method of accounting for process costs.

ANALYTICAL Q&A

The weighted average cost per equivalent unit for April is $10. There were 3,800 units completed and transferred out during April and 750 units in EWIP, 40 percent complete. Calculate the cost of goods transferred out and the cost assigned to EWIP.

Answers on pages 711 to 715.

Step 1: Physical Flow Analysis

The purpose of step 1 is to trace the physical units of production. Physical units are not equivalent units; they are units that may be in any stage of completion. The **physical flow schedule,** like the one shown by Cornerstone 6-5 for Healthblend's picking department, provides an analysis of the physical flow of units. To construct the schedule from the information given in the example, two calculations are needed.

CORNERSTONE 6-5

The HOW and WHY of Preparing a Physical Flow Schedule

Information:

Production:	
Units in process, July 1, 75 percent complete	20,000 litres
Units completed and transferred out	50,000 litres
Units in process, July 31, 25 percent complete	10,000 litres

Required:

Prepare a physical flow schedule.

Solution:

Units started and completed = Units completed − Units, BWIP
= 50,000 − 20,000
= 30,000

Units started = Units started and completed + Units, EWIP
= 30,000 + 10,000
= 40,000

Physical flow schedule:		
Units to account for:		
Units in BWIP (75 percent complete)	20,000	
Units started during the period	40,000	
Total units to account for	60,000	
Units accounted for:		
Units completed and transferred out:		
Started and completed	30,000	
From beginning work in process	20,000	50,000
Units in EWIP (25 percent complete)		10,000
Total units accounted for		60,000

WHY:

In order to allocate the costs to the production units, we must understand how the *physical units* flow through the department. These do not represent equivalent units but the number of actual units so that we will know that we have accounted for all of them at the end of the cost assignment process.

- Units started and completed in this period are obtained by subtracting the units in BWIP from the total units completed.
- The units started are obtained by adding the units started and completed to the units in EWIP.

ANALYTICAL Q&A

The following data are provided for the month of April:

Units in process, April 1, 40 percent complete	6,000 cases
Units completed and transferred out	20,000 cases

How many units were started and completed during April?

Answers on pages 711 to 715.

Notice that the "Total units to account for" must equal the "Total units accounted for." The physical flow schedule is important because it contains the information needed to calculate equivalent units (step 2).

Step 2: Calculation of Equivalent Units Given the information in the physical flow schedule, the weighted average equivalent units for July can be calculated as follows:

Units completed	50,000
Add: Units in ending work in process × Fraction complete (10,000 units × 25 percent)	2,500
Equivalent units of output	52,500

Notice that July's output is measured as 52,500 units, 50,000 units completed and transferred out and 2,500 equivalent units from ending inventory (10,000 × 25 percent). What about beginning inventory? There were 20,000 units in beginning inventory, 75 percent complete. These units are included in the 50,000 units completed and transferred out during the month. Thus, the weighted average method treats beginning inventory units as if they were started and completed during the current period. Because of this, the equivalent unit schedule shown in step 2 shows only the total units completed. There is no need to show whether the units completed are from July or from BWIP as was done by Cornerstone 6-4.

ANALYTICAL Q&A

During June, 5,000 units were completed and transferred out, and there were 1,500 units in EWIP, 80 percent complete. How many equivalent units were completed in June, using the weighted average method?

Answers on pages 711 to 715.

Step 3: Computation of Unit Cost In addition to July output, July manufacturing costs are needed to compute a unit cost. The weighted average method rolls back and includes the manufacturing costs associated with the units in BWIP and counts these costs as if they belong to July. Thus, as Cornerstone 6-4 illustrated, these costs are pooled to define total manufacturing costs for July as $13,650 ($3,525 + $10,125). The manufacturing costs carried over from the prior period ($3,525) are treated as if they were current period costs. The unit cost for July is July's pooled costs divided by the equivalent output for July:

$$\text{Unit cost} = \frac{\$13,650}{52,500}$$
$$= \$0.26 \text{ per equivalent unit}$$

Step 4: Valuation of Inventories Cornerstone 6-4 also showed how to value goods transferred out and EWIP. Using the unit cost of $0.26, we value the two inventories as follows:

- Cost of goods transferred to the encapsulating department is $13,000 (50,000 units × $0.26 per unit)
- Cost of EWIP is $650 (2,500 equivalent units × $0.26 per unit).

Notice that units completed (from step 1), equivalent units in EWIP (from step 2), and the unit cost (from step 3) were all needed to value both goods transferred out and EWIP.

ANALYTICAL Q&A

June had the following costs to account for:
BWIP: $4,000
Incurred in June: $27,000
There were 6,200 equivalent units produced in June. What is the unit cost for June using the weighted average method?

Answers on pages 711 to 715.

Step 5: Cost Reconciliation The total manufacturing costs assigned to inventories are as follows:

Goods transferred out	$13,000
Goods in EWIP	650
Total costs accounted for	$13,650

The manufacturing costs to account for are also $13,650.

BWIP	$ 3,525
Incurred during the period	10,125
Total costs to account for	$13,650

Thus, **cost reconciliation** checks to see if the costs to account for are exactly assigned to inventories. Remember, the total costs assigned to goods transferred out and to EWIP must agree with the total costs in BWIP and the manufacturing costs incurred during the current period.

Production Report

Steps 1 through 5 provide all of the information needed to prepare a production report for the picking department for July. The method for preparing this report is shown in Cornerstone 6-6.

CORNERSTONE 6-6

The HOW and WHY of Preparing a Production Report: Weighted Average Method

Information:
Steps 1 to 5 of the Healthblend Company example.

Required:
Prepare a production report.

Solution:

Healthblend Company
Picking Department
Production Report For July 2011
(Weighted Average Method)

UNIT INFORMATION

Physical Flow

Units to account for:		Units accounted for:	
Units in beginning work in process	20,000	Units completed	50,000
Units started	40,000	Units in ending work in process	10,000
Total units to account for	60,000	Total units accounted for	60,000

Equivalent Units

Units completed	50,000
Units in ending work in process	2,500
Total equivalent units	52,500

COST INFORMATION

Costs to account for:	
Beginning work in process	$ 3,525
Incurred during the period	10,125
Total costs to account for	$13,650
Cost per equivalent unit	$ 0.26

	Transferred Out	Ending Work in Process	Total
Costs accounted for:			
Goods transferred out ($0.26 × 50,000)	$13,000	—	$13,000
Goods in ending work in process ($0.26 × 2,500)	—	$650	650
Total costs accounted for	$13,000	$650	$13,650

WHY:
The production report brings together all five steps that we follow in calculating the costs of each type of inventory for the period. It allows us to ensure that all costs and all units are properly accounted for.

Evaluation of the Weighted Average Method

The major benefit of the weighted average method is simplicity. By treating units in BWIP as belonging to the current period, all equivalent units belong to the same category when it comes to calculating unit costs. Thus, unit cost computations are simplified. The main disadvantage of this method is reduced accuracy in computing unit costs for current period output and for units in BWIP. If the unit cost in a process is relatively stable from one period to the next, the weighted average method is reasonably accurate. However, if the price of manufacturing inputs increases significantly from one period to the next, the unit cost of current output is understated, and the unit cost of BWIP units is overstated. If greater accuracy in computing unit costs is desired, a company should use the FIFO method to determine unit costs.

Multiple Inputs, Multiple Departments, and Hybrid Costing

OBJECTIVE 4
Explain how nonuniform inputs and multiple processing departments affect process costing.

Accounting for production under process costing is complicated by nonuniform application of manufacturing inputs and the presence of multiple processing departments. How process-costing methods address these complications will now be discussed.

Nonuniform Application of Manufacturing Inputs

Up to this point, we have assumed that WIP being 60 percent complete meant that 60 percent of materials, labour, and manufacturing overhead needed to complete the process have been used and that another 40 percent are needed to finish the units. In other words, we have assumed that manufacturing inputs are applied uniformly as the manufacturing process unfolds.

Assuming uniform application of conversion costs (direct labour and manufacturing overhead) is not unreasonable. Direct labour input is usually needed throughout the process, and manufacturing overhead is normally assigned on the basis of direct labour hours. Direct materials, on the other hand, are not as likely to be applied uniformly. In many instances, materials are added at either the beginning or the end of the process.

For example, look at the differences in Healthblend's three departments. In the picking and encapsulating departments, all materials are added at the beginning of the process. However, in the bottling department, materials are added both at the beginning (filled capsules and bottles) and at the end (bottle caps and boxes).

WIP in the picking department that is 50 percent complete with respect to conversion inputs would be 100 percent complete with respect to the material inputs. But WIP in bottling that is 50 percent complete with respect to conversion would be 100 percent complete with respect to bottles and transferred-in capsules, but 0 percent complete with respect to bottle caps and boxes.

Different percentage completion figures for manufacturing inputs pose a problem for the calculation of equivalent units, unit cost, and valuation of EWIP (steps 2–4). Fortunately, the solution is relatively simple. Equivalent unit calculations are done for each category of manufacturing input. Thus, equivalent units are calculated for each category of materials and for conversion cost. Next, a unit cost for each category is computed. The individual category costs are then used in step 4 to cost out EWIP. The total unit cost is used to calculate the cost of goods transferred out in the same way as when there was only one input category. Cornerstone 6-7 shows how to calculate steps 2 through 4 with nonuniform inputs, using the weighted average method.

For illustrative purposes, a production report, based on Cornerstone 6-7, is shown in Exhibit 6-4. As the example shows, applying manufacturing inputs at different stages of a process poses no serious problems. However, the effort required has increased.

CORNERSTONE 6-7

The HOW and WHY of Calculating Equivalent Units and Unit Costs, and Valuing Inventories with Nonuniform Inputs

Information:
The picking department of Healthblend has the following data for September:

Production:	
Units in process, September 1, 50 percent complete*	10,000
Units completed and transferred out	60,000
Units in process, September 30, 40 percent complete*	20,000
Costs:	
WIP, September 1:	
Materials	$ 1,600
Conversion costs	200
Total	$ 1,800
Current costs:	
Materials	$12,000
Conversion costs	3,200
Total	$15,200

* With respect to conversion costs, all materials are added at the beginning of the process.

Required:
Calculate steps 2 through 4 using the weighted average method.

Solution:
Step 2: Calculation of equivalent units, nonuniform application:

	Materials	Conversion
Units completed	60,000	60,000
Add: Units in ending work in process ×		
Fraction complete:		
20,000 × 100 percent	20,000	—
20,000 × 40 percent	—	8,000
Equivalent units of output	80,000	68,000

Step 3: Calculation of unit costs:

$$\begin{aligned}\text{Unit materials cost} &= (\$1,600 + \$12,000)/80,000 \\ &= \$0.17 \\ \text{Unit conversion cost} &= (\$200 + \$3,200)/68,000 \\ &= \$0.05 \\ \text{Total unit cost} &= \text{Unit materials cost} + \text{Unit conversion cost} \\ &= \$0.17 + \$0.05 \\ &= \$0.22 \text{ per completed unit}\end{aligned}$$

Step 4: Valuation of EWIP and goods transferred out:

The cost of EWIP is as follows:

Materials: $0.17 × 20,000	$3,400
Conversion: $0.05 × 8,000	400
Total cost	$3,800

Valuation of goods transferred out:

Cost of goods transferred out = $0.22 × 60,000 = $13,200

WHY:
In most manufacturing processes the inputs are not added at the same rate over the entire process. Therefore, we must be able to distinguish between the inputs to account for the different rate at which the inputs are added. The equivalent units for each input will be the basis for allocating the cost of that input.

CORNERSTONE 6-7 *(continued)*

Exhibit 6-4

Production Report: Weighted Average Method

Healthblend Company
Picking Department
Production Report for September 2011
(Weighted Average Method)

UNIT INFORMATION

Units to account for:		Units accounted for:	
Units in beginning work in process	10,000	Units completed	60,000
Units started during the period	70,000	Units in ending work in process	20,000
Total units to account for	80,000	Total units accounted for	80,000

	Equivalent Units	
	Materials	**Conversion Cost**
Units completed	60,000	60,000
Units in ending work in process	20,000	8,000
Total equivalent units	80,000	68,000

COST INFORMATION

	Materials	**Conversion Cost**	**Total**
Costs to account for:			
Beginning work in process	$ 1,600	$ 200	$ 1,800
Incurred during the period	12,000	3,200	15,200
Total costs to account for	$13,600	$3,400	$17,000
Cost per equivalent unit	$ 0.17	$ 0.05	$ 0.22

	Transferred Out	**Ending Work in Process**	**Total**
Costs accounted for:			
Goods transferred out ($0.22 × 60,000)	$13,200	—	$13,200
Goods in ending work in process:			
Materials ($0.17 × 20,000)	—	$3,400	3,400
Conversion ($0.05 × 8,000)	—	400	400
Total costs accounted for	$13,200	$3,800	$17,000

Multiple Departments

In process manufacturing, some departments receive partially completed goods from prior departments. The usual approach is to treat transferred-in goods as a separate material category when calculating equivalent units. Thus, the department receiving transferred-in goods would have *three* input categories: one for the transferred-in materials, one for materials added, and one for conversion costs.

In dealing with transferred-in goods, two important points should be remembered. First, the cost of this material is the cost of the goods transferred out as computed in the prior department. Second, the units started in the subsequent department correspond to the units transferred out from the prior department (assuming that there is a one-to-one relationship between the output measures of both departments). Cornerstone 6-8 shows how to calculate the first three process-costing steps when there are transferred-in goods, where steps 2 and 3 are restricted to the transferred-in category.

The only additional complication introduced in the analysis for a subsequent department is the presence of the transferred-in category. As has just been shown, dealing with this category is similar to handling any other category. However, it must be remembered that the current cost of this special type of raw material is the cost of the units transferred in from the prior process and that the units transferred in are the units started.

ANALYTICAL Q&A

A mixing process produced 200 equivalent units of material and 500 equivalent units of conversion activity during the month. If the materials cost was $400 and the conversion cost was $1,000, what is the cost per equivalent unit for the month?

Answers on pages 711 to 715.

CONCEPT Q&A

How are transferred-in goods viewed and treated by the department receiving them?

Answers on pages 711 to 715.

Hybrid Costing

Hybrid costing is a combination of job-order costing (perhaps on a batch basis) and process costing. In some instances, a company will produce the basic product on a process costing basis and then add unique elements to certain of their products before they are completed. An example could be an automobile manufacturing plant, where the basic model is produced and then additional components, such as an upgraded stereo system or heavy-duty suspension, are added to the luxury version of the model. In these instances, elements of both process costing and job-order costing are used.

The HOW and WHY of Calculating the Physical Flow Schedule, Equivalent Units, and Unit Costs with Transferred-In Goods

CORNERSTONE 6-8

Information:

For September, Healthblend's encapsulating department had 15,000 units in beginning inventory (with transferred-in costs of $3,000) and completed 70,000 units during the month. Further, the picking department completed and transferred out 60,000 units at a cost of $13,200 in September.

Required:

1. Prepare a physical flow schedule with transferred-in goods.
2. Calculate equivalent units for the transferred-in category.
3. Calculate unit cost for the transferred-in category.

Solution:

1. In constructing a physical flow schedule for the encapsulating department, its dependence on the picking department must be considered:

Units to account for:	
Units in BWIP	15,000
Units transferred in during September	60,000
Total units to account for	75,000
Units accounted for:	
Units completed and transferred out:	
Started and completed	55,000
From BWIP	15,000
Units in EWIP	5,000
Total units accounted for	75,000

2. Equivalent units for the transferred-in category only:

Transferred in:	
Units completed	70,000
Add: Units in EWIP × Fraction complete (5,000 × 100 percent)*	5,000
Equivalent units of output	75,000

* Remember that the EWIP is 100 percent complete with respect to transferred-in costs, not to all costs of the encapsulating department.

3. To find the unit cost for the transferred-in category, we add the cost of the units transferred in from picking in September to the transferred-in costs in BWIP and divide by transferred-in equivalent units:

$$\text{Unit cost (transferred-in category)} = (\$13,200 + \$3,000)/75,000$$
$$= \$16,200/75,000$$
$$= \$0.216$$

WHY:

The nature of manufacturing processes is that products move from department to department. As a product moves from one department to the next, the cost incurred in the previous department(s) must be included in the total cost of the units, but these costs represent fully completed units from the previous processes so they must be accounted for separately.

Summary of Learning Objectives

LO1. Describe the basic characteristics and cost flows associated with process manufacturing.

- Cost flows under process costing are similar to those under job-order costing.
- Raw materials are purchased and debited to the raw materials account.
- Direct materials used in production, direct labour, and applied manufacturing overhead are charged to the WIP account.
- In a production process with several processes, there is a WIP account for each department or process. Goods completed in one department are transferred out to the next department.
- When units are completed in the final department or process, their cost is credited to Work in Process and is debited to Finished Goods.

LO2. Define *equivalent units* and explain their role in process costing. Explain the differences between the weighted average method and the FIFO method of accounting for process costs.

- Equivalent units of production are the complete units that could have been produced given the total amount of manufacturing effort expended during the period.
- The number of physical units is multiplied by the percentage of completion to calculate equivalent units.
- The weighted average costing method combines beginning inventory costs to compute unit costs.
- The FIFO costing method separates units in beginning inventory from those produced during the current period.

LO3. Prepare a departmental production report using the weighted average method.

- The production report summarizes the manufacturing activity occurring in a department for a given period.
- It discloses information concerning the physical flow of units, equivalent units, unit costs, and the disposition of the manufacturing costs associated with the period.

LO4. Explain how nonuniform inputs and multiple processing departments affect process costing.

- Nonuniform inputs and multiple departments are easily handled by process-costing methods.
- When inputs are added nonuniformly, equivalent units and unit cost are calculated for each separate input category.
- The adjustment for multiple departments is also relatively simple.
- The goods transferred from a prior department to a subsequent department are treated as a material added at the beginning of the process. Thus, there is a separate transferred-in materials category, where the equivalent units and unit cost are calculated.

CORNERSTONES FOR CHAPTER 6

CORNERSTONE 6-1 The HOW and WHY of calculating cost flows without work in process, page 247

CORNERSTONE 6-2 The HOW and WHY of calculating equivalent units of production: no beginning work in process, page 250

CORNERSTONE 6-3 The HOW and WHY of measuring output and assigning costs: no beginning work in process, page 251

CORNERSTONE 6-4 The HOW and WHY of measuring output and assigning costs: weighted average method, page 252

CORNERSTONE 6-5 The HOW and WHY of preparing a physical flow schedule, page 254

CORNERSTONE 6-6 The HOW and WHY of preparing a production report: weighted average method, page 256

Key Terms

Cost reconciliation, 255
Equivalent units of output, 249
FIFO costing method, 250
Parallel processing, 245
Physical flow schedule, 253
Production report, 246
Sequential processing, 244
Transferred-in costs, 246
Weighted average costing method, 249

Appendix: Production Report—First-In, First-Out Costing

OBJECTIVE 5
Prepare a departmental production report using the FIFO method.

Under the FIFO costing method, the equivalent units and manufacturing costs in BWIP are excluded from the current period unit cost calculation. This method recognizes that the work and costs carried over from the prior period legitimately belong to that period.

Differences between the First-In, First-Out and Weighted Average Methods

If changes occur in the prices of the manufacturing inputs from one period to the next, then FIFO produces a more accurate (i.e., more current) unit cost than does the weighted average method. A more accurate unit cost means better cost control, better pricing decisions, and so on. Keep in mind that if the period is as short as a week or a month, however, the unit costs calculated under the two methods are not likely to differ much. In that case, the FIFO method has little, if anything, to offer over the weighted average method. Perhaps for this reason, many firms use the weighted average method.

Since FIFO excludes prior-period work and costs, it is necessary to create two categories of completed units. FIFO assumes that units in BWIP are completed first, before any new units are started. Thus, one category of completed units is BWIP units. The second category is for those units started and completed during the current period.

For example, assume that a department had 20,000 units in BWIP and completed and transferred out a total of 50,000 units. Of the 50,000 completed units, 20,000 are the units initially found in WIP. The remaining 30,000 were started and completed during the current period.

These two categories of completed units are needed in the FIFO method so that each category can be costed correctly. For the units started and completed, the unit cost is obtained by dividing total current manufacturing costs by the current period equivalent output. However, for the BWIP units, the total associated manufacturing costs are the sum of the prior period costs plus the costs incurred in the current period to finish the units.

Example of the First-In, First-Out Method

Cornerstone 6-9 shows how FIFO handles output and cost calculations. The computations of Cornerstone 6-9 are based on the same Healthblend data used for the weighted average method (Cornerstone 6-4). Using the same data highlights the differences between the two methods. Cornerstone 6-9 shows that the equivalent unit calculation measures only the output for the current period. Cornerstone 6-9 also reveals that costs from the current period and costs carried over from June (beginning inventory costs) are not pooled to calculate July's unit cost. The unit cost calculation uses only July (current period) costs. The five steps to cost out production follow.

CORNERSTONE 6-9

The HOW and WHY of Calculating Output and Cost Assignments: First-In, First-Out Method

Information:

Production:	
Units in process, July 1, 75 percent complete	20,000 litres
Units completed and transferred out	50,000 litres
Units in process, July 31, 25 percent complete	10,000 litres
Costs:	
Work in process, July 1	$3,525
Costs added during July	10,125

Required:

1. Calculate the output measure for July.
2. Assign costs to units transferred out and EWIP using the FIFO method.

Solution:

1. Equivalent units:

Key:  = 10,000 units completed

 = 10,000 units, 25% complete

Output for July:
60,000 total units ⟶ Become 37,500 equivalent units

BWIP: To be completed (20,000 × 25%):

 = 5,000

\+ Units started and completed:

 = 30,000

\+ EWIP: Started but not completed
(10,000 × 0.25)

 = 2,500
= 37,500

2. Cost assignment:
Costs for July:

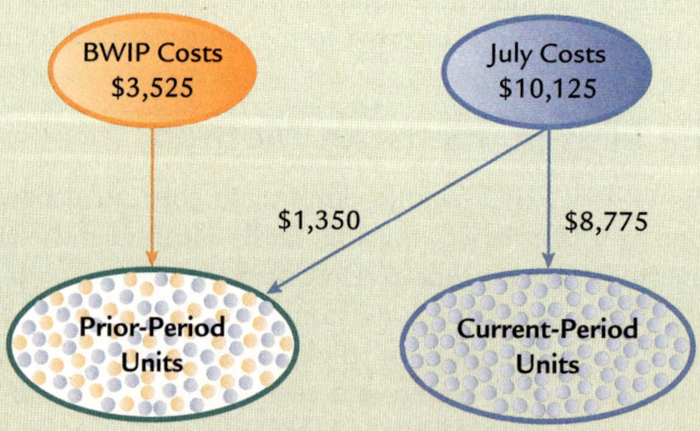

Cost/unit = $10,125/37,500 = $0.27	
Transferred out:	
Cost from BWIP (prior period carryover)	$ 3,525
To complete BWIP ($0.27 × 5,000)	1,350
Started and completed ($0.27 × 30,000)	8,100
Total	$12,975
EWIP ($0.27 × 2,500)	675
Total cost assigned	$13,650

CORNERSTONE 6-9 *(continued)*

WHY:
Inventory can be measured on the first-in, first-out basis. Under this approach, the partially completed units in opening work in process will maintain the costs incurred in previous periods and the cost to complete these units in the current period will be added to calculate the total cost of these units. Therefore, units transferred out of the department in the current period will be valued at two different amounts depending on whether they were in process at the beginning of the period or were started and completed in the current period.

Step 1: Physical Flow Analysis The purpose of step 1 is to trace the physical units of production. As with the weighted average method, in the FIFO method, a physical flow schedule is prepared. This schedule is identical for both methods and for convenience is presented again in Exhibit 6-5. (See Cornerstone 6-5 for details on how to prepare this schedule.)

Step 2: Calculation of Equivalent Units Cornerstone 6-9 illustrates the calculation of equivalent units under the FIFO method and is summarized as follows without the graphic detail.

Units started and completed	30,000
Add: Units in BWIP × Fraction to be completed (20,000 × 25 percent)	5,000
Add: Units in EWIP × Fraction complete (10,000 × 25 percent)	2,500
Equivalent units of output	37,500

From the equivalent unit computation, one difference between weighted average and FIFO becomes immediately apparent. Under FIFO, the equivalent units in BWIP (work done in the prior period) are not counted as part of the total equivalent work. Only the equivalent work to be completed this period is counted. The equivalent work to be completed for the units from the prior period is computed by multiplying the number of units in BWIP by the percentage of work remaining. Since in this example the percentage of work done in the prior period is 75 percent, the percentage left to

Exhibit 6-5

Physical Flow Schedule

Units to account for:		
Units in beginning work in process (75 percent complete)		20,000
Units started during the period		40,000
Total units to account for		60,000
Units accounted for:		
Units completed:		
Started and completed	30,000	
From beginning work in process	20,000	50,000
Units in ending work in process (25 percent complete)		10,000
Total units accounted for		60,000

ANALYTICAL Q&A

For August, there are 40,000 units in BWIP that are 30 percent complete and 20,000 units in EWIP that are 60 percent complete. There were 80,000 units started and completed. How many equivalent units were produced in August using the FIFO method?

Answers on pages 711 to 715.

be completed this period is 25 percent, or an equivalent of 5,000 additional units of work.

The effect of excluding prior period effort is to produce the current period equivalent output. Recall that under the weighted average method, 52,500 equivalent units were computed for this month. Under FIFO, only 37,500 units are calculated for the same month. These 37,500 units represent current period output. The difference, of course, is explained by the fact that the weighted average method rolls back and counts the 15,000 equivalent units of prior period work (20,000 units BWIP × 75 percent) as belonging to this period.

Step 3: Computation of Unit Cost The additional manufacturing costs incurred in the current period are $10,125. Thus, the current period unit manufacturing cost is $10,125/37,500, or $0.27. Notice that the costs of beginning inventory are excluded from this calculation. Only current period manufacturing costs are used.

Step 4: Valuation of Inventories Cornerstone 6-9 shows FIFO values for EWIP and goods transferred out. Since all equivalent units in ending work in process are current period units, the cost of EWIP is simply $0.27 × 2,500, or $675, the same value that the weighted average method would produce. However, when it comes to valuing goods transferred out, a significant difference emerges between the weighted average method and FIFO.

Under weighted average, the cost of goods transferred out is simply the unit cost times the units completed. Under FIFO, however, there are two sources of completed units: 20,000 units from beginning inventory and 30,000 units started and completed. The cost of the 30,000 units that were started and completed in the current period and transferred out is $8,100 ($0.27 × 30,000). For these units, the use of the current period unit cost is entirely appropriate. However, the cost of the BWIP units that were transferred out is another matter. These units started the period with $3,525 of manufacturing costs already incurred and 15,000 units of equivalent output already completed. To finish these units, the equivalent of 5,000 units were needed. The cost of finishing the units in BWIP is $1,350 ($0.27 × 5,000). Adding this $1,350 to the $3,525 in cost carried over from the prior period gives a total manufacturing cost for these units of $4,875. The unit cost of these 20,000 units, then, is about $0.244 ($4,875/20,000).

CONCEPT Q&A

The FIFO cost per equivalent unit for July was $12. The BWIP had 25,000 units, 20 percent complete, with $50,000 of costs carried over from June. What is the total cost that these 25,000 units will contribute to the cost of goods transferred out?

Answers on pages 711 to 715.

Step 5: Cost Reconciliation The total costs assigned to production are as follows:

Goods transferred out:	
Units in BWIP	$ 4,875
Units started and completed	8,100
Goods in EWIP	675
Total costs accounted for	$13,650

The total manufacturing costs to account for during the period are:

BWIP	$ 3,525
Incurred during the period	10,125
Total costs to account for	$13,650

The costs assigned, thus, equal the costs to account for. With the completion of step 5, the production report can be prepared. Cornerstone 6-10 shows how to prepare this report for FIFO.

The HOW and WHY of Preparing a Production Report: First-In, First-Out Method

CORNERSTONE 6-10

Information:

The five steps for the Healthblend Company.

Required:

Prepare a production report for July 2011 (FIFO method).

Solution:

Healthblend Company
Picking Department
Production Report For July 2011
(FIFO Method)

UNIT INFORMATION

Units to account for:	
Units in beginning work in process	20,000
Units started during the period	40,000
Total units to account for	60,000

	Physical Flow	Equivalent Units
Units accounted for:		
Units started and completed	30,000	30,000
Units completed from beginning work in process	20,000	5,000
Units in ending work in process	10,000	2,500
Total units accounted for	60,000	37,500

COST INFORMATION

Costs to account for:	
Beginning work in process	$ 3,525
Incurred during the period	10,125
Total costs to account for	$13,650
Cost per equivalent unit	$ 0.27

	Transferred Out	Ending Work in Process	Total
Costs accounted for:			
Units in beginning work in process:			
From prior period	$ 3,525	—	$ 3,525
From current period ($0.27 × 5,000)	1,350	—	1,350
Units started and completed ($0.27 × 30,000)	8,100	—	8,100
Goods in ending work in process ($0.27 × 2,500)	—	$675	675
Total costs accounted for	$12,975	$675	$13,650

WHY:

The production report brings together all five steps that we follow in calculating the costs of each type of inventory for the period. Under the FIFO method of inventory valuation, it isolates the costs assigned to completing the units that were in Opening WIP from the cost of units started and completed in the current period. It also allows us to ensure that all costs and all units are properly accounted for.

Appendix: Summary of Learning Objectives

A production report prepared according to the FIFO method separates the cost of BWIP from the cost of the current period. BWIP is assumed to be completed and transferred out first. Costs from BWIP are not pooled with the current period costs in computing unit cost. Additionally, equivalent units of production exclude work done in the prior period. When calculating the cost of goods transferred out, the prior period costs are added to the costs of completing the units in BWIP, and then these costs are added to the costs of units started and completed.

CORNERSTONES FOR APPENDIX

CORNERSTONE 6-9 The HOW and WHY of calculating output and cost assignments: first-in, first-out method, page 264

CORNERSTONE 6-10 The HOW and WHY of preparing a production report: first-in, first-out method, page 267

Review Problems

I. Process Costing

Springville Company, which uses the weighted average method, produces a product that passes through two departments: Blending and Cooking. In the blending department, all materials are added at the beginning of the process. All other manufacturing inputs are added uniformly. The following information pertains to the blending department for February:

a. BWIP, May 1: 100,000 kilograms, 40 percent complete with respect to conversion costs. The costs assigned to this work are as follows:

Materials	$20,000
Labour	10,000
Overhead	30,000

b. EWIP, May 31: 50,000 kilograms, 60 percent complete with respect to conversion costs.

c. Units completed and transferred out: 370,000 kilograms. The following costs were added during the month:

Materials	$211,000
Labour	100,000
Overhead	270,000

Required:

1. Prepare a physical flow schedule.
2. Prepare a schedule of equivalent units.
3. Compute the cost per equivalent unit.
4. Compute the cost of goods transferred out and the cost of EWIP.
5. Prepare a cost reconciliation.

Solution:

1. Physical flow schedule:

Units to account for:	
Units in BWIP	100,000
Units started	320,000
Total units to account for	420,000

Units accounted for:		
Units completed and transferred out:		
Started and completed	270,000	
From BWIP	100,000	370,000
Units in EWIP		50,000
Total units accounted for		420,000

2. Schedule of equivalent units:

	Materials	Conversion
Units completed	370,000	370,000
Units in EWIP × Fraction complete:		
Materials (50,000 × 100 percent)	50,000	—
Conversion (50,000 × 60 percent)	—	30,000
Equivalent units of output	420,000	400,000

3. Cost per equivalent unit:

Materials unit cost = ($20,000 + $211,000)/420,000
= $0.550
Conversion unit cost = ($40,000 + $370,000)/400,000
= $1.025
Total unit cost = $1.575 per equivalent unit

4. Cost of goods transferred out and cost of EWIP:

Cost of goods transferred out = $1.575 × 370,000
= $582,750
Cost of EWIP = ($0.550 × 50,000) + ($1.025 × 30,000)
= $58,250

5. Cost reconciliation:

Costs to account for:	
BWIP	$ 60,000
Incurred during the period	581,000
Total costs to account for	$641,000
Costs accounted for:	
Goods transferred out	$582,750
WIP	58,250
Total costs accounted for	$641,000

II. Process Costing

Now suppose that Springville Company uses the FIFO method for inventory valuations. Springville produces a product that passes through two departments: Blending and Cooking. In the blending department, all materials are added at the beginning of the process. All other manufacturing inputs are added uniformly. The following information pertains to the blending department for February:

a. BWIP, February 1: 100,000 kilograms, 40 percent complete with respect to conversion costs. The costs assigned to this work are as follows:

Materials	$20,000
Labour	10,000
Overhead	30,000

b. EWIP, February 28: 50,000 kilograms, 60 percent complete with respect to conversion costs.

c. Units completed and transferred out: 370,000 pounds. The following costs were added during the month:

Materials	$211,000
Labour	100,000
Overhead	270,000

Required:

1. Prepare a physical flow schedule.
2. Prepare a schedule of equivalent units.
3. Compute the cost per equivalent unit.
4. Compute the cost of goods transferred out and the cost of EWIP.

Solution:

1. Physical flow schedule:

Units to account for:		
Units in BWIP	100,000	
Units started	320,000	
Total units to account for	420,000	
Units accounted for:		
Units completed and transferred out:		
Started and completed	270,000	
From BWIP	100,000	370,000
Units in EWIP		50,000
Total units accounted for		420,000

2. Schedule of equivalent units:

	Direct Materials	Conversion Costs
Units started and completed	270,000	270,000
Units, BWIP × Percentage to complete	—	60,000
Units, EWIP × Percentage complete:		
Direct materials (50,000 × 100 percent)	50,000	—
Conversion costs (50,000 × 60 percent)	—	30,000
Equivalent units of output	320,000	360,000

3. Cost per equivalent unit:

DM unit cost $211,000/320,000	$0.659*
CC unit cost $370,000/360,000	1.028
Total cost per equivalent unit	$1.687

* Rounded.

4. Cost of goods transferred out and cost of EWIP:

Cost of goods transferred out = ($1.687 × 270,000) + ($1.028 × 60,000) + $60,000 = $577,170

Cost of EWIP = ($0.659 × 50,000) + ($1.028 × 30,000) = $63,790

Note: Difference of $40.00 between total cost incurred ($60,000 + $581,000) and total cost assigned ($577,170 + $63,790) due to rounding.

Discussion Questions

1. Distinguish between sequential processing and parallel processing.
2. Describe the differences between process costing and job-order costing.

3. What are equivalent units? Why are they needed in a process-costing system?
4. Under the weighted average method, how are prior period costs and output treated? How are they treated under the FIFO method?
5. Under what conditions will the weighted average and FIFO methods give the same results?
6. How is the equivalent unit calculation affected when materials are added at the beginning or end of the process rather than uniformly throughout the process?
7. Explain why transferred-in costs are a special type of raw material for the receiving department.
8. What are the similarities in and differences between the manufacturing cost flows for job-order firms and process firms?
9. What journal entry would be made as goods are transferred out from one department to another department? From the final department to the warehouse?
10. Describe the five steps in accounting for the manufacturing activity of a processing department, and explain how they interrelate.
11. What is a production report? What purpose does this report serve?
12. In assigning costs to goods transferred out, how do the weighted average and FIFO methods differ?
13. Describe the effect of automation on the process accounting system.
14. How does the adoption of a JIT approach to manufacturing affect process costing?
15. How would process costing for services differ from process costing for manufactured goods?

Multiple-Choice Exercises

6-1 Process costing works well whenever

a. heterogeneous products pass through a series of processes and receive similar doses of materials, labour, and manufacturing overhead.
b. homogeneous products pass through a series of processes and receive similar amounts of materials, labour, and manufacturing overhead.
c. homogeneous products pass through a series of processes and receive similar doses of conversion inputs and different doses of material inputs.
d. material cost is accumulated by process and conversion cost is accumulated by process.
e. none of the above.

6-2 Operation costing works well whenever

a. heterogeneous products pass through a series of processes and receive similar doses of materials, labour, and manufacturing overhead.
b. homogeneous products pass through a series of processes and receive similar doses of materials, labour, and manufacturing overhead.
c. homogeneous products pass through a series of processes and receive similar doses of conversion inputs and different doses of material inputs.
d. material cost is accumulated by process and conversion cost is accumulated by process.
e. none of the above.

6-3 Sequential processing is characterized by

a. a pattern where partially completed units are worked on simultaneously.
b. a pattern where different partially completed units must pass through parallel processes before being brought together in a final process.
c. a pattern where partially completed units must pass through one process before they can be worked on in later processes.
d. a pattern where partially completed units must be purchased from outside suppliers and delivered to the final process in a sequential time mode.
e. none of the above.

6-4 To record the transfer of costs from a prior process to a subsequent process, the following entry would be made:

a. Debit Finished Goods and credit Work in Process.
b. Debit Work in Process (subsequent department) and credit Transferred-In Materials.
c. Debit Work in Process (prior department) and credit Work in Process (subsequent department).
d. Debit Work in Process (subsequent department) and credit Conversion Cost Control.
e. None of the above.

6-5 The costs transferred from a prior process to a subsequent process

a. are treated as another type of material cost.
b. are referred to as transferred-in costs (for the receiving department).
c. are referred to as the cost of goods transferred out (for the transferring department).
d. all of the above.
e. none of the above.

6-6 During the month of May, the grinding department produced and transferred out 2,000 units. EWIP had 500 units, 60 percent complete. There was no BWIP. The equivalent units of output for May are

a. 2,000.
b. 2,500.
c. 2,300.
d. 2,200.
e. none of the above.

Use the following information for Multiple-Choice Exercises 6-7 through *6-9.*
The drilling department incurred $24,000 of manufacturing costs during the month of October. The department transferred out 2,000 units and had 400 equivalent units in EWIP. There was no BWIP.

6-7 The unit cost for the month of October is

a. $12.
b. $10.
c. $24.
d. $120.
e. $100.

6-8 The cost of goods transferred out is

a. $20,000.
b. $24,000.
c. $28,800.
d. $18,000.
e. None of the above.

6-9 The cost of EWIP is

a. $400.
b. $4,800.
c. $4,000.
d. $8,800.
e. none of the above.

6-10 During May, Kimbrell Manufacturing completed and transferred out 100,000 units. In EWIP, there were 25,000 units, 80 percent complete. Using the weighted average method, the equivalent units are

a. 100,000 units.
b. 125,000 units.
c. 105,000 units.
d. 110,000 units.
e. 120,000 units.

6-11 During June, Kimbrell Manufacturing completed and transferred out 100,000 units. In EWIP, there were 25,000 units, 40 percent complete. Using the weighted average method, the equivalent units are

a. 100,000 units.
b. 125,000 units.
c. 105,000 units.
d. 110,000 units.
e. 120,000 units.

6-12 For August, Kimbrell Company has costs in BWIP equal to $50,000. During August, the cost incurred was $450,000. Using the weighted average method, Kimbrell had 125,000 equivalent units for August. There were 100,000 units transferred out during the month. The cost of goods transferred out is

a. $500,000.
b. $400,000.
c. $450,000.
d. $360,000.
e. $50,000.

6-13 For September, Murphy Company has manufacturing costs in BWIP equal to $100,000. During September, the manufacturing costs incurred were $650,000. Using the weighted average method, Murphy had 100,000 equivalent units for September. The equivalent unit cost for September is

a. $1.00.
b. $7.50.
c. $6.50.
d. $6.00.
e. $6.62.

6-14 During June, Faust Manufacturing started and completed 80,000 units. In BWIP, there were 25,000 units, 60 percent complete. In EWIP, there were 25,000 units, 40 percent complete. Using FIFO, the equivalent units are

a. 80,000 units.
b. 100,000 units.
c. 90,000 units.
d. 105,000 units.
e. 85,000 units.

6-15 During July, Faust Manufacturing started and completed 80,000 units. In BWIP, there were 25,000 units, 20 percent complete. In EWIP, there were 25,000 units, 80 percent complete. Using FIFO, the equivalent units are

a. 80,000 units.
b. 85,000 units.
c. 65,000 units.
d. 120,000 units.
e. 100,000 units.

6-16 Assume for August that Faust Manufacturing has manufacturing costs equal to $80,000. During August, the cost incurred was $720,000. Using the

FIFO method, Faust had 120,000 equivalent units for August. The cost per equivalent unit for August is

a. $6.12.
b. $6.50.
c. $5.60.
d. $6.67.
e. $6.00.

6-17 For August, Lanny Company had 25,000 units in BWIP, 40 percent complete, with costs equal to $36,000. During August, the cost incurred was $450,000. Using the FIFO method, Lanny had 125,000 equivalent units for August. There were 100,000 units transferred out during the month. The cost of goods transferred out is

a. $500,000.
b. $400,000.
c. $450,000.
d. $360,000.
e. $50,000.

6-18 When materials are added either at the beginning or the end of the process, a unit cost should be calculated for the

a. materials and labour categories.
b. materials category only.
c. materials and conversion categories.
d. conversion category only.
e. labour category only.

6-19 With nonuniform inputs, the cost of EWIP is calculated by

a. multiplying the unit cost in each input category by the equivalent units of each input found in EWIP.
b. subtracting the cost of goods transferred out from the total cost of materials.
c. adding the materials cost to the conversion cost.
d. multiplying the total unit cost by the units in EWIP.
e. none of the above.

6-20 Transferred-in goods are treated by the receiving department as

a. units started for the period.
b. a material added at the beginning of the process.
c. a category of materials separate from conversion costs.
d. All of the above.
e. None of the above.

Cornerstone Exercises

OBJECTIVE 1
CORNERSTONE 6-1

Cornerstone Exercise 6-21 BASIC COST FLOWS

Sabor Company produces 500-gram boxes of an oat cereal. Sabor uses three departments: Mixing, Cooking, and Packaging. During the month of August, Sabor produced 150,000 boxes with the following costs:

	Mixing Department	Cooking Department	Packaging Department
Direct materials	$225,000	$75,000	$60,000
Direct labour	30,000	15,000	45,000
Applied overhead	45,000	22,500	67,500

Required:

1. Calculate the costs transferred out of each department.
2. Prepare journal entries that reflect these cost transfers.

Cornerstone Exercise 6-22 EQUIVALENT UNITS, NO BEGINNING WORK IN PROCESS

OBJECTIVE 2
CORNERSTONE 6-2

Thomas Manufacturing produces cylinders used in internal combustion engines. During June, Thomas' welding department had the following data:

Units in BWIP	—
Units completed	20,000
Units in EWIP (40 percent complete)	3,000

Required:

Calculate June's output for the welding department in equivalent units of production.

Cornerstone Exercise 6-23 UNIT COST, VALUING GOODS TRANSFERRED OUT AND EWIP

OBJECTIVE 2
CORNERSTONE 6-3

During the month of April, the moulding department of Paterson Foundry completed and transferred out 28,000 units. At the end of April, there were 10,000 units in process, 60 percent complete. Paterson incurred manufacturing costs totalling $408,000.

Required:

1. Calculate the unit cost.
2. Calculate the cost of goods transferred out and the cost of EWIP.

Cornerstone Exercise 6-24 WEIGHTED AVERAGE METHOD, UNIT COST, VALUING INVENTORIES

OBJECTIVE 3
CORNERSTONE 6-4

Buckner Enterprises produces premier strawberry jam. Output is measured in litres. Bucker uses the weighted average method. During January, the company had the following production data:

Units in process, January 1, 60 percent complete	12,000 litres
Units completed and transferred out	80,000 litres
Units in process, January 31, 40 percent complete	25,000 litres
Costs:	
Work in process, January 1	$ 18,000
Costs added during January	117,000

Required:

1. Using the weighted average method, calculate the equivalent units for January.
2. Calculate the unit cost for January.
3. Assign costs to units transferred out and EWIP.

Cornerstone Exercise 6-25 PHYSICAL FLOW SCHEDULE

OBJECTIVE 3
CORNERSTONE 6-5

Lawson Inc. just finished its second month of operations. Lawson mass produces integrated circuits. The following production information is provided for the month of November:

Units in process, November 1, 80 percent complete	75,000
Units completed and transferred out	450,000
Units in process, November 30, 60 percent complete	50,000

Required:

Prepare a physical flow schedule.

OBJECTIVE 3
CORNERSTONE 6-6

Cornerstone Exercise 6-26 PRODUCTION REPORT, WEIGHTED AVERAGE

Kinnamon Inc. manufactures bicycle frames in two departments: Cutting and Welding. Kinnamon uses the weighted average method. Manufacturing costs are added uniformly throughout the process. The following are cost and production data for the cutting department for October:

Production:	
Units in process, October 1, 40 percent complete	5,000
Units completed and transferred out	34,000
Units in process, October 31, 60 percent complete	10,000
Costs:	
WIP, October 1	$ 40,000
Costs added during October	760,000

Required:

Prepare a production report for the cutting department.

OBJECTIVE 4
CORNERSTONE 6-7

Cornerstone Exercise 6-27 NONUNIFORM INPUTS, WEIGHTED AVERAGE

Jackson Inc. had the following production and cost information for its fabrication department during the month of March (materials are added at the beginning of the fabrication process):

Production:	
Units in process, March 1, 50 percent complete with respect to conversion	5,000
Units completed	32,600
Units in process, March 31, 40 percent complete	6,000
Costs:	
Work in process, March 1:	
Materials	$ 10,000
Conversion costs	7,500
Total	$ 17,500
Current costs:	
Materials	$ 62,500
Conversion costs	105,000
Total	$167,500

Jackson uses the weighted average method.

Required:

1. Prepare an equivalent units schedule.
2. Calculate the unit cost.
3. Calculate the cost of units transferred out and the cost of EWIP.

OBJECTIVE 4
CORNERSTONE 6-8

Cornerstone Exercise 6-28 TRANSFERRED-IN COST

Energetics Inc. produces an energy drink. The product is sold by the litre. The company has two departments: Mixing and Bottling. For July, the bottling department had 40,000 litres in beginning inventory (with transferred-in costs of $142,000) and completed 175,000 litres during the month. Further, the mixing department completed and transferred out 160,000 litres at a cost of $458,000 in July.

Required:

1. Prepare a physical flow schedule for the bottling department.
2. Calculate equivalent units for the transferred-in category.
3. Calculate the unit cost for the transferred-in category.

Cornerstone Exercise 6-29 **(APPENDIX) FIRST-IN, FIRST-OUT METHOD; EQUIVALENT UNITS**

OBJECTIVE 5
CORNERSTONE 6-9

Bebida Inc. produces soft drinks. Mixing is the first department and its output is measured in litres. Bebida uses the FIFO method. All manufacturing costs are added uniformly. For August, the mixing department provided the following information:

Production:	
Units in process, August 1, 80 percent complete	20,000 litres
Units completed and transferred out	138,000 litres
Units in process, August 31, 75 percent complete	16,000 litres
Costs:	
Work in process, August 1	$ 19,200
Costs added during August	180,900

Required:

1. Calculate the equivalent units for August.
2. Calculate the unit cost.
3. Assign costs to units transferred out and EWIP using the FIFO method.

Cornerstone Exercise 6-30 **(APPENDIX) FIFO; PRODUCTION REPORT**

OBJECTIVE 5
CORNERSTONE 6-10

Refer to the data in **Cornerstone Exercise 6-29**.

Required:

Prepare a cost of production report.

Exercises

Exercise 6-31 **BASIC COST FLOWS**

OBJECTIVE 1

Gardner Company produces a common machine component for industrial equipment. The component is produced in three departments: moulding, grinding, and finishing. The following data are available for the month of September:

	Moulding Department ($)	Grinding Department ($)	Finishing Department ($)
Direct materials	30,800	3,800	2,450
Direct labour	2,300	5,600	3,800
Applied overhead	3,500	27,200	3,800

During September, 3,000 components were completed. There is no beginning or ending WIP in any department.

Required:

1. Prepare a schedule showing, for each department, the cost of direct materials, direct labour, applied overhead, product transferred in from a prior department, and total manufacturing cost.
2. Calculate the unit cost.

Exercise 6-32 **JOURNAL ENTRIES, BASIC COST FLOWS**

OBJECTIVE 1

In October, Gardner Company had the following cost flows:

	Moulding Department ($)	Grinding Department ($)	Finishing Department ($)
Direct materials	35,800	5,000	3,600
Direct labour	3,000	5,800	4,800
Applied overhead	3,200	29,200	4,600

	Moulding Department ($)	Grinding Department ($)	Finishing Department ($)
Transferred-in cost:			
From Moulding		42,000	
From Grinding	—	—	82,000
Total cost	42,000	82,000	95,000

Required:

Prepare the journal entries to transfer costs from (a) Moulding to Grinding, (b) Grinding to Finishing, and (c) Finishing to Finished Goods.

OBJECTIVE 2

Exercise 6-33 EQUIVALENT UNITS, UNIT COST, VALUATION OF GOODS TRANSFERRED OUT AND ENDING WORK IN PROCESS

The mixing department had the following data for the month of December:

Units in BWIP	—
Units completed	5,850
Units in EWIP (30 percent complete)	500
Total manufacturing costs	$3,900

Required:

1. What is the output in equivalent units for December?
2. What is the unit manufacturing cost for December?
3. Calculate the cost of goods transferred out for December.
4. Calculate the value of December's EWIP.

OBJECTIVE 3

Exercise 6-34 WEIGHTED AVERAGE METHOD, EQUIVALENT UNITS

Lawson Company produces a product where all manufacturing inputs are applied uniformly. The company produced the following physical flow schedule for March:

Units to account for:	
Units in BWIP (40 percent complete)	15,000
Units started	35,000
Total units to account for	50,000
Units accounted for:	
Units completed:	
From BWIP	10,000
Started and completed	32,000
	42,000
Units, EWIP (75 percent complete)	8,000
Total units accounted for	50,000

Required:

Prepare a schedule of equivalent units using the weighted average method.

OBJECTIVE 3

Exercise 6-35 WEIGHTED AVERAGE METHOD, UNIT COST, VALUING INVENTORIES

Milton Inc. manufactures products that pass through two or more processes. During April, equivalent units were computed using the weighted average method:

Units completed	18,000
Units in EWIP × Fraction complete (12,000 × 60 percent)	7,200
Equivalent units of output	25,200

April's costs to account for are as follows:

BWIP (40 percent complete)	$ 3,360
Materials	30,000
Conversion cost	12,000
Total	$45,360

Required:

1. Calculate the unit cost for April using the weighted average method.
2. Using the weighted average method, determine the cost of EWIP and the cost of the goods transferred out.

Exercise 6-36 WEIGHTED AVERAGE METHOD, UNIT COSTS, VALUING INVENTORIES

OBJECTIVE 3

Walser Inc. produces a product that passes through two processes. During February, equivalent units were calculated using the weighted average method:

Units completed	150,000
Add: Units in EWIP × Fraction complete (50,000 × 40 percent)	20,000
Equivalent units of output (weighted average)	170,000
Less: Units in BWIP × Fraction complete (25,000 × 70 percent)	17,500
Equivalent units of output (FIFO)	152,500

The costs that Walser had to account for during the month of February were as follows:

BWIP	$ 105,000
Costs added	993,000
Total	$1,098,000

Required:

1. Using the weighted average method, calculate unit cost.
2. Under the weighted average method, what is the total cost of units transferred out? What is the cost assigned to units in ending inventory?

Exercise 6-37 PHYSICAL FLOW SCHEDULE

OBJECTIVE 3

The following information was obtained for the first department of LPZ Company for April:

a. BWIP had 30,500 units, 30 percent complete with respect to manufacturing costs.
b. EWIP had 8,400 units, 25 percent complete with respect to manufacturing costs.
c. LPZ started 33,000 units in April.

Required:

Prepare a physical flow schedule.

Exercise 6-38 PHYSICAL FLOW, WEIGHTED AVERAGE METHOD

OBJECTIVE 3

Nelrok Company manufactures fertilizer. Department 1 mixes the chemicals required for the fertilizer. The following data are for the year:

BWIP (40 percent complete)	25,000
Units started	142,500
Units in EWIP (60 percent complete)	35,000

Required:

Prepare a physical flow schedule.

Exercise 6-39 PRODUCTION REPORT, WEIGHTED AVERAGE

OBJECTIVE 3

Mino Inc. manufactures chocolate syrup in three departments: Cooking, Mixing, and Bottling. Mino uses the weighted average method. The following are cost and production data for the cooking department for April (assume that units are measured in litres):

Production:	
Units in process, April 1, 60 percent complete	20,000
Units completed and transferred out	50,000
Units in process, April 30, 20 percent complete	10,000
Costs:	
WIP, April 1	$ 93,600
Costs added during April	314,600

Required:

Prepare a production report for the cooking department.

OBJECTIVE 4

Exercise 6-40 NONUNIFORM INPUTS, EQUIVALENT UNITS

Terry Linens Inc. manufactures bed and bath linens. The bath linens department sews terry cloth into towels of various sizes. Terry uses the weighted average method. All materials are added at the beginning of the process. The following data are for the bath linens department for August:

Production:	
Units in process, August 1, 25 percent complete*	10,000
Units completed and transferred out	60,000
Units in process, August 31, 60 percent complete	20,000

* With respect to conversion costs.

Required:

Calculate equivalent units of production for the bath linens department for August.

OBJECTIVE 4

Exercise 6-41 UNIT COST AND COST ASSIGNMENT, NONUNIFORM INPUTS

Loran Inc. had the following equivalent units schedule and cost for its fabrication department during the month of September:

	Materials	Conversion
Units completed	180,000	180,000
Add: Units in ending WIP × Fraction complete (60,000 × 60%)	60,000	36,000
Equivalent units of output	240,000	216,000

Costs:	
Work in process, September 1:	
Materials	$ 147,000
Conversion costs	7,875
Total	$ 154,875
Current costs:	
Materials	$1,053,000
Conversion costs	236,205
Total	$1,289,205

Required:

1. Calculate the unit cost for materials, for conversion, and in total for the fabrication department for September.
2. Calculate the cost of units transferred out and the cost of EWIP.

OBJECTIVE 4

Exercise 6-42 NONUNIFORM INPUTS, TRANSFERRED-IN COST

Drysdale Dairy produces a variety of dairy products. In Department 12, cream (transferred in from Department 6) and other materials (sugar and flavourings) are mixed and churned to make ice cream. The following data are for Department 12 for August:

Production:	
Units in process, August 1, 25 percent complete*	40,000
Units completed and transferred out	120,000
Units in process, August 31, 60 percent complete*	30,000

* With respect to conversion costs.

Required:

1. Prepare a physical flow schedule for the month.
2. Calculate equivalent units for the following categories: transferred-in, materials, and conversion.

Exercise 6-43 TRANSFERRED-IN COST

OBJECTIVE 4

Golding's finishing department had the following data for the month of July:

	Transferred-In	Materials	Conversion
Units transferred out	60,000	60,000	60,000
Units in EWIP	15,000	15,000	9,000
Equivalent units	75,000	75,000	69,000
Costs:			
Work in process, July 1:			
Transferred-in from fabricating	$ 2,100		
Materials	1,500		
Conversion costs	3,000		
Total	$ 6,600		
Current costs:			
Transferred-in from fabricating	$30,900		
Materials	22,500		
Conversion costs	45,300		
Total	$98,700		

Required:

1. Calculate unit costs for the following categories: transferred-in, materials, and conversion.
2. Calculate total unit cost.

Exercise 6-44 (APPENDIX) FIRST-IN, FIRST-OUT METHOD; EQUIVALENT UNITS

OBJECTIVE 5

Lawson Company produces a product where all manufacturing inputs are applied uniformly. The company produced the following physical flow schedule for March:

Units to account for:	
Units in BWIP (40 percent complete)	15,000
Units started	35,000
Total units to account for	50,000
Units accounted for:	
Units completed:	
From BWIP	10,000
Started and completed	32,000
	42,000
Units, EWIP (75 percent complete)	8,000
Total units accounted for	50,000

Required:

Prepare a schedule of equivalent units using the FIFO method.

OBJECTIVE 5

Exercise 6-45 (APPENDIX) FIRST-IN, FIRST-OUT METHOD; UNIT COST; VALUING INVENTORIES

Loren Inc. manufactures products that pass through two or more processes. During April, equivalent units were computed using the FIFO method:

Units started and completed	4,600
Units in BWIP × Fraction to complete (60 percent)	840
Units in EWIP × Fraction complete (4,000 × 60 percent)	2,400
Equivalent units of output (FIFO)	7,840
April's costs to account for are as follows:	
BWIP (40 percent complete)	$ 1,120
Materials	10,000
Conversion cost	4,000
Total	$15,120

Required:

1. Calculate the unit cost for April using the FIFO method. Round to two decimal places.
2. Using the FIFO method, determine the cost of EWIP and the cost of the goods transferred out.

Problems

OBJECTIVE 1 2

Problem 6-46 BASIC FLOWS, EQUIVALENT UNITS

Karsen Company produces a pain medication that passes through two departments: Mixing and Tableting. Karsen uses the weighted average method. Data for November for Mixing is as follows: BWIP was zero; EWIP had 2,400 units, 50 percent complete; and 28,000 units were started.

Tableting's data for November is as follows: BWIP was 1,600 units, 20 percent complete; and 800 units were in EWIP, 40 percent complete.

Required:

1. For Mixing, calculate the following:
   a. Number of units transferred to Tableting.
   b. Equivalent units of production.
2. For Tableting, calculate the number of units transferred out to Finished Goods.
3. Suppose that the units in the mixing department are measured in grams, while the units in Tableting are measured in bottles of 100 tablets, with a total weight of eight grams (excluding the bottle). Decide how you would treat units that are measured differently, and then repeat Requirement 2 using this approach.

OBJECTIVE 1 2 3 4

Problem 6-47 STEPS IN PREPARING A COST OF PRODUCTION REPORT

Stillwater Designs is expanding its market by becoming an original equipment supplier to DaimlerChrysler. DaimlerChrysler will offer a high-end Kicker audio package for its Dodge Neon SRT4 line. As part of this effort, Stillwater Designs will produce the plastic cabinet prototypes that will house the Kicker speakers and amplifiers. After producing the prototype cabinets, their production will be outsourced. However, assembly will remain in-house. Stillwater Designs will assemble the product by placing the speakers and amplifiers (produced according to specifications by outside manufacturers) in the plastic cabinets. Plastic cabinets and Kicker speaker and amplifier components are added at the beginning of the assembly process.

Assume that Stillwater Designs uses the weighted average method to cost out the audio package. The following are cost and production data for the assembly process for April:

Production:	
Units in process, April 1, 60 percent complete	40,000
Units completed and transferred out	100,000
Units in process, April 30, 20 percent complete	20,000
Costs:	
WIP, April 1:	
Plastic cabinets	$ 800,000
Kicker components	8,400,000
Conversion costs	3,600,000
Costs added during April:	
Plastic cabinets	$ 1,600,000
Kicker components	16,800,000
Conversion costs	5,760,000

Required:

1. Prepare a physical flow analysis for the assembly department for the month of April.
2. Calculate equivalent units of production for the assembly department for the month of April.
3. Calculate unit cost for the assembly department for the month of April.
4. Calculate the cost of units transferred out and the cost of EWIP inventory.
5. Prepare a cost reconciliation for the assembly department for the month of April.

Problem 6-48 STEPS FOR A COST OF PRODUCTION REPORT

OBJECTIVE 1 3

The owner of Stillwater Designs was pleased with the prospect of becoming an original equipment supplier to DaimlerChrysler. Stillwater will provide an audio package for the Dodge Neon SRT4 line. Assembling the plastic cabinets, speakers, and amplifiers for this audio package will be done in-house.

Assume that Stillwater Designs uses the weighted average method to cost out the audio package. The following are cost and production data for the assembly process for April:

Production:	
Units in process, April 1, 60 percent complete	40,000
Units completed and transferred out	100,000
Units in process, April 30, 20 percent complete	20,000
Costs:	
WIP, April 1:	
Plastic cabinets	$ 800,000
Kicker components	8,400,000
Conversion costs	3,600,000
Costs added during April:	
Plastic cabinets	$ 1,600,000
Kicker components	16,800,000
Conversion costs	5,760,000

Required:

1. Prepare a cost of production report for the assembly department for the month of April.
2. Write a one-page report that compares the purpose and content of the cost of production report with the job-order cost sheet.

OBJECTIVE 1 2 3 4

Problem 6-49 EQUIVALENT UNITS, UNIT COST, WEIGHTED AVERAGE

Fino Linens Inc. manufactures bed and bath linens. The bath linens department sews terry cloth into towels of various sizes. Fino uses the weighted average method. All materials are added at the beginning of the process. The following data are for the bath linens department for August:

Production:	
Units in process, August 1, 60 percent complete	20,000
Units completed and transferred out	60,000
Units in process, August 31, 60 percent complete	20,000
Costs:	
WIP, August 1	$11,520
Current costs	72,000
Total	$83,520

Required:

1. Prepare a physical flow analysis for the bath linens department for August.
2. Calculate equivalent units of production for the bath linens department for August.
3. Calculate the unit cost for the bath linens department for August.
4. Show that the cost per unit calculated in Requirement 3 is a weighted average of the cost per equivalent unit in BWIP and the current (FIFO) cost per equivalent unit. (*Hint:* The weights are in proportion to the number of units from each source.)

OBJECTIVE 3

Problem 6-50 COST OF PRODUCTION REPORT

The owner of Fino Linens Inc., a manufacturer of bed and bath linens, insisted on a formal report that provided all the details of the weighted average method. In the manufacturing process, all materials are added at the beginning. The following data are for the bath linens department for August:

Production:	
Units in process, August 1, 60 percent complete	20,000
Units completed and transferred out	60,000
Units in process, August 31, 60 percent complete	20,000
Costs:	
WIP, August 1	$11,520
Current costs	72,000
Total	$83,520

Required:

Prepare a cost of production report for the bath linens department for August using the weighted average method.

OBJECTIVE 1 2 3

Problem 6-51 WEIGHTED AVERAGE METHOD, PHYSICAL FLOW, EQUIVALENT UNITS, UNIT COSTS, COST ASSIGNMENT

Yomasca Inc. manufactures various Halloween masks. Each mask is shaped from a piece of rubber in the moulding department. The masks are then transferred to the finishing department, where they are painted and have elastic bands attached. Yomasca uses the weighted average method. In April, the moulding department reported the following data:

a. BWIP consisted of 6,000 units, 20 percent complete. Cost in beginning inventory totalled $552.
b. Costs added to production during the month were $8,698.
c. At the end of the month, 18,000 units were transferred out to Finishing. Then, 2,000 units remained in EWIP, 25 percent complete.

Required:

1. Prepare a physical flow schedule.
2. Calculate equivalent units of production.
3. Compute unit cost.
4. Calculate the cost of goods transferred to Finishing at the end of the month. Calculate the cost of ending inventory.
5. Assume that the masks are inspected at the end of the moulding process. Of the 18,000 units inspected, 1,000 are rejected as faulty and are discarded. Thus, only 17,000 units are transferred to the finishing department. The manager of Yomasca considers all such spoilage as abnormal and does not want to assign any of this cost to the 17,000 good units produced and transferred to finishing. Your task is to determine the cost of this spoilage of 1,000 units and then to discuss how you would account for this spoilage cost. Now suppose that the manager feels that this spoilage cost is just part of the cost of producing the good units transferred out. Therefore, he wants to assign this cost to the good production. Explain how this would be handled. (*Hint:* Spoiled units are a type of output, and equivalent units of spoilage can be calculated.)

Problem 6-52 WEIGHTED AVERAGE METHOD, SINGLE-DEPARTMENT ANALYSIS

OBJECTIVE 1 2 3

Jbooth Company produces a product that passes through an assembly process and a finishing process. All manufacturing costs are added uniformly for both processes. The following information was obtained for the assembly department for March:

a. WIP, March 1, had 48,000 units (60 percent completed) and the following costs:

Direct materials	$186,256
Direct labour	64,864
Overhead applied	34,400

b. During March, 138,400 units were completed and transferred to the finishing department, and the following costs were added to production:

Direct materials	$267,880
Direct labour	281,280
Overhead applied	117,144

c. On March 31, there were 21,600 partially completed units in process. These units were 70 percent complete.

Required:

Prepare a production report for the assembly department for March using the weighted average method of costing. The report should disclose the physical flow of units, equivalent units, and unit costs and should track the disposition of manufacturing costs.

Problem 6-53 FIRST-IN, FIRST-OUT METHOD; SINGLE-DEPARTMENT ANALYSIS; ONE COST CATEGORY

OBJECTIVE 1 2 3

Jbooth Company produces a product that passes through an assembly process and a finishing process. All manufacturing costs are added uniformly for both processes. The following information was obtained for the assembly department for March:

a. WIP, March 1, had 48,000 units (60 percent completed) and the following costs:

Direct materials	$186,256
Direct labour	64,864
Overhead applied	34,400

b. During March, 138,400 units were completed and transferred to the finishing department, and the following costs were added to production:

Direct materials	$267,880
Direct labour	281,280
Overhead applied	117,144

c. On March 31, there were 21,600 partially completed units in process. These units were 70 percent complete.

Required:

Prepare a production report for the assembly department for March using the FIFO method of costing. (Carry the unit cost computation to four decimal places.)

OBJECTIVE 1 2 3

Problem 6-54 WEIGHTED AVERAGE METHOD, SEPARATE MATERIALS COST

Tyrone Company produces a variety of stationery products. One product, sealing wax sticks, passes through two processes: blending and moulding. The weighted average method is used to account for the costs of production. After blending, the resulting product is sent to the moulding department, where it is poured into moulds and cooled. The following information relates to the blending process for August:

a. WIP, August 1, had 20,000 kilograms, 20 percent complete. Costs associated with partially completed units were:

Materials	$220,000
Direct labour	30,000
Overhead applied	10,000

b. WIP, August 31, had 30,000 kilograms, 70 percent complete.

c. Units completed and transferred out totalled 500,000 kilograms. Costs added during the month were (all inputs are added uniformly):

Materials	$5,610,000
Direct labour	3,877,500
Overhead applied	1,292,500

Required:

1. Prepare (a) a physical flow schedule and (b) an equivalent unit schedule.
2. Calculate the unit cost. Round to four decimal places.
3. Compute the cost of EWIP and the cost of goods transferred out.
4. Prepare a cost reconciliation.
5. Suppose that the materials added uniformly in blending are paraffin and pigment and that the manager of the company wants to know how much each of these materials costs per equivalent unit produced. The costs of the materials in BWIP are as follows:

Paraffin	$120,000
Pigment	100,000

The costs of the materials added during the month are also given:

Paraffin	$3,060,000
Pigment	2,550,000

Prepare an equivalent unit schedule with cost categories for each material. Calculate the cost per unit for each type of material.

Problem 6-55 WEIGHTED AVERAGE METHOD, JOURNAL ENTRIES

OBJECTIVE 1 2 3 4

Seacrest Company uses a process-costing system. The company manufactures a product that is processed in two departments, A and B. As work is completed, it is transferred out. The following summarizes the production activity and costs for November:

	Department A	Department B
Beginning inventories:		
Physical units	5,000	8,000
Costs:		
Transferred in	—	$45,320
Direct materials	$10,000	—
Conversion costs	$6,900	$16,800
Current production:		
Units started	25,000	?
Units transferred out	28,000	33,000
Costs:		
Transferred in	—	?
Direct materials	$57,800	$37,950
Conversion costs	$95,220	$128,100
Percentage completion:		
Beginning inventory	40%	50%
Ending inventory	80%	50%

Required:

1. Using the weighted average method, prepare the following for Department A:
   a. A physical flow schedule.
   b. An equivalent unit calculation.
   c. Calculation of unit costs. Round to two decimal places.
   d. Cost of EWIP and cost of goods transferred out.
   e. A cost reconciliation.
2. Prepare journal entries that show the flow of manufacturing costs for Department A. Use a conversion cost control account for conversion costs. Many firms are now combining direct labour and manufacturing overhead costs into one category. They are not tracking direct labour separately. Offer some reasons for this practice.

Problem 6-56 WEIGHTED AVERAGE METHOD, NONUNIFORM INPUTS, MULTIPLE DEPARTMENTS

OBJECTIVE 1 2 3 4

Benson Pharmaceuticals uses a process-costing system to compute the unit costs of the over-the-counter cold remedies that it produces. It has three departments: Picking, Encapsulating, and Bottling. In Picking, the ingredients for the cold capsules are measured, sifted, and blended. The mix is transferred out in litre containers. The encapsulating department takes the powdered mix and places it in capsules. One litre of powdered mix converts into 1,500 capsules. After the capsules are filled and polished, they are transferred to Bottling, where they are placed in bottles that are then affixed with a safety seal, lid, and label. Each bottle receives 50 capsules.

During March, the following results are available for the first two departments:

	Picking	Encapsulating
Beginning inventories:		
Physical units	10 litres	4,000
Costs:		
Materials	$252	$32
Labour	$282	$20
Overhead	?	?
Transferred in	—	$140

	Picking	Encapsulating
Current production:		
Transferred out	140 litres	208,000
Ending inventory	20 litres	6,000
Costs:		
Materials	$3,636	$1,573
Transferred in	—	?
Labour	$4,618	$1,944
Overhead	?	?
Percentage of completion:		
Beginning inventory	40%	50%
Ending inventory	50%	40%

Overhead in both departments is applied as a percentage of direct labour costs. In the picking department, overhead is 200 percent of direct labour. In the encapsulating department, the overhead rate is 150 percent of direct labour.

Required:

1. Prepare a production report for the picking department using the weighted average method. Follow the five steps outlined in the chapter. Round to two decimal places for the unit cost.
2. Prepare a production report for the encapsulating department using the weighted average method. Follow the five steps outlined in the chapter. Round to four decimal places for the unit cost.
3. Explain why the weighted average method is easier to use than FIFO. Explain when weighted average will give about the same results as FIFO.

OBJECTIVE 3

Problem 6-57 PRODUCTION REPORT, ETHICAL BEHAVIOUR

Consider the following conversation between Gary Means, manager of a division that produces industrial machinery, and his controller, Donna Simpson, a certified management accountant and chartered accountant:

Gary: Donna, we have a real problem. Our operating cash is too low, and we are in desperate need of a loan. As you know, our financial position is marginal, and we need to show as much income as possible—and our assets need bolstering as well.

Donna: I understand the problem, but I don't see what can be done at this point. This is the last week of the fiscal year, and it looks like we'll report income just slightly above break even.

Gary: I know all this. What we need is some creative accounting. I have an idea that might help us, and I wanted to see if you would go along with it. We have 200 partially finished machines in process, about 20 percent complete. That compares with the 1,000 units that we completed and sold during the year. When you computed the per-unit cost, you used 1,040 equivalent units, giving us a manufacturing cost of $1,500 per unit. That per-unit cost gives us cost of goods sold equal to $1.5 million and ending work in process worth $60,000. The presence of the work in process gives us a chance to improve our financial position. If we report the units in work in process as 80 percent complete, this will increase our equivalent units to 1,160. This, in turn, will decrease our unit cost to about $1,345 and cost of goods sold to $1.345 million. The value of our work in process will increase to $215,200. With those financial stats, the loan would be a cinch.

Donna: Gary, I don't know. What you're suggesting is risky. It wouldn't take much auditing skill to catch this one.

Gary: You don't have to worry about that. The auditors won't be here for at least six to eight more weeks. By that time, we can have those partially completed units completed and sold. I can bury the labour cost by having some of our more loyal workers work overtime for some bonuses. The overtime will never be reported. And, as you know, bonuses come out of the corporate budget and are assigned to overhead—next year's overhead. Donna, this will work. If we look good and get the loan to boot, corporate headquarters will treat us well. If we don't do this, we could lose our jobs.

Required:

1. Should Donna agree to Gary's proposal? Why or why not? To assist in deciding, review the corporate code of ethics standards described in Chapter 1. Do any apply?
2. Assume that Donna refuses to cooperate and that Gary accepts this decision and drops the matter. Does Donna have any obligation to report the divisional manager's behaviour to a superior? Explain.
3. Assume that Donna refuses to cooperate; however, Gary insists that the changes be made. Now what should she do? What would you do?
4. Suppose that Donna is age 63 and that the prospects for employment elsewhere are bleak. Assume again that Gary insists that the changes be made. Donna also knows that his supervisor, the owner of the company, is his father-in-law. Under these circumstances, would your recommendations for Donna differ?

Problem 6-58 (APPENDIX) FIRST-IN, FIRST-OUT METHOD; JOURNAL ENTRIES

OBJECTIVE 1 2 4 5

Seacrest Company uses a process-costing system. The company manufactures a product that is processed in two departments, A and B. As work is completed, it is transferred out. The following summarizes the production activity and costs for November:

	Department A	Department B
Beginning inventories:		
Physical units	5,000	8,000
Costs:		
Transferred in	—	$45,320
Direct materials	$10,000	—
Conversion costs	$6,900	$16,800
Current production:		
Units started	25,000	?
Units transferred out	28,000	33,000
Costs:		
Transferred in	—	?
Direct materials	$57,800	$37,950
Conversion costs	$95,220	$128,100
Percentage completion:		
Beginning inventory	40%	50%
Ending inventory	80%	50%

Required:

1. Using the FIFO method, prepare the following for Department A:
   a. A physical flow schedule.
   b. An equivalent unit calculation.
   c. Calculation of unit costs. Round to two decimal places.
   d. Cost of EWIP and cost of goods transferred out.
   e. A cost reconciliation.
2. Prepare journal entries that show the flow of manufacturing costs for Department A. Use a conversion cost control account for conversion costs. Many firms are now combining direct labour and manufacturing overhead costs into one category. They are not tracking direct labour separately. Offer some reasons for this practice.

Problem 6-59 (APPENDIX) FIRST-IN, FIRST-OUT METHOD

OBJECTIVE 5

Benson Pharmaceuticals uses a process-costing system to compute the unit costs of the over-the-counter cold remedies that it produces. It has three departments: Picking, Encapsulating, and Bottling. In Picking, the ingredients for the cold capsules are measured, sifted, and blended. The mix is transferred out in litre containers. The encapsulating department takes the powdered mix and places it in capsules. One litre of powdered mix converts into 1,500 capsules. After the capsules are filled and polished, they are transferred to Bottling, where they are placed in bottles that are then affixed with a safety seal, lid, and label. Each bottle receives 50 capsules.

During March, the following results are available for the first two departments:

	Picking	Encapsulating
Beginning inventories:		
Physical units	10 litres	4,000
Costs:		
Materials	$252	$32
Labour	$282	$20
Overhead	?	?
Transferred in	—	$140
Current production:		
Transferred out	140 litres	208,000
Ending inventory	20 litres	6,000
Costs:		
Materials	$3,636	$1,573
Transferred in	—	?
Labour	$4,618	$1,944
Overhead	?	?
Percentage of completion:		
Beginning inventory	40%	50%
Ending inventory	50%	40%

Overhead in both departments is applied as a percentage of direct labour costs. In the picking department, overhead is 200 percent of direct labour. In the encapsulating department, the overhead rate is 150 percent of direct labour.

Required:

Prepare a production report for each department using the FIFO method. (*Hint:* For the second department, you must convert litres to capsules.)

Problem 6-60 WEIGHTED AVERAGE COST METHOD, NONUNIFORM INPUTS

Sherbrooke Toboggan Company manufactures toboggans for the Canadian market. The product goes through three manufacturing processes: Forming, Sealing, and Assembly. In the forming department, the wood is shaped into the proper form; in the sealing department, a lacquer is applied to seal the wood and give it a satin finish; in the assembly department, the wood is assembled into the final product and cushions and rope are attached to the toboggan.

The company uses the weighted average cost method to calculate production costs, and materials are added in the sealing department at the very beginning of the process. During the month of August, the following information was determined for the sealing department:

BWIP:	
Units	2,000
Percentage complete	60%
Costs:	
Transferred in	$105,000
Material	$3,950
Conversion	$ 12,350
Current production	
Units started	15,000

Costs:	
Transferred in	$750,000
Material	$ 30,000
Conversion	$125,500
EWIP:	
Units	5,000
Percentage complete	35%

Required:

1. Prepare a cost of production report for the sealing department for the month of August, including all five steps. (Take all calculations to four decimal places).
2. Determine the unit cost in the previous period in the sealing department.

Problem 6-61 FIFO COST METHOD, NONUNIFORM INPUTS

Sherbrooke Toboggan Company manufactures toboggans for the Canadian market. The product goes through three manufacturing processes: Forming, Sealing, and Assembly. In the forming department, the wood is shaped into the proper form; in the sealing department, a lacquer is applied to seal the wood and give it a satin finish; in the assembly department, the wood is assembled into the final product and cushions and rope are attached to the toboggan.

The Company uses the FIFO method of costing to calculate production costs, and materials are added in the sealing department at the very beginning of the process. During the month of August, the following information was determined for the sealing department:

BWIP:	
Units	2,000
Percentage complete	60%
Costs:	
Transferred in	$105,000
Material	$ 3,950
Conversion	$ 12,350
Current production	
Units started	15,000
Costs:	
Transferred in	$750,000
Material	$ 30,000
Conversion	$125,500
EWIP:	
Units	5,000
Percentage complete	35%

Required:

1. Prepare a cost of production report for the sealing department for the month of August, including all five steps. (Take all calculations to four decimal places.)
2. Explain how the calculations are different in this problem as compared to **Problem 6-60.**

Cases

Case 6-62 PROCESS COSTING VERSUS ALTERNATIVE COSTING METHODS, IMPACT ON RESOURCE ALLOCATION DECISION

OBJECTIVE 1 2 3 4

Golding Manufacturing, a division of Farnsworth Sporting Inc., produces two different models of bows and eight models of knives. The bow-manufacturing process involves the production of two major subassemblies: the limbs and the handles. The limbs pass through four sequential processes before reaching final assembly: layup, moulding, fabricating, and finishing. In the layup department, limbs are created by laminating layers of wood. In the moulding department, the limbs are heat-treated, under pressure, to form strong resilient limbs. In the fabricating department, any protruding glue or other processing residue is removed. Finally, in the finishing department, the limbs are cleaned with acetone, dried, and sprayed with the final finishes.

The handles pass through two processes before reaching final assembly: pattern and finishing. In the pattern department, blocks of wood are fed into a machine that is set to shape the handles. Different patterns are possible, depending on the machine's setting. After coming out of the machine, the handles are cleaned and smoothed. They then pass to the finishing department, where they are sprayed with the final finishes. In final assembly, the limbs and handles are assembled into different models using purchased parts such as pulley assemblies, weight-adjustment bolts, side plates, and string.

Golding, since its inception, has been using process costing to assign product costs. A predetermined overhead rate is used based on direct labour dollars (80 percent of direct labour dollars). Recently, Golding has hired a new controller, Karen Jenkins. After reviewing the product-costing procedures, Karen requested a meeting with the divisional manager, Aaron Suhr. The following is a transcript of their conversation.

Karen: Aaron, I have some concerns about our cost accounting system. We make two different models of bows and are treating them as if they were the same product. Now I know that the only real difference between the models is the handle. The processing of the handles is the same, but the handles differ significantly in the amount and quality of wood used. Our current costing does not reflect this difference in material input.

Aaron: Your predecessor is responsible. He believed that tracking the difference in material cost wasn't worth the effort. He simply didn't believe that it would make much difference in the unit cost of either model.

Karen: Well, he may have been right, but I have my doubts. If there is a significant difference, it could affect our views of which model is more important to the company. The additional bookkeeping isn't very stringent. All we have to worry about is the pattern department. The other departments fit what I view as a process-costing pattern.

Aaron: Why don't you look into it? If there is a significant difference, go ahead and adjust the costing system.

After the meeting, Karen decided to collect cost data on the two models: the Deluxe model and the Econo model. She decided to track the costs for one week. At the end of the week, she had collected the following data from the pattern department:

a. There were a total of 2,500 bows completed: 1,000 Deluxe models and 1,500 Econo models.
b. There was no BWIP; however, there were 300 units in EWIP: 200 Deluxe and 100 Econo models. Both models were 80 percent complete with respect to conversion costs and 100 percent complete with respect to materials.
c. The pattern department experienced the following costs:

Direct materials	$114,000
Direct labour	45,667

d. On an experimental basis, the requisition forms for materials were modified to identify the dollar value of the materials used by the Econo and Deluxe models:

Econo model	$30,000
Deluxe model	84,000

Required:

1. Compute the unit cost for the handles produced by the pattern department assuming that process costing is totally appropriate. Round unit cost to two decimal places.
2. Compute the unit cost of each handle using the separate cost information provided on materials. Round unit cost to two decimal places.

3. Compare the unit costs computed in Requirements 1 and 2. Is Karen justified in her belief that a pure process-costing relationship is not appropriate? Describe the costing system that you would recommend.
4. In the past, the marketing manager has requested more money for advertising the Econo line. Aaron has repeatedly refused to grant any increase in this product's advertising budget because its per-unit profit (selling price less manufacturing cost) is so low. Given the results in Requirements 1 through 3, was Aaron justified in his position?

Case 6-63 EQUIVALENT UNITS; VALUATION OF WORK-IN-PROCESS INVENTORIES; FIRST-IN, FIRST-OUT VERSUS WEIGHTED AVERAGE

OBJECTIVE 1 2 3 4

AKL Foundry manufactures metal components for different kinds of equipment used by the aerospace, commercial aircraft, medical equipment, and electronics industries. The company uses investment casting to produce the required components. Investment casting consists of creating, in wax, a replica of the final product and pouring a hard shell around it. After removing the wax, molten metal is poured into the resulting cavity. What remains after the shell is broken is the desired metal object ready to be put to its designated use.

Metal components pass through eight processes: gating, shell creating, foundry work, cutoff, grinding, finishing, welding, and strengthening. Gating creates the wax mould and clusters the wax pattern around a sprue (a hole through which the molten metal will be poured through the gates into the mould in the foundry process), which is joined and supported by gates (flow channels) to form a tree of patterns. In the shell-creating process, the wax moulds are alternately dipped in a ceramic slurry and a fluidized bed of progressively coarser refractory grain until a sufficiently thick shell (or mould) completely encases the wax pattern. After drying, the mould is sent to the foundry process. Here, the wax is melted out of the mould, and the shell is fired, strengthened, and brought to the proper temperature. Molten metal is then poured into the dewaxed shell. Finally, the ceramic shell is removed, and the finished product is sent to the cutoff process, where the parts are separated from the tree by the use of a band saw. The parts are then sent to the grinding process, where the gates that allowed the molten metal to flow into the ceramic cavities are ground off using large abrasive grinders. In the finishing process, rough edges caused by the grinders are removed by small handheld pneumatic tools. Parts that are flawed at this point are sent to welding for corrective treatment. The last process uses heat to treat the parts to bring them to the desired strength.

In 2011, the two partners who owned AKL Foundry decided to split up and divide the business. In dissolving their business relationship, they were faced with the problem of dividing the business assets equitably. Since the company had two plants—one in Manitoba and one in Saskatchewan—a suggestion was made to split the business on the basis of geographic location. One partner would assume ownership of the plant in Manitoba, and the other would assume ownership of the plant in Saskatchewan. However, this arrangement had one major complication: the amount of WIP inventory located in the Saskatchewan plant.

The Saskatchewan facilities had been in operation for more than a decade and were full of WIP. The Manitoba facility had been operational for only two years and had much smaller WIP inventories. The partner located in Manitoba argued that to disregard the unequal value of the WIP inventories would be grossly unfair.

Unfortunately, during the entire business history of AKL Foundry, WIP inventories had never been assigned any value. In computing the cost of goods sold each year, the company had followed the policy of adding depreciation to the out-of-pocket costs of direct labour, direct materials, and overhead. Accruals for the company are nearly nonexistent, and there are hardly ever any ending inventories of materials.

During 2011, the Saskatchewan plant had sales of $2,028,670. The cost of goods sold is itemized as follows:

Direct materials	$378,000
Direct labour	530,300
Overhead	643,518

Upon request, the owners of AKL provided the following supplementary information (percentages are cumulative):

Costs Used by Each Process as a Percentage of Total Cost

	Direct Materials (%)	Direct Total Labour Cost (%)
Gating	23	35
Shell creating	70	50
Foundry work	100	70
Cutoff	100	72
Grinding	100	80
Finishing	100	90
Welding	100	93
Strengthening	100	100

Gating had 10,000 units in BWIP, 60 percent complete. Assume that all materials are added at the beginning of each process. During the year, 50,000 units were completed and transferred out. The ending inventory had 11,000 unfinished units, 60 percent complete.

Required:

1. The partners of AKL want a reasonable estimate of the cost of WIP inventories. Using the gating department's inventory as an example, prepare an estimate of the cost of the EWIP. What assumptions did you make? Did you use the FIFO or weighted average method? Why? Round unit cost to two decimal places.
2. Assume that the shell-creating process has 8,000 units in BWIP, 20 percent complete. During the year, 50,000 units were completed and transferred out. (All 50,000 units were sold; no other units were sold.) The EWIP inventory had 8,000 units, 30 percent complete. Compute the value of the shell-creating department's EWIP. What additional assumptions had to be made?

CMA Problem*

CMA Problem 6-1 PROCESS COSTING, EQUIVALENT UNITS—DELPHI CORPORATION

Delphi Corporation is a manufacturer that uses process costing to account for costs of production. Delphi manufactures a product in three separate departments: moulding, assembly, and finishing. The following information was obtained for the assembling department for the month of June:

Work-in-process, June 1—1,000 units made up of:

	Amount	Degree of Completion
Moulding department costs transferred in	$32,000	100%
Costs added by the assembly department		
Direct materials	20,000	100
Direct labour	7,200	60
Manufacturing overhead	5,500	50
Work-in-process, June 1	$64,700	

During the month of June, 5,000 units were transferred in from the moulding department at a cost of $160,000. The assembly department added the following $150,000 of costs:

Direct materials	$ 96,000
Direct labour	36,000
Manufacturing overhead	18,000
	$150,000

Four thousand units were completed and transferred to the finishing department.

At June 30, 2,000 units were still in WIP. The degree of completion of WIP at June 30 was:

Direct materials	90%
Direct labour	70
Manufacturing overhead	35

Required:

Calculate the cost of the units transferred out to the finishing department and the value of the ending WIP assuming that Delphi Corporation used (a) the weighted average method and (b) the FIFO method.

Chapter 7

Activity-Based Costing and Management

After studying Chapter 7, you should be able to:

1. Explain why functional (or volume)-based costing approaches may produce distorted costs.
2. Explain how an activity-based costing system works for product costing.
3. Describe activity-based customer costing and activity-based supplier costing.
4. Explain how activity-based management can be used for cost reduction.

JIM WEST/ALAMY/GETSTOCK

Tim Hortons and Cold Stone Creamery

Experts believe that ice cream as we currently know it was invented in the 1600s and was popularized in part by Charles I of England, who made it a staple of the royal table. Ice cream remains as popular as ever today. However, trips to the local ice cream parlour have changed dramatically over the past quarter century.

Tim Hortons has formed a new international partnership with American ice cream giant **Cold Stone Creamery**. The co-branding partnership between the two companies was established in 2009 when Tim Hortons franchises were added to 50 Cold Stone Creamery locations in the United States. Following the success of 12 test locations in Canada in the summer of 2009, the companies announced they would be opening between 60 and 80 Cold Stone Creamery franchises in Tim Hortons locations in Canada. The stores will be co-branded and not co-owned, in much the same way that the Tim Hortons and Wendy's partnership was created.

Cold Stone Creamery has helped lead this development with its innovative new business model focused on making the ice cream trip an entertainment experience for the entire family. Cold Stone operates 1,500 stores worldwide, with another 1,000 franchises in the works. Cold Stone executives must understand and control the company's complex cost structure in order to profitably manage its ice cream empire. For example, its most popular product line—ice cream with "mix in" ingredients—boasts 16 basic ice cream flavours with 30 different ingredients and three sizes, which represents a total of over 1,400 possible ice cream product options! These impressively numerous selection opportunities are great for customers with varied tastes but are quite challenging for Cold Stone to manage given the different types of activities associated with different types of product orders. Therefore, Cold Stone adopted activity-based costing (ABC), first to identify the activity drivers associated with each type of ice cream order and then to estimate the costs of these activities.

Two important drivers of costs for Cold Stone are ingredients and time, both of which vary significantly across different ice cream product orders. With the insights gained from its ABC analysis, Cold Stone understands the cost of various orders' preparation times, which are measured in seconds. In addition to labour, Cold Stone's ABC system considers the costs associated with training, uniforms, and employee benefits when estimating the cost of each second required in making each product. When combined with other costs, the ABC analysis provides an estimate of profit margin by product type. If a particular product is not making its expected margin, Cold Stone managers know to look at the activities involved in creating the product and to fine-tune that activity. Understanding its complex cost structure provides Cold Stone managers with a significant challenge. However, it is the mastery of this costing challenge that has provided Cold Stone with a valuable competitive advantage to become one of the most profitable and fastest-growing franchises in the world.

Here's The Real Kicker

For Stillwater Designs, and Audio Inc., warranty work is a significant cost. Warranty work associated with defective products is typically labelled a non-value-added cost. Stillwater Designs recognizes the non-value-added nature of this activity and takes measures to eliminate the causes of the defective units. The company tracks return failures (over time) and provides this information to its research and development (R&D) department. R&D then uses this information to make design improvements on existing models (running changes) as well to change the design on future models. The objective of the design changes is to reduce the demand for the warranty activity, thus reducing warranty cost.

When products are returned, customer service decides whether or not the problem is covered under warranty. Sometimes, problems are covered even though they are not attributable to a defective product. When the company decides to replace a non-defective product, it is making a conscious decision to increase customer satisfaction and brand loyalty. This part of the warranty cost is a "marketing warranty cost" and could be classified as a value-added cost. For example, customers sometimes buy amplifiers that are more powerful than the subwoofers can handle, resulting in burnt voice coils. By replacing the product (even though technically it's the customer's fault), the customer will be more likely to buy again and to provide good word-of-mouth advertising for Kicker products

KICKER®

OBJECTIVE 1
Explain why functional (or volume)-based costing approaches may produce distorted costs.

Limitations of Functional-Based Cost Accounting Systems

Plantwide and departmental rates based on direct labour hours, machine hours, or other volume-based measures have been used for decades to assign overhead costs to products and continue to be used successfully by many organizations. However, for many settings, this approach to costing is equivalent to an averaging approach and may produce distorted or inaccurate costs. Distorted costs can be a real problem in extremely competitive environments like the automobile industry, where in 2007 **General Motors**, for the first time in 76 years, lost its spot as the world's largest automaker as a result of unrelenting competition from an increasing number of competitors like **Toyota**. To understand why average costing can cause difficulties, consider the case where two individuals go out for dinner. One orders steak and lobster, costing \$40, and the other orders a chef salad, costing \$10. Thus, the total cost of the food is \$50. If the bill were split evenly between the two, each individual would pay \$25. The \$25 would be the average cost of the meals, but it wouldn't represent well the actual cost of each meal. One meal is overstated by \$15, and the other is understated by \$15. If it is important to know the cost of each meal (e.g., so that the one ordering steak and lobster can be reimbursed by his company), then the averaging approach will not be suitable.

In the same way, plantwide and departmental rates can produce average costs that severely under- or overstate individual product costs. Product cost distortions can be damaging, particularly for those firms whose business environment is characterized by intense or increasing competitive pressures (often on a worldwide level), small profit margins, continuous improvement, total quality management, total customer satisfaction, and sophisticated technology. Firms operating in theses types of business environments in particular need accurate cost information in order to make effective decisions. In order for accurate cost information to be produced, it is important that the firm's cost system accurately reflect the firm's underlying business, or economic, reality. However, as firms operating in an intensely competitive environment (or the other environments mentioned above) adopt new strategies to achieve competitive excellence, their cost accounting systems often must change to keep pace. Unfortunately, due to the time commitment and costs required to change cost systems, some firms do not change their systems when their business environment changes. Cost distortions subsequently result due to the poor matching between the firm's business reality and the cost system's representation of that reality. Thus it is important that the managerial accountant continually ask the question, "How well does the cost system's *representation* of my business match the economic *reality* of my business?" If the answer is "not very well," then it is likely that the cost system needs to be changed.

Therefore, in much the same way that financial statements must be transparent for external users, the cost system must be transparent in its assignment of costs for internal users.

The need for more accurate product costs has forced many companies to take a serious look at their costing procedures. At least two major factors can impair the ability of unit-based plantwide and departmental rates to assign overhead costs accurately: (1) the proportion of non-unit-related overhead costs to total overhead costs is large, and (2) the degree of product diversity is great.

Non-Unit-Related Overhead Costs

The use of either plantwide rates or departmental rates assumes that a product's consumption of overhead resources is related strictly to the units produced. For **unit-level activities**—activities that are performed each time a unit is produced—this assumption makes sense. Traditional, volume-based cost systems label the costs associated with these activities as variable in nature, because they increase or decrease in direct proportion to increases or decreases in the levels of these unit-level activities. All other costs (i.e., ones that are not unit-level) are considered fixed by volume-based cost systems.

But what if there are *non-unit-level activities*—activities that are not performed each time a unit of product is produced? The costs associated with these non-unit-level activities are unlikely to vary (i.e., increase or decrease) with units produced. However, sometimes these costs vary with some other factor(s), besides units, and identifying such factor(s) is very helpful in predicting and managing these costs. Proponents of activity-based costing (ABC) refer to the ABC cost hierarchy that categorizes costs either as *unit-level* (i.e., vary with output volume), *batch-level* (i.e., vary with the number of groups or batches that are run), *product-sustaining* (i.e., vary with the diversity of the product or service line), or *facility-sustaining* (i.e., do not vary with any factor but are necessary in operating the plant).[1] Exhibit 7-1 shows the activity-based costing hierarchy. ABC is discussed in detail later in this chapter, but the ABC cost hierarchy is identified at this point to illustrate its usefulness in helping managers realize that certain costs associated with non-unit-level activities are driven by other factors.

Consider the following two examples of non-unit-level activities: setting up equipment and re-engineering products. Often, the same equipment is used to produce different products. Setting up equipment means preparing it for the particular type of product being made. For example, a vat may be used to dye t-shirts. After completing a batch of 1,000 red t-shirts, the vat must be carefully cleaned before a batch of 3,000 green t-shirts is produced. Thus,

Exhibit 7-1

ABC Hierarchy

Type of Cost	Description of Cost Driver	Example
Unit-level	Varies with output volume (e.g., units); traditional variable costs	Cost of indirect materials for labelling each bottle of **Victoria's Secret** perfume
Batch-level	Varies with the number of batches produced	Cost of setting up laser engraving equipment for each batch of **Epilog** key chains
Product-sustaining	Varies with the number of product lines	Cost of inventory handling and warranty servicing of different brands carried by **Best Buy** electronics store
Facility-sustaining	Necessary to operate the plant facility but does not vary with units, batches, or product lines	Cost of General Motors plant manager salary

[1] R. Cooper, Cost Classification in Unit-Based and Activity-Based Manufacturing Cost Systems, *Journal of Cost Management for the Manufacturing Industry* (Fall 1990): 4–14.

setup costs are incurred each time a batch of products is produced. A batch may consist of 1,000 or 3,000 units, and the cost of setup is the same. Yet as more setups are done, setup costs increase. The number of setups (a batch-level cost), not the number of units produced (a unit-level cost), is a much better measure of the consumption of the setup activity.

At times, based on customer feedback, firms face the necessity of redesigning their products. This product re-engineering activity is authorized by a document called an *engineering work order*. For example, **Rio Novo**, a Brazilian appliance manufacturer, may issue engineering work orders to correct design flaws in its refrigerators, freezers, and washers. Product re-engineering costs may depend on the number of different engineering work orders (a product-sustaining cost) rather than on the units produced of any given product. Thus, *non-unit-level drivers* such as setups and engineering orders are needed for accurate cost assignment of non-unit-level activities. Also, **JetBlue**'s decision to add a second type of jet, the Embraer 190, to its existing fleet of Airbus A320s, caused it to incur significant additional product-sustaining costs that it would not have incurred had it stayed with only one type of plane. These additional product-sustaining costs included the costs for doubling the spare parts inventory, maintenance programs, and separate pilot-training tracks.[2] Therefore, **non-unit-level activity drivers** (i.e., batch, product-sustaining, and facility-sustaining) are factors that measure the consumption of non-unit-level activities by products and other cost objects, whereas **unit-level activity drivers** measure the consumption of unit-level activities. **Activity drivers**, then, are factors that measure the consumption of activities by products and other cost objects and can be classified as either *unit-level* or *non-unit-level*.

CONCEPT Q&A

One department inspects each product produced. A second department inspects a small sample of each batch of products produced. Which inspection activity is unit-level, and which is non-unit-level?

Answers on pages 711 to 715.

Using only unit-based activity drivers to assign non-unit-related overhead costs can create distorted product costs. The severity of this distortion depends on what proportion of total overhead costs these non-unit-based costs represent. For many companies, this percentage can be significant. This possibility suggests that some care should be exercised in assigning non-unit-based overhead costs. If non-unit-based overhead costs are only a small percentage of total overhead costs, then the distortion of product costs will be quite small. In such a case, using unit-based activity drivers to assign overhead costs is acceptable.

Product Diversity

The presence of significant non-unit overhead costs is a necessary but not sufficient condition for plantwide and departmental rate failure (i.e., distorted costs). For example, if products consume the non-unit-level overhead activities in the same proportion as the unit-level overhead activities, then no product-costing distortion will occur (with the use of traditional overhead assignment methods). The presence of product diversity is also necessary for product cost distortion to occur. **Product diversity** means that products consume overhead activities in systematically different proportions. This may occur for several reasons. For example, differences in product size, product complexity, setup time, and size of batches all can cause products to consume overhead at different rates. Regardless of the nature of the product diversity, product cost will be distorted whenever the quantity of unit-based overhead that a product consumes does not vary in direct proportion to the quantity consumed of non-unit-based overhead. The proportion of each activity consumed by a product is defined as the **consumption ratio**. How non-unit-level overhead costs and product diversity can produce distorted product costs is discussed next.

Illustrating the Failure of Plantwide or Departmental Rates

To illustrate how traditional unit-based overhead rates can distort product costs, consider a Nova Inc. plant that produces two models of washers: a deluxe and a regular model. The

[2] S. Carey, "Balancing Act: Amid JetBlue's rapid ascent, CEO adopts big rivals' traits," *The Wall Street Journal* (August 25, 2005).

Exhibit 7-2

Product-Costing Data

	Activity Usage Measures		
	Deluxe	Regular	Total
Units produced	10	100	110
Prime costs	$800	$8,000	$8,800
Direct labour hours	20	80	100
Machine hours	10	40	50
Setup hours	3	1	4
Number of moves	6	4	10

Activity	Activity Cost Data (Overhead Activities) Activity Cost
Setting up equipment	$1,200
Moving goods	800
Machining	1,500
Assembly	500
Total	$4,000

detailed data are provided in Exhibit 7-2. Because the quantity of regular models produced is 10 times greater than that of the deluxe, we can label the regular model a high-volume product and the deluxe model a low-volume product. The models are produced in batches.

Remember that prime costs represent direct materials and direct labour. Given that these costs are direct in nature, they can be traced to each individual unit produced. It is the indirect, or overhead, costs that typically are treated differently by different types of cost systems. Usually, activity-based cost systems generate more accurate cost data than unit-based cost systems because of their more appropriate treatment of overhead costs. For simplicity, only four types of overhead activities, performed by four distinct support departments, are assumed: setting up the equipment for each batch (different configurations are needed for the electronic components associated with each model), moving a batch, machining, and assembly. Assembly is performed after each department's operations.

Problems with Cost Distortion The activity usage data in Exhibit 7-2 reveal some serious problems with either plantwide or departmental rates for assigning overhead costs. The main problem with either procedure is the assumption that unit-level drivers such as machine hours or direct labour hours drive or cause all overhead costs.

From Exhibit 7-2, it can be seen that regular models, the high-volume product, use four times as many direct labour hours as deluxe models, the low-volume product (80 hours vs. 20 hours). Thus, if a plantwide rate is used, the regular models will be assigned four times more overhead cost than the deluxe models. But is this reasonable? Do unit-based drivers explain the consumption of all overhead activities? In particular, is it reasonable to assume that each product's consumption of overhead increases in direct proportion to the direct labour hours used? Now consider the four overhead activities to see if the unit-level drivers accurately reflect the demands of regular and deluxe model production.

The data in Exhibit 7-2 suggest that a significant portion of overhead costs is not driven or caused by direct labour hours. Each product's demands for setup and material-moving activities are more logically related to the setup hours and the number of moves, respectively. These non-unit activities represent 50 percent ($2,000/$4,000) of the total overhead costs—a significant percentage. Notice that the low-volume

ANALYTICAL Q&A

The activity driver for the receiving activity is number of orders processed. Product A uses 10 orders, and Product B uses 30 orders. Calculate the consumption ratios for Product A and Product B.

Answers on pages 711 to 715.

CORNERSTONE 7-1

The HOW and WHY of Calculating Consumption Ratios

Information:
Activity usage information, Exhibit 7-2.

Required:
Calculate the consumption ratios for each product.

Solution:
First, we must identify the activity driver for each activity. Next, divide the amount of driver used for each product by the total driver quantity. We obtain the following:

	Consumption Ratios		
Overhead Activity	**Deluxe Model**	**Regular Model**	**Activity Driver**
Setting up equipment	0.75[a]	0.25[a]	Setup hours
Moving goods	0.60[b]	0.40[b]	Number of moves
Machining	0.20[c]	0.80[c]	Machine hours
Assembly	0.20[d]	0.80[d]	Direct labour hours

[a] 3/4 (deluxe) and 1/4 (regular).
[b] 6/10 (deluxe) and 4/10 (regular).
[c] 10/50 (deluxe) and 40/50 (regular).
[d] 20/100 (deluxe) and 80/100 (regular).

WHY:
Because different products or services require different amounts of resources to be completed. Therefore one has to calculate the ratios (proportion) of each activity spent on each product/service produced.

product, deluxe models, uses three times more setup hours than the regular models (3/1) and one and a half as many moves (6/4). However, using a plantwide rate based on direct labour hours, a unit-based activity driver assigns four times more setup and material moving costs to the regular models than to the deluxe. Thus, product diversity exists, and we should expect product cost distortion because the quantity of unit-based overhead that each product consumes does not vary in direct proportion to the quantity consumed of non-unit-based overhead.

Cornerstone 7-1 illustrates how to calculate the consumption ratios for the two products. Consumption ratios represent the proportion of each activity consumed by a product. The consumption ratios suggest that a plantwide rate based on direct labour hours will overcost the regular models and undercost the deluxe models.

Solving the Problem of Cost Distortion The cost distortion just described can be solved by the use of activity rates. That is, rather than assigning the overhead costs by using a single, plantwide rate, why not calculate a rate for each overhead activity and then use these activity rates to assign overhead costs? Cornerstone 7-2 shows how to calculate these rates.

To assign overhead costs, the amount of activity consumed by each product is needed along with the activity rates. Cornerstone 7-3 shows how to calculate the unit cost for each product by using activity rates. A visual summary is provided in Exhibit 7-3 (page 305).

ANALYTICAL Q&A

Inspecting provides 4,000 inspection hours and costs $80,000 per year. What is the activity rate for inspecting?

Answers on pages 711 to 715.

Comparison of Functional-Based and Activity-Based Product Costs A plantwide rate based on direct labour hours is calculated by dividing the total overhead costs by the total direct labour hours: $4,000/100 = $40 per direct

The HOW and WHY of Calculating Activity Rates

CORNERSTONE 7-2

Information:
(from Exhibit 7-2)

Activity	Activity Cost ($)	Driver	Driver Quantity
Setting up equipment	1,200	Setup hours	4
Moving goods	800	Number of moves	10
Machining	1,500	Machine hours	50
Assembly	500	Direct labour hours	100

Required:
Calculate activity rates.

Solution:
The rates are obtained by dividing the activity cost by the total driver quantity:

Setup rate:	$1,200/4 setup hours = $300 per setup hour
Materials handling rate:	$800/10 moves = $80 per move
Machining rate:	$1,500/50 machine hours = $30 per machine hour
Assembly rate:	$500/100 direct labour hours = $5 per direct labour hour

WHY:
Because different activities consume organizations' resources at different amounts/rates. It is important to determine the consumption rates for each activity a firm is involved with using different and pertinent drivers for each activity.

labour hour. The product cost for each product using this single unit-level overhead rate is calculated as follows:

	Deluxe	Regular
Prime costs	$ 800	$ 8,000
Overhead costs:		
$40 × 20	800	
$40 × 80		3,200
Total cost	$1,600	$11,200
Units produced	÷ 10	÷ 100
Unit cost	$ 160	$ 112

Now compare these product costs with the activity-based cost of Cornerstone 7-3. This comparison clearly illustrates the effects of using only unit-based activity drivers to assign overhead costs. The activity-based cost assignment reflects the pattern of overhead consumption and is, therefore, the most accurate. Activity-based product costing reveals that functional-based costing undercosts the low-volume deluxe models and overcosts the high-volume regular models. In fact, the ABC assignment increases the reported cost of the deluxe models by $98 per unit and decreases the reported cost of the regular models by almost $10 per unit—a movement in the right direction given the pattern of overhead consumption. In a diverse product environment, activity-based costing promises greater accuracy, and given the importance of making decisions based on accurate facts, a detailed look at activity-based costing is certainly merited.

ANALYTICAL Q&A

Producing 5,000 units of a DVD player requires $150,000 of prime costs, uses 1,000 machine hours, and takes 600 setup hours. The activity rates are $20 per machine hour and $50 per setup hour. What is the unit cost of a DVD player?

Answers on pages 711 to 715.

CORNERSTONE 7-3

The HOW and WHY of Calculating Activity-Based Unit Costs

Information:

	Deluxe	Regular	Activity Rate ($)
Units produced per year	10	100	
Prime costs	$800	$8,000	
Setup hours	3	1	$300
Number of moves	6	4	$ 80
Machine hours	10	40	$ 30
Direct labour hours	20	80	$ 5

Required:

Calculate the unit cost for deluxe and regular models.

Solution:

	Deluxe	Regular
Prime costs	$ 800	$ 8,000
Overhead costs:		
Setups:		
$300 × 3 setup hours	900	
$300 × 1 setup hour		300
Moving materials:		
$80 × 6 moves	480	
$80 × 4 moves		320
Machining:		
$30 × 10 machine hours	300	
$30 × 40 machine hours		1,200
Assembly:		
$5 × 20 direct labour hours	100	
$5 × 80 direct labour hours		400
Total manufacturing costs	$2,580	$10,220
Units produced	÷ 10	÷ 100
Unit cost (Total costs/Units)	$ 258	$102.20

WHY:

Because a firm needs product/service cost per unit information to price inventories, price products competitively, prepare financial statements, and so on. Adding together the cost per unit of each activity and dividing it by the total number of units produced allows us to calculate the per-unit-of-product cost.

ETHICS One of the ethical standards of the Society of Management Accountants requires that its members maintain professional expertise by continually developing knowledge and skills. An interesting issue is whether accounting professionals who resist learning different cost management methods are exhibiting ethical behaviour. At the very least, cost accounting professionals should learn about different approaches and assess whether the benefit-cost trade-offs justify their use.◆

OBJECTIVE 2
Explain how an activity-based costing system works for product costing.

Activity-Based Costing (ABC)

In the past, the vast majority of departments used direct labour hours as the only cost driver for applying costs to products and services. But in modern, highly automated

Exhibit 7-3

Visual Summary of Cornerstones 7-2 and 7-3

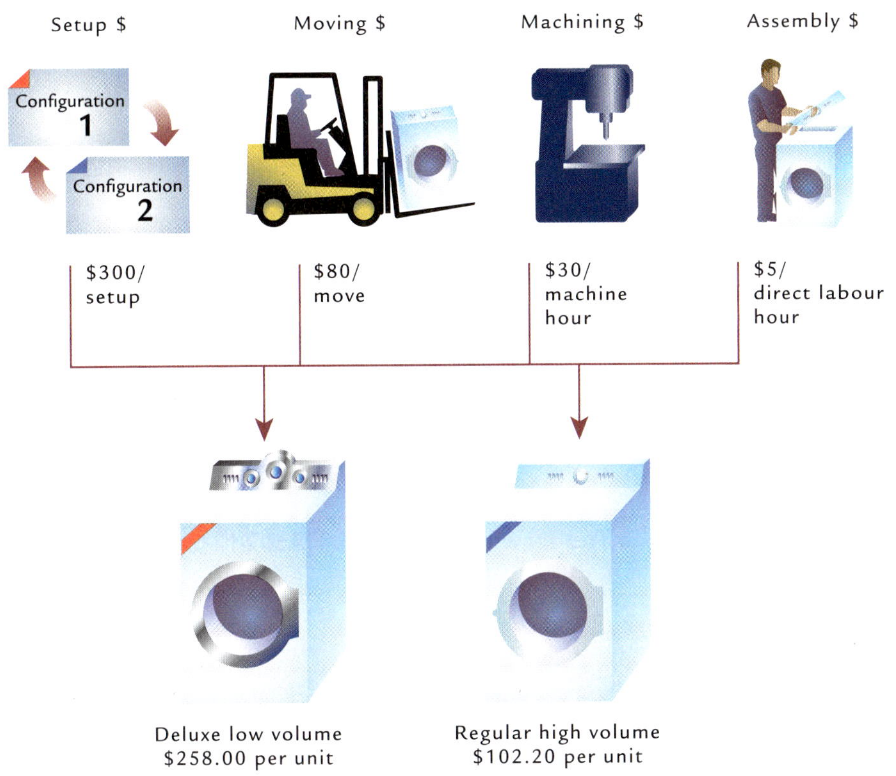

organizations, direct labour hours are not a good measure of the cause of costs. Labour-related costs in an automated system may be only a small percentage of the total costs and often are not related to the causes of most overhead costs. Therefore, many companies are beginning to use machine hours or other cost-allocation bases. Using direct labour hours or cost, or machine hours, as the only cost driver seldom meets the cause/effect criterion desired in cost allocation. However, most managers in modern manufacturing firms and automated service companies believe it is inappropriate to allocate all costs based on measures of volume such as direct labour hours or cost, or machine hours. A single cost driver seldom meets the cause/effect criterion desired in cost allocation. If many costs are caused by non-volume-based cost drivers, activity-based costing (ABC) should be considered.

Activity-based costing (ABC) accumulates overhead costs for each of the organization's activities and then assigns the costs of activities to the products, services, or other cost objects that caused those activities. To establish a cause/effect relationship between an activity and a cost object, cost drivers are identified for each activity. For example

Activity	Cost Driver
Production setup	Number of production runs
Engineering	Number of engineering change orders
Maintenance	Number of machine hours
Power	Number of kilowatt hours
Cleaning	Number of squares metres to be cleaned

Consider the billing department (BD) of a mobile phone company. The BD is engaged in providing account billing, account verification, account inquiries, and e-mail correspondence.

Activity Centre	Cost Driver
Account billing	Number of lines
Account verification	Number of accounts
Account inquiry	Number of labour hours
E-mails	Number of e-mails

Activity-based accounting systems can turn many indirect manufacturing overhead costs into direct costs because each activity cost is caused by its cost drivers, and therefore costs can be traced to those activities (direct costs). Appropriate selection of activities and cost drivers allows managers to trace many manufacturing overhead costs to each activity. Because activity-based accounting systems classify more costs as direct than do traditional systems, managers have greater confidence in the costs of products and services those systems report.

Consider the following visual explanation of activity-based costing, this one for a manufacturing company:

Visual Explanation of a Top-Down Structure and Activity-Based Costing

A. Business Functions

- Research and Development
- Product Design
- Manufacturing
- Marketing
- Distribution

B. Production Departments

The manufacturing function has three departments:

- Machining
- Assembly
- Forging

C. Activities

The assembly department involves four activities:

- Material Handling
- Machine Inserting
- Testing
- Packaging

According to bottom-up activity-based costing:

First, calculate the cost of the activities in the assembly department. To establish a cause/effect relationship between an activity and a cost object, cost drivers are identified for each activity.

Second, repeat the same for the departments of machining and forging. The total cost to manufacture the product is the sum of costs in the three departments.

Third, build in the same fashion (Steps 1 and 2) all the other costs of the other business functions.

Set of Key Questions Interview questions can be used to identify activities and activity attributes needed for costing purposes. The information derived from these questions serves as the basis for constructing an activity dictionary as well as providing data helpful for assigning resource costs to individual activities. The list is not exhaustive but serves to illustrate the nature of the information gathering process.

1. How many employees are in your department? (Activities consume labour.)
2. What do they do (please describe)? (Activities are people doing things for other people.)
3. Do customers outside your department use any equipment? (Activities also can be equipment working for other people. In other words, the equipment provides the service for someone by itself).
4. What resources are used by each activity (equipment, materials, energy)? (Activities consume resources in addition to labour.)
5. What are the outputs of each activity? (Helps to identify activity drivers.)
6. Who or what uses the activity output? (Identifies the cost object: products, other activities, customers, etc.)
7. How much time do workers spend on each activity? Time on each activity by equipment? (Information needed to assign the cost of labour and equipment to activities.)

Activity-based cost assignment consists of the following three steps:

1. *Identify and define activities using interviews and surveys.* Then build a list of activities (i.e., an **activity dictionary**). This dictionary lists **activity attributes**—that is, financial and nonfinancial information that describes the activities. For example:
   - Activity name—usually consists of an action verb and an object.
   - A description of the tasks that make up the activity.
   - Classification as a *primary activity* (activity consumed by a product or customer) or a *secondary activity* (activity consumed by other primary or secondary activities).
   - Activity driver—a measure of activity output.

2. *Assign costs to activities.* Determine the cost of resources (such as materials, labour, and capital) consumed by each activity:
   - If the resource is exclusive to the activity (such as materials), use direct tracing.
   - If the resource is shared by several activities, use drivers to trace and measure the consumption of resources by each activity.
   - The costs of secondary activities are ultimately assigned to primary activities using activity drivers.

3. *Assign costs to products.* After the cost of primary activities is calculated, assign the cost of these activities to products based on usage of the activity as measured by activity drivers. Costs assigned to products are calculated as follows:

   Cost assigned to product = Predetermined activity rate × Actual usage of activity

ABC costing has several shortcomings:

First, ABC does not conform to GAAP. ABC suggests that some nonproduct costs (such as those for R&D) *should* be allocated to products, whereas certain other product costs (such as factory building depreciation) should *not* be allocated to products. Therefore, most companies use ABC for internal reporting but continue to prepare their external financial statements with the more traditional system: job-order or process costing. This dual costing system may incur additional costs.

Second, ABC requires a significant amount of time and, thus, cost to implement. Substantial time is needed to properly identify and analyze the activities taking place, trace costs to those activities, and determine the cost drivers.

Third, substantial support is needed throughout the firm to overcome a variety of barriers: individual (people need to learn new skills), organizational (people resist change), and environmental (regulatory agencies may not accept ABC data). Support for the status quo (i.e., traditional costing systems) may be strong.

Value-Added Activities and Non-Value-Added Activities

All activities require some resource consumption, and resource consumption inevitably drives costs higher. Higher costs cannot always be passed on to customers because most prices are set by the marketplace. This suggests that if prices are fixed, then in order to reduce costs, organizations that want to achieve higher profits have no choice but to reduce or eliminate activities. Well-run organizations try to identify such activities.

A *value-added activity* increases the value of a product or service to a customer and is one for which the customer is willing to pay. Besides improving customer value and enhancing profitability, value-added activities result in more efficient production methods, continuous operating improvements, better operational control, and reduced times for completing the operational cycle.

A *non-value-added activity (NVA)* increases the time and/or cost spent on a product or service, but without increasing its worth. NVA activities may include warehousing materials or components until needed for production and/or hiring employees with the necessary skills to make a product or provide a service. NVAs may be necessary from a business perspective but not from a customer's. Thus, every effort should be made to reduce or eliminate NVA activities in ways that do not affect the value or quality of the product or service.

The most effective way to determine the value provided by an activity is to take a zero-based budgeting perspective—that is, ask *why* the activity is necessary and identify valid business reasons. "Valid" here means that the activity actually adds value.

This approach may result in identifying some activities that are essential to business operations but for which customers are not willing to pay. These activities are indeed NVA. For example, a company must prepare a sales invoice to document a sale. A reasonable customer will understand that this activity must occur, that it adds to the cost of doing business, and that the selling price must cover the costs of this activity. However, because invoice preparation adds no direct value to products and services, customers would rather not pay for this activity.

The actual time it takes to perform all *necessary* functions to manufacture a product or provide a service is referred to as *processing or service time;* this sort of time adds value. Idle time, transfer time, and inspection time are theoretically NVA activities. Storage time and time spent waiting for a production operation to begin are considered NVA *idle time.* The moving of raw material, WIP inventory, and finished goods or components from one place to another constitutes NVA *transfer time.* Performing quality control is NVA *inspection time.*

Although few companies can eliminate NVA completely, managers strive to minimize it. Managers should focus on reducing or eliminating those NVA activities that generate the highest costs and add the least value. This may require a change in management philosophy, physical plant layout, human resource policies, and so on.

The length of time from ordering to selling an item in a retail environment is called *cycle time.* NVA activities in retail include shipping time from the supplier, delays in the receiving department in order to count the merchandise, and any storage time between receipt and sale. In a service company, cycle time refers to the time between service order and service completion. All time spent on activities that do not enhance service performance, such as delays in starting work on service orders, is considered NVA. Just-in-time methods eliminate a significant amount of idle time (especially in storage) and increase manufacturing cycle time. JIT also has a positive impact on engineering, purchasing, receiving, warehousing, accounting, human resources, and marketing.

Constructing a value chart for every product or service could indicate where a company is losing time and money through NVA activities. The costs of such activities can be approximated by estimating storage facility depreciation, property taxes, insurance charges, wages for warehouse employees, and the cost of working capital funds tied up in stored inventory.

NVA activities can be attributed to systemic, physical, and human factors. For example, a *systemic* factor is the need to manufacture products in large batches to minimize setup costs; a *physical* factor is the plant layout, which may not provide the most efficient transfer of products; and a *human* factor is employees who have improper skills or who received inadequate training. Attempts to reduce NVA activities should address all of these causes.

Assigning Costs to Activities

Once activities are identified and described, the next task is to determine how much it costs to perform each activity. This determination requires identification of the resources being consumed by each activity. Some cost system experts consider this task to be the most difficult one in creating an accurate cost system. Activities consume resources such as labour, materials, energy, and capital. The cost of these resources is found in the general ledger, but the money spent on each activity is not revealed. Thus, it becomes necessary to assign the resource costs to activities by using direct and driver tracing. For labour resources, a ***work distribution matrix*** often is used. A work distribution matrix identifies the amount of labour consumed by each activity and is derived from the interview process (or a written survey). Exhibit 7-5 provides an example of a work distribution matrix supplied by the manager of the credit card department for individual activities (refer to Question 7 on page 307).

We know that both direct tracing and driver tracing are used to assign resource costs to activities. For this example, the time spent on each activity is the basis for assigning the labour costs to the activity. If the time is 100 percent, then labour is exclusive to the activity, and the assignment method is direct tracing. If the resource is shared by several activities (as is the case of the clerical resource), then the assignment is driver tracing, and the drivers are called *resource drivers.* **Resource drivers** are factors that measure the consumption of resources by activities. Once resource drivers are identified, then the costs of the resource can be assigned to the activity. Cornerstone 7-4 shows how resource drivers and direct tracing are used to assign labour cost to the credit department activities.

CONCEPT Q&A

How are resource costs assigned to activities?

Answers on pages 711 to 715.

Labour, of course, is not the only resource consumed by activities. Activities also consume materials, capital, and energy. The interview, for example, reveals that the activities within the credit card department use computers (capital), phones (capital), desks (capital), and paper (materials). The automatic teller activity uses the automatic teller (capital) and energy. The cost of these other resources must also be assigned to the various activities. They are assigned in the same way as was described for labour (using direct tracing and resource drivers). The cost of computers could be assigned by using direct tracing (for the supervising activity) and hours of usage for the remaining activities. From the interview, we know the relative usage of computers by each activity. The general ledger reveals that the cost per computer is \$1,200 per year. Thus, an additional \$6,000 (5 × \$1,200) would be assigned to three activities based on relative usage: 70 percent to processing transactions (\$4,200), 20 percent to preparing statements (\$1,200), and 10 percent to answering questions (\$600). Repeating this process for all resources, the total cost of each activity can be calculated. Exhibit 7-6 gives the cost of the activities associated with the credit card department under the assumption that all resource costs have been assigned (these numbers are assumed because all resource data are not given for their calculation).

Exhibit 7-5

Work Distribution Matrix

Activity	Percentage of Time on Each Activity
Processing transactions	40%
Preparing statements	30%
Answering questions	30%

CORNERSTONE 7-4

The HOW and WHY of Assigning Resource Costs to Activities by Using Direct Tracing and Resource Drivers

Information:

Assume that each clerk is paid a salary of $30,000 ($150,000 total clerical cost for five clerks). Refer also to the work distribution matrix of Exhibit 7-5.

Required:

Assign the cost of labour to each of the activities in the credit department.

Solution:

The amount of labour cost assigned to each activity is given below. The percentages come from the work distribution matrix.

Processing transactions	$60,000 (0.4 × $150,000)
Preparing statements	$45,000 (0.3 × $150,000)
Answering questions	$45,000 (0.3 × $150,000)

WHY:

Because costs usually are assigned by financial accounting entries to different categories, such as material and labour costs. Each activity absorbs only a portion of these costs. Under activity-based costing, one has to determine what portion of, say, labour is used by each activity. Thus total labour cost is allocated/prorated to each activity according to how heavily it uses labour resources.

ANALYTICAL Q&A

A company has three inspectors, each earning a salary of $50,000. One inspector works exclusively on inspecting parts received from outside suppliers, while the other two spend 30 percent of their time inspecting parts and 70 percent of their time inspecting final products. How much labour cost should be assigned to the activity of inspecting parts?

Answers on pages 711 to 715.

Assigning Costs to Products

From Cornerstone 7-3, we know that activity costs are assigned to products by multiplying a predetermined activity rate by the usage of the activity, as measured by activity drivers. Exhibit 7-4 identified the activity drivers for each of the four credit card activities: number of transactions for processing transactions, number of statements for preparing statements, number of calls for answering questions, and number of teller transactions for the activity of providing automatic tellers. To calculate an activity rate, the practical capacity of each activity must be determined. To assign costs, the amount of each activity consumed by each product must also be known. Assuming that the practical activity capacity is equal to the total activity usage by all products, the following actual data have been collected for the credit card example:

Exhibit 7-6

Activity Costs, First Stage: Credit Card Department

Processing transactions	$130,000
Preparing statements	102,000
Answering questions	92,400
Providing automatic tellers	250,000

Exhibit 7-7

Assigning Costs: Final Stage

	Classic	Gold	Platinum
Processing transactions:			
$0.13 × 600,000	$ 78,000		
$0.13 × 300,000		$ 39,000	
$0.13 × 100,000			$ 13,000
Preparing statements:			
$0.85 × 60,000	51,000		
$0.85 × 36,000		30,600	
$0.85 × 24,000			20,400
Answering questions:			
$3.08 × 10,000	30,800		
$3.08 × 12,000		36,960	
$3.08 × 8,000			24,640
Providing automatic tellers:			
$1.25 × 15,000	18,750		
$1.25 × 3,000		3,750	
$1.25 × 2,000			2,500
Total costs	$ 178,550	$ 110,310	$ 60,540
Units	÷ 5,000	÷ 3,000	÷ 2,000
Unit cost	$ 35.71	$ 36.77	$ 30.27

	Classic Card	Gold Card	Platinum Card	Total
Number of cards	5,000	3,000	2,000	10,000
Transactions processed	600,000	300,000	100,000	1,000,000
Number of statements	60,000	36,000	24,000	120,000
Number of calls	10,000	12,000	8,000	30,000
Number of teller transactions*	15,000	3,000	2,000	20,000

* The number of teller transactions for the cards is 10 percent of the total transactions from all sources. Thus, teller transactions total 20,000 (0.10 × 200,000).

Applying Cornerstone 7-2 by using the data and costs from Exhibit 7-6, the activity rates are calculated as follows:

Rate calculations:

Processing transactions:	$130,000/1,000,000 = $0.13 per transaction
Preparing statements:	$102,000/120,000 = $0.85 per statement
Answering questions:	$92,400/30,000 = $3.08 per call
Providing automatic tellers:	$250,000/200,000 = $1.25 per transaction

These rates provide the cost of each activity usage. Using these rates, costs are assigned as shown in Exhibit 7-7. Also, we now know the whole story behind the development of the activity rates and usage measures. Furthermore, the banking setting emphasizes the utility of ABC in service organizations.

Activity-Based Customer Costing and Activity-Based Supplier Costing

OBJECTIVE 3
Describe activity-based customer costing and activity-based supplier costing.

ABC systems originally became popular for their ability to improve product-costing accuracy by tracing activity costs to the products that consume the activities. However, since the beginning of the 21st century, the use of ABC has expanded into areas upstream (i.e., before the production section of the value chain—research and development, prototyping, etc.) and downstream (i.e., after the production section of the value chain—marketing, distribution, customer service, etc.) from production.

Exhibit 7-8

The Whale Curve of Cumulative Customer Profitability

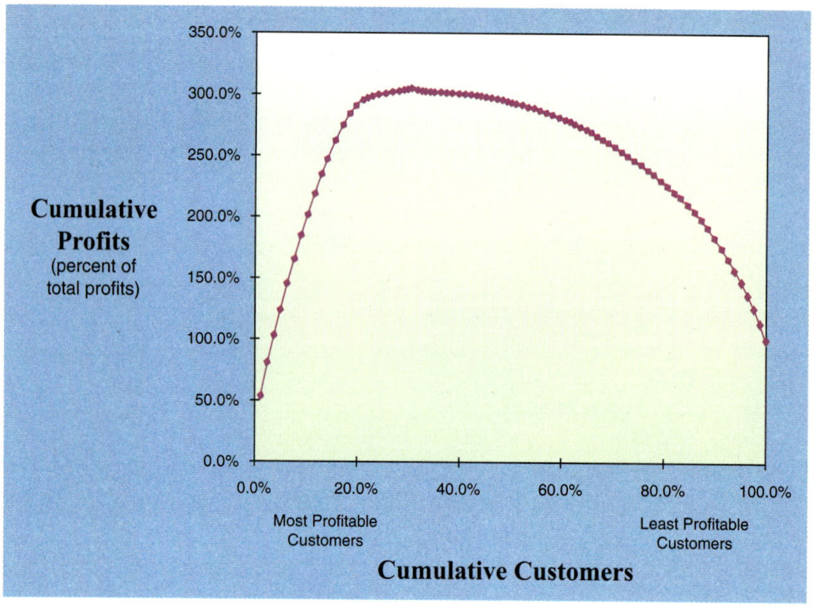

Specifically, ABC often is used to more accurately determine the upstream costs of suppliers and the downstream costs of customers. Knowing the costs of suppliers and customers can be vital information for improving a company's profitability.

LSI Logic, a high-tech producer of semiconductors, implemented ABC customer costing and discovered that 10 percent of its customers were responsible for about 90 percent of its profits. LSI also discovered that it was actually losing money on about 50 percent of its customers. It worked to convert its unprofitable customers into profitable ones and invited those who would not provide a fair return to take their business elsewhere. As a consequence, LSI's sales decreased, but its profit tripled.[3] Exhibit 7-8 depicts this interesting yet common relationship between customers and their contributions to company profitability. Some managers refer to this graph as the "whale curve" of customer profitability, likely because of its resemblance to the shape of a whale cresting at the water's surface. The important observation from the curve is that the customers to the left of the hump, or peak, increase the company's profitability, while the customers to the right decrease the company's profitability. Therefore, activity-based customer costing is helpful in determining where each customer falls on the curve and, subsequently, how each customer should therefore be treated given its position on the curve. Of particular interest are those customers to the far right because they severely decrease the company's profitability and need either to be terminated as unacceptably bad customers or altered in some way so as to become profitable customers for the company.

Activity-Based Customer Costing

Customers are cost objects of fundamental interest. As the LSI Logic experience illustrates, customer management can produce significant gains in profit. It is possible to have customer diversity, just as it is possible to have product diversity. Customers can consume customer-driven activities in different proportions. Sources of customer diversity include order frequency, delivery frequency, geographic distance, sales and promotional support, and engineering support requirements. Knowing how much it costs to service different customers can be vital information for such purposes as setting pricing, determining customer mix, and improving profitability. Furthermore,

[3]Gary Cokins, "Are All of Your Customers Profitable (To You)?" (June 14, 2001): http://www.bettermanagment.com/Library (accessed January 2004).

because of diversity of customers, multiple drivers are needed to trace costs accurately. This outcome means that ABC can be useful to organizations that may have only one product, homogeneous products, or a just-in-time (JIT) structure where direct tracing diminishes the value of ABC for product costing.

Customer Costing versus Product Costing Assigning the costs of customer service to customers is done in the same way that manufacturing costs are assigned to products. Customer-driven activities such as order entry, order picking, shipping, making sales calls, and evaluating a client's credit are identified and listed in an activity dictionary. The cost of the resources consumed is assigned to activities, and the cost of the activities is assigned to individual customers. The same model and procedures that apply to products apply to customers as well. Cornerstone 7-5 illustrates how ABC assigns costs to customers.

The activity-based cost assignments reveal a much different picture of the cost of servicing each type of customer. The smaller customer is costing more, attributable to smaller, more frequent orders and the evident need for the sales force to engage in more negotiations to make a sale.

What does this analysis tell management that it didn't know before? First, the large customer costs much less to service than the smaller customers and perhaps should be charged less. Second, it raises some significant questions relative to the smaller customers. For example, is it possible to encourage larger, less frequent orders? Perhaps offering discounts for larger orders would be appropriate. Why is it more difficult to sell to the smaller customers? Why are more calls needed? Are they less informed than the larger customer about the products? Can we improve profits by influencing our customers to change their buying behaviour?

CONCEPT Q&A

How are costs assigned to customers by using the ABC approach?

Answers on pages 711 to 715.

Activity-Based Supplier Costing

ABC can also help a manager to identify the true cost of a firm's suppliers. The cost of a supplier is much more than the purchase price of the components or materials acquired. Just like customers, suppliers can affect many internal activities of a firm and significantly increase the cost of purchasing. A more correct view is one where the costs associated with quality, reliability, and late deliveries are added to the purchase costs. Managers are then required to evaluate suppliers based on total cost, not just purchase price. ABC is the key to tracing costs relating to purchase, quality, reliability, and delivery performance to suppliers.

Supplier Costing Methodology Assigning the costs of supplier-related activities to suppliers follows the same pattern as ABC product and customer costing. Supplier-driven activities such as purchasing, receiving, inspection of incoming components, reworking products (because of defective components), expediting products (because of late deliveries of suppliers), and warranty work (due to defective supplier components) are identified and listed in an activity dictionary. The cost of the resources consumed is assigned to these activities, and the cost of the activities is assigned to individual suppliers. Cornerstone 7-6 illustrates how to use ABC for supplier costing.

The example in Cornerstone 7-6 shows that Murray, the "low-cost" supplier (as measured by the purchase price of the two parts), actually costs more when the supplier-related activities of repairing and expediting are considered. If all costs are considered, then the choice becomes clear: Plata Associates is the better supplier with a higher-quality product, more on-time deliveries, and, consequently, a lower overall cost per unit.

CONCEPT Q&A

How are costs assigned to suppliers by using the ABC approach?

Answers on pages 711 to 715.

Process-Value Analysis

OBJECTIVE 4
Explain how activity-based management can be used for cost reduction.

Process-value analysis is fundamental to **activity-based management**. It focuses on cost reduction instead of cost assignment and emphasizes the maximization of

CORNERSTONE 7-5

The HOW and WHY of Calculating Activity-Based Customer Costs

Information:

Milan Company produces precision parts for 11 major buyers. Of the 11 customers, one accounts for 50 percent of the sales, with the remaining 10 accounting for the rest of the sales. The 10 smaller customers purchase parts in roughly equal quantities. Orders placed by the smaller customers are about the same size. Data concerning Milan's customer activity follow:

	Large Customer	Ten Smaller Customers
Units purchased	500,000	500,000
Orders placed	2	200
Number of sales calls	10	210
Manufacturing costs	\$3,000,000	\$3,000,000
Order filling costs allocated*	\$202,000	\$202,000
Sales force costs allocated*	\$110,000	\$110,000

* Allocated based on sales volume.

Currently, customer-driven costs are assigned to customers based on units sold, a unit-level driver.

Required:

Assign costs to customers by using an ABC approach.

Solution:

The appropriate drivers are orders placed and number of sales calls. The activity rates are:

\$404,000/202 orders = \$2,000 per order
\$220,000/220 calls = \$1,000 per call

Using this information, the customer-driven costs can be assigned to each group of customers as follows:

	Large Customer	Ten Smaller Customers
Order filling costs:		
(\$2,000 × 2)	\$ 4,000	
(\$2,000 × 200)		\$400,000
Sales force costs:		
(\$1,000 × 10)	10,000	
(\$1,000 × 210)		210,000
	\$14,000	\$610,000

WHY:

Because a typical firm has many customers. Some purchase a lot of the firm's products, and some a little; some place orders frequently, some not; some buy at large quantities, some in small quantities. Clearly, the cost per client is different, driven by the frequency and size of orders as well as by demands for service. This suggests different corresponding order-filling costs. So it is wise to know the cost of doing business with each of the firm's customers.

systemwide performance. As the model in Exhibit 7-9 illustrates, process-value analysis is concerned with (1) *driver analysis,* (2) *activity analysis,* and (3) *performance measurement.*

The HOW and WHY of Calculating Activity-Based Supplier Costs

CORNERSTONE 7-6

Information:

Assume that a purchasing manager uses two suppliers, Murray Inc. and Plata Associates, as the source of two machine parts: Part A1 and Part B2. Consider two activities: repairing products (under warranty) and expediting products. Repairing products occurs because of part failure (bought from suppliers). Expediting products occurs because suppliers are late in delivering needed parts. Activity cost information and other data needed for supplier costing follow:

I. Activity Costs Caused by Suppliers (e.g., failed parts or late delivery)

Activity	Costs ($)
Repairing products	800,000
Expediting products	200,000

II. Supplier Data

	Murray Inc.		Plata Associates	
	Part A1	Part B2	Part A1	Part B2
Unit purchase price	$20	$52	$24	$56
Units purchased	80,000	40,000	10,000	10,000
Failed units	1,600	380	10	10
Late shipments	60	40	0	0

Required:

Determine the cost of each supplier by using ABC.

Solution:

Using the above data, the activity rates for assigning costs to suppliers are computed as follows:

$$\text{Repair rate} = \$800,000/2,000^{*}$$
$$= \$400 \text{ per failed part}$$

*(1,600 + 380 + 10 + 10)

$$\text{Expediting rate} = \$200,000/100^{**}$$
$$= \$2,000 \text{ per late delivery}$$

**(60 + 40)

Using these rates and the activity data, the total purchasing cost per unit of each component is computed:

	Murray Inc.		Plata Associates	
	Part A1	Part B2	Part A1	Part B2
Purchase cost:				
$20 × 80,000	$1,600,000			
$52 × 40,000		$2,080,000		
$24 × 10,000			$240,000	
$56 × 10,000				$560,000

	Murray Inc.		Plata Associates	
	Part A1	Part B2	Part A1	Part B2
Repairing products:				
$400 × 1,600	640,000			
$400 × 380		152,000		
$400 × 10			4,000	
$400 × 10				4,000
Expediting products:				
$2,000 × 60	120,000			
$2,000 × 40		80,000		
Total costs	$2,360,000	$2,312,000	$ 244,000	$ 564,000
Units	÷ 80,000	÷ 40,000	÷ 10,000	÷ 10,000
Total unit cost	$ 29.50	$ 57.80	$ 24.40	$ 56.40

WHY:

Because not all suppliers are made equal. Some are more reliable than others, delivering orders when they promise (JIT delivery); others do so with undesirable delays. Such delays often necessitate extra expediting costs (e.g., expensive overnight delivery, extra shifts to complete work on time). Similarly, some suppliers produce higher quality products that result in fewer repairing costs under warranty. It is sensible, then, for an organization to know the costs per unit for expediting production and repairing defective units. The lowest cost per unit of such "failures" for each supplier suggests the most reliable supplier.

Driver Analysis: The Search for Root Causes

Managing activities requires an understanding of what causes activity costs. Every activity has inputs and outputs. **Activity inputs** are the resources consumed by the activity in producing its output. **Activity output** is the result or product of an activity. For example, if the activity is moving materials, the inputs would be such things as a forklift, a forklift driver, fuel (for the forklift), and crates. The output would be moved goods and materials. An **activity output measure** is the number of times the activity is performed. It is the quantifiable measure of the output. For example, the number of moves or distance moved are possible output measures for the material moving activity.

The output measure effectively is a measure of the demands placed on an activity and is what we have been calling an *activity driver*. As the demands for an activity change, the cost of the activity can change. For example, as the number of programs written increases, the activity of writing programs may need to consume more inputs (labour, disks, paper, and so on). However, output measures, such as the number of programs, may not (and usually do not) correspond to the root causes of activity costs; rather, they are the consequences of the activity being performed. The purpose of driver analysis is to reveal root causes. Thus, **driver analysis** is the effort expended to identify those factors that are the root causes of activity costs. For example, an analysis may reveal that the root cause of the cost of moving materials is plant layout.

Exhibit 7-9

Process-Value Analysis Model

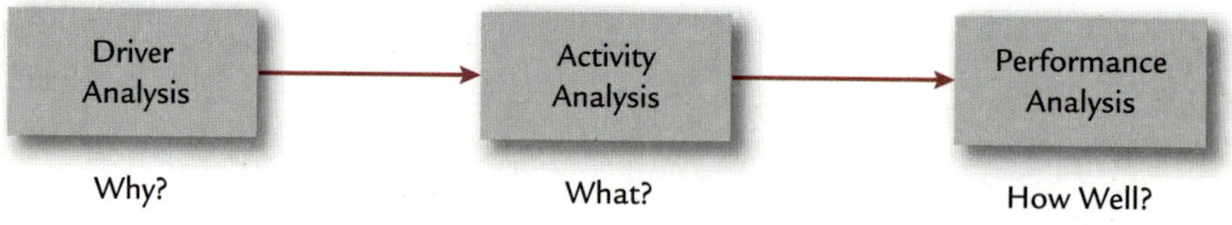

Once the root cause is known, then action can be taken to improve the activity. Specifically, reorganizing plant layout can reduce the cost of moving materials.

Often, the root cause of the cost of an activity is also the root cause of other related activities. For example, the costs of inspecting purchased parts and reordering may both be caused by poor supplier quality. By working with suppliers to reduce the number of defective components supplied (or choosing suppliers that have fewer defects), the demand for both activities may then decrease, allowing the company to save money.

Activity Analysis: Identifying and Assessing Value Content

The heart of process-value analysis is activity analysis. **Activity analysis** is the process of identifying, describing, and evaluating the activities that an organization performs. Activity analysis should produce four outcomes: (1) what activities are done; (2) how many people perform the activities; (3) the time and resources required to perform the activities; and (4) an assessment of the value of the activities to the organization, including a recommendation to select and keep only those that add value. Steps 1 through 3 have been described earlier and are common to the information needed for determining and assigning activity costs. Knowing how much an activity costs is clearly an important part of activity-based management. Step 4, determining the value-added content of activities, is concerned with cost reduction rather than cost assignment. Thus, some managerial accountants feel that this is the most important part of activity analysis. Activities can be classified as *value-added* or *non-value-added.*

CONCEPT Q&A

What is the purpose of driver analysis?

Answers on pages 711 to 715.

Value-Added Activities

Those activities necessary to remain in business are called **value-added activities**. Some activities—required activities—are necessary to comply with legal mandates. Activities needed to comply with the reporting requirements of the Ontario Securities Commission and the filing requirements of the Canada Revenue Agency are examples. These activities are value-added by *mandate*. The remaining activities in the firm are *discretionary.* A discretionary activity is classified as value-added provided it simultaneously satisfies three conditions: (1) the activity produces a change of state, (2) the change of state was not achievable by preceding activities, and (3) the activity enables other activities to be performed.

For example, consider the production of rods used in hydraulic cylinders. The first activity, cutting rods, cuts long rods into the correct lengths for the cylinders. Next, the cut rods are welded to cut plates. The cutting rod activity is value-added because (1) it causes a change of state—uncut rods become cut rods, (2) no prior activity was supposed to create this change of state, and (3) it enables the welding activity to be performed. Though the value-added properties are easy to see for an operational activity like cutting rods, what about a more general activity like supervising production workers? A managerial activity is specifically designed to manage other value-added activities—to ensure that they are performed in an efficient and timely manner. Supervision certainly satisfies the enabling condition. Is there a change in state? There are two ways of answering in the affirmative. First, supervising can be viewed as an enabling resource that is consumed by the operational activities that do produce a change of state. Thus, supervising is a secondary activity that serves as an input that is needed to help bring about the change of state expected for value-added primary activities. Second, it could be argued that the supervision brings order by changing the state from uncoordinated activities to coordinated activities. Once value-added activities are identified, we can define value-added costs. **Value-added costs** are the costs to perform value-added activities with perfect efficiency.

CONCEPT Q&A

What is a value-added activity?

Answers on pages 711 to 715.

Non-Value-Added Activities

All activities other than those that are absolutely essential to remain in business, are referred to as **non-value-added activities**. A non-value-added activity can be identified by its failure to satisfy any one of the three previous defining conditions. Violation of the first two is the usual case for non-value-added activities. Inspecting cut rods (for correct length), for example, is a non-value-added activity. Inspection is a state-detection activity, not a state-changing activity (it tells us the state of the cut rod—whether it is the right length or not). Thus, it fails the first condition. Consider the activity of reworking goods or subassemblies. Rework is designed to bring a good from a nonconforming state to a conforming state. Thus, a change of state occurs. Yet the activity is non-value-added because it repeats work; it is doing something that should have been done by preceding activities (Condition 2 is violated).

CONCEPT Q&A

How can a value-added activity have non-value-added costs?

Answers on pages 711 to 715.

Non-value-added costs are costs that are caused either by non-value-added activities or by the inefficient performance of valued-added activities. For non-value-added activities, the non-value-added cost is the cost of the activity itself. For inefficient value-added activities, the activity cost must be broken into its value-added and non-value-added components. For example, if Receiving should use 10,000 receiving orders but uses 20,000, then half the cost of Receiving is value-added and half is non-value-added. The value-added component is the waste-free component of the value-added activity and is, therefore, the *value-added standard*. Due to increased competition, many firms are attempting to eliminate non-value-added activities because they add unnecessary cost and impede performance; firms are also striving to optimize value-added activities. Thus, activity analysis identifies and eventually eliminates all unnecessary activities and, simultaneously, increases the efficiency of necessary activities.

The theme of activity analysis is waste elimination. As waste is eliminated, costs are reduced. The cost reduction *follows* the elimination of waste. Note the value of managing the causes of the costs rather than the costs themselves. Though managing costs may increase the efficiency of an activity, if the activity is unnecessary, what does it matter if it's performed efficiently? An unnecessary activity is wasteful and should be eliminated. For example, moving raw materials and partially finished goods is often cited as a non-value-added activity. Installing an automated materials handling system may increase the efficiency of this activity, but changing to cellular manufacturing with on-site, just-in-time delivery of raw materials could virtually eliminate the activity. It's easy to see which is preferable.

Examples of Non-Value-Added Activities

Reordering parts, expediting production, and rework because of defective parts are all examples of non-value-added activities. Other examples include warranty work, handling customer complaints, and reporting defects. Non-value-added activities can exist anywhere in the organization. In the manufacturing operation, five major activities are often cited as wasteful and unnecessary:

1. *Scheduling*. An activity that uses time and resources to determine when different products have access to processes (or when and how many setups must be done) and how much will be produced.
2. *Moving*. An activity that uses time and resources to move raw materials, work in process, and finished goods from one department to another.
3. *Waiting*. An activity in which raw materials or work in process use time and resources by waiting on the next process.
4. *Inspecting*. An activity in which time and resources are spent ensuring that the product meets specifications.
5. *Storing*. An activity that uses time and resources while a good or raw material is held in inventory.

None of these activities adds any value for the customer. (Note that inspection would not be necessary if the product were produced correctly the first time and, therefore, adds no value for the customer.) The challenge of activity analysis is to find ways to produce the good without using any of these activities.

Cost Reduction

Activity management carries with it the objective of cost reduction. Competitive conditions dictate that companies must deliver customer-desired products on time and at the lowest possible cost. These conditions mean that an organization must continually strive for cost improvement. Activity management can reduce costs in four ways:[4]

1. Activity elimination
2. Activity selection
3. Activity reduction
4. Activity sharing

Activity elimination focuses on non-value-added activities. Once activities that fail to add value are identified, measures must be taken to rid the organization of these activities. For example, the activity of inspecting incoming parts seems necessary to ensure that the product using the parts functions according to specifications. Use of a bad part can produce a bad final product. Yet this activity is necessary only because of the poor quality performance of the supplying firms. Selecting suppliers who are able to supply high-quality parts or who are willing to improve their quality performance to achieve this objective will eventually allow the elimination of incoming inspection. Cost reduction then follows.

Activity selection involves choosing among different sets of activities that are caused by competing strategies. Different strategies cause different activities. Different product design strategies, for example, can require significantly different activities. Activities, in turn, cause costs. Each product design strategy has its own set of activities and associated costs. All other things being equal, the lowest-cost design strategy should be chosen. In a continual improvement environment, redesign of existing products and processes can lead to a different, cheaper set of activities. Thus activity selection can have a significant effect on cost reduction.

Activity reduction decreases the time and resources required by an activity. This approach to cost reduction should be primarily aimed at improving the efficiency of necessary activities or a short-term strategy for improving non-value-added activities until they can be eliminated. Setup activity is a necessary activity that is often cited as an example for which less time and fewer resources need to be used. Finding ways to reduce setup time—and thus lower the cost of setups—is another example of the concept of gradual reductions in activity costs.

Activity sharing increases the efficiency of necessary activities by using economies of scale. Specifically, the quantity of the cost driver is increased without increasing the total cost of the activity itself. This lowers the per-unit cost of the cost driver and the amount of cost traceable to the products that consume the activity. For example, a new product can be designed to use components already being used by other products. By using existing components, the activities associated with these components already exist, and the company avoids the creation of a whole new set of activities.

Cornerstone 7-7 shows how to determine the non-value-added cost of activities. Determining the cost is followed by a root-cause analysis and then by the selection of an approach to reduce the waste found in the activity. For example, defective products cause warranty work. Defective products, in turn, are caused by such factors as defective internal processes, poor product design, and defective supplier components. Correcting the causes will lead to the elimination of the warranty activity. Inefficient purchasing could be attributable to such root causes as poor product design (too many components), orders that are incorrectly filled out, and defective supplier components (producing additional orders). Correcting the causes will reduce the demand for the purchasing activity, and as the activity is reduced, cost reduction will follow.

Reasons for Adopting ABC Costing

Because activity-based accounting systems are more complex and costly than traditional systems, not all companies use them. However, more and more organizations in both manufacturing and nonmanufacturing industries are adopting activity-based systems for a variety of reasons:

[4] Peter B. B. Turney, "How Activity-Based Costing Helps Reduce Cost," *Journal of Cost Management* (Winter 1991): 29–35.

CORNERSTONE 7-7

The HOW and WHY of Assessing Non-Value-Added Costs

Information:

Consider the following two activities: (1) Performing warranty work, cost: \$120,000. The warranty cost of the most efficient competitor is \$20,000. (2) Purchasing components, cost: \$200,000 (10,000 purchase orders). A benchmarking study reveals that the most efficient level will use 5,000 purchase orders and entail a cost of \$110,000.

Required:

Determine the non-value-added cost of each activity.

Solution:

Determine the value content of each activity: Is the activity non-value-added or value-added? Performing warranty work is non-value-added; it is done to correct something that wasn't done right the first time. Thus, the non-value-added cost of performing warranty work is \$120,000. The cost of the competitor is also non-value-added and has no bearing on the analysis. Root causes for warranty work are defective products. Purchasing components is necessary so that materials are available to produce products and, thus, is value-added. However, the activity is not performed efficiently, as revealed by the benchmarking study. The non-value-added cost is \$90,000 (\$200,000 − \$110,000).

WHY:

Because a firm engages in value-added and non-value-added activities. For example, inspection to determine whether products are produced to specifications and rework costs to bring defective products to established specifications are considered non-value-added costs. The idea is that all those costs can be avoided if things are done right in the first place, without the need for inspection or rework. So assessing the non-value-added costs is important, as they eat way an organization's profits and may in the long run render the firm uncompetitive.

- Fierce global competition has resulted in shrinking profit margins. Companies may know their overall margin, but they often do not trust the accuracy of the margins for *individual* products or services. ABC costing better allows firms to trace the profitability for each product or service.
- There is wide diversity in the types of products and services, in customer classes, and in consumption of resources consumed by each product. ABC costing allows for better tracking of consumption of a company's shared resources among different products and customers.
- Indirect costs are far more important in today's modern business world, sometimes surpassing 50 percent of total cost. This promotes ABC costing, which turns indirect overhead costs into direct costs.
- Computer technology has reduced the costs of developing and operating cost systems. This allows for tracking many activities and their costs.

Is ABC Costing Suitable for Your Company?

Direct labour hours or direct machine hours used in calculating plantwide overheard rates or departmental overhead rates provide inadequate cost information. A great deal of valuable information can be lost when activity and cost relationships are not considered. But does this mean that ABC is suitable for your organization? Some questions that companies must consider before adopting ABC include the following:

- Are the costs in each cost pool driven by and proportional to the company's activities?
- Are diverse products and/or services being produced?

- Do different products or services use different degrees of support services?
- Do some products or services generate substantially higher overhead costs than others? (e.g., do some require more advertising than others?)

One way or another, all organizations strive to eliminate non-value-added activities. Activity-based costing promotes understanding of cost drivers and identifies non-value-added activities; in this sense, continuous improvement and ABC costing go hand in hand.

Activity Performance Measurement

Assessing how well activities (and processes) are performed is fundamental to management's efforts to improve profitability. Activity performance measures exist in both financial and nonfinancial forms. These measures are designed to assess how well an activity was performed and the results achieved. They are also designed to reveal if constant improvement is being realized. Measures of activity performance centre on three major dimensions: (1) efficiency, (2) quality, and (3) time.

Efficiency focuses on the relationship of activity inputs to activity outputs. For example, one way to improve activity efficiency is to produce the same activity output with lower cost for the inputs used. Thus cost and trends in cost become important measures of efficiency. *Quality* is concerned with doing the activity right the first time it is performed. If the activity output is defective, then the activity may need to be repeated, causing unnecessary cost and reduction in efficiency. Quality cost management is a major topical area and is discussed in more detail later in this chapter. The *time* required to perform an activity is also critical. Longer times usually mean more resource consumption and less ability to respond to customer demands. Time measures of performance tend to be nonfinancial, whereas efficiency and quality measures are both financial and nonfinancial.

Cycle time and *velocity* are two operational measures of time-based performance. Cycle time can be applied to any activity or process that produces an output, and it measures how long it takes to produce an output from start to finish. Consider the manufacturing process. In this case, **cycle time** is the length of time that it takes to produce a unit of output from the time raw materials are received (starting point of the cycle) until the good is delivered to finished goods inventory (finishing point of the cycle). Thus, cycle time is the time required to produce one unit of a product (time/units produced). **Velocity** is the number of units of output that can be produced in a given period of time (units produced/time). Notice that velocity is the reciprocal of cycle time. For the cycle time example, the velocity is two units per hour. Cornerstone 7-8 demonstrates how to compute cycle time and velocity.

CONCEPT Q&A

What are the three dimensions of performance for activities? Explain why they are important.

Answers on pages 711 to 715.

Quality Cost Management

Activity-based management also is useful for understanding how quality costs can be managed. Quality costs can be substantial *in size* and a source of significant savings *if managed effectively.* Improving quality can produce significant improvements in profitability and overall efficiency. Quality improvement can increase profitability in two ways: (1) by increasing customer demand *and thus sales revenues* and (2) by decreasing costs. For example, when Toyota sold more cars and trucks than General Motors for the first time ever in 2007, some automotive industry experts attributed this crowning achievement to Toyota's long-time commitment to quality-related issues, such as quality cost management.[5]

Quality-linked activities are those activities performed because poor quality may or does exist. The costs of performing these activities are referred to as **costs of quality**. Thus, the costs of quality are associated with two subcategories of quality-related

[5] D. Jones, "Toyota's success pleases proponents of 'lean'," *USA Today* (May 3, 2007): 2B.

CORNERSTONE 7-8

The HOW and WHY of Calculating Cycle Time and Velocity

Information:
Assume that a company takes 10,000 hours to produce 20,000 units of a product.

Required:
What is the velocity in hours? Cycle time in hours? Cycle time in minutes?

Solution:
Velocity = 20,000/10,000 = 2 units per hour;
Cycle time = 10,000/20,000 = 1/2 hour.
= 10,000(60 minutes)/20,000 = 30 minutes.

WHY:
Because time is money. In managerial accounting, we assign value to time by calculating how long it takes to produce a product or deliver a service; the shorter the better. Given the time constraints of a firm (e.g., eight hours per shift), one can calculate how many units can be produced given the capacity per hour. In addition, it can be calculated how long it takes (cycle time) from the beginning to the end to complete a product.

activities: *control activities* and *failure activities.* **Control activities** are performed by an organization to prevent or detect poor quality (because poor quality may exist). **Control costs** are the costs of performing control activities. Control activities are made up of prevention and appraisal activities.

Prevention costs are incurred to prevent poor quality in the products or services being produced. As prevention costs increase, we would expect the costs of failure to decrease. Examples of prevention costs are quality engineering, quality training programs, quality planning, quality reporting, supplier evaluation and selection, quality audits, quality circles, field trials, and design reviews.

Appraisal costs are incurred to determine whether products and services are conforming to their requirements or customer needs. Examples include inspecting and testing raw materials, packaging inspection, supervising appraisal activities, product acceptance, process acceptance, measurement (inspection and test) equipment, and outside endorsements. The main objective of the appraisal function is to prevent nonconforming goods from being shipped to customers.

Failure activities are performed by an organization or its customers in response to poor quality (poor quality does exist). **Failure costs** are the costs incurred by an organization because failure activities are performed. Notice that the definitions of *failure activities* and *failure costs* imply that customer response to poor quality can impose costs on an organization. The definitions of *quality-related activities* also imply four categories of quality costs: (1) prevention costs, (2) appraisal costs, (3) internal failure costs, and (4) external failure costs.

Internal failure costs are incurred when products and services do not conform to specifications or customer needs. This nonconformance is detected *before* the bad products or services (nonconforming, unreliable, not durable, and so on) are shipped or delivered to outside parties. These are the failures detected by appraisal activities. Examples of internal failure costs are scrap, rework, downtime (due to defects), reinspection, retesting, and design changes. These costs disappear if no defects exist.

External failure costs are incurred when products and services fail to conform to requirements or satisfy customer needs *after* being delivered to customers. Of all the costs of quality, this category can be the most devastating. For example, costs of recalls can run into the hundreds of millions of dollars. Other examples include lost sales because of poor product performance, returns and allowances because of poor quality, warranties, repairs, product liability, customer dissatisfaction, lost market share, and complaint adjustment.

Just-in-Time (JIT) Systems

Attempts to minimize non-value-added costs have led many organizations to adopt just-in-time systems to eliminate waste and improve quality. In a *just-in-time (JIT) production system*, an organization purchases materials and parts and produces components just when they are needed in the production process. Goods are not produced until it is time for them to be shipped to a customer. The goal is to have zero inventories, because holding inventory is a non-value-added activity. Customer orders drive the production process. An order triggers the immediate delivery of materials, followed by production and delivery of the goods. Instead of producing inventory and hoping orders will come, a JIT system produces products directly for received orders. JIT systems emphasize *total quality control (TQC)* and *continuous improvement in quality*. If all employees strive for zero defects, non-value-added activities such as inspection and rework of defective items are minimized. This shortens production *cycle time* (the time from initiating production to delivery of goods to the customer). Keeping production cycle times short allows timely response to customer orders and reduces the level of inventories. Fluctuations in production rates inevitably lead to delays in delivery to customers and excess inventories. To achieve smooth production flow, JIT companies simplify the production process with the goal of reducing the possibilities of delay. They also develop close relations with suppliers to ensure timely delivery and high quality of purchased materials, and they perform routine maintenance on equipment to prevent costly breakdowns.

Many companies help achieve these objectives by improving the physical layout of their plants. In conventional manufacturing, similar machines (lathes, moulding machines, drilling machines, etc.) are grouped together. Workers specialize on only one machine operation. There are at least two negative effects of such a layout. First, products must be moved from one area of the plant to another for required processing. This increases material handling costs and results in work-in-process inventories that can be substantial. This is a non-value-added activity that increases costs. Second, the specialized labour resource is often idle while it waits for work in process. This wasted resource—idle labour time—is also non-value-added. Work-in-process inventories are reduced or eliminated with JIT because there is no need to move and store inventory. Idle time is also reduced or eliminated because workers are capable of moving from idle machine activities to needed activities. As a result, production cycle times are reduced.

Environmental Cost Management

For many organizations, management of environmental costs is becoming a matter of high priority and a significant competitive issue. Many executives now believe that improving environmental quality may actually reduce environmental costs rather than increase them. For example, between 1992 and 1999, **Baxter International Inc.**, a producer of medical products, reduced toxic wastes emitted to air, water, and soil; increased recycling activity; and, as a consequence, reported environmental savings for the seven-year period of $98 million.[6]

Before environmental cost information can be provided to management, environmental costs must be defined. Various possibilities exist; however, an appealing approach is to adopt a definition consistent with a total environmental quality model. Accordingly, environmental costs can be referred to as *environmental quality costs*. Similar to product quality, environmentally linked activities are those activities performed because poor environmental quality may or does exist. The costs of performing these activities are referred to as *environmental costs*. As with quality costs, **environmental costs** are associated with two subcategories of environmentally related activities: *control activities* and *failure activities*. In other words, environmental costs are associated with the creation, detection, remediation, and prevention of environmental degradation. With this definition, environmental costs are also classified into four analogous categories: prevention costs, detection costs, internal failure costs, and

[6]Baxter Environmental Financial Statement, 1999, at http://www.baxter.com/sustainability (accessed October 2006).

external failure costs. External failure costs, in turn, can be subdivided into realized and unrealized categories.

Environmental prevention costs are the costs of activities carried out to prevent the production of contaminants and/or waste that could cause damage to the environment. Examples of prevention activities include the following: evaluating and selecting suppliers, evaluating and selecting equipment to control pollution, designing processes and products to reduce or eliminate contaminants, training employees, studying environmental impacts, auditing environmental risks, undertaking environmental research, developing environmental management systems, and recycling products.

Environmental detection costs are the costs of activities executed to determine if products, processes, and other activities within the firm are in compliance with appropriate environmental standards. The environmental standards and procedures that a firm seeks to follow are defined in three ways: (1) regulatory laws of governments, (2) voluntary standards developed by private organizations, and (3) environmental policies developed by management. Examples of detection activities are auditing environmental activities, inspecting products and processes (for environmental compliance), developing environmental performance measures, carrying out contamination tests, verifying supplier environmental performance, and measuring levels of contamination.

Environmental internal failure costs are costs of activities performed because contaminants and waste have been produced but not discharged into the environment. Thus, internal failure costs are incurred to eliminate and manage contaminants or waste once produced. Internal failure activities have one of two goals: (1) to ensure that the contaminants and waste produced are not released to the environment or (2) to reduce the level of contaminants released to an amount that complies with environmental standards. Examples of internal failure activities include operating equipment to minimize or eliminate pollution, treating and disposing of toxic materials, maintaining pollution equipment, licensing facilities for producing contaminants, and recycling scrap.

Environmental external failure costs are the costs of activities performed after discharging contaminants and waste into the environment. **Realized external failure costs** are those incurred and paid for by the firm. **Unrealized external failure costs**, or **societal costs**, are caused by the firm but are incurred and paid for by parties outside the firm. Examples of realized external failure activities are cleaning up a polluted lake, cleaning up oil spills, cleaning up contaminated soil, using materials and energy inefficiently, settling personal injury claims from environmentally unsound practices, settling property damage claims, restoring land to its natural state, and losing sales from a bad environmental reputation. Examples of societal costs include receiving medical care because of polluted air (individual welfare), losing a lake for recreational use because of contamination (degradation), losing employment because of contamination (individual welfare), and damaging ecosystems from solid waste disposal (degradation).

CONCEPT Q&A

Why are there two categories of external failure costs?

Answers on pages 711 to 715

Summary of Learning Objectives

LO1. Explain why functional (or volume)-based costing approaches may produce distorted costs.

- Overhead costs have increased in significance over time and in many firms represent a much higher percentage of product costs than direct labour.
- Many overhead activities are unrelated to the units produced.
- Functional-based costing systems are not able to assign the costs of these non-unit-based overhead activities properly.

- Non-unit-based overhead activities often are consumed by products in different proportions than are unit-based overhead activities. Because of this nonproportionality, assigning overhead by using only unit-based drivers can distort product costs.
- If the non-unit-based overhead costs are a significant proportion of total overhead costs, the inaccuracy in cost assignments can be a serious matter.

LO2. Explain how an activity-based costing system works for product costing.

- Activities are identified and defined through the use of interviews and surveys. This information allows an activity dictionary to be constructed.
- The activity dictionary lists activities and potential activity drivers, classifies activities as primary or secondary, and provides any other attributes deemed to be important.
- Resource costs are assigned to activities by using direct tracing and resource drivers.
- The costs of secondary activities are ultimately assigned to primary activities by using activity drivers.
- Finally, the costs of primary activities are assigned to products, customers, and other cost objects.
- The cost assignment process is described by the following general steps: (1) identifying the major activities and building an activity dictionary, (2) determining the cost of those activities, (3) identifying a measure of consumption for activity costs (activity drivers), (4) calculating an activity rate, (5) measuring the demands placed on activities by each product, and (6) calculating product costs.

LO3. Describe activity-based customer costing and activity-based supplier costing.

- Tracing customer-driven costs to customers can provide significant information to managers.
- Accurate customer costs allow managers to make better pricing decisions, customer-mix decisions, and other customer-related decisions that improve profitability.
- Tracing supplier-driven costs to suppliers can enable managers to choose the true low-cost suppliers, producing a stronger competitive position and increased profitability.

LO4. Explain how activity-based management can be used for cost reduction.

- Assigning costs accurately is vital for good decision making.
- Assigning the costs of an activity accurately does not address the issue of whether or not the activity should be performed or whether it is being performed efficiently.
- Activity-based management focuses on process-value analysis.
- Process-value analysis has three components: driver analysis, activity analysis, and performance evaluation. These three steps determine what activities are being done, why they are being done, and how well they are done.
- Understanding the root causes of activities provides the opportunities to manage activities so that costs can be reduced.
- Quality and environmental activities are particularly susceptible to activity-based management.
- Quality costs are costs that are incurred because poor product quality exists or may exist.
- Environmental costs are costs that are incurred because environmental degradation exists or may exist.

CORNERSTONES FOR CHAPTER 7

Key Terms

Review Problems

I. Plantwide Rates

Gee Company produces two types of stereo units: deluxe and regular. For the most recent year, Gee reports the following data:

Budgeted overhead	$180,000
Expected activity (in direct labour hours)	50,000
Actual activity (in direct labour hours)	51,000
Actual overhead	$200,000

	Deluxe	Regular
Units produced	5,000	50,000
Prime costs	$40,000	$300,000
Direct labour hours	5,000	46,000

Required:

1. Calculate a predetermined overhead rate based on direct labour hours.
2. What is the applied overhead?
3. What is the under- or overapplied overhead?
4. Calculate the unit cost of each stereo unit.

Solution:

1. Rate = $180,000/50,000 = $3.60 per direct labour hour
2. Applied overhead = $3.60 × 51,000 = $183,600
3. Overhead variance = $200,000 – $183,600 = $16,400 underapplied
4. Unit cost:

	Deluxe	Regular
Prime costs	$ 40,000	$ 300,000
Overhead costs:		
$3.60 × 5,000	18,000	
$3.60 × 46,000		165,600
Total manufacturing costs	$ 58,000	$ 465,600
Units produced	÷ 5,000	÷ 50,000
Unit cost (total costs/units)	$ 11.60	$ 9.31*

* Rounded.

II. Departmental Rates

Gee Company gathers the following departmental data for a second year. Two types of stereo units are produced: deluxe and regular.

	Fabrication	Assembly
Budgeted overhead	$120,000	$60,000
Expected and actual usage (direct labour hours):		
Deluxe	3,000	2,000
Regular	3,000	43,000
	6,000	45,000

	Fabrication	Assembly
Expected and actual usage (machine hours):		
Deluxe	2,000	5,000
Regular	18,000	5,000
	20,000	10,000

In addition to the departmental data, the following information is provided:

	Deluxe	Regular
Units produced	5,000	50,000
Prime costs	$40,000	$300,000

Required:

1. Calculate departmental overhead rates by using machine hours for fabrication and direct labour hours for assembly.
2. Calculate the applied overhead by department.
3. Calculate the applied overhead by product.
4. Calculate unit costs.

Solution:

1. Departmental rates
   Fabrication: $120,000/20,000 = $6.00 per machine hour
   Assembly: $60,000/45,000 = $1.33* per direct labour hour
   *Rounded.
2. Applied overhead (by department):
   Fabrication: $6.00 × 20,000 = $120,000
   Assembly: $1.33 × 45,000 = $59,850
3. Applied overhead (by product):
   Deluxe: ($6.00 × 2,000) + ($1.33 × 2,000) = $14,660
   Regular: ($6.00 × 18,000) + ($1.33 × 43,000) = $165,190
4. Unit cost (rounded to the nearest cent):
   Deluxe: ($40,000 + $14,660)/5,000 = $10.93
   Regular: ($300,000 + $165,190)/50,000 = $9.30

III. Activity-Based Rates

Gee Company produces two types of stereo units: deluxe and regular. Activity data follow:

	Product-Costing Data		
Activity Usage Measures	**Deluxe**	**Regular**	**Total**
Units produced per year	5,000	50,000	55,000
Prime costs	$39,000	$369,000	$408,000
Direct labour hours	5,000	45,000	50,000
Machine hours	10,000	90,000	100,000
Production runs	10	5	15
Number of moves	120	60	180

Activity Cost Data (Overhead Activities)

Activity	Cost
Setups	$ 60,000
Material handling	30,000
Power	50,000
Testing	40,000
Total	$180,000

Required:

1. Calculate the consumption ratios for each activity.
2. Group activities based on the consumption ratios.
3. Calculate a rate for each pooled group of activities.
4. Using the pool rates, calculate unit product costs.

Solution:

1. Consumption ratios:

Overhead Activity	Deluxe	Regular	Activity Driver
Setups	0.67[a]	0.33[a]	Production runs
Material handling	0.67[b]	0.33[b]	Number of moves
Power	0.10[c]	0.90[c]	Machine hours
Testing	0.10[d]	0.90[d]	Direct labour hours

[a] 10/15 (deluxe) and 5/15 (regular)
[b] 120/180 (deluxe) and 60/180 (regular)
[c] 10,000/100,000 (deluxe) and 90,000/100,000 (regular)
[d] 5,000/50,000 (deluxe) and 45,000/50,000 (regular)

2. Batch-level: setups and material handling
   Unit-level: power and testing

3.

Batch-Level Pool		Unit-Level Pool	
Setups	$60,000	Power	$ 50,000
Material handling	30,000	Testing	40,000
Total	$90,000	Total	$ 90,000
Runs	÷ 15	Machine hours	÷100,000
Pool rate	$ 6,000 per run	Pool rate	$ 0.90 per machine hour

4. Unit Costs: Activity-Based Costing

	Deluxe	Regular
Prime costs	$ 39,000	$ 369,000
Overhead costs:		
Batch-level pool:		
($6,000 × 10)	60,000	
($6,000 × 5)		30,000
Unit-level pool:		
($0.90 × 10,000)	9,000	
($0.90 × 90,000)		81,000
Total manufacturing costs	$ 108,000	$ 480,000
Units produced	÷ 5,000	÷ 50,000
Unit cost (total costs/units)	$ 21.60	$ 9.60

IV. Environmental Costs

At the beginning of 2011, Kleaner Company initiated a program to improve its environmental performance. Efforts were made to reduce the production and emission of contaminating gaseous, solid, and liquid residues. By the end of the year, in an executive meeting, the environmental manager indicated that the company had made significant improvement in its environmental performance, reducing the emission of contaminating residues of all types. The president of the company was pleased with the reported success but wanted an assessment of the financial consequences of the environmental improvements. To satisfy this request, the following financial data were collected for 2010 and 2011 (all changes in costs are a result of environmental improvements):

	2010 ($)	2011 ($)
Sales	20,000,000	20,000,000
Evaluating and selecting suppliers	0	600,000
Treating and disposing of toxic materials	1,200,000	800,000
Inspecting processes (environmental objective)	200,000	300,000
Land restoration (annual fund contribution)	1,600,000	1,200,000
Maintaining pollution equipment	400,000	300,000
Testing for contaminants	150,000	100,000

Required:

Classify the costs as prevention, detection, internal failure, or external failure.

Solution:

Prevention costs: evaluating and selecting suppliers; detection costs: testing for contaminants and inspecting processes; internal failure: maintaining pollution equipment and treating and disposing of toxic materials; and external failure: land restoration.

Discussion Questions

1. Describe the two-stage process associated with plantwide overhead rates.
2. Describe the two-stage process for departmental overhead rates.
3. What are non-unit-level overhead activities? Non-unit-based cost drivers? Give some examples.
4. What is meant by "product diversity"?
5. What is an overhead consumption ratio?
6. What is activity-based product costing?
7. What is an activity dictionary?
8. Explain how costs are assigned to activities.
9. Describe the value of activity-based customer costing.
10. Explain how ABC can help a firm identify its true low-cost suppliers.
11. What is driver analysis? What role does it play in process-value analysis?
12. What are value-added activities? Value-added costs?
13. What are non-value-added activities? Non-value-added costs? Give an example of each.
14. Identify and define four different ways to manage activities so that costs can be reduced.
15. What is cycle time? Velocity?

Multiple-Choice Exercises

7-1 A unit-level driver is consumed by a product each and every time that

a. a batch of products is produced.
b. a purchase order is issued.
c. a unit is produced.
d. a customer complains.
e. None of the above.

7-2 Which of the following is a non-unit-level driver?

a. direct labour hours
b. machine hours
c. setup hours
d. direct materials
e. assembly hours

7-3 Consider the information given on two products and their activity usage:

	Laser Printer	Dot Matrix Printer
Units produced	1,000	4,000
Setup hours	800	400
Inspection hours	500	500
Machine hours	200	1,000

The consumption ratios for the setup activity for each product are

a. 0.167; 0.833.
b. 0.333; 0.667.
c. 0.500; 0.500.
d. 0.20; 0.80.
e. none of the above.

7-4 Refer to the data for Multiple-Choice Exercise 7-3. Suppose that machine hours are used to assign all overhead costs to the two products. Select the best answer from the following:

a. Laser printers are undercosted, and dot matrix printers are overcosted.
b. Laser printers and dot matrix printers are accurately costed.
c. Laser printers are overcosted, and dot matrix printers are undercosted.
d. Using inspection hours to assign overhead costs is the most accurate approach.
e. None of the above.

7-5 The first stage of ABC entails the assignment of

a. resource costs to departments.
b. activity costs to products or customers.
c. resource costs to a plantwide pool.
d. resource costs to individual activities.
e. resource costs to distribution channels.

7-6 The second stage of ABC entails the assignment of

a. resource costs to departments.
b. activity costs to products or customers.
c. resource costs to a plantwide pool.
d. resource costs to individual activities.
e. resource costs to distribution channels.

7-7 Interview questions are asked to determine

a. what activities are being performed.
b. who performs the activities.
c. the relative amount of time spent on each activity by individual workers.
d. possible activity drivers for assigning costs to products.
e. all of the above.

7-8 The receiving department employs one worker, who spends 75 percent of his time on the receiving activity and 25 percent of his time on inspecting products. His salary is $40,000. The amount of cost assigned to the receiving activity is

a. $34,000.
b. $40,000.
c. $10,000.
d. $30,000.
e. none of the above.

7-9 Assume that the moving activity has an expected cost of $80,000. Expected direct labour hours are 20,000, and expected number of moves is 40,000. The best activity rate for moving is

a. $4 per move.
b. $1.33 per hour-move.
c. $4 per hour.
d. $2 per move.
e. none of the above.

7-10 Which of the following is a true statement about activity-based customer costing?

a. Customer diversity requires multiple drivers to trace costs accurately to customers.
b. Customers can consume customer-driven activities in different proportions.
c. It often produces changes in the company's customer mix.
d. It often improves profitability.
e. All of the above are true.

7-11 Which of the following is a true statement about activity-based supplier costing?

a. The cost of a supplier is the purchase price of the components or materials acquired.
b. Suppliers can affect many internal activities of a firm and significantly increase the cost of purchasing.
c. It encourages managers to evaluate suppliers based on purchase cost.
d. It encourages managers to increase the number of suppliers.
e. All of the above are true.

7-12 This year, Lambert Company will ship 1,500,000 kilograms of goods to customers at a cost of $1,200,000. If a customer orders 10,000 kilograms and produces $200,000 of revenue (total revenue is $20 million), the amount of shipping cost assigned to the customer by using ABC would be

a. indeterminate.
b. $24,000 (2 percent of the shipping cost).
c. $8,000 ($0.80 per kilograms shipped).
d. $12,000 (1 percent of the shipping cost).
e. none of the above.

7-13 Lambert Company has two suppliers: Deming and Leming. The cost of warranty work due to defective components is $2,000,000. The total units repaired under warranty average 100,000, of which 90,000 have components from Deming and 10,000 have components from Leming. Select the items below that represent true statements.

a. Components purchased from Deming cost $200,000 more than their purchase price.
b. Components purchased from Leming cost $1,800,000 more than their purchase price.
c. Components from Deming appear to be of higher quality.
d. All of the above are true.
e. None of the above is true.

7-14 A forklift and its driver used for moving materials are examples of

a. activity outputs.
b. activity output measures.
c. resource drivers.
d. activity inputs.
e. root causes.

7-15 Which of the following are non-value-added activities?

a. Moving goods.
b. Storing goods.
c. Inspecting finished goods.
d. Reworking a defective product.
e. All of the above.

7-16 **Suppose that a company is spending $50,000 per year for inspecting, $40,000 for purchasing, and $60,000 for reworking products. A good estimate of non-value-added costs would be**

a. $110,000.
b. $50,000.
c. $60,000.
d. $90,000.
e. $100,000.

7-17 **The cost of inspecting incoming parts is most likely to be reduced by**

a. activity sharing.
b. activity selection.
c. activity reduction.
d. activity elimination.
e. none of the above.

7-18 **Thom Company produces 100 units in 5 hours. The cycle time for Thom**

a. is 20 units per hour.
b. is 5 hours per unit.
c. is 3 minutes per unit.
d. is 1 hour per 20 units.
e. cannot be calculated.

7-19 **Thom Company produces 100 units in 5 hours. The velocity for Thom**

a. is 20 units per hour.
b. is 5 hours per unit.
c. is 3 minutes per unit.
d. is 1 hour per 20 units.
e. cannot be calculated.

7-20 **Striving to produce the same activity output with lower costs for the input used is concerned with which of the following dimensions of activity performance?**

a. quality
b. time
c. activity sharing
d. efficiency
e. effectiveness

7-21 **Which of the following is a quality prevention cost?**

a. quality planning
b. supplier evaluation and selection
c. quality audits
d. field trials
e. all of the above

7-22 **Which of the following is an appraisal cost (quality)?**

a. design reviews
b. quality reporting
c. manager of an inspection team
d. warranties
e. retesting

7-23 **Which of the following is an internal failure cost (quality)?**

a. supplier evaluation and selection
b. scrapped units

OBJECTIVE 1 2

Exercise 7-40 ACTIVITY-BASED PRODUCT COSTING

Suppose that a surgical ward has gathered the following information for four nursing activities and two types of patients:

		Patient Category		
	Driver	Normal	Intensive	Activity Rate ($)
Treating patients	Treatments	4,000	20,000	8.00
Providing hygienic care	Hygienic hours	3,000	11,000	10.00
Responding to requests	Requests	20,000	50,000	4.00
Monitoring patients	Monitoring hours	15,000	180,000	1.50

Required:

1. Determine the total nursing costs assigned to each patient category.
2. Output is measured in patient days. Assuming that the normal patient category uses 10,000 patient days and that the intensive patient category uses 8,000 patient days, calculate the nursing cost per patient day for each type of patient.

OBJECTIVE 2

Exercise 7-41 ASSIGNING COSTS TO ACTIVITIES, RESOURCE DRIVERS

Receiving has three activities: unloading, counting goods, and inspecting. Unloading uses a forklift that is leased for $12,000 per year. The forklift is used only for unloading. The fuel for the forklift is $2,400 per year. Other operating costs (maintenance) for the forklift total $1,000 per year. Inspection uses some special testing equipment that has a depreciation of $800 per year and an operating cost of $500. Receiving has three employees who have an average salary of $40,000 per year. The work distribution matrix for the receiving personnel is as follows:

Activity	Percentage of Time on Each Activity (%)
Unloading	40
Counting	25
Inspecting	35

No other resources are used for these activities.

Required:

1. Calculate the cost of each activity.
2. Explain the two methods used to assign costs to activities.

OBJECTIVE 2

Exercise 7-42 ACTIVITY-BASED CUSTOMER-DRIVEN COSTS

Suppose that Stillwater Designs has two classes of distributors: JIT distributors and non-JIT distributors. The JIT distributor places small, frequent orders, and the non-JIT distributor tends to place larger, less frequent orders. Both types of distributors are buying the same product. Stillwater Designs provides the following information about customer-related activities and costs for the most recent quarter:

	JIT Distributors	Non-JIT Distributors
Sales orders	200	20
Sales calls	20	20
Service calls	100	50
Average order size	500	5,000
Manufacturing cost/unit	$100	$100
Customer costs:		
Processing sales orders	$ 880,000	
Selling goods	320,000	
Servicing goods	300,000	
Total	$1,500,000	

Required:

1. Calculate the total revenues per distributor category, and assign the customer costs to each distributor type by using revenues as the allocation base. Selling price for one unit is $125.
2. Calculate the customer cost per distributor type using activity-based cost assignments. Discuss the merits of offering the non-JIT distributors a $3 price decrease (assume that they are agitating for a price concession).
3. Assume that the JIT distributors are simply imposing the frequent orders on Stillwater Designs. No formal discussion has taken place between JIT customers and Stillwater Designs regarding the supply of goods on a JIT basis. The sales pattern has evolved over time. As an independent consultant, what would you suggest to Stillwater Designs' management?

Exercise 7-43 ACTIVITY-BASED SUPPLIER COSTING

OBJECTIVE 3

Estia Company manufactures heating systems. Estia produces all the parts necessary for its product except for one electronic component, which is purchased from two local suppliers: Wood Inc. and Forest Company. Both suppliers are reliable and seldom deliver late; however, Wood sells the component for $48 per unit, while Forest sells the same component for $43. Estia purchases 80 percent of its components from Forest because of its lower price. The total annual demand is 2,000,000 components.

To help assess the cost effect of the two components, the following data were collected for supplier-related activities and suppliers:

I. Activity Data

	Activity Cost ($)
Inspecting components (sampling only)	240,000
Reworking products (due to failed component)	3,042,000
Warranty work (due to failed component)	4,800,000

II. Supplier Data

	Wood Inc.	Forest Company
Unit purchase price	$48	$43
Units purchased	400,000	1,600,000
Sampling hours*	40	1,960
Rework hours	180	2,820
Warranty hours	400	7,600

* Sampling inspection for Wood's product has been reduced because the reject rate is so low.

Required:

1. Calculate the cost per component for each supplier, taking into consideration the costs of the supplier-related activities and using the current prices and sales volume. Round the unit cost to two decimal places.
2. Suppose that Estia loses $2,000,000 in sales per year because of the reputation effect of defective units attributable to failed components. Using warranty hours, assign the cost of lost sales to each supplier. By how much would this change the cost of each supplier's component?

Exercise 7-44 NON-VALUE-ADDED COSTS

OBJECTIVE 4

The following six situations are independent.

a. A manual insertion process takes 30 minutes and 8 kilograms of material to produce a product. Automating the insertion process requires 15 minutes of machine time and 7.5 kilograms of material. The cost per labour hour is $12, the cost per machine hour is $8, and the cost per kilogram of materials is $10.
b. With its original design, a gear requires eight hours of setup time. By redesigning the gear so that the number of different grooves needed is reduced by 50 percent, the setup time is reduced by 75 percent. The cost per setup hour is $50.

c. A product currently requires six moves. By redesigning the manufacturing layout, the number of moves can be reduced from six to zero. The cost per move is $20.

d. Inspection time for a plant is 16,000 hours per year. The cost of inspection consists of salaries of eight inspectors, totalling $320,000. Inspection also uses supplies costing $5 per inspection hour. The company eliminated most defective components by eliminating low-quality suppliers. The number of production errors was reduced dramatically by installing a system of statistical process control. Further quality improvements were realized by redesigning the products, making them easier to manufacture. The net effect was to achieve a close to zero-defect state and eliminate the need for any inspection activity.

e. Each unit of a product requires six components. The average number of components is 6.5 due to component failure, requiring rework and extra components. Developing relations with the right suppliers and increasing the quality of the purchased component can reduce the average number of components to six components per unit. The cost per component is $500.

f. A plant produces 100 different electronic products. Each product requires an average of eight components that are purchased externally. The components are different for each part. By redesigning the products, it is possible to produce the 100 products so that they all have four components in common. This will reduce the demand for purchasing, receiving, and paying bills. Estimated savings from the reduced demand are $900,000 per year.

Required:

Estimate the non-value-added cost for each situation.

OBJECTIVE 4

Exercise 7-45 DRIVER ANALYSIS

Refer to the six situations in **Exercise 7-44**.

Required:

For each situation, identify the possible root cause(s) of the activity cost (such as plant layout, process design, and product design).

OBJECTIVE 4

Exercise 7-46 TYPE OF ACTIVITY MANAGEMENT

Refer to the six situations in **Exercise 7-44**.

Required:

For each situation, identify the cost reduction measure: activity elimination, activity reduction, activity sharing, or activity selection.

OBJECTIVE 4

Exercise 7-47 CYCLE TIME AND VELOCITY

A manufacturing cell produces 90,000 stereo speakers per quarter. A total of 15,000 production hours are used within the cell per quarter.

Required:

1. Calculate the velocity (per hour).
2. Calculate the cycle time (minutes per unit produced).

OBJECTIVE 1 2

Exercise 7-48 PRODUCT-COSTING ACCURACY, CONSUMPTION RATIOS

Plata Company produces two products: a mostly handcrafted soft leather briefcase sold under the label Maletin Elegant and a leather briefcase produced largely through automation and sold under the label Maletin Fina. The two products use two overhead activities, with the following costs:

Setting up equipment	$ 3,000
Machining	$18,000

The controller has collected the expected annual prime costs for each briefcase, the machine hours, the setup hours, and the expected production.

	Elegant	Fina
Direct labour	$9,000	$3,000
Direct materials	$3,000	$3,000
Units	3,000	3,000
Machine hours	500	4,500
Setup hours	100	100

Required:

1. Do you think that the direct labour costs and direct materials costs are accurately traced to each briefcase? Explain.
2. Calculate the consumption ratios for each activity.
3. Calculate the overhead cost per unit for each briefcase by using a plantwide rate based on direct labour costs. Comment on this approach to assigning overhead.
4. Calculate the overhead cost per unit for each briefcase by using overhead rates based on machine hours and setup hours. Explain why these assignments are more accurate than using the direct labour costs.

Exercise 7-49 PRODUCT-COSTING ACCURACY, CONSUMPTION RATIOS, ACTIVITY RATES, ACTIVITY COSTING

OBJECTIVE 1 2

Tristar Manufacturing produces two types of battery-operated toy soldiers: infantry and special forces. The soldiers are produced by using one continuous process. Four activities have been identified: machining, setups, receiving, and packing. Resource drivers have been used to assign costs to each activity. The overhead activities, their costs, and the other related data are as follows:

Product	Machine Hours	Setups	Receiving Orders	Packing Orders
Infantry	20,000	300	900	1,600
Special forces	20,000	100	100	800
Costs	$80,000	$24,000	$18,000	$30,000

Required:

1. Calculate the total overhead assigned to each product by using only machine hours to calculate a plantwide rate.
2. Calculate consumption ratios for each activity.
3. Calculate a rate for each activity by using the associated driver.
4. Assign the overhead costs to each product by using the activity rates computed in Requirement 3.
5. Comment on the difference between the assignment in Requirement 1 and the activity-based assignment.

Exercise 7-50 FORMATION OF AN ACTIVITY ANALYSIS

OBJECTIVE 2

A hospital is in the process of implementing an ABC system. A pilot study is being done to assess the effects of the costing changes on specific products. Of particular interest is the cost of caring for patients who receive in-patient recovery treatment for illness, surgery (noncardiac), and injury. These patients are housed on the third and fourth floors of the hospital (the floors are dedicated to patient care and have only nursing stations and patient rooms). A partial transcript of an interview with the hospital's nursing supervisor is as follows:

1. How many nurses are in the hospital?
   There are 101 nurses, including me.

2. Of these 100 nurses, how many are assigned to the third and fourth floors?
   Fifty nurses are assigned to these two floors.

3. What do these nurses do (please describe)?
   Provide nursing care for patients, which, as you know, means answering questions, changing bandages, administering medicine, changing clothes, etc.

4. And what do you do?
I supervise and coordinate all the nursing activity in the hospital. This includes surgery, maternity, the emergency room, and the two floors you mentioned.

5. What other lodging and care activities are done for the third and fourth floors by persons other than the nurses?
The patients must be fed. The hospital cafeteria delivers meals. The laundry department picks up dirty clothing and bedding once each shift. The floors also have a physical therapist assigned to provide care on a physician-directed basis.

6. Do patients use any equipment?
Yes. Mostly monitoring equipment.

7. Who or what uses the activity output?
Patients. But there are different kinds of patients. On these two floors, we classify patients into three categories according to severity: intensive care, intermediate care, and normal care. The more severe the illness, the more activity is used. Nurses spend much more time with intermediate care patients than with normal care. The more severe patients tend to use more of the laundry service as well. Their clothing and bedding need to be changed more frequently. On the other hand, severe patients use less food. They eat fewer meals. Typically, we measure each patient type by the number of days of hospital stay. And you have to realize that the same patient contributes to each type of product.

Required:

Prepare an activity analysis with three categories: activity name, activity description, and activity driver.

OBJECTIVE 1 2

Exercise 7-51 PLANTWIDE RATE AND ACTIVITY-BASED COSTING

The controller for Vitrina Inc. has established the following activity cost pools and cost drivers.

Activity Cost Pool	Budgeted Overhead Cost	Cost Driver	Budgeted Level for Cost Driver
Machine setups	$200,000	Number of setups	160
Material handling	100,000	Weight of material	50,000 kilograms
Waste control	50,000	Weight of chemicals	10,000 kilograms
Quality control	75,000	Number of inspections	300
Other overhead costs	200,000	Machine hours	20,000

Each order must be a minimum of 1,000 boxes of film chemicals.
The production requirements for each minimum order are as follows:

Machine setups	5 setups
Material handling	1,500 kilograms
Waste control	200 kilograms
Quality control	5 inspections
Other overhead costs	500 machine hours

Required:

1. Calculate the overhead that should be assigned to each minimum order of film chemicals using the above data.
2. Calculate the overhead that should be assigned to each minimum order of film chemicals if Vitrina decides to use a single predetermined overhead rate based on machine hours.

Exercise 7-52 DEPARTMENTAL PLANTWIDE RATE

OBJECTIVE 1 2

Axia Metals Inc. has two production departments with the following characteristics:

	Department A	Department B	Total
Direct labour hours per month	10,000	10,000	20,000
Machine hours per month	–	10,000	10,000
Floor space in square metres	1,000	29,000	30,000
Production equipment amortization	–	$50,000	
Power cost	$ 100	$ 4,900	

Some of the company's products are produced exclusively in Department A and others require activity only in Department B. The following costs are budgeted for the month and form the basis for computing the predetermined overhead rate.

Building costs	$33,000
Power cost	5,000
Production equipment amortization	50,000
Total	$88,000

Required:

1. Calculate a single predetermined overhead rate for the company based on direct labour hours.
2. Calculate an overhead rate for each production department, based on two different cost drivers: direct labour hours in Department A and machine hours in Department B.

Exercise 7-53 PLANTWIDE RATE AND ACTIVITY-BASED COSTING

OBJECTIVE 1 2

Kanis Manufacturing Inc. has four categories of overhead. The expected overhead costs for each of the categories for the next year are as follows:

	Costs	Cost Driver	Expected Activity
Maintenance	$510,000	Machine hours	60,000
Material handling	250,000	Material moves	20,000
Setups	60,000	Setups	3,000
Inspection	21,000	Inspections	12,000

Currently, the company applies overhead using a predetermined overhead rate based upon budgeted direct labour hours of 100,000.

The company has been asked to submit a bid on a proposed job. Usually bids are based upon full manufacturing costs plus a percentage of 10 percent.

Estimates for the proposed job are as follows:

Direct materials	$30,000
Direct labour	$24,000
Number of direct labour hours	8,000
Number of material moves	100
Number of inspections	120
Number of setups	24
Number of machine hours	4,000

Required:

1. If the company used activity-based cost drivers to assign overhead, calculate the bid price of the proposed job.
2. If the company used direct labour hours as the cost driver, calculate the bid price of the proposed job.

OBJECTIVE 2 3

Exercise 7-54 PLANTWIDE RATE AND ACTIVITY-BASED COSTING: BID PRICE OF JOB

Gonies Manufacturing Inc. has four categories of overhead. The expected overhead costs for each of the categories for the next year are as follows:

	Costs	Cost Driver	Expected Activity
Maintenance	$120,000	Machine hours	5,000
Material handling	18,000	Material moves	600
Setups	16,000	Setups	200
Inspection	60,000	Inspections	1,000

Currently, the company applies overhead using a predetermined overhead rate based on budgeted direct labour hours of 20,000.

The company has been asked to bid on a proposed job. Usually bids are based on full manufacturing costs plus a percentage of 15 percent.

Estimates for the proposed job are as follows:

Direct materials	$2,000
Direct labour	$6,000
Number of direct labour hours	600
Number of material moves	4
Number of inspections	6
Number of setups	8
Number of machine hours	80

Required:

1. If the company used direct labour hours as the cost driver, calculate the bid price of the proposed job.
2. If the company used activity-based cost drivers to assign overhead, calculate the bid price of the proposed job.

OBJECTIVE 2

Exercise 7-55 PLANTWIDE RATE AND ACTIVITY-BASED COSTING

Oikos Textile Inc. manufactures two products: sweatshirts and t-shirts. The manufacturing process involves two activities: cutting and sewing. Expected overhead costs and cost drivers are as follows:

	Cutting	Sewing
Overhead costs	$160,000	$350,000
Machine hours	800,000	50,000
Direct labour hours	40,000	20,000

Required:

1. Calculate the activity-based overhead rates. Use machine hours for the cutting activity and direct labour hours for the sewing activity. Round to two decimal points.
2. Calculate a plantwide overhead rate using direct labour hours as the cost driver.
3. Assume the activities for sweatshirts are as follows:

	Cutting	Sewing
Machine hours	4	2
Direct labour hours	2	4

   Calculate the overhead costs allocated to sweatshirts based on the activity-based overhead rates calculated in Requirement 1.
4. Using the assumptions given in Requirment 3, calculate the overhead costs allocated to sweatshirts using the plantwide overhead rate in Requirement 2.

Exercise 7-56 PLANTWIDE RATE AND DEPARTMENTAL RATES

Omikron Inc. has two manufacturing departments: cutting and folding. The company has been using a plantwide predetermined rate based on direct labour cost. The following data are for the current year:

	Cutting	Folding	Total
Budgeted overhead	$240,000	$180,000	$420,000
Budgeted direct labour hours	30,000	12,000	42,000
Budgeted machine hours	9,000	10,000	19,000
Actual overhead	$220,000	$215,000	$435,000
Actual direct labour hours	31,000	13,000	44,000
Actual machine hours	9,000	11,000	20,000
Prime costs	$145,000	$155,000	$300,000

Required:

1. Calculate a plantwide predetermined overhead rate using direct labour hours.
2. Calculate applied overhead using the plantwide predetermined overhead rate.
3. Calculate the overhead variance and label the variance as underapplied or overapplied overhead.
4. Calculate separate departmental overhead rates using direct labour hours for cutting and machine hours for folding.
5. Calculate the total amount of applied overhead for each department.

Exercise 7-57 ACTIVITY-BASED COSTING

Gefyra Corporation manufactures a variety of office chairs. The costing system was designed using an activity-based approach. The company produced two styles of chairs in December. The production data are as follows:

	Units	Direct Materials	Direct Labour Hours	Number of Parts
Style A	5,000	$600,000	7,500	100,000
Style B	100	$ 25,000	500	3,500

Three activities have been identified. Resource drivers are used to assign costs to each activity. The overhead activities, activity costs, and other related data are as follows:

	Budgeted Costs	Cost Drivers	Cost Allocation Rate
Material handling	$ 200,000	Parts	0.25
Cutting	2,160,000	Parts	2.5
Assembly	2,000,000	Direct labour hours	25

There is no beginning and ending inventory. The direct labour rate is $20 per hour.

Required:

1. Calculate the December total manufacturing costs.
2. Calculate the unit costs for the Style A and Style B chairs.

Exercise 7-58 ACTIVITY-BASED COSTING

Flex Company uses activity-based costing to determine the costs of its products. The estimated total cost and expected activity for each of the company's three activity cost pools are as follows:

Activity Cost Pools	Estimated Costs	Expected Activity Product A	Product B	Total
Receiving materials	$19,800	800	300	1,100
Inspecting goods	16,000	2,200	1,800	4,000
Shipping goods	14,000	400	300	700

Required:

Calculate the overhead that should be assigned to Product A and Product B.

OBJECTIVE 2

Exercise 7-59 ACTIVITY RATES AND ACTIVITY-BASED PRODUCT COSTING

Hammer Company produces a variety of electronic equipment. One of its plants produces two laser printers: the deluxe and the regular. At the beginning of the year, the following data were prepared for this plant:

	Deluxe	Regular
Quantity	100,000	800,000
Selling price	$900	$750
Unit prime cost	$529	$483

In addition, the following information was provided so that overhead costs could be assigned to each product:

Activity Name	Activity Driver	Activity Cost ($)	Deluxe	Regular
Setups	Number of setups	2,000,000	300	200
Machining	Machine hours	80,000,000	100,000	300,000
Engineering	Engineering hours	6,000,000	50,000	100,000
Packing	Packing orders	1,000,000	100,000	400,000

Required:

1. Calculate the overhead rates for each activity.
2. Calculate the per-unit product cost for each product.

OBJECTIVE 4

Exercise 7-60 VALUE- AND NON-VALUE-ADDED COSTS

Waterfun Technology produces engines for recreational boats. Because of competitive pressures, the company was making an effort to reduce costs. As part of this effort, management implemented an activity-based management system and began focusing its attention on processes and activities. Purchasing was among the processes (activities) that were carefully studied. The study revealed that the number of purchase orders was a good driver for purchasing costs. During the past year, the company incurred fixed receiving costs of $630,000 (salaries of 15 employees). These fixed costs provide a capacity of processing 72,000 receiving orders (7,200 per employee at practical capacity). Management decided that the efficient level for purchasing should use 36,000 receiving orders.

Required:

1. Explain why receiving would be viewed as a value-added activity. List all possible reasons. Also, list some possible reasons that explain why the demand for purchasing is more than the efficient level of 36,000 orders.
2. Break the cost of receiving into its value-added and non-value-added components.

Problems

OBJECTIVE 1 2

Problem 7-61 FUNCTIONAL-BASED VERSUS ACTIVITY-BASED COSTING

For years, Tamarindo Company produced only one product: backpacks. Recently, the company decided to add a line of duffel bags. With this addition, the company began assigning overhead costs by using departmental rates. (Prior to this, the company used a predetermined plantwide rate based on units produced.) Departmental rates meant that overhead costs had to be assigned to each producing department in order to create overhead pools so that predetermined departmental rates could be calculated. Surprisingly, after the addition of the duffel-bag line and the switch to departmental rates, the costs to produce the backpacks increased, and their profitability dropped.

The marketing manager and the production manager both complained about the increase in the production cost of backpacks. The marketing manager was concerned because the increase in unit costs led to pressure to increase the unit price of backpacks. She was resisting this pressure because she was certain that the increase would harm the company's market share. The production manager was receiving pressure to cut costs also, yet he was convinced that nothing different was being done in the way the backpacks were produced. He was also convinced that further efficiency in the manufacture of the backpacks was unlikely. After some discussion, the two managers decided that the problem had to be connected to the addition of the duffel-bag line.

Upon investigation, they were informed that the only real change in product costing procedures was in the way overhead costs were being assigned. A two-stage procedure was now in use. First, overhead costs were assigned to the two producing departments, Patterns and Finishing. Some overhead costs are assigned to the producing departments by using direct tracing, and some were assigned by using driver tracing. For example, the salaries of the producing department's supervisors were assigned by using direct tracing, whereas the costs of the factory's accounting department were assigned by using driver tracing (the driver being the number of transactions processed for each department). Second, the costs accumulated in the producing departments were assigned to the two products by using direct labour hours as a driver (the rate in each department is based on direct labour hours). The managers were assured that great care was taken to associate overhead costs with individual products. So that they could construct their own example of overhead cost assignment, the controller provided them with the information necessary to show how accounting costs were being assigned to products:

	Department		
	Patterns	Finishing	Total
Accounting cost	$48,000	$72,000	$120,000
Transactions processed	32,000	48,000	80,000
Total direct labour hours	10,000	20,000	30,000
Direct labour hours per backpack*	0.10	0.20	0.30
Direct labour hours per duffel bag*	0.40	0.80	1.20

* Hours required to produce one unit of each product.

The controller remarked that the cost of operating the accounting department had doubled with the addition of the new product line. The increase came because of the need to process additional transactions, which had also doubled in number.

During the first year of producing duffel bags, the company produced and sold 100,000 backpacks and 25,000 duffel bags. The 100,000 backpacks matched the prior year's output for that product.

Required:

1. Calculate the amount of accounting cost assigned to a backpack before the duffel-bag line was added by using a plantwide rate approach based on units produced. Is this assignment accurate? Explain.
2. Suppose that the company decided to assign the accounting costs directly to the product lines by using the number of transactions as the activity driver. What is the accounting cost per unit of backpacks? Per unit of duffel bags?
3. Calculate the amount of accounting cost assigned to each backpack and duffel bag by using departmental rates based on direct labour hours.
4. Which way of assigning overhead does the best job—the functional-based approach by using departmental rates or the activity-based approach by using transactions processed for each product? Explain. Discuss the value of ABC before the duffel-bag line was added.

OBJECTIVE ➤ 1 2

Problem 7-62 PLANTWIDE VERSUS DEPARTMENTAL RATES, PRODUCT-COSTING ACCURACY: ACTIVITY-BASED COSTING

Ramsey Company produces speakers (Model A and Model B). Both products pass through two producing departments. Model A's production is much more labour-intensive than that of Model B. Model B is also the more popular of the two speakers. The following data have been gathered for the two products:

	Product Data	
	Model A	Model B
Units produced per year	30,000	300,000
Prime costs	$100,000	$1,000,000
Direct labour hours	140,000	300,000
Machine hours	20,000	200,000
Production runs	40	60
Inspection hours	800	1,200
Maintenance hours	10,000	90,000
Overhead costs:		
Setup costs	$180,000	
Inspection costs	140,000	
Machining	160,000	
Maintenance	180,000	
Total	$660,000	

Required:

1. Calculate the overhead cost per unit for each product by using a plantwide rate based on direct labour hours. Round to two decimal places.
2. Calculate the overhead cost per unit for each product by using ABC. Round to two decimal places.
3. Suppose that Ramsey decides to use departmental overhead rates. There are two departments: Department 1 (machine intensive) with a rate of $2.33 per machine hour and Department 2 (labour intensive) with a rate of $0.60 per direct labour hour. The consumption of these two drivers is as follows:

	Department 1 Machine Hours	Department 2 Direct Labour Hours
Model A	10,000	130,000
Model B	170,000	270,000

Calculate the overhead cost per unit for each product by using departmental rates. Round to two decimal places.

4. Using the activity-based product costs as the standard, comment on the ability of departmental rates to improve the accuracy of product costing. (Did the departmental rates do better than the plantwide rate?)

OBJECTIVE ➤ 1 2

Problem 7-63 PRODUCTION-BASED COSTING VERSUS ACTIVITY-BASED COSTING, ASSIGNING COSTS TO ACTIVITIES, RESOURCE DRIVERS

Willow Company produces lawn mowers. One of its plants produces two versions of mowers: a basic model and a deluxe model. The deluxe model has a sturdier frame, a higher horsepower engine, a wider blade, and mulching capability. At the beginning of the year, the following data were prepared for this plant:

	Basic Model	Deluxe Model
Expected quantity	40,000	20,000
Selling price	$180	$360
Prime costs	$80	$160
Machine hours	5,000	5,000
Direct labour hours	10,000	10,000
Engineering support (hours)	1,500	4,500
Receiving (orders processed)	250	500
Materials handling (number of moves)	1,200	4,800
Purchasing (number of requisitions)	100	200
Maintenance (hours used)	1,000	3,000
Paying suppliers (invoices processed)	250	500
Setting up equipment (number of setups)	16	64

Additionally, the following overhead activity costs are reported:

Maintaining equipment	$114,000
Engineering support	120,000
Materials handling	?
Setting up equipment	96,000
Purchasing materials	60,000
Receiving goods	40,000
Paying suppliers	30,000
Providing space	20,000
Total	$?

Facility-level costs are allocated in proportion to machine hours (provides a measure of time the facility is used by each product). Materials handling uses three inputs: two forklifts, gasoline to operate the forklift, and three operators. The three operators are paid a salary of $40,000 each. The operators spend 25 percent of their time on the receiving activity and 75 percent on moving goods (materials handling). Gasoline costs $3 per move. Depreciation amounts to $6,000 per forklift per year.

Required:

Round answers to two decimal places.

1. Calculate the cost of the materials handling activity. Label the cost assignments as driver tracing or direct tracing. Identify the resource drivers.
2. Calculate the cost per unit for each product by using direct labour hours to assign all overhead costs.
3. Calculate activity rates, and assign costs to each product. Calculate a unit cost for each product, and compare these costs with those calculated in Requirement 2.
4. Calculate consumption ratios for each activity.
5. Explain how the consumption ratios calculated in Requirement 4 can be used to reduce the number of rates. Calculate the rates that would apply under this approach.

Problem 7-64 ACTIVITY COSTING, ASSIGNING RESOURCE COSTS, PRIMARY AND SECONDARY ACTIVITIES

OBJECTIVE 1 2

Trinity Clinic has identified three activities for daily maternity care: occupancy and feeding, nursing, and nursing supervision. The nursing supervisor oversees 150 nurses, 25 of whom are maternity nurses (the other nurses are located in other care areas such as the emergency room and intensive care). The nursing supervisor has three assistants, a secretary, several offices, computers, phones, and furniture. The three assistants spend 75 percent of their time on the supervising activity and 25 percent of their time as surgical nurses. They each receive a salary of $48,000. The nursing supervisor has a salary of $70,000. She spends 100 percent of her time supervising. The secretary receives a salary of $22,000 per year. Other costs directly traceable to the supervisory activity (depreciation, utilities, phone, etc.) average $100,000 per year.

Daily care output is measured as "patient days." The clinic has traditionally assigned the cost of daily care by using a daily rate (a rate per patient day). Different kinds of daily care are provided, and rates are structured to reflect these differences. For example, a higher daily rate is charged for an intensive care unit than for a maternity care unit. Within units, however, the daily rates are the same for all patients. Under the traditional, functional approach, the daily rate is computed by dividing the annual costs of occupancy and feeding, nursing, and a share of supervision by the unit's capacity expressed in patient days. The cost of supervision is assigned to each care area based on the number of nurses. A single driver (patient days) is used to assign the costs of daily care to each patient.

A pilot study has revealed that the demands for nursing care vary within the maternity unit, depending on the severity of a patient's case. Specifically, demand for nursing services per day increases with severity. Assume that the maternity unit has three levels of increasing severity: normal patients, cesarean patients, and patients with complications. The pilot study provided the following activity and cost information:

Activity	Annual Cost ($)	Activity Driver	Annual Quantity
Occupancy and feeding	1,000,000	Patient days	10,000
Nursing care (maternity)	950,000	Hours of nursing care	50,000
Nursing supervision	?	Number of nurses	150

The pilot study also revealed the following information concerning the three types of patients and their annual demands:

Patient Type	Patient Days Demanded	Nursing Hours Demanded
Normal	7,000	17,500
Cesarean	2,000	12,500
Complications	1,000	20,000
Total	10,000	50,000

Required:

1. Calculate the cost per patient day by using a functional-based approach.
2. Calculate the cost per patient day by using an activity-based approach.
3. The hospital processes 1,000,000 pounds of laundry per year. The cost for the laundering activity is $500,000 per year. In a functional-based cost system, the cost of the laundry department is assigned to each user department in proportion to the kilograms of laundry produced. Typically, maternity produces 200,000 kilograms per year. How much would this change the cost per patient day calculated in Requirement 1? Now, describe what information you would need to modify the calculation made in Requirement 2. Under what conditions would this activity calculation provide a more accurate cost assignment?

OBJECTIVE ➤ 1 2 3

Problem 7-65 CUSTOMERS AS A COST OBJECT

Security National Bank has requested an analysis of chequing account profitability by customer type. Customers are categorized according to the size of their account: low balances, medium balances, and high balances. The activities associated with the three different customer categories and their associated annual costs are as follows:

Opening and closing accounts	$ 200,000
Issuing monthly statements	300,000
Processing transactions	2,050,000
Customer inquiries	400,000
Providing automatic teller machine (ATM) services	1,120,000
Total cost	$4,070,000

Additional data concerning the usage of the activities by the various customers are also provided:

	Account Balance		
	Low	Medium	High
Number of accounts opened/closed	15,000	3,000	2,000
Number of statements issued	450,000	100,000	50,000
Processing transactions	18,000,000	2,000,000	500,000
Number of telephone minutes	1,000,000	600,000	400,000
Number of ATM transactions	1,350,000	200,000	50,000
Number of chequing accounts	38,000	8,000	4,000

Required:

Round answers to two decimal places.

1. Calculate a cost per account per year by dividing the total cost of processing and maintaining chequing accounts by the total number of accounts. What is the average fee per month that the bank should charge to cover the costs incurred because of chequing accounts?
2. Calculate a cost per account by customer category by using activity rates.
3. Currently, the bank offers free chequing to all of its customers. The interest revenues average $90 per account; however, the interest revenues earned per account by category are $80, $100, and $165 for the low-, medium-, and high-balance accounts, respectively. Calculate the average profit per account (average revenue less average cost from Requirement 1). Then calculate the profit per account by using the revenue per customer type and the unit cost per customer type calculated in Requirement 2.
4. After the analysis in Requirement 3, a vice president recommended eliminating the free chequing feature for low-balance customers. The bank president expressed reluctance to do so, arguing that the low-balance customers more than made up for the loss through cross-sales. He presented a survey that showed that 50 percent of the customers would switch banks if a chequing fee were imposed. Explain how you could verify the president's argument by using ABC.

Problem 7-66 ACTIVITY-BASED COSTING AND CUSTOMER-DRIVEN COSTS

OBJECTIVE 2 3

Aero Manufacturing produces several types of bolts used in aircrafts. The bolts are produced in batches according to customer orders. Although there are a variety of bolts, they can be grouped into three product families. Because the product families are used in different kinds of aircraft, customers also can be grouped into three categories, corresponding to the product family that they purchase. The number of units sold to each customer class is the same. The selling prices for the three product families range from $0.50 to $0.80 per unit. Historically, the costs of order entry, processing, and handling were expensed and not traced to individual customer groups. These costs are not trivial and totalled $4,500,000 for the most recent year. Furthermore, these costs had been increasing over time. Recently, the company started emphasizing a cost reduction strategy; however, any cost reduction decisions had to contribute to the creation of a competitive advantage.

Because of the magnitude and growth of order-filling costs, management decided to explore the causes of these costs. They discovered that order-filling costs were driven by the number of customer orders processed. Further investigation revealed the following cost behaviour for the order-filling activity:

Step-fixed cost component: $50,000 per step (2,000 orders define a step)*
Variable cost component: $20 per order

* Aero currently has sufficient steps to process 100,000 orders.

The expected customer orders for the year total 100,000. The expected usage of the order-filling activity and the average size of an order by customer category follow:

	Category I	Category II	Category III
Number of orders	50,000	30,000	20,000
Average order size	600	1,000	1,500

As a result of cost behaviour analysis, the marketing manager recommended the imposition of a charge per customer order. The president of the company concurred. The charge was implemented by adding the cost per order to the price of each order (computed by using the projected ordering costs and expected orders). This ordering cost was then reduced as the size of the order increased and was eliminated as the order size reached 2,000 units (the marketing manager indicated that any penalties imposed for orders greater than this size would lose sales from some of the smaller customers). Within a short period of communicating this new price information to customers, the average order size for all three product families increased to 2,000 units.

Required:

1. Aero traditionally has expensed order-filling costs. What is the most likely reason for this practice?
2. Calculate the cost per order for each customer category. Round to two decimal places.
3. Calculate the reduction in order-filling costs produced by the change in pricing strategy (assume that resource spending is reduced as much as possible and that the total units sold remain unchanged). Explain how exploiting customer activity information produced this cost reduction. Would any other internal activities benefit from this pricing strategy?

OBJECTIVE 2 3

Problem 7-67 ACTIVITY-BASED SUPPLIER COSTING

Levy Inc. manufactures tractors for agricultural usage. Levy purchases the engines needed for its tractors from two sources: Johnson Engines and Watson Company. The Johnson engine is the more expensive of the two sources and has a price of $1,000. The Watson engine is $900 per unit. Levy produces and sells 22,000 tractors. Of the 22,000 engines needed for the tractors, 4,000 are purchased from Johnson Engines, and 18,000 are purchased from Watson Company. The production manager, Jamie Murray, prefers the Johnson engine. However, Jan Booth, purchasing manager, maintains that the price difference is too great to buy more than the 4,000 units currently purchased. Booth also wants to maintain a significant connection with the Johnson source just in case the less expensive source cannot supply the needed quantities. Even though Jamie understands the price argument, he is convinced that the quality of the Johnson engine is worth the price difference.

Frank Wallace, the controller, has decided to use activity costing to resolve the issue. The following activity cost and supplier data have been collected:

Activity	Cost ($)
Replacing engines[a]	800,000
Expediting orders[b]	1,000,000
Repairing engines[c]	1,800,000

[a] All units are tested after assembly, and some are rejected because of engine failure. The failed engines are removed and replaced, with the supplier replacing any failed engine. The replaced engine is retested before being sold. Engine failure often causes collateral damage, and other parts often need to be replaced.
[b] Due to late or failed delivery of engines.
[c] Repair work is for units under warranty and almost invariably is due to engine failure. Repair usually means replacing the engine. This cost plus labour, transportation, and other costs make warranty work very expensive.

	Watson	Johnson
Engines replaced by source	1,980	20
Late or failed shipments	198	2
Warranty repairs (by source)	2,440	60

Required:

1. Calculate the activity-based supplier cost per engine (acquisition cost plus supplier-related activity costs). Which of the two suppliers is the low-cost supplier? Explain why this is a better measure of engine cost than the usual purchase costs assigned to the engines.

2. Consider the supplier cost information obtained in Requirement 1. Suppose further that Johnson can only supply a total of 20,000 units. What actions would you advise Levy to undertake with its suppliers?

Problem 7-68 ACTIVITY-BASED MANAGEMENT, NON-VALUE-ADDED COSTS

OBJECTIVE 4

Danna Martin, president of Mays Electronics, was concerned about the end-of-the year marketing report that she had just received. According to Larry Savage, marketing manager, a price decrease for the coming year was again needed to maintain the company's annual sales volume of integrated circuit boards (CBs). This would make a bad situation worse. The current selling price of $18 per unit was producing a $2-per-unit profit—half the customary $4-per-unit profit. Foreign competitors kept reducing their prices. To match the latest reduction would reduce the price from $18 to $14. This would put the price below the cost to produce and sell it. How could these firms sell for such a low price? Determined to find out if there were problems with the company's operations, Danna decided to hire a consultant to evaluate the way in which the CBs were produced and sold. After two weeks, the consultant had identified the following activities and costs:

Setting up equipment	$ 125,000
Materials handling	180,000
Inspecting products	122,000
Engineering support	120,000
Handling customer complaints	100,000
Filling warranties	170,000
Storing goods	80,000
Expediting goods	75,000
Using materials	500,000
Using power	48,000
Manual insertion labour[a]	250,000
Other direct labour	150,000
Total costs	$1,920,000[b]

[a] Diodes, resistors, and integrated circuits are inserted manually into the circuit board.
[b] This total cost produces a unit cost of $16 for last year's sales volume.

The consultant indicated that some preliminary activity analysis shows that per-unit costs can be reduced by at least $7. Since the marketing manager had indicated that the market share (sales volume) for the boards could be increased by 50 percent if the price could be reduced to $12, Danna became quite excited.

Required:

1. What is activity-based management? What phases of activity analysis did the consultant provide? What else remains to be done?
2. Identify as many non-value-added costs as possible. Calculate the cost savings per unit that would be realized if these costs were eliminated. Was the consultant correct in his preliminary cost reduction assessment? Discuss actions that the company can take to reduce or eliminate the non-value-added activities.
3. Calculate the unit cost required to maintain current market share, while earning a profit of $4 per unit. Now calculate the unit cost required to expand sales by 50 percent. How much cost reduction would be required to achieve each unit cost?
4. Assume that further activity analysis revealed the following: switching to automated insertion would save $60,000 of engineering support and $90,000 of direct labour. Now, what is the total potential cost reduction per unit available from activity analysis? With these additional reductions, can Mays achieve the unit cost to maintain current sales? To increase it by 50 percent? What form of activity analysis is this: reduction, sharing, elimination, or selection?
5. Calculate income based on current sales, prices, and costs. Then calculate the income by using a $14 price and a $12 price, assuming that the maximum cost reduction possible is achieved (including Requirement 4's reduction). What price should be selected?

OBJECTIVE 3 4

Problem 7-69 NON-VALUE-ADDED COSTS, ACTIVITY COSTS, ACTIVITY COST REDUCTION

John Thomas, vice president of Mallett Company (a producer of a variety of plastic products), has been supervising the implementation of an ABC management system. One of John's objectives is to improve process efficiency by improving the activities that define the processes. To illustrate the potential of the new system to the president, John has decided to focus on two processes: production and customer service.

Within each process, one activity will be selected for improvement: materials usage for production and sustaining engineering for customer service (sustaining engineers are responsible for redesigning products based on customer needs and feedback). Value-added standards are identified for each activity (the level of efficiency so that no waste exists). For materials usage, the value-added standard calls for six kilograms per unit of output (although the plastic products differ in shape and function, their size—as measured by weight—is uniform). The value-added standard is based on the elimination of all waste due to defective moulds. The standard price of materials is $5 per kilogram. For sustaining engineering, the standard is 58 percent of current practical activity capacity. This standard is based on the fact that about 42 percent of the complaints have to do with design features that could have been avoided or anticipated by the company.

Current practical capacity (at the end of 2009) is defined by the following requirements: 6,000 engineering hours for each product group that has been on the market or in development for five years or less and 2,400 hours per product group of more than five years. Four product groups have less than five years' experience, and 10 product groups have more. Each of the 24 engineers is paid a salary of $60,000. Each engineer can provide 2,000 hours of service per year. No other significant costs are incurred for the engineering activity.

Actual materials usage for 2010 was 25 percent above the level called for by the value-added standard; engineering usage was 46,000 hours. A total of 80,000 units of output were produced. John and the operational managers have selected some improvement measures that promise to reduce non-value-added activity usage by 40 percent in 2011. Selected actual results achieved for 2011 are as follows:

Units produced	80,000
Materials used	584,800
Engineering hours	35,400

The actual prices paid for materials and engineering hours are identical to the standard or budgeted prices.

Required:

1. For 2010, calculate the non-value-added usage and costs for materials usage and sustaining engineering.
2. Using the budgeted improvements, calculate the expected activity usage levels for 2011. Now, calculate the 2011 usage variances (the difference between the expected and actual values), expressed in both physical and financial measures, for materials and engineering. Comment on the company's ability to achieve its targeted reductions. In particular, discuss what measures the company must take to capture any realized reductions in resource usage.

OBJECTIVE 4

Problem 7-70 CYCLE TIME, VELOCITY, PRODUCT COSTING

Goldman Company has a JIT system in place. Each manufacturing cell is dedicated to the production of a single product or major subassembly. One cell, dedicated to the production of telescopes, has four operations: machining, finishing, assembly, and qualifying (testing).

For the coming year, the telescope cell has the following budgeted costs and cell time (both at theoretical capacity):

Budgeted conversion costs	$7,500,000
Budgeted raw materials	$9,000,000
Cell time	12,000 hours
Theoretical output	90,000 telescopes

During the year, the following actual results were obtained:

Actual conversion costs	$7,500,000
Actual materials	$7,800,000
Actual cell time	12,000 hours
Actual output	75,000 telescopes

Required:

1. Calculate the velocity (number of telescopes per hour) that the cell can theoretically achieve. Now, calculate the theoretical cycle time (number of hours or minutes per telescope) that it takes to produce one telescope.
2. Calculate the actual velocity and the actual cycle time.
3. Calculate the budgeted conversion costs per minute. Using this rate, calculate the conversion costs per telescope if theoretical output is achieved. Using this measure, calculate the conversion costs per telescope for actual output. Does this product costing approach provide an incentive for the cell manager to reduce cycle time? Explain.

Problem 7-71 CLASSIFICATION OF ENVIRONMENTAL COSTS

OBJECTIVE 4

Consider the following independent environmental activities:

a. A company takes actions to reduce the amount of material in its packages.
b. After its useful life, a soft-drink producer returns the activated carbon used for purifying water for its beverages to the supplier. The supplier reactivates the carbon for a second use in nonfood applications. As a consequence, many tonnes of material are prevented from entering landfills.
c. An evaporator system is installed to treat wastewater and to collect usable solids for other uses.
d. The inks used to print snack packages (for chips) contain heavy metals.
e. Processes are inspected to ensure compliance with environmental standards.
f. Delivery boxes are used five times and then recycled. This prevents 50 million kilograms of cardboard from entering landfills and saves two million trees per year.
g. Scrubber equipment is installed to ensure that air emissions are less than the level permitted by law.
h. Local residents are incurring medical costs from illnesses caused by air pollution from automobile exhaust pollution.
i. As part of implementing an environmental perspective for a balanced performance measurement system, environmental performance measures are developed.
j. Because of liquid and solid residues being discharged into a local lake, it is no longer fit for swimming, fishing, and other recreational activities.
k. To reduce energy consumption, magnetic ballasts are replaced with electronic ballasts, and more efficient light bulbs and lighting sensors are installed. As a result, 2.3 million kilowatt-hours of electricity are saved per year.
l. Because of a legal settlement, a chemical company must spend $20,000,000 to clean up contaminated soil.
m. A soft-drink company uses the following practice: In all bottling plants, packages damaged during filling are collected and recycled (glass, plastic, and aluminum).
n. Products are inspected to ensure that the gaseous emissions produced during operation follow legal and company guidelines.
o. Costs are incurred to operate pollution-control equipment.
p. An internal audit is conducted to verify that environmental policies are being followed.

Required:

Classify these environmental activities as prevention, detection, internal failure, or external failure costs. For external failure costs, classify the costs as societal or private. Also, label those activities that are compatible with sustainable development with "SD."

Problem 7-72 ACTIVITY-BASED COSTING

Attica has identified the following overhead activities, costs, and activity drivers for the coming year:

Activity	Expected Cost ($)	Activity Driver	Activity Capacity
Setting up	60,000	Number of setups	300
Inspecting	45,000	Inspection hours	4,500
Grinding	90,000	Machine hours	18,000
Receiving	25,000	Number of parts	50,000

The company produces several different machine subassemblies used by other manufacturers. Information on separate batches for two of these subassemblies follows:

	A	B
Direct materials	$850	$950
Direct labour	$600	$600
Units completed	100	50
Number of setups	1	1
Inspection hours	4	2
Machine hours	20	30
Parts used	20	40

The company's normal activity is 4,000 direct labour hours. Each batch uses 50 hours of direct labour.

Required:

1. Upon investigation, you discover that Receiving employs one worker, who spends half her time on the receiving activity and half her time on inspecting products. Her salary is $40,000. Receiving also uses a forklift, at a cost of $5,000 per year for amortization and fuel. The forklift is used only in receiving.
   a. Verify the cost of the receiving activity given above.
   b. What resource driver was used?
2. Determine the unit cost for each product using direct labour hours to apply overhead.
3. Determine the unit cost for each product using the four activity drivers.

Problem 7-73 ACTIVITY-BASED COSTING

Olympus produces two types of jackets for equipment. Information concerning the two products follows:

	Jacket 1	Jacket 2
Units completed	100	50
Direct labour hours	40	60
Grinding hours	20	30
Number of setups	5	5
Inspection hours	4	2
Number of orders	15	25
Prime costs	$145,000	$155,000

Additionally, the following overhead costs are reported for the activities associated with the two products:

Setting up	$ 60,000
Inspecting	45,000
Grinding	90,000
Receiving	25,000
Total	$220,000

Required:

1. Calculate the total cost per unit of each jacket using a plantwide rate based on direct labour hours to assign overhead.
2. Calculate the total overhead of each jacket using activity-based costing methods appropriate to the information provided.

Cases

Case 7-74 ACTIVITY-BASED COSTING, DISTORTED PRODUCT COSTS

OBJECTIVE 2 3 4

Sharp Paper Inc. has three paper mills, one of which is located in Timmins, Ontario. The mill produces 300 different types of coated and uncoated specialty printing papers. This large variety of products was the result of a full-line marketing strategy adopted by Sharp's management. Management was convinced that the value of variety more than offset the extra costs of the increased complexity.

During 2010, the Timmins mill produced 120,000 tons of coated paper and 80,000 tons of uncoated paper. Of the 200,000 tons produced, 180,000 were sold. Sixty products account for 80 percent of the tons sold. Thus, 240 products are classified as low-volume products.

Lightweight lime hopsack in cartons (LLHC) is one of the low-volume products. LLHC is produced in rolls, converted into sheets of paper, and then sold in cartons. In 2010, the cost to produce and sell one tonne of LLHC was as follows:

Direct materials:		
Furnish (3 different pulps)	2,225 kilograms	$ 450
Additives (11 different items)	200 kilograms	500
Tub size	75 kilograms	10
Recycled scrap paper	(296 kilograms)	(20)
Total direct materials		$ 940
Direct labour		$ 450
Overhead:		
Paper machine ($100 per tonne × 2,500 kilograms)		$ 125
Finishing machine ($120 per tonne × 2,500 kilograms)		150
Total overhead		$ 275
Shipping and warehousing		$ 30
Total manufacturing and selling cost		$1,695

Overhead is applied by using a two-stage process. First, overhead is allocated to the paper and finishing machines by using the direct method of allocation with carefully selected cost drivers. Second, the overhead assigned to each machine is divided by the budgeted tonnes of output. These rates are then multiplied by the number of kilograms required to produce one good tonne.

In 2010, LLHC sold for $2,400 per tonne, making it one of the most profitable products. A similar examination of some of the other low-volume products revealed that they also had very respectable profit margins. Unfortunately, the performance of the high-volume products was less impressive, with many showing losses or very low profit margins. This situation led Ryan Chesser to call a meeting with his marketing vice president, Jennifer Woodruff, and his controller, Kaylin Penn.

Ryan: The above-average profitability of our low-volume specialty products and the poor profit performance of our high-volume products make me believe that we should switch our marketing emphasis to the low-volume line. Perhaps we should drop some of our high-volume products, particularly those showing a loss.

Jennifer: I'm not convinced that the solution you are proposing is the right one. I know our high-volume products are of high quality, and I am convinced that we are as efficient in our production as other firms. I think that somehow our costs are not being assigned correctly. For example, the shipping and warehousing costs are assigned by dividing these costs by the total tonnes of paper sold. Yet . . .

Kaylin: Jennifer, I hate to disagree, but the $30-per-tonne charge for shipping and warehousing seems reasonable. I know that our method to assign these costs is identical to a number of other paper companies.

Jennifer: Well, that may be true, but do these other companies have the variety of products that we have? Our low-volume products require special handling and processing, but when we assign shipping and warehousing costs, we average these special costs across our entire product line. Every tonne produced in our mill passes through our mill shipping department and is either sent directly to the customer or to our distribution centre and then eventually to customers. My records indicate quite clearly that virtually all of the high-volume products are sent directly to customers, whereas most of the low-volume products are sent to the distribution centre. Now, all of the products passing through the mill shipping department should receive a share of the $2,000,000 annual shipping costs. I am not convinced, however, that all products should receive a share of the receiving and shipping costs of the distribution centre as currently practiced.

Ryan: Kaylin, is this true? Does our system allocate our shipping and warehousing costs in this way?

Kaylin: Yes, I'm afraid it does. Jennifer may have a point. Perhaps we need to re-evaluate our method to assign these costs to the product lines.

Ryan: Jennifer, do you have any suggestions concerning how the shipping and warehousing costs should be assigned?

Jennifer: It seems reasonable to make a distinction between products that spend time in the distribution centre and those that do not. We should also distinguish between the receiving and shipping activities at the distribution centre. All incoming shipments are packed on pallets and weigh one tonne each (there are 14 cartons of paper per pallet). In 2010, the receiving department processed 56,000 tonnes of paper. Receiving employs 15 people at an annual cost of $600,000. Other receiving costs total about $500,000. I would recommend that these costs be assigned by using tonnes processed.

Shipping, however, is different. There are two activities associated with shipping: picking the order from inventory and loading the paper. We employ 30 people for picking and 10 for loading, at an annual cost of $1,200,000. Other shipping costs total $1,100,000. Picking and loading are more concerned with the number of shipping items than with tonnage. That is, a shipping item may consist of two or three cartons instead of pallets. Accordingly, the shipping costs of the distribution centre should be assigned by using the number of items shipped. In 2010, for example, we handled 190,000 shipping items.

Ryan: These suggestions have merit. Kaylin, I would like to see what effect Jennifer's suggestions have on the per-unit assignment of shipping and warehousing for LLHC. If the effect is significant, then we will expand the analysis to include all products.

Kaylin: I'm willing to compute the effect, but I'd like to suggest one additional feature. Currently, we have a policy to carry about 25 tonnes of LLHC in inventory. Our current costing system totally ignores the cost of carrying this inventory. Since it costs us $1,665 to produce each tonne of this product, we are tying up a lot of money in inventory—money that could be invested in other productive opportunities. In fact, the return lost is about 16 percent per year. This cost should also be assigned to the units sold.

Ryan: Kaylin, this also sounds good to me. Go ahead and include the carrying cost in your computation.

To help in the analysis, Kaylin gathered the following data for LLHC for 2010:

Tonnes sold	10
Average cartons per shipment	2
Average shipments per tonne	7

Required:

1. Identify the flaws associated with the current method of assigning shipping and warehousing costs to Sharp's products.
2. Calculate the shipping and warehousing cost per tonne of LLHC sold by using the new method suggested by Jennifer and Kaylin.
3. Using the new costs computed in Requirement 2, calculate the profit per tonne of LLHC. Compare this with the profit per tonne computed by using the old method. Do you think that this same effect would be realized for other low-volume products? Explain.
4. Comment on Ryan's proposal to drop some high-volume products and place more emphasis on low-volume products. Discuss the role of the accounting system in supporting this type of decision making.
5. After receiving the analysis of LLHC, Ryan decided to expand the analysis to all products. He also had Kaylin reevaluate the way in which mill overhead was assigned to products. After the restructuring was completed, Ryan took the following actions: (a) the prices of most low-volume products were increased, (b) the prices of several high-volume products were decreased, and (c) some low-volume products were dropped. Explain why his strategy changed so dramatically.

Case 7-75 ACTIVITY-BASED PRODUCT COSTING AND ETHICAL BEHAVIOUR

OBJECTIVE 2 3 4

Consider the following conversation between Leonard Bryner, president and manager of a firm engaged in job manufacturing, and Chuck Davis, certified management accountant, the firm's controller.

Leonard: Chuck, as you know, our firm has been losing market share over the past three years. We have been losing more and more bids, and I don't understand why. At first, I thought that other firms were undercutting simply to gain business, but after examining some of the public financial reports, I believe that they are making a reasonable rate of return. I am beginning to believe that our costs and costing methods are at fault.

Chuck: I can't agree with that. We have good control over our costs. Like most firms in our industry, we use a normal job-costing system. I really don't see any significant waste in the plant.

Leonard: After talking with some other managers at a recent industrial convention, I'm not so sure that waste by itself is the issue. They talked about activity-based management, activity-based costing, and continuous improvement. They mentioned the use of something called "activity drivers" to assign overhead. They claimed that these new procedures can help to produce more efficiency in manufacturing, better control of overhead, and more accurate product costing. A big deal was made of eliminating activities that added no value. Maybe our bids are too high because these other firms have found ways to decrease their overhead costs and to increase the accuracy of their product costing.

Chuck: I doubt it. For one thing, I don't see how we can increase product costing accuracy. So many of our costs are indirect costs. Furthermore, everyone uses some measure of production activity to assign overhead costs. I imagine that what they are calling "activity drivers" is just some new buzzword for measures of production volume. Fads in costing come and go. I wouldn't worry about it. I'll bet that our problems with decreasing sales are temporary. You might recall that we experienced a similar problem about 12 years ago—it was 2 years before it straightened out.

Required:

1. Do you agree or disagree with Chuck and the advice that he gave Leonard? Explain.
2. Was there anything wrong or unethical in the behaviour that Chuck displayed? Explain your reasoning.
3. Do you think that Chuck was well informed—that he was aware of the accounting implications of ABC and that he knew what was meant by cost drivers? Should he have been well informed? Review (in Chapter 1) the first category of the standards of ethical conduct for management accountants. Do any of these standards apply in Chuck's case?

CMA Problem*

CMA Problem 7-1 ACTIVITY-BASED COSTING—OINEON CORPORATION

Oineon Corporation manufactures several different types of printed circuit boards; however, two of the boards account for the majority of the company's sales. The first board, a television circuit board, has been a standard in the industry for several years. The market for this type of board is competitive and, therefore, price sensitive. Oineon plans to sell 65,000 of the TV boards in 2012 at a price of $150 per unit. The second high-volume product, a personal computer (PC) circuit board, is a recent addition to Oineon's product line. Because the PC board incorporates the latest technology, it can be sold at a premium price; the 2012 plans include the sale of 40,000 PC boards at $300 per unit.

Oineon's management group is meeting to discuss strategies for 2012 and the current topic of conversation is how to spend the sales and promotion dollars for next year. The sales manager believes the market share for the TV board could be expanded by concentrating Oineon's promotional efforts in this area. In response to this suggestion, the production manager said, "Why don't you go after a bigger market for the PC board? The cost sheets I get show the contribution from the PC board is more than double the contribution from the TV board. I know we get a premium price for the PC board, so selling it should help overall profitability."

Oineon uses a standard cost system and the following data apply to the TV and PC boards.

	TV Board	PC Board
Direct material	$80	$140
Direct labour	1.5 hours	4 hours
Machine time	.5 hours	1.5 hours

Variable factory overhead is applied on the basis of direct labour hours. For 2012, variable factory overhead is budgeted at $1,120,000 and direct labour hours are estimated at 280,000. The hourly rates for machine time and direct labour are $10 and $14, respectively. Oineon applies a material handling charge at 10 percent of material cost. This material handling charge is not included in variable factory overhead. Total 2012 expenditures for material are budgeted at $10,600,000.

Ed Welch, Oineon's controller, believes that before management proceeds with the discussion about allocating sales and promotional dollars to individual products, it might be worthwhile to look at the products on the basis of the activities involved in their production. As Welch explained to the group, "Activity-based costing integrates the cost of all activities, known as cost drivers, into individual product costs rather than including these costs in overhead pools." Welch has prepared the schedule shown on the next page to help management understand this concept.

Budgeted Cost		Cost Driver	Annual Activity for Cost Driver
Material overhead:			
Procurement	$ 400,000	Number of parts	4,000,000 parts
Production scheduling	220,000	Number of boards	110,000 boards
Packaging and shipping	440,000	Number of boards	110,000 boards
	$1,060,000		
Variable overhead:			
Machine setup	$ 446,000	Number of setups	278,750 setups
Hazardous waste disposal	48,000	Kilograms of waste	16,000 kilograms
Quality control	560,000	Number of inspections	160,000 inspections
General supplies	66,000	Number of boards	110,000 boards
	$1,120,000		
Manufacturing:			
Machine insertion	$1,200,000	Number of parts	3,000,000 parts
Manual insertion	4,000,000	Number of parts	1,000,000 parts
Wave soldering	132,000	Number of boards	110,000 boards
	$5,332,000		

Required Per Unit	TV Board	PC Board
Parts	25	55
Machine insertions	24	35
Manual insertions	1	20
Machine setups	2	3
Hazardous waste	0.02 kg	0.35 kg
Inspections	1	2

"Using this information," Welch explained, "we can calculate an activity-based cost for each TV and PC board and then compare it to the standard cost we have been using. The only cost that remains the same for both cost methods is the cost of direct material. The cost drivers will replace the direct labour, machine time and overhead costs in the standard cost."

Required:

Prepare an Activity-Based Costing report for the TV and PC boards, and comment on the differences with the current standard costs.

Chapter 8

Absorption and Variable Costing, and Inventory Management

After studying Chapter 8, you should be able to:

1. Explain the difference between absorption and variable costing.
2. Prepare segmented income statements.
3. Discuss inventory management under the economic order quantity and just-in-time (JIT) models.

© RYAN STINER

Experience Managerial Decisions

with Zingerman's

Often people think of income statements in the form learned in financial accounting—with all of the sales and expenses shown for the company as a whole. This may be sufficient for external parties, such as investors and banks. However, companies with more than one business segment need to know how each segment is performing as well. **Zingerman's** deli has eight separate businesses. Seven of these segments—the Delicatessen, Mail Order, Bakehouse, ZingTrain, Roadhouse Restaurant, Creamery, and Coffee Company—sell to external customers. The eighth segment, ZingNet, provides payroll, accounting, and human resources services to the other seven segments.

In looking at the segments, it is easy to see that each has both variable and fixed costs. For example, Roadhouse Restaurant has variable costs of food, beverages, paper products, and some labour. Direct fixed costs for Roadhouse include rent/depreciation for the building, furniture, and equipment. In addition, there are common costs.

All seven external customer–oriented Zingerman businesses use ZingNet (part of the Zingerman conglomerate of businesses) to provide support services, such as human resources, payroll, organizational marketing, graphics brand design, information technology, administration, accounting, and office rental. The allocation of the ZingNet costs is done on the basis of revenues for each business. Zingerman executives note that this method of allocation can occasionally cause problems among the other businesses–especially those that do not use much of the ZingNet services, but have high sales (thereby getting a larger share of ZingNet cost allocation). The use of variable costing and segmented income statements can help to overcome this kind of problem, since a properly developed segmented income statement separates direct fixed costs from common fixed costs. Treating the ZingNet costs as common fixed costs would also be consistent with Zingerman's belief that ZingNet costs are an investment in future profitability.

Zingerman's

Here's The Real Kicker

Inventory management is an important activity at Kicker. Because many of the speakers are made overseas, Kicker must schedule production and shipments to match demand. Demand for speakers is seasonal. Imagine a typical Kicker customer. He's a young man, aged 16–24, who wants great, loud sound in his car or truck. He drives around with the volume up and the windows down. From this description, we can see why sales decrease by 15 percent during the winter months. But in mid-March, sales ramp up. California, Florida, and New York are major markets. Spring and summer will start earlier in the first two states and continue into May and June in the latter. It's vital that Kicker have the units available for customers when they want speakers.

Now let's focus on the production side. Many speakers are made in China. The Chinese New Year typically begins in late January or early February. There are major festivals and the speaker factory closes down for a month. Since Kicker sales increase during the spring months, they need a fair amount of inventory on hand early in the year to meet demand and coordinate with production shutdown. Inventory is a fact of life for Kicker in the spring and can range as high as 50 to 100 percent of anticipated sales. In essence, Kicker has a sizable safety stock. The executive team hates lost sales. In fact, that was emphasized in their discussion of inventory policy. They did have previous stockouts, and vividly remember the lost sales.

In summary, stockouts are a problem to be avoided. The cost of lost sales is high. Production and sales are seasonal. Overall, Kicker believes that the traditional reasons for holding inventory are best solved by substantial inventory.

KICKER®

OBJECTIVE 1
Explain the difference between absorption and variable costing.

Variable and Absorption Income Statements

Many companies are composed of separate business units called profit centres. It is important for these companies to determine the overall performance of the business as well as the performance of the individual profit centres. The overall income statement is useful for looking at overall company performance. However, this income statement is of little use for determining the viability of the individual business units or segments. Instead, it is important to develop a segmented income statement for each profit centre. Two methods of computing income have been developed: one based on variable costing and the other based on full or absorption costing. These are costing methods because they refer to the way in which product costs are determined. Recall that *product costs* are inventoried; they include direct materials, direct labour, and overhead. *Period costs*, such as selling and administrative expense, are expensed in the period incurred. The difference between variable and absorption costing hinges on the treatment of one particular cost: fixed factory overhead.

Absorption costing assigns *all* manufacturing costs to the product. Direct materials, direct labour, variable overhead, and fixed overhead define the cost of a product. Thus, under absorption costing, fixed overhead is viewed as a product cost, not a period cost. Under this method, fixed overhead is assigned to the product through the use of a predetermined fixed overhead rate and is not expensed until the product is sold. In other words, fixed overhead is an inventoriable cost.

Variable costing assigns only variable manufacturing costs to the product; these costs include direct materials, direct labour, and variable overhead. Fixed overhead is treated as a period expense and is *excluded* from the product cost. Variable costing stresses the difference between fixed and variable manufacturing costs. The rationale for this is that fixed overhead is a cost of capacity, or staying in business. Once the period is over, any benefits provided by capacity have expired and should not be inventoried. Under variable costing, fixed overhead of a period is seen as expiring in that period and is charged in total against the revenues of the period. Exhibit 8-1 illustrates the classification of costs as product or period costs under absorption and variable costing.

Generally accepted accounting principles (GAAP) require absorption costing for external reporting. The Canada Revenue Agency (CRA) and other regulatory bodies do not accept variable costing as a product-costing method for external reporting. Yet variable costing can supply vital cost information for decision making and control,

Exhibit 8-1

Classification of Costs under Absorption and Variable Costing as Product or Period Costs

	Absorption Costing	Variable Costing
Product costs	Direct materials Direct labour Variable overhead Fixed overhead	Direct materials Direct labour Variable overhead
Period costs	Selling expenses Administrative expenses	Fixed overhead Selling expenses Administrative expenses

information not supplied by absorption costing. For *internal* application, variable costing is an important managerial tool.

Inventory Valuation

Inventory is valued at cost (product or manufacturing cost). (Recall that inventory cost *never* includes the period costs of selling or administration.) Under absorption costing, that product cost includes direct materials, direct labour, variable overhead, and fixed overhead. Under variable costing, the product cost includes only direct materials, direct labour, and variable overhead. Cornerstone 8-1 shows how to compute inventory cost under absorption costing.

Notice that the inventory cost computed under absorption costing is the traditional product cost used for external financial statements and for GAAP. Each unit includes all variable manufacturing costs as well as a portion of fixed factory overhead. Cornerstone 8-2 shows how to calculate inventory cost under variable costing.

Looking carefully at Cornerstones 8-1 and 8-2, we can see that the only difference between the two approaches is the treatment of fixed factory overhead. Thus, the unit product cost under absorption costing is always greater than the unit product cost under variable costing. Exhibit 8-2 shows this difference pictorially for a simplified example.

Income Statements Using Variable and Absorption Costing

Because unit product costs are the basis for cost of goods sold, the variable and absorption costing methods can lead to different operating income figures. The difference arises because of the amount of fixed overhead recognized as an expense under the two methods. Cornerstone 8-3 shows how to develop cost of goods sold and income statements for absorption costing.

As we see in Cornerstone 8-3, the cost of goods sold includes some but not all fixed factory overhead. Total fixed factory overhead is \$250,000 (\$25 × 10,000 units produced). However, only \$200,000 (\$25 × 8,000 units sold) of fixed overhead was expensed in cost of goods sold. Where did the other \$50,000 of fixed overhead go? It is included in the cost of ending inventory.

Cornerstone 8-4 shows how to prepare a variable-costing income statement.

Let's compare Cornerstones 8-3 and 8-4. Operating income under absorption costing is \$500,000 whereas operating income under variable costing is only \$450,000. Remember that \$50,000 of current period product cost in fixed factory overhead went into inventory under absorption costing. However, all of the fixed factory overhead is included in the costs for variable costing. Notice that selling and administrative expenses are never included in product cost. They are always expensed on the income statement and never appear on the balance sheet.

ANALYTICAL Q&A

Suppose that unit product costs include direct materials of \$6, direct labour of \$7, and variable overhead of \$2. Total fixed overhead is \$75,000 and typically 25,000 units are produced. What is the cost of one unit under variable costing? What is the cost of one unit under absorption costing?

Answers on pages 711 to 715.

CORNERSTONE 8-1

The HOW and WHY of Computing Inventory Cost under Absorption Costing

Information:

During the most recent year, Fairchild Company had the following data associated with the product it makes:

Units in beginning inventory	—
Units produced	10,000
Units sold ($300 per unit)	8,000
Variable costs per unit:	
Direct materials	$50
Direct labour	$100
Variable overhead	$50
Fixed costs:	
Fixed overhead per unit produced	$25
Fixed selling and administrative	$100,000

Required:

1. How many units are in ending inventory?
2. Using absorption costing, calculate the per-unit product cost.
3. What is the value of ending inventory?

Solution:

1. Units in ending inventory = Units in beginning inventory + Units produced − Units sold
   = 0 + 10,000 − 8,000
   = 2,000

2. Absorption costing unit cost:

Direct materials	$ 50
Direct labour	100
Variable overhead	50
Fixed overhead	25
Unit product cost	$225

3. Value of ending inventory = Units in ending inventory × Absorption unit product cost
   = 2,000 × $225
   = $450,000

WHY:

Because pricing the inventory is necessary to state accurately the total assets of a firm, the gross margin, and the net profit margin.

Production, Sales, and Income Relationships

The relationship between variable-costing income and absorption-costing income changes as the relationship between production and sales changes. If more is sold than was produced, variable-costing income is greater than absorption-costing income. This situation is just the opposite of that for the Fairchild example. Selling more than was produced means that beginning inventory and units produced are being sold. Under absorption costing, units coming out of inventory have attached to them fixed overhead from a prior period. In addition, units produced and sold

The HOW and WHY of Computing Inventory Cost under Variable Costing

CORNERSTONE 8-2

Information:

During the most recent year, Fairchild Company had the following data associated with the product it makes:

Units in beginning inventory	—
Units produced	10,000
Units sold ($300 per unit)	8,000
Variable costs per unit:	
Direct materials	$50
Direct labour	$100
Variable overhead	$50
Fixed costs:	
Fixed overhead per unit produced	$25
Fixed selling and administrative	$100,000

Required:

1. How many units are in ending inventory?
2. Using variable costing, calculate the per-unit product cost.
3. What is the value of ending inventory?

Solution:

1. Units in ending inventory = Units in beginning inventory + Units produced − Units sold
   = 0 + 10,000 − 8,000
   = 2,000

2. Variable costing unit cost:

Direct materials	$ 50
Direct labour	100
Variable overhead	50
Unit product cost	$200

3. Value of ending inventory = Units in ending inventory × Variable unit product cost
   = 2,000 × $200
   = $400,000

WHY:

Because pricing the inventory under variable costing allows us to accurately calculate the variable cost of goods sold and the contribution margin for a firm.

Exhibit 8-2

Product Cost under Absorption and Variable Costing

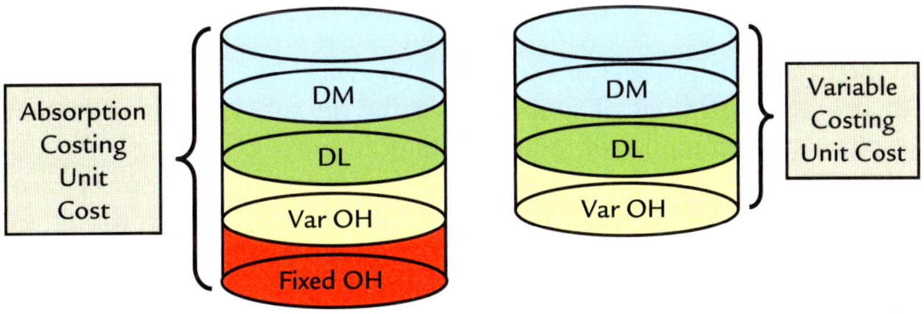

CORNERSTONE 8-3

The HOW and WHY of Preparing an Absorption-Costing Income Statement

Information:
During the most recent year, Fairchild Company had the following data:

Units in beginning inventory	—
Units produced	10,000
Units sold ($300 per unit)	8,000
Variable costs per unit:	
Direct materials	$50
Direct labour	$100
Variable overhead	$50
Fixed costs:	
Fixed overhead per unit produced	$25
Fixed selling and administrative	$100,000

Required:
1. Calculate the cost of goods sold under absorption costing.
2. Prepare an income statement using absorption costing.

Solution:
1. Cost of goods sold = Absorption unit product cost × Units sold
= $225 × 8,000
= $1,800,000

2.

Fairchild Company
Absorption-Costing Income Statement

Sales ($300 × 8,000)	$2,400,000
Less: Cost of goods sold	1,800,000
Gross margin	$ 600,000
Less: Selling and administrative expenses	100,000
Operating income	$ 500,000

WHY:
Because it is expected by the CRA for reporting purposes.

have all of the current period's fixed overhead attached. Thus, the amount of fixed overhead expensed by absorption costing is greater than the current period's fixed overhead by the amount of fixed overhead flowing out of beginning inventory. Accordingly, variable-costing income is greater than absorption-costing income by the amount of fixed overhead flowing out of beginning inventory.

If production and sales are equal, of course, no difference exists between the two reported incomes. Since the units produced are all sold, absorption costing, like variable costing, will recognize the total fixed overhead of the period as an expense. No fixed overhead flows into or out of inventory.

The relationships between production, sales, and the two reported incomes are summarized in Exhibit 8-3. Note that if production is greater than sales, then inventory has increased. If production is less than sales, then inventory must have decreased. If production is equal to sales, then the number of units in beginning inventory is equal to the number of units in ending inventory.

The difference between absorption and variable costing centres on the recognition of expense associated with fixed factory overhead. Under absorption costing, fixed factory overhead must be assigned to units produced. This presents two problems that we

The HOW and WHY of Preparing a Variable-Costing Income Statement

CORNERSTONE 8-4

Information:

During the most recent year, Fairchild Company had the following data:

Units in beginning inventory	—
Units produced	10,000
Units sold ($300 per unit)	8,000
Variable costs per unit:	
Direct materials	$50
Direct labour	$100
Variable overhead	$50
Fixed costs:	
Fixed overhead per unit produced	$25
Fixed selling and administrative	$100,000

Required:

1. Calculate the cost of goods sold under variable costing.
2. Prepare an income statement using variable costing.

Solution:

1. Cost of goods sold = Variable unit product cost × Units sold
   = $200 × 8,000
   = $1,600,000

2.

Fairchild Company
Variable-Costing Income Statement

Sales ($300 × 8,000)		$2,400,000
Less variable expenses:		
Variable cost of goods sold		1,600,000
Contribution margin		$ 800,000
Less fixed expenses:		
Fixed overhead	$250,000	
Fixed selling and administrative	100,000	350,000
Operating income		$ 450,000

WHY:

Because a variable costing income statement facilitates, among other things, a cost-volume-profit analysis.

Exhibit 8-3

Production, Sales, and Income Relationships

	If	Then
1.	Production > Sales	Absorption income > Variable income
2.	Production < Sales	Absorption income < Variable income
3.	Production = Sales	Absorption income = Variable income

have not explicitly considered. First, how do we convert factory overhead applied on the basis of direct labour hours or machine hours into factory overhead applied to units produced? Second, what is done when actual factory overhead does not equal applied factory overhead? The solution to these problems is reserved for a more advanced accounting course.

Reasons for Using Variable Costing

Why do many companies use variable costing for internal statements? One reason is that absorption-costing income is affected by production volume while variable-costing income is not.

Suppose the evaluation of a manager's performance is based heavily on operating income. If the company uses the absorption-costing approach, a manager might be tempted to produce unneeded units just to increase reported operating income, for the increase in inventory would absorb some of the overhead costs (i.e., those costs would not be expensed). No such temptation exists with variable costing.

Companies also choose variable or absorption costing based on which system they believe gives a better signal about performance. A sales-oriented company may prefer variable costing because its income is affected primarily by the level of sales. In contrast, a production-oriented company (e.g., a company that can easily sell all the units it produces) might prefer absorption costing. Why? Because additional production increases the operating income with absorption costing but not with variable costing.

Comparing Variable and Absorption Costing

The *contribution approach* (variable or direct costing) is a method of internal reporting that emphasizes the distinction between variable and fixed costs for decision-making purposes. The income statement provides a *contribution margin*, which is computed after deducting all variable costs, including variable selling and administrative costs. This approach makes it easier to see the impact of changes in sales demand on operating income. It also dovetails neatly with the cost-volume-profit analysis.

The *absorption approach* (absorption or full costing) is the traditional approach of external reporting. It considers all factory overhead, fixed and variable, to be product, inventoriable costs and therefore to be expensed only when the products are sold. This is the approach taken by most companies.

For decision purposes, the major difference between the contribution approach and the absorption approach is that the former emphasizes the distinction between variable and fixed costs. Thus, costs are classified primarily by variable and fixed *cost behaviour patterns*, not by *business functions*. These methods also differ in one primary conceptual respect: fixed manufacturing overhead is excluded from the cost of products under *variable costing* but is included in the cost of products under *absorption costing*. In other words, variable costing signifies that fixed factory overhead is not inventoried. In contrast, absorption costing indicates that inventory values include fixed factory overhead.

In addition, variable costing is affected only by the level of sales. Variable costs of goods sold and variable selling and administrative expense are a function of sales. Absorption costing, by contrast, is a function of both sales and production.

Furthermore, an absorption-costed income statement separates costs into manufacturing and nonmanufacturing categories. By contrast, a variable-costed income statement separates costs into fixed and variable.

Gross Margin/Contribution Margin

The difference between the gross margin (from the absorption approach) and the contribution margin (from the contribution approach) is striking in manufacturing companies.

Fixed factory overhead does not appear as a separate line in an absorption-costing income statement. Instead, the fixed factory overhead is included in two places: as part of the cost of goods sold and as a *production volume variance*. A *production volume variance* appears whenever actual production deviates from the expected volume of production used in computing the fixed overhead rate:

$$\text{Production volume variance} = (\text{Actual volume} - \text{Expected volume}) \times \text{Fixed overhead rate}$$

The fixed overhead rate or the amount of fixed manufacturing overhead applied to each unit of production is determined by dividing the budgeted fixed overhead by the budgeted volume of production.

Variable costing for internal reporting requires in effect *two* systems, since external reporting must be done when an absorption-costing method is used.

Absorption costing is more widely used than variable costing. However, the growing use of the contribution approach in performance measurement and cost analysis has led to the increasing use of variable costing for internal reporting purposes. Keep in mind that advocates of the contribution approach do not maintain that fixed costs are unimportant or irrelevant; they simply stress that the distinctions between the behaviours of variable and fixed costs are crucial for certain decisions.

Variable costing, which allocates both variable and fixed overheads to inventory, and absorption costing are both accepted by the CRA as methods for costing inventory, although only absorption costing is accepted for tax reporting purposes. This means that a method allowed to be used for financial statement purposes (variable costing) need not be consistent with the method of inventory valuation method used for tax reporting purposes (absorption costing).

Despite the important differences between the two approaches, firms increasingly are not concerned with the choice between variable and absorption costing. The adoption of just-in-time production methods has sharply reduced inventory levels, and as a result, there is no difference between variable-costing and absorption-costing income if the inventory level does not change.

Reconciliation of Variable Costing and Absorption Costing Remember that the relationship between sales and production is what determines the difference between variable-costing and absorption-costing income. Whenever sales exceed production—that is, when inventory decreases—variable-costing income is greater than absorption-costing income. Whenever production exceeds sales—that is, when inventory increases—variable-costing income is less than absorption-costing income. See Exhibit 8-4. The difference in income also equals the difference in the total amount of fixed manufacturing overhead charged as expense during a given year. The difference is explained by multiplying the fixed-overhead product-costing rate by the *change* in the total units in the beginning and ending inventories.

Evaluating Profit-Centre Managers

The evaluation of managers is often tied to the profitability of the units that they control. How income changes from one period to the next and how actual income compares with planned income are frequently used as signals of managerial ability. To be meaningful signals, however, income should reflect managerial effort. For example, if a manager has worked hard and increased sales while holding costs in check, income should increase over the prior period, signalling success. In general terms, if income performance is expected to reflect managerial performance, then managers have the right to expect the following:

1. As sales revenue increases from one period to the next, all other things being equal, income should increase.
2. As sales revenue decreases from one period to the next, all other things being equal, income should decrease.
3. As sales revenue remains unchanged from one period to the next, all other things being equal, income should remain unchanged.

Variable costing ensures that the above relationships hold; however, absorption costing may not.

Segmented Income Statements Using Variable Costing

OBJECTIVE 2
Prepare segmented income statements.

A **segment** is a subunit of a company of sufficient importance to warrant the production of performance reports. Segments can be divisions, departments, product lines, customer classes, and so on. Variable costing is useful in preparing segmented income statements because it gives useful information on variable and fixed expenses.

Exhibit 8-4

Variable and Absorption Costing Models

Variable Costing Model

Types of costs incurred	**INCOME STATEMENT**
	Revenue
	less
Product costs	
Direct material (DM)	
Direct labour (DL)	
Variable manufacturing overhead (VOH)	Variable costs of goods sold
	equals Product contribution margin
	less
Period costs	
Variable nonmanufacturing expenses	Variable selling expenses
	Variable administrative expenses
	equals Total contribution margin
	less
Fixed manufacturing overhead	Fixed manufacturing expenses
Fixed nonmanufacturing overhead	Fixed selling expenses
	Fixed administrative expenses
	equals EBT (Earning Before Taxes)

Absorption Costing Model

Types of costs incurred	**INCOME STATEMENT**
	Revenue
	less
Product costs	
Direct material (DM)	
Direct labour (DL)	
Variable manufacturing overhead (VOH)	Costs of goods sold
Fixed manufacturing overhead	
	equals Gross margin
	less
Period costs	
Nonmanufacturing expenses	Selling expenses
	Administrative expenses
	equals EBT (Earnings Before Taxes)

In segmented income statements, fixed expenses are broken down into two categories: *direct fixed expenses* and *common fixed expenses.* This additional subdivision highlights controllable versus noncontrollable costs and enhances the manager's ability to evaluate each segment's contribution to overall firm performance.

CONCEPT Q&A

Consider a department store. Suppose that the store decides to drop a department, such as the furniture department. What are the direct fixed costs involved? What are the common fixed costs that would not be reduced if the department is dropped?

Answers on pages 711 to 715.

Direct fixed expenses are fixed expenses that are directly traceable to a segment. These are sometimes referred to as *avoidable fixed expenses* or *traceable fixed expenses* because they vanish if the segment is eliminated. For example, if the segments were sales regions, a direct fixed expense for each region would be the rent for the sales office, salary of the sales manager of each region, and so on. If one region were to be eliminated, then those fixed expenses would disappear.

Common fixed expenses are jointly caused by two or more segments. These expenses persist even if one of the segments to which they are common is eliminated. For example, depreciation on the corporate headquarters building, the salary of the CEO, and the cost of printing and distributing the annual report to shareholders are common fixed expenses for **Walt Disney Company**. If Walt Disney Company were to sell a theme park or open a new one, those common expenses would not be affected.

The HOW and WHY of Preparing a Segmented Income Statement

CORNERSTONE 8-5

Information:

Audiomatronics Inc. produces MP3 players and DVD players in a single factory. The following information was provided for the coming year.

	MP3 Players	DVD Players
Sales	$400,000	$290,000
Variable cost of goods sold	200,000	150,000
Direct fixed overhead	30,000	20,000

A sales commission of 5 percent of sales is paid for each of the two product lines. Direct fixed selling and administrative expense was estimated to be $10,000 for the MP3 line and $15,000 for the DVD line.

Common fixed overhead for the factory was estimated to be $100,000; common selling and administrative expense was estimated to be $20,000.

Required:

Prepare a segmented income statement for Audiomatronics Inc. for the coming year, using variable costing.

Solution:

Audiomatronics Inc.
Segmented Income Statement
For the Coming Year

	MP3 Players	DVD Players	Total
Sales	$ 400,000	$ 290,000	$ 690,000
Variable cost of goods sold	(200,000)	(150,000)	(350,000)
Variable selling expense*	(20,000)	(14,500)	(34,500)
Contribution margin	$ 180,000	$ 125,500	$ 305,500
Less direct fixed expenses:			
Direct fixed overhead	(30,000)	(20,000)	(50,000)
Direct selling and administrative	(10,000)	(15,000)	(25,000)
Segment margin	$ 140,000	$ 90,500	$ 230,500
Less common fixed expenses:			
Common fixed overhead			(100,000)
Common selling and administrative			(20,000)
Operating income			$ 110,500

* Variable selling expense for MP3 players = 0.05 × Sales = 0.05 × $400,000 = $20,000
Variable selling expense for DVD players = 0.05 × Sales = 0.05 × $290,000 = $14,500

WHY:

Because it is often necessary to calculate net income per division or department and to available segment performance.

Cornerstone 8-5 shows how to prepare a segmented income statement where the segments are product lines. In the example, Audiomatronics produces both MP3 players and DVD players.

Notice that Cornerstone 8-5 shows that both MP3 players and DVD players have large positive contribution margins ($180,000 for MP3 players and $125,500 for DVD players). Both products are providing revenue above variable costs that can be used to help cover the firm's fixed costs. However, some of the firm's fixed costs are

CONCEPT Q&A

Has a store ever been out of an item that you wanted to buy? What did you do? What is the impact of the stockout on the store?

Answers on pages 711 to 715.

The first question needs to be addressed before the second can be answered. Assume that demand is known. In choosing an order quantity, managers need to be concerned only with ordering and carrying costs. The formulas for calculating these are as follows:

$$\text{Total inventory-related cost} = \text{Ordering cost} + \text{Carrying cost}$$

$$\text{Ordering cost} = \text{Number of orders per year} \times \text{Cost of placing an order}$$

$$\text{Average number of units in inventory} = \frac{\text{Units in order}}{2}$$

$$\text{Carrying cost} = \text{Average number of units in inventory} \times \text{Cost of carrying one unit in inventory}$$

The cost of carrying inventory can be computed for any organization that carries inventories, including retail, service, and manufacturing organizations. Cornerstone 8-6 illustrates the application for a service organization and shows how to calculate total ordering cost, carrying cost, and inventory cost.

The total carrying cost for the year is calculated by multiplying the average number of units on hand by the cost of carrying one unit in inventory for a year. But what is the

CORNERSTONE 8-6

The HOW and WHY of Calculating Ordering Cost, Carrying Cost, and Total Inventory-Related Cost

Information:

Mall-o-Cars Inc. sells a number of automotive brands and provides service after the sale for those brands. Part X7B is used in the repair of water pumps (the part is purchased from external suppliers). Each year, 10,000 units of Part X7B are used; they are currently purchased in lots of 1,000 units. It costs Mall-o-Cars $25 to place the order, and carrying cost is $2 per part per year.

Required:

1. How many orders for Part X7B does Mall-o-Cars place per year?
2. What is the total ordering cost of Part X7B per year?
3. What is the total carrying cost of Part X7B per year?
4. What is the total cost of Mall-o-Cars' inventory policy for Part X7B per year?

Solution:

1. Number of orders = Annual number of units used/Number of units in an order
   = 10,000/1,000
   = 10 orders per year
2. Total ordering cost = Number of orders × Cost per order
   = 10 orders × $25
   = $250
3. Total carrying cost = Average number of units in inventory × Cost of carrying one unit in inventory
   = (1,000/2) × $2
   = $1,000
4. Total inventory-related cost = Total ordering cost + Total carrying cost
   = $250 + $1,000
   = $1,250

WHY:

Because it allows for the efficient management of inventories and improvement of performance measures.

Exhibit 8-7

Beginning, Ending, and Average Inventory

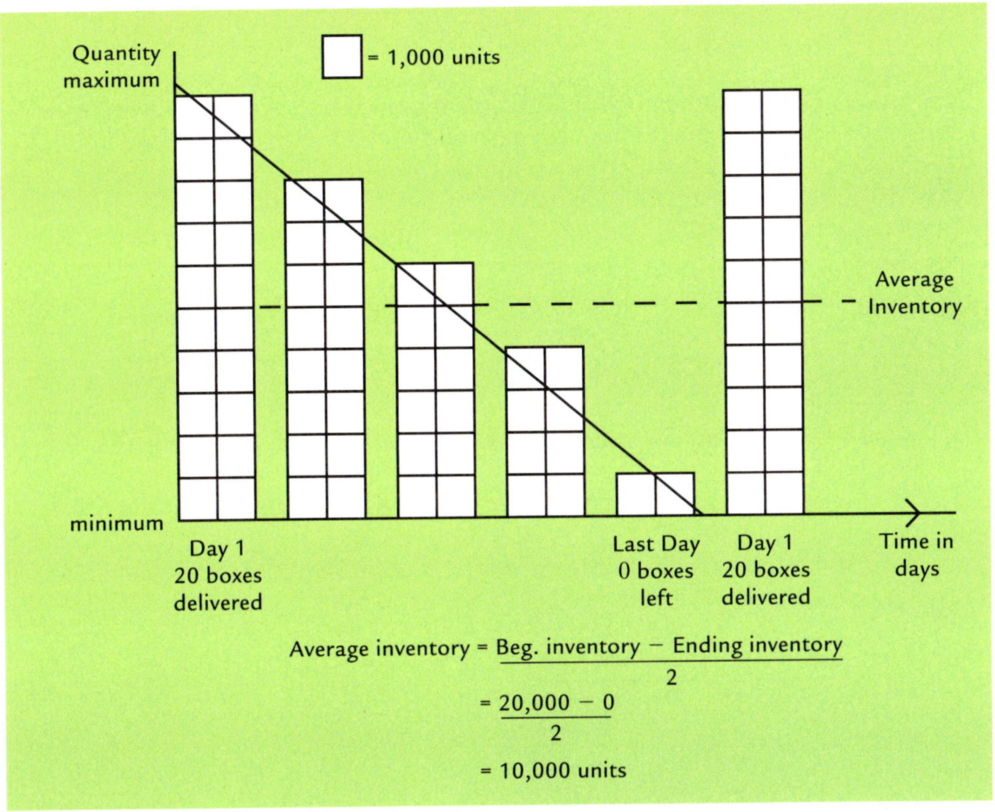

average number of units on hand? Given the policy of ordering 1,000 units at a time, the maximum number on hand would be 1,000 units—the amount on hand just after an order is delivered. The minimum amount on hand would be zero, ideally, the amount seconds before the new order arrives. Therefore, the average amount in inventory is the maximum plus the minimum divided by two. See Exhibit 8-7 for an illustration of this concept.

The total cost of Mall-o-Cars' current policy is \$1,250 (\$250 + \$1,000). An order quantity of 1,000 with a total cost of \$1,250, however, may not be the best choice. Some other order quantity may produce a lower total cost. The objective is to find the order quantity that minimizes the total cost. The number of units in the optimal size order quantity is called the **economic order quantity (EOQ)**.

The Economic Order Quantity

Since EOQ is the quantity that minimizes total inventory-related costs, a formula[1] for computing it is as follows.

$$EOQ = \sqrt{2 \times CO \times D/CC}$$

where:

EOQ = The optimal number of units to be ordered at one time
CO = The cost of placing one order
D = The annual demand for the item in units
CC = The cost of carrying one unit in inventory for a year

Cornerstone 8-7 shows how to use the EOQ formula.

Look carefully at Cornerstone 8-7. Notice that at the EOQ, the carrying cost equals the ordering cost. This is always true for the simple EOQ model described here. Now compare Cornerstone 8-7 with Cornerstone 8-6. The EOQ order quantity of 500 is less costly than an order quantity of 1,000 (\$1,000 vs. \$1,250).

[1] This formula is derived by using calculus. Its derivation is reserved for a later course.

CORNERSTONE 8-7

The HOW and WHY of Calculating the Economic Order Quantity (EOQ)

Information:
Mall-o-Cars Inc. sells a number of automotive brands and provides service after the sale for a variety of automotive makes and models. Part X7B is used in the repair of water pumps (the part is purchased from external suppliers). Each year, 10,000 units of Part X7B are used; they are currently purchased in lots of 1,000 units. It costs Mall-o-Cars $25 to place the order, and carrying cost is $2 per part per year.

Required:
1. What is the EOQ for Part X7B?
2. How many orders per year for Part X7B will Mall-o-Cars place under the EOQ policy?
3. What is the total annual ordering cost of Part X7B for a year under the EOQ policy?
4. What is the total annual carrying cost of Part X7B per year under the EOQ policy?
5. What is the total annual inventory-related cost for Part X7B under the EOQ?

Solution:

1. $EOQ = \sqrt{2 \times CO \times D/CC}$

   $EOQ = \sqrt{2 \times \$25 \times 10{,}000/\$2}$

   $= \sqrt{500{,}000/2}$

   $= 500$ units

2. Number of orders = Annual number of units used/Number of units in an order
   = 10,000/500
   = 20 orders per year

3. Total ordering cost = Number of orders × Cost per order
   = 20 orders × $25
   = $500

4. Total carrying cost = Average number of units in inventory × Cost of carrying one unit in inventory
   = (500/2) × $2
   = $500

5. Total inventory-related cost = Total ordering cost + Total carrying cost
   = $500 + $500
   = $1,000

WHY:
Because the EOQ determines the ideal order quantity that minimizes the inventory-related costs.

Reorder Point

The EOQ answers the question of how much to order (or produce). Knowing when to place an order (or set up for production) is also an essential part of any inventory policy.

The **reorder point** is the point in time when a new order should be placed (or setup started). It is a function of the EOQ, the lead time, and the rate at which inventory is used.

The HOW and WHY of Calculating the Reorder Point

CORNERSTONE 8-8

Information:
Mall-o-Cars Inc. sells a number of automotive brands and provides service after the sale for those brands. Part X7B is used in the repair of water pumps (the part is purchased from external suppliers). Each year, 10,000 units of Part X7B are used; they are used at the rate of 40 parts per day. It takes Mall-o-Cars five days from the time of order to the time of the arrival of the order.

Required:
Calculate the reorder point.

Solution:
Reorder point = Daily usage × Lead time
Reorder point = 40 × 5 days = 200

WHY:
Because it allows a firm to avoid stockout situations.

Lead time is the time required to receive the economic order quantity once an order is placed or a setup is started.

To avoid stockout costs and to minimize carrying costs, an order should be placed so that it arrives just as the last item in inventory is used. Knowing the rate of usage and lead time allows us to compute the reorder point that accomplishes these objectives:

$$\text{Reorder point} = \text{Rate of usage} \times \text{Lead time}$$

Cornerstone 8-8 shows how to calculate the reorder point when usage is known with certainty.

Thus, when Mall-o-Cars' supply of Part X7B drops to 200 parts, it is time to reorder.

If the demand for the part or product is not known with certainty, a stockout may occur. For example, if 45 units of the part were used per day instead of 40, the firm would use 200 parts after nearly four and a half days. Since the new order would not arrive until the end of the fifth day, production would be idled for half a day. To avoid this problem, organizations often choose to carry safety stock.

Safety stock is extra inventory carried to serve as insurance against changes in demand. Safety stock is computed by multiplying the lead time by the difference between the maximum rate of usage and the average rate of usage. Cornerstone 8-9 shows how to calculate safety stock and the reorder point with safety stock.

Economic Order Quantity and Inventory Management

The EOQ model is very useful in identifying the optimal trade-off between inventory ordering costs and carrying costs. It also is useful in helping to deal with uncertainty by using safety stock. The historical importance of the EOQ model in many industries can be better appreciated by understanding the nature of the traditional manufacturing environment. This environment has been characterized by the mass production of a few standardized products that typically have a very high setup cost. The high setup cost encouraged a large batch size. Thus, production runs for these firms tended to be quite long, and the excess production was placed in inventory.

Just-in-Time Approach to Inventory Management

The economic environment for many traditional, large-batch, high-setup-cost firms has changed dramatically in the past 10 to 20 years. Advances in transportation and communication have contributed significantly to the creation of global competition. Advances in technology have contributed to shorter life cycles for products, and product diversity has increased. These competitive pressures have led many firms to

CORNERSTONE 8-9

The HOW and WHY of Calculating Safety Stock and the Reorder Point with Safety Stock

Information:

Mall-o-Cars Inc. sells a number of automotive brands and provides service after the sale for those brands. Part X7B is used in the repair of water pumps (the part is purchased from external suppliers). Each year, 10,000 units of Part X7B are used; they are used at an average rate of 40 parts per day. However, some days as many as 50 parts are used. It takes Mall-o-Cars five days from the time of order to the time of the arrival of the order.

Required:

1. Calculate the amount of safety stock.
2. Calculate the reorder point with safety stock.

Solution:

1. Safety stock = (Maximum daily usage − Average daily usage) × Lead time
   = (50 − 40) × 5 days
   = 50

2. Reorder point = Maximum daily usage × Lead time
   Reorder point = 50 × 5 days = 250

   Or

   Reorder point = (Average daily usage × Lead time) + Safety stock
   Reorder point = (40 × 5 days) + 50 = 250

WHY:

Because the safety stock calculation assists a firm in determining the potential cost or lost sales from stockout situations.

abandon the EOQ model in favour of a just-in-time (JIT) approach. In this way, the costs of ordering and carrying inventory are simply not incurred. However, it is still necessary to solve the underlying problems of uncertainty.

The **just-in-time (JIT)** approach maintains that goods should be pulled through the system by present demand rather than being pushed through on a fixed schedule based on anticipated demand. Many fast-food restaurants, such as **McDonald's**, use a pull system to control their finished goods inventory. When a customer orders a hamburger, it is taken from the rack. When the number of hamburgers gets too low, the cooks make new hamburgers. Customer demand pulls the materials through the system. This same principle is used in manufacturing settings. Each operation produces only what is necessary to satisfy the demand of the succeeding operation. The material or subassembly arrives just in time for production to occur so that demand can be met.

Benefits of JIT

The hallmark of JIT is to reduce all inventories to very low levels. The pursuit of insignificant levels of inventories is vital to the success of JIT. This idea of pursuing insignificant inventories, however, necessarily challenges the traditional reasons for holding inventories (Exhibit 8-6).

According to the traditional view, inventories solve some underlying problems related to each of the reasons listed in Exhibit 8-6. For example, the problem of resolving the conflict between ordering or setup costs and carrying costs is solved by selecting an inventory level that minimizes the sum of these costs. If demand is greater than expected or if production is reduced by breakdowns and production inefficiencies, then inventories serve as buffers, providing products to customers that may otherwise not have been available. Similarly, inventories can prevent shutdowns caused by late deliveries of materials, defective parts, and failures of machines used to produce subassemblies. Finally, inventories are often the solution to the problem of buying the best raw materials for the least cost through the use of quantity discounts. JIT inventory management offers alternative solutions that do not require high inventories.

Ordering costs are reduced by developing close relationships with suppliers. Negotiating long-term contracts for the supply of outside materials will obviously reduce the number of orders and the associated ordering costs. Some retailers have reduced ordering costs by allowing the manufacturer to handle inventory management for the retailer. The manufacturer tells the retailer when and how much stock to reorder. The retailer reviews the recommendation and approves the order if it makes sense. The **Hudson's Bay Company** and **Canadian Tire Corporation** for example, use this arrangement to reduce inventories as well as stockout problems.

Uncertainty in demand is approached by reducing setup times. Then, manufacturers can literally produce to order. Most shutdowns occur for one of three reasons: machine failure, defective material or subassembly, and unavailability of a raw material or subassembly. Holding inventories is one traditional solution to all three problems. Those espousing the JIT approach claim that inventories do not solve these problems but rather cover up or hide them. JIT solves the three problems by emphasizing total preventive maintenance and total quality control and by building the right kind of relationship with suppliers.

Traditionally, inventories are carried so that a firm can take advantage of quantity discounts and hedge against future price increases of the items purchased. The objective is to lower the cost of inventory. JIT achieves the same objective without carrying inventories. The JIT solution is to negotiate long-term contracts with a few chosen suppliers located as close to the production facility as possible and to establish more extensive supplier involvement. Suppliers are not selected on the basis of price alone. Performance—the quality of the component and the ability to deliver as needed—and commitment to JIT purchasing are vital considerations. Other benefits of long-term contracts exist. They stipulate prices and acceptable quality levels. Long-term contracts also reduce dramatically the number of orders placed, which helps drive down the ordering cost.

Limitations of JIT

JIT does have limitations. It is often referred to as a program of simplification—yet this does not imply that JIT is simple or easy to implement. Time is required, for example, to build sound relationships with suppliers. Insisting on immediate changes in delivery times and quality may not be realistic and may cause difficult confrontations between a company and its suppliers. Workers also may be affected by JIT. Studies have shown that sharp reductions in inventory buffers may cause a regimented workflow and high levels of stress among production workers. If the workers perceive JIT as a way of simply squeezing more out of them, then JIT efforts may be doomed. Perhaps a better strategy for JIT implementation is one where inventory reductions follow the process improvements that JIT offers. It requires careful and thorough planning and preparation. Companies should expect some struggle and frustration.

The most glaring deficiency of JIT is the absence of inventory to buffer production interruptions. Current sales are constantly being threatened by an unexpected interruption in production. In fact, if a problem occurs, JIT's approach consists of trying to find and solve the problem before any further production activity occurs. Retailers who use JIT tactics also face the possibility of shortages. (JIT retailers order what they need now, not what they expect to sell; the idea is to flow goods through the channel as late as possible, keeping inventories low and decreasing the need for markdowns.) If demand increases well beyond the retailer's supply of inventory, then the retailer may be unable to make order adjustments quickly enough to avoid lost sales and irritated customers. The JIT manufacturing company is also willing to place current sales at risk to achieve assurance of future sales. This assurance comes from higher quality, quicker response time, and less operating costs. Even so, we must recognize that a sale lost today is a sale lost forever. Installing a JIT system so that it operates with little interruption is not a short-run project. Thus, losing sales is a real cost of installing a JIT system.

Here's The Real Kicker

Stillwater Designs has 14 departments. Each department is given a budget for the coming fiscal year. The budgeting process begins with a sales forecast prepared by the president and vice presidents. The fiscal year for the company is October 1 through September 30. The budget is prepared during August and September, the last two months of the fiscal year. The fiscal year is driven by the seasonal nature of the business. In January of each year, there is a consumer electronics show in Las Vegas, Nevada. New products are introduced, and initial orders from distributors are taken. The sales season starts earnestly in March, reaches its peak in June or July, and drops to its lowest level in the fall. The sales season is driven by the anticipation of warm weather. The young men buying the Kicker speakers and amplifiers want to drive with windows down—with the apparent hope of impressing the girls!

Each department is given a percentage of sales as its expense budget. The amount ultimately decided upon is not simply a top-down decision. Department managers submit a request for their desired budget. Negotiation takes place between the department managers and their associated vice presidents (each departmental manager is answerable to a specific vice president). Whether or not the desired levels are provided depends on how well the departmental manager can justify the expenditures. An important criterion is the notion that resources are expended to make profits.

The budget is reviewed monthly. Any large deviations from the budget are investigated (usually more than a 10 percent deviation is required for an investigation). However, no formal incentive system is tied to budgetary performance. The budget is viewed as a guideline. If more resources are needed, then they can be obtained provided the request is backed up with a good idea and a promising payout.

KICKER®

OBJECTIVE 1

Define budgeting and discuss its role in planning, control, and decision making.

Description of Budgeting

All businesses should prepare budgets; all large businesses do. Business entities come in a variety of forms: sole proprietorships (single-owner businesses), partnerships, and corporations. Even small, professional corporations like sole-practitioner lawyers, dentists, and doctors can benefit from the planning and control provided by budgets.

Budgeting and Planning and Control

Planning and control are tied together in an important and vital way. *Planning* is looking ahead to see what actions should be taken to realize particular goals. *Control* is looking backward, determining what actually happened, and comparing it with the previously planned outcomes. This comparison can then be used to adjust the budget, looking forward once more. Exhibit 9-1 illustrates the cycle of planning, control, and budgets.

Budgets are financial plans for the future and are a key component of planning. They identify objectives and the actions needed to achieve them. Before a budget is prepared, an organization should develop a strategic plan. The **strategic plan** identifies strategies for future activities and operations, generally covering at least five years. The organization can translate the overall strategy into long- and short-term objectives. These objectives form the basis of the budget. The budget and the strategic plan should be tightly linked. Since budgets, especially one-year plans, are short run in nature, this linkage is important because it helps management ensure that not all attention is focused on the short run. For example, on May 14, 2007, private equity firm **Cerberus Capital Management** announced it would buy an 80.1 percent stake in **Chrysler** from its German parent **DaimlerChrysler** for $7.41 billion.[1] Managers at Cerberus undoubtedly performed detailed budgetary analyses of Chrysler's expected future cash inflows and outflows, as well as earnings. Short-run analyses were especially important to Cerberus as auto analysts speculated that Cerberus would attempt to make Chrysler leaner through cost cutting before turning around and selling it to another company for a profit shortly thereafter. However, Cerberus's analyses also needed to demonstrate sufficient cash flows and earnings for Chrysler over the long term as well, in case its anticipated plan to unload the company in the near term did not materialize.

[1] Gail Edmondson, "Why Daimler Gave Chrysler to Cerberus," *Business Week* (May 15, 2007): http://www.msnbc.msn.com/id/18680299/, accessed on March 17, 2008.

Exhibit 9-1

Planning, Control, and Budgets

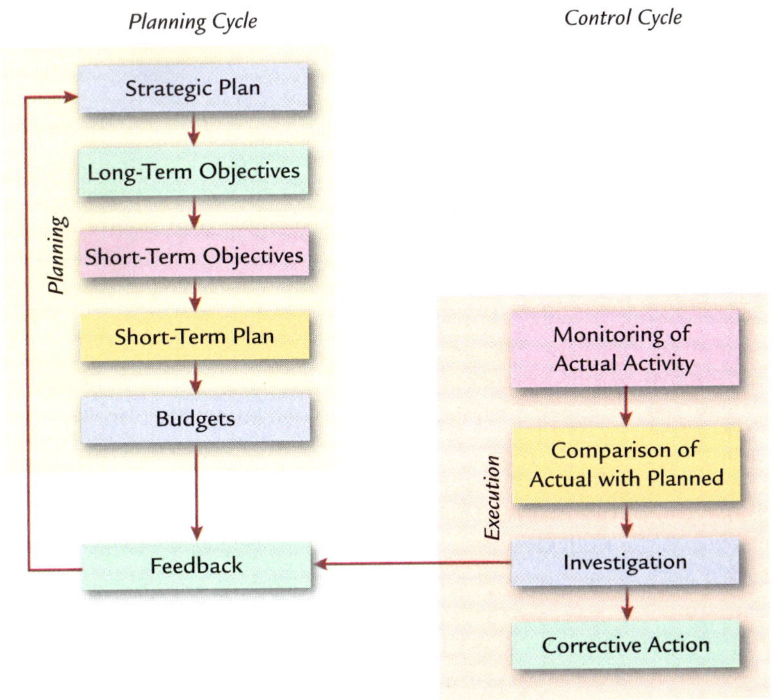

Advantages of Budgeting

A budgetary system gives an organization several advantages.

1. It forces managers to plan.
2. It provides information that can be used to improve decision making.
3. It provides a standard for performance evaluation.
4. It improves communication and coordination.

Budgeting forces management to plan for the future. It encourages managers to develop an overall direction for the organization, foresee problems, and develop future policies.

Budgets improve decision making. For example, a restaurant owner who knows the expected revenues and the costs of meat, vegetables, cheeses, and so on might make menu changes that play up the less expensive items and reduce the use of more expensive ingredients. These better decisions, in turn, may keep customers happy while still providing a profitable living for the chefs, waiters, and others who work at the restaurant.

Budgets set standards that can control the use of a company's resources and motivate employees. A vital part of the budgetary system, **control** is achieved by comparing actual results with budgeted results on a periodic basis (e.g., monthly). A large difference between actual and planned results is feedback revealing that the system is out of control. Steps should be taken to find out why and then to correct the situation. For example, if a pizza restaurant knows how much cheese should be used on a pizza and what the cost should be, the owner can evaluate the amount of cheese actually used. If more cheese is being used than expected, the owner may discover that the workers are careless when preparing the pizzas such that some pizzas get less than their share of cheese and others get much more. Extra care in preparing the pizzas will produce savings and will convince customers that a consistent product will result each time. The same principle applies to other resources used by the corporation. In total, the savings could be significant.

CONCEPT Q&A

How can a budget help in planning and control?

Answers on pages 711 to 715.

Budgets also serve to communicate and coordinate. Budgets formally communicate the plans of the organization to each employee. Accordingly, all employees can be aware of their particular role in achieving those objectives. Since budgets for the various areas and activities of the organization must all work together to achieve organizational objectives, coordination is promoted. Managers can see the needs of other areas and are encouraged to subordinate their individual interests to those of the organization. The role of communication and coordination becomes more significant as an organization increases in size.

The Master Budget

The **master budget** is the comprehensive financial plan for the organization as a whole. Typically, the master budget is for a one-year period, corresponding to the fiscal year of the company. Yearly budgets are broken down into quarterly and monthly budgets. The use of smaller time periods allows managers to compare actual data with budgeted data more frequently, so that problems may be noticed and resolved sooner.

Some organizations have developed a continuous budgeting philosophy. A **continuous budget** is a moving 12-month budget. As a month expires in the budget, an additional month in the future is added so that the company always has a 12-month plan on hand. Proponents of continuous budgeting maintain that it forces managers to plan ahead constantly.

Directing and Coordinating Most organizations prepare the master budget for the coming year during the last four or five months of the current year. The **budget committee** reviews the budget, provides policy guidelines and budgetary goals, resolves differences that arise as the budget is prepared, approves the final budget, and monitors the actual performance of the organization as the year unfolds. The president of the organization appoints the members of the committee, who are usually the president, vice president for marketing, vice president for manufacturing, other vice presidents, and the controller. The controller usually serves as the **budget director**, the person responsible for directing and coordinating the organization's overall budgeting process.

Major Components of the Master Budget A master budget can be divided into operating and financial budgets. **Operating budgets** describe the income-generating activities of a firm: sales, production, and finished goods inventories. The ultimate outcome of the operating budgets is a pro forma or budgeted income statement. **Financial budgets** detail the inflows and outflows of cash and the overall financial position. Planned cash inflows and outflows appear in the cash budget. The expected financial position at the end of the budget period is shown in a budgeted, or pro forma, balance sheet. Since many of the financing activities are not known until the operating budgets are known, the operating budget is prepared first. Describing and illustrating the individual budgets that make up the master budget will make apparent the interdependencies of the component budgets. A diagram displaying these interrelationships is shown in Exhibit 9-2. Details of the capital budget are covered in a separate chapter.

CONCEPT Q&A

What is the main objective of continuous budgeting?

Answers on pages 711 to 715.

OBJECTIVE 2
Define and prepare the operating budget, identify its major components, and explain the interrelationships of its various components.

Preparing the Operating Budget

The operating budget consists of a budgeted income statement accompanied by the following supporting schedules:

1. Sales budget
2. Production budget
3. Direct materials purchases budget
4. Direct labour budget
5. Manufacturing overhead budget
6. Selling and administrative expenses budget
7. Ending finished goods inventory budget
8. Cost of goods sold budget

Exhibit 9-2

The Master Budget and Its Interrelationships

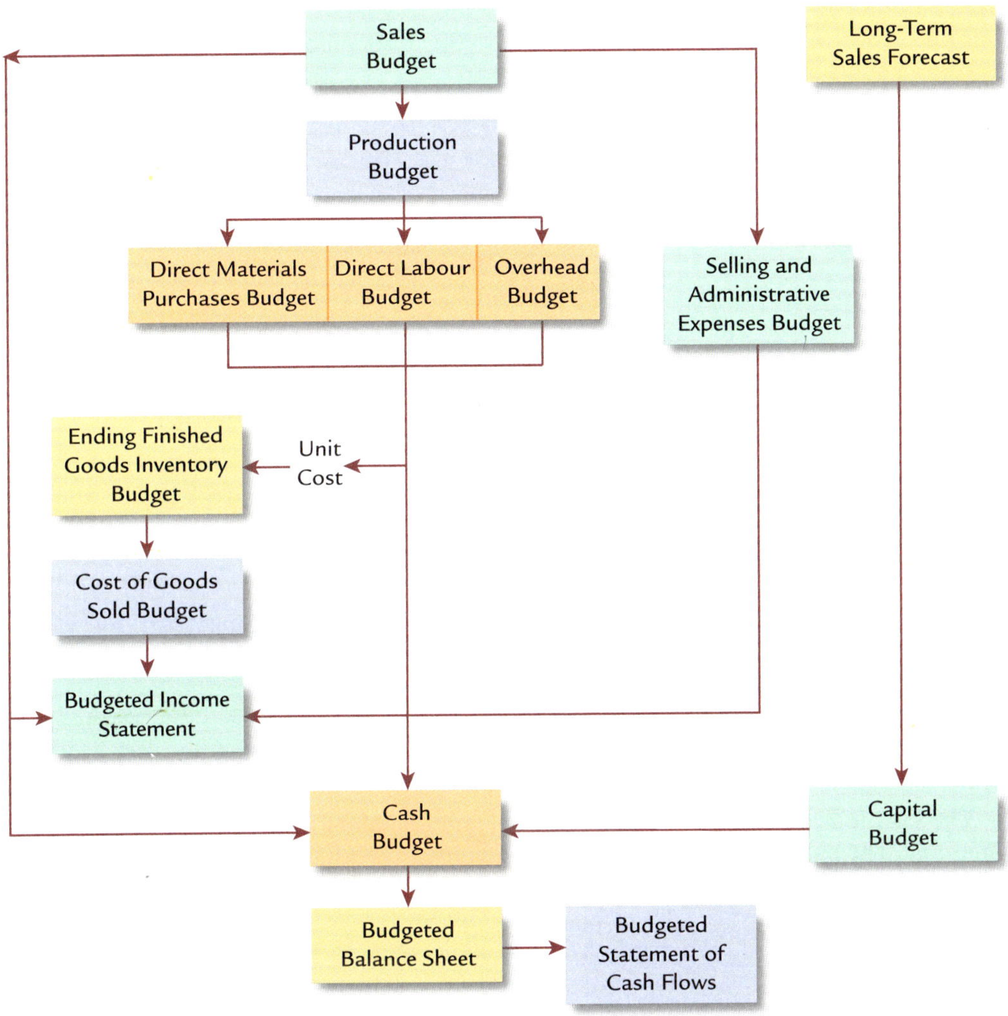

We illustrate the master budgeting process with an example based on the activities of Moose Patties Inc., a trendy restaurant in northern Ontario that sells t-shirts with the Moose Patties logo (a moose that engages in a variety of adventures while eating the hamburgers for which the restaurant is known). The example focuses on the Moose Patties clothing manufacturing plant.

Sales Budget

The **sales budget** is approved by the budget committee and describes expected sales in units and dollars. Because the sales budget is the basis for all of the other operating budgets and most of the financial budgets, it is important that it be as accurate as possible.

The first step in creating a sales budget is to develop the sales forecast. This is usually the responsibility of the marketing department. One approach to forecasting sales is the *bottom-up approach*, which requires individual salespeople to submit sales predictions. These are aggregated to form a total sales forecast. The accuracy of this sales forecast may be improved by considering other factors such as the general economic climate, competition, advertising, pricing policies, and so on. Some companies use more formal approaches, such as time-series analysis, correlation analysis, and econometric modelling. For example, the regression technique studied in the Appendix of Chapter 3 can be applied to forecasting sales, in addition to costs.

CORNERSTONE 9-1

The HOW and WHY of Preparing a Sales Budget

Information:
Budgeted units to be sold for each quarter: 1,000, 1,200, 1,500, and 2,000. Selling price is $10 per t-shirt.

Required:
Prepare a sales budget for each quarter and for the year.

Solution:

Moose Patties Inc.
Sales Budget
For the Year Ending December 31, 2010

	Quarter				
	1	**2**	**3**	**4**	**Year**
Units	1,000	1,200	1,500	2,000	5,700
Unit selling price	× $10	× $10	× $10	× $10	× $10
Budgeted sales	$10,000	$12,000	$15,000	$20,000	$57,000

WHY:
Because the sales budget is the starting point for every budgeting exercise. All the other budgets flow from this one set of assumptions.

The sales forecast is just the initial estimate, and it is often adjusted by the budget committee. The budget committee may decide that the forecast is too pessimistic or too optimistic and revise it appropriately. For example, **Nintendo**, according to a videogame analyst, set very conservative sales estimates for 2008. However, the company had to increase its sales forecast. Wii hardware sales alone were so robust that sales were expected to increase by one million units more than the company's original forecast.[2]

Cornerstone 9-1 shows how to prepare the sales budget for Moose Patties' standard t-shirt line. For simplicity, we assume that Moose Patties has only one product: a standard short-sleeved t-shirt with the Moose Patties logo screen printed on the back. (For a multiple-product firm, the sales budget reflects sales for each product in units and sales dollars.)

Notice that the sales budget in Cornerstone 9-1 reveals that Moose Patties' sales fluctuate seasonally. Most sales take place in the summer and fall quarters. This is due to the popularity of the t-shirts in the summer and the sales promotions that Moose Patties puts on for "back to school" and Christmas.

CONCEPT Q&A

Why is the sales budget not necessarily the same as the sales forecast?

Answers on pages 711 to 715.

Production Budget

The **production budget** tells how many units must be produced to meet sales needs and to satisfy ending inventory requirements. The Moose Patties production budget would show how many t-shirts are needed to satisfy sales demand for each quarter and for the year. If there were no beginning or ending inventories, the t-shirts to be produced would exactly equal the units to be sold. This would be the case in a just-in-time (JIT) firm. However, many firms use inventories as a buffer against uncertainties in demand or production. Thus, they need to plan for inventory levels as well as sales.

[2] "Pachter finds Nintendo's Sales Forecast Too Humble." Posted January 31, 2008 at 02:57 pm by Pulkit Chandna: http://www.gamertell.com/gaming/comment/analyst-nintendos-forecasts-remain-too-low/, accessed March 16, 2008.

The HOW and WHY of Preparing a Production Budget

CORNERSTONE 9-2

Information:

Budgeted units to be sold for each quarter: 1,000, 1,200, 1,500, and 2,000. Assume that company policy requires 20 percent of the next quarter's sales in ending inventory and that beginning inventory of t-shirts for the first quarter of the year was 180. Assume also that sales for the first quarter of 2011 are estimated at 1,000 units.

Required:

1. Calculate the desired ending inventory in units for each quarter of the year. What is the ending inventory in units for the year?
2. Prepare a production budget for each quarter and for the year.

Solution:

1. Ending inventory, quarter 1 = 0.20 × 1,200 units = 240
   Ending inventory, quarter 2 = 0.20 × 1,500 units = 300
   Ending inventory, quarter 3 = 0.20 × 2,000 units = 400
   Ending inventory, quarter 4 = 0.20 × 1,000 units = 200
   Ending inventory for the year = Ending inventory for quarter 4 = 200 units

2.

Moose Patties Inc.
Production Budget
For the Year Ending December 31, 2010

	Quarter 1	Quarter 2	Quarter 3	Quarter 4	Year
Sales in units	1,000	1,200	1,500	2,000	5,700
Desired ending inventory*	240	300	400	200	200
Total needs	1,240	1,500	1,900	2,200	5,900
Less: Beginning inventory**	(180)	(240)	(300)	(400)	(180)
Units to be produced	1,060	1,260	1,600	1,800	5,720

*Ending inventory for each quarter is calculated in part 1.

**Recall that the beginning inventory for one quarter is equal to the ending inventory of the preceding quarter.

WHY:

Because the production budget allows us to translate the requirements of the sales budget into the actual units that need to be produced to meet the needs of the company's operations, including inventory levels as set by corporate policy.

To compute the units to be produced, both unit sales and units of beginning and ending finished goods inventory are needed:

Units to be produced = Expected unit sales + Units in desired ending inventory (EI) − Units in beginning inventory (BI)

Cornerstone 9-2 shows how to prepare a production budget using this formula. Consider the first column (quarter 1) of the budget in Cornerstone 9-2. Moose Patties anticipates sales of 1,000 t-shirts. In addition, the company wants 240 t-shirts in ending inventory at the end of the first quarter (0.20 × 1,200). Thus, 1,240 t-shirts are needed

ANALYTICAL Q&A

Assume that the expected sales for January and February are 2,000 units and 2,500 units, respectively. The desired ending inventory is 20 percent of the next month's expected sales. If the inventory on hand at the beginning of January is 150 units, how many units should be budgeted for production in January?

Answers on pages 711 to 715.

during the first quarter. Where will these 1,240 t-shirts come from? Beginning inventory can provide 180 of them, leaving 1,060 to be produced during the quarter. Notice that the production budget is expressed in terms of units.

Two important points should be emphasized. First, the beginning inventory for one quarter is always equal to the ending inventory of the previous quarter. For quarter 2, the beginning inventory is 240 t-shirts, which is identical to the desired ending inventory for quarter 1. Second, the column for the year is not simply the addition of the amounts for the four quarters. Notice that the desired ending inventory for the year is 200 t-shirts, which is, of course, equal to the desired ending inventory for the fourth quarter.

Direct Materials Purchases Budget

After the production budget is completed, the budgets for direct materials, direct labour, and overhead can be prepared. The **direct materials purchases budget** tells the amount and cost of raw materials to be purchased in each time period; it depends on the expected use of materials in production and the raw materials inventory needs of the firm. The company needs to prepare a separate direct materials purchases budget for every type of raw material used. The formula used for calculating purchases is as follows:

$$\begin{aligned}\text{Purchases} = {} & \text{Direct materials needed for production} \\ & + \text{Direct materials in desired ending inventory} \\ & - \text{Direct materials in beginning inventory}\end{aligned}$$

The quantity of direct materials in inventory is determined by the firm's inventory policy.

Moose Patties uses two types of raw materials: plain t-shirts and ink. The direct materials purchases budgets for these two materials are presented in Cornerstone 9-3. Notice how similar the direct materials purchases budget is to the production budget. Consider the first quarter, starting with the plain t-shirts. It takes one plain t-shirt for every logo t-shirt, so the 1,060 logo t-shirts to be produced are multiplied by one to obtain the number of plain t-shirts needed for production. Next, the desired ending inventory of 126 (10 percent of the next quarter's production needs) is added. Thus, 1,186 plain t-shirts are needed during the first quarter. Of this total, 58 are already in beginning inventory, meaning that the remaining 1,128 must be purchased. Multiplying the 1,128 plain t-shirts by the cost of $3 each gives Moose Patties the $3,384 expected cost of plain t-shirt purchases for the first quarter of the year.

The second section of the direct materials purchases budget is for ink. Again using the first quarter, every logo t-shirt uses 5 grams of ink; so the 1,060 logo t-shirts to be produced are multiplied by 5 to obtain the 5,300 grams of ink needed for production. Next, the desired ending inventory of 630 grams (10 percent of the next quarter's production needs) is added, yielding a requirement of 5,930 grams of ink for the first quarter. Of this total, 390 grams are already in beginning inventory, meaning that the remaining 5,540 grams must be purchased. Multiplying the 5,540 grams of ink by the cost of $0.20 per gram gives Moose Patties the $1,108 expected cost of ink purchases for the first quarter of the year.

The total direct materials purchases of $4,492 for the first quarter are the sum of the $3,384 plain t-shirt purchases and the $1,108 ink purchases. As you can see, there is a separate direct materials purchases budget for each type of raw material in a firm.

Direct Labour Budget

The **direct labour budget** shows the total direct labour hours and the direct labour cost needed for the number of units in the production budget. As with direct materials, the budgeted hours of direct labour are determined by the relationship between labour and output.

The HOW and WHY of Preparing a Direct Materials Purchases Budget

CORNERSTONE 9-3

Information:

Budgeted units to be produced for each quarter: 1,060, 1,260, 1,600, and 1,800. Plain t-shirts cost $3 each, and ink (for the screen printing) costs $0.20 per gram. On a per-unit basis, the factory needs one plain t-shirt and five grams of ink for each logo t-shirt that it produces. Moose Patties' policy is to have 10 percent of the following quarter's production needs in ending inventory. The factory has 58 plain t-shirts and 390 grams of ink on hand on January 1. At the end of the year, the desired ending inventory is 106 plain t-shirts and 530 grams of ink.

Required:

1. Calculate the ending inventory of plain t-shirts and of ink for quarters 2 and 3.
2. Prepare a direct materials purchases budget for plain t-shirts and for ink.

Solution:

1. Ending inventory plain t-shirts, quarter 2 = 0.10 × (1,600 units × 1 t-shirt) = 160
   Ending inventory plain t-shirts, quarter 3 = 0.10 × (1,800 units × 1 t-shirt) = 180
   Ending inventory ink, quarter 2 = 0.10 × (1,600 units × 5 grams) = 800
   Ending inventory ink, quarter 3 = 0.10 × (1,800 units × 5 grams) = 900
2.

Moose Patties Inc.
Direct Materials Purchases Budget
For the Year Ending December 31, 2010

Plain t-shirts	Quarter 1	Quarter 2	Quarter 3	Quarter 4	Year
Units to be produced	1,060	1,260	1,600	1,800	5,720
Direct materials per unit	× 1	× 1	× 1	× 1	× 1
Production needs	1,060	1,260	1,600	1,800	5,720
Desired ending inventory	126	160	180	106	106
Total needs	1,186	1,420	1,780	1,906	5,826
Less: Beginning inventory	(58)	(126)	(160)	(180)	(58)
Direct materials to be purchased	1,128	1,294	1,620	1,726	5,768
Cost per t-shirt	× $3	× $3	× $3	× $3	× $3
Total purchase cost plain t-shirts	$3,384	$3,882	$4,860	$5,178	$17,304

Ink	Quarter 1	Quarter 2	Quarter 3	Quarter 4	Year
Units to be produced	1,060	1,260	1,600	1,800	5,720
Direct materials per unit	× 5	× 5	× 5	× 5	× 5
Production needs	5,300	6,300	8,000	9,000	28,600
Desired ending inventory	630	800	900	530	530
Total needs	5,930	7,100	8,900	9,530	29,130
Less: Beginning inventory	(390)	(630)	(800)	(900)	(390)
Direct materials to be purchased	5,540	6,470	8,100	8,630	28,740
Cost per gram	×$0.20	×$0.20	×$0.20	×$0.20	×$0.20
Total purchase cost of ink	$1,108	$1,294	$1,620	$1,726	$ 5,748
Total direct materials purchase cost	$4,492	$5,176	$6,480	$6,904	$23,052

WHY:

Because once the level of production has been established, these objectives must be expressed in terms of how much material needs to be purchased in order to allow the production operation to meet the goals.

CORNERSTONE 9-4

The HOW and WHY of Preparing a Direct Labour Budget

Information:
Recall from Cornerstone 9-2 that budgeted units to be produced for each quarter are: 1,060, 1,260, 1,600, and 1,800. It takes 0.12 hour to produce one t-shirt. The average wage cost per hour is $10.

Required:
Prepare a direct labour budget.

Solution:

Moose Patties Inc.
Direct Labour Budget
For the Year Ending December 31, 2010

	Quarter 1	Quarter 2	Quarter 3	Quarter 4	Year
Units to be produced	1,060	1,260	1,600	1,800	5,720
Direct labour time per unit in hours	× 0.12	× 0.12	× 0.12	× 0.12	× 0.12
Total hours needed	127.2	151.2	192.0	216.0	686.4
Average wage per hour	× $10	× $10	× $10	× $10	× $10
Total direct labour cost	$ 1,272	$ 1,512	$ 1,920	$ 2,160	$ 6,864

WHY:
Because direct labour is a key component of the production operation and factory workers will have a target level of units to be produced for each hour of labour. These targets will then be translated into the number of direct labour hours needed to meet the production requirements established in the production budget and the company will be able to make arrangements to ensure that it has the proper work-force available to meet its needs.

Suppose that it takes 0.12 direct labour hours to produce a single t-shirt, and that the average wage rate is $10 per direct labour hour. The direct labour budget for Moose Patties is shown in Cornerstone 9-4.

Overhead Budget

ANALYTICAL Q&A

Assume that a product uses two hours of direct labour per unit. Expected production for the year is 1,250 units. The average wage cost per hour is $8. What is the budget for direct labour cost?

Answers on pages 711 to 715.

The **overhead budget** shows the expected cost of all production costs other than direct materials and direct labour. Many companies use direct labour hours as the driver for overhead. Then costs that vary with direct labour hours are pooled and called variable overhead. The remaining overhead items are pooled into fixed overhead. For the Moose Patties example, the variable overhead rate is $5 per direct labour hour. Fixed overhead is $1,645 per quarter (this amount includes $540 per quarter for depreciation). The method for preparing an overhead budget using this approach to cost behaviour is shown in Cornerstone 9-5.

Ending Finished Goods Inventory Budget

The **ending finished goods inventory budget** supplies information needed for the balance sheet and also serves as an important input for the preparation of the cost of goods sold budget. To prepare this budget, the unit cost of producing each t-shirt

The HOW and WHY of Preparing an Overhead Budget

CORNERSTONE 9-5

Information:
Refer to Cornerstone 9-4 for the direct labour budget. The variable overhead rate is $5 per direct labour hour; fixed overhead is budgeted at $1,645 per quarter.

Required:
Prepare an overhead budget.

Solution:

Moose Patties Inc.
Overhead Budget
For the Year Ending December 31, 2010

	Quarter 1	Quarter 2	Quarter 3	Quarter 4	Year
Budgeted direct labour hours	127.2	151.2	192.0	216.0	686.4
Variable overhead rate	× $5	× $5	× $5	× $5	× $5
Budgeted variable overhead	$ 636	$ 756	$ 960	$1,080	$ 3,432
Budgeted fixed overhead*	1,645	1,645	1,645	1,645	6,580
Total overhead	$2,281	$2,401	$2,605	$2,725	$10,012

* Includes $540 of depreciation in each quarter.

WHY:
Because manufacturing overhead must be incurred in order to provide the appropriate level of support for the production operations. Being able to predict the overhead requirements will allow the company to ensure that it has arrangements in place to supply these requirements to the production process.

must be calculated by using information from the direct materials, direct labour, and overhead budgets. The way to calculate the unit cost of a t-shirt and the cost of the planned ending inventory is shown in Cornerstone 9-6.

Cost of Goods Sold Budget

Assuming that the beginning finished goods inventory is valued at $1,251, the budgeted cost of goods sold schedule can be prepared using information from Cornerstones 9-3 to 9-6. The **cost of goods sold budget** reveals the expected cost of the goods to be sold and is shown in Cornerstone 9-7.

Selling and Administrative Expenses Budget

The next budget to be prepared, the **selling and administrative expenses budget**, outlines planned expenditures for nonmanufacturing activities. As with overhead, selling and administrative expenses can be broken down into fixed and variable components. Such items as sales commissions, freight, and supplies vary with sales activity. The

ANALYTICAL Q&A

Assume that the budget formula for overhead costs (OH) is OH = $2,000 + $3X, where X = total direct labour hours. If the company expects to work 5,000 direct labour hours, what is the budgeted variable overhead? Budgeted fixed overhead? Budgeted total overhead?

Answers on pages 711 to 715.

CONCEPT Q&A

What operating budgets are needed to calculate a budgeted unit cost?

Answers on pages 711 to 715.

CORNERSTONE 9-6

The HOW and WHY of Preparing an Ending Finished Goods Inventory Budget

Information:

Refer to Cornerstones 9-3, 9-4, and 9-5 for the direct materials, direct labour, and overhead budgets.

Required:

1. Calculate the unit product cost.
2. Prepare an ending finished goods inventory budget.

Solution:

1. Unit cost computation:

Direct materials:		
Plain t-shirt	$3	
Ink	1	$4.00
Direct labour (0.12 hr. @ $10)		1.20
Overhead:		
Variable (0.12 hr. @ $5)		0.60
Fixed (0.12 hr. @ $9.59*)		1.15
Total unit cost		$6.95

* Budgeted fixed overhead/Budgeted direct labour hours = $6,580/686.4 = $9.59.

2.

Moose Patties Inc.
Ending Finished Goods Inventory Budget
For the Year Ending December 31, 2010

Logo t-shirts	200
Unit cost	× $6.95
Total ending inventory	$1,390

WHY:

Because part of the production budget calculation was a determination of the finished goods inventory in units throughout the process. At this point we need to translate the units of finished goods inventory into a dollar value that represents the investment required by the company and that can be used in our financial statement presentations.

CORNERSTONE 9-7

The HOW and WHY of Preparing a Cost of Goods Sold Budget

Information:

Refer to Cornerstones 9-3 through 9-6 for the direct materials, direct labour, overhead, and ending finished goods budgets.

Required:

Prepare a cost of goods sold budget.

Solution:

CORNERSTONE 9-7 (continued)

Moose Patties Inc.
Cost of Goods Sold Budget
For the Year Ending December 31, 2010

Direct materials used (Cornerstone 9-3)*	$22,880
Direct labour used (Cornerstone 9-4)	6,864
Overhead (Cornerstone 9-5)	10,012
Budgeted manufacturing costs	$39,756
Beginning finished goods	1,251
Goods available for sale	$41,007
Less: Ending finished goods (Cornerstone 9-6)	(1,390)
Budgeted cost of goods sold	$39,617

* Production needs = (5,720 plain t-shirts × $3) + (28,600 oz. ink × $0.20).

WHY:

Because the cost of goods sold is one of the fundamental amounts used to calculate corporate profitability. Certain financial ratios are calculated using cost of goods sold, and a company can determine whether it will meet its objectives in this area if the budget remains unchanged.

selling and administrative expenses budget is illustrated in Cornerstone 9-8 (page 418).

Budgeted Income Statement

With the completion of the budgeted cost of goods sold schedule and the budgeted selling and administrative expenses budget, Moose Patties has all the operating budgets needed to prepare an estimate of *operating* income. The way to prepare this budgeted income statement is shown in Cornerstone 9-9 (page 419). The eight budgets already prepared, along with the budgeted operating income statement, define the operating budget for Moose Patties.

Operating income is *not* equivalent to the net income of a firm. To yield net income, interest expense and taxes must be subtracted from operating income. The interest expense deduction is taken from the cash budget for Moose Patties (Cornerstone 9-12), a budget discussed in the section on financial budgets. The taxes owed depend on the current federal and provincial tax laws. For simplicity, a combined rate of 40 percent is assumed.

ANALYTICAL Q&A

Assume that the budgeted cost of goods sold is $700. There is no beginning finished goods inventory. Budgeted manufacturing costs are $1,000. What is the budgeted finished goods inventory?

Answers on pages 711 to 715.

ANALYTICAL Q&A

Assume that sales agents are paid a commission of 2 percent of sales revenue. Further, the only fixed selling expense is advertising, which is expected to be $10,000. If sales revenue is budgeted at $500,000, what is the budgeted selling expense?

Answers on pages 711 to 715.

Preparing the Financial Budget

OBJECTIVE 3
Define and prepare the financial budget, identify its major components, and explain the interrelationships of its various components.

The remaining budgets found in the master budget are the financial budgets. The usual financial budgets prepared are:

1. The cash budget
2. The budgeted balance sheet
3. The budget for capital expenditures

The master budget also contains a plan for acquiring long-term assets—that is, assets that have a time horizon that extends beyond the one-year operating period. Some of these assets may be purchased during the coming year; plans to pur-

CONCEPT Q&A

Why is it not possible to prepare a budgeted income statement by using only operating budgets?

Answers on pages 711 to 715.

CORNERSTONE 9-8

The HOW and WHY of Preparing a Selling and Administrative Expenses Budget

Information:

Refer to Cornerstone 9-1 for the sales budget. Variable expenses are $0.10 per unit sold. Salaries average $1,420 per quarter; utilities, $50 per quarter; and depreciation, $150 per quarter. Advertising for quarters 1 through 4 is $100, $200, $800, and $500, respectively.

Required:

Prepare a selling and administrative expenses budget.

Solution:

Moose Patties Inc.
Selling and Administrative Expenses Budget
For the Year Ending December 31, 2010

	Quarter				
	1	**2**	**3**	**4**	**Year**
Planned sales in units (Cornerstone 9-1)	1,000	1,200	1,500	2,000	5,700
Variable selling and administrative expenses per unit	×$0.10	×$0.10	×$0.10	×$0.10	×$0.10
Total variable expenses	$100	$120	$150	$200	$570
Fixed selling and administrative expenses:					
Salaries	$1,420	$1,420	$1,420	$1,420	$5,680
Utilities	50	50	50	50	200
Advertising	100	200	800	500	1,600
Depreciation	150	150	150	150	600
Total fixed expenses	$1,720	$1,820	$2,420	$2,120	$8,080
Total selling and administrative expenses	$1,820	$1,940	$2,570	$2,320	$8,650

WHY:

Because the nature of our operations as determined in the previous budgets will determine the size and type of organization needed to meet our objectives. The company must ensure that it has the resources in place, or can acquire the resources, to meet these needs.

chase others may be detailed for future periods. This part of the master budget is typically referred to as the *capital budget*. Decision making for capital expenditures is considered in Chapter 14. Accordingly, only the cash budget and the budgeted balance sheet will be illustrated here.

Cash Budget

Understanding cash flows is critical in managing a business. Often, a business successfully produces and sells products but fails because of timing problems associated with cash inflows and outflows. Examples include the smallest entrepreneurs, who are required by suppliers to pay cash up front but must sell to their customers on credit, as well as large corporations like **Sears**. In early 2008, Sears acknowledged that available cash had dropped by nearly 60 percent over 2007. A cash crunch was leading Sears to consider selling assets.[3]

By knowing when cash inflows and outflows are likely to occur, a manager can plan to borrow cash when needed and to repay the loans during periods of excess cash. Because cash flow is the lifeblood of an organization, the cash budget is one of the most important budgets in the master budget. The basic structure of a **cash budget** includes cash receipts, disbursements, any excess or deficiency of cash, and financing. At its simplest, a cash budget is cash inflows minus cash outflows. Suppose, for example, that a company expects $3,000 in the cash account on June 1. During

Cash budget
Cash inflow
− Cash outflows

[3] Gary McWilliams, "Profit Down, Sears May Hold Yard Sale," *The Wall Street Journal* (February 29, 2008): A13.

The HOW and WHY of Preparing a Budgeted Income Statement

CORNERSTONE 9-9

Information:
Refer to Cornerstones 9-1, 9-7, 9-8, and 9-12 for the sales budget, the cost of goods sold budget, the selling and administrative expenses budget, and the cash budget. Assume that the tax rate is 40 percent.

Required:
Prepare a budgeted income statement.

Solution:

Moose Patties Inc.
Budgeted Income Statement
For the Year Ending December 31, 2010

Sales (Cornerstone 9-1)	$ 57,000
Less: Cost of goods sold (Cornerstone 9-7)	(39,617)
Gross margin	$ 17,383
Less: Selling and administrative expenses (Cornerstone 9-8)	(8,650)
Operating income	$ 8,733
Less: Interest expense (Cornerstone 9-12)	(60)
Income before taxes	$ 8,673
Less: Income taxes (0.40 × $8,673)	(3,469)
Net income	$ 5,204

WHY:
Because the budgeted income statement can be prepared by reference to each of the component costs already calculated. The budgeted income statement will indicate to the company management whether the current budget assumptions will allow the company to achieve its financial targets. If not, the budgeting process will have to be reviewed and adjustments made.

June, cash sales of $45,000 are predicted, as are cash disbursements of $39,000. The resulting cash budget for June is illustrated in Exhibit 9-3.

Cash available consists of the beginning cash balance and the expected cash receipts. Expected cash receipts include all sources of cash for the period being considered. The principal source of cash is from sales. Since a large proportion of sales is usually on account, a major task of an organization is to determine the pattern of collection for its accounts receivable. If a company has been in business for a while, it can use past experience in creating an accounts receivable aging schedule. In other words, the company can determine, on average, what percentages of its accounts receivable are paid in the months following sales.

Cornerstone 9-10 shows how to create an accounts receivable aging schedule for Moose Patties. From past experience, Moose Patties expects 25 percent of all sales to be for cash, and the remaining 75 percent to be on credit. Of the credit sales, 90 percent are paid

Exhibit 9-3

The Cash Budget

Expected beginning balance	$ 3,000
Add cash receipts	45,000
Cash available	$48,000
Less disbursements	39,000
Expected ending balance	$ 9,000

CORNERSTONE 9-10

The HOW and WHY of Preparing an Accounts Receivable Collections Schedule

Information:

Moose Patties expects that, on average, 25 percent of total sales are cash and 75 percent of total sales are on credit. Of the credit sales, Moose Patties expects that 90 percent will be paid in cash during the quarter of sale, and the remaining 10 percent will be paid in the following quarter. Recall from Cornerstone 9-1 that Moose Patties expects the following total sales:

Quarter 1	$10,000
Quarter 2	$12,000
Quarter 3	$15,000
Quarter 4	$20,000

The balance in accounts receivable as of the last quarter of 2009 was $1,350. This will be collected in cash during the first quarter of 2010.

Required:

1. Calculate cash sales expected in each quarter of 2010.
2. Prepare a schedule showing cash receipts from sales expected in each quarter of 2010.

Solution:

1. Cash sales expected in Quarter 1 = $10,000 × 0.25 = $2,500
   Cash sales expected in Quarter 2 = $12,000 × 0.25 = $3,000
   Cash sales expected in Quarter 3 = $15,000 × 0.25 = $3,750
   Cash sales expected in Quarter 4 = $20,000 × 0.25 = $5,000
2. Cash from credit sales:

	Quarter			
Source	**1**	**2**	**3**	**4**
Cash sales	$ 2,500	$ 3,000	$ 3,750	$ 5,000
Received on account from:				
Quarter 4, 2009	1,350			
Quarter 1, 2010	6,750[a]	750[b]		
Quarter 2, 2010		8,100[c]	900[d]	
Quarter 3, 2010			10,125[e]	1,125[f]
Quarter 4, 2010				13,500[g]
Total cash receipts	$10,600	$11,850	$14,775	$19,625

[a] ($10,000 × 0.75)(0.9)
[b] ($10,000 × 0.75)(0.1)
[c] ($12,000 × 0.75)(0.9)
[d] ($12,000 × 0.75)(0.1)
[e] ($15,000 × 0.75)(0.9)
[f] ($15,000 × 0.75)(0.1)
[g] ($20,000 × 0.75)(0.9)

WHY:

Because cash collections from customers represent the primary source of cash to the company, and this is dependent on how long it takes the customers, on average, to pay their bills. Accounts receivable aging allows us to predict when amounts will be received.

in the same quarter as the sale. The remaining 10 percent are paid in the following quarter. While Moose Patties expects no bad debts expense, that may not be the case for all firms. If a firm expects less than 100 percent of the credit sales to be received in cash, then it expects

The HOW and WHY of Determining Cash Payments on Accounts Payable

CORNERSTONE 9-11

Information:

Moose Patties purchases all raw materials on account; 80 percent of purchases are paid for in the quarter of purchase. The remaining 20 percent are paid for in the following quarter. The purchases for the fourth quarter of 2009 were $5,000. Cornerstone 9-3 shows total expected purchases of raw materials for each quarter of 2010. These are shown here.

Quarter 1	$4,492
Quarter 2	$5,176
Quarter 3	$6,480
Quarter 4	$6,904

Required:

Prepare a schedule showing anticipated payments for accounts payable for materials.

Solution:

Cash needed for payments on account:

	Quarter			
Source	**1**	**2**	**3**	**4**
Quarter 4, 2009	1,000[a]			
Quarter 1, 2010	3,594[b]	898[c]		
Quarter 2, 2010		4,141[d]	1,035[e]	
Quarter 3, 2010			5,184[f]	1,296[g]
Quarter 4, 2010				5,523[h]
Total cash needed	$4,594	$5,039	$6,219	$6,819

[a] ($5,000 × 0.20)
[b] ($4,492 × 0.80)
[c] ($4,492 × 0.20)
[d] ($5,176 × 0.80)
[e] ($5,176 × 0.20)
[f] ($6,480 × 0.80)
[g] ($6,480 × 0.20)
[h] ($6,904 × 0.80)

WHY:

Because offsetting the cash receipts calculated previously, a company must make payments of various amounts to its suppliers. Establishing a policy of how suppliers will be paid allows a company to predict, with reasonable accuracy, how cash will be paid out. These payments will represent the major cash outflows for the company.

some bad debts. For example, if a firm expected to be repaid 98 percent of credit sales, then it expects 2 percent bad debts. In other words, not everyone pays for their credit sales. This 2 percent is ignored for purposes of cash budgeting since it will not be received in cash. Different firms have different accounts receivable repayment experiences.

The cash disbursements section lists all planned cash outlays for the period. All expenses that do not require a cash outlay are *excluded* from the list (e.g., depreciation is never included in the disbursements section). Just as sources of cash may require an accounts receivable aging schedule to calculate cash expected from credit sales, the disbursements section may require care in handling payments on account. Cornerstone 9-11 shows how to handle timing differences arising from paying for items on account.

A disbursement that is typically not included in the disbursements section is interest on short-term borrowing. This interest expenditure is reserved for the section on loan repayments.

The cash excess or deficiency line compares the cash available with the cash needed. Cash needed is the total cash disbursements plus the minimum cash balance required by company policy. The minimum cash balance is simply the lowest amount of cash on hand that the firm finds acceptable. Consider your own chequing account. You probably try to keep at least some cash in the account, perhaps because by having a minimum balance you avoid service charges, or because a minimum balance allows you to make an unplanned purchase. Similarly, companies also require minimum cash balances. The amount varies from firm to firm and is determined by each company's particular needs and policies. If the total cash available is less than the cash needed, a deficiency exists. In such a case, a short-term loan will be needed. On the other hand, with a cash excess (cash available is greater than the firm's cash needs), the firm has the ability to repay loans and perhaps to make some temporary investments.

The final section of the cash budget consists of borrowings and repayments. If there is a deficiency, this section shows the necessary amount to be borrowed. When excess cash is available, this section shows planned repayments, including interest expense.

The last line of the cash budget is the planned ending cash balance. Remember that the company wishes to maintain a minimum cash balance, so the ending cash balance line must equal or exceed this minimum required level. The way to prepare a cash budget is illustrated in Cornerstone 9-12.

Cornerstone 9-12 reveals that much of the information needed to prepare the cash budget comes from the operating

CONCEPT Q&A

Why would a company want a minimum cash balance? Suppose that the minimum cash balance is $1,000 and that the projected cash surplus is $500. What would a company have to do to achieve the desired minimum?

Answers on pages 711 to 715.

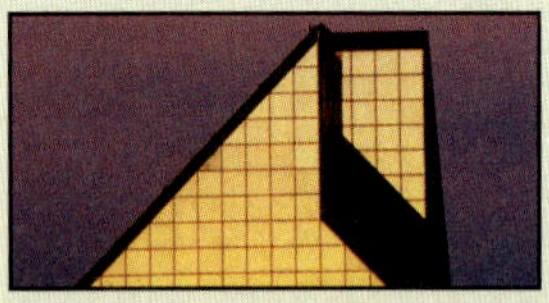

CORNERSTONE 9-12

The HOW and WHY of Preparing a Cash Budget

Information:

Refer to Cornerstones 9-1, 9-3, 9-4, 9-5, 9-8, 9-9, 9-10, and 9-11 as well as the following details:

a. A $1,000 minimum cash balance is required for the end of each quarter. Money can be borrowed and repaid in multiples of $1,000. Interest is 12 percent per year. Interest payments are made only for the amount of the principal being repaid. All borrowing takes place at the beginning of a quarter, and all repayment takes place at the end of a quarter.
b. Budgeted depreciation is $540 per quarter for overhead and $150 per quarter for selling and administrative expenses (Cornerstones 9-5 and 9-8).
c. The capital budget for 2010 revealed plans to purchase additional screen printing equipment. The cash outlay for the equipment, $6,500, will take place in the first quarter. The company plans to finance the acquisition of the equipment with operating cash, supplementing it with short-term loans as necessary.
d. Corporate income taxes are approximately $3,469 and will be paid at the end of the fourth quarter (Cornerstone 9-9).
e. Beginning cash balance equals $5,200.
f. All amounts in the budget are rounded to the nearest dollar.

Required:

Prepare a cash budget for Moose Patties.

Solution:

CORNERSTONE 9-12 (continued)

Moose Patties Inc.
Cash Budget
For the Year Ending December 31, 2010

	Quarter 1	Quarter 2	Quarter 3	Quarter 4	Year	Source*
Beginning cash balance	$ 5,200	$ 1,023	$ 1,611	$ 3,762	$ 5,200	e
Cash sales and collections on account:	10,600	11,850	14,775	19,625	56,850	10
Total cash available	$ 15,800	$ 12,873	$ 16,386	$ 23,387	$ 62,050	
Less disbursements:						
Payments for:						
Raw materials	$ (4,594)	$ (5,039)	$ (6,219)	$ (6,819)	$(22,671)	11
Direct labour	(1,272)	(1,512)	(1,920)	(2,160)	(6,864)	4
Overhead	(1,741)	(1,861)	(2,065)	(2,185)	(7,852)	b,5
Selling and administrative	(1,670)	(1,790)	(2,420)	(2,170)	(8,050)	b,8
Income taxes	—	—	—	(3,469)	(3,469)	d,9
Equipment	(6,500)	—	—	—	(6,500)	c
Total disbursements	$(15,777)	$(10,202)	$(12,624)	$(16,803)	$(55,406)	
Excess (deficiency) of cash available over needs	$ 23	$ 2,671	$ 3,762	$ 6,584	$ 6,644	
Financing:						
Borrowings	1,000	—	—	—	1,000	
Repayments	—	(1,000)	—	—	(1,000)	a
Interest**	—	(60)	—	—	(60)	a
Total financing	$ 1,000	$ (1,060)	—	—	$ (60)	
Ending cash balance***	$ 1,023	$ 1,611	$ 3,762	$ 6,584	$ 6,584	

* Letters refer to the detailed information above. Numbers refer to Cornerstone schedules.
**Interest payment is 6/12 × 0.12 × $1,000. Since borrowings occur at the beginning of the quarter and repayments at the end of the quarter, the principal repayment takes place after six months.
*** Total cash available minus total disbursements plus (or minus) total financing.

WHY:
The cash budget will indicate to the company when cash receipts will occur and when cash disbursements will be required. The compilation of all cash receipts and cash disbursements will allow a company to determine, in advance, when it might need to acquire additional cash resources from outside parties and when these funds will be able to be repaid.

budgets and from the schedules for cash receipts on accounts receivable and cash payments on accounts payable.

The cash budget underscores the importance of breaking down the annual budget into smaller time periods. The cash budget for the year gives the impression that sufficient operating cash will be available to finance the acquisition of the new equipment. Quarterly information, however, shows the need for short-term borrowing ($1,000) because of both the acquisition of the new equipment and the timing of the firm's cash flows. Most firms prepare monthly cash budgets, and some even prepare weekly and daily budgets.

CONCEPT Q&A

Sales for a month totalled $10,000. Cash receipts for the same month were $15,000. How is it possible for cash receipts to be more than sales?

Answers on pages 711 to 715.

Another significant piece of information emerges from Moose Patties' cash budget. By the end of the third quarter, the firm has more cash ($3,762) than necessary to meet operating needs. Moose Patties management should consider investing the excess cash in an interest-bearing account. Once plans are finalized for use of the excess cash, the cash budget should be revised to reflect those plans. Budgeting is a dynamic process. As the budget is developed, new information becomes available, and better plans can be formulated.

Budgeted Balance Sheet

The budgeted balance sheet depends on information contained in the current balance sheet and in the other budgets in the master budget. Exhibit 9-4 shows the budgeted balance sheets as of December 31, 2009 and December 31, 2010. Explanations for the budgeted figures are provided in the footnotes.

OBJECTIVE 4
Describe the behavioural dimension of budgeting.

Using Budgets for Performance Evaluation

Budgets are often used to judge the performance of managers. Bonuses, salary increases, and promotions are all affected by a manager's ability to achieve or beat budgeted goals. Since a manager's financial status and career can be affected, budgets can have a significant behavioural effect. Whether that effect is positive or negative depends in large part on how budgets are used.

Positive behaviour occurs when the goals of each manager are aligned with the goals of the organization and each manager has the drive to achieve them. The alignment of managerial and organizational goals is often referred to as **goal congruence**. If the budget is improperly administered, subordinate managers may subvert the organization's goals. **Dysfunctional behaviour** is individual behaviour that is in basic conflict with the goals of the organization.

CONCEPT Q&A

In the last quarter of the fiscal year, a divisional manager chose to delay budgeted preventive maintenance expenditures so that the budgeted income goals could be achieved. Is this an example of goal congruent behaviour or dysfunctional behaviour?

Answers on pages 711 to 715.

An ideal budgetary system is one that achieves complete goal congruence and, simultaneously, creates a drive in managers to achieve the organization's goals in an ethical manner. While an ideal budgetary system probably does not exist, research and practice have identified some key features that promote a reasonable degree of positive behaviour. These features include frequent feedback on performance, monetary and nonmonetary incentives, participative budgeting, realistic standards, controllability of costs, and multiple measures of performance.

Frequent Feedback on Performance

Managers need to know how they are doing as the year unfolds. Providing them with frequent, timely performance reports allows them to know how successful their efforts have been, to take corrective actions, and to change plans as necessary.

Monetary and Nonmonetary Incentives

A sound budgetary system encourages goal-congruent behaviour. The means an organization uses to influence a manager to exert effort to achieve an organization's goals are called **incentives**. Traditional organizational theory assumes that employees are primarily motivated by monetary rewards, that they resist work, and that they are inefficient and wasteful. Thus, **monetary incentives** are used to control a manager's tendency to shirk and waste resources by relating budgetary performance to salary increases, bonuses, and promotions. The threat of dismissal is the ultimate economic sanction for poor performance. In reality, employees are motivated by more than

Exhibit 9-4

Budgeted Balance Sheet

Moose Patties Inc.
Balance Sheet
December 31, 2009

Assets		
Current assets:		
Cash	$ 5,200	
Accounts receivable	1,350	
Raw materials inventory	252	
Finished goods inventory	1,251	
Total current assets		$ 8,053
Property, plant, and equipment (PP&E):		
Land	$ 1,100	
Building and equipment	30,000	
Accumulated depreciation	(5,000)	
Total PP&E		26,100
Total assets		$34,153
Liabilities and Owner's Equity		
Current liabilities:		
Accounts payable		$ 1,000
Owner's equity:		
Retained earnings		33,153
Total liabilities and owner's equity		$34,153

Moose Patties Inc.
Budgeted Balance Sheet
December 31, 2010

Assets		
Current assets:		
Cash	$ 6,584[a]	
Accounts receivable	1,500[b]	
Raw materials inventory	424[c]	
Finished goods inventory	1,390[d]	
Total current assets		$ 9,898
Property, plant, and equipment (PP&E):		
Land	$ 1,100[e]	
Building and equipment	36,500[f]	
Accumulated depreciation	(7,760)[g]	
Total PP&E		29,840
Total assets		$39,738
Liabilities and Owner's Equity		
Current liabilities:		
Accounts payable		$ 1,381[h]
Owner's equity:		
Retained earnings		38,357[i]
Total liabilities and owner's equity		$39,738

[a] Ending balance from Cornerstone 9-12.
[b] Ten percent of fourth-quarter credit sales (0.75 × $20,000)—see Cornerstones 9-1 and 9-12.
[c] From Cornerstone 9-3 [(106 × $3) + (530 × $0.20)].
[d] From Cornerstone 9-6.
[e] From the December 31, 2009, balance sheet.
[f] December 31, 2009, balance ($30,000) plus new equipment acquisition of $6,500 (see the 2009 ending balance sheet and Cornerstone 9-12).
[g] From the December 31, 2009, balance sheet, Cornerstone 9-5, and Cornerstone 9-8 ($5,000 + $2,160 + $600).
[h] Twenty percent of fourth-quarter purchases (0.20 × $6,904)—see Cornerstones 9-3 and 9-12.
[i] $33,153 + $5,204 (December 31, 2009, balance plus net income from Cornerstone 9-9).

economic factors. Employees are also motivated by intrinsic psychological and social factors, such as the satisfaction of a job well done, recognition, responsibility, self-esteem, and the nature of the work itself. Thus **nonmonetary incentives**, including job enrichment, increased responsibility and autonomy, recognition programs, and so on, can be used to enhance a budgetary control system.

Participative Budgeting

CONCEPT Q&A

Assume that a company evaluates and rewards its managers based on their ability to achieve budgeted goals. Why would the same company ask its managers to participate in setting their budgeted standards?

Answers on pages 711 to 715.

Rather than imposing budgets on subordinate managers, **participative budgeting** allows subordinate managers considerable say in how the budgets are established. Typically, overall objectives are communicated to the manager, who helps develop a budget that will accomplish these objectives. Participative budgeting communicates a sense of responsibility to subordinate managers and fosters creativity. Since the subordinate manager creates the budget, the budget's goals will more likely become the manager's personal goals, resulting in greater goal congruence. The increased responsibility and challenge inherent in the process provide nonmonetary incentives that lead to a higher level of performance.

Participative budgeting has three potential problems:

1. Setting standards that are either too high or too low
2. Building slack into the budget (often referred to as padding the budget)
3. Pseudoparticipation

Some managers may tend to set the budget either too loose or too tight. Since budgeted goals tend to become the manager's goals when participation is allowed, making this mistake in setting the budget can result in decreased performance levels. If goals are too easily achieved, a manager may lose interest, and performance may actually drop. Feeling challenged is important to aggressive and creative individuals. Similarly, setting the goals too high ensures failure to achieve the standards and frustrates the manager. This frustration, too, can lead to poorer performance. The trick is to get managers in a participative setting to set high but achievable goals. (Exhibit 9-5).

The second problem with participative budgeting is the opportunity for managers to build slack into the budget. **Budgetary slack** (or *padding the budget*) exists when a manager deliberately underestimates revenues or overestimates costs in an effort to make the future period appear less attractive in the budget than they think it will be in

Exhibit 9-5

The Art of Standard Setting

Standard Set Too Loose
Goals Too Easily Achieved

Standard Set Too Tight
Frustration

reality. Either approach increases the likelihood that the manager will achieve the budget and consequently reduces the risk that the manager faces. Top management should carefully review budgets proposed by subordinate managers and provide input, where needed, in order to decrease the effects of building slack into the budget. Furthermore, the act of padding the budget is questionable when considering what is viewed as ethical professional practice. Padding the budget is certainly not communicating information fairly and objectively and constitutes a violation of the credibility standard. The motive for such behaviour is also not consistent with the professional responsibility to exhibit integrity.

The third problem with participation occurs when top management assumes total control of the budgeting process, seeking only superficial participation from lower-level managers. This practice is termed **pseudoparticipation**. Top management is simply obtaining formal acceptance of the budget from subordinate managers, not seeking real input. Accordingly, none of the behavioural benefits of participation will be realized.

Realistic Standards

Budgeted objectives are used to gauge performance; accordingly, they should be based on realistic conditions and expectations. Budgets should reflect operating realities such as actual levels of activity, seasonal variations, efficiencies, and general economic trends. Flexible budgets are used to ensure that budgeted costs can be realistically compared with costs for actual levels of activity. Interim budgets should reflect seasonal effects. **Toys "R" Us**, for example, would expect much higher sales in the quarter that includes Christmas than in other quarters. Budgetary cuts should be based on *planned* increases in efficiency and not simply arbitrary across-the-board reductions. Across-the-board cuts without any formal evaluation may impair the ability of some units to carry out their missions. General economic conditions also need to be considered. Budgeting for a significant increase in sales when a recession is projected is not only foolish but also potentially dangerous.

Controllability of Costs

Ideally, managers are held accountable only for costs that they can control. **Controllable costs** are costs whose level a manager can influence. For example, divisional managers have no power to authorize such corporate-level costs as research and development and salaries of top managers. Therefore, they should not be held accountable for the incurrence of those costs. If noncontrollable costs are put in the budgets of subordinate managers to help them understand that these costs also need to be covered, then they should be separated from controllable costs and labelled as *noncontrollable.*

Multiple Measures of Performance

Often, organizations make the mistake of using budgets as their only measure of managerial performance. While financial measures of performance are important, overemphasis can lead to a form of dysfunctional behaviour called *milking the firm* or *myopia*. **Myopic behaviour** occurs when a manager takes actions that improve budgetary performance in the short run but bring long-run harm to the firm. For example, to meet budgeted cost objectives or profits, managers can delay promoting deserving employees or reducing expenditures for preventive maintenance, advertising, and new product development. Using measures that are both financial and nonfinancial and that are long term and short term can alleviate this problem. For example, **Starwood Hotels** incurs considerable costs every year to research consumer trends and to train its hotel staff members to help ensure sustainable growth in room revenue for its luxury St. Regis brand. Budgetary measures alone cannot prevent myopic behaviour.

OBJECTIVE 3
CORNERSTONE 9-12

Cornerstone Exercise 9-32 PREPARING A CASH BUDGET

TNT Pizzeria provided the following information for the month of October:

a. Sales are budgeted to be $120,000. About 15 percent of sales are cash; the remainder are on account.
b. TNT expects that, on average, 70 percent of credit sales will be paid in the month of sale, and 26 percent will be paid in the following month.
c. Food purchases, all on account, are expected to be $83,000. TNT pays 25 percent in the month of purchase and 75 percent in the month following purchase.
d. Most of the work is done by the owners, who typically withdraw $6,000 a month from the business as their salary. (The $6,000 is a payment in total to the two owners, not per person.) Various part-time workers cost $4,400 per month. They are paid for their work weekly, so on average 90 percent of their wages are paid in the month incurred and the remaining 10 percent in the next month.
e. Utilities average $5,200 per month. Rent on the building is $3,600 per month.
f. Insurance is paid quarterly; the next payment of $900 is due in October.
g. September sales were $130,000 and purchases of food in September equalled $98,000.
h. The cash balance on October 1 is $7,680.

Required:

1. Calculate the cash receipts expected in October. (Hint: Remember to include both cash sales and payments from credit sales.)
2. Calculate the cash needed in October to pay for food purchases.
3. Prepare a cash budget for the month of October.

Exercises

OBJECTIVE 1

Exercise 9-33 PLANNING AND CONTROL

a. Dr. Jones, a dentist, wants to increase the size and profitability of his business by building a reputation for quality and timely service.
b. To achieve this, he plans on adding a dental laboratory to his building so that crowns, bridges, and dentures can be made in-house.
c. To add the laboratory, he needs additional money, which he decides must be obtained by increasing revenues. After some careful calculation, Dr. Jones concludes that annual revenues must be increased by 10 percent.
d. Dr. Jones finds that his fees for fillings and crowns are below the average in his community and decides that the 10 percent increase can be achieved by increasing these fees.
e. He then identifies the quantity of fillings and crowns expected for the coming year, the new per-unit fee, and the total fees expected.
f. As the year unfolds (on a month-by-month basis), Dr. Jones compares the actual revenues received with the budgeted revenues. For the first three months, actual revenues were less than planned.
g. Upon investigating, he discovered that he had some reduction in the number of patients because he had also changed his available hours of operation.
h. He returned to his old schedule and found out that the number of patients was restored to the original expected levels.
i. However, to make up the shortfall, he also increased the price of some of his other services.

Required:

Match each statement with the following planning and control elements (a letter may be matched to more than one item):

1. Corrective action
2. Budgets
3. Feedback
4. Investigation

(Continued)

5. Short-term plan
6. Comparison of actual with planned
7. Monitoring of actual activity
8. Strategic plan
9. Short-term objectives
10. Long-term objectives

Exercise 9-34 SALES BUDGET

OBJECTIVE 1 2

Stillwater Designs produces two automotive subwoofers: S12L7 and S12L5. The S12L7 sells for $475, and the S12L5 sells for $300. Projected sales (number of speakers) for the coming five quarters are as follows:

	S12L7	S12L5
First quarter, 2010	1,600	500
Second quarter, 2010	2,100	1,000
Third quarter, 2010	8,350	4,200
Fourth quarter, 2010	4,300	2,400
First quarter, 2011	1,650	750

The vice president of sales believes that the projected sales are realistic and can be achieved by the company.

Required:

1. Prepare a sales budget for each quarter of 2010 and for the year in total. Show sales by product and in total for each time period.
2. How will Stillwater Designs use this sales budget?

Exercise 9-35 PRODUCTION BUDGET

OBJECTIVE 2

Stillwater Designs produces two automotive subwoofers: S12L7 and S12L5. Projected sales (number of speakers) for the coming five quarters are as follows:

	S12L7	S12L5
First quarter, 2010	1,600	500
Second quarter, 2010	2,100	1,000
Third quarter, 2010	8,350	4,200
Fourth quarter, 2010	4,300	2,400
First quarter, 2011	1,650	750

The vice president of sales believes that the projected sales are realistic and can be achieved by the company.

Stillwater Designs needs a production budget for each product (representing the amount that must be outsourced to manufacturers located in Asia). Beginning inventory of S12L7 for the first quarter of 2010 was 500 speakers. The company's policy is to have 30 percent of the next quarter's sales of S12L7 in ending inventory. Beginning inventory of S12L5 was 200 speakers. The company's policy is to have 40 percent of the next quarter's sales of S12L5 in ending inventory.

Required:

Prepare a production budget for each quarter for 2010 and for the year in total.

Exercise 9-36 PRODUCTION BUDGET AND DIRECT MATERIALS PURCHASES BUDGETS

OBJECTIVE 2

Seafood Inc. produces shrimp in cans. The sales budget for the first four months of the year is as follows:

	Unit Sales	Dollar Sales ($)
January	200,000	150,000
February	240,000	180,000
March	220,000	165,000
April	200,000	150,000

Company policy requires that ending inventories for each month be 35 percent of next month's sales. At the beginning of January, the inventory of shrimp is 36,000 cans.

Each can of shrimp needs two raw materials: 125 grams of shrimp and one can. Company policy requires that ending inventories of raw materials for each month be 20 percent of the next month's production needs. That policy was met on January 1.

Required:

1. Prepare a production budget for the first quarter of the year. Show the number of cans that should be produced each month as well as for the quarter in total.
2. Prepare separate direct materials purchases budgets for cans and for shrimp for the months of January and February.

OBJECTIVE 2

Exercise 9-37 PRODUCTION BUDGET

Jimison Inc. produces spiral-bound notebooks. The unit sales for the first four months of the year for this product is as follows:

	Unit Sales
January	150,000
February	200,000
March	220,000
April	200,000

Company policy requires that ending inventories for each month be 15 percent of next month's sales. However, at the beginning of January, due to greater sales in December than anticipated, the beginning inventory of notebooks is only 12,000.

Required:

Prepare a production budget for the first quarter of the year. Show the number of units that should be produced each month as well as for the quarter in total.

OBJECTIVE 2

Exercise 9-38 DIRECT MATERIALS PURCHASES BUDGET

Lester Company produces a variety of labels, including iron-on name labels, which are sold to parents of camp-bound children. (The camps require campers to have their name on each article of clothing.) The labels are sold in a roll of 1,000, which requires about 25 metres of paper strip. Each metre of paper strip costs $0.17. Lester has budgeted production of the label rolls for the next four months as follows:

	Units
March	5,000
April	25,000
May	35,000
June	6,000

Inventory policy requires that sufficient paper strip be in ending monthly inventory to satisfy 20 percent of the following month's production needs. The inventory of paper strip at the beginning of March equals exactly the amount needed to satisfy the inventory policy.

Required:

Prepare a direct materials purchases budget for March, April, and May, showing purchases in units and in dollars for each month and in total.

OBJECTIVE 2

Exercise 9-39 DIRECT LABOUR BUDGET

Pendel Company produces a variety of garden tools. The production budget for rakes is shown for the following months:

	Units
March	50,000
April	60,000
May	30,000
June	28,000

Each rake produced requires (on average) 0.15 direct labour hour. The average cost of direct labour is $18 per hour.

Required:

Prepare a direct labour budget for March, April, and May, showing the hours needed and the direct labour cost for each month and in total.

Exercise 9-40 SALES BUDGET

OBJECTIVE 2

Norton Inc. manufactures six models of leaf blowers and weed eaters. Norton's budgeting team is finalizing the sales budget for the coming year. Sales in units and dollars for last year follow:

Product	Number Sold	Price ($)	Revenue
LB-1	16,800	29	$ 487,200
LB-2	18,000	15	270,000
WE-6	25,200	13	327,600
WE-7	16,200	10	162,000
WE-8	2,400	22	52,800
WE-9	1,000	26	26,000
Total			$1,325,600

In looking over the previous year's sales figures, Norton's sales budgeting team recalled the following:

a. Model LB-1 is a newer version of the leaf blower with a gasoline engine. The LB-1 is mounted on wheels instead of being carried. This model is designed for the commercial market and did better than expected in its first year. As a result, the number of units of Model LB-1 to be sold was forecast at 300 percent of the previous year's units.
b. Models WE-8 and WE-9 were introduced on October 1 of last year. They are lighter versions of the traditional weed eater and are designed for smaller households or condo units. Norton estimates that demand for both models will continue at the previous year's rate.
c. A competitor has announced plans to introduce an improved version of model WE-6, Norton's traditional weed eater. Norton believes that the model WE-6 price must be cut 20 percent to maintain unit sales at the previous year's level.
d. It was assumed that unit sales of all other models would increase by 10 percent, prices remaining constant.

Required:

Prepare a sales budget by product and in total for Norton Inc. for the coming year.

Exercise 9-41 PRODUCTION BUDGET AND DIRECT MATERIALS PURCHASES BUDGET

OBJECTIVE 2

Raylene Webber, owner of Raylene's Flowers and Gifts, produces gift baskets for various special occasions. Each gift basket includes fruit or assorted small gifts (e.g., a coffee mug, deck of cards, novelty cocoa mixes, scented soap) in a basket that is wrapped in colourful cellophane. Raylene has estimated the following unit sales of the standard gift basket for the rest of the year and for January of next year.

September	200
October	150
November	180
December	250
January	100

Raylene likes to have 10 percent of the next month's sales needs on hand at the end of each month. This requirement was met on August 31.

Two materials are needed for each fruit basket:

Fruit	1 kilogram
Small gifts	5 items

The materials inventory policy is to have 5 percent of the next month's fruit needs on hand and 50 percent of the next month's production needs of small gifts. (The relatively low inventory amount for fruit is designed to prevent spoilage.) Materials inventory on September 1 met this company policy.

Required:

1. Prepare a production budget for September, October, November, and December for gift baskets.
2. Prepare a direct materials purchases budget for the two types of materials used in the production of gift baskets for the months of September, October, and November. (Round answers to the nearest whole unit.)

OBJECTIVE 3

Exercise 9-42 ACCOUNTS RECEIVABLE AGING SCHEDULE AND CASH BUDGET

Kotari Inc. found that about 15 percent of its sales during the month were for cash. Kotari has the following accounts receivable payment experience:

Percent paid in the month of sale	20
Percent paid in the month after the sale	70
Percent paid in the second month after the sale	8

Kotari's anticipated sales for the next few months are as follows:

April	$200,000
May	240,000
June	230,000
July	246,000
August	250,000

Required:

1. Calculate credit sales for May, June, July, and August.
2. Prepare a schedule of cash receipts for July and August.

OBJECTIVE 3

Exercise 9-43 ACCOUNTS RECEIVABLE AGING SCHEDULE AND CASH BUDGET

Janzen Inc. sells all of its product on account. Janzen has the following accounts receivable payment experience:

Percent paid in the month of sale	20
Percent paid in the month after the sale	60
Percent paid in the second month after the sale	15

To encourage payment in the month of sale, Janzen gives a 2 percent cash discount. Janzen's anticipated sales for the next few months are as follows:

April	$200,000
May	220,000
June	230,000
July	210,000
August	250,000

Required:

1. Prepare a schedule of cash receipts for July.
2. Prepare a schedule of cash receipts for August.

Exercise 9-44 CASH PAYMENTS SCHEDULE

OBJECTIVE 3

Boger Company provided the following information relating to cash payments:

a. Boger purchased direct materials on account in the following amounts:

June	$40,000
July	45,000
August	50,000

b. Boger pays 30 percent of accounts payable in the month of purchase and the remaining 70 percent in the following month.
c. In July, direct labour cost is $39,000. August direct labour cost was $48,000. The company finds that typically 90 percent of direct labour cost is paid in cash during the month, with the remainder paid in the following month.
d. August overhead amounted to $73,700, including $6,100 of depreciation.
e. Boger had taken out a loan of $112,000 on May 1. Interest, due with payment of principal, accrued at the rate of 12 percent per year. The loan and all interest were repaid on August 31.

Required:

Prepare a schedule of cash payments for Boger Company for the month of August.

Exercise 9-45 CASH BUDGET

OBJECTIVE 3

The owner of a small mining supply company has requested a cash budget for June. After examining the records of the company, you find the following:

a. Cash balance on June 1 is $830.
b. Actual sales for April and May are as follows:

	April	May
Cash sales	$10,000	$15,000
Credit sales	25,000	35,000
Total sales	$35,000	$50,000

c. Credit sales are collected over a three-month period: 50 percent in the month of sale, 30 percent in the second month, and 15 percent in the third month. The sales collected in the third month are subject to a 1 percent late fee, which is paid by those customers in addition to what they owe. The remaining sales are uncollectible.
d. Inventory purchases average 75 percent of a month's total sales. Of those purchases, 20 percent are paid for in the month of purchase. The remaining 80 percent are paid for in the following month.
e. Salaries and wages total $8,700 per month, including a $4,500 salary paid to the owner.
f. Rent is $1,340 per month.
g. Taxes to be paid in June are $5,500.

The owner also tells you that he expects cash sales of $15,000 and credit sales of $50,000 for June. No minimum cash balance is required. The owner of the company does not have access to short-term loans.

Required:

1. Prepare a cash budget for June. Include supporting schedules for cash collections and cash payments.
2. Did the business show a negative cash balance for June? Assuming that the owner has no hope of establishing a line of credit for the business, what recommendations would you give the owner for dealing with a negative cash balance?

b. Each month, 30 percent of sales are for cash and 70 percent are on credit. The collection pattern for credit sales is 20 percent in the month of sale, 50 percent in the following month, and 30 percent in the second month following the sale.
c. Each month, the ending inventory exactly equals 50 percent of the cost of next month's sales. The markup on goods is 25 percent of cost.
d. Inventory purchases are paid for in the month following the purchase.
e. Recurring monthly expenses are as follows:

Salaries and wages	$10,000
Depreciation on plant and equipment	4,000
Utilities	1,000
Other	1,700

f. Property taxes of $15,000 are due and payable on July 15, 2010.
g. Advertising fees of $6,000 must be paid on August 20, 2010.
h. A lease on a new storage facility is scheduled to begin on September 2, 2010. Monthly payments are $5,000.
i. The company has a policy to maintain a minimum cash balance of $10,000. If necessary, it will borrow to meet its short-term needs. All borrowing is done at the end of the month. All payments on principal and interest are also made at the end of a month. The annual interest rate is 9 percent. The company must borrow in multiples of $1,000.
j. A partially completed balance sheet as of June 30, 2010, follows. (Accounts payable is for inventory purchases only.)

Cash	$?	
Accounts receivable	?	
Inventory	?	
Plant and equipment	425,000	
Accounts payable		$?
Common shares		210,000
Retained earnings		268,750
Total	$?	$?

Required:

1. Complete the balance sheet given in item j.
2. Prepare a cash budget for each month in the third quarter and for the quarter in total (the third quarter begins on July 1). Provide a supporting schedule of cash collections.
3. Prepare a pro forma balance sheet as of September 30, 2010.
4. Form a group with two or three other students. Discuss why a bank might require a cash budget for businesses that are seeking short-term loans. Determine what other financial reports might be useful for a loan decision. Also, discuss how the reliability of cash budgets and other financial information can be determined.

OBJECTIVE 1 4

Problem 9-49 PARTICIPATIVE BUDGETING, NOT-FOR-PROFIT SETTING

Dwight D. Eisenhower was the 34th president of the United States and the Supreme Commander of the Allied Forces during the second world war. Much of his army career was spent in planning. He once said that "planning is everything; the plan is nothing." What do you think he meant by this? Consider his comment with respect to the master budget. Do you agree or disagree? Be sure to include the impact of the master budget on planning and control.

OBJECTIVE 3

Problem 9-50 CASH BUDGET

The controller of Pratesh Company is gathering data to prepare the cash budget for July. He plans to develop the budget from the following information:

a. Of all sales, 35 percent are cash sales.

b. Of credit sales, 60 percent are collected within the month of sale. Half of the credit sales collected within the month receive a 2 percent cash discount (for accounts paid within 10 days). Twenty percent of credit sales are collected in the following month; remaining credit sales are collected the month thereafter. There are virtually no bad debts.

c. Sales for the second two quarters of the year follow. (The first three months are actual sales, and the last three months are estimated sales.)

	Sales ($)
April	450,000
May	580,000
June	900,000
July	1,140,000
August	1,200,000
September	1,134,000

d. The company sells all that it produces each month. The cost of raw materials equals 22 percent of each sales dollar. The company requires a monthly ending inventory equal to the coming month's production requirements. Of raw materials purchases, 50 percent are paid for in the month of purchase. The remaining 50 percent is paid for in the following month.

e. Wages total $105,000 each month and are paid in the month incurred.

f. Budgeted monthly operating expenses total $336,000, of which $45,000 is depreciation and $6,000 is expiration of prepaid insurance (the annual premium of $72,000 is paid on January 1).

g. Dividends of $130,000, declared on June 30, will be paid on July 15.

h. Old equipment will be sold for $25,200 on July 4.

i. On July 13, new equipment will be purchased for $173,000.

j. The company maintains a minimum cash balance of $20,000.

k. The cash balance on July 1 is $27,000.

Required:

Prepare a cash budget for July. Give a supporting schedule that details the cash collections from sales.

Problem 9-51 MASTER BUDGET, COMPREHENSIVE REVIEW

OBJECTIVE 1 2 3

Optima Company is a high-technology organization that produces a mass-storage system. The design of Optima's system is unique and represents a breakthrough in the industry. The units Optima produces combine positive features of both compact and hard disks. The company is completing its fifth year of operations and is preparing to build its master budget for the coming year (2010). The budget will detail each quarter's activity and the activity for the year in total. The master budget will be based on the following information:

a. Fourth-quarter sales for 2009 are 55,000 units.

b. Unit sales by quarter (for 2010) are projected as follows:

First quarter	65,000
Second quarter	70,000
Third quarter	75,000
Fourth quarter	90,000

The selling price is $400 per unit. All sales are credit sales. Optima collects 85 percent of all sales within the quarter in which they are realized; the other 15 percent is collected in the following quarter. There are no bad debts.

c. There is no beginning inventory of finished goods. Optima is planning the following ending finished goods inventories for each quarter:

First quarter	13,000 units
Second quarter	15,000 units
Third quarter	20,000 units
Fourth quarter	10,000 units

The production schedule for the six-month period beginning with October reflects the company's policy of maintaining a stable year-round work force by scheduling overtime to meet the following production schedules:

October (actual)	90,000
November (actual)	90,000
December (estimated)	90,000
January (estimated)	90,000
February (estimated)	100,000
March (estimated)	100,000

The bats are made from wooden blocks that cost $6 each. Ten bats can be produced from each block. The blocks are acquired one year in advance so they can be properly aged. Calydon pays the supplier one-twelfth of the cost of this material each month until the obligation is retired. The monthly payment is $60,000.

The plant is normally scheduled for a 40-hour, five-day work week. During the busy production season, however, the work week may be increased to six 10-hour days. Workers can produce 7.5 bats per hour. Normal monthly output is 75,000 bats. Factory employees are paid $15 per hour for regular time and time and one-half for overtime.

Other manufacturing costs include variable overhead of $0.30 per unit and annual fixed overhead of $280,000. Depreciation charges totalling $40,000 are included among the fixed overhead. Selling expenses include variable costs of $0.20 per unit and annual fixed costs of $60,000. Fixed administrative costs are $120,000 annually. All fixed costs are incurred uniformly throughout the year.

The controller has accumulated the following additional information:

1. The balances of selected accounts as of November 30, 2012 are:

Cash	$ 12,000
Marketable securities, at market value	40,000
Accounts receivable	96,000
Prepaid expenses	4,800
Accounts payable (arising from raw material purchases)	300,000
Accrued vacation pay	9,500
Equipment note payable	102,000
Accrued income taxes payable	50,000

2. Interest to be received from the company's temporary investments is estimated at $500 for December.
3. Prepaid expenses of $3,600 will expire during December and the balance of the prepaid account is estimated at $4,200 for the end of December.
4. Calydon purchased new machinery in 2012 as part of a plant modernization program. The machinery was financed by a 24-month note of $144,000. The terms call for equal principal payments over the next 24 months with interest paid at the rate of 1 percent per month on the unpaid balance at the first of the month. The first payment was made on May 1, 2012.
5. Old equipment, which has a book value of $8,000, is to be sold during December for $7,500.
6. Each month the company accrues $1,700 for vacation pay by charging vacation pay expense and crediting accrued vacation pay. The plant closes for two weeks in June when all plant employees take a vacation.
7. Quarterly dividends of $0.20 per share will be paid on December 15 to shareholders of record. Calydon Corporation has authorized 10,000 shares. The company has issued 7,500 shares and 500 of these are classified as treasury stock.
8. The quarterly income taxes payment of $50,000 is due on December 15, 2012.

Required:

Prepare a schedule that forecasts the cash position at December 31, 2012. What action, if any, will be required to maintain a $10,000 cash balance?

Chapter 10

Standard Costing: A Managerial Control Tool

After studying Chapter 10, you should be able to:

1. Explain how unit standards are set and why standard cost systems are adopted.
2. Explain the purpose of a standard cost sheet.
3. Describe the basic concepts underlying variance analysis, and explain when variances should be investigated.
4. Compute the materials variances, and explain how they are used for control.
5. Compute the labour variances, and explain how they are used for control.
6. (Appendix) Prepare journal entries for materials and labour variances.

© NAVISTAR

Experience Managerial Decisions
with Navistar

Understanding an income statement is a relatively easy task. However, understanding the causes underlying net income represents a far more challenging task, especially for Fortune 300 companies like **Navistar International Truck and Engine Corporation**, whose truck assembly plant is in Chatham, Ontario. Navistar's annual net income typically falls in the neighbourhood of several hundred million dollars. Navistar uses variance analysis as an important tool for understanding the many causes of its net income. This type of analysis helps managers at Navistar to learn which parts of the company are contributing to net income as expected and which parts are not contributing to net income as expected and, as such, will require careful attention to improve in the future. For example, Navistar recently reported that its monthly production cost was $48 million to manufacture 1,228 actual units—considerably higher than its budgeted production cost of only $41 million to produce 883 expected units. If you were the manager in charge of Navistar's production, what would you do after receiving the news that actual costs were $7 million greater (or approximately 17 percent more than the budgeted total production cost) than expected?

Before Navistar's management took any rash actions, it performed an in-depth variance analysis on all of its key production factors to try and understand what had caused the unfavourable static budget variance between its actual costs at month-end and its budgeted costs at the beginning of the month. These key production factors included direct and indirect materials, direct and indirect labour, benefits, utilities, depreciation, and information technology expense. As you might expect, variance analysis revealed that the $7 million unfavourable static budget variance was comprised of numerous smaller variances, some favourable and others unfavourable, involving many of Navistar's key production factors. Most importantly, Navistar's managers were happy to learn that when adjusting the total budgeted costs for the higher production volume, total production costs should have increased by over $11 million, much more than the actual cost increase of $7 million. In fact, effective management of labour and materials purchasing—both of which had large favourable flexible budget variances—actually helped Navistar to save $4 million. Without variance analysis, Navistar would have a much harder time understanding the causes of its net income and taking the appropriate action when components of income are different than expected.

Here's The Real Kicker

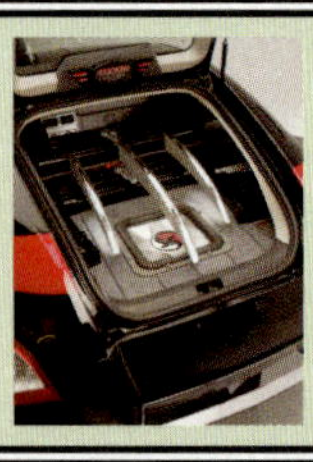

About 15 percent of the defective Kicker speakers returned to Stillwater Designs can be rebuilt. The other 85 percent are sold as metal scrap. Speakers are candidates for rebuilding if the cost of direct materials and labour is less than the sum of the speaker's purchase cost, shipping cost, and duty (the production of Kicker speakers is outsourced to mostly Asian producers). This is true, for example, of the square S12L7 speakers.

To rebuild a square S12L7, the returned speaker is torn down to its basic structures, chemical and glue residues are removed, and the speaker is demagnetized so that it is possible to get rid of metal shavings and pieces. After this preparatory work, recone kits are used to replace the stripped-out components. The rebuilt woofer is then placed in a cabinet and sealed. The completed unit undergoes two tests—one to ensure that the power is hooked up correctly and a second that checks for air leaks.

Every two years, standard costs for materials and labour are set. Time studies are used to determine the time required for rebuilding, and, thus, the labour content. The cost of the recone kit is the major material cost. These standard costs are used for two purposes: (1) to determine if rebuilding is feasible for a given model and (2) to assign costs to the rebuilt product on an ongoing basis if rebuilding is the decision.

KICKER®

OBJECTIVE 1

Explain how unit standards are set and why standard cost systems are adopted.

Unit Standards

Most operating managers recognize the need to control costs. Cost control often means the difference between success and failure or between above-average profits and lesser profits. For example, as healthcare costs skyrocket due to the large and aging baby boomer generation, the growing complexity of medical treatments, and the growing number of uninsured patients, most healthcare facilities are desperately trying to budget and control costs more effectively. Usually, cost control means that managers must be cost conscious and assume responsibility for this important objective.

In Chapter 9, we learned that budgets set standards that are used to control and evaluate managerial performance. However, budgets are aggregate measures of performance; they identify the revenues and costs in total that an organization should experience if plans are executed as expected. By comparing the actual costs and actual revenues with the corresponding budgeted amounts at the same level of activity, a measure of managerial efficiency emerges.

Although the process just described provides significant information for control, developing standards for unit amounts, as well as for total amounts, can enhance control. To determine the unit standard cost for a particular input, two decisions must be made: (1) the amount of input that *should* be *used* per unit of output (the quantity decision) and (2) the amount that *should* be *paid* for the quantity of the input to be used (the pricing decision). The quantity decision produces **quantity standards**, and the pricing decision produces **price standards**. The unit standard cost can be computed by multiplying these two standards: Quantity standard × Price standard.

ANALYTICAL Q&A

If the unit quantity standard for a raw material is 10 kilograms per unit, and the cost per kilogram of this material is $8, what is the standard cost per unit of product for the material?

Answers on pages 711 to 715.

For example, a soft-drink bottling company may decide that 300 grams of fructose should be used for every 1 litre bottle of cola (the quantity standard), and the price of the fructose should be $0.20 per 100 grams (the price standard). The standard cost of the fructose per bottle of cola is then $0.60 (3 × $0.20). The standard cost per unit of fructose can be used to predict what the total cost of fructose should be as the activity level varies; thus, it becomes a flexible budget formula. If 10,000 bottles of cola are produced, then the total expected cost of fructose is $6,000 ($0.60 × 10,000); if 15,000 bottles are produced, then the total expected cost of fructose is $9,000 ($0.60 × 15,000).

How Standards Are Developed

Historical experience, engineering studies, and input from operating personnel are three potential sources of quantitative standards. Although historical experience may provide an initial guideline for setting standards, it should be used with caution. Often, processes are operating inefficiently; adopting input–output relationships from the past thus perpetuates these inefficiencies. Engineering studies can determine the most efficient way to operate and can provide rigorous guidelines; however, engineered standards often are too rigorous. They may not be achievable by operating personnel. Since operating personnel are accountable for meeting standards, they should have significant input in setting standards. The same principles governing participative budgeting pertain to setting unit standards.

Price standards are the joint responsibility of operations, purchasing, personnel, and accounting. Operating personnel determine the quality of the inputs required; personnel and purchasing have the responsibility of acquiring the labour and materials quality requested at the lowest price. Market forces, trade unions, and other external forces limit the range of choices for price standards. In setting price standards, purchasing must consider discounts, freight, and quality; personnel, on the other hand, must consider payroll taxes, fringe benefits, and qualifications. Accounting is responsible for recording the price standards as well as for preparing reports that compare actual performance with the standard.

Types of Standards

Standards are generally classified as either *ideal* or *currently attainable*. **Ideal standards** demand maximum efficiency and can be achieved only if everything operates perfectly. No machine breakdowns, slack, or lack of skill (even momentarily) are allowed. **Currently attainable standards** can be achieved under efficient operating conditions. Allowance is made for normal breakdowns, interruptions, less than perfect skill, and so on. These standards are demanding but achievable. Exhibit 10-1 provides a visual and conceptual portrayal of the two standards.

CONCEPT Q&A

What is the difference between an ideal standard and a currently attainable standard?

Answers on pages 711 to 715.

Exhibit 10-1

Types of Standards

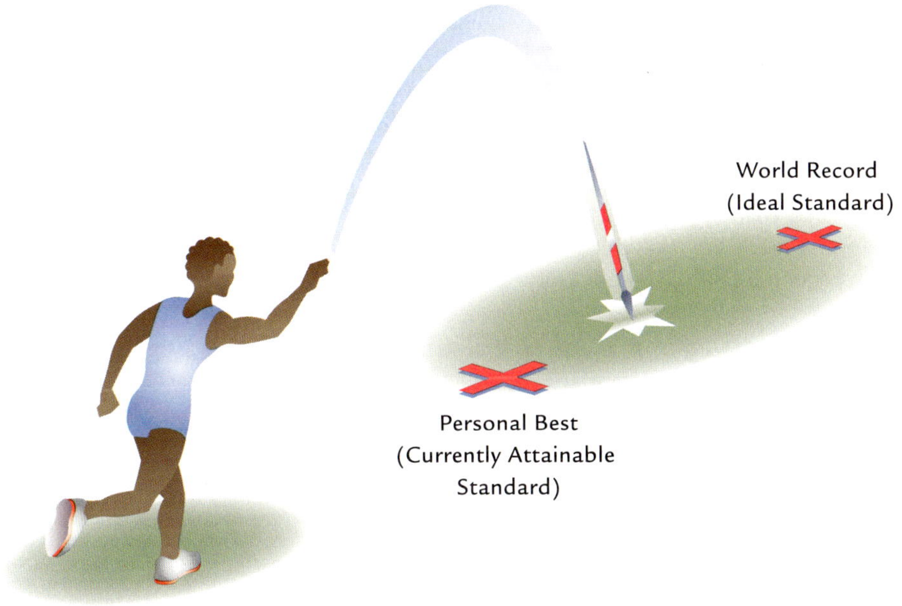

Of the two types, currently attainable standards offer the most behavioural benefits. If standards are too tight and never achievable, workers become frustrated and performance levels decline. However, challenging but achievable standards tend to extract higher performance levels—particularly when the individuals subject to the standards have participated in their creation.

Why Standard Cost Systems Are Adopted

Two reasons for adopting a standard cost system are frequently mentioned: to improve planning and control and to facilitate product costing.

Planning and Control Standard costing systems enhance planning and control and improve performance measurement. Unit standards are a fundamental requirement for a flexible budgeting system, which is a key feature of a meaningful planning and control system. Budgetary control systems compare actual costs with budgeted costs by computing *variances*, the difference between the actual and planned costs for the actual level of activity. By developing unit price and quantity standards, an overall variance can be decomposed into a price variance and a usage or efficiency variance.

Performing this decomposition provides a manager with additional information beyond that of the overall variance. For example, if the variance is unfavourable, this decomposition can inform a manager whether it is attributable to discrepancies between planned prices and actual prices, to discrepancies between planned usage and actual usage, or to both. Since operating managers have more control over the usage of inputs than over their prices, efficiency variances provide specific signals regarding the need for corrective action and where that action should be focused. Thus, in principle, the use of efficiency variances enhances operational control. Additionally, by breaking out the price variance, over which operating managers potentially have less control, the system provides an improved measure of managerial efficiency.

The benefits of operational control, however, may not extend to the manufacturing environments that are emphasizing continuous improvement and just-in-time (JIT) purchasing and manufacturing. The use of a standard cost system for operational control in these settings can produce dysfunctional behaviour. For example, materials price variance reporting may encourage the purchasing department to buy in large quantities in order to take advantage of discounts. Yet this practice might lead to holding significant inventories, something not desired by JIT firms. Therefore, the detailed computation of variances—at least at the operational level—is discouraged in this new environment. Nonetheless, standards in this newer manufacturing environment are still useful for planning, such as in the creation of bids. Also, variances may still be computed and presented in reports to higher-level managers so that the financial dimension can be monitored. In addition, other incentives, such as a fee charged to managers for holding excessive inventories, can be created to discourage managers from allowing inventories to grow beyond the level desired by JIT systems.

Finally, it should be mentioned that many firms operate with conventional manufacturing systems. Standard cost systems are widely used. According to one survey, 87 percent of the firms responding used a standard cost system.[1] Furthermore, the survey revealed that significant numbers of respondents were calculating variances at the operational level. For example, about 40 percent of the firms using a standard costing system reported labour variances for small work crews or individual workers.

Product Costing In a *standard* costing system, costs are assigned to products using quantity and price standards for all three manufacturing costs: direct materials, direct labour, and overhead. At the other end of the cost assignment spectrum, an *actual*

[1] Bruce R. Gaumnitz and Felix P. Kollaritsch, "Manufacturing Variances: Current Practice and Trends," *Journal of Cost Management* (Spring 1991): 59–64. Similar widespread usage is also reported by Carole B. Cheatham and Leo R. Cheatham, "Redesigning Cost Systems: Is Standard Costing Obsolete?" *Accounting Horizons* (December 1996): 23–31. Furthermore, a survey of UK firms revealed that 76 percent of them use a standard cost system; see Colin Drury, "Standard Costing: A Technique at Variance with Modern Management," *Management Accounting* (London, November 1999): 56–58.

Exhibit 10-2

Cost Assignment Approaches

	Manufacturing Costs		
	Direct Materials	**Direct Labour**	**Overhead**
Actual costing system	Actual	Actual	Actual
Normal costing system	Actual	Actual	Budgeted
Standard costing system	Standard	Standard	Standard

costing system assigns the actual costs of all three manufacturing inputs to products. In the middle of this spectrum is a *normal* costing system, which predetermines overhead costs for the purpose of product costing but assigns direct materials and direct labour to products by using actual costs. Thus, a normal costing system assigns actual direct costs to products but allocates budgeted indirect costs to products using a budgeted rate and actual activity levels. Exhibit 10-2 summarizes these three cost assignment approaches. Standard product costing has several advantages over normal costing and actual costing. One, of course, is the greater capacity for control. Standard costing systems also provide readily available unit cost information that can be used for pricing decisions at any time throughout the period because actual costs (either direct or indirect) do not need to be known. This ability is particularly helpful for companies that do a significant amount of bidding and that are paid on a cost-plus basis.

Other simplifications also are possible. For example, if a process-costing system uses standard costing to assign product costs, there is no need to compute a unit cost for each equivalent unit cost category. A standard unit cost would exist for each category. Additionally, there is no need to distinguish between the first-in, first-out (FIFO) and weighted average methods of accounting for beginning inventory costs. Usually, a standard process-costing system will follow the equivalent unit calculation of the FIFO approach. That is, current equivalent units of work are calculated. By calculating current equivalent work, current actual production costs can be compared with standard costs for control purposes.

CONCEPT Q&A

Why would a firm adopt a standard costing system?

Answers on pages 711 to 715.

Standard Product Costs

OBJECTIVE 2
Explain the purpose of a standard cost sheet.

In manufacturing firms, standard costs are developed for direct materials, direct labour, and overhead. Using these costs, the **standard cost per unit** is computed. The **standard cost sheet** provides the production data needed to calculate the standard unit cost. To illustrate, a standard cost sheet will be developed for a 500-gram bag of corn chips produced by Crunchy Chips Inc. The production of corn chips begins by steaming and soaking corn kernels overnight in a lime solution. This process softens the kernels so that they can be shaped into a sheet of dough. The dough is then cut into small triangular chips. Next, the chips are toasted in an oven and are dropped into a deep fryer. After cooking, the chips pass under a salting device and are inspected for quality. Substandard chips are sorted and discarded; the chips that pass inspection are bagged by a packaging machine. The bagged chips are manually packed into boxes for shipping.

Four materials are used to process corn chips: yellow corn, cooking oil, salt, and lime. The package in which the chips are placed is also classified as a direct material. Crunchy Chips has two types of direct labourers: machine operators and inspectors (or sorters). Variable overhead is made up of three costs: gas, electricity, and water. Both variable and fixed overhead are applied by using direct labour hours. The standard cost sheet is given in Exhibit 10-3. Note that it should cost \$1.61 to produce a 500-gram package of corn chips. Also notice that the company should use 550 grams of corn to produce a 500-gram package of chips. There are two reasons for this 50 grams difference. First, some chips are discarded during the inspection process. The company

Exhibit 10-3

Standard Cost Sheet for Corn Chips (500 g package)

Description	Standard Price	Standard Usage	Standard Cost*	Subtotal
Direct materials:				
Yellow corn	$ 0.018**	550 g	$0.10	
Cooking oil	0.30**	50 g	.15	
Salt	1.00**	25 g	.25	
Lime	0.50**	100 g	.50	
Bags	0.05	1 bag	.05	
Total direct materials				$1.05
Direct labour:				
Inspection	8.00	0.01 hr.	$0.08	
Machine operators	10.00	0.01 hr.	0.10	
Total direct labour				0.18
Overhead:				
Variable overhead	4.00	0.02 hr.	$0.08	
Fixed overhead	15.00	0.02 hr.	0.30	
Total overhead				0.38
Total standard unit cost				$1.61

*Calculated by multiplying price times usage. Yellow corn is rounded.
**Prices are per 100 grams.

plans on a normal amount of waste. Second, the company wants to have more than 500 grams in each package to increase customer satisfaction with its product and to avoid any problems with fair packaging laws.

Exhibit 10-3 also reveals other important insights. The standard usage for variable and fixed overhead is tied to the direct labour standards. For variable overhead, the rate is $4.00 per direct labour hour. Since one package of corn chips should use 0.02 hours of direct labour per unit, the variable overhead cost assigned to a package of corn chips is $0.08 ($4.00 × 0.02). For fixed overhead, the rate is $15.00 per direct labour hour, making the fixed overhead cost per package of corn chips $0.30 ($15.00 × 0.02). About twenty percent of the cost of production is fixed, indicating a capital-intensive production effort. Indeed, much of the operation is mechanized.

The standard cost sheet also reveals the quantity of each input that should be used to produce one unit of output. The unit quantity standards can be used to compute the total amount of inputs allowed for the actual output. This computation is an essential component in computing efficiency variances. A manager should be able to compute the **standard quantity of materials allowed (*SQ*)** and the **standard hours allowed (*SH*)** for the actual output. This computation must be done for every class of direct material and every class of direct labour. Cornerstone 10-1 shows how to compute these quantities by using one type of material and one class of labour.

ANALYTICAL Q&A

A product is allowed 100 grams of silver per unit and 0.5 hour of labour. If 3,000 units are produced, what is the standard quantity of silver allowed? Standard quantity of labour?

Answers on pages 711 to 715.

OBJECTIVE 3
Describe the basic concepts underlying variance analysis, and explain when variances should be investigated.

Variance Analysis: General Description

It is possible to calculate the costs that should have been incurred for the actual level of activity. This figure is obtained by multiplying the amount of input allowed (either materials or labour) for the actual output by the standard price of the input. Letting *SP* be the standard unit price of an input and *SQ* the standard quantity of input allowed for the actual output, the planned or budgeted input cost is *SP* × *SQ*. The actual input cost is *AP* × *AQ*, where *AP* is the actual price per unit of the input and *AQ* is the actual quantity of input used. The **total budget variance** is the difference

The HOW and WHY of Computing Standard Quantities Allowed (*SQ* and *SH*)

CORNERSTONE 10-1

Information:
Assume that 100,000 packages of corn chips are produced during the first week of March. The unit quantity standard is 550 grams of yellow corn per package (Exhibit 10-3). The unit quantity standard for machine operators is 0.01 hour per package produced (Exhibit 10-3).

Required:
How much yellow corn and how many operator hours should be used for the actual output of 100,000 packages?

Solution:
Corn allowed:

$$\begin{aligned} SQ &= \text{Unit quantity standard} \times \text{Actual output} \\ &= 550 \times 100{,}000 \\ &= 55{,}000{,}000 \text{ grams} \end{aligned}$$

Operator hours allowed:

$$\begin{aligned} SH &= \text{Unit labour standard} \times \text{Actual output} \\ &= 0.01 \times 100{,}000 \\ &= 1{,}000 \text{ direct labour hours} \end{aligned}$$

WHY:
Once quantity standards have been set for each unit of output, these must be translated into the quantities of units allowed for the level of output achieved, if the production operations were meeting the standards. These will be calculated for each component of input for the units produced.

between the actual cost of the input and its planned cost. As will be explained in Chapter 11, this variance is formally called the static budget variance. However, for now, the total budget variance will simply be called the *total variance*:

$$\begin{aligned} \text{Total variance} &= \text{Actual cost} - \text{Planned cost} \\ &= (AP \times AQ) - (SP \times SQ) \end{aligned}$$

Because responsibility for deviations from planned prices tends to be located in the purchasing or personnel department and responsibility for deviations from planned usage of inputs tends to be located in the production department, it is important to separate the total variance into price and usage (quantity) variances.

Price and Usage Variances

Exhibit 10-4 provides a general model for calculating price and quantity variances for materials and labour.[2] For labour, the price variance is usually called a *rate variance*, and the usage (quantity) variance is called an *efficiency variance*. **Price (rate) variance** is the difference between the actual and standard unit price of an input multiplied by the number of inputs used: $(AP - SP)AQ$. **Usage (efficiency) variance** is the difference between the actual and standard quantity of inputs multiplied by the standard unit price of the input: $(AQ - SQ)SP$.

Unfavourable (*U*) variances occur whenever actual prices or actual usage of inputs are greater than standard prices or standard usage. When the opposite occurs, **favourable (*F*) variances** are obtained. Favourable and unfavourable variances are

[2] Overhead variance analysis is discussed in Chapter 11 .

Exhibit 10-4

Variance Analysis: General Description

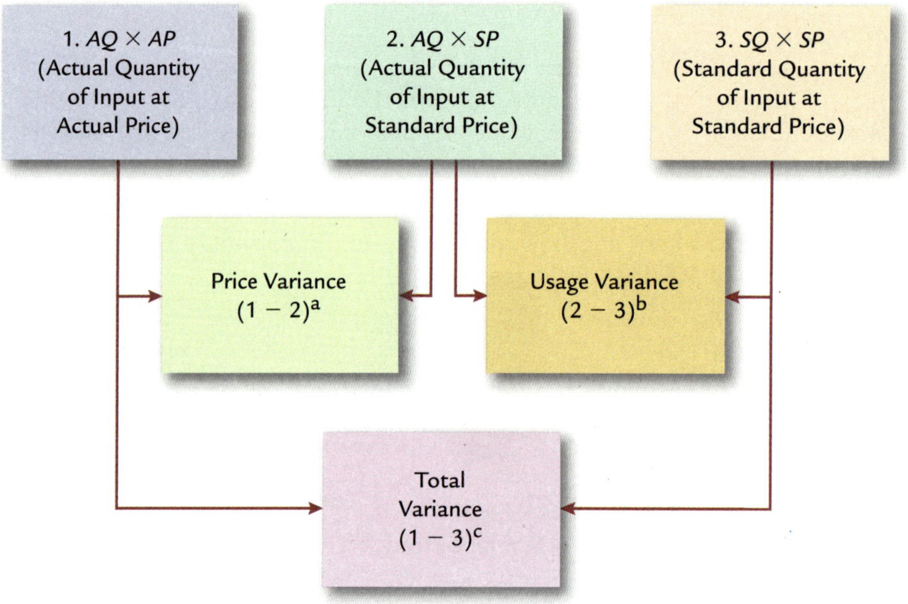

[a]Price variance = $(AQ \times AP) - (AQ \times SP) = (AP - SP)AQ$
[b]Usage variance = $(AQ \times SP) - (SQ \times SP) = (AQ - SQ)SP$
[c]Total variance = $(AQ \times AP) - (SQ \times SP)$

not equivalent to good and bad variances. The terms merely indicate the relationship of the actual prices (or quantities) to the standard prices (or quantities). Whether or not the variances are good or bad depends on why they occurred. Determining the cause of a variance requires managers to do some investigation.

The Decision to Investigate

Rarely will actual performance exactly meet the established standards, and management does not expect it to do so. Random variations around the standard are expected. As a result, management should have in mind an acceptable range of performance. When variances are within this range, they are assumed to be caused by random factors. When a variance falls outside of this range, the deviation is likely to be caused by nonrandom factors, either factors that managers can control or factors they cannot control. In the noncontrollable case, managers need to revise the standard. In addition, it is possible that a variance that is too small to warrant investigation might be the result of two much larger but offsetting variances, each of which work in the opposite direction. For example, a $5,000 unfavourable total variance for materials might be comprised of a $100,000 unfavourable price variance and a $95,000 favourable usage variance, both of which likely warrant investigation on their own. Detailed analysis allows managers to recognize such offsetting variance situations.

An example from the pharmaceutical industry may drive home the importance of variance investigation.[3] Drugs must contain a certain amount of the active ingredient, plus or minus a small percent (e.g., aspirin claiming to have five grains per tablet must really have somewhere between 90 and 110 percent of the specified amount). The Food and Drug Administration (FDA) is responsible for ensuring the safety and efficacy of drugs manufactured in the United States and abroad. An anonymous letter alerted the FDA to manufacturing problems with an antibiotic produced by the Canadian firm, **Novopharm Ltd**. Basically, the drug was too strong and could potentially destroy beneficial bacteria along with the harmful bacteria. Upon investigation, the FDA found the blending process to be "out of control." The result was that the firm stopped shipping

[3]The examples given here are taken from an article by Christopher Drew, "Medicines from Afar Raise Safety Concerns," *The New York Times* (October 29, 1995): A1 and A16.

that drug until the process could be corrected. Another FDA investigation centred on **Haimen Pharmaceutical Factory** in China. In this case, the FDA found the samples of an antileukemia drug to be too weak. Again, large variances from the standard triggered an investigation. Interestingly, the question of what to do about the company and the drug was not clear-cut. In this case, the FDA did not withdraw its approval because the drug was in short supply.

CONCEPT Q&A

Suppose that the actual labour rate paid is $12 per hour, while the standard labour rate is $11.50. Will the labour rate variance be favourable or unfavourable?

Answers on pages 711 to 715.

ETHICS The earlier two examples also illustrate the strong ethical content of variance analysis. Significant deviations from standard in these examples can cause physical harm to the users of the product, by being either too potent or not potent enough. It is critical that a strong control system be in place and function as intended. Competence is the guiding ethical standard. Clearly, the consumers of these products are interested in those individuals responsible to perform their professional duties in accordance with the relevant laws, regulations, and technical standards.◆

Now that we understand why variance investigation is important, we need to understand when to investigate. Investigating the cause of variances and taking corrective action, like all activities, have costs associated with them. As a general principle, an investigation should be undertaken only if the expected benefits are greater than the expected costs. Assessing the costs and benefits of a variance investigation is not an easy task, however. A manager must consider whether a variance will recur. If so, the process may be permanently out of control, meaning that continuing savings may be achieved if corrective action is taken. But how is it possible to know if the variance is going to recur unless an investigation is conducted? And how is it possible to know the cost of corrective action unless the cause of the variance is known?

Because it is difficult to assess the costs and benefits of variance analysis on a case-by-case basis, many firms adopt the general guideline of investigating variances only if they fall outside of an acceptable range. They are not investigated unless they are large enough to be of concern. They must be large enough to be caused by something other than random factors and large enough (on average) to justify the costs of investigating and taking corrective action.

How do managers determine whether variances are significant? How is the acceptable range established? The acceptable range is the standard, plus or minus an allowable deviation. The top and bottom measures of the allowable range are called the **control limits**. The upper control limit is the standard plus the allowable deviation, and the lower control limit is the standard minus the allowable deviation. Current practice sets the control limits subjectively: Based on past experience, intuition, and judgment, management determines the allowable deviation from standard.[4] The actual deviations from standard often are plotted over time against the upper and lower limits to allow managers to see the significance of the variance. Cornerstone 10-2 shows how control limits are used to trigger an investigation. The control chart graphically illustrates the concept of control limits. The assumed standard is $100,000, and the allowable deviation is plus or minus $10,000. The upper limit is $110,000, and the lower limit is $90,000. Investigation occurs whenever an observation falls outside of these limits (as would be the case for the sixth observation). Trends can also be important.

The control limits often are expressed both as a percentage of the standard and as an absolute dollar amount. For example, the allowable deviation may be expressed as the lesser of 10 percent of the standard amount, or $10,000.

In other words, management will not accept a deviation of more than $10,000 even if that deviation is less than 10 percent of the standard. Alternatively, even if the dollar amount is less than $10,000, an investigation is required if the deviation is more than 10 percent of the standard amount.

CONCEPT Q&A

Refer to the control chart in Cornerstone 10-2. What action would you take for an actual value of $89,750?

Answers on pages 711 to 715.

[4] Gaumnitz and Kollaritsch, "Manufacturing Variances: Current Practices and Trends," reports that about 45 to 47 percent of the firms use dollar or percentage control limits. Most of the remaining firms use judgment rather than any formal identification of limits.

CORNERSTONE 10-2

The HOW and WHY of Using Control Limits to Trigger a Variance Investigation

Information:

Standard cost: $100,000; allowable deviation: ±10,000; actual costs for six months:

June	$ 97,500	September	$102,500
July	105,000	October	107,500
August	95,000	November	112,500

Required:

Plot the actual costs over time against the upper and lower control limits. Determine when a variance should be investigated.

Solution:

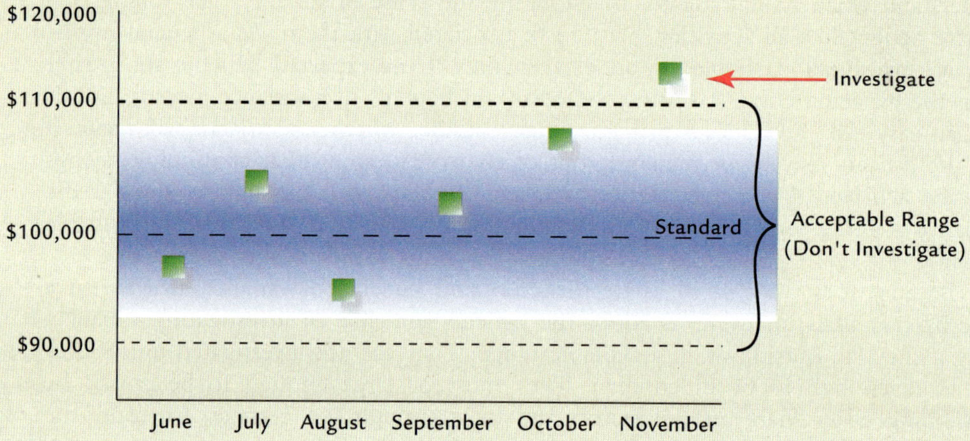

The control chart reveals that the last variance should be investigated. The chart also reveals a short-term increasing trend that suggests the process is moving out of control. A nongraphical approach is to calculate the difference between the actual cost and the upper or lower limit and see if it exceeds $10,000.

WHY:

Not all variances warrant follow-up, so a mechanism must be established to determine which variances will be investigated further and which ones will not.

OBJECTIVE 4
Compute the materials variances, and explain how they are used for control.

Variance Analysis: Materials

The total variance for materials measures the difference between the actual costs of materials and their budgeted costs for the actual level of activity. Cornerstone 10-3 illustrates how to calculate the total variance for materials by using selected data from Crunchy Chips for the first week of March. To keep the example simple, only one material (corn) is illustrated.

Direct Materials Variances

To help control the cost of materials, price and usage variances are calculated. However, the sum of the price and usage variances will add up to the total materials

The HOW and WHY of Calculating the Total Variance for Materials

CORNERSTONE 10-3

Information:

Unit standards from Exhibit 10-3; the actual results for the first week in March:

Actual production	48,500 bags of corn chips
Actual cost of corn	27,000,000 grams at $0.02 per 100 g = $5,400

Required:

Calculate the total variance for corn for the first week in March.

Solution:

	Actual Costs	Budgeted Costs*	Total Variance
	AQ × *AP*	*SQ* × *SP*	(*AQ* × *AP*) – (*SQ* × *SP*)
Corn	$5,400	$4,801.50	$598.50 *U*

* The standard quantities for materials and labour are computed as unit quantity standards from Exhibit 10-3:

Corn: SQ = 550 × 48,500 = 26,675,000 grams

Multiplying these standard quantities by the unit standard prices given in Exhibit 10-3 produces the budgeted amounts appearing in this column:

Corn: $0.018 per 100 g × 266750 = $4,801.50

WHY:

We must calculate the total variance for materials to help us explain why actual results are different from expected results.

AQ = Actual quantity used.
AP = Actual price per unit.

variance calculated in Cornerstone 10-3 *only if the materials purchased equal the materials used.* The materials price variance is computed by using the actual quantity of materials purchased, and the materials usage variance is computed by using the actual quantity of materials used.

Since it is better to have information on variances earlier rather than later, the materials price variance uses the actual quantity of materials purchased rather than the actual quantity of materials used. The more timely the information, the more likely that proper managerial action can be taken. Old information often is useless information. Materials may sit in inventory for weeks or months before they are needed in production. By the time the materials price variance is computed, signalling a problem, it may be too late to take corrective action. Or, even if corrective action is still possible, the delay may cost the company thousands of dollars. For example, suppose a new purchasing agent is unaware of the availability of a quantity discount on a raw material. If the materials price variance that ignores the discount is computed when a new purchase is made, the resulting unfavourable signal would lead to quick corrective action. (In this case, the action would be to use the discount for future purchases.) If the materials price variance is not computed until the material is issued to production, it may be several weeks or even months before the problem is discovered.

Materials price and usage variances normally should be calculated using variance formulas. However, the three-pronged (columnar) approach is used when the materials purchased equal the materials used. Cornerstone 10-4 shows how to use the materials variance formulas, which we now specifically state and define.

CONCEPT Q&A

When is the total materials variance the sum of the price variance and the usage variance?

Answers on pages 711 to 715.

CORNERSTONE 10-4

The HOW and WHY of Calculating Materials Variances: Formula and Columnar Approaches

Information:

Unit standards from Exhibit 10-3; the actual results for the first week in March:

Actual production	48,500 bags of corn chips
Actual cost of corn	27,000,000 grams @ \$0.02 per 100 grams

Required:

Calculate the materials price and usage variances by using the three-pronged (columnar) and formula approaches.

Solution:

1. Formulas (recommended approach for materials variances because materials purchased may differ from materials used):

$$MPV = (AP - SP)AQ$$
$$= (\$0.02 - \$0.018)\ 270{,}000$$
$$= \$540\ U$$

$$MUV = (AQ - SQ)SP$$
$$= (270{,}000 - 266{,}750)\ (\$0.018)$$
$$= \$58.50\ U$$

2. Columnar (this approach is possible only if the materials purchased equal materials used):

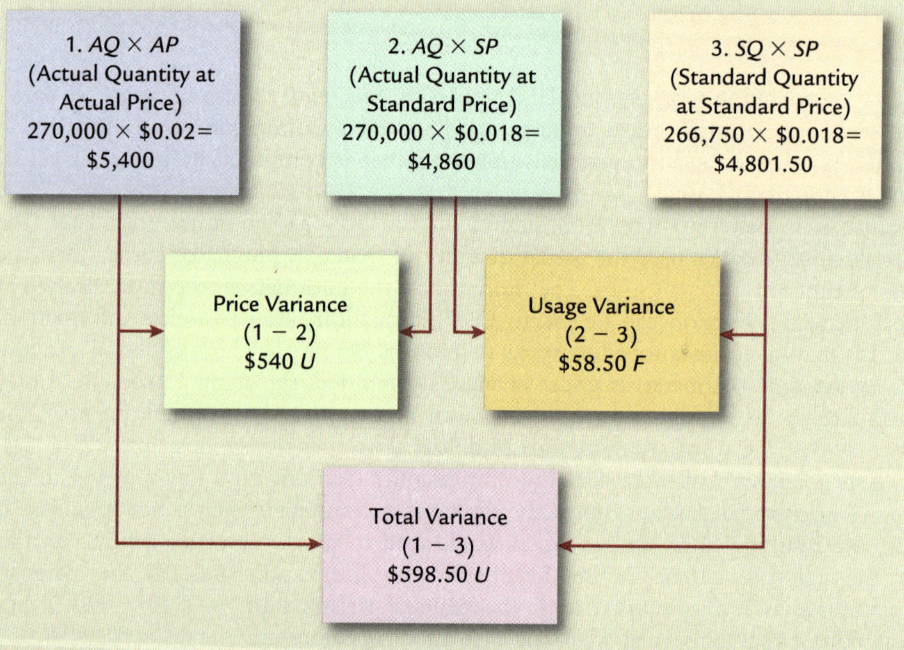

WHY:

The total variance for materials is of limited value, so we must further analyze it into price and usage variances to be able to identify the specific type of corrective action that needs to be taken. There are two approaches that could be used.

The **materials price variance (*MPV*)** measures the difference between what should have been paid for raw materials and what was actually paid. The formula for computing this variance is:

$$MPV = (AP \times AQ) - (SP \times AQ)$$

or, factoring, we have:

$$MPV = (AP - SP)AQ$$

where

AP = The actual price per unit

SP = The standard price per unit

AQ = The actual quantity of material purchased

It should be noted that the *MPV* formula uses the ***actual*** quantity purchased, rather than the standard amount that should have been purchased, because purchasing managers typically influence the amount of materials actually purchased. Likewise, the *MPV* uses material ***purchased***, rather than used, because purchasing managers typically do not control the amount of material actually used in production. Thus, the *MPV* contains items over which purchasing managers likely have control, which is helpful given that their bonuses often are affected by the *MPV*.

The **materials usage variance (*MUV*)** measures the difference between the direct materials actually used and the direct materials that should have been used for the actual output. The formula for computing this variance is:

$$MUV = (SP \times AQ) - (SP \times SQ)$$

or, factoring:

$$MUV = (AQ - SQ)SP$$

where

AQ = The actual quantity of materials used

SQ = The standard quantity of materials allowed for the actual output

SP = The standard price per unit

It should be noted that the *MUV* formula uses the ***standard*** price that should have been paid, rather than the actual price that was paid, because production managers typically do not influence the actual price paid for materials. Using the standard price in the *MUV*—a variance for which production managers typically are held accountable—prevents them from unfairly being affected by the actual price. Cornerstone 10-4 shows how to calculate the materials price and usage variances using either a columnar approach or a formula approach for the Crunchy Chips example (for corn only).

ANALYTICAL Q&A

Assume that $SP = \$3$ and $AP = \$2$. If 100 units are purchased, what is the materials price variance?

Answers on pages 711 to 715.

Using Materials Variance Information

Calculating materials variances is only the first step. Using the variance information to exercise control is fundamental to a standard cost system. Responsibility must be assigned, variance significance must be assessed, and the variances must be accounted for and disposed of at the end of the year.

Responsibility for the Materials Price Variance The responsibility for controlling the materials price variance usually belongs to the purchasing agent. Admittedly, the price of materials is largely beyond his or her control; however, the price variance can be influenced by such factors as quality, quantity discounts, distance of the source from the plant, and so on. These factors often are under the control of the agent.

Using the price variance to evaluate the performance of purchasing has some limitations. Emphasis on meeting or beating the standard can produce some undesirable outcomes. For example, if the purchasing agent feels pressured to produce favourable price variances, materials of lower quality than desired may be purchased or too much inventory may be acquired to take advantage of quantity discounts.

Analysis of the Materials Price Variance The first step in variance analysis is deciding whether or not the variance is significant. If it is judged insignificant, no further steps are needed. The materials price variance is $3,900 unfavourable, which is about 45 percent of standard cost ($3,900/$8,730). Most managers would judge this variance to be significant. The next step is to find out why it occurred.

For the Crunchy Chips example, the investigation revealed that a higher-quality corn was purchased because of a shortage of the usual grade in the market. Once the reason is known, corrective action can be taken if necessary—and if possible. In this case, no corrective action is needed. The firm has no control over the supply shortage; it will simply have to wait until market conditions improve.

Responsibility for the Materials Usage Variance The production manager is generally responsible for materials usage. Minimizing scrap, waste, and rework are all ways in which the manager can ensure that the standard is met. However, at times, the cause of the variance is attributable to others outside of the production area, as the next section shows.

As with the price variance, using the usage variance to evaluate performance can lead to undesirable behaviour. For example, a production manager feeling pressure to produce a favourable usage variance might allow a defective unit to be transferred to finished goods. While this transfer avoids the problem of wasted materials, it may create customer relations problems.

Analysis of the Materials Usage Variance The materials usage variance is approximately 11 percent of standard cost ($930/$8,730). A deviation greater than 10 percent likely is to be judged significant. Thus, investigation is needed. Investigation revealed that the favourable materials usage variance was the result of the higher-quality corn acquired by the purchasing department. In this case, the favourable variance is essentially assignable to purchasing. Since the materials usage variance is favourable—but smaller than the unfavourable price variance—the overall result of the change in purchasing is unfavourable. In the future, management should try to resume purchasing of the normal-quality corn.

If the overall variance had been favourable, a different response would be expected. If the favourable variance were expected to persist, the higher-quality corn should be purchased regularly and the price and quantity standards revised to reflect it. As this possibility reveals, standards are not static. As improvements in production take place and conditions change, standards may need to be revised to reflect the new operating environment. The importance of evaluating current business conditions and updating standards to reflect any changes in these conditions cannot be overemphasized.

Accounting and Disposition of Materials Variances Recognizing the price variance for materials at the point of purchase also means that the raw materials inventory is carried at standard cost. In general, materials variances are not inventoried. Typically, materials variances are added to cost of goods sold if unfavourable and are subtracted from cost of goods sold if favourable. The journal entries associated with the purchase and usage of raw materials for a standard cost system are illustrated in the Appendix.

OBJECTIVE 5
Compute the labour variances, and explain how they are used for control.

Variance Analysis: Direct Labour

The total labour variance measures the difference between the actual costs of labour and their budgeted costs for the actual level of activity. Cornerstone 10-5 illustrates how to calculate the total variance for labour by using selected data from Crunchy

CORNERSTONE 10-5

The HOW and WHY of Calculating the Total Variance for Labour

Information:
Unit standards from Exhibit 10-3; the actual results for the first week in March:

Actual production	48,500 bags of corn chips
Actual cost of inspection labour	360 hours @ \$8.35 = \$ 3,006

Required:
Calculate the total variance for inspection labour for the first week in March.

Solution:

	Actual Costs	Budgeted Costs*	Total Variance
	$AR \times AH$	$SR \times SH$	$(AR \times AH) - (SR \times SH)$
Inspection labour	\$3,006	\$3,880	\$874 *F*

* The standard quantities for inspection labour are computed as unit quantity standards from Exhibit 10-3:

Labour: $SH = 0.01 \times 48{,}500 = 485$ hours

Multiplying these standard quantities by the unit standard prices given in Exhibit 10-3 produces the budgeted amounts appearing in this column:

Labour: $\$8.00 \times 485 = \$3{,}880$

WHY:
We must calculate the total variance for labour to help us explain why actual results are different than the expected results.

Chips for the first week of March. To keep the example simple, only inspection labour is illustrated.

Direct Labour Variances

Labour hours cannot be purchased and stored for future use as can be done with materials (i.e., there can be no difference between the amount of labour purchased and the amount of labour used). Therefore, unlike the total materials variance, the labour rate and labour efficiency variances always will add up to the total labour variance, as calculated in Cornerstone 10-5. Thus, the rate (price) and efficiency (usage) variances for labour can be calculated by using either the columnar approach or the associated formulas. Which technique to use is a matter of preference. The formulas are adapted to reflect the specific terms used for labour prices (rates) and usage (efficiency).

The **labour rate variance (*LRV*)** computes the difference between what was paid to direct labourers and what should have been paid:

$$LRV = (AR \times AH) - (SR \times AH)$$

or, factoring:

$$LRV = (AR - SR)\,AH$$

where

AR = The actual hourly wage rate
SR = The standard hourly wage rate
AH = The actual direct labour hours used

The **labour efficiency variance (*LEV*)** measures the difference between the labour hours that were actually used and the labour hours that should have been used:

$$LEV = (AH \times SR) - (SH \times SR)$$

or, factoring:

$$LEV = (AH - SH)SR$$

where

$AH =$ The actual direct labour hours used

$SH =$ The standard direct labour hours that should have been used

$SR =$ The standard hourly wage rate

Cornerstone 10-6 shows how to calculate the labour rate and efficiency variances for the Crunchy Chips example (for inspection labour only) using both a columnar approach and a formula approach.

Using Labour Variance Information

As with materials variances, calculating labour variances initiates the feedback process. Using the labour variance information to exercise control is fundamental. Responsibility must be assigned, variance significance must be assessed, and the variances must be accounted for and disposed of at the end of the year.

Responsibility for the Labour Rate Variance Labour rates are largely determined by such external forces as labour markets and union contracts. The actual wage rate rarely departs from the standard rate. When labour rate variances do occur, they usually do so because an average wage rate is used for the rate standard and because more skilled and more highly paid labourers are used for less skilled tasks. Unexpected overtime also can be the cause of a labour rate variance.

Wage rates for a particular labour activity often differ among workers because of differing levels of seniority. Rather than selecting labour rate standards reflecting those different levels, an average wage rate often is chosen. As the seniority mix of workers changes, the average rate changes. This rate change will give rise to a labour rate variance; it also calls for a new standard to reflect the new seniority mix. Controllability is not assignable for this cause of a labour rate variance.

However, the use of labour is controllable by the production manager. The use of more skilled workers to perform less skilled tasks (or vice versa) is a decision that a production manager consciously makes. For this reason, responsibility for the labour rate variance generally is assigned to the individuals who decide how labour will be used.

ANALYTICAL Q&A

Assume that $AH = 100$ hours and $SH = 80$ hours, with $SR = \$10$. What is the labour efficiency variance?

Answers on pages 711 to 715.

Analysis of the Labour Rate Variance The labour rate variance is only 3 percent of the standard cost ($126/$3,880). Although a 3 percent variance is not likely to be judged significant, for illustrative purposes, assume that an investigation is conducted. The cause of the variance is found to be the use of more highly paid and skilled machine operators as inspectors, which occurred because two inspectors quit without formal notice. The corrective action is to hire and train two new inspectors.

Responsibility for the Labour Efficiency Variance Generally speaking, production managers are responsible for the productive use of direct labour. However, as is true of all variances, once the cause is discovered, responsibility may be assigned elsewhere. For example, frequent breakdowns of machinery may cause interruptions

The HOW and WHY of Calculating Labour Variances: Formula and Columnar Approaches

CORNERSTONE 10-6

Information:

Unit standards from Exhibit 10-3; the actual results for the first week in March:

Actual production	48,500 bags of corn chips
Actual cost of inspection labour	360 hours @ $8.35

Required:

Calculate the labour rate and efficiency variances by using the three-pronged (columnar) and formula approaches.

Solution:

Formulas:

$$LRV = (AR - SR)AH = (\$8.35 - \$8.00)360 = \$126U$$

$$LEV = (AH - SH)SR = (360 - 485)(\$8.00) = \$1{,}000F$$

Columnar:

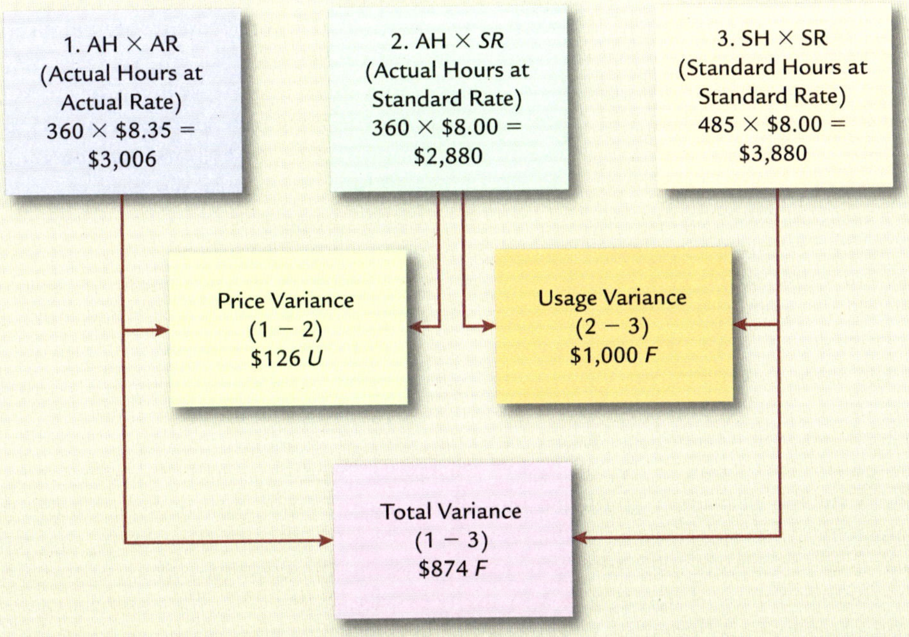

WHY:

The total variance for labour is of limited value so we must further analyse it into price and usage variances to be able to identify the specific type of corrective action that needs to be taken. There are two approaches that could be used.

and nonproductive use of labour. But the responsibility for these breakdowns may be faulty maintenance. If so, the maintenance manager should be charged with the unfavourable labour efficiency variance.

Production managers may be tempted to engage in dysfunctional behaviour if too much emphasis is placed on the labour efficiency variance. For example, to avoid losing hours or using additional hours because of possible rework, a production manager could deliberately transfer defective units to finished goods.

Analysis of the Labour Efficiency Variance The labour efficiency variance is 26 percent of standard cost ($1,000/$3,880). This favourable variance is judged to be significant, and an investigation is undertaken. Investigation revealed that inspections flowed more smoothly because of the higher quality of materials. This additional benefit of the higher-quality materials should be factored into whether Crunchy should return to purchasing the normal-quality corn when it becomes available or whether the higher-quality material should again be purchased. In this case, even with this additional benefit, the materials price variance is so large that the correct action is to acquire the normal-quality material when it again becomes available.

Additional Cost Management Practices: Kaizen Costing and Target Costing

In addition to standard costing, some companies choose to employ other cost management practices, such as kaizen costing and target costing. Kaizen costing focuses on the continuous reduction of the *manufacturing* costs of existing products and processes. Kaizen is a Japanese word meaning continuous improvement. The philosophy in a standard costing system is that the budgeted expectation, or standard, should be met each period. However, as the phrase "continuous improvement" suggests, the philosophy in a kaizen costing system is that the budgeted expectation, or kaizen standard, of the current period should exceed the improvement accomplished the previous period. Using this philosophy, each period's kaizen standard is set based on prior periods' improvements, thereby locking in these improvements to push for even greater improvements in the future. Typically, continuous cost improvements are achieved by identifying a large number of relatively small cost-reducing opportunities (e.g., repositioning factory work space, placing or transporting work-in-process inventory in such a way that the next worker can immediately access the inventory and begin working on it, etc.). For example, **Honda** uses kaizen costing practices to help its engineers implement the product design improvements identified by its shop floor workers.

Target costing focuses on the reduction of the *design* costs of existing and future products and processes. Increasingly, companies such as **Toyota**, **Boeing**, and **Olympus** are emphasizing cost management in the design stage as they begin to recognize that an astonishingly large percentage (somewhere between 75 to 90 percent) of a product's total costs are "locked in" or "committed to" by the time it finishes the design stage and moves into the manufacturing stage.[5] A **target cost** is the difference between the sales price needed to capture a predetermined market share and the desired per-unit profit (i.e., target cost per unit = expected sales price per unit − desired profit per unit). The sales price reflects the product specifications or functions valued by the customer. If the target cost is *less* than the current actual cost, then management must find cost reductions that decrease the actual cost to the target cost. Some managers refer to this process as closing the cost gap, which is the difference between current actual cost and the necessary target cost. Closing this cost gap is the principal challenge of target costing and usually requires the participation of suppliers and other business partners outside of the company over a period of several years. If this cost gap is not closed to zero (i.e., the actual cost is not reduced to the target cost) by the date the new product is planned to launch, then most target costing proponents will follow the cardinal rule of target costing and delay the product launch date until the gap is closed. The reason for the delay is that many managers feel that once the product launches, the incentive to reduce the actual cost falls significantly and, thus, the likelihood of the actual cost eventually decreasing to the target cost level necessary to generate the desired profit margin becomes unacceptably small. **Caterpillar** is famous for adhering to this rule even though the launch delay means that the company must forego significant sales revenues during the delay period.

As you might have noticed, target costing is more than just cost control, because it includes expected sales revenues and desired profit margins in the calculation of the target cost. For this reason, target costing often is referred to as a profit planning

[5] See *Julie H Hertenstein and Marjorie B Platt. Management Accounting.* Apr 1998. Vol. 79, Iss. 10; p. 50 (6 pages).

technique. In addition, target costing is more of a long-term approach to cost reduction, whereas kaizen costing is more of a continuous, short-term approach to cost reduction. Finally, given that target and kaizen costing practices focus on different segments of the value chain, they can serve as effective complements as an organization strives to reduce its costs along the entire value chain.

Summary of Learning Objectives

LO1. Explain how unit standards are set and why standard cost systems are adopted.

- A standard cost system budgets quantities and costs on a unit basis. These unit budgets are for labour, materials, and overhead. Standard costs, therefore, are the amount that should be expended to produce a product or service.
- Standards are set by using historical experience, engineering studies, and input from operating personnel, marketing, and accounting.
- Currently attainable standards are those that can be achieved under efficient operating conditions.
- Ideal standards are those achievable under maximum efficiency, or ideal operating conditions.
- Standard cost systems are adopted to improve planning and control and to facilitate product costing. By comparing actual outcomes with standards and breaking the variance into price and quantity components, detailed feedback is provided to managers. This information allows managers to exercise a greater degree of cost control than that found in a normal or actual cost system.

LO2. Explain the purpose of a standard cost sheet.

- The standard cost sheet provides the details for computing the standard cost per unit. It shows the standard costs for materials, labour, and variable and fixed overhead.
- The standard cost sheet also reveals the quantity of each input that should be used to produce one unit of output. By using these unit quantity standards, the standard quantity of materials allowed and the standard hours allowed can be computed for the actual output.

LO3. Describe the basic concepts underlying variance analysis, and explain when variances should be investigated.

- The total variance is the difference between actual costs and planned costs.
- In a standard costing system, the total variance is broken down into price and usage variances. By breaking the total variances into price and usage variances, managers are better able to analyze and control the total variance.
- Variances should be investigated if they are material (i.e., significant) and if the benefits of corrective action are greater than the costs of investigation. Because of the difficulty of assessing cost and benefits on a case-by-case basis, many firms set up formal control limits—either a dollar amount, a percentage, or both. Other firms use judgment to assess the need to investigate.

LO4. Compute the materials variances, and explain how they are used for control.

- The materials price and usage variances are computed by using either a three-pronged (columnar) approach or formulas.
- The materials price variance is the difference between what was actually paid for materials (generally associated with the purchasing activity) and what should have been paid.
- The materials usage variance is the difference between the actual amount of materials used (generally associated with the production activity) and the amount of materials that should have been used.
- When a significant variance is signalled, an investigation is undertaken to find the cause. Corrective action is taken, if possible, to put the system back in control.

LO5. Compute the labour variances, and explain how they are used for control.

- The labour variances are computed by using either a three-pronged approach or formulas.
- The labour rate variance is caused by the actual wage rate differing from the standard wage rate. It is the difference between the wages that were paid and those that should have been paid.
- The labour efficiency variance is the difference between the actual amount of labour that was used and the amount of labour that should have been used.
- When a significant variance is signalled, investigation is called for, and corrective action should be taken, if possible, to put the system back in control.
- Kaizen costing focuses on continuous short-term improvements in manufacturing costs, while target costing focuses on long-term improvements in design costs. Target cost is the difference between the targeted revenue and the targeted profit.

Summary of Important Equations

1. $MPV = (AP - SP)AQ$
2. $MUV = (AQ - SQ)SP$
3. $LRV = (AR - SR)AH$
4. $LEV = (AH - SH)SR$

CORNERSTONES FOR CHAPTER 10

Key Terms

Appendix: Accounting for Variances

OBJECTIVE 6
Prepare journal entries for materials and labour variances.

To illustrate recording variances, we will assume that the materials price variance is computed at the time materials are purchased. With this assumption, we can state a general rule for a firm's inventory accounts: All inventories are carried at standard cost. As a result, actual costs are not entered into an inventory account. Instead, applied standard costs flow through inventory and eventually to cost of goods sold. As illustrated in this appendix, the accounts containing the variances between applied standard costs and actual costs are closed, which allows the amount of actual costs to ultimately impact the final cost of goods sold number that appears in the financial statements. In recording variances, unfavourable variances always are debits, and favourable variances always are credits.

Entries for Direct Materials Variances

Materials Price Variance The entry to record the purchase of materials follows (assuming an unfavourable *MPV* and that *AQ* is materials purchased):

Materials	***SP* × *AQ***	
Materials Price Variance	**(*AP* − *SP*)*AQ***	
Accounts Payable		***AP* × *AQ***

For example, if *AP* is $0.0069 per gram of corn, *SP* is $0.0060 per gram, and 780,000 grams of corn are purchased, the entry would be:

Materials	4,680	
Materials Price Variance	702	
Accounts Payable		5,382

Notice that the raw materials are carried in the inventory account at standard cost.

Materials Usage Variance The general form for the entry to record the issuance and usage of materials, assuming a favourable *MUV*, is as follows:

Work in Process	***SQ* × *SP***	
Materials Usage Variance		**(*AQ* − *SQ*)*SP***
Materials		***AQ* × *SP***

Here, *AQ* is the materials issued and used, not necessarily equal to the materials purchased. Notice that only standard quantities and standard prices are used to assign costs to Work in Process; no actual costs enter this account.

For example, if *AQ* is 780,000 grams of corn, *SQ* is 873,000 grams, and *SP* is $0.006, then the entry would be:

Work in Process	5,238	
Materials Usage Variance		558
Materials		4,680

Notice that the favourable usage variance appears as a credit entry.

Entries for Direct Labour Variances

Unlike the materials variances, the entry to record both types of labour variances is made simultaneously. The general form of this entry follows (assuming an unfavourable labour rate variance and an unfavourable labour efficiency variance).

Direct materials (1 recon kit @ $150.00)	$150.00
Direct materials (1 cabinet @ $50)	50.00
Direct labour (6 hrs. @ $12)	72.00

Required:

1. Compute the standard hours allowed for a volume of 5,000 rebuilt units.
2. Compute the standard number of kits and cabinets allowed for a volume of 5,000 rebuilt units.

OBJECTIVE 3

Exercise 10-27 INVESTIGATION OF VARIANCES

Sommers Company uses the following rule to determine whether materials usage variances should be investigated: A materials usage variance will be investigated anytime the amount exceeds the lesser of $12,000 or 10 percent of the standard cost. Reports for the past five weeks provided the following information:

Week	*MUV* ($)	Standard Materials Cost ($)
1	10,500 *F*	120,000
2	10,700 *U*	100,500
3	9,000 *F*	120,000
4	13,500 *U*	127,500
5	10,500 *U*	103,500

Required:

1. Using the rule provided, identify the cases that will be investigated.
2. Suppose investigation reveals that the cause of an unfavourable materials usage variance is the use of lower-quality materials than are normally used. Who is responsible? What corrective action would likely be taken?
3. Suppose investigation reveals that the cause of a significant unfavourable materials usage variance is attributable to a new approach to manufacturing that takes less labour time but causes more material waste. Examination of the labour efficiency variance reveals that it is favourable and larger than the unfavourable materials usage variance. Who is responsible? What action should be taken?

OBJECTIVE 4 5

Exercise 10-28 BUDGET VARIANCES, MATERIALS AND LABOUR

Bolsa Corporation produces high-quality leather belts. The company uses a standard cost system and has set the following standards for materials and labour:

Leather (3 strips @ $4)	$12.00
Direct labour (0.75 hr. @ $12)	9.00
Total prime cost	$21.00

During the year, Bolsa produced 40,000 belts. Actual leather purchased was 122,000 strips at $3.96 per strip. There were no beginning or ending inventories of leather. Actual direct labour was 31,200 hours at $12.50 per hour.

Required:

1. Compute the costs of leather and direct labour that should be incurred for the production of 40,000 leather belts.
2. Compute the total budget variances for materials and labour.

OBJECTIVE 4

Exercise 10-29 MATERIALS VARIANCES

Refer to the data provided in **Exercise 10-28**.

Required:

Break down the total variance for materials into a price variance and a usage variance using the columnar and formula approaches.

Exercise 10-30 LABOUR VARIANCES

OBJECTIVE 5

Refer to the data provided in **Exercise 10-28**.

Required:

Break down the total variance for labour into a rate variance and an efficiency variance using the columnar and formula approaches.

Exercise 10-31 MATERIALS VARIANCES

OBJECTIVE 4

Legumbre Company produces vegetable juices, sold in litres. Recently, the company adopted the following material standard for one litre of its tomato juice:

Direct materials (128 grams @ $0.06) = $7.68

During the first week of operation, the company experienced the following results:

a. Litre units produced: 20,000.
b. Grams of materials purchased and used: 2,600,000 grams at $0.07.
c. No beginning or ending inventories of raw materials.

Required:

1. Compute the materials price variance.
2. Compute the materials usage variance.

Exercise 10-32 LABOUR VARIANCES

OBJECTIVE 5
CORNERSTONE 10-6

Verde Company produces wheels for bicycles. During the year, 330,000 wheels were produced. The actual labour used was 180,000 hours at $9.25 per hour. Verde has the following labour standard: 0.5 hour at $10.

Required:

1. Compute the labour rate variance.
2. Compute the labour efficiency variance.

Exercise 10-33 MATERIALS AND LABOUR VARIANCES

OBJECTIVE 4 5

At the beginning of the year, Shults Company had the following standard cost sheet for one of its plastic products:

Direct materials (5 kg @ $4.00)	$20.00
Direct labour (2 hrs. @ $11.25)	22.50
Standard prime cost per unit	$42.50

The actual results for the year are as follows:

a. Units produced: 175,000.
b. Materials purchased: 930,000 kilograms @ $4.10.
c. Materials used: 925,000 kilograms.
d. Direct labour: 362,500 hours @ $11.15.

Required:

1. Compute price and usage variances for materials.
2. Compute the labour rate and labour efficiency variances.

Exercise 10-34 VARIANCES, EVALUATION, AND BEHAVIOUR

OBJECTIVE 1

Jackie Iverson was furious. She was about ready to fire Tom Rich, her purchasing agent. Just a month ago, she had given him a salary increase and a bonus for his performance. She had been especially pleased with his ability to meet or beat the price standards. But now, she found out that it was because of a huge purchase of raw materials. It would take months to use that inventory, and there was hardly space to store it. In the meantime, where could the other materials supplies be put that would be ordered and processed on a regular basis? Additionally, it was a lot of capital to tie up in inventory—money that could have been used to help finance the cash needs of the new product just coming on line.

Her interview with Tom was frustrating. He was defensive, arguing that he thought she wanted those standards met and that the means were not that important. He also pointed out that quantity purchases were the only way to meet the price standards. Otherwise, an unfavourable variance would have been realized.

Required:

1. Why did Tom Rich purchase the large quantity of raw materials? Do you think that this behaviour was the objective of the price standard? If not, what is the objective(s)?
2. Suppose that Tom is right and that the only way to meet the price standards is through the use of quantity discounts. Also, assume that using quantity discounts is not a desirable practice for this company. What would you do to solve this dilemma?
3. Should Tom be fired? Explain.

OBJECTIVE 4 5

Exercise 10-35 MATERIALS AND LABOUR VARIANCES

Camisa Company produces single-coloured t-shirts. Materials for the shirts are dyed in large vats. After dying the materials for a given colour, the vats must be cleaned and prepared for the next batch of materials to be coloured. The following standards for changeover for a given batch have been established:

Direct materials (2.5 kg @ $0.90)	$2.25
Direct labour (0.75 hr. @ $7.00)	5.25
Standard prime cost	$7.50

During the year, 53,000 kilograms of material were purchased and used for the changeover activity. There were 20,000 batches produced, with the following actual prime costs:

Direct materials	$42,000
Direct labour	102,000 (for 14,900 hrs.)

Required:

Compute the materials and labour variances associated with the changeover activity, labelling each variance as favourable or unfavourable.

OBJECTIVE 6

Exercise 10-36 (APPENDIX) JOURNAL ENTRIES

Refer to the data provided in **Exercise 10-35**.

Required:

1. Prepare a journal entry for the purchase of raw materials.
2. Prepare a journal entry for the issuance of raw materials.
3. Prepare a journal entry for the addition of labour to Work in Process.
4. Prepare a journal entry for the closing of variances to Cost of Goods Sold.

OBJECTIVE 4 6

Exercise 10-37 (APPENDIX) MATERIALS VARIANCES, JOURNAL ENTRIES

Esteban Products produces instructional aids. Among the company's products are white boards, which use coloured markers instead of chalk. They are particularly popular for conference rooms in educational institutions and executive offices of large corporations. The standard cost of materials for this product is 12 kilograms at $8.25 per kilogram.

During the first month of the year, 3,200 boards were produced. Information concerning actual costs and usage of materials follows:

Materials purchased	38,000 kg @ $8.35
Materials used	37,500 kg

Required:

1. Compute the materials price and usage variances.
2. Prepare journal entries for all activity relating to materials.

Exercise 10-38 (APPENDIX) LABOUR VARIANCES, JOURNAL ENTRIES

OBJECTIVE 5 6

Escuchar Products, a producer of DVD players, has established a labour standard for its product—direct labour: 2 hrs at $9.65 per hour. During January, Escuchar produced 12,800 boards. The actual direct labour used was 25,040 hours at a total cost of $245,392.

Required:

1. Compute the labour rate and efficiency variances.
2. Prepare journal entries for all activities relating to labour.

Problems

Problem 10-39 SETTING STANDARDS AND ASSIGNING RESPONSIBILITY

OBJECTIVE 1

Cabanarama Inc. designs and manufactures easy-to-set-up beach cabanas. The cabanas come in a kit that includes canvas, lacing, and aluminum support poles. Families can easily transport the cabanas to the beach, set them up, and have a protected place to change clothing, store picnic hampers, and so on. Cabanarama has expanded rapidly from a two-person operation to one involving over a hundred employees. The founder and owner of Cabanarama, Frank Love, understands that a more formal approach to standard setting and control is needed to ensure that the consistent quality for which the company is known continues.

Frank and Annette Wilson, his financial vice president, divided the company into departments and designated each department as a cost centre. Sales, Quality Control, and Design report directly to Frank. Production, Shipping, Finance, and Accounting report to Annette. In the production department, one of the supervisors was assigned the materials purchasing function; the job included purchasing all raw materials, overseeing inventory handling (receiving, storage, etc.), and tracking materials purchases and use.

Frank felt that control would be better achieved if there were a way for his employees to continue to perform in such a way that quality was maintained and cost reduction was achieved. Annette suggested that Cabanarama institute a standard costing system. Variances for materials and labour could then be calculated and reported directly to her, and she could alert Frank to any problems or opportunities for improvement.

Required:

1. a. When Annette designs the standard costing system for Cabanarama, who should be involved in setting the standards for each cost component?
   b. What factors should be considered in establishing the standards for each cost component?
2. Assume that Cabanarama develops the standards for materials use, materials price, labour use, and labour wages. Who will be assigned responsibility for each and for any resulting variances? Why?

Problem 10-40 BASICS OF VARIANCE ANALYSIS, VARIABLE INPUTS

OBJECTIVE 3 4 5

Guanamo Waste Disposal Company has a long-term contract with several large cities to collect garbage and trash from residential customers. To facilitate the collection, Guanamo places a large plastic container with each household. Because of wear and tear, growth, and other factors, Guanamo places about 200,000 new containers each year (about 20 percent of the total households). Several years ago, Guanamo decided to manufacture its own containers as a cost-saving measure. A strategically located plant involved in this type of manufacturing was acquired. To help ensure cost efficiency, a standard cost system was installed in the plant. The following standards have been established for the product's variable inputs:

	Standard Quantity	Standard Price (rate in $)	Standard Cost ($)
Direct materials	12 kg	$ 3.00	$36.00
Direct labour	1.60 hrs.	10.00	16.00
Variable overhead	1.60 hrs.	2.50	4.00
Total			$56.00

The purchasing agent located a new source of slightly higher quality plastic, and this material was used during the first week in January. Also, a new manufacturing process was implemented on a trial basis. The new process required a slightly higher level of skilled labour. The higher quality material has no effect on labour utilization. However, the new manufacturing process was expected to reduce materials usage by 0.25 kilograms per can.

During the first week, the company had the following actual results:

Units produced	4,000
Actual labour costs	$70,000
Actual labour hours	6,600
Materials purchased and used	46,000 kg @ $3.05
Actual variable overhead costs	$26,500

Required:

1. Compute the materials price and usage variances. Assume that the 0.25 kilogram per can reduction of materials occurred as expected and that the remaining effects are all attributable to the higher quality material. Would you recommend that the purchasing agent continue to buy this quality, or should the usual quality be purchased? Assume that the quality of the end product is not affected significantly.
2. Compute the labour rate and efficiency variances. Assuming that the labour variances are attributable to the new manufacturing process, should it be continued or discontinued? In answering, consider the new process's materials reduction effect as well. Explain.
3. Refer to Requirement 2. Suppose that the industrial engineer argued that the new process should not be evaluated after only one week. His reasoning was that it would take at least a week for the workers to become efficient with the new approach. Suppose that the production is the same the second week and that the actual labour hours were 6,000 and the labour cost was $62,000. Should the new process be adopted? Assume the variances are attributable to the new process. Assuming production of 4,000 units per week, what would be the projected annual savings? (Include the materials reduction effect.)

OBJECTIVE 1 4 5

Problem 10-41 SETTING STANDARDS, MATERIALS AND LABOUR VARIANCES

Tom Belford and Tony Sorrentino own a small business devoted to kitchen and bath granite installations. Recently, building contractors have insisted on up-front bid prices for a house rather than the cost-plus system that Tom and Tony used. They worry because natural flaws in the granite make it impossible to tell in advance exactly how much granite will be used on a particular job. In addition, granite can be easily broken, meaning that Tom or Tony could ruin a slab and would need to start over with a new one. Sometimes the improperly cut pieces could be used for smaller installations, sometimes not. All their accounting is done by a local chartered accounting firm headed by Charlene Davenport. Charlene listened to their concerns and suggested that it might be time to implement tighter controls by setting up a standard costing system.

Charlene reviewed the invoices pertaining to a number of Tom and Tony's previous jobs to determine the average amount of granite and glue needed per square metre. She then updated prices on both materials to reflect current conditions. The standards she developed for one square metre of counter installed were as follows:

Granite, per square metre	$50.00
Glue (10 g @ $0.15)	1.50
Direct labour hours:	
Cutting labour (0.10 hr. @ $15)	1.50
Installation labour (0.25 hr. @ $25)	6.25

These standards assumed that one seamless counter requires one sink cut (the space into which the sink will fit) as well as cutting the counter to fit the space available.

Charlene tracked the actual costs incurred by Tom and Tony for granite installation for the next six months. She found that they completed 50 jobs with an average of 3.2 square metres of granite installed in each one. The following information on actual amounts used and cost was gathered:

Granite purchased and used (1,640 sq. metres)	$79,048
Glue purchased and used (16,000 grams)	$ 2,560
Actual hours cutting labour	180
Actual hours installation labour	390

The actual wage rate for cutting and installation labour remained unchanged from the standard rate.

Required:

1. Calculate the materials price variances and materials usage variances for granite and for glue for the past six months.
2. Calculate the labour rate variances and labour efficiency variances for cutting labour and for installation labour for the past six months.
3. Would it be worthwhile for Charlene to establish standards for atypical jobs (e.g., those with more than one sink cut or wider than normal)?

Problem 10-42 SETTING A DIRECT LABOUR STANDARD, LEARNING CURVE EFFECTS, SERVICE COMPANY

OBJECTIVE 1 2 5

Mantenga Company provides routine maintenance services for heavy moving and transportation vehicles. Although the vehicles vary, the maintenance services provided follow a fairly standard pattern. Recently, a potential customer has approached the company, requesting a new maintenance service for a radically different type of vehicle. New servicing equipment and some new labour skills will be needed to provide the maintenance service. The customer is placing an initial order to service 150 vehicles and has indicated that if the service is satisfactory, several additional orders of the same size will be placed every three months over the next three to five years.

Mantenga uses a standard costing system and wants to develop a set of standards for the new part. The usage standards for direct materials such as oil, lubricants, and transmission fluids were easily established. The usage standard is 25 litres per servicing, with a standard cost of $4 per litre. Management has also decided on standard rates for labour and overhead: The standard labour rate is $15 per direct labour hour, the standard variable overhead rate is $8 per direct labour hour, and the standard fixed overhead rate is $12 per hour. The only remaining decision is the standard for labour usage. To assist in developing this standard, the engineering department has estimated the following relationship between units serviced and average direct labour hours used:

Units Serviced	Cumulative Average Time per Unit (hours)
40	2.500
80	2.000
160	1.600
320	1.280
640	1.024

As the workers learn more about servicing the new vehicles, they become more efficient, and the average time needed to service one unit declines. Engineering estimates that all of the learning effects will be achieved by the time that 320 units are produced. No further improvement will be realized past this level.

Required:

1. Assume that the average labour time is 0.768 hour per unit after the learning effects are achieved. Using this information, prepare a standard cost sheet that details the standard service cost per unit. Round costs to two decimal places.

2. Given the per-unit labour standard set, would you expect a favourable or an unfavourable labour efficiency? Explain. Calculate the labour efficiency variance for servicing the first 320 units.
3. Assuming no further improvement in labour time per unit is possible past 320 units, explain why the cumulative average time per unit at 640 is lower than the time at 320 units. Show that the standard labour time should be 0.768 hour per unit. Explain why this value is a good choice for the per-unit labour standard.

OBJECTIVE 2 4 5

Problem 10-43 UNIT COSTS, MULTIPLE PRODUCTS, VARIANCE ANALYSIS, SERVICE SETTING

The maternity wing of the city hospital has two types of patients: normal and cesarean. The standard quantities of labour and materials per delivery for 2011 are:

	Normal	Cesarean
Direct materials (kg)	8	20
Nursing labour (hrs.)	2	4

The standard price paid per kilogram of direct materials is $10. The standard rate for labour is $16. Overhead is applied on the basis of direct labour hours. The variable overhead rate for maternity is $30 per hour, and the fixed overhead rate is $40 per hour.

Actual operating data for 2011 are as follows:

a. Patient days produced: normal, 3,500; cesarean, 7,000.
b. Direct materials purchased and used: 172,000 kilograms at $9.50—30,000 for normal maternity patients and 142,000 for the cesarean patients; no beginning or ending raw materials inventories.
c. Nursing labour: 36,500 hours—7,200 hours for normal patients and 29,300 hours for the cesarean; total cost of labour, $580,350.

Required:

1. Prepare a standard cost sheet showing the unit cost per patient day for each type of patient.
2. Compute the materials price and usage variances for each type of patient.
3. Compute the labour rate and efficiency variances.
4. Assume that you know only the total direct materials used for both procedures and the total direct labour hours used for both procedures. Can you compute the total materials usage and labour efficiency variances? Explain.
5. Standard costing concepts have been applied in the health care industry. For example, diagnostic-related groups (DRGs) are used for prospective payments for Medicare patients. Select a search engine (such as Yahoo! or Google), and conduct a search to see what information you can obtain about DRGs. You might try "Medicare DRGs" as a possible search topic. Write a memo that answers the following questions:
   a. What is a DRG?
   b. How are DRGs established?
   c. How many DRGs are used?
   d. How does the DRG concept relate to standard costing concepts discussed in the chapter? Can hospitals use DRGs to control their costs? Explain.

OBJECTIVE 3 4 5

Problem 10-44 CONTROL LIMITS, VARIANCE INVESTIGATION

Goodsmell Company produces a well-known cologne. The standard manufacturing cost of the cologne is described by the following standard cost sheet:

Direct materials:	
Liquids (4.2 decilitres @ $0.25)	$1.05
Bottles (1 @ $0.05)	0.05
Direct labour (0.2 hr. @ $12.50)	2.50

Variable overhead (0.2 hr. @ $4.70)	0.94
Fixed overhead (0.2 hr. @ $1.00)	0.20
Standard cost per unit	$4.74

Management has decided to investigate only those variances that exceed the lesser of 10 percent of the standard cost for each category or $20,000.

During the past quarter, 250,000 four decilitre bottles of cologne were produced. Descriptions of actual activity for the quarter follow:

a. A total of 1.15 million decilitres of liquids was purchased, mixed, and processed. Evaporation was higher than expected (no inventories of liquids are maintained). The price paid per decilitre averaged $0.27.
b. Exactly 250,000 bottles were used. The price paid for each bottle was $0.048.
c. Direct labour hours totalled 48,250, with a total cost of $622,425.

Normal production volume for Goodsmell is 250,000 bottles per quarter. The standard overhead rates are computed by using normal volume. All overhead costs are incurred uniformly throughout the year.

Required:

1. Calculate the upper and lower control limits for each manufacturing cost category.
2. Compute the total materials variance, and break it into price and usage variances. Would these variances be investigated?
3. Compute the total labour variance, and break it into rate and efficiency variances. Would these variances be investigated?

Problem 10-45 CONTROL LIMITS, VARIANCE INVESTIGATION

OBJECTIVE 3 4 5

The management of Golding Company has determined that the cost to investigate a variance produced by its standard cost system ranges from $2,000 to $3,000. If a problem is discovered, the average benefit from taking corrective action usually outweighs the cost of investigation. Past experience from the investigation of variances has revealed that corrective action is rarely needed for deviations within 8 percent of the standard cost. Golding produces a single product, which has the following standards for materials and labour:

Direct materials (8 kg @ $0.25)	$2
Direct labour (0.4 hr. @ $7.50)	3

Actual production for the past three months with the associated actual usage and costs for materials and labour follow. There were no beginning or ending raw materials inventories.

	April	May	June
Production (units)	90,000	100,000	110,000
Direct materials:			
Cost	$189,000	$218,000	$230,000
Usage (kg)	723,000	870,000	885,000
Direct labour:			
Cost	$270,000	$323,000	$360,000
Usage (hrs.)	36,000	44,000	46,000

Required:

1. What upper and lower control limits would you use for materials variances? For labour variances?
2. Compute the materials and labour variances for April, May, and June. Identify those that would require investigation.
3. Let the horizontal axis be time and the vertical axis be variances measured as a percentage deviation from standard. Draw horizontal lines that identify upper and lower control limits. Plot the labour and material variances for April, May, and June.

Prepare a separate graph for each type of variance. Explain how you would use these graphs (called *control charts*) to assist your analysis of variances.

OBJECTIVE 2 4 5

Problem 10-46 STANDARD COSTING, PLANNED VARIANCES

Ogundipe Company manufactures a plastic toy cell phone. The following standards have been established for the toy's materials and labour inputs:

	Standard Quantity	Standard Price (rate in $)	Standard Cost ($)
Direct materials	0.5 kg	1	0.50
Direct labour	0.1 hr.	10	1.00

During the first week of July, the company had the following results:

Units produced	40,000
Actual labour costs	$42,000
Actual labour hours	4,100
Materials purchased and used	19,500 kg @ $1.05 per kg

Other information: The purchasing agent located a new source of slightly higher quality plastic, and this material was used during the first week in July. Also, a new manufacturing layout was implemented on a trial basis. The new layout required a slightly higher level of skilled labour. The higher quality material has no effect on labour utilization. Similarly, the new manufacturing approach has no effect on material usage.

Required:

1. Compute the materials price and usage variances. Assuming that the materials variances are essentially attributable to the higher quality of materials, would you recommend that the purchasing agent continue to buy this quality, or should the usual quality be purchased? Assume that the quality of the end product is not affected significantly.
2. Compute the labour rate and efficiency variances. Assuming that the labour variances are attributable to the new manufacturing layout, should it be continued or discontinued? Explain.
3. Refer to Requirement 2. Suppose that the industrial engineer argued that the new layout should not be evaluated after only one week. His reasoning was that it would take at least a week for the workers to become efficient with the new approach. Suppose that the production is the same the second week and that the actual labour hours were 3,900 and the labour cost was $39,000. Should the new layout be adopted? Assume the variances are attributable to the new layout. If so, what would be the projected annual savings?

OBJECTIVE 1 4 5

Problem 10-47 STANDARD COSTING

Whitecotton Company produces plastic bottles. The unit for costing purposes is a case of 18 bottles. The following standards for producing one case of bottles have been established:

Direct materials (5 kg @ $0.80)	$ 4
Direct labour (1.5 hours @ $16.00)	24
Standard prime cost	$28

During December, 52,000 kilograms of material were purchased and used in production. There were 10,000 cases produced, with the following actual prime costs:

Direct materials	$40,000
Direct labour	236,910 (for 14,900 hrs.)

Required:

1. Compute the materials variances.
2. Compute the labour variances.
3. What are the advantages and disadvantages that can result from the use of a standard costing system?

Problem 10-48 (APPENDIX) VARIANCE ANALYSIS, REVISION OF STANDARDS, JOURNAL ENTRIES

OBJECTIVE 4 5 6

The Chatham plant of Morril's Small Motor Division produces a major subassembly for a 6.0 horsepower motor for lawn mowers. The plant uses a standard costing system for production costing and control. The standard cost sheet for the subassembly follows:

Direct materials (6.0 kg @ $5.00)	$30.00
Direct labour (1.6 hrs. @ $12.00)	19.20

During the year, the Chatham plant had the following actual production activity:

a. Production of motors totalled 50,000 units.
b. A total of 260,000 kilograms of raw materials was purchased at $4.70 per kilogram.
c. There were 60,000 kilograms of raw materials in beginning inventory (carried at $5 per kg). There was no ending inventory.
d. The company used 82,000 direct labour hours at a total cost of $1,066,000.

The Chatham plant's practical activity is 60,000 units per year. Standard overhead rates are computed based on practical activity measured in standard direct labour hours.

Required:

1. Compute the materials price and usage variances. Of the two materials variances, which is viewed as the most controllable? To whom would you assign responsibility for the usage variance in this case? Explain.
2. Compute the labour rate and efficiency variances. Who is usually responsible for the labour efficiency variance? What are some possible causes for this variance?
3. Assume that the purchasing agent for the small motors plant purchased a lower-quality raw material from a new supplier. Would you recommend that the plant continue to use this cheaper raw material? If so, what standards would likely need revision to reflect this decision? Assume that the end product's quality is not significantly affected.
4. Prepare all possible journal entries.

Cases

Case 10-49 ESTABLISHMENT OF STANDARDS, VARIANCE ANALYSIS

OBJECTIVE 1 2 4

Paul Golding and his wife, Nancy, established Crunchy Chips in 1938. (Nancy sold her piano to help raise capital to start the business.) Paul assumed responsibility for buying potatoes and selling chips to local grocers; Nancy assumed responsibility for production. Since Nancy was already known for her delicious thin potato chips, the business prospered.

Over the next 60 years, the company established distribution channels in all ten provinces, with production facilities in BC, Ontario, and Nova Scotia. In 1980, Paul Golding died, and his son, Edward, took control of the business. By 2009, the company was facing stiff competition from multinational snack-food companies. Edward was advised that the company's plants needed to gain better control over production costs. To assist in achieving this objective, he hired a consultant to install a standard costing system. To help the consultant in establishing the necessary standards, Edward sent her the following memo:

To:	Diana Craig, Certified Management Accountant
From:	Edward Golding, President, Crunchy Chips
Subject:	Description and Data Relating to the Production of Our Plain Potato Chips
Date:	September 28, 2009

The manufacturing process for potato chips begins when the potatoes are placed into a large vat in which they are automatically washed. After washing, the potatoes flow directly to an automatic peeler. The peeled potatoes then pass by inspectors, who manually cut out deep eyes or other blemishes. After inspection, the potatoes are automatically sliced and are dropped into the cooking oil. The frying process is closely monitored by an employee. After the chips are cooked, they pass under a salting device and then pass by more inspectors, who sort out the unacceptable finished chips (those that are discoloured or too small). The chips then continue on the conveyor belt to a bagging machine that bags them in 500 gram bags. After bagging, the bags are placed in a box and shipped. The box holds 15 bags.

The raw potato pieces (eyes and blemishes), peelings, and rejected finished chips are sold to animal feed producers for $0.16 per kilogram. The company uses this revenue to reduce the cost of potatoes; we would like this reflected in the price standard relating to potatoes.

Crunchy Chips purchases high-quality potatoes at a cost of $0.245 per kilogram. Each potato averages 135 grams. Under efficient operating conditions, it takes four potatoes to produce one 500-gram bag of plain chips. Although we label bags as containing 500 grams, we actually place 520 grams in each bag. We plan to continue this policy to ensure customer satisfaction. In addition to potatoes, other raw materials are the cooking oil, salt, bags, and boxes. Cooking oil costs $0.04 per gram, and we use 3.3 grams of oil per bag of chips. The cost of salt is so small that we add it to overhead. Bags cost $0.11 each and boxes $0.52 each.

Our plant produces 8.8 million bags of chips per year. A recent engineering study revealed that we would need the following direct labour hours to produce this quantity if our plant operates at peak efficiency:

Raw potato inspection	3,200
Finished chip inspection	12,000
Frying monitor	6,300
Boxing	16,600
Machine operators	6,300

I'm not sure that we can achieve the level of efficiency advocated by the study. In my opinion, the plant is operating efficiently for the level of output indicated if the hours allowed are about 10 percent higher.

The hourly labour rates agreed upon with the union are:

Raw potato inspectors	$15.20
Finished chip inspectors	10.30
Frying monitor	14.00
Boxing	11.00
Machine operators	13.00

Overhead is applied on the basis of direct labour dollars. We have found that variable overhead averages about 116 percent of our direct labour cost. Our fixed overhead is budgeted at $1,135,216 for the coming year.

Required:

1. Discuss the benefits of a standard costing system for Crunchy Chips.
2. Discuss the president's concern about using the result of the engineering study to set the labour standards. What standard would you recommend?

3. Form a group with two or three other students. Develop a standard cost sheet for Crunchy Chips' plain potato chips.
4. Suppose that the level of production was 8.8 million bags of potato chips for the year as planned. If 4.8 million kilograms of potatoes were used, compute the materials usage variance for potatoes.

Case 10-50 STANDARD COSTING, ETHICAL BEHAVIOUR, USEFULNESS OF STANDARD COSTING

Pat James, the purchasing agent for a local plant of the Oakden Electronics Division, was considering the possible purchase of a component from a new supplier. The component's purchase price, $0.90, compared favourably with the standard price of $1.10. Given the quantity that would be purchased, Pat knew that the favourable price variance would help to offset an unfavourable variance for another component. By offsetting the unfavourable variance, his overall performance report would be impressive and good enough to help him qualify for the annual bonus. More importantly, a good performance rating this year would help him to secure a position at division headquarters at a significant salary increase.

Purchase of the part, however, presented Pat with a dilemma. Consistent with his past behaviour, Pat made inquiries regarding the reliability of the new supplier and the part's quality. Reports were basically negative. The supplier had a reputation for making the first two or three deliveries on schedule but being unreliable from then on. Worse, the part itself was of questionable quality. The number of defective units was only slightly higher than that for other suppliers, but the life of the component was 25 percent less than what normal sources provided.

If the part were purchased, no problems with deliveries would surface for several months. The problem of shorter life would cause eventual customer dissatisfaction and perhaps some loss of sales, but the part would last at least 18 months after the final product began to be used. If all went well, Pat expected to be at headquarters within six months. He saw little personal risk associated with a decision to purchase the part from the new supplier. By the time any problems surfaced, they would belong to his successor. With this rationalization, Pat decided to purchase the component from the new supplier.

Required:

1. Do you agree with Pat's decision? Why or why not? How important was Pat's assessment of his personal risk in the decision? Should it be a factor?
2. Do you think that the use of standards and the practice of holding individuals accountable for their achievement played major roles in Pat's decision?
3. Review the discussion on corporate ethical standards in Chapter 1. Identify the standards that might apply to Pat's situation. Should every company adopt a set of ethical standards that apply to its employees, regardless of their specialty?
4. The usefulness of standard costing has been challenged in recent years. Some claim that its use is an impediment to the objective of continuous improvement (an objective that many feel is vital in today's competitive environment). Write a short paper (individually or in a small group with two or three other students) that analyzes the role and value of standard costing in today's manufacturing environment. Address the following questions:

   a. What are the major criticisms of standard costing?
   b. Will standard costing disappear, or is there still a role for it in the new manufacturing environment? If so, what is the role?
   c. Given the criticisms, can you explain why its use continues to be so prevalent? Will this use eventually change?

In preparing your paper, the following references may be useful; however, do not restrict your literature search to these references. They are simply to help you get started.

- Robin Cooper and Robert S. Kaplan, "Activity-Based Systems: Measuring the Costs of Resource Usage," *Accounting Horizons* (September 1992): 1–13.

- Forrest B. Green and Felix E. Amenkhienan, "Accounting Innovations: A Cross-Sectional Survey of Manufacturing Firms," *Journal of Cost Management* (Spring 1992): 59–64.
- Bruce R. Gaumnitz and Felix P. Kollaritsch, "Manufacturing Variances: Current Practice and Trends," *Journal of Cost Management* (Spring 1991): 59–64.
- Chris Guilding, Dane Lamminmaki, and Colin Drury, "Budgeting and Standard Costing Practices in New Zealand and the United Kingdom," *Journal of International Accounting*, Vol. 33, No. 5 (1998): 569–588.

CMA Problem*

CMA Problem 10-1 FLEXIBLE BUDGET VARIANCES—PELLA INC.

The controller of Pella Inc. created standards for variable costs for one of its products as:

	Per Unit
Direct material	$2.00
Direct labour	5.60
Variable overhead	1.25

At the beginning of the year, Pella Inc. estimated the average selling price to be $15 per unit and, at this price, estimated sales to be 70,000 units. Annual fixed costs were estimated to be $180,000.

Subsequent to year-end, the controller determined actual results to be sales of 75,000 units at an average price of $13.50 per unit. Total variable costs were $660,000 and total fixed costs were $192,000. There was no beginning or ending inventory.

Required:

Calculate the estimated results based on the revised estimated volume and compare them to the expected results using the original level of estimated sales. Compare the results.

Integrative Exercise 2

Cost System Choices, Budgeting, and Variance Analyses for Sacred Heart Hospital

Chapters	Objectives	Cornerstones
7	7-1	7-2
9	7-2	7-3
10	7-4	10-1
	9-1	10-3
	10-1	10-4
	10-3	10-5
	10-4	10-6
	10-5	

The purpose of this integrated exercise is to demonstrate how a change in the cost system's allocation base can result in significantly different reported costs for control purposes (e.g., the cost of various service lines), as well as significantly different budgeted costs for planning purposes (e.g., flexible budgets and variance analyses).

The Two Cost Systems

Sacred Heart Hospital (SHH) faces skyrocketing nursing costs, all of which relate to its two biggest nursing service lines—the Emergency Room (ER) and the Operating Room (OR). SHH's current cost system assigns total nursing costs to the ER and OR based on the number of patients serviced by each line. Total hospital annual nursing costs for these two lines are expected to equal $300,000. The table below shows expected patient volume for both lines.

Measure	ER	OR	Total
Number of patients (ER visits or OR surgeries)	1,000	1,000	2,000
Number of vital signs checks	2,000	4,000	6,000
Number of nursing hours	10,000	5,000	15,000

Required:

1. Using the current cost system, calculate the hospital-wide rate based on number of patients.
2. Calculate the amount of nursing costs that the current cost system assigns to the ER and to the OR.
3. Using the results from Requirement 2, calculate the cost per OR nursing hour under the current cost system.

After discussion with several experienced nurses, Jack Bauer (SHH's accountant) decided that assigning nursing costs to the two service lines based on the number of times that nurses must check patients' vital signs might more closely match the underlying use of costly hospital resources. Therefore, for comparative purposes, Jack decided to develop a second cost system on his computer that assigns total nursing costs to the ER and OR based on the number of times nurses check patients' vital signs. This system is referred to as the "vital-signs costing system." The earlier table also shows data for vital sign checks for lines.

4. Using the vital-signs costing system, calculate the hospital-wide rate based on the number of vital sign checks.
5. Calculate the amount of nursing costs that the vital-signs costing system assigns to the ER and to the OR.
6. Using the results from Requirement 5, calculate the cost per OR nursing hour under the vital-signs costing system.

Budgeting and Variance Analysis

In an effort to better plan for and control OR costs, SHH management asked Jack to calculate the flexible budget variance (i.e., flexible budget costs–actual costs) for OR nursing costs, including the price variance and efficiency variance that make up the flexible budget variance for OR nursing costs. Given that Jack is interested in comparing the reported costs of both systems, he decided to prepare the requested OR variance analysis for both the current cost system and the vital-signs costing system. In addition, Jack chose to use each cost system's estimate of the cost per OR nursing hour as the standard cost per OR nursing hour. Jack collected the following additional information for use in preparing the flexible budget variance for both systems:

Actual number of surgeries performed = 950

Standard number of nursing hours allowed for each OR surgery = 5

Actual number of OR nursing hours used = 5,000

Actual OR nursing costs = 190,000

7. For the OR service line, use the information above and the cost per OR nursing hour under the current cost system to calculate the:
   a. Flexible budget variance (Hint: Use your answer to Requirement 3 as the standard cost per OR nursing hour for the current cost system.)
   b. Price variance
   c. Efficiency variance
8. For the OR service line, use the information above and the cost per OR nursing hour under the vital signs cost system to calculate the:
   a. Flexible budget variance (Hint: Use your answer to Requirement 6 as the standard cost per OR nursing hour for the vital-signs cost system.)
   b. Price variance
   c. Efficiency variance

Discussion of Reported Costs and Variances from the Two Systems

9. Consider SHH's need to control its skyrocketing costs, Jack's discussion with experienced nurses regarding their use of hospital resources, and the reported costs that you calculated from each cost system. Based on these considerations, which cost system (current or vital signs) would you choose to implement if you were Jack? Briefly explain the reasoning behind your choice.
10. What does each of the calculated variances suggest to Jack regarding actions that he should or should not take with respect to investigating and improving each variance? Also, briefly explain why the variances differ between the two cost systems.

Chapter 11

Flexible Budgets and Overhead Analysis

After studying Chapter 11, you should be able to:

1. Prepare a flexible budget, and use it for performance reporting.
2. Calculate the variable overhead variances, and explain their meaning.
3. Calculate the fixed overhead variances, and explain their meaning.
4. Prepare an activity-based flexible budget.

Experience Managerial Decisions

with The Second City

The Second City has been North America's premiere live improvisational and sketch comedy theatre company for the past 50 years. Many famous Canadian stars began their careers at The Second City, including John Candy, Mike Myers, Eugene Levy, Catherine O'Hara, Dave Thomas, Dan Ackroyd, Martin Short, and Rick Moranis. More than just The Second City Television (SCTV), The Second City includes training centres, national touring companies, media and entertainment offshoots, and a corporate communication division. As you might imagine, The Second City is an entrepreneurial organization, as evidenced most recently by its decision to provide comedy theatre aboard Norwegian Cruise Line ships. Given the nature of its businesses, The Second City is extremely dependent on overhead costs. These overhead costs must be allocated to each business to create accurate budgets, which is followed by variance analyses when actual overhead costs are very different from budgeted overhead costs. Its fixed overhead costs are associated with capacity and, as such, relate more to its resident stages and training centre facilities in Chicago, Toronto, and Hollywood. Examples of The Second City's fixed overhead costs include salaries, stage and other facilities rent, facilities maintenance, depreciation, taxes, and insurance. These overhead costs then are assigned to individual business budgets by using allocation bases such as square footage, number of employees, and percentage of earnings. The Second City then uses overhead cost variances to "red flag" potential problems that might not be self-correcting and need managerial attention.

For example, The Second City Theatricals might have a slow year because the producers are too busy with other ventures to mount a new production, while at the same time, The Second City Training Center might have a surge in enrollment. Such a scenario likely would lead The Second City financial executives to shift some assigned overhead costs from the theatrical business to the training centre business. Also, The Second City uses flexible budgeting to adjust budgets for its businesses that experience sporadic volumes, such as the seasonality present in some of its travelling and cruise activities. While the managerial accountants likely do not intentionally provide too many jokes, they do provide the critical function of budgeting and examining variances for overhead costs, which allows the comic talent of The Second City to continue to do what it does best—make us laugh!

Here's The Real Kicker

Stillwater Designs has a Product Steering Committee whose charge is to decide on the timing for upgrades and redesigns for its various Kicker speaker models. About every four years, a complete redesign is done for a Kicker speaker. A complete redesign takes about 16 to 18 months. A specification workshop is held that identifies features, benefits, customers, and competitors. Additionally, the costs of the new model, including the design costs (research and development), acquisition costs, freight, and duties, are estimated for various sales volumes. During this phase, the company will work closely with the manufacturers to control the design so that manufacturing costs are carefully set. A financial analysis is run over the expected life cycle of the new product (two to three years) to see what the profit potential is. Thus, both expected revenues and costs for various levels of activity are assessed. This before-the-fact flexible budgeting analysis is especially important for those products with which the company has less experience. At times, a new product may be produced even if at the most likely volume the product is not expected to be profitable. The reason? The new product may complete a line or may enhance the overall image of the Kicker speakers.

KICKER®

OBJECTIVE 1
Prepare a flexible budget, and use it for performance reporting.

Using Budgets for Performance Evaluation

Budgets are useful for both planning and control. As well, they are often used as benchmarks for performance evaluation. Determining how budgeted amounts should be compared with actual results is a major consideration that must be addressed.

Static Budgets versus Flexible Budgets

In Chapter 8, we learned how companies prepare a master budget based on their best estimate of the level of sales and production activity for the coming period (the best estimate is the budgeted level for the period). We also discussed some behavioural issues associated with performance reporting. However, no detailed discussion was provided on how to prepare budgetary *performance reports.* A **performance report** compares actual costs with budgeted costs. Two possibilities exist for making this comparison: (1) comparison of actual costs with the budgeted costs for the budgeted level of activity and (2) comparison of actual costs with the actual level of activity. The first choice is a report based on *static budgets*, whereas the second choice is for a report based on *flexible budgets.* The two approaches for variance calculation are illustrated in Exhibit 11-1.

Exhibit 11-1

Static and Flexible Budget Variances

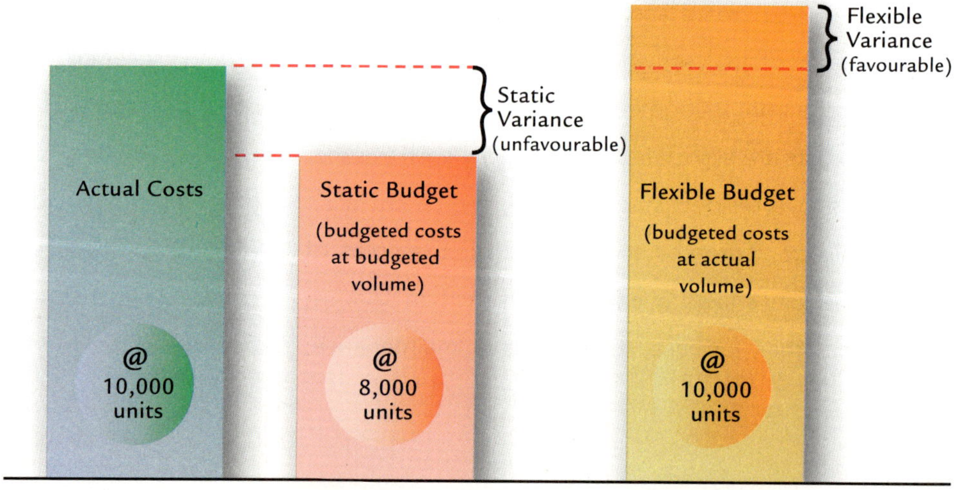

The HOW and WHY of Preparing a Performance Report Based on a Static Budget (Using Budgeted Production)

CORNERSTONE 11-1

Information:

Relationships from the Master Budget

Budgeted production for Quarter 1: 1,060
Materials:
  1 plain t-shirt @ $3.00
  5 grams of ink @ $0.20
Labour: 0.12 hr. @ $10.00
Variable overhead:
  Maintenance: 0.12 hr. @ $3.75
  Power: 0.12 hr. @ $1.25
  Fixed overhead:
    Grounds keeping: $1,200 per quarter
    Depreciation: $600 per quarter

Actual Data for Quarter 1

Production: 1,200 units
Materials cost: $4,830
Labour cost: $1,500
Maintenance cost: $535
Power cost: $170
Grounds keeping: $1,050
Depreciation: $600

Required:
Prepare a performance report using a budget based on expected production.

Solution:

	Actual	Budgeted	Variance
Units produced	1,200	1,060	140 F[a]
Direct materials cost	$4,830	$4,240[b]	$590 U[c]
Direct labour cost	1,500	1,272[d]	228 U
Variable overhead:			
Maintenance	535	477[e]	58 U
Power	170	159[f]	11 U
Fixed overhead:			
Grounds keeping	1,050	1,200	(150) F
Depreciation	600	600	0
Total	$8,685	$7,948	$737 U

[a] F means the variance is favourable.
[b] Budgeted units (t-shirt cost + ink cost) = 1,060[($3 + (5 g × $0.20)].
[c] U means the variance is unfavourable.
[d] Budgeted units (number of direct labour hours × cost per hour) = 1,060(0.12 × $10.00).
[e] Budgeted units (number of direct labour hours × variable maintenance rate) = 1,060(0.12 × $3.75).
[f] Budgeted units (number of direct labour hours × variable power rate) = 1,060(0.12 × $1.25).

WHY:
The starting point for every budgeting exercise, the static budget, should be prepared before the accounting period begins. This budget, which is prepared using expected volumes of sales and output, is the budget that management usually identifies with, and we must be able to relate actual results to it.

Static Budgets and Performance Reports A **static budget** is a budget for a particular level of activity usually prepared at the beginning of the period. Master budgets are generally created for a particular level of activity. Thus, one way to prepare a performance report is to compare the actual costs with the budgeted costs from the master budget. As an example, the production of Cool-U screen-printed t-shirts will be considered. In setting up the master budget for the first quarter of the year, Cool-U expected to produce 1,060 t-shirts. When the quarter had ended, Cool-U found that it had actually produced 1,200 t-shirts. Cornerstone 11-1 shows how to prepare a performance report based on a static budget for the Cool-U clothing manufacturing plant for its first quarter of operations. For simplicity, the report only considers production costs.

According to the report, there were unfavourable variances for direct materials, direct labour, maintenance, and power. However, there is something fundamentally wrong with the report. Actual costs for production of 1,200 t-shirts are being compared with planned costs for production of 1,060. Because direct materials, direct labour, and variable overhead are variable costs, they should be greater at a higher level of production. Thus, even if cost control were perfect for the production of 1,200 units, unfavourable variances would be produced for at least some of the variable costs. To create a meaningful performance report, actual costs and expected costs must be compared at the *same* level of activity. Since actual output often differs from planned output, a method is needed to compute what the costs should have been for the actual output level.

ETHICS If a company were to insist on using the budget for planned output as the benchmark for performance evaluation, it would invite potential abuse by managers subject to this approach. Although unethical, a manager could manipulate the performance report by deliberately producing less than the planned output—producing, for example, 1,000 t-shirts instead of the planned 1,060. By producing less, the costs will be less than the budgeted amounts, creating a favourable performance outcome. Using flexible budgeting allows the benchmark to be adjusted to reflect the expected costs for the actual level of output.◆

Flexible Budgets A **flexible budget** enables a firm to compute expected costs for a range of activity levels. The key to flexible budgeting is knowledge of fixed and variable costs. The two types of flexible budgets are:

1. *Before-the-fact.* This type of flexible budget helps managers deal with uncertainty by allowing them to see the expected outcomes for a range of activity levels. It can be used to generate financial results for a number of plausible scenarios.
2. *After-the-fact.* This flexible budget is the budget for the actual level of activity achieved in the period. This type of budget is used to compute what costs should have been for the actual level of activity. Those expected costs are then compared with the actual costs in order to assess performance.

Flexible budgeting is the key to providing the frequent feedback that managers need to exercise control and effectively carry out the plans of an organization.

CONCEPT Q&A

Why are static budgets usually not a good choice for benchmarks in preparing a performance report?

Answers on pages 711 to 715.

To illustrate the before-the-fact capability of flexible budgeting, suppose that the management of Cool-U wants to know the cost of producing 1,000 t-shirts, 1,200 t-shirts, and 1,400 t-shirts. To compute the expected cost for these different levels of output, the cost behaviour pattern of each item in the budget needs to be known. Knowing the variable cost per unit and the total fixed costs allows the calculation of the expected costs for various levels of activity. Cornerstone 11-2 shows how budgets can be prepared for different levels of activity, using cost formulas for each item.

Notice in Cornerstone 11-2 that total budgeted production costs increase as the production level increases. Budgeted costs change because total variable costs go up as output increases. Because of this, flexible budgets are sometimes referred to as **variable budgets**. Since Cool-U has a mix of variable and fixed costs, the overall cost of producing one t-shirt goes *down* as production goes *up*. This makes sense. As production increases, there are more units over which to spread the fixed production costs.

It should also be pointed out that the flexible budget formulas often are based on some level of input activity instead of units. This level of activity could be direct labour hours, direct machine hours, direct material costs, or some other measure that can be directly traced to output. In our example, we will use direct labour hours, but it could be another measure of input. This is easy to do because direct labour hours are correlated with units produced. For example, the variable cost formulas for variable overhead are \$3.75 and \$1.25 per direct labour hour (\$5.00 per direct labour hour in total) for maintenance and power, respectively. When standard hours are used, we need to convert units into direct labour hours. For the Cool-U example, the production of 1,000

The HOW and WHY of Preparing a Flexible Production Budget

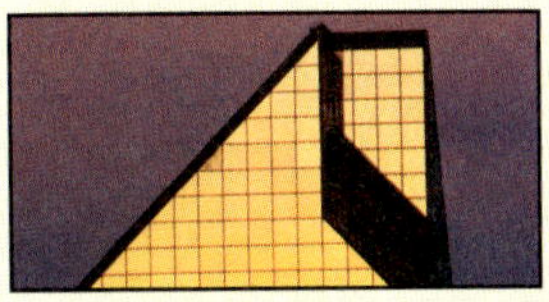

CORNERSTONE 11-2

Information:

Levels of output: 1,000, 1,200, and 1,400.

Materials:

1 plain t-shirt @ $3.00

5 grams of ink @ $0.20

Labour:

0.12 hr. @ $10.00

Variable overhead:

Maintenance: 0.12 hr. @ $3.75

Power: 0.12 hr. @ $1.25

Fixed overhead:

Grounds keeping: $1,200 per quarter

Depreciation: $600 per quarter

Required:

Prepare a budget for three levels of output: 1,000, 1,200, and 1,400 units.

Solution:

Production Costs	Variable Cost per Unit	Range of Production (units)		
		1,000	1,200	1,400
Variable:				
Direct materials	$4.00[a]	$4,000[b]	$4,800	$5,600
Direct labour	1.20[c]	1,200[d]	1,440	1,680
Variable overhead:				
Maintenance	0.45[e]	450[f]	540	630
Power	0.15[g]	150[h]	180	210
Total variable costs	$5.80	$5,800	$6,960	$8,120
Fixed overhead:				
Grounds keeping		$1,200	$1,200	$1,200
Depreciation		600	600	600
Total fixed costs		$1,800	$1,800	$1,800
Total production costs		$7,600	$8,760	$9,920

[a] t-shirt cost + ink cost = [($3.00 × 1 t-shirt) × ($0.20 × 5 g)].
[b] ($4 × 1,000 units)
[c] ($10.00 per direct labour hour × 0.12 direct labour hours per unit).
[d] ($1.20 × 1,000 units)
[e] ($3.75 per direct labour hour × 0.12 direct labour hours per unit).
[f] ($0.45 × 1,000 units)
[g] ($1.25 per direct labour hour × 0.12 direct labour hours per unit).
[h] ($0.15 × 1,000 units)

WHY:

A flexible budget is a representation of the original budget, the static budget, adjusted to reflect actual sales/output achieved. This prevents the distortions that would arise due to volume differences between the budgeted level of activity and the level actually achieved.

budgeted units means that 120 direct labour hours will be needed (0.12 direct labour hours per unit × 1,000 budgeted units).

Flexible budgets are powerful control tools because they allow management to compute what the costs should be for the level of *output that actually occurred.* Recall that Cool-U thought that 1,060 units would be produced, and budgeted for that amount. However, actual production was 1,200 units. It does not make sense to compare the

CORNERSTONE 11-3

The HOW and WHY of Preparing a Performance Report Using a Flexible Budget

Information:

For convenience, the actual costs for 1,200 units (Cornerstone 11-1) and the budgeted costs for the actual level of activity (Cornerstone 11-2) are repeated here.

	Actual Costs	Budgeted Costs
Units produced	1,200	1,200
Direct materials cost	$4,830	$4,800
Direct labour cost	1,500	1,440
Variable overhead:		
Maintenance	535	540
Power	170	180
Fixed overhead:		
Grounds keeping	1,050	1,200
Depreciation	600	600

Required:

Prepare a performance report using budgeted costs for the actual level of activity.

Solution:

	Actual	Budget	Variance
Units produced	1,200	1,200	—
Production costs:			
Direct materials	$4,830	$4,800	$ 30 U
Direct labour	1,500	1,440	60 U
Variable overhead:			
Maintenance	535	540	(5) F
Power	170	180	(10) F
Total variable costs	$7,035	$6,960	$ 75 U
Fixed overhead:			
Grounds keeping	$1,050	$1,200	$(150) F
Depreciation	600	600	(0)
Total fixed costs	$1,650	$1,800	$(150) F
Total production costs	$8,685	$8,760	$ (75) F

WHY:

The performance report, using flexible budget values that are based on actual activity levels achieved, will highlight the operational differences between expected performance and actual performance. This will assist us in identifying what explanations are required and, possibly, what corrective actions need to be taken.

ANALYTICAL Q&A

What is the budgeted cost of maintenance if 2,000 t-shirts are produced?

Answers on pages 711 to 715.

actual costs for 1,200 t-shirts to the budgeted costs for 1,060 t-shirts. Management will need a useful performance report, one that compares actual and budgeted costs for the actual level of activity. This is the second type of flexible budget and preparation of this report is shown in Cornerstone 11-3. The revised performance report in Cornerstone 11-3 paints a much different picture than the one in Cornerstone 11-1. All of the variances are fairly small. Had they been larger, management would have searched for the cause and tried to correct the problems.

A difference between the actual amount and the flexible budget amount is the **flexible budget variance**. The flexible budget provides a measure of the efficiency of a manager. In other words, given the level of production achieved, how well did the manager control costs? To measure whether or not a manager accomplishes his or her goals, the static budget is used. The static budget represents certain goals that the firm wants to achieve. A manager is effective if the goals described by the static budget are achieved or exceeded. In the Cool-U example, production volume was 140 units greater than the original budgeted amount; the manager exceeded the original budgeted goal. Therefore, the effectiveness of the manager is not in question.

Flexible Budget Sales Variances

The sales component of a flexible budget will reveal the difference between the level of sales actually achieved and the level of sales indicated by the master budget. There can be several reasons for this difference, and only by isolating the differences as a result of the volume of units sold and the volume anticipated can the causes of the problem be understood. A sales price variance can be calculated by looking at the actual units sold and the expected (budgeted) revenues at that volume. Any difference will be explained by a selling price variance.

Variable Overhead Analysis

OBJECTIVE 2
Calculate the variable overhead variances, and explain their meaning.

In Chapter 10, total variances for direct materials and direct labour were broken down into price and efficiency variances. In a standard cost system, the total overhead variance, which is the difference between applied and actual overhead, is also broken down into component variances. The number of component variances computed depends on the method of variance analysis used. The four-variance method is described in this chapter. First, overhead is divided into fixed and variable categories. Next, two variances are calculated for each category. The total variable overhead variance is divided into the variable overhead spending variance and the variable overhead efficiency variance. Similarly, the total fixed overhead variance is divided into the fixed overhead spending variance and the fixed overhead volume variance.

Total Variable Overhead Variance

To illustrate the variable overhead variances, the first quarter data for Cool-U will be used. The unit prices and quantities used for the flexible budget are assumed to be the standards associated with Cool-U's standard cost system. Cornerstone 11-4 illustrates how to calculate the total variable overhead variance. The total variable overhead variance is simply the difference between the total *actual variable overhead* and *applied variable overhead*. Variable overhead is applied by using hours allowed in a standard cost system. The total variable overhead variance can be divided into spending and efficiency variances. Variable overhead spending and efficiency variances can be calculated by using either the three-pronged (columnar) approach or formulas. The best approach is a matter of preference. However, the formulas first need to be expressed specifically for variable overhead.

Because the equations for variable overhead variances can be long if expressed in words, abbreviations are often used. Here are some common abbreviations that you will find in the rest of this section:

AH = actual direct labour hours

SH = standard direct labour hours that *should have been worked* for actual units produced

$AVOR$ = actual variable overhead rate

$SVOR$ = standard variable overhead rate

CORNERSTONE 11-4

The HOW and WHY of Calculating the Total Variable Overhead Variance

Information:

Standard variable overhead rate (*SVOR*)	$5.00 per direct labour hour
Actual variable overhead costs	$705
Standard hours allowed per unit	0.12 hour
Actual direct labour hours worked	150 hours
Actual production	1,200 units

Required:

1. Calculate the actual variable overhead rate (*AVOR*).
2. Calculate the total variable overhead variance.

Solution:

1. Actual variable overhead rate = Actual overhead cost/Actual direct labour hours
   AVOR = $705/150 hours
   AVOR = $4.70

2.

Actual variable overhead (*AH* × *AVOR*)	$705
Applied variable overhead (*SH* × *SVOR*)*	720
Total variable overhead variance [(*AH* × *AVOR*) − (*SH* × *SVOR*)]	$ (15) F

* *SH* × *SVOR* = 0.12 × 1,200 × $5.

WHY:

Overhead has become an increasingly important component of cost, and we must fully understand how we are incurring these overhead costs.

Variable Overhead Spending Variance

The **variable overhead spending variance** measures the aggregate effect of differences between the actual variable overhead rate (*AVOR*) and the standard variable overhead rate (*SVOR*). The actual variable overhead rate is computed as follows:

$$AVOR = \frac{\text{Actual variable overhead}}{\text{Actual hours}}$$

As shown by Cornerstone 11-4, this rate is $4.70 per hour, computed as actual variable overhead cost of $705 divided by 150 actual direct labour hours. The formula for computing the variable overhead spending variance is:

$$\begin{aligned}\text{Variable overhead spending variance} &= (AVOR \times AH) - (SVOR \times AH) \\ &= (AVOR - SVOR)AH\end{aligned}$$

Variable Overhead Efficiency Variance

Variable overhead is assumed to vary as the production volume changes. Thus, variable overhead changes in proportion to changes in the direct labour hours used. The **variable overhead efficiency variance** measures the change in the actual variable overhead that occurs because of efficient (or inefficient) use of direct labour. The efficiency variance is computed by using the following formula:

$$\text{Variable overhead efficiency variance} = (AH - SH)SVOR$$

ANALYTICAL Q&A

If actual hours equal 100, standard hours equal 90, and the standard variable overhead rate is $6, what is the variable overhead efficiency variance?

Answers on pages 711 to 715.

The HOW and WHY of Calculating Variable Overhead Spending and Efficiency Variances: Columnar and Formula Approaches

CORNERSTONE 11-5

Information:

Standard variable overhead rate (*SVOR*)	$5.00 per direct labour hour
Actual variable overhead rate (*AVOR*)	$4.70
Actual hours worked (*AH*)	150 hours
Number of t-shirts produced	1,200 units
Hours allowed for production (*SH*)	144 hours[a]

[a] 0.12 × 1,200.

Required:
Calculate the variable overhead spending and efficiency variances.

Solution:
Columnar:

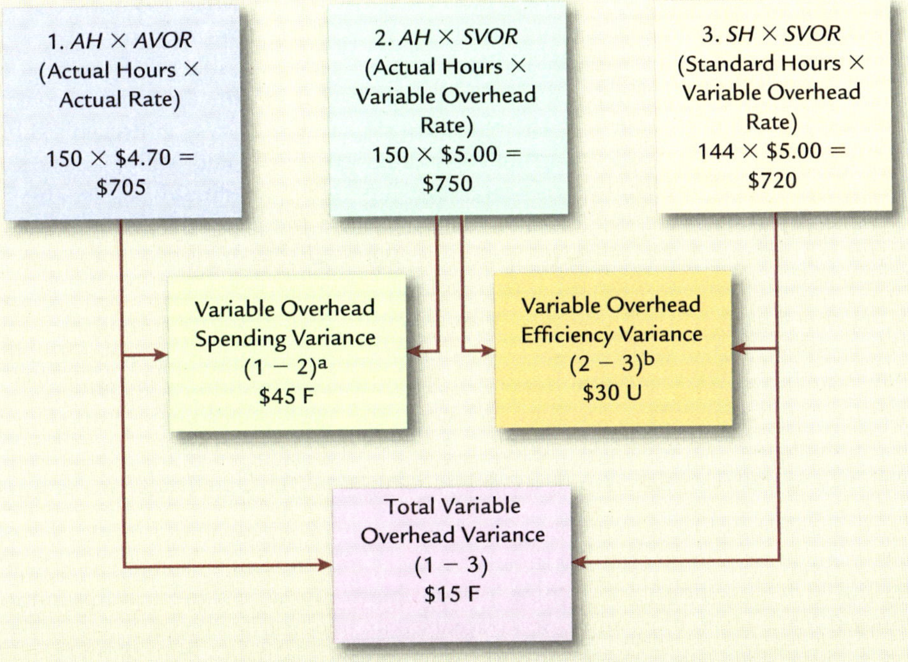

Formulas:

[a]*VOH* spending variance = (*AVOR* − *SVOR*)*AH*
= ($4.70 − $5.00)150
= $45 F

[b]*VOH* efficiency variance = (*AH* − *SH*)*SVOR*
= (150 − 144)($5.00)
= $30 U

WHY:
Variable overhead is a key component of overhead costs and must be divided into understandable components: spending and efficiency variances. There are two approaches that will help us understand these variances: columnar and formula.

How to calculate the variable overhead variances using either a columnar or formula approach is shown for the Cool-U example in Cornerstone 11-5.

Comparison of the Variable Overhead Spending Variance with the Price Variances of Materials and Labour

The variable overhead spending variance is similar but not identical to the price variances of materials and labour; there are some conceptual differences. Variable overhead is not a single input—it is made up of a large number of individual items, such as indirect materials, indirect labour, electricity, maintenance, and so on. The standard variable overhead rate represents the weighted cost per direct labour hour that should be incurred for all variable overhead items. The difference between what should have been spent per hour and what actually was spent per hour is a type of price variance.

A variable overhead spending variance can arise because prices for individual variable overhead items have increased or decreased. Assume, for the moment, that the price changes of individual overhead items are the only cause of the spending variance. If the spending variance is unfavourable, price increases for individual variable overhead items are the cause; if the spending variance is favourable, price decreases are dominating.

If the only source of the variable overhead spending variance were price changes, then it would be just like the price variances of materials and labour. Unfortunately, the spending variance is also affected by how efficiently overhead is used. Waste or inefficiency in the use of variable overhead increases the actual variable overhead cost. This increased cost, in turn, is reflected in an increased actual variable overhead rate. Thus, even if the actual prices of the individual overhead items were equal to the budgeted or standard prices, an unfavourable variable overhead spending variance could still take place. For example, more kilowatt-hours of power may be used than should be, yet this is not captured by any change in direct labour hours. However, the effect is reflected by an increase in the total cost of power and, thus, the total cost of variable overhead. Similarly, efficiency can decrease the actual variable overhead cost and decrease the actual variable overhead rate. Efficient use of variable overhead items contributes to a favourable spending variance. If the waste effect dominates, then the net contribution will be unfavourable; if efficiency dominates, then the net contribution is favourable. Therefore, the variable overhead spending variance is the result of both price and efficiency.

CONCEPT Q&A

How does the variable overhead spending variance differ from the materials and labour price variances?

Answers on pages 711 to 715.

Responsibility for the Variable Overhead Spending Variance

Many variable overhead items are affected by several responsibility centres. For example, utilities are a joint cost. To the extent that consumption of variable overhead can be traced to a responsibility centre, responsibility can be assigned. Consumption of indirect materials is an example of a traceable variable overhead cost.

Controllability is a prerequisite for assigning responsibility. Price changes of variable overhead items are essentially beyond the control of supervisors. If price changes are small (as they often are), then the spending variance is primarily a matter of the efficient use of overhead in production. This is controllable by production supervisors. Accordingly, responsibility for the variable overhead spending variance is generally assigned to production departments.

Responsibility for the Variable Overhead Efficiency Variance

The variable overhead efficiency variance is directly related to the direct labour efficiency or usage variance. If variable overhead is truly proportional to direct labour consumption, then like the labour usage variance, the variable overhead efficiency variance is caused by efficient, or inefficient use of direct labour. If more (or fewer) direct labour hours are used than the standard calls for, then the total variable overhead cost will increase (or decrease). The validity of the measure depends on the validity of the relationship between variable overhead costs and direct labour hours. In other words, do variable overhead costs really change in proportion to changes in direct labour hours? If so, responsibility for the variable overhead efficiency variance should be assigned to the individual who has responsibility for the use of direct labour: the production manager.

The HOW and WHY of Preparing a Performance Report for the Variable Overhead Variances

CORNERSTONE 11-6

Information:

Standard variable overhead rate (*SVOR*)	$5.00 per direct labour hour
Actual costs:	
Maintenance	$535
Power	$170
Actual hours worked (*AH*)	150 hours
Number of t-shirts produced	1,200 units
Hours allowed for production (*SH*)	144 hours[a]
Variable overhead:	
Maintenance	0.12 hr. @ $3.75
Power	0.12 hr. @ $1.25

[a] 0.12 × 1,200.

Required:
Prepare a performance report that shows the variances on an item-by-item basis.

Solution:

Performance Report
For the Quarter Ended March 31, 2010

Cost	Cost Formula[a]	Actual Costs	Budget for Actual Hours[b]	Spending Variance[c]	Budget for Standard Hours[d]	Efficiency Variance[e]
Maintenance	$3.75	$535	$562.50	$27.50 F	$540	$22.50 U
Power	1.25	170	187.50	17.50 F	180	7.50 U
Total	$5.00	$705	$750.00	$45.00 F	$720	$30.00 U

[a] Per direct labour hour.
[b] Computed using the cost formula and 150 actual hours.
[c] Spending variance = Actual costs − Budget for actual hours.
[d] Computed using the cost formula and an activity level of 144 standard hours.
[e] Efficiency variance = Budget for actual hours − Budget for standard hours.

WHY:
Reporting variable overhead variances will allow managers to understand where the potential problem areas are and who should be queried about their operations.

A Performance Report for the Variable Overhead Spending and Efficiency Variances

Cornerstone 11-5 showed a favourable $45 variable overhead spending variance and an unfavourable $30 variable overhead efficiency variance. The $45 F spending variance means that overall Cool-U spent less than expected on variable overhead. The reasons for the $30 unfavourable variable overhead efficiency variance are the same as those offered for an unfavourable labour usage variance. An unfavourable variance means that more hours were used than called for by the standard. Even if the total variable overhead spending and efficiency variances are insignificant, they reveal nothing about how well costs of *individual* variable overhead items were controlled. It is possible for two large variances of opposite sign to cancel each other out. Control of variable overhead requires line-by-line analysis for each item. Cornerstone 11-6 shows how to prepare a performance report

CONCEPT Q&A

Why are the labour efficiency and variable overhead efficiency variances similar in nature?

Answers on pages 711 to 715.

that supplies the line-by-line information essential for detailed analysis of the variable overhead variances.

The analysis on a line-by-line basis reveals no unusual problems such as two large individual item variances with opposite signs. No individual item variance is greater than 10 percent of its budgeted amount. Thus, no variance at the individual item level appears to be of a large enough magnitude to be of concern.

OBJECTIVE 3
Calculate the fixed overhead variances, and explain their meaning.

Fixed Overhead Analysis

Fixed overhead costs are capacity costs that are acquired in advance of usage. Examples include the property, plant, and equipment needed to manufacture the product. Recall from Chapter 5 that the predetermined overhead rate is calculated at the beginning of the year by dividing budgeted overhead by the budgeted amount of the base (e.g., direct labour hours). Now, however, we need to divide that predetermined overhead rate into variable and fixed overhead rates. It was easy to find the variable overhead rate since that rate is unchanged even though the number of units produced, and thus direct labour hours, changes. However, the fixed overhead rate changes as the underlying activity changes. To keep a stable fixed overhead rate throughout the year, companies typically use practical capacity to determine the number of direct labour hours in the denominator of the fixed overhead rate.

Suppose that Cool-U can produce 1,500 t-shirts per quarter under efficient operating conditions, then practical capacity measured in standard hours (SH_p) is calculated by the following formula:

$$SH_p = \text{Unit standard} \times \text{Units of practical capacity}$$

$$= 0.12 \times 1{,}500$$
$$= 180 \text{ hours}$$

ANALYTICAL Q&A

If the budgeted fixed overhead is $10,000 and the standard fixed overhead rate is $100 per direct labour hour (calculated using practical capacity), what is the practical capacity, measured in direct labour hours?

Answers on pages 711 to 715.

Recall from Cornerstone 11-2 that Cool-U's total fixed costs per quarter equal $1,800. The standard fixed overhead rate (SFOR) is calculated as follows:

$$SFOR = \frac{\text{Budgeted fixed overhead costs}}{\text{Practical capacity}}$$

$$SFOR = \frac{\$1{,}800}{180}$$
$$= \$10 \text{ per direct labour hour}$$

Some firms use average or expected capacity instead of practical capacity to calculate fixed overhead rates. In this case, the standard hours used to calculate the fixed overhead rate will typically be less than the standard direct labour hours at practical capacity.

Total fixed overhead can be calculated by multiplying the fixed overhead rate by the number of direct labour hours at capacity (if direct labour hours are the overhead application base used).

Total Fixed Overhead Variances

The total fixed overhead variance is the difference between actual fixed overhead and applied fixed overhead, when applied fixed overhead is obtained by multiplying the standard fixed overhead rate times the standard hours allowed for the actual output. Thus, the applied fixed overhead is:

$$\text{Applied fixed overhead} = SFOR \times SH$$

The total fixed overhead variance is the difference between the actual fixed overhead and the applied fixed overhead:

$$\text{Total variance} = \text{Actual fixed overhead} - \text{Applied fixed overhead}$$

CORNERSTONE 11-7

The HOW and WHY of Calculating the Total Fixed Overhead Variance

Information:

Standard fixed overhead rate (*SFOR*)	\$10.00 per direct labour hour
Actual fixed overhead costs	\$1,650
Standard hours allowed per unit	0.12 hour
Actual production	1,200 units

Required:

1. Calculate the standard hours for actual units produced.
2. Calculate the total applied fixed overhead.
3. Calculate the total fixed overhead variance.

Solution:

1. SH = Actual units × Standard hours allowed per unit
   = 1,200 units × 0.12 hour
   = 144 hours

2. Applied fixed overhead = $SH \times SFOR$
   = 144 × \$10
   = \$1,440

3.

Actual fixed overhead cost	\$1,650
Applied fixed overhead	1,440
Total variance	\$ 210 U

WHY:
Fixed overhead is a critical component of overhead costs and must be analyzed separately from variable overhead costs. Since fixed costs do not vary, irrespective of volume, there is no difference between the static budget amount for fixed overhead and the flexible budget amount for fixed overhead.

Cornerstone 11-7 illustrates how to calculate the total fixed overhead variance, using the Cool-U example. The total fixed overhead variance can be divided into spending and volume variances. Spending and volume variances can be calculated by using either the three-pronged (columnar) approach or formulas. The best approach to use is a matter of preference. However, the formulas first need to be expressed specifically for fixed overhead.

Fixed Overhead Spending Variance

The **fixed overhead spending variance** is defined as the difference between the actual fixed overhead (*AFOH*) and the budgeted fixed overhead (*BFOH*):

$$FOH \text{ spending variance} = AFOH - BFOH$$

Fixed Overhead Volume Variance

The **fixed overhead volume variance** is the difference between budgeted fixed overhead and applied fixed overhead:

$$\text{Volume variance} = \text{Budgeted fixed overhead} - \text{Applied fixed overhead}$$
$$= \text{Budgeted fixed overhead} - (SH \times SFOR)$$

The volume variance measures the effect of the actual output differing from the output used at the beginning of the year to compute the predetermined standard fixed overhead rate. If you think of the output used to calculate the fixed overhead rate as the capacity acquired (practical capacity) and the actual output as the capacity used, then the volume variance is the cost of unused capacity. Cornerstone 11-8 illustrates how to calculate the fixed overhead variances using either a columnar or a formula approach.

Responsibility for the Fixed Overhead Spending Variance

Fixed overhead is made up of items such as salaries, depreciation, taxes, and insurance. Many fixed overhead items—long-run investments, for instance—are not subject to change in the short run; consequently, fixed overhead costs are often beyond the immediate control of management. Since many fixed overhead costs are affected primarily by long-run decisions, and not by changes in production levels, the budget variance is usually small. For example, actual depreciation, salaries, taxes, and insurance costs are not likely to be much different from planned costs.

Analysis of the Fixed Overhead Spending Variance

Because fixed overhead is made up of many individual items, a line-by-line comparison of budgeted costs with actual costs provides more information concerning the causes of the spending variance. The fixed overhead section of Cornerstone 11-3 provides such a report. The report reveals that the fixed overhead spending variance is out of line with expectations. Less was spent on grounds keeping than expected. In fact, the entire spending variance is attributable to this one item. Since the amount is more than 10 percent of budget, it merits an investigation. An investigation, for example, might reveal that the weather was especially wet and thus reduced the cost of watering for the period involved. In this case, no action is needed, as a natural correction would be forthcoming.

Responsibility for the Fixed Overhead Volume Variance

Assuming that volume variance measures capacity utilization implies that the general responsibility for this variance should be assigned to the production department. At times, however, investigation into the reasons for a significant volume variance may reveal the cause to be factors beyond the control of production. In this instance, specific responsibility may be assigned elsewhere. For example, if the purchasing department buys lower-quality raw materials than usual, significant rework time may result. This will cause lower production and an unfavourable volume variance. In this case, responsibility for the variance rests with purchasing, not production.

Analysis of the Volume Variance

The \$360 U variance (Cornerstone 11-8) occurs because the production capacity is 180 hours and only 144 hours should have been used. Why the company failed to use all of its capacity is not known. Given that unused capacity is about 20 percent of the total, investigation seems merited. Exhibit 11-2 graphically illustrates the volume variance. Notice that the volume variance occurs because fixed overhead is treated as if it were a variable cost. In reality, fixed costs do not change as activity changes, as a predetermined fixed overhead rate would imply.

The total of the variable overhead and fixed overhead variances will equal the total over- or under-absorbed overhead in an accounting period.

Sales variances can be calculated by comparing the budgeted sales volume in dollars with the actually achieved sales volume. Such a variance can be analyzed in terms of the difference in the number of units sold and the average price per unit. In more advanced texts, these variances will be further analyzed in several different ways.

The HOW and WHY of Calculating Fixed Overhead Variances: Columnar and Formula Approaches

CORNERSTONE 11-8

Information:

Standard fixed overhead rate (*SFOR*)	$10.00 per direct labour hour
Budgeted fixed overhead (*BFOH*)	$1,800
Number of t-shirts produced	1,200 units
Hours allowed for production (*SH*)	144 hours[a]

[a] 0.12 × 1,200.

Required:

Calculate the fixed overhead spending and volume variances.

Solution:

Columnar:

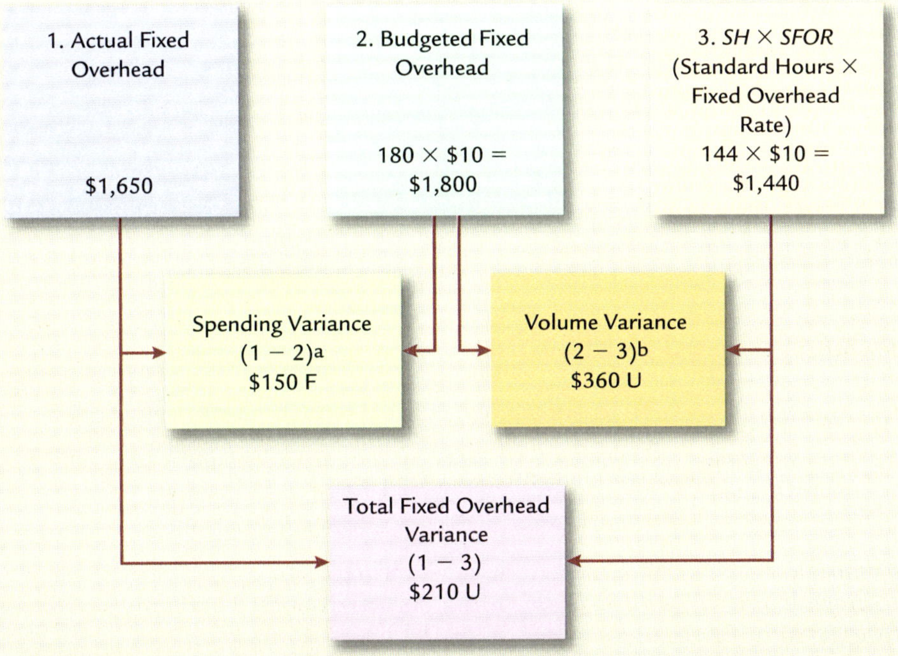

Formulas:

[a]FOH spending variance = Actual fixed overhead − Budgeted fixed overhead
= $1,650 − $1,800
= $150 F

[b]FOH volume variance = Budgeted fixed overhead – Applied fixed overhead
= Budgeted fixed overhead – (*SH* × *SFOR*)
= $1,800 – (144 × $10)
= $1,800 – $1,440
= $360 U

WHY:

Fixed overhead variances should be further divided into spending and volume variances to provide more useful information for further investigation. There are two approaches that can assist in this process: columnar and formula.

Exhibit 11-2

Graphical Analysis of the Volume Variance

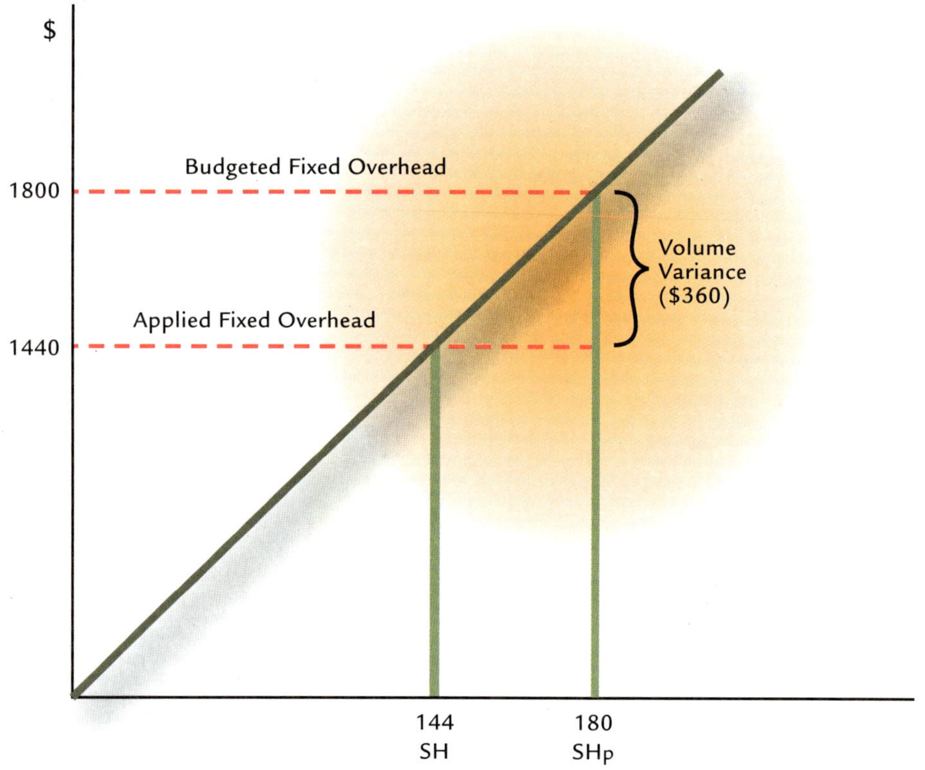

OBJECTIVE 4
Prepare an activity-based flexible budget.

Activity-Based Budgeting

The traditional approach to budgeting (explained in Chapter 8) emphasizes:

1. the estimation of revenues and costs by organizational units (e.g., departments, plants), and
2. the use of a single unit-based driver such as direct labour hours.

Companies that have implemented an activity-based costing (ABC) system may also wish to install an *activity-based budgeting system.* An **activity-based budgeting system (ABB)** focuses on:

1. estimating the costs of activities rather than the costs of departments and plants, and
2. the use of multiple drivers, both unit-based and non-unit-based.

The activity-based budgeting approach supports continuous improvement and process management. Because activities consume resources (which cause cost), activity-based budgeting can be used to reduce cost through the elimination of wasteful activities and improving the efficiency of necessary activities.

Static Activity Budgets

Assuming that activity-based costing has been implemented, the major emphasis for ABB is estimating the workload (demand) for each activity and then determining the resources required for this workload. The workload for each activity must be set to support the sales and production activities expected for the coming period.

As with traditional budgeting, ABB begins with sales and production budgets. Direct materials and direct labour budgets are also compatible with an activity-based costing framework because these inputs can be directly traced to the individual products. The major differences between functional and activity-based budgeting are found in the overhead and selling and administration categories. In a functional-based

The HOW and WHY of Preparing a Static Budget for an Activity

CORNERSTONE 11-9

Information:

1. Demand for purchase orders based on materials requirements: 15,000 purchase orders.
2. Resources needed:
   a. Five purchasing agents, each capable of processing 3,000 orders per year; salary, $40,000 each.
   b. Supplies (forms, paper, stamps, envelopes, etc.), projected to cost $1.00 per purchase order.
   c. Desks and computers: depreciation, $5,000 per year.
   d. Office space, rent, and utilities, $6,000.

Required:

Prepare a budget for the purchasing activity.

Solution:

Purchasing budget:

Salaries	$200,000
Depreciation	5,000
Supplies	15,000
Occupancy	6,000
Total	$226,000

WHY:

Activity-based budgeting is an important tool for managers to use. Preparing a static budget for any activity will help managers understand the underlying principles used for the budgeting process.

approach, budgets within these categories are typically detailed by cost categories. These cost categories are classified as variable or fixed, using production or sales output measures as the basis for determining cost behaviour. Furthermore, these budgets are usually constructed by budgeting for a cost item within a department (function) and then rolling these items up into the master overhead budget. For example, the cost of supervision in an overhead budget is the sum of all the supervision costs of the various departments. ABB, on the other hand, identifies the overhead, selling, and administrative *activities* and then builds a budget for each activity, based on the resources needed to provide the required activity output levels. Costs are classified as variable or fixed with respect to the *activity* output measure.

Consider, for example, purchasing materials. The demand for this activity is a function of the materials requirements for the various products and services produced. An activity driver, such as number of purchase orders, measures the activity output demand. Cornerstone 11-9 illustrates how to prepare a budget at the activity level for the purchasing activity.

Of the resources consumed by the purchasing activity in Cornerstone 11-9, supplies is a variable cost, and the other resources are fixed costs (a step-fixed cost behaviour in the case of salaries and depreciation). However, one important difference should be mentioned: Fixed and variable purchasing costs are defined with respect to the *number of purchase orders* and not direct labour hours or units produced or other measures of production output. In budgeting at the activity level, the cost behaviour of each activity is defined with respect to *its* output measure (which is often different from the production-based drivers used in functional-based budgeting). Knowing the output

CONCEPT Q&A

What are the main differences between ABB and traditional budgeting?

Answers on pages 711 to 715.

measure provides significant insights for controlling activity costs. In an activity framework, controlling costs results from managing activities. For example, by redesigning products so that they use more common components, the number of purchase orders can be decreased. By decreasing the number of purchase orders demanded, flexible resource demand is reduced; furthermore, decreasing the number of purchase orders demanded also reduces the activity capacity needed. Thus, activity costs will decrease.

Activity Flexible Budgeting

Understanding the relationship between changes in activity costs and changes in activity drivers allows managers to more carefully plan and monitor activity improvements. **Activity flexible budgeting** is the prediction of what activity costs will be as related output changes. Variance analysis within an activity framework makes it possible to improve traditional budgetary performance reporting, and enhances the ability to manage activities.

In a functional-based approach, budgeted costs for the actual level of activity are obtained by assuming that a single unit-based driver (e.g., units of product or direct labour hours) drives all costs. A cost formula is developed for each cost item as a function of units produced or direct labour hours. Cornerstone 11-2 illustrated a traditional flexible budget for production based on direct labour hours. If, however, costs vary with respect to more than one cost driver, and the drivers are not highly correlated with direct labour hours, then the predicted costs can be misleading.

The solution is to build flexible budget formulas for more than one cost driver. Cost estimation procedures (high-low method, the method of least squares, and so on) can be used to estimate cost formulas for each activity. This multiple-formula approach allows managers to predict more accurately what costs should be for different levels of activity, as measured by the cost drivers. These costs can then be compared with the actual costs to help assess budgetary performance. Cornerstone 11-10 illustrates how to prepare an activity flexible budget. Notice that flexible budgets are computed for *each cost driver.*

Notice that the activity-based performance report shown in Cornerstone 11-11 compares the budgeted costs for the actual activity usage levels with the actual costs. The five items are mixed costs. The net outcome is a favourable variance of $22,500. The performance report in Cornerstone 11-11 compares total budgeted costs for the actual level of activity with the total actual costs for each activity. The preparation of the performance report follows the pattern and approach in Cornerstone 11-3. The difference is that the comparison is for *each* activity.

CONCEPT Q&A

Why does activity-based flexible budgeting provide a more accurate prediction of costs?

Answers on pages 711 to 715.

One can also compare the actual fixed activity costs with the budgeted fixed activity costs and the actual variable activity costs with the budgeted variable costs. For example, assume that the actual fixed inspection costs are $82,000 (due to a midyear salary adjustment, reflecting a more favourable union agreement than anticipated) and that the actual variable inspection costs are $43,500. The variable and fixed budget variances for the inspection activity are computed as follows:

Activity	Actual Cost	Budgeted Cost	Variance
Inspection			
Fixed	$ 82,000	$ 80,000	$2,000 U
Variable	43,500	52,500	9,000 F
Total	$125,500	$132,500	$7,000 F

Breaking each variance into fixed and variable components provides more insight into the source of the variation in planned and actual expenditures.

The HOW and WHY of Preparing an Activity Flexible Budget

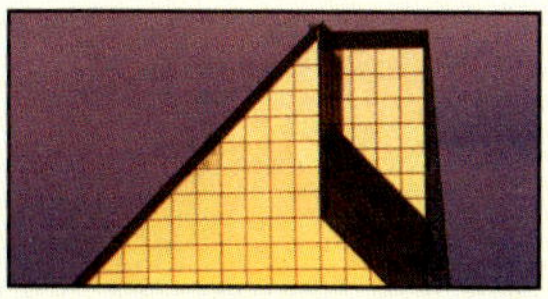

CORNERSTONE 11-10

Information:

Information on four overhead activities for a company is given below.

Activity	Driver	Fixed Cost	Variable Rate
Maintenance	Machine hours	$ 20,000	$ 5.50
Machining	Machine hours	15,000	2.00
Setting up	Setups	—	1,800
Inspection	Setups	80,000	2,100
Purchasing	Purchase orders	211,000	1.00

Required:

Prepare an activity-based flexible budget for the following production levels:

Driver	32,000 units	64,000 units
Machine hours	8,000	16,000
Setups	25	30
Purchase orders	15,000	25,000

Solution:

Steps in forming the activity-based flexible budget include:

1. Set up a table showing the activities under their related driver.
2. Calculate total activity cost by multiplying the variable rate times the driver level and adding the fixed amount. For example, at 8,000 machine hours,

   Maintenance = $20,000 + ($5.50 × 8,000 machine hours) = $64,000

   And at 16,000 machine hours,

   Maintenance = $20,000 + ($5.50 × 16,000 machine hours) = $108,000

			Required for	
			32,000 units	**64,000 units**
Driver: Machine Hours				
	Fixed	**Variable**	**8,000**	**16,000**
Maintenance	$20,000	$5.50	$64,000	$108,000
Machining	15,000	2.00	31,000	47,000
Subtotal	$35,000	$7.50	$95,000	$155,000
Driver: Number of Setups				
	Fixed	**Variable**	**25**	**30**
Setups	$ —	$1,800	$ 45,000	$ 54,000
Inspections	80,000	2,100	132,500	143,000
Subtotal	$80,000	$3,900	$177,500	$197,000
Driver: Number of Orders				
	Fixed	**Variable**	**15,000**	**25,000**
Purchasing	$211,000	$1.00	$226,000	$236,000
Total			$498,500	$588,000

WHY:

Converting the static budget based on activities to a flexible budget will enable managers to eliminate the distortions in the results that may be caused by different levels of activity achieved as compared to the expected levels of activity.

CORNERSTONE 11-11

The HOW and WHY of Preparing an Activity-Based Performance Report

Information:

Actual activity level is the first one for each activity listed in Cornerstone 11-10. For example, budgeted costs for maintenance would be based on 8,000 machine hours and would equal $64,000.

Actual costs:

Maintenance	$ 55,000
Machining	29,000
Setups	46,500
Inspections	125,500
Purchasing	220,000

Required:

Prepare an activity-based performance report.

Solution:

Note, for this performance report, just input the actual costs as given above. Then input the budgeted costs for the activity levels required. The budget variance is the difference between the actual costs and the budgeted costs. If actual costs are greater than budgeted costs, the budget variance is unfavourable (U). If actual costs are less than budgeted costs, the budget variance is favourable (F).

	Actual Costs	Budgeted Costs	Budget Variance
Maintenance	$ 55,000	$ 64,000	$ 9,000 F
Machining	29,000	31,000	2,000 F
Inspections	125,500	132,500	7,000 F
Setups	46,500	45,000	1,500 U
Purchasing	220,000	226,000	6,000 F
Total	$476,000	$498,500	$22,500 F

WHY:

Performance reports based on activity levels will help managers determine which activities need further attention.

Summary of Learning Objectives

LO1. Prepare a flexible budget, and use it for performance reporting.

- Static budgets provide expected cost for a given level of activity. If the actual level of activity differs from the level associated with the static budget level, then comparing actual costs with budgeted costs does not make any sense. The solution is flexible budgeting.
- Flexible budgets divide costs into those that vary with units of production (or direct labour hours) and those that are fixed with respect to these unit-level drivers. These relationships allow the identification of a cost formula for each item in the budget.

- Cost formulas are the means for calculating expected costs for various levels of activity. There are two applications of flexible budgets: before-the-fact and after-the-fact.
  - Before-the-fact applications allow managers to see what costs will be for different levels of activity (sensitivity analysis), thus helping in planning.
  - After-the-fact applications allow managers to see what the cost should have been for the actual level of activity achieved in the period. Knowing these after-the-fact expected or budgeted costs then provides the opportunity to evaluate efficiency by comparing actual costs with budgeted costs.

LO2. Calculate the variable overhead variances, and explain their meaning.

- Overhead costs are often a significant proportion of costs in a budget.
- Comparing actual variable and fixed overhead costs with applied overhead costs yields a total overhead variance.
- In a standard cost system, it is possible to break down these overhead variances into component variances.
- For variable overhead, the two component variances are the spending variance and the efficiency variance.
- The spending variance is the result of comparing the actual costs with budgeted costs.
- The variable overhead efficiency variance is the result of efficient or inefficient use of labour because variable overhead is assumed to vary with direct labour hours.

LO3. Calculate the fixed overhead variances, and explain their meaning.

- For fixed overhead, the two component variances are the spending variance and the volume variance.
- The spending variance is the result of comparing the actual costs with budgeted costs.
- The fixed overhead volume variance is the result of producing a level different than that used to calculate the predetermined fixed overhead rate. It can be interpreted as a measure of capacity utilization.

LO4. Prepare an activity-based flexible budget.

- Activity-based budgeting (ABB) is done at the activity level.
- First, demand for products is assessed.
- Next, the level of activity output needed to support the expected production level is estimated.
- Finally, the resources needed to support the required activity output are estimated. This then becomes the activity budget.
- Activity flexible budgets differ from traditional flexible budgets because the cost formulas are based on the activity drivers for the respective activities rather than being based only on a single unit-based driver, such as direct labour hours.

Summary of Important Equations

Abbreviations:

AH = actual direct labour hours

SH = standard direct labour hours that *should have been worked* for actual units produced

AVOR = actual variable overhead rate

SVOR = standard variable overhead rate

SFOR = standard fixed overhead rate

1. Variable overhead spending variance $= (AVOR \times AH) - (SVOR \times AH)$

   $= (AVOR - SVOR)AH$

2. Variable overhead efficiency variance $= (AH - SH)SVOR$

Chapter 12

Performance Evaluation and Decentralization

After studying Chapter 12, you should be able to:

1. Explain how and why firms choose to decentralize.
2. Compute and explain return on investment.
3. Compute and explain residual income and economic value added.
4. Explain the role of transfer pricing in a decentralized firm.
5. Explain the uses of the Balanced Scorecard, and compute cycle time, velocity, and manufacturing cycle efficiency.

HERMAN MILLER, INC.

Experience Managerial Decisions

with Herman Miller

When the Vancouver Aquarium conducted a two-phase expansion in 2004, including the opening of a Discovery Learning Centre, it showed that it was committed to the goals of sustainability and conservation. It wanted to equip its facility with the "greenest" furniture it could find. Its search for the right partner led it to **Herman Miller Inc.**, a furniture manufacturer with business activities in more than 100 countries. With enterprises as large as Herman Miller's, performance evaluation is critical to success. The goal of performance evaluation is to provide information useful for assessing the effectiveness of past decisions so that future decisions can be improved. As you might guess, this goal is difficult to achieve because of the sheer quantity of information present in organizations and the complexity of the business environment in which most decisions are made. Herman Miller uses an increasingly popular performance evaluation technique—economic value added (EVA)—to help it make better decisions. For example, the entire office furniture market experienced a devastating slump in the early 2000s as a result of the dot-com bust and the 9/11 disaster. EVA measures provided Herman Miller with information beyond traditional accounting performance metrics that was critical to its dramatic and quick recovery from the negative operating margins it experienced during the slump to the near double-digit positive margins it enjoyed only a few years later. EVA identifies the return generated by the company's assets and then subtracts the cost of all capital, both debt (e.g., money raised from loans, leases, and bonds) and equity (e.g., money raised from investors), used by the company to finance those assets in order to determine whether value is being created or destroyed. More specifically, EVA helps Herman Miller to quantify the long-term financial benefits of carrying less inventory and employing fewer fixed assets in its business. As a result of such EVA analyses, Herman Miller makes fundamentally different strategic and operating decisions involving its furniture production processes than it would if it relied solely on traditional accounting metrics. The ability to impact decisions in such a positive fashion has catapulted EVA into a position of prominence in Herman Miller's successful performance evaluation system.

HermanMiller

HERMAN MILLER INC.

Here's The Real Kicker

Kicker's top management is closely involved in all aspects of the company, from design and development through production, sales, delivery, and aftermarket activities. Profit performance, as measured by periodic income statements, is an important measure. In addition, Kicker keeps track of a number of other measures of performance.

For example, financial information is very important. Financial statements are presented to the president and vice presidents every month. These are reviewed carefully for trends and are compared with the budgeted amounts. Worrisome increases in expenses or decreases in revenue are analyzed to see what the underlying factors might be. This leads to the next perspective.

Customer satisfaction is also continually measured. Kicker has two major types of customers—dealers who sell Kicker products and end users who have Kicker speakers installed in the car. Each customer type has specific needs. For example, dealers have the exclusive right to sell Kicker products. Theoretically, you must buy from a dealer to get a new set of speakers, amplifier, and so on. Kicker offers a one-year warranty on speakers sold through a dealer. However, end users want as low a price as possible. Speakers are available on the Internet, which are called "grey market" speakers (that is, the seller is not authorized to sell them). In the past, no warranty was available on non-dealer-sold speakers. Problems arose when customers purchased obviously new products through the Internet, something went wrong, and they were not covered under warranty. It was very difficult to explain the no-warranty policy. Finally, Kicker decided to offer a shorter warranty for new products sold by unauthorized sellers. The objective of keeping the customer base happy and increasing satisfaction was achieved.

Kicker focuses on strategic objectives for the long term. For example, engineers in R&D take continuing education to stay current in their fields. When Kicker approached producing and selling original equipment manufacture (OEM) speakers to a major automobile maker, a number of employees had to learn International Organization for Standardization (ISO) quality concepts quickly. They took classes, met with consultants, and travelled to the site of other ISO-qualified firms to learn how to meet quality standards.

KICKER®

OBJECTIVE 1
Explain how and why firms choose to decentralize.

Decentralization and Responsibility Centres

In general, a company is organized along lines of responsibility. The traditional organizational chart, with its pyramid shape, illustrates the lines of responsibility flowing from the chief executive officer down through the vice presidents to middle- and lower-level managers. As organizations grow larger, these lines of responsibility become longer and more numerous. The structure becomes cumbersome. Contemporary practice is moving toward a flattened hierarchy. This structure—emphasizing teams—is consistent with decentralization. **GE Capital**, for example, is essentially a group of smaller businesses. A strong link exists between the structure of an organization and its responsibility accounting system. Ideally, the responsibility accounting system mirrors and supports the structure of an organization.

Firms with multiple responsibility centres usually choose one of two decision-making approaches to manage their diverse and complex activities: *centralized* or *decentralized*. In centralized decision making, decisions are made at the very top level, and lower-level managers are charged with implementing these decisions. On the other hand, decentralized decision making allows managers at lower levels to make and implement key decisions pertaining to their areas of responsibility. **Decentralization** is the practice of delegating decision-making authority to the lower levels of management in a company. Exhibit 12-1 illustrates the difference between centralized and decentralized companies.

Organizations range from highly centralized to strongly decentralized. Most firms fall somewhere in between, with the majority tending toward decentralization. The reasons for the popularity of decentralization and the ways in which a company may choose to decentralize are discussed next.

Reasons for Decentralization

Firms decide to decentralize for several reasons, including (1) ease of gathering and using local information; (2) focusing of central management; (3) training and motivating of segment managers; and (4) enhanced competition, exposing segments to market forces.

Exhibit 12-1

Centralization and Decentralization

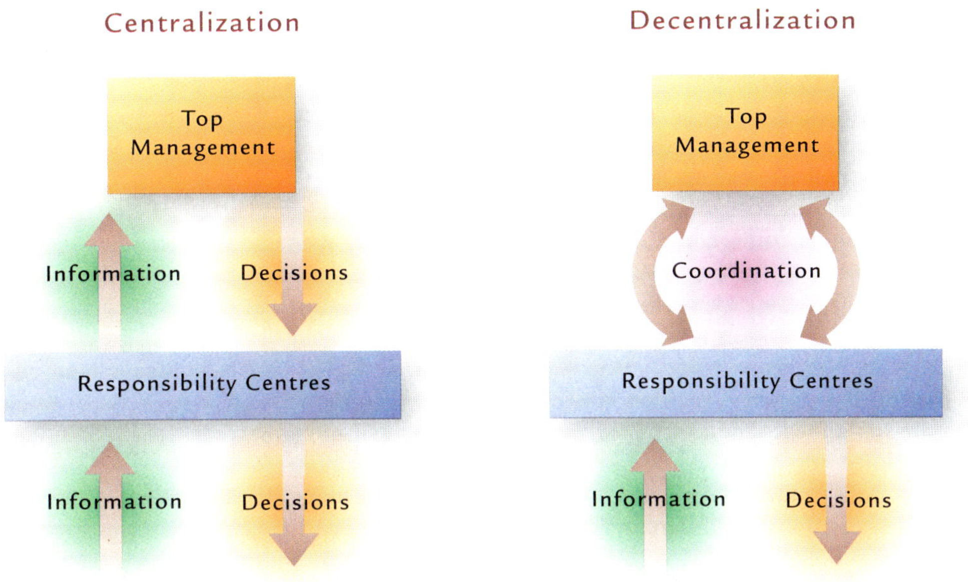

Gathering and Using Local Information The quality of decisions is affected by the quality of information available. As a firm grows in size and operates in different markets and regions, central management may not understand local conditions. Lower-level managers, however, are in contact with immediate operating conditions (such as the strength and nature of local competition, the nature of the local labour force, and so on). As a result, they often are better positioned to make local decisions. For example, **McDonald's** has restaurants around the world. The tastes of people in China or France differ from those of people in Canada. So, McDonald's tailors its menu to different countries. The result is that the McDonald's in each country can differentiate to meet the needs of its local market.

Focusing of Central Management By decentralizing the operating decisions, central management is free to engage in strategic planning and decision making. The long-run survival of the organization should be of more importance to central management than day-to-day operations.

Training and Motivating of Managers Organizations always need well-trained managers to replace higher-level managers who leave to take advantage of other opportunities. What better way to prepare a future generation of higher-level managers than by providing them the opportunity to make significant decisions? These opportunities also enable top managers to evaluate local managers' capabilities. Those who make the best decisions are the ones who can be promoted.

Enhanced Competition In a highly centralized company, overall profit margins can mask inefficiencies within the various subdivisions. Large companies now find that they cannot afford to keep a noncompetitive division. One of the best ways to improve performance of a division or factory is to expose it more fully to market forces. At **Koch Industries Inc.**, each unit is expected to act as an autonomous business unit and to set prices both externally and internally. Units whose services are not required by other Koch units may face possible elimination.

Divisions in the Decentralized Firm

Decentralization involves a cost-benefit trade-off. As a firm becomes more decentralized, it passes more decision authority down the managerial hierarchy. As a result, managers in a decentralized firm make and implement more decisions than do managers in a centralized firm. The benefit of decentralization is that decisions are more likely to be made by managers who possess the specific local knowledge—not possessed by high-level managers—to use the firm's resources in the best way possible to maximize firm value. However, the cost of decentralization is that lower-level managers who have the knowledge to make the best decisions with the firm's resources are less likely to possess the same incentive as high-level managers to maximize firm value. Stated differently, as compared to high-level managers, lower-level managers are more likely to use the firm's resources for personal gain than for increasing the firm's share value. Therefore, decentralization requires the use of particular incentives, such as profit sharing and stock options, to try and motivate lower-level managers to make decisions that maximize firm value. **Starbucks**, for example, is famous for offering incentives, such as health care benefits and stock options, even to its part-time employees. Successful decentralized firms manage this trade-off in an effective fashion.

Decentralization usually is achieved by creating units called *divisions.* One way in which divisions are differentiated may be by the types of goods or services produced. For example, divisions of **PepsiCo** include the Snack Ventures Europe Division (a joint venture with **General Mills**), **Frito-Lay Inc.**, and **Tropicana**, as well as its flagship soft-drink division. Exhibit 12-2 shows decentralized divisions of PepsiCo. These divisions are organized on the basis of product lines. Notice that some divisions depend on other divisions. For example, PepsiCo spun off its restaurant divisions to **YUMBrands**. As a result, the cola you drink at **Pizza Hut**, **Taco Bell**, and **KFC** will be Pepsi—not Coke. In a decentralized setting, some interdependencies usually exist; otherwise, a company would merely be a collection of totally separate entities.

Divisions may also be created along geographic lines. For example, **UAL Inc.** (parent of **United Airlines**) has a number of regional divisions: Asian/Pacific, Caribbean, European, Latin American, and North American. The presence of divisions spanning one or more regions creates the need for performance evaluation that can take into account differences in divisional environments.

Exhibit 12-2

Decentralized Divisions

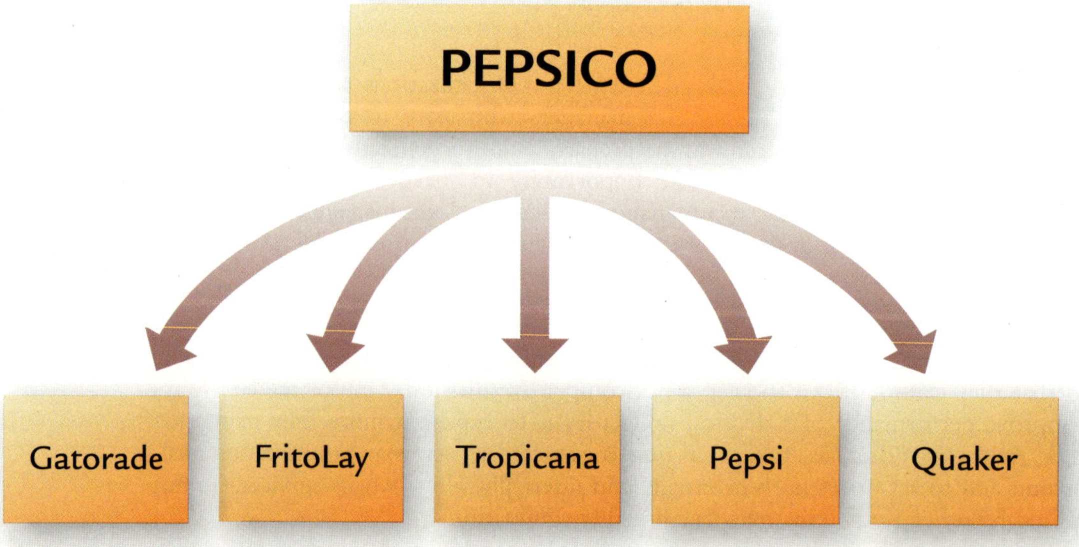

A third way divisions differ is by the type of responsibility given to the divisional manager. As a firm grows, top management typically creates areas of responsibility, known as responsibility centres, and assigns subordinate managers to those areas. A **responsibility centre** is a segment of the business whose manager is accountable for specified sets of activities. The results of each responsibility centre can be measured according to the information that managers need to operate their centres. The four major types of responsibility centres are as follows:

1. **Cost centre:** A responsibility centre in which a manager is responsible only for costs.
2. **Revenue centre:** A responsibility centre in which a manager is responsible only for generating sales, or revenue.
3. **Profit centre:** A responsibility centre in which a manager is responsible for both revenues and costs.
4. **Investment centre:** A responsibility centre in which a manager is responsible for revenues, costs, and investments.

The choice of responsibility centre typically mirrors the actual situation and the type of information available to the manager. Information is the key to appropriately holding managers responsible for outcomes. For example, a production department manager is held responsible for departmental costs but not for sales. This responsibility choice occurs because the production department manager understands and directly controls some production costs but does not set selling prices. Any difference between actual and expected costs can best be explained at this level.

The marketing department manager sets the price and projected sales. Therefore, the marketing department may be evaluated as a revenue centre. Direct costs of the marketing department and overall sales are the responsibility of the sales manager.

In some companies, plant managers are given the responsibility for manufacturing and marketing their products. These plant managers control both costs and revenues, putting them in control of a profit centre. Operating income is an important performance measure for profit centre managers.

Finally, divisions sometimes are cited as examples of investment centres. In addition to having control over cost and pricing decisions, divisional managers may have the power to make investment decisions such as plant closings and openings and decisions to keep or drop a product line. As a result, both operating income and some type of ROI are important performance measures for investment centre managers. Exhibit 12-3 displays these centres along with the type of information that managers need to manage their operations. As the exhibit shows, investment centres represent the greatest degree of decentralization (followed by profit centres and finally by cost and revenue centres) because their managers have the freedom to make the greatest variety of decisions.

It is important to realize that while the responsibility centre manager has responsibility only for the activities of that centre, decisions made by that manager can affect

CONCEPT Q&A

Think about summer jobs that you and your friends have held. To what extent did you or your friends work in a centralized or decentralized decision-making environment?

Answers on pages 711 to 715.

Exhibit 12-3

Types of Responsibility Centres and Accounting Information Used to Measure Performance

	Cost	Sales	Capital Investment	Other
Cost centre	X			
Revenue centre		X		
Profit centre	X	X		
Investment centre	X	X	X	X

other responsibility centres. For example, the sales force at a floor care products firm routinely offers customers price discounts at the end of the month. Sales increase dramatically, which is good for revenue and the sales force. However, the factory is forced to institute overtime shifts to keep up with demand. These overtime shifts increase the costs of the factory as well as the cost per unit of product.

Organizing divisions as responsibility centres creates the opportunity to control the divisions through the use of responsibility accounting. Revenue centre control is achieved by evaluating the efficiency and the effectiveness of divisional managers on the basis of sales revenue. Cost centre control is based on control of costs and frequently employs variance analysis, as described in Chapters 9 and 10. This chapter will focus on the evaluation of profit centres and investment centres.

OBJECTIVE 2
Compute and explain return on investment.

Measuring the Performance of Investment Centres by Using Return on Investment

Typically, investment centres are evaluated on the basis of return on investment (ROI). Other measures, such as residual income and economic value added, are discussed in the following section.

Return on Investment

Divisions that are investment centres will have an income statement and a balance sheet. So, could those divisions be ranked on the basis of income? Suppose, for example, that a company has two divisions—Alpha and Beta. Alpha's operating income is $100,000, and Beta's operating income is $200,000. Did Beta perform better than Alpha? What if Alpha used an investment of $500,000 to produce the contribution of $100,000, while Beta used an investment of $2 million to produce the $200,000 contribution? Does your response change? Clearly, relating the reported operating profits to the assets used to produce them is a more meaningful measure of performance.

One way to relate operating profits to assets employed is to compute the **return on investment (ROI)**, which is the profit earned per dollar of investment. ROI is the most common measure of performance for an investment centre. It can be defined as follows:

$$\text{ROI} = \frac{\text{Operating income}}{\text{Average operating assets}}$$

Operating income refers to earnings before interest and taxes. **Operating assets** are all assets acquired to generate operating income, including cash, receivables, inventories, land, buildings, and equipment. The figure for average operating assets is computed as follows:

$$\text{Average operating assets} = \frac{(\text{Beginning assets} + \text{Ending assets})}{2}$$

Opinions vary regarding how long-term assets (plant and equipment) should be valued (e.g., gross book value vs. net book value or historical cost vs. current cost). Most firms use historical cost and net book value.[1]

Going back to our example, Alpha's ROI is 0.20 ($100,000/$500,000), while Beta's ROI is only 0.10 ($200,000/$2,000,000). The formula for ROI is quick and easy to use. However, the decomposition of ROI into margin and turnover ratios gives additional information. Cornerstone 12-1 shows how to calculate these ratios.

[1] There is no one correct way to calculate ROI. The important thing is to be sure that one method is applied consistently, which allows the company to compare the ROIs among divisions and over time.

The HOW and WHY of Calculating Average Operating Assets, Margin, Turnover, and Return on Investment

CORNERSTONE 12-1

Information:
Celimar Company's Ontario Division earned operating income last year as shown in the following income statement:

Sales	$480,000
Cost of goods sold	222,000
Gross margin	$258,000
Selling and administrative expense	210,000
Operating income	$ 48,000

At the beginning of the year, the value of operating assets was $277,000. At the end of the year, the value of operating assets was $323,000.

Required:
For the Ontario Division, calculate:

1. Average operating assets
2. Margin
3. Turnover
4. Return on investment

Solution:

1. Average operating assets = (Beginning assets + Ending assets)/2
   = ($277,000 + $323,000)/2
   = $300,000
2. Margin = Operating income/Sales = $48,000/$480,000
   = 0.10, or 10 percent
3. Turnover = Sales/Average operating assets = $480,000/$300,000 = 1.6
4. *ROI* = Margin × Turnover = 0.10 × 1.6 = 0.16, or 16 percent

Alternatively,

ROI = Operating income/Average operating assets
= $48,000/$300,000
= 0.16, or 16 percent

WHY:
Performance measures are critical to any system of management. Understanding how to calculate these important measures will enable managers to properly implement appropriate control measures.

Margin and Turnover

A second way to calculate ROI is to separate the formula (Operating income/Average operating assets) into margin and turnover.

$$\text{ROI} = \underbrace{\frac{\text{Operating income}}{\text{Sales}}}_{\textbf{Margin}} \times \underbrace{\frac{\text{Sales}}{\text{Average operating assets}}}_{\textbf{Turnover}}$$

Notice that "Sales" in the above formula can be cancelled out to yield the original ROI formula of Operating income/Average operating assets.

Margin is the ratio of operating income to sales. It tells how many cents of operating income result from each dollar of sales; it expresses the portion of sales that is available for interest, taxes, and profit. Some managers also refer to margin as return on sales. **Turnover** is a different measure; it is found by dividing sales by average operating assets. Turnover tells how many dollars of sales result from every dollar invested in operating assets; it shows how productively assets are being used to generate sales.

Suppose, for example, that Alpha had sales of $400,000. Then, margin would be 0.25 ($100,000/$400,000), and turnover would be 0.80 ($400,000/$500,000). Alpha's ROI would still be 0.20 (0.25 × 0.80).

While both approaches yield the same ROI, the calculation of margin and turnover gives a manager valuable information. To illustrate this additional information, consider the data presented in Exhibit 12-4. The Electronics Division improved its ROI from 18 percent in year 1 to 20 percent in year 2. The Medical Supplies Division's ROI, however, dropped from 18 percent to 15 percent. Computing the margin and turnover ratios for each division gives a better picture of what caused the change in rates. As with variance analysis, understanding the causes of managerial accounting measures (i.e., variances, margins, turnover, etc.) helps managers take actions to improve the division. These ratios also are presented in Exhibit 12-4.

Notice that the margins for both divisions dropped from year 1 to year 2. In fact, the divisions experienced the *same* percentage of decline (16.67 percent). A declining margin could be explained by increasing expenses, by competitive pressures (forcing a decrease in selling prices), or both.

CONCEPT Q&A

Think about some stores in your town, such as a jewellery store, fast-food outlet, and grocery store. How do you suppose their margins and turnover ratios compare with each other? Explain your thinking.

Answers on pages 711 to 715.

Exhibit 12-4

Comparison of Divisional Performance

	Comparison of ROI	
	Electronics Division	Medical Supplies Division
Year 1:		
Sales	$30,000,000	$117,000,000
Operating income	1,800,000	3,510,000
Average operating assets	10,000,000	19,500,000
ROI[a]	18%	18%
Year 2:		
Sales	$40,000,000	$117,000,000
Operating income	2,000,000	2,925,000
Average operating assets	10,000,000	19,500,000
ROI[a]	20%	15%

	Margin and Turnover Comparisons			
	Electronics Division		Medical Supplies Division	
	Year 1	Year 2	Year 1	Year 2
Margin[b]	6.0%	5.0%	3.0%	2.5%
Turnover[c]	× 3.0	× 4.0	× 6.0	× 6.0
ROI	18.0%	20.0%	18.0%	15.0%

[a] Operating income divided by average operating assets.
[b] Operating income divided by sales.
[c] Sales divided by average operating assets.

Despite the declining margin, the Electronics Division was able to increase its rate of return. The reason is that the increase in turnover more than compensated for the decline in margin. One explanation for the increased turnover could be a deliberate policy to reduce inventories.

(Notice that the average assets employed remained the same for the Electronics Division even though sales increased by $10 million.)

The experience of the Medical Supplies Division was less favourable. Because its turnover rate remained unchanged, its ROI dropped. This division, unlike the Electronics Division, could not overcome the decline in margin.

Advantages of Return on Investment

At least three positive results stem from the use of ROI:

1. It encourages managers to focus on the relationships among sales, expenses, and investment, as should be the case for a manager of an investment centre.
2. It encourages managers to focus on cost efficiency.
3. It encourages managers to focus on operating asset efficiency.

These advantages are illustrated by the following three scenarios.

Focus on Return on Investment Relationships Della Barnes, manager of the Plastics Division, is mulling over a suggestion from her marketing vice president to increase the advertising budget by $100,000. The marketing vice president is confident that this increase will boost sales by $200,000. Della realizes that the increased sales will also raise expenses. She finds that the increased variable cost will be $80,000.

The division also will need to purchase additional machinery to handle the increased production. The equipment will cost $50,000 and will add $10,000 of depreciation expense. As a result, the proposal will add $10,000 ($200,000 – $80,000 – $10,000 – $100,000) to operating income. Currently, the division has sales of $2 million, total expenses of $1,850,000, and operating income of $150,000. Operating assets equal $1 million.

	Without Increased Advertising	With Increased Advertising
Sales	$2,000,000	$2,200,000
Less: Expenses	1,850,000	2,040,000
Operating income	$ 150,000	$ 160,000
Average operating assets	$1,000,000	$1,050,000
ROI:		

$150,000/$1,000,000 = 0.15, or 15 percent
$160,000/$1,050,000 = 0.1524, or 15.24 percent

The ROI without the additional advertising is 15 percent; the ROI with the additional advertising and $50,000 investment in assets is 15.24 percent. Since ROI is increased by the proposal, Della decides to authorize the increased advertising. In effect, the current ROI, without the proposal, is the *hurdle rate*. This term is frequently used to indicate the minimum ROI necessary to accept an investment.

Focus on Cost Efficiency Kyle Chugg, manager of Turner's Battery Division, groaned as he reviewed the projections for the last half of the current fiscal year. The recession was hurting his division's performance. Adding the projected operating income of $200,000 to the actual operating income of the first half produced expected annual earnings of $425,000. Kyle then divided the expected operating income by the division's average operating assets to obtain an expected ROI of 12.15 percent. "This is awful," muttered Kyle. "Last year our ROI was 16 percent. And I'm looking at a couple more bad years before business returns to normal. Something has to be done to improve our performance."

Kyle directed all operating managers to identify and eliminate non-value-added activities. As a result, lower-level managers found ways to reduce costs by $150,000 for the remaining half of the year. This reduction increased the annual operating income from $425,000 to $575,000, increasing ROI from 12.15 percent to 16.43 percent as a result. Interestingly, Kyle found that some of the reductions could be maintained after business returned to normal.

Focus on Operating Asset Efficiency The Electronic Storage Division prospered during its early years. In the beginning, the division developed portable external disk drives for storing data; sales and ROI were extraordinarily high. However, during the past several years, competitors had developed competing technology, and the division's ROI had plunged from 30 to 15 percent. Cost cutting had helped initially, but all of the fat had been removed, making further improvements from cost reductions impossible. Moreover, any increase in sales was unlikely—competition was too stiff. The divisional manager searched for some way to increase the ROI by at least 3 to 5 percent. Only by raising the ROI so that it compared favourably with that of the other divisions could the division expect to receive additional capital for research and development (R&D).

The divisional manager initiated an intensive program to reduce operating assets. Most of the gains were made in the area of inventory reductions; however, one plant was closed because of a long-term reduction in market share. By installing a just-in-time purchasing and manufacturing system, the division was able to reduce its asset base without threatening its remaining market share. Finally, the reduction in operating assets meant that operating costs could be decreased still further. The end result was a 50 percent increase in the division's ROI, from 15 percent to more than 22 percent.

Disadvantages of the Return on Investment Measure

Overemphasis on ROI can produce myopic behaviour. Two negative aspects associated with ROI frequently are mentioned:

1. It can produce a narrow focus on divisional profitability at the expense of profitability for the overall firm.
2. It encourages managers to focus on the short run at the expense of the long run.

These disadvantages are illustrated by the following two scenarios:

Narrow Focus on Divisional Profitability A Cleaning Products Division has the opportunity to invest in two projects for the coming year. The outlay required for each investment, the dollar returns, and the ROI are as follows:

	Project I	Project II
Investment	$10,000,000	$4,000,000
Operating income	1,300,000	640,000
ROI	13%	16%

The division currently earns ROI of 15 percent, with operating assets of $50 million and operating income on current investments of $7.5 million. The division has approval to request up to $15 million in new investment capital. Corporate headquarters requires that all investments earn at least 10 percent (this rate represents the corporation's cost of acquiring the capital). Any capital not used by a division is invested by headquarters, and it earns exactly 10 percent.

The division manager has four alternatives: (1) invest in Project I, (2) invest in Project II, (3) invest in both Projects I and II, or (4) invest in neither project. The divisional ROI was computed for each alternative.

	Alternatives			
	Select Project I	Select Project II	Select Both Projects	Select Neither Project
Operating income	$8,800,000	$8,140,000	$9,440,000	$7,500,000
Operating assets	$60,000,000	$54,000,000	$64,000,000	$50,000,000
ROI	14.67%	15.07%	14.75%	15.00%

The divisional manager chose to invest only in Project II, since it would boost ROI from 15.00 percent to 15.07 percent.

While the manager's choice maximized divisional ROI, it did not maximize the profit the company could have earned. If Project I had been selected, the company would have earned $1.3 million in profits. By not selecting Project I, the $10 million in capital is invested at 10 percent, earning only $1 million (0.10 × $10,000,000). The single-minded focus on divisional ROI, then, cost the company $300,000 in profits ($1,300,000 − $1,000,000).

Encourages Short-Run Optimization Ruth Lunsford, manager of a Small Tools Division, was displeased with her division's performance during the first three quarters. Given the expected income for the fourth quarter, the ROI for the year would be 13 percent, at least two percentage points below where she had hoped to be. Such an ROI might not be strong enough to justify the early promotion she wanted. With only three months left, drastic action was needed. Increasing sales for the last quarter was unlikely. Most sales were booked at least two to three months in advance. Emphasizing extra sales activity would benefit next year's performance. What was needed were some ways to improve this year's performance.

After careful thought, Ruth decided to take the following actions:

1. Lay off five of the highest paid salespeople.
2. Cut the advertising budget for the fourth quarter by 50 percent.
3. Delay all promotions within the division for three months.
4. Reduce the preventive maintenance budget by 75 percent.
5. Use cheaper raw materials for fourth-quarter production.

In the aggregate, these steps would reduce expenses, increase income, and raise the ROI to about 15.2 percent for the current year.

While Ruth's actions increase the profits and ROI in the short run, they have some long-run negative consequences. Laying off the highest paid (and possibly the best) salespeople may harm the division's future sales-generating capabilities. Future sales could also be hurt by cutting back on advertising and using cheaper raw materials. Delaying promotions could hurt employee morale, which could, in turn, lower productivity and future sales. Finally, reducing preventive maintenance will likely increase downtime and decrease the life of the productive equipment.

ETHICS Ethical considerations also come into play when managers attempt to "game" ROI. Ruth's five top-earning salespeople probably were her best salespeople. Letting them go meant that sales would probably decrease, an outcome not in the best interests of the firm. Thus, her action is directly contrary to her obligation to take actions in the best interests of the company. The layoffs may also violate the implicit contract a company has with workers that outstanding work will lead to continued employment.◆

Measuring the Performance of Investment Centres by Using Residual Income and Economic Value Added

OBJECTIVE 3
Compute and explain residual income and economic value added.

To compensate for the tendency of ROI to discourage investments that are profitable for the company but that lower a division's ROI, some companies have adopted alternative performance measures such as residual income. Economic value added is an alternative way to calculate residual income that is being used in a number of companies, such as Herman Miller.

CORNERSTONE 12-2

The HOW and WHY of Calculating Residual Income

Information:

Celimar Company's Ontario Division earned operating income last year as shown in the following income statement:

Sales	$480,000
Cost of goods sold	222,000
Gross margin	$258,000
Selling and administrative expense	210,000
Operating income	$ 48,000

At the beginning of the year, the value of operating assets was $277,000. At the end of the year, the value of operating assets was $323,000. Celimar Company requires a minimum rate of return of 12 percent.

Required:

For the Ontario Division, calculate:

1. Average operating assets
2. Residual income

Solution:

1. Average operating assets = (Beginning assets + Ending assets)/2
   = ($277,000 + $323,000)/2
   = $300,000
2. Residual income = Operating income − (Minimum rate of return × Average operating assets
   = $48,000 − (0.12 × $300,000)
   = $48,000 − $36,000
   = $12,000

WHY:

Residual income is a measure that many companies prefer to use to motivate managers to make the right decisions. It tends to correct some of the shortcomings of return on investment as a measurement tool.

Residual Income

Residual income is the difference between operating income and the minimum dollar return required on a company's operating assets:

Residual income = Operating income − (Minimum rate of return × Average operating assets)

Cornerstone 12-2 shows how to calculate residual income.

The minimum rate of return is set by the company and is the same as the hurdle rate mentioned in the section on ROI. If residual income is greater than zero, then the division is earning more than the minimum required rate of return (or hurdle rate). If residual income is less than zero, then the division is earning less than the minimum required rate of return. Finally, if residual income equals zero, then the division is earning precisely the minimum required rate of return.

Advantage of Residual Income Recall that the manager of the Cleaning Products Division rejected Project I because it would have reduced divisional ROI; however, that decision cost the company $300,000 in profits. The use of residual income as the performance measure would have prevented this loss. The residual income for each project is computed as follows:

Project I

Residual income = Operating income − (Minimum rate of return × Average operating assets)
= $1,300,000 − (0.10 × $10,000,000)
= $1,300,000 − $1,000,000
= $300,000

Project II

Residual income = $640,000 − (0.10 × $4,000,000)
= $640,000 − $400,000
= $240,000

Notice that both projects have positive residual income. For comparative purposes, the divisional residual income for each of the four alternatives identified are as follows:

	Alternatives			
	Select Only Project I	Select Only Project II	Select Both Projects	Select Neither Project
Operating assets	$60,000,000	$54,000,000	$64,000,000	$50,000,000
Operating income	$ 8,800,000	$ 8,140,000	$ 9,440,000	$ 7,500,000
Minimum return*	$ 6,000,000	$ 5,400,000	$ 6,400,000	$ 5,000,000
Residual income	$ 2,800,000	$ 2,740,000	$ 3,040,000	$ 2,500,000

* 0.10 × Operating assets.

As shown above, selecting both projects produces the greatest increase in residual income. The use of residual income encourages managers to accept any project that earns a return that is above the minimum rate.

Disadvantages of Residual Income Residual income, like ROI, can encourage a short-run orientation. If Ruth Lunsford were being evaluated on the basis of residual income, she could have taken the same actions.

Another problem with residual income is that, unlike ROI, it is an absolute measure of profitability. Thus, direct comparison of the performance of two different investment centres becomes difficult, as the level of investment may differ. For example, consider the residual income computations for Division A and Division B, where the minimum required rate of return is 8 percent.

	Division A	Division B
Average operating assets	$15,000,000	$2,500,000
Operating income	$ 1,500,000	$ 300,000
Minimum return[a]	(1,200,000)	(200,000)
Residual income	$ 300,000	$ 100,000
Residual return[b]	2%	4%

[a] 0.08 × Operating assets.
[b] Residual income divided by operating assets.

It is tempting to claim that Division A is outperforming Division B since its residual income is three times higher. Notice, however, that Division A is considerably larger than Division B and has six times as many assets. One possible way to correct this disadvantage is to compute both ROI and residual income and to use both measures for performance evaluation. ROI could then be used for interdivisional comparisons.

Economic Value Added

A specific way of calculating residual income is *economic value added.* **Economic value added (EVA)**[2] is net income (operating income minus taxes) minus the total annual cost of capital. Basically, EVA is residual income with the minimum rate of return equal to the actual cost of capital for the firm (as opposed to some minimum rate of return desired by the company for other reasons). It is said that if EVA is positive, then the company has increased its wealth during the period; if EVA is negative, then the company has decreased its wealth during the period. Consider the old saying, "It takes money to make money." EVA helps the company to determine whether the money it makes is more than the money it takes to make it. Over the long term, only those companies creating capital, or wealth, can survive.

As a form of residual income, EVA is a dollar figure, not a percentage rate of return. However, it does bear a resemblance to rates of return such as ROI because it links net income (return) to capital employed. The key feature of EVA is its emphasis on *after-tax* operating profit and the *actual* cost of capital. Residual income, on the other hand, uses a minimum expected rate of return. Investors like EVA because it relates profit to the amount of resources needed to achieve it. A number of companies have been evaluated on the basis of EVA. In 2003, for example, economic value added for **General Electric** was $5.98 billion, for **Wal-Mart Stores** it was $2.93 billion, and for **Merck & Co.** it was $3.87 billion.[3] Among large companies showing negative EVA were **IBM** at ($8.03) billion, **Verizon Communications** at ($5.61) billion, and **Disney Company** at ($2.07) billion. Smaller companies also differed in terms of their economic value added. **Pixar**'s was positive at $31 million while **Jetblue Airways Corp**. came in at $15 million.

Some companies adjust after-tax operating income in the EVA calculation to eliminate the impact of expenditures that have long-term beneficial impact on the company, such as brand advertising, research and development costs, training, and similar items. Senior management wants these expenditures to continue even if eliminating them would improve short-term performance.

CONCEPT Q&A

What are the differences and similarities between the basic residual income calculation and EVA?

Answers on pages 711 to 715.

Calculating Economic Value Added

EVA is after-tax operating income minus the dollar cost of capital employed. The dollar cost of capital employed is the actual percentage cost of capital[4] multiplied by the total capital employed. The equation for EVA is expressed as follows:

$$EVA = \text{After-tax operating income} - (\text{Actual percentage cost of capital} \times \text{Total capital employed})$$

Cornerstone 12-3 shows how to calculate EVA.

Behavioural Aspects of Economic Value Added

A number of companies have discovered that EVA helps to encourage the right kind of behaviour from their divisions in a way that emphasis on operating income alone cannot. The underlying reason is EVA's reliance on the true cost of capital. In some companies, the responsibility for investment decisions rests with corporate management. As a result, the cost of capital is considered a corporate expense rather than an expense attributable to particular divisions. If a division builds inventories and investment, the cost of financing that investment is passed along to the overall income statement and does not show up as a reduction from that division's operating income as it would under

[2] EVA was developed by Stern Stewart & Co. in the 1990s. More information can be found on the firm's website, http://www.sternstewart.com/evaabout/whatis.php.

[3] Stephen Taub, "MVPs of MVA," *CFO Magazine* (July 1, 2003), http://www.cfo.com/article/1,5309,9854%7C22%7CA%7C14%7C,00.html (accessed December 13, 2006).

[4] The computation of a company's actual cost of capital is reserved for advanced accounting courses.

The HOW and WHY of Calculating Economic Value Added

CORNERSTONE 12-3

Information:
Celimar Company's Ontario Division earned net income last year as shown in the following income statement:

Sales	$480,000
Cost of goods sold	222,000
Gross margin	$258,000
Selling and administrative expense	210,000
Operating income	$ 48,000
Less: Income taxes (@ 30%)	14,400
Net income	$ 33,600

Total capital employed equalled $300,000. Celimar Company's actual cost of capital is 10 percent.

Required:
Calculate EVA for the Ontario Division.

Solution:

EVA = After-tax operating income − (Actual percentage cost of capital × Total capital employed)
= $33,600 − (0.10 × $300,000)
= $33,600 − $30,000
= $3,600

WHY:
Economic value added is a measurement tool that some companies employ to allow them to reflect the actual cost of capital in the residual income type of calculation.

an EVA analysis. Without an EVA analysis, the result is to make investment seem free to the divisions, and of course, they want more. Not surprisingly, research indicates that more firms continue to adopt EVA measures as part of their overall performance evaluation package.[5] It should be cautioned, however, that research also shows that some firms that collect EVA measures struggle to integrate these relatively complex measures into managerial decision making without considerable training for the managers.[6]

Transfer Pricing

OBJECTIVE 4
Explain the role of transfer pricing in a decentralized firm.

In many decentralized organizations, the output of one division is used as the input of another. For example, assume that one division of **Sony** manufactures batteries for its VAIO computers, which in turn sells the batteries to another Sony division that uses them to complete the computer manufacturing process. This internal transfer between two divisions within Sony raises an accounting issue. How is the transferred

[5] Stern Stewart Research, "Stern Stewart's EVA Clients Outperform the Market and Their Peers," *EVAluation: Special Report* (October 2002).

[6] Alexander Mersereau, "Pushing the Art of Management Accounting," *CMA Management,* Volume 79, Issue 9 (February 1, 2006).

perspective, the internal business process perspective, and the learning and growth (infrastructure) perspective. The **financial perspective** describes the economic consequences of actions taken in the other three perspectives. The **customer perspective** defines the customer and market segments in which the business unit will compete. The **internal business process perspective** describes the internal processes needed to provide value for customers and owners. Finally, the **learning and growth (infrastructure) perspective** defines the capabilities that an organization needs to create long-term growth and improvement. This last perspective is concerned with three major *enabling factors*: employee capabilities, information systems capabilities, and employee attitudes (motivation, empowerment, and alignment). Exhibit 12-6 shows a Balanced Scorecard for a typical hotel based on questionnaire data provided by a research survey of three- and four-star hotels.[8] The scorecard includes the four basic scorecard categories and objectives with key measures for each category.

Exhibit 12-6

Balanced Scorecard for Ashley Hotel*

Objective	*Measure*
Financial Perspective	
Operating Revenues	• Total daily operating revenue • Revenue per available room
Operating Costs	• Operating expenses relative to budget • Cost per occupant
Customer Perspective	
Customer Satisfaction	• Customer satisfaction ratings • Number of monthly complaints
Customer Loyalty	• Number of new reward club members • Percent of returning guests
Internal Perspective	
Employee Turnover	• Employee turnover rate • Number of employee complaints
Response to Customer Complaints	• Percentage of complaints receiving response • Average response time
Learning and Growth	
New Market Identification	• Growth in reward club membership for new demographic segments
Employee Training and Advancement	• Percentage of employees participating in training courses • Survey scores pre- and post-training sessions

*Measures are based on survey data reported from actual hotels—N. Evans, "Assessing the Balanced Scorecard as a Management Tool for Hotels," *International Journal of Contemporary Hospitality Management*. Vol. 17 (Issue 4/5): 376–390.

[8] N. Evans, "Assessing the Balanced Scorecard as a Management Tool for Hotels," *International Journal of Contemporary Hospitality Management*, Vol. 17 (Issue 4/5, 2005): 376–390.

Strategy Translation

Strategy, according to the creators of the Balanced Scorecard framework, is defined as:[9]

> choosing the market and customer segments the business unit intends to serve, identifying the critical internal and business processes that the unit must excel at to deliver the value propositions to customers in the targeted market segments, and selecting the individual and organizational capabilities required for the internal, customer, and financial objectives.

Strategy specifies management's desired relationships among the four perspectives. *Strategy translation*, on the other hand, means specifying objectives, measures, targets, and initiatives for each perspective. Consider, for example, the financial perspective. For the financial perspective, a company's *objective* may be to grow revenues by introducing new products. The *performance measure* may be the percentage of revenues from the sale of new products. The *target* or *standard* for the coming year for the measure may be 20 percent (i.e., 20 percent of the total revenues for the coming year *must* be from the sale of new products). The *initiative* describes *how* this is to be accomplished. The "how," of course, involves the other three perspectives. The company must now identify the customer segments, internal processes, and individual and organizational capabilities that will permit the realization of the revenue growth objective. This illustrates the fact that the financial objectives serve as the focus for the objectives, measures, and initiatives of the other three perspectives.

The Role of Performance Measures The Balanced Scorecard is not simply a collection of critical performance measures. The performance measures are derived from a company's vision, strategy, and objectives. These measures must be *balanced* between performance driver measures (i.e., lead indicators of future financial performance) and outcome measures (i.e., lagged indicators of financial performance), between objective and subjective measures, between external and internal measures, and between financial and nonfinancial measures. The performance measures must also be carefully *linked* to the organization's strategy. Doing so creates significant advantages for an organization. For example, each quarter, **Analog Devices**' senior managers gather to discuss Balanced Scorecard results for the various divisions. On one occasion, managers noted problems with their new-product ratios—used to measure the effectiveness of R&D spending. They quickly discovered that one division lagged in developing new products. The division's manager focused heavily on R&D by investing more money and exploring new market segments, new product sales, and marketing strategies. Analog Devices' corporate vice president for marketing, quality, and planning noted that they wouldn't have been able to catch the problem so early if they just looked at financials.[10] Other companies, such as **Bank of Montreal**, **Hilton Hotels Corporation**, Verizon Communications, **Duke University Children's Hospital**, **NatWest Bancorp**, and **AT&T Canada LDS**, have had similar success. The rapid and widespread adoption of this strategic management system is a strong testimonial of its worth. For example, companies like General Electric, Verizon, and **Microsoft** have adapted their initial Balanced Scorecards into risk dashboards that contain key financial and nonfinancial measures pertaining to the important risks that threaten organizational success.[11] In addition, other organizations, like Wal-Mart, adapt their Balanced Scorecards to include measures that help their suppliers focus on increasingly important sustainability issues like using less packaging materials and more effective packaging techniques.[12]

[9] Robert S. Kaplan and David P. Norton, *The Balanced Scorecard* (Boston: Harvard Business School Press, 1996), p. 37.

[10] Joel Kurtzman, "Is Your Company Off Course: Now You Can Find Out Why," *Fortune* (February 17, 1997), http://money.cnn.com/magazines/fortune/fortune_archive/1997/02/17/222180/index.htm (accessed December 13, 2006).

[11] Ante Spencer, "Giving the Boss the Big Picture," *Business Week* (February 13, 2006).

[12] "Getting Leaner—Ahead of the Pack: Suppliers Adjust to New Packaging Priorities," *Retailing Today* (2006): 16–18.

Linking Performance Measures to Strategy Balancing outcome measures with performance drivers is essential to linking with the organization's strategy. Performance drivers make things happen and are indicators of how the outcomes are going to be realized. Thus, they tend to be unique to a particular strategy. Outcome measures are also important because they reveal whether the strategy is being implemented successfully with the desired economic consequences. For example, if the number of defective products is decreased, does this produce a greater market share? Does this, in turn, produce more revenues and profits? These questions suggest that the most important principle of linkage is the usage of cause-and-effect relationships. In fact, a **testable strategy** can be defined as a set of linked objectives aimed at an overall goal. The testability of the strategy is achieved by restating the strategy into a set of cause-and-effect hypotheses that are expressed by a sequence of if-then statements.[13] Consider, for example, the following sequence of if-then statements that link quality training with increased profitability:

> If design engineers receive quality training, then they can redesign products to reduce the number of defective units; if the number of defective units is reduced, then customer satisfaction will increase; if customer satisfaction increases, then market share will increase; if market share increases, then sales will increase; if sales increase, then profits will increase.

Exhibit 12-7 illustrates the quality improvement strategy described by a sequence of if-then statements. First, notice how each of the four perspectives is linked through the cause-and-effect relationships hypothesized. The learning and growth perspective is present through the training dimension; the process perspective is represented by the redesign and manufacturing processes; the customer perspective is represented by customer satisfaction and market share; and, finally, the financial perspective is present because of revenues and profits. Second, viability of the strategy is testable. Strategic feedback is available that allows managers to test the reasonableness of the strategy. Hours of training, the number of products redesigned, the number of defective units,

Exhibit 12-7

Testable Strategy Illustrated

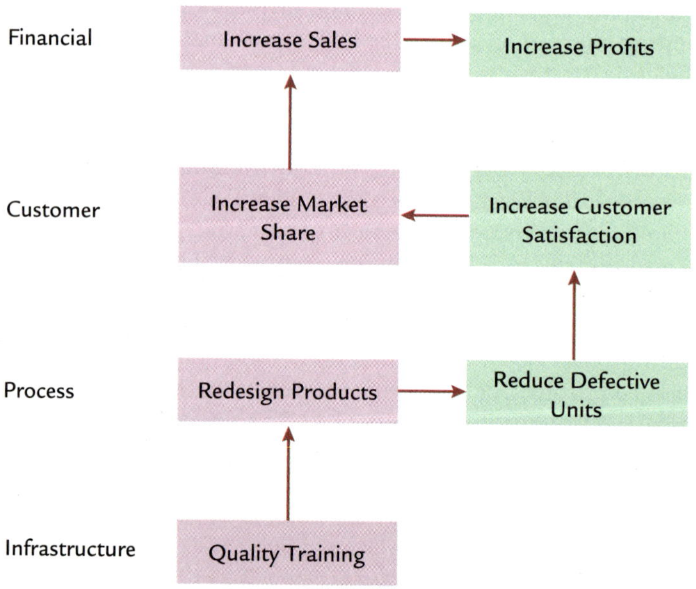

[13] Robert S. Kaplan and David P. Norton, *The Balanced Scorecard* (Boston: Harvard Business School Press, 1996), p. 149. (Kaplan and Norton describe the sequence of if-then statements only as a strategy. Calling it a testable strategy distinguishes it from the earlier, more general definition offered, and, in our opinion, properly so.)

customer satisfaction, market share, revenues, and profits are all observable measures. Thus, the claimed relationships can be checked to see if the strategy produces the expected results. If not, it could be due to one of two causes: (1) implementation problems or (2) an invalid strategy. First, it is possible that key *performance drivers* such as training and redesign of products did not achieve their targeted levels (i.e., fewer hours of training and fewer products redesigned than planned). In this case, the failure to produce the targeted *outcomes* for defects, customer satisfaction, market share, revenues, and profits could be merely an implementation problem. On the other hand, if the targeted levels of performance drivers were achieved and the expected outcomes did not materialize, then the problem could very well lie with the strategy itself. This is an example of *double-loop feedback*. **Double-loop feedback** occurs whenever managers receive information about both the *effectiveness* of strategy implementation as well as the *validity* of the assumptions underlying the strategy. In a functional-based responsibility accounting system, typically only *single-loop feedback* is provided. **Single-loop feedback** emphasizes only effectiveness of implementation. In single-loop feedback, actual results deviating from planned results are a signal to take corrective action so that the plan (strategy) can be executed as intended. The validity of the assumptions underlying the plan is usually not questioned.

The Four Perspectives and Performance Measures

The four perspectives define the strategy of an organization. Furthermore, the example of if-then statements illustrates that the four perspectives provide the structure or framework for developing an integrated, cohesive set of performance measures. These measures, once developed, become the means for articulating and communicating the strategy of the organization to its employees and managers. The measures also serve the purpose of aligning individual objectives and actions with organizational objectives and initiatives. Given the role the four perspectives play in development of performance measures, a more detailed examination of the perspectives is warranted.

The Financial Perspective

The financial perspective establishes the long- and short-term financial performance objectives. The financial perspective is concerned with the global financial consequences of the other three perspectives. Thus, the objectives and measures of the other perspectives must be linked to the financial objectives. The financial perspective has three strategic themes: revenue growth, cost reduction, and asset utilization. These themes serve as the building blocks for the development of specific operational objectives and measures.

Revenue Growth Several possible objectives are associated with revenue growth, including (1) increase the number of new products, (2) create new applications for existing products, (3) develop new customers and markets, and (4) adopt a new pricing strategy. Once operational objectives are known, performance measures can be designed. For example, possible measures for the above list of objectives (in the order given) are percentage of revenue from new products, percentage of revenue from new applications, percentage of revenue from new customers and market segments, and profitability by product or customer.

Cost Reduction Reducing the cost per unit of product, per customer, or per distribution channel are examples of cost reduction objectives. The appropriate measure is obvious: the cost per unit of the particular cost object. Trends in this measure will tell whether the costs are being reduced or not. For these objectives, the accuracy of cost assignments is especially important. Activity-based costing can play an essential measurement role, especially for selling and administrative costs—costs not usually assigned to cost objects like customers and distribution channels.

Asset Utilization Improving asset utilization is the principal objective. Financial measures such as return on investment and economic value added are used. The objectives and measures for the financial perspective are summarized in Exhibit 12-8.

Exhibit 12-8

Summary of Objectives and Measures: Financial Perspective

Objectives	Measures
Revenue Growth:	
Increase the number of new products	Percentage of revenue from new products
Create new applications	Percentage of revenue from new applications
Develop new customers and markets	Percentage of revenue from new sources
Adopt a new pricing strategy	Product and customer profitability
Cost Reduction:	
Reduce unit product cost	Unit product cost
Reduce unit customer cost	Unit customer cost
Reduce distribution channel cost	Cost per distribution channel
Asset Utilization:	
Improve asset utilization	Return on investment
	Economic value added

Customer Perspective The customer perspective is the source of the revenue component for the financial objectives. This perspective defines and selects the customer and market segments in which the company chooses to compete.

Core Objectives and Measures Once the customers and segments are defined, then *core objectives and measures* are developed. **Core objectives and measures** are those that are common across all organizations. The five key core objectives are to (1) increase market share, (2) increase customer retention, (3) increase customer acquisition, (4) increase customer satisfaction, and (5) increase customer profitability. Possible core measures for these objectives, respectively, are market share (percentage of the market), percentage growth of business from existing customers and percentage of repeating customers, number of new customers, ratings from customer satisfaction surveys, and individual and segment profitability. Activity-based costing is a key tool in assessing customer profitability (Chapter 7). Notice that customer profitability is the only financial measure among the core measures. This measure, however, is critical because it emphasizes the importance of the *right* kind of customers. What good is it to have customers if they are not profitable? The obvious answer spells out the difference between being customer focused and customer obsessed.

Customer Value In addition to the core measures and objectives, measures are needed that drive the creation of *customer value* and, thus, drive the core outcomes. For example, increasing customer value builds customer loyalty (increases retention) and increases customer satisfaction. **Customer value** is the difference between realization and sacrifice, where realization is what the customer receives and sacrifice is what is given up in return. Realization includes such things as product functionality (features), product quality, reliability of delivery, delivery response time, image, and reputation. Sacrifice includes product price, time to learn to use the product, operating cost, maintenance cost, and disposal cost. The costs incurred by the customer *after* purchase are called **postpurchase costs**.

The attributes associated with the realization and sacrifice value propositions provide the basis for the objectives and measures that will lead to improving the core outcomes. The objectives for the sacrifice value proposition are the simplest: decrease price and decrease postpurchase costs. Selling price and postpurchase costs are important measures of value creation. Decreasing these costs decreases customer sacrifice and, thus, increases customer value. Increasing customer value should impact favourably on most of the core objectives. Similar favourable effects can be obtained by increasing realization. Realization objectives, for example, would include the following: improve product functionality, improve product quality, increase delivery reliability, and improve product image and reputation. Possible measures for these objectives include, respectively, feature satisfaction ratings, percentage of returns, on-time delivery percentage, and product recognition ratings. Of these objectives and measures, delivery reliability will be used to illustrate how measures can affect managerial behaviour, indicating the need to be careful in the choice and use of performance measures.

Delivery reliability means that output is delivered on time. On-time delivery is a commonly used operational measure of reliability. To measure on-time delivery, a firm sets delivery dates and then calculates on-time delivery performance by dividing the orders delivered on time by the total number of orders delivered. The goal, of course, is to achieve a ratio of 100 percent. Some, however, have found that use of this measure may produce undesirable behavioural consequences.[14] Specifically, plant managers were giving priority to filling orders not yet late over orders that were already late. The performance measure was encouraging managers to have one very late shipment rather than several moderately late shipments! A chart measuring the age of late deliveries could help mitigate this problem. Exhibit 12-9 summarizes the objectives and measures for the customer perspective.

Process Perspective

Processes are the means for creating customer and shareholder value. Thus, the process perspective entails the identification of the processes needed to achieve the customer and financial objectives. To provide the framework needed for this perspective, a *process value chain* is defined. The **process value chain** is made up of three processes: the *innovation process*, the *operations process*, and the *postsales service process*. The **innovation process** anticipates the emerging and potential needs of customers and creates new products and services to satisfy those needs. It represents what is called the *long-wave* of value creation. The **operations process** produces and delivers *existing* products and services to customers. It begins with a customer order and ends with the delivery of the product or service. It is the *short-wave* of value creation. The **postsales service process** provides critical and responsive services to customers after the product or service has been delivered.

Innovation Process: Objectives and Measures

Objectives for the innovation process include the following: (1) increase the number of new products, (2) increase

Exhibit 12-9

Summary of Objectives and Measures: Customer Perspective

Objectives	Measures
Core:	
Increase market share	Market share (percentage of market)
Increase customer retention	Percentage growth of business from existing customers
	Percentage of repeating customers
Increase customer acquisition	Number of new customers
Increase customer satisfaction	Ratings from customer surveys
Increase customer profitability	Customer profitability
Performance Value:	
Decrease price	Price
Decrease postpurchase costs	Postpurchase costs
Improve product functionality	Ratings from customer surveys
Improve product quality	Percentage of returns
Increase delivery reliability	On-time delivery percentage
	Aging schedule
Improve product image and reputation	Ratings from customer surveys

[14] Joseph Fisher, "Nonfinancial Performance Measures," *Journal of Cost Management* (Spring 1992): 31–38.

CORNERSTONE 12-5

The HOW and WHY of Computing Cycle Time and Velocity

Information:
A company has the following data for one of its manufacturing cells:

Maximum units produced in a quarter (3-month period): 200,000 units
Actual units produced in a quarter: 160,000 units
Productive hours in one quarter: 40,000 hours

Required:
1. Compute the theoretical cycle time (in minutes).
2. Compute the actual cycle time (in minutes).
3. Compute the theoretical velocity in units per hour.
4. Compute the actual velocity in units per hour.

Solution:
1. Theoretical cycle time = (40,000 hours)(60 minutes per hour)/200,000 units
   = 12 minutes per unit
2. Actual cycle time = (40,000 hours)(60 per hour)/160,000 units
   = 15 minutes per unit
3. Theoretical velocity = 60 minutes per hour/12 minutes per unit
   = 5 units per hour
4. Actual velocity = 60 minutes per hour/15 minutes per unit
   = 4 units per hour

WHY:
Cycle time and velocity are two important concepts in analyzing a company's performance. These results can assist managers in understanding where the manufacturing process is performing well or poorly and lead to corrective actions being taken.

percentage of revenue from proprietary products, and (3) decrease the time to develop new products. Associated measures are actual new products developed versus planned products, percentage of total revenues from new products, percentage of revenues from proprietary products, and development cycle time (time to market).

Operations Process: Objectives and Measures The three operations process objectives that are almost always mentioned and emphasized include the following: (1) increase process quality, (2) increase process efficiency, and (3) decrease process time. Examples of process quality measures are quality costs, output yields (good output/good input), and percentage of defective units (good output/total output). Measures of process efficiency are concerned mainly with process cost and process productivity. Activity-based costing and process-value analysis facilitate measuring and tracking process costs. Common process time measures are cycle time, velocity, and manufacturing cycle effectiveness (MCE).

Cycle Time and Velocity

The time to respond to a customer order is referred to as *responsiveness. Cycle time* and *velocity* are two operational measures of responsiveness. **Cycle time** is the length of time it takes to produce a unit of output from the time raw materials are received (starting point of the cycle) until the good is delivered to finished goods inventory (finishing point of the cycle). Thus, cycle time is the time required to produce a product (time/units produced). **Velocity** is the number of units of output that can be produced in a given period of time (units produced/time). Cornerstone 12-5 shows how to compute cycle time and velocity.

Incentives can be used to encourage operational managers to reduce manufacturing cycle time or to increase velocity, thus improving delivery performance. A natural way to accomplish this objective is to tie product costs to cycle time and reward operational managers for reducing product costs. For example, in a just-in-time (JIT) firm, conversion costs of the cell can be assigned to products on the basis of the time that it takes a product to move through the cell. Using the theoretical productive time available for a period (in minutes), a value-added standard cost per minute can be computed.

$$\text{Standard cost per minute} = \frac{\text{Cell conversion costs}}{\text{Minutes available}}$$

To obtain the conversion cost per unit, this standard cost per minute is multiplied by the actual cycle time used to produce the units during the period. By comparing the unit cost computed using the actual cycle time with the unit cost possible using the theoretical or optimal cycle time, a manager can assess the potential for improvement. Note that the more time it takes a product to move through the cell, the greater the unit product cost. With incentives to reduce product cost, this approach to product costing encourages operational managers and cell workers to find ways to decrease cycle time or increase velocity.

Manufacturing Cycle Efficiency

Another time-based operational measure calculates **MCE (manufacturing cycle efficiency)**. MCE is measured as value-added time divided by total time. Total time includes both value-added time (the time spent efficiently producing the product) and non-value-added time (such as move time, inspection time, and waiting time). The formula for computing MCE is:

$$MCE = \frac{\text{Processing time}}{\text{Processing time} + \text{Move time} + \text{Inspection time} + \text{Waiting time}}$$

In this equation, processing time is the time that it takes to convert raw materials into a finished good. The other activities and their times are viewed as wasteful, and the goal is to reduce those times to zero. If this is accomplished, the value of MCE will be 1.0, or 100 percent. As MCE improves (moves toward 1.0), cycle time decreases. Furthermore, since the only way MCE can improve is by decreasing waste, cost reduction must also follow. Cornerstone 12-6 shows how to calculate MCE.

Actually, Cornerstone 12-6 illustrates a fairly efficient process, as measured by MCE. Many manufacturing companies have MCEs less than 0.05.[15]

Postsales Service Process: Objectives and Measures

Increasing quality, increasing efficiency, and decreasing process time are also objectives that apply to the postsales service process. Service quality, for example, can be measured by first-pass yields, where first-pass yields are defined as the percentage of customer requests resolved with a single service call. Efficiency can be measured by cost trends and productivity measures. Process time can be measured by cycle time, where the starting point of the cycle is defined as the receipt of a customer request, and the finishing point is when the customer's problem is solved. The objectives and measures for the process perspective are summarized in Exhibit 12-10.

Learning and Growth Perspective

The learning and growth perspective is the source of the capabilities that enable the accomplishment of the other three perspectives' objectives. This perspective has three major objectives: (1) increase employee capabilities; (2) increase motivation, empowerment, and alignment; and (3) increase information systems capabilities.

Employee Capabilities

Three core *outcome* measurements for employee capabilities are employee satisfaction ratings, employee turnover percentages, and employee productivity (e.g., revenue per employee). Examples of lead measures or performance drivers for employee capabilities are hours of training and strategic job coverage ratios (percentage

[15] Robert S. Kaplan and David P. Norton, *The Balanced Scorecard* (Boston: Harvard Business School Press, 1996), p. 117.

CORNERSTONE 12-6

The HOW and WHY of Calculating Manufacturing Cycle Efficiency

Information:

A company provided the following information:

Maximum units produced in a quarter (3-month period): 200,000 units
Actual units produced in a quarter: 160,000 units
Productive hours in one quarter: 40,000 hours
Actual cycle time = 15 minutes
Theoretical cycle time = 12 minutes

Required:

1. Calculate the amount of processing time and the amount of nonprocessing time.
2. Calculate MCE.

Solution:

1. Processing time is equal to theoretical cycle time. That is, if everything goes smoothly and there is no wasted time, it takes 12 minutes to produce one unit. Nonprocessing time, therefore, must be the difference between actual cycle time (which includes some waste) and theoretical cycle time.

   Processing time = Theoretical cycle time = 12 minutes

   Nonprocessing time = Actual cycle time − Theoretical cycle time
   = 15 − 12 = 3 minutes

2. MCE = Processing time/(Processing time + Nonprocessing time)
   = 12/(12 + 3) = 0.8, or 80 percent

WHY:

Manufacturing cycle efficiency will tell us how closely we are tracking the objectives of the production process. This knowledge helps managers pinpoint problem areas.

Exhibit 12-10

Summary of Objectives and Measures: Process Perspective

Objectives	Measures
Innovation:	
Increase the number of new products	Number of new products vs. planned
Increase proprietary products	Percentage revenue from proprietary products
Decrease new product development time	Time to market (from start to finish)
Operations:	
Increase process quality	Quality costs
	Output yields
	Percentage of defective units
Increase process efficiency	Unit cost trends
	Output/input(s)
Decrease process time	Cycle time and velocity
	MCE
Postsales Service:	
Increase service quality	First-pass yields
Increase service efficiency	Cost trends
	Output/input
Decrease service time	Cycle time

Exhibit 12-11

Summary of Objectives and Measures: Learning and Growth Perspective

Objectives	Measures
Increase employee capabilities	Employee satisfaction ratings Employee turnover percentages Employee productivity (revenue/employee) Hours of training Strategic job coverage ratio (percentage of critical job requirements filled)
Increase motivation and alignment	Suggestions per employee Suggestions implemented per employee
Increase information systems capabilities	Percentage of processes with real-time feedback capabilities Percentage of customer-facing employees with online access to customer and product information

of critical job requirements filled). As new processes are created, new skills are often required. Training and hiring are sources of these new skills. Furthermore, the percentage of the employees needed in certain key areas with the requisite skills signals the capability of the organization to meet the objectives of the other three perspectives.

Motivation, Empowerment, and Alignment Employees must not only have the necessary skills, but they must also have the freedom, motivation, and initiative to use those skills effectively. The number of suggestions per employee and the number of suggestions implemented per employee are possible measures of motivation and empowerment. Suggestions per employee provide a measure of the degree of employee involvement, whereas suggestions implemented per employee signal the quality of the employee participation. The second measure also signals to employees whether or not their suggestions are being taken seriously.

Information Systems Capabilities Increasing information system capabilities means providing more accurate and timely information to employees so that they can improve processes and effectively execute new processes. Measures should be concerned with the *strategic information availability*. For example, possible measures include percentage of processes with real-time feedback capabilities and percentage of customer-facing employees with online access to customer and product information. Exhibit 12-11 summarizes the objectives and measures for the learning and growth perspective.

Summary of Learning Objectives

LO1. Explain how and why firms choose to decentralize.

- In a decentralized organization, lower-level managers make and implement decisions. In a centralized organization, lower-level managers are responsible only for implementing decisions.
- Reasons why companies decentralize:
  - Local managers can make better decisions using local information.
  - Local managers can provide a more timely response.
  - It is impossible for any one central manager to be fully knowledgeable about all products and markets.
- Decentralization can train and motivate local managers and free top management from day-to-day operating conditions so that they can spend time on

Here's The Real Kicker

Some time ago, the loan officer at Kicker's bank left for another job out of province. This was an excellent time for Kicker to re-evaluate its banking relationship. The company took a number of bids from the four major banks in town. In the process, Kicker executives learned a great deal about various banking services and the way that banks charged for them. Some examples include Internet service, loan rates, credit card transactions, returned cheque fees, and wire transfer fees. Qualitative factors played a role in the ultimate decision. For example, how quickly does the bank respond? Does Kicker feel comfortable with its banking officer (is she or he knowledgeable about the speaker and electronics industry and attuned to Kicker's special needs)? After weighing both the monetary and nonmonetary factors, Kicker switched banks.

KICKER®

Decision making is a key part of management. Often, it is useful to consider decision making as either long run or short run. Long-run decision making, often involving investment in property, plant, and equipment, is referred to as *capital budgeting*. That topic is covered in Chapter 14. The use of cost and revenue data in making short-run decisions, such as the acceptance of special orders or choosing to outsource the production of parts rather than make them in-house, is the focus of this chapter.

OBJECTIVE 1

Describe the short-run decision-making model, and explain how cost behaviour affects the information used to make decisions.

Short-Run Decision Making

Short-run decision making consists of choosing among alternatives with an immediate or limited end in view. Accepting a special order for less than the normal selling price to utilize idle capacity and to increase this year's profits is an example. Thus, some decisions tend to be *short run* in nature; however, it should be emphasized that short-run decisions often have long-run consequences. Consider a second example. Suppose that a company is thinking about producing a component instead of buying it from suppliers. The immediate objective may be to lower the cost of making the main product. Yet this decision may be a small part of the overall strategy of establishing a cost leadership position for the firm. Therefore, short-run decisions are often *small-scale actions* that serve a larger purpose.

The Decision-Making Model

How does a company go about making good short-run decisions? A **decision model**, a specific set of procedures that produces a decision, can be used to structure the decision maker's thinking and to organize the information to make a good decision. The following is an outline of one decision-making model.

1. Recognize and define the problem.
2. Identify alternatives as possible solutions to the problem; eliminate alternatives that clearly are not feasible.
3. Identify the costs and benefits associated with each feasible alternative. Classify costs and benefits as relevant or irrelevant, and eliminate irrelevant ones from consideration.
4. Estimate the relevant costs and benefits for each alternative.
5. Assess qualitative factors.
6. Make the decision by selecting the alternative with the greatest overall net benefit.

The decision-making model described has six steps. Nothing is special about this particular listing. You may find it more useful to break the steps into 8 or 10 segments. Alternatively, you may find it useful to aggregate them into a shorter list. For example, you could use a three-step model: (1) identify the decision, (2) identify alternatives and their associated relevant costs, and (3) make the decision. The key point is to find a comfortable way for you to remember the important steps in the decision-making model.

To illustrate the decision-making model, consider Audio-Blast Inc., a company that manufactures speaker systems for new automobiles. Recently, Audio-Blast was approached by a major automobile manufacturer about the possibility of installing 20,000 of Audio-Blast's main product—the mega-blast speaker system—into its new sports car. That way, Audio-Blast speakers would be installed at the factory. Suppose that Audio-Blast Inc. decides to pursue the speaker order from the automobile manufacturer. Currently, the company does not have sufficient productive and storage capacity to fulfill the order. How might the decision-making model help Audio-Blast find the best way of obtaining that capacity?

Step 1: Define the Problem

The first step is to recognize and define a specific problem. For example, the members of Audio-Blast's management team recognized the need for additional productive capacity as well as increased space for raw materials and finished goods inventories. The number of workers and the amount of space needed, the reasons for the need, and how the additional space would be used are all important dimensions of the problem. However, the central question is *how* to acquire the additional capacity.

Step 2: Identify the Alternatives

The second step is to list and consider possible solutions. Suppose that the production head and the consulting engineer identified the following possible solutions:

1. Build a new factory with sufficient capacity to handle current and foreseeable needs.
2. Lease a larger facility, and sublease its current facility.
3. Lease an additional, similar facility.
4. Institute a second shift in the main factory, and lease an additional building that would be used for storage of raw materials and finished goods inventories only, thereby freeing up space for expanded production.
5. Outsource production to another company, and resell the speakers to the auto manufacturer.

As part of this step, Audio-Blast's upper management team met to discuss and eliminate alternatives that clearly were not feasible. The first alternative was eliminated because it carried too much risk for the company. The order had not even been secured, and the popularity of the new sports car model was not proven. Audio-Blast's president refused to "bet the company" on such a risky proposition. The second alternative was rejected because the economy in Audio-Blast's small town was such that subleasing a facility of its size was not possible. The third alternative was eliminated because it went too far in solving the space problem and, presumably, was too expensive. The fourth and fifth alternatives were feasible; they were within the cost and risk constraints and solved the needs of the company. Notice that the president linked the short-run decision (increase productive capacity) to the company's overall growth strategy by rejecting alternatives that involved too much risk at this stage of the company's development.

Step 3: Identify the Costs and Benefits Associated with Each Feasible Alternative

In the third step, the costs and benefits associated with each feasible alternative are identified. At this point, clearly irrelevant costs can be eliminated from consideration. (It is fine to include irrelevant costs and benefits in the analysis as long as they are included for all alternatives. The reason we usually do not include them is that focusing only on the relevant costs and benefits reduces the amount of data to be collected.) Typically, the controller is responsible for gathering necessary data.

Assume that Audio-Blast determines that the costs of making the 20,000 speakers include the following:

Direct materials	$ 60,000
Direct labour	110,000
Variable overhead	10,000
Total variable production cost	$180,000

In addition, a second shift must be put in place and a warehouse must be leased to store raw materials and finished goods inventories if Audio-Blast continues to manufacture the speakers internally. Additional costs of the second shift, including a production supervisor and part-time maintenance and engineering, amount to $90,000 per year. A building that could serve as a warehouse is sitting empty across the street and can be rented for $20,000 per year. Costs of operating the building for inventory storage, including telephone and Internet access as well as salaries of materials handlers, would amount to $80,000 per year. The second alternative is to purchase the speakers externally and use the freed-up production space for inventory. An outside supplier has offered to supply sufficient volume for $360,000 per year.

It should be mentioned that when the cash flow patterns become complicated for competing alternatives, it becomes difficult to produce a stream of equal cash flows for each alternative. In such a case, more sophisticated procedures can and should be used for the analysis. These procedures are discussed in Chapter 14, which deals with the long-run investment decisions referred to as *capital expenditure decisions.*

Step 4: Estimate the Relevant Costs and Benefits for Each Feasible Alternative

We now see that the fourth alternative—continuing to produce internally and leasing more space—costs $370,000, while the fifth alternative—purchasing outside and using internal space—costs $360,000. The comparison follows:

Alternative 4		Alternative 5	
Variable cost of production	$180,000	Purchase price	$360,000
Added second shift costs	90,000		
Building lease and operating costs	100,000		
Total	$370,000		

The **differential cost** is the difference between the summed costs of two alternatives in a decision. Notice that the differential cost is $10,000 in favour of the fifth alternative. Typically, a differential cost compares the sum of each alternative's *relevant* costs only, as in the differential cost comparison of alternatives 4 and 5. Emphasis on differential cost allows decision makers to occasionally include irrelevant costs in the alternatives if they choose to do so. However, the inclusion of irrelevant costs is acceptable *only if all irrelevant costs are included for each alternative.* For example, suppose that the controller had included fixed manufacturing cost that must be paid whether or not the speakers are made internally or externally. Then, the total cost of each alternative would increase, but the differential cost would still be $10,000. Again, as noted earlier in the chapter, it is recommended to compare only relevant costs because the inclusion of irrelevant costs often adds unnecessary data collection expenses and confusion in communicating additional information that is not relevant to the given analysis.

Step 5: Assess the Qualitative Factors

While the costs and revenues associated with the alternatives are important, they do not tell the whole story. Qualitative factors can significantly affect the manager's decision. Qualitative factors are simply those factors that are hard to put a number on.

For example, companies like **Ford Motor Company** and **Levi's** that relocate some or all of their U.S. manufacturing facilities to countries outside of the U.S. with cheaper labour often face stiff political pressure in the United States as a result of such offshoring decisions. Some managers worry that such political pressure from customers can have long-term negative effects on sales that more than offset the labour cost savings that spurred the decision to offshore. Product safety represents another key qualitative factor for outsourcing organizations, as illustrated by the trouble **Mattel** encountered when it was discovered that its Chinese suppliers used illegal lead paint on thousands of its toys.

Returning to Audio-Blast, its president likely would be concerned with qualitative considerations such as the quality of the speakers purchased externally, the reliability of supply sources, the expected stability of prices over the next several years, labour relations, community image, and so on. To illustrate the possible impact of qualitative factors on Audio-Blast's decision, consider the first two factors, quality and reliability of supply. If the quality of speakers is significantly less when purchased externally from what is available internally, then the quantitative advantage from purchasing may be more fictitious than real. Reselling lower-quality speakers to such a high-profile buyer could permanently damage Audio-Blast's reputation. Because of this possibility, Audio-Blast may choose to continue to produce the speakers internally. Similarly, if supply sources are not reliable, production schedules could be interrupted, and customer orders could arrive late. These factors can increase labour costs and overhead and hurt sales. Again, depending on the perceived trade-offs, Audio-Blast may decide that producing the speakers internally is better than purchasing them, even if relevant cost analysis gives the initial advantage to purchasing.

How should qualitative factors be handled in the decision-making process? First, they must be identified. Secondly, the decision maker should try to quantify them. Often, qualitative factors are simply more difficult to quantify, not impossible. For example, possible unreliability of the outside supplier might be quantified as the probable number of late delivery days multiplied by the penalty Audio Blast would be charged by the auto manufacturer for later delivery. More difficult measurement challenges exist. For example, **Mobil Corporation** decided to implement a strategic change of focusing on a new target audience, including "road warriors" (employees who drive a lot), "true blues" (affluent, loyal customers), and generation F3 (yuppies on the go who want fuel, want food, and want them fast).[1] However, successful implementation required that the company find a way to measure the experience of new target customers at newly designed Mobil gas pumps and convenience stores. After considerable thought, an innovative manager developed one of the first recognized "secret shopper" programs in which Mobil employees secretly dressed as customers in order to live the Mobil gas station "experience." These secret shoppers then recorded numerous aspects of their experience on quantitative scales for feedback to station managers. Without such evaluative data, it would have been extremely difficult for Mobil managers to assess the causes of success or failure of the new strategy implementation. Finally, truly qualitative factors, such as the impact of late orders on customer relations, must be taken into consideration in the final step of the decision-making model—the selection of the alternative with the greatest overall benefit.

CONCEPT Q&A

Apply the decision-making model outlined in this section to a problem you have faced. For example, the problem might be whether or not to go to university or which car to buy. Include all of the steps. Will the application of the decision-making model help you to make the decision? Why or why not?

Answers on pages 711 to 715.

Step 6: Make the Decision

Once all relevant costs and benefits for each alternative have been assessed and the qualitative factors weighed, a decision can be made.

[1] Marc Epstein and Bill Birchard, *Counting What Counts: Turning Corporate Accountability to Competitive Advantage*. Perseus Books, New York, NY. 2000.

Ethics in Decision Making

ETHICS Ethical concerns revolve around the way in which decisions are implemented and the possible sacrifice of long-run objectives for short-run gain. Relevant costs are used in making short-run decisions. However, decision makers should always maintain an ethical framework. Reaching objectives is important, but how you get there is perhaps more important. Unfortunately, many managers have the opposite view. Part of the reason for the problem is the extreme pressure to perform that many managers face. Often, the individual who is not a top performer may be laid off or demoted. Under such conditions, the temptation is often great to engage in questionable behaviour today and to let the future take care of itself. Unfortunately, as the recent historic banking regulatory upheaval demonstrates, many U.S. financial services institutions in the mid-2000s yielded to unethical temptations to lend excessive amounts of money to prospective homeowners who in the end could not afford such loans. Whenever relevant costing is used, it is important to include all costs that are relevant—including those involving ethical ramifications.◆

Relevant Costs Defined

The decision-making approach just described emphasized the importance of identifying and using relevant costs. **Relevant costs** possess two characteristics: (1) they are *future* costs and (2) they *differ* across alternatives. All pending decisions relate to the future; accordingly, only future costs can be relevant to decisions. However, to be relevant, a cost must not only be a future cost but must also differ from one alternative to another. If a future cost is the same for more than one alternative, then it has no effect on the decision. Such a cost is *irrelevant*. The same relevance characteristics also apply to benefits. One alternative may produce an amount of future benefits different from another alternative (e.g., differences in future revenues). If future benefits differ across alternatives, then they are relevant and should be included in the analysis. The ability to identify relevant and irrelevant costs (and revenues) is a very important decision-making skill.

Relevant Costs Illustrated

To illustrate the concept of relevant costs, consider Audio-Blast's make-or-buy alternatives. The cost of direct labour to produce the additional 20,000 speakers is $110,000. Is the direct labour cost a future cost that differs across the two alternatives? It is certainly a future cost. Producing the speakers for the auto manufacturer requires the services of direct labourers who must be paid. But does it differ across the two alternatives? If the speakers are purchased from an external supplier, then a second shift, with its direct labour, will not be needed. Thus, the cost of direct labour differs across alternatives ($110,000 for the make alternative and $0 for the buy alternative). Therefore, it is a relevant cost.

Implicit in this analysis is the use of a past cost to estimate a future cost. The most recent cost of direct labour has averaged $5.50 per speaker; for 20,000 speakers, the direct labour will cost $110,000. This past cost was used as the estimate of next year's cost. Although past costs are never relevant, they often are used to predict what future costs will be.

Another type of relevant cost is opportunity cost. **Opportunity cost** is the benefit sacrificed or forgone when one alternative is chosen over another. Therefore, an opportunity cost is relevant because it is both a future cost and one that differs across alternatives. While an opportunity cost is never an accounting cost, because accountants do not record the cost of what might happen in the future (i.e., they do not appear in financial statements), it is an important consideration in decision making. For example, if you are deciding whether to work full time or to go to school full time, the opportunity cost of going to school would be the wages you give up by not working. Companies also include opportunity costs in many of their decision analyses. When **Ernst & Young** estimates the net benefit of sending thousands of its accountants to week-long training courses, it includes the opportunity cost of the tens of millions of dollars in lost revenue that it forgoes by not being able to bill clients for the time accountants spend in training. Oftentimes, opportunity costs are quite challenging to estimate. However, their inclusion can change the final result of the analysis, such as whether or not to accept a special sales opportunity or to outsource a product rather than make it in-house. Therefore, managerial accountants have the ability to add significant value to relevant decision making by finding ways to measure particularly challenging opportunity costs.

Irrelevant Past Cost Illustrated Audio-Blast uses large power saws to cut the lumber that forms the housings for speakers. These saws were purchased three years ago and are being depreciated at an annual rate of $25,000. Is this $25,000 a relevant cost? In other words, is depreciation a future cost that differs across the two alternatives?

Depreciation represents an allocation of a cost already incurred. It is a **sunk cost**, a cost that cannot be affected by any future action. Although we allocate this sunk cost to future periods and call that allocation depreciation, none of the original cost is avoidable. Sunk costs are always the same across alternatives and, therefore, always irrelevant.

Thus, depreciation costs, like all sunk costs, fail to possess the two characteristics required of relevant costs and, therefore, always are irrelevant. In choosing between the two alternatives, the original cost of the power saws and their associated depreciation are not relevant factors. However, it should be noted that salvage value of the machinery is a relevant cost for certain decisions. For example, if Audio-Blast decides to transform itself into a distributor, not a producer, of speakers, the amount that can be realized from the sale of the power equipment will be relevant and will be included as a benefit of the switch to distributor status.

Finally, it is important to note the psychology behind managers' treatment of sunk costs. Although managers *should ignore* sunk costs for relevant decisions, such as whether or not to continue funding a particular product in the future, it unfortunately is human nature to allow sunk costs to affect these decisions. For example, **Toshiba** and its HD DVD product team engaged in a fierce, multi-year battle with **Sony** and its Blu-ray product team for recognition as the universally accepted format in the growing next-generation high-definition DVD market. Throughout the battle, both sides spent millions of dollars developing, manufacturing, and advertising its own format. However, Sony's Blu-ray sales trounced Toshiba's HD DVD sales one Christmas shopping season, which prompted Hollywood giant **Warner Bros.** to decide to release its films only on Sony's Blu-ray format, rather than on both formats as it had done previously (the other major production companies had already sided with Sony as well). Around the same time, **Blockbuster Video** announced that it would only carry DVDs with the Blu-ray format. To objective entertainment business experts outside of Toshiba, these decisions by Warner Bros. and Blockbuster were the final blow to Toshiba's format and it was obvious that the HD DVD product line should be discontinued immediately to cut its losses and stop the financial bleeding. However, rather than ignore its significant sunk costs by cutting its future losses, Toshiba announced that it was "unwilling to concede defeat in the next-generation-DVD battle" and decided to launch an "aggressive advertising campaign to promote its [Toshiba's] HD DVD players and slash prices about 50%."[2] Therefore, not only did Toshiba continue to spend money developing, manufacturing, and marketing its failed product, it expected to earn only about half of the regular sales revenue per unit sold! Eventually, even Toshiba recognized the handwriting on the wall and dropped its HD DVD format, but only after throwing away a considerable amount of money on a product that most experts believed should have been dropped much earlier.

Another classic example of inappropriately honouring sunk costs is **Coca-Cola**'s New Coke debacle in the mid-1980s. The development and launching of New Coke was very costly and also an undeniably huge failure. However, Coca-Cola unwisely elected to continue to spend money to advertise and maintain its failed new product simply because it had already spent so much money on the product in the past. As business experts repeatedly noted, no amount of advertising cost was going to change the company's past expenditures to develop and launch New Coke and the company would have been far better off to scrap New Coke as soon as its failure was apparent.

[2] Michelle Kessler, "Toshiba Turns Up Heat in DVD War," *USA Today* (January 15, 2008): 4B.

The **XFL** football league in 2001 and the Concorde supersonic jet over a period of 20 years are additional examples of companies that failed to cut their losses and drop their product or service and instead continued to pour money into past failed ideas because of their large associated sunk costs.

Irrelevant Future Cost Illustrated Suppose that Audio-Blast currently pays an Internet provider $5,000 per year to store its website on the server. Since Audio-Blast intends to keep the Web page no matter what is decided regarding the potential speaker order, that cost is not relevant to the decision.

The same concepts apply to benefits. One alternative may produce an amount of future benefits different from another alternative (e.g., differences in future revenues). If future benefits differ across alternatives, then they are relevant and should be included in the analysis.

Cost Behaviour and Relevant Costs

Most short-run decisions require extensive consideration of cost behaviour. It is easy to fall into the trap of believing that variable costs are relevant and fixed costs are not. But this assumption is not true. For example, the variable costs of production were relevant to Audio-Blast's decision. The fixed costs associated with the existing factory were not relevant. However, the additional fixed cost of the supervisor for a second shift was relevant to the decision.

The key point is that changes in supply and demand for resources must be considered when assessing relevance. If changes in demand and supply for resources across alternatives bring about changes in spending, then the changes in resource spending are the relevant costs that should be used in assessing the relative desirability of the two alternatives.

Flexible resources can be easily purchased in the amount needed and at the time of use. For example, electricity used to run stoves that boil fruit in the production of jelly is a resource that can be acquired as used and needed. Thus, if the jelly manufacturer wants to increase production of jelly, electricity will increase just enough to satisfy that demand. This type of resource is typically referred to as a strictly variable cost.

Some resources are purchased before they are used. Clearly, investment in a factory of a particular size falls into this category; so does a year-to-year lease of office space or equipment. These costs usually are treated as fixed costs. If the decision covers a situation shorter than the time period for which the resource is fixed, then this cost usually is irrelevant.

Still other resources are acquired in advance of usage through implicit contracting; they are usually acquired in lumpy amounts. In Chapter 3, these costs were shown as step costs. This category may include an organization's salaried and hourly employees. The implicit understanding is that the organization will maintain employment levels even though there may be temporary downturns in the quantity of an activity used. This understanding means that an activity may have unused capacity available. Recall that the relevant range is important in considering step costs. As long as a company remains within the relevant range, it will not go up or down a step, so the cost is fixed for all intents and purposes. For example, assume that a company has three purchasing agents who can process 15,000 purchase orders a year. This assumption means that the existing staff can handle 45,000 purchase orders a year. If the company is processing only 40,000 purchase orders, then there is some unused capacity in purchasing. If the company is considering a special order that will require an additional 2,000 purchase orders, then there is no increased cost to purchasing. However, if the company considers an expansion that will require an additional 8,000 purchase orders per year, then additional staffing will be needed in purchasing.

OBJECTIVE 2
Apply relevant costing and decision-making concepts in a variety of business situations.

Some Common Relevant Cost Applications

Relevant costing is of value in solving many different types of problems. Traditionally, these applications include decisions to make or buy a component, to keep or drop a segment or product line, to accept a special order at less than the usual price, and to further process joint products or sell them at the split-off point. Though by no means an exhaustive list, many of the same decision-making principles apply to a variety of problems.

Make-or-Buy Decisions

Managers often are faced with the decision of whether to make a particular product or service or to buy it from an outside supplier. A manufacturer may need to consider whether to make or buy components used in manufacturing. A manager of a service firm may need to decide whether to provide a service in-house or to outsource it. Many services traditionally performed within the company, such as payroll processing, individual income tax form preparation, or human resources, are now being outsourced. **Make-or-buy decisions** are those decisions involving a choice between internal and external production. Exhibit 13-1 illustrates the make-or-buy decision.

To illustrate more fully the cost analysis of a make-or-buy problem, assume that Swasey Manufacturing currently produces an electronic component used in one of its printers. In one year, Swasey will switch production to another type of printer, and the electronic component will not be used. However, for the coming year, Swasey must produce 10,000 of these parts to support the production requirements for the old printer.

A potential supplier has approached Swasey about the component. The supplier will build the electronic component to Swasey's specifications for $4.75 per unit. The offer sounds very attractive since the full manufacturing cost per unit is $8.20. Should Swasey Manufacturing make or buy the component?

The problem and the feasible alternatives are both readily identifiable. Since the horizon for the decision is only one period, there is no need to be concerned about periodically recurring costs. Relevant costing is particularly useful for short-run analysis. We simply need to identify the relevant costs, total them, and make a choice (assuming no overriding qualitative concerns).

The full absorption cost of the component is computed as follows:

	Total Cost	Unit Cost
Direct materials	$10,000	$1.00
Direct labour	20,000	2.00
Variable overhead	8,000	0.80
Fixed overhead	44,000	4.40
Total	$82,000	$8.20

Fixed overhead consists of common factory costs that are allocated to each product line. No matter what happens to the component line, overall fixed overhead will not be affected. As a result, the fixed overhead is irrelevant; it can be safely ignored in structuring the problem.

Exhibit 13-1

Make or Buy

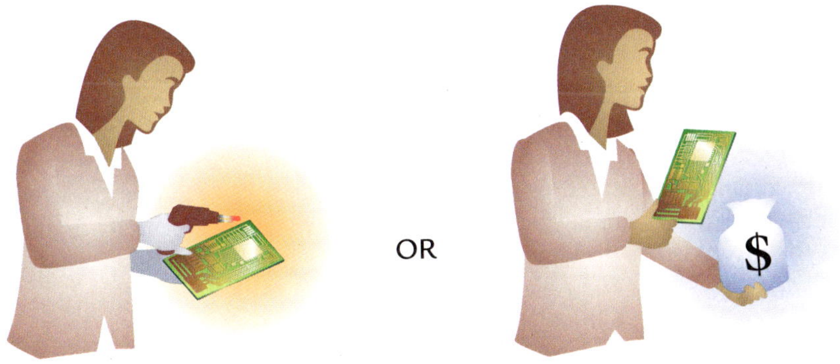

All other costs are relevant. The costs of direct materials and direct labour are relevant because they will not be needed if the part is bought externally. Similarly, variable overhead is relevant, because its cost would not be incurred if the component were bought externally.

Now, what about the purchase of the component? Of course, the purchase price is relevant. If the component were made, this cost would not be incurred. Are there any other costs associated with an outside purchase? A check with the purchasing department and receiving dock confirmed that there was sufficient slack in the system to easily handle the additional purchase. Cornerstone 13-1 shows how to structure this make-or-buy problem.

Be sure to read the analysis in Cornerstone 13-1 carefully. At first, the fixed overhead remains whether or not the component is made internally. In this case, fixed overhead is not relevant, and making the product is $9,500 cheaper than buying it. Later, in Requirement 4, part of the fixed overhead is avoidable. This condition means that purchasing the component externally will save $10,000 in fixed cost (i.e., Swasey can avoid $10,000 of fixed overhead if it buys the component). Now, the $10,000 of fixed cost is relevant—it is a future cost and it differs between the two alternatives—and the offer of the supplier should be accepted; it is $500 cheaper to buy the component.

The same analysis can be performed on a unit-cost basis. Once the relevant costs are identified, relevant unit costs can be compared. For this example, these costs are $3.80 ($38,000/10,000) for the make alternative and $4.75 ($47,500/10,000) for the buy alternative.

CONCEPT Q&A

You also have make-or-buy decisions to make. For example, do you change the oil in your car yourself, or do you take it to the shop? Do you make your own clothing or complete home improvement projects? Choose one such decision, and explain why you have chosen to "make it" or "buy it." What factors could influence you to change your mind?

Answers on pages 711 to 715.

One type of relevant cost that is becoming increasingly large due to globalization and the green environmental movement concerns the disposal costs associated with electronic waste (or e-waste). Increasingly government agencies are assessing manufacturers of computers, televisions, digital music devices, etc., a costly fee at production to cover product disposal costs that public landfills eventually incur once the products reach the end of their life cycle, become obsolete, and are thrown out to pollute the environment. **Hewlett-Packard Co.** has taken a strategic leadership position by recycling approximately 10 percent of its sales as a more cost-effective means than incurring the aforementioned governmental fees at production.[3] The failure to include relevant life cycle costs can cause the make side of the make-or-buy analysis to appear more attractive (i.e., less costly) than it is in reality.

Special-Order Decisions

From time to time, a company may consider offering a product or service at a price different from the usual price. For example, bid prices can vary to customers in the same market, and firms often have the opportunity to consider special orders from potential customers in markets not ordinarily served. For example, **General Motors** contracted with the U.S. Pentagon to use excess production capacity to manufacture its popular 4-wheel drive pickup truck for use by U.S. troops in desert combat situations, except that these trucks were altered to include bulletproof windows, mounts for machine guns, and night vision capability. A potentially important qualitative factor in this example is that certain customer segments might hold strong opinions about General Motors' association with combat activities. Such opinions might help or hurt regular sales, but their effect should be estimated and included in the relevant analysis if they are deemed to be significant. **Special-order decisions** focus on whether a specially priced order should be accepted or rejected. These orders often can be attractive, especially when the firm is operating below its maximum productive capacity. Exhibit 13-2 illustrates the special-order decision.

[3] Lorraine Woellert, "HP Wants Your Old PCs Back," *BusinessWeek Online* (April 10, 2006).

The HOW and WHY of Structuring a Make-or-Buy Problem

CORNERSTONE 13-1

Information:

Swasey Manufacturing needed to determine if it would be cheaper to make 10,000 units of a component in-house or to purchase them from an outside supplier for $4.75 each. Cost information on internal production includes the following:

	Total Cost	Unit Cost
Direct materials	$10,000	$1.00
Direct labour	20,000	2.00
Variable overhead	8,000	0.80
Fixed overhead	44,000	4.40
Total	$82,000	$8.20

Fixed overhead will continue whether the component is produced internally or externally. No additional costs of purchasing will be incurred beyond the purchase price.

4.75 each.

Required:

1. What are the alternatives for Swasey Manufacturing?
2. List the relevant cost(s) of internal production and of external purchase.
3. Which alternative is more cost effective and by how much?
4. Now assume that the fixed overhead includes $10,000 of cost that can be avoided if the component is purchased externally. Which alternative is more cost effective and by how much?

Solution:

1. There are two alternatives: make the component in-house or purchase it externally.
2. Relevant costs of making the component in-house include direct materials, direct labour, and variable overhead. Relevant costs of purchasing the component externally include the purchase price.
3.

	Alternatives		Differential Cost to Make
	Make	Buy	
Direct materials	$10,000	—	$ 10,000
Direct labour	20,000	—	20,000
Variable overhead	8,000	—	8,000
Purchase cost	—	$47,500	(47,500)
Total relevant cost	$38,000	$47,500	$ (9,500)

It is cheaper to make the component in-house. This alternative is cheaper by $9,500.

4.

	Alternatives		Differential Cost to Make
	Make	Buy	
Direct materials	$10,000	—	$ 10,000
Direct labour	20,000	—	20,000
Variable overhead	8,000	—	8,000
Avoidable fixed overhead	10,000	—	10,000
Purchase cost	—	$47,500	(47,500)
Total relevant cost	$48,000	$47,500	$ 500

CORNERSTONE 13-1 *(continued)*

Now it is cheaper to purchase the component. This alternative is cheaper by $500.

WHY:

Make-or-buy decisions are among the most common decisions faced by management, and structuring the analysis of such a decision is critical to arriving at the most appropriate one. If the problem is not structured properly, the result can be faulty or overcomplicated analysis.

Suppose, for example, that an ice cream company produces only premium ice cream. Its factory has a capacity of 20 million 1 litre units but only plans to produce 16 million units. The total costs associated with producing and selling 16 million units are as follows (in thousands of dollars):

	Total	Unit Cost
Variable costs:		
Ingredients	$15,200	$0.95
Packaging	3,200	0.20
Direct labour	4,000	0.25
Variable overhead	1,280	0.08
Selling commission	320	0.02
Total variable costs	$24,000	$1.50
Total fixed costs	1,552	0.097
Total costs	$25,552	$1.597
Selling price		$2.00

An ice cream distributor from a geographic region not normally served by the company has offered to buy 2 million units at $1.55 per unit, provided its own label can be attached to the product. Since the distributor approached the company directly, there is no sales commission. As the manager of the ice cream company, would you accept or reject this order?

The offer of $1.55 is well below the normal selling price of $2.00; in fact, it is even below the total unit cost. Even so, accepting the order may be profitable. The company has idle capacity, and the order will not replace, or cannibalize, other units being produced to sell at the normal price. Additionally, many of the costs are not relevant; fixed costs will continue regardless of whether the order is accepted or rejected.

If the order is accepted, a benefit of $1.55 per unit will be realized that otherwise wouldn't be. However, all of the variable costs except for commissions ($0.02) also

Exhibit 13-2

Accept or Reject a Special Order

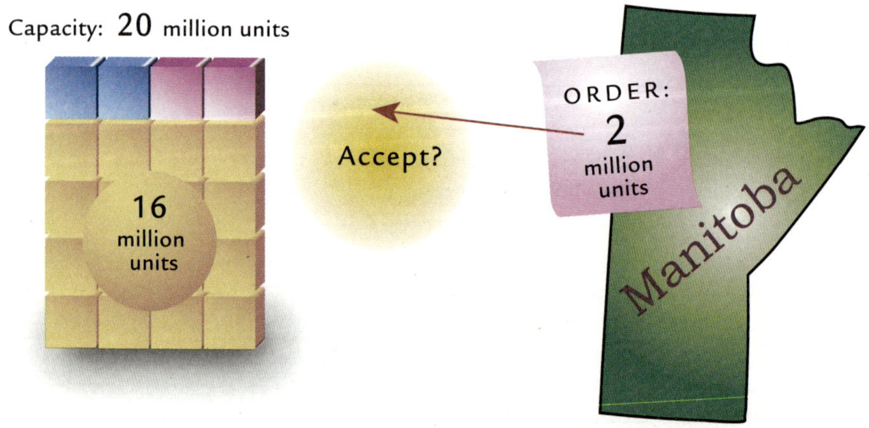

will be incurred, producing a cost of $1.48 per unit. The net benefit is $0.07 ($1.55 − $1.48) per unit. The relevant cost analysis can be summarized as follows:

	Accept	Reject	Differential Benefit to Accept
Revenues	$ 3,100,000	$—	$ 3,100,000
Ingredients	(1,900,000)	—	(1,900,000)
Packaging	(400,000)	—	(400,000)
Direct labour	(500,000)	—	(500,000)
Variable overhead	(160,000)	—	(160,000)
Profit	$ 140,000	$ 0	$ 140,000

We see that for this company, accepting the special order will increase profits by $140,000 ($0.07 × 2,000,000).

Cornerstone 13-2 shows how to apply relevant costing to a special-order problem.

Keep-or-Drop Decisions

Often, a manager needs to determine whether or not a segment, such as a product line, should be kept or dropped. Keep-or-drop decisions can be relatively small scale in nature, such as when **Nike** decides what to do with particular existing celebrity- and athlete-sponsored clothing or equipment lines. On the other hand, these decisions can be very large scale in nature, such as when Ford Motor Company contemplated the sale of its luxury Jaguar and Land Rover automobile lines. Segmented reports prepared on a variable-costing basis provide valuable information for these **keep-or-drop decisions**. Both the segment's contribution margin and its segment margin are useful in evaluating the performance of segments. However, while segmented reports provide useful information for keep-or-drop decisions, relevant costing describes how the information should be used to arrive at a decision.

To illustrate, consider Norton Materials Inc., which produces concrete blocks, bricks, and roofing tile. The controller has prepared the following estimated segment income statement for next year (in thousands of dollars):

	Blocks	Bricks	Tile	Total
Sales revenue	$500	$800	$150	$1,450
Less: Variable expenses	250	480	140	870
Contribution margin	$250	$320	$ 10	$ 580
Less direct fixed expenses:				
Advertising	(10)	(10)	(10)	(30)
Salaries	(37)	(40)	(35)	(112)
Depreciation	(53)	(40)	(10)	(103)
Segment margin	$150	$230	$ (45)	$ 335

The projected performance of the roofing tile line shows a negative segment margin. This occurrence would be the third consecutive year of poor performance for that line. The president of Norton Materials, Tom Blackburn—concerned about this poor performance—is trying to decide whether to drop or keep the roofing tile line.

His first reaction is to try to increase the sales revenue of roofing tiles, possibly through an aggressive sales promotion coupled with an increase in the selling price. The marketing manager thinks that this approach would be fruitless since the market is saturated, and the level of competition is too keen to hold out any hope for increasing the firm's market share.

Increasing the product line's profits through cost cutting is not feasible either. Costs were cut the past two years to reduce the loss to its present anticipated level. Any further reductions would lower the quality of the product and adversely affect sales.

With no hope for improving the profit performance of the line beyond its projected level, Tom has decided to drop it. He reasons that the firm will lose a total of $10,000 in contribution margin but will save $45,000 by dismissing the line's

CORNERSTONE 13-2

The HOW and WHY of Structuring a Special-Order Problem

Information:

Leibnitz Company has been approached by a new customer with an offer to purchase 20,000 units of model TR8 at a price of $9 each. The new customer is geographically separated from the company's other customers, and existing sales would not be affected. Leibnitz normally produces 100,000 units of TR8 per year but only plans to produce and sell 75,000 in the coming year. The normal sales price is $14 per unit. Unit cost information for the normal level of activity is as follows:

Direct materials	$3.00
Direct labour	2.80
Variable overhead	1.50
Fixed overhead	2.00
Total	$9.30

Fixed overhead will not be affected by whether or not the special order is accepted.

Required:

1. What are the relevant costs and benefits of the two alternatives (accept or reject the special order)?
2. By how much will operating income increase or decrease if the order is accepted?

Solution:

1. Relevant costs and benefits of accepting the special order include the sales price of $9, direct materials, direct labour, and variable overhead. No relevant costs or benefits are attached to rejecting the order.
2. If the problem is analyzed on a unit basis:

	Accept	Reject	Differential Benefit to Accept
Price	$ 9.00	$—	$ 9.00
Direct materials	(3.00)	—	(3.00)
Direct labour	(2.80)	—	(2.80)
Variable overhead	(1.50)	—	(1.50)
Increase in operating income	$ 1.70	$ 0	$ 1.70

Operating income will increase by $34,000 ($1.70 × 20,000 units) if the special order is accepted.

WHY:

Special-order situations require careful analysis. Many different factors must be considered before the decision is made, so we must structure the analysis to properly consider all decision factors.

supervisor and eliminating its advertising budget. (The depreciation cost of $10,000 is not relevant because it represents an allocation of a sunk cost.) Thus, dropping the product line has a $35,000 advantage over keeping it. Cornerstone 13-3 shows how to structure this information as a keep-or-drop product line problem.

A merger between companies is another type of keep-or-drop decision that requires managerial accountants to estimate relevant costs, such as which costs would go away when two companies merge and which costs would remain. For example, when **XM Satellite Radio** and **Sirius Satellite Radio** considered merging into one giant satellite radio company, proponents argued that the merger would create significant cost

The HOW and WHY of Structuring a Keep-or-Drop Product Line Problem

CORNERSTONE 13-3

Information:
Shown below is a segmented income statement for Norton Materials Inc.'s three product lines:

	Blocks	Bricks	Tile	Total
Sales revenue	$500	$800	$150	$1,450
Less: Variable expenses	250	480	140	870
Contribution margin	$250	$320	$ 10	$ 580
Less direct fixed expenses:				
Advertising	(10)	(10)	(10)	(30)
Salaries	(37)	(40)	(35)	(112)
Depreciation	(53)	(40)	(10)	(103)
Segment margin	$150	$230	$ (45)	$ 335

The roofing tile line has a contribution margin of $10,000 (sales of $150,000 less total variable costs of $140,000). All variable costs are relevant. Relevant fixed costs associated with this line include $10,000 in advertising and $35,000 in supervision.

Required:
1. List the alternatives being considered with respect to the roofing tile line.
2. List the relevant benefits and costs for each alternative.
3. Which alternative is more cost effective and by how much?

Solution:
1. The two alternatives are to keep the roofing tile line or to drop it.
2. The relevant benefits and costs of keeping the roofing tile line include sales of $150,000, variable costs of $140,000, advertising cost of $10,000, and supervision cost of $35,000.
   None of the relevant benefits and costs of keeping the roofing tile line would occur under the drop alternative.
3.

	Keep	Drop	Differential Amount to Keep
Sales	$150,000	$—	$150,000
Less: Variable expenses	140,000	—	140,000
Contribution margin	$ 10,000	$—	$ 10,000
Less: Advertising	(10,000)	—	(10,000)
Cost of supervision	(35,000)	—	(35,000)
Total relevant benefit (loss)	$ (35,000)	$ 0	$ (35,000)

The difference is $35,000 in favour of dropping the roofing tile line.

WHY:
Every company faces the question of whether it should keep or drop a particular product or division. The analysis must consider a variety of factors, especially since the conclusions are not readily available from the raw data.

savings to the new company that could be passed along to consumers in the form of lower prices.[4] They reasoned that many of the costs that XM and Sirius incurred as separate companies would either decrease or be eliminated because the new combined company would need only one research and development group, one marketing

[4] Kim Peterson, "XM Plus Sirius Doesn't Equal Monopoly?" (March 24, 2008): accessed April 5, 2008, from http://blogs.moneycentral.msn.com/topstocks/archive/2008/03/24/xm-plus-sirius-doesn-t-equal-monopoly-feds-say.aspx.

CORNERSTONE 13-4

The HOW and WHY of Structuring a Keep-or-Drop Product Line Problem with Complementary Effects

Information:

Refer to Norton Material's segmented income statement in Cornerstone 13-3. Assume that dropping the product line reduces sales of blocks by 10 percent and sales of bricks by 8 percent. All other information remains the same.

Required:

1. If the roofing tile line is dropped, what is the contribution margin for the block line? For the brick line?
2. Which alternative (keep or drop the roofing tile line) is now more cost effective and by how much?

Solution:

1. Previous contribution margin of blocks was $250,000. A 10 percent decrease in sales implies a 10 percent decrease in total variable costs, so the contribution margin decreases by 10 percent.

   New contribution margin for blocks = $250,000 − 0.10($250,000) = $225,000

   The reasoning is the same for the brick line, but the decrease is 8 percent.

   New contribution margin for bricks = $320,000 − 0.08($320,000) = $294,400.

   Therefore, if the roofing tile product line were dropped, the resulting total contribution margin for Norton would equal $519,400 ($225,000 + $294,400).

2.

	Keep	Drop	Differential Amount to Keep
Contribution margin	$ 580,000	$519,400	$ 60,600
Less: Advertising	(30,000)	(20,000)	(10,000)
Cost of supervision	(112,000)	(77,000)	(35,000)
Total	$ 438,000	$422,400	$ 15,600

Notice that the contribution margin for the drop alternative equals the new contribution margins of the block and brick lines ($225,000 + $294,400). Also, advertising and supervision remain relevant across these alternatives.

Now the analysis favours keeping the roofing tile line. In fact, company income will be $15,600 higher if all three lines are kept as opposed to dropping the roofing tile line.

WHY:

A complication of any keep-or-drop question is the implications such a decision may have on other aspects of the business. We must analyze these implications carefully before making a final decision.

department, etc. Any costs that would decrease or go away after the merger would be relevant costs for the merger analysis, while any costs that would remain unchanged after the merger would be irrelevant.

Keep or Drop with Complementary Effects Suppose that dropping the roofing tile line would lower sales of blocks by 10 percent and bricks by 8 percent, as many customers buy roofing tile at the same time that they purchase blocks or bricks. Some customers will go elsewhere if they cannot buy both products at the same location. How does this information affect the keep-or-drop decision? Cornerstone 13-4 shows the impact on all product lines.

The example provides some insights beyond the simple application of the decision model. The initial analysis, which focused on two feasible alternatives, led to a tentative decision to drop the product line. Additional information provided by the marketing manager led to a reversal of the first decision. Perhaps other feasible alternatives exist as well. These additional alternatives would require still more analyses.

Further Processing of Joint Products

Joint products have common processes and costs of production up to a split-off point. At that point, they become distinguishable as separately identifiable products. For example, certain minerals such as copper and gold may both be found in a given ore. The ore must be mined, crushed, and treated before the copper and gold are separated. The point of separation is called the **split-off point**. The costs of mining, crushing, and treatment are common to both products.

Many joint products are sold at the split-off point. However, sometimes it is more profitable to process a joint product further, beyond the split-off point, prior to selling it. A **sell-or-process-further decision** is an important relevant decision that a manager must make.

To illustrate, consider Appletime Corporation, a large corporate farm that specializes in growing apples. Each plot produces approximately one ton of apples. The trees in each plot must be sprayed, fertilized, watered, and pruned. When the apples are ripened, workers are hired to pick them. The apples are then transported to a warehouse, where they are washed and sorted. The approximate cost of all these activities (including processing) is \$300 per tonne per year.

Apples are sorted into three grades (A, B, and C), determined by size and blemishes. Large apples without blemishes (bruises, cuts, wormholes, and so on) are sorted into one bin and classified as Grade A. Small apples without blemishes are sorted into a second bin and classified as Grade B. All remaining apples are placed in a third bin and classified as Grade C. Every ton of apples produces, on average, 400 kilograms of Grade A, 300 kilograms of Grade B, and 300 kilograms of Grade C.

Grade A apples are sold to large supermarkets for \$0.80 per kilogram. Grade B apples are packaged in 2 kilogram bags and sold to supermarkets for \$1.25 per bag. (The cost of each bag is \$0.05.) Grade C apples are processed further and made into applesauce. The sauce is sold in 0.5 kilogram cans for \$0.75 each. The cost of processing is \$0.10 per kilogram of apples. The final output is 500 0.5 kilogram cans.

A large supermarket chain recently requested that Appletime supply 0.5 kilogram cans of apple pie filling for which the chain is willing to pay \$0.90 per can. Appletime determined that the Grade B apples would be suitable for this purpose and estimated that it would cost \$0.24 per kilogram to process the apples into pie filling. The output would be 500 cans. Exhibit 13-3 illustrates the decision to sell grade B apples at the split-off point or to process them further into pie filling.

Exhibit 13-3

Further Processing of Joint Products

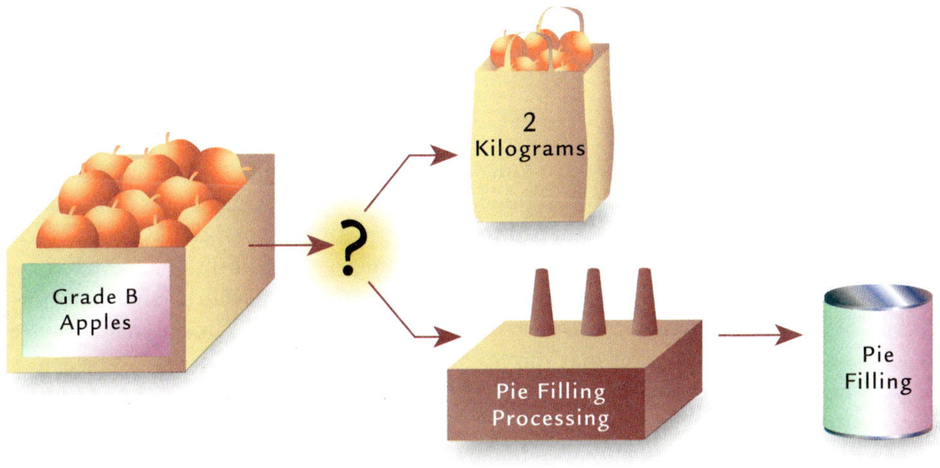

CORNERSTONE 13-5

The HOW and WHY of Structuring the Sell-or-Process-Further Decision

Information:

Appletime grows apples and then sorts them into one of three grades, A, B, or C, based on their condition. Appletime must decide whether to sell the Grade B apples at split-off or to process them into apple pie filling. The company normally sells the Grade B apples in 120 two-kilogram bags at a per-unit price of \$1.25. If the apples are processed into pie filling, the result will be 500 cans of filling with additional costs of \$0.24 per can. The buyer will pay \$0.90 per can.

Required:

1. What is the contribution to income from selling the Grade B apples in two-kilogram bags?
2. What is the contribution to income from processing the Grade B apples into pie filling?
3. Should Appletime continue to sell the Grade B apples in bags or process them further into pie filling?

Solution:

1. Revenue from apples in bags = (\$1.25 × 120) = \$150.
2. Revenue from further processing = \$0.90 × 500 = \$450.
   Further processing cost = \$0.24 × 500 = \$120.
   Income from further processing = \$450 − \$120 = \$330.
3. Appletime should process the Grade B apples into pie filling because the company will make \$330 versus the \$150 it would make by selling the apples in bags.

WHY:

Products that share common processes at the initial stages must be analyzed separately as to whether or not they should be processed further or sold immediately. The overriding principle is that action should be taken that maximizes company profit.

In deciding whether to sell Grade B apples at split-off or to process them further and sell them as pie filling, the common costs of spraying, pruning, and so on are not relevant. The company must pay the \$300 per tonne for these activities regardless of whether it sells at split-off or processes further. However, the revenues earned at split-off are likely to differ from the revenues that would be received if the Grade B apples were further processed and sold as pie filling. Therefore, revenues are a relevant consideration. Similarly, the processing costs occur only if further processing takes place. Hence, processing costs are relevant. Cornerstone 13-5 shows how to structure the sell-or-process-further decision for the Grade B apples.

OBJECTIVE 3
Choose the optimal product mix when faced with one constrained resource.

Product Mix Decisions

Most of the time, organizations have wide flexibility in choosing their product mix. Decisions about product mix can have a significant impact on an organization's profitability.

Each mix represents an alternative that carries with it an associated profit level. A manager should choose the alternative that maximizes total profits. Since fixed costs do not vary with activity level, the total fixed costs of a firm will be the same for all possible mixes and, therefore, are not relevant to the decision. Thus, a manager needs to choose the alternative that maximizes total contribution margin.

Assume, for example, that Jorgenson Company produces two types of gears: X and Y, with unit contribution margins of \$25 and \$10, respectively. If the firm possesses unlimited resources and the demand for each product is unlimited, then the

The HOW and WHY of Determining the Optimal Product Mix with One Constrained Resource

CORNERSTONE 13-6

Information:

Jorgenson Company produces two types of gears, X and Y, with unit contribution margins of $25 and $10, respectively. Each gear must be notched by a special machine. The firm owns eight machines that together provide 40,000 hours of machine time per year. Gear X requires two hours of machine time, and Gear Y requires 0.5 hour of machine time. There are no other constraints.

Required:

1. What is the contribution margin per hour of machine time for each gear?
2. What is the optimal mix of gears?
3. What is the total contribution margin earned for the optimal mix?

Solution:

1.

	Gear X	Gear Y
Contribution margin per unit	$ 25.00	$ 10
Required machine time per unit	÷ 2	÷0.5
Contribution margin per hour of machine time	$ 12.50	$ 20

2. Since Gear Y yields $20 of contribution margin per hour of machine time, all machine time should be devoted to the production of Gear Y.

   Units Gear Y = 40,000 total hours/0.5 hour per Gear Y = 80,000 units

   The optimal mix is Gear Y—80,000 units and Gear X—0 units.

3. Total contribution margin of optimal mix = (80,000 units Gear Y)$10
   = $800,000

WHY:

A company often faces a situation where one of its processes (or resources) cannot handle all the demands placed on it. Therefore, a company must decide how best to allocate this scarce resource to production operations in order to maximize company profit.

product mix decision is simple—produce an infinite number of each product. Unfortunately, every firm faces limited resources and limited demand for each product. These limitations are called **constraints**. A manager must choose the optimal mix given the constraints found within the firm.

Assuming that Jorgenson can sell all that is produced, some individuals might argue that only Gear X should be produced and sold—it has the larger contribution margin. However, this solution is not necessarily the best choice. The selection of the optimal mix can be significantly affected by the relationships of the constrained resources to the individual products. These relationships affect the quantity of each product that can be produced and, consequently, the total contribution margin that can be earned. This point is most vividly illustrated when faced with one resource constraint. Cornerstone 13-6 shows how to determine the optimal product mix with one constrained resource.

Cornerstone 13-6 clearly illustrates a fundamentally important point involving relevant decision making with a constrained resource. This point is that the contribution margin *per unit* of each product is not the critical concern when deciding how much of each product type to produce and sell. Instead, the contribution margin *per unit of the scarce resource* is the deciding factor, which means that the product yielding the highest contribution margin per unit of the scarce resource should be selected. Returning to Cornerstone 13-6, Gear X earns contribution margin per unit of $25, which is 2.5 times greater than the $10 contribution margin per unit earned by Gear Y. However,

CORNERSTONE 13-7

The HOW and WHY of Determining the Optimal Product Mix with One Constrained Resource and a Sales Constraint

Information:

Jorgenson Company produces two types of gears, X and Y, with unit contribution margins of $25 and $10, respectively. Each gear must be notched by a special machine. The firm owns eight machines that together provide 40,000 hours of machine time per year. Gear X requires two hours of machine time, and Gear Y requires 0.5 hour of machine time. A maximum of 60,000 units of each gear can be sold.

Required:

1. What is the contribution margin per hour of machine time for each gear?
2. What is the optimal mix of gears?
3. What is the total contribution margin earned for the optimal mix?

Solution:

1.

	Gear X	**Gear Y**
Contribution margin per unit	$ 25.00	$ 10
Required machine time per unit	÷ 2	÷ 0.5
Contribution margin per hour of machine time	$ 12.50	$ 20

2. Since Gear Y yields $20 of contribution margin per hour of machine time, the first priority is to produce all of Gear Y that the market will take (i.e., demands).

   Machine time required for maximum amount of Gear Y = 60,000 × 0.5 machine hours required for each Gear Y unit
   = 30,000 hours needed to manufacture 60,000 Gear Y units

   Remaining machine time for Gear X = 40,000 − 30,000
   = 10,000 hours

   Units of Gear X to be produced in remaining 10,000 hours = 10,000/2
   = 5,000 units

   Now the optimal mix is 60,000 units of Gear Y and 5,000 units of Gear X. This mix will precisely exhaust the machine time available.

3. Total contribution margin of optimal mix = (60,000 units Gear Y × $10)
   + (5,000 units Gear X × $25)
   = $725,000

WHY:

A complication of the scarce resource question arises when there is also a sales constraint that indicates the maximum sales that can be achieved. Keeping both the constrained resource and the sales constraint in mind is essential if the best decision is to be made.

each Gear X unit requires *more* than 2.5 times as much machine time (the constrained factor) to produce than does each Gear Y unit, thereby making Gear Y more attractive financially than Gear X. Specifically, Gear X earns $12.50 of contribution margin per machine hour ($25/2), but Gear Y earns $20 of contribution margin per machine hour ($10/0.5). Thus, Gear Y is the more attractive product and the optimal mix is 80,000 units of Gear Y and no units of Gear X.

Suppose, however, that there is also a demand constraint. Only 60,000 units of Gear Y can be sold. Cornerstone 13-7 shows how to incorporate this additional constraint. Coffee chain **Caribou Coffee**, as well as other retail businesses, pay careful attention to profitability and sales per square metre of café floor space, which often is the most important constrained resource. The importance of this metric explains why fast-food restaurants like **McDonald's** push their drive-through service—customers using the drive-through option do not require any internal store floor space. In fact, some restaurants generate more than 80% of sales from this service!

CONCEPT Q&A

Consider your, or a friend's, cell phone plan. Often, there are different types of minutes—priced at different levels. For example, a plan might include 300 "anytime" minutes and 1,000 "night and weekend minutes." Discuss these different types of minutes as constraints. What do they constrain? Do these constraints affect the decision to call a friend?

Answers on pages 711 to 715.

Multiple Constrained Resources

The presence of only one constrained resource might not be realistic. Organizations often face multiple constraints: limitations of raw materials, limitations of skilled labour, limited demand for each product, and so on. The solution of the product mix problem in the presence of multiple constraints is considerably more complicated and requires the use of a specialized mathematical technique known as *linear programming*, which is reserved for advanced cost management courses.

The Use of Costs in Pricing Decisions

OBJECTIVE 4
Explain the impact of cost on pricing decisions.

One of the more difficult decisions faced by a company is pricing. This section examines the impact of cost on price and the role of the accountant in gathering the needed information.

Cost-Based Pricing

Demand is one side of the pricing equation; supply is the other side. Since revenue must cover all costs for the firm to make a profit, many companies start with cost to determine price. That is, they calculate product cost and add the desired profit. The mechanics of this approach are straightforward. Usually, there is some cost base and a markup. The **markup** is a percentage applied to the base cost; it includes desired profit and any costs not included in the base cost. Companies that bid for jobs routinely base bid price on cost. Law firms and public accounting firms are service organizations that use cost-plus pricing to bid for clients. Cornerstone 13-8 shows how to apply a markup percentage to cost to obtain price.

Notice in Cornerstone 13-8 that the markup of 20 percent is not pure profit. Instead, it includes other costs not specified, such as overhead (including Elvin's offices and management salaries) as well as any marketing and administrative expenses. The markup percentage can be calculated using a variety of bases.

Retail stores often use markup pricing, and typical markup is 100 percent of cost. Thus, if Graham Department Store purchases a sweater for \$24, the retail price marked is \$48 [\$24 + (1.00 × \$24)]. Again, the 100 percent markup is not pure profit—it goes toward the salaries of the clerks, payment for space and equipment (cash registers, furniture, and fixtures), utilities, advertising, and so on. A major advantage of markup pricing is that standard markups are easy to apply. Consider the difficulty of setting a price for every piece of merchandise in a hardware or department store. It is much simpler to apply a uniform markup to cost and then to adjust prices as needed if demand is less than anticipated.

Several important observations are in order at this point concerning the relationship between the base cost, the markup percentage, and the firm's cost system. First, when the firm includes relatively few costs in the base cost (rather than a large number of costs), it usually becomes very important that the firm selects a large enough markup percentage to ensure that the markup covers all of the remaining costs not included in the base cost. Covering more costs with the markup requires significant judgment and cost estimation. Second, on a related note, the effectiveness of cost-plus pricing relies heavily on the accuracy of the cost system and pricing managers'

Here's The Real Kicker

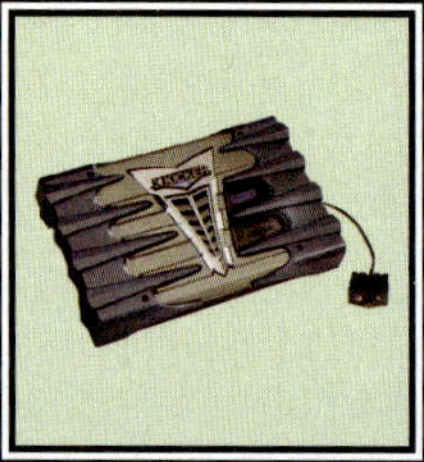

During the period 2001–2003, Stillwater Designs experienced high sales of their Kicker products. As a consequence, the levels of inventory filled all storage areas to capacity. Consequently, Stillwater Designs began plans to add another building on existing property with 50,000 square feet of capacity. This new facility had an estimated construction cost between $1 million and $1.5 million. During this preliminary planning phase, a shipping strike placed extra storage demands on existing facilities, and Stillwater Designs began looking for a warehousing facility that could be leased on a short-term basis.

They identified a large 250,000-square-foot facility, housed on 22 acres, that was owned by Moore Business Forms. This facility not only was an attractive leasing option, but it also quickly became a competing alternative to adding the 50,000-square-foot facility to Stillwater's current complex of buildings. In fact, the company began looking at the possibility of buying and renovating the Moore facility and moving all of its operations into the one facility. Renovation required such actions as installing a new HVAC system, bringing the building up to current fire codes, painting and resealing the floor, and adding a large number of offices. After careful financial analysis, Stillwater Designs decided that the buy-and-renovate option was more profitable than adding the 50,000-square-foot building to its current complex of buildings. Two economic factors affecting the decision were (1) selling the current complex of five buildings would help pay for the needed renovations, and (2) the purchase cost of the nonrenovated Moore facility was less than the cost of building the 50,000-square-foot facility.

KICKER®

OBJECTIVE 1
Explain the meaning of *capital investment decisions*, and distinguish between independent and mutually exclusive capital investment decisions.

Types of Capital Investment Decisions

Organizations often are faced with the opportunity (or need) to invest in assets or projects that represent long-term commitments. New production systems, new plants, new equipment, and new product development are examples of assets and projects that fit this category. Usually, many alternatives are available. For example, an organization may be faced with the decision of whether or not to invest in a new plant, or whether to invest in a flexible manufacturing system or to continue with an existing traditional manufacturing system. These long-range decisions are examples of *capital investment decisions.*

Capital investment decisions are concerned with the process of planning, setting goals and priorities, arranging financing, and using certain criteria to select long-term assets. Because capital investment decisions place large amounts of resources at risk for long periods of time and simultaneously affect the future development of the firm, they are among the most important decisions made by managers. Every organization has limited resources, which should be used to maintain or enhance its long-run profitability. Poor capital investment decisions can be disastrous. For example, a failure to invest in automated manufacturing when other competitors do so may result in significant losses in market share because of the inability to compete on the basis of quality, cost, and delivery time. Competitors with more modern facilities may produce more output at lower cost and higher quality. Thus, making the right capital investment decisions is absolutely essential for long-term survival.

The process of making capital investment decisions often is referred to as **capital budgeting**. Two types of capital budgeting projects will be considered: *independent projects* and *mutually exclusive projects.* **Independent projects** are projects that, if accepted or rejected, do not affect the cash flows of other projects. For example, a decision by **General Motors** to build a new plant for production of the Cadillac line is not affected by its decision to build a new plant for the production of its truck line. These are independent capital investment decisions. The second type of capital budgeting project requires a firm to choose among competing alternatives that provide the same basic service. Acceptance of one option precludes the acceptance of another. Thus, **mutually exclusive projects** are those projects that, if accepted, preclude the acceptance of all other competing projects. For example, some time ago, **Monsanto**'s Fibers Division decided to automate its Pensacola, Florida, plant. Thus, Monsanto was faced with the choice of continuing with its existing manual production operation or replacing it with an automated system. In all likelihood, part of the company's deliberation concerned different types of automated systems. If three different automated systems were being considered, this would produce four alternatives: the current system plus the three potential new systems. Once one system is chosen, the other three are excluded; they are mutually exclusive.

Notice that one of the competing alternatives in the Monsanto example is that of maintaining the status quo (the manual system). This point emphasizes the fact that new investments replacing existing investments must prove to be economically superior. Of course, at times, replacement of the old system is mandatory and not discretionary if the firm wishes to remain in business (e.g., equipment in the old system may be worn out, making the old system not a viable alternative). In such a situation, going out of business could be a viable alternative, especially if none of the new investment alternatives is profitable.

Capital investment decisions often are concerned with investments in long-term capital assets. With the exception of land, these assets depreciate over their lives, and the original investment is used up as the assets are employed. In general terms, a sound capital investment will earn back its original capital outlay over its life and, at the same time, provide a reasonable return on the original investment. Therefore, managers must decide whether or not a capital investment will earn back its original outlay and provide a reasonable return. By making this assessment, a manager can decide on the acceptability of independent projects and compare competing projects on the basis of their economic merits.

But what is meant by reasonable return? It is generally agreed that any new project must cover the opportunity cost of the funds invested. For example, if a company takes money from a money market fund that is earning 6 percent and invests it in a new project, then the project must provide at least a 6 percent return (the return that could have been earned had the money been left in the money market fund). Of course, in reality, funds for investment often come from different sources—each representing a different opportunity cost. The return that must be earned is a blend of the opportunity costs of the different sources. Thus, if a company uses two sources of funds, one with an opportunity cost of 4 percent and the other with an opportunity cost of 6 percent, then the return that must be earned is somewhere between 4 and 6 percent, depending on the relative amounts used from each source. Furthermore, it is usually assumed that managers should select projects that promise to maximize the wealth of the owners of the firm.

To make a capital investment decision, a manager must estimate the quantity and timing of cash flows, assess the risk of the investment, and consider the impact of the project on the firm's profits. One of the most difficult tasks is to estimate the cash flows. Projections must be made years into the future, and forecasting is far from a perfect science. Obviously, as the accuracy of cash flow forecasts increases, the reliability of the decision improves. In making projections, managers must identify and quantify the benefits associated with the proposed project(s). For example, an automated cash deposit system can produce the following benefits (relative to a manual system): bank charge reductions, productivity gains, greater data integrity, lower training costs, and savings in time required to audit and do bank/cash reconciliations. The dollar value of these benefits must be assessed. Although forecasting future cash flows is a critical part of the capital investment process, forecasting methods will not be considered here. Furthermore, the cash flows projected must be *after-tax cash flows.* Taxes have an important role in developing cash flow assessments. However, taxes will not be explicitly considered. Tax effects either are assumed away or the cash flows can be thought of as after-tax cash flows. Forecasting methodologies are issues that are left for more advanced studies. Consequently, after-tax cash flows are assumed to be known; the focus will be on making capital investment decisions *given* these cash flows.

Managers must set goals and priorities for capital investments. They also must identify some basic criteria for the

CONCEPT Q&A

What is the difference between independent and mutually exclusive investments?

Answers on pages 711 to 715.

acceptance or rejection of proposed investments. In this chapter, we will study four basic methods to guide managers in accepting or rejecting potential investments. The methods include both nondiscounting and discounting decision approaches (two methods are discussed for each approach). The discounting methods are applied to investment decisions involving both independent and mutually exclusive projects.

OBJECTIVE 2
Compute the payback period and accounting rate of return for a proposed investment, and explain their roles in capital investment decisions.

Nondiscounting Models

The basic capital investment decision models can be classified into two major categories: *nondiscounting models* and *discounting models.* **Nondiscounting models** ignore the time value of money, whereas **discounting models** explicitly consider it. Although many accounting theorists disparage the nondiscounting models because they ignore the time value of money, many firms continue to use these models in making capital investment decisions. However, the use of discounting models has increased over the years, and few firms use only one model; indeed, most firms seem to use both types.[1] This pattern suggests that both categories—nondiscounted and discounted—supply useful information to managers as they struggle to make capital investment decisions.

Payback Period

One type of nondiscounting model is the *payback period.* The **payback period** is the time required for a firm to recover its original investment. If the cash flows of a project are an equal amount each period, then the following formula can be used to compute its payback period:

$$\text{Payback period} = \frac{\text{Original investment}}{\text{Annual cash flow}}$$

If, however, the cash flows are unequal, the payback period is computed by adding the annual cash flows until such time as the original investment is recovered. If a fraction of a year is needed, it is assumed that cash flows occur evenly within each year. Cornerstone 14-1 shows how payback analysis is done for both even and uneven cash flows.

One way to use the payback period is to set a maximum payback period for all projects and to reject any project that exceeds this level. Why would a firm use the payback period in this way? Some analysts suggest that the payback period can be used as a rough measure of risk, with the notion that the longer it takes for a project to pay for itself, the riskier it is. Also, firms with riskier cash flows in general could require a shorter payback period than normal. Additionally, firms with liquidity problems would be more interested in projects with quick paybacks. Another critical concern is obsolescence. In some industries, the risk of obsolescence is high; firms within these industries, such as computer and MP3 player manufacturers, would be interested in recovering funds rapidly.

Another reason, less beneficial to the firm, may also be involved. Many managers in a position to make capital investment decisions may choose investments with quick payback periods out of self-interest. If a manager's performance is measured using such short-run criteria as annual net income, he or she may choose projects with quick paybacks to show improved net income and cash flow as quickly as possible. Consider that divisional managers often are responsible for making capital investment decisions and are evaluated on divi-

ANALYTICAL Q&A

Suppose that a project requires an investment of $30,000 and produces $8,000 cash per year. What is the payback period?

Answers on pages 711 to 715.

[1] From the mid-1950s to 1988, surveys reveal that the use of discounting models as the primary evaluation method for capital projects went from about 9 to 80 percent. See A. Robichek and J. G. McDonald, "Financial Planning in Transition, Long Range Planning Service," Report No. 268 (Stanford Research Institute, Menlo Park, CA: January 1966); and T. Klammer, B. Koch, and N. Wilner, "Capital Budgeting Practices—A Survey of Corporate Use," published in the Proceedings of Decision Sciences National Meeting, November 21-24, 1988, North Texas State University.

The HOW and WHY of Calculating Payback

CORNERSTONE 14-1

Information:

Suppose that a new car wash facility requires an investment of \$100,000 and either has:

a. Even cash flows of \$50,000 per year or
b. The following expected annual cash flows: \$30,000, \$40,000, \$50,000, \$60,000, and \$70,000.

Required:

Calculate the payback period for each case.

Solution:

a. Even cash flows:

Payback period = Original investment/Annual cash flow
= \$100,000/\$50,000 = 2 years

b. Uneven cash flows:

Year	Unrecovered Investment (\$) (beginning of year)	Annual Cash Flow (\$)	Time Needed for Payback (years)
1	100,000	30,000	1.0
2	70,000	40,000	1.0
3	30,000	50,000	0.6*
4	0	60,000	0.0
5	0	70,000	0.0
			2.6

* At the beginning of year 3, \$30,000 is needed to recover the investment. Since a net cash flow of \$50,000 is expected, only 0.6 year (\$30,000/\$50,000) is needed to recover the remaining \$30,000, assuming a uniform cash inflow throughout the year.

WHY:

Payback is a simple concept that calculates how long it takes to recover the value of the money initially invested from the cash flow of a project. Sometimes it is the initial starting point in evaluating a project.

sional profit. The tenure of divisional managers, however, is typically short—three to five years on average. Consequently, the incentive for such managers is to shy away from investments that promise healthy long-run returns but relatively meagre returns in the short run. New products and services that require time to develop a consumer following fit this description particularly well. Corporate budgeting policies and a budget review committee can eliminate these problems.

The payback period can be used to choose among competing alternatives. Under this approach, the investment with the shortest payback period is preferred over investments with longer payback periods. However, this use of the payback period is less defensible because this measure suffers from two major deficiencies: (1) it ignores the cash flow performance of the investments beyond the payback period, and (2) it ignores the time value of money.

These two significant deficiencies are easily illustrated. Assume that an engineering firm is considering two different types of computer-aided design (CAD) systems: CAD-A and CAD-B. Each system requires an initial outlay of \$150,000, has a five-year life, and displays the following annual cash flows:

Investment	Year 1	Year 2	Year 3	Year 4	Year 5
CAD-A	\$90,000	\$60,000	\$50,000	\$50,000	\$50,000
CAD-B	40,000	110,000	25,000	25,000	25,000

Both investments have payback periods of two years. In other words, if a manager uses the payback period to choose among competing investments, the two investments would be equally desirable. In reality, however, the CAD-A system should be preferred over the CAD-B system for two reasons. First, the CAD-A system provides a much larger dollar return for the years 3, 4, and 5 beyond the payback period ($150,000 vs. $75,000). Second, the CAD-A system returns $90,000 in the first year, while B returns only $40,000. The extra $50,000 that the CAD-A system provides in the first year could be put to productive use, such as investing in another project. It is better to have a dollar now than to have it one year from now, because the dollar on hand can be invested to provide a return one year from now.

In summary, the payback period provides information to managers that can be used as follows:

1. To help control the risks associated with the uncertainty of future cash flows.
2. To help minimize the impact of an investment on a firm's liquidity problems.
3. To help control the risk of obsolescence.
4. To help control the effect of the investment on performance measures.

However, the method suffers significant deficiencies: It ignores a project's total profitability and the time value of money. While the computation of the payback period may be useful to a manager, relying on it solely for a capital investment decision would be foolish.

Accounting Rate of Return

The *accounting rate of return* is the second commonly used nondiscounting model. The **accounting rate of return** (ARR) measures the return on a project in terms of income, as opposed to using a project's cash flow. The accounting rate of return is computed by the following formula:

$$\text{Accounting rate of return} = \frac{\text{Average income}}{\text{Initial investment}}$$

Income is not equivalent to cash flows because of accruals and deferrals used in its computation. The average income of a project is obtained by adding the net income for each year of the project and then dividing this total by the number of years. Cornerstone 14-2 shows how to calculate the accounting rate of return.

Unlike the payback period, the accounting rate of return does consider a project's profitability; like the payback period, it ignores the time value of money. Ignoring the time value of money is a critical deficiency in this method as well; it can lead a manager to choose investments that do not maximize profits. The ARR and payback models are referred to as *nondiscounting models* because they ignore the time value of money. Discounting models use **discounted cash flows**, which are future cash flows expressed in terms of their present value. The use of discounting models requires an understanding of the present value concepts. Present value concepts are reviewed in Appendix 14-A. You should review these concepts and make sure that you understand them before studying capital investment discount models. Present value tables (Exhibits 14B-1 and 14B-2) are presented in Appendix 14-B at the end of this chapter. These tables are referred to and used throughout the rest of this chapter.

In addition to ignoring the time value of money, the ARR has other potential drawbacks because it is dependent upon net income, which is the financial measure most likely to be manipulated by managers. Some of the reasons for manipulating net income include debt contracts (i.e., debt covenants) and bonuses. Often, debt contracts require that a firm maintain certain financial accounting ratios, which can be affected by the income reported and by the level of long-term assets. Accordingly, the accounting rate of return may be used as a screening measure to ensure that any new investment will

CONCEPT Q&A

Why would a manager choose only investments that return the highest income per dollar invested?

Answers on pages 711 to 715.

The HOW and WHY of Calculating the Accounting Rate of Return

CORNERSTONE 14-2

Information:

An investment requires an initial outlay of $100,000 and has a five-year life with no salvage value. The yearly cash flows are $50,000, $50,000, $60,000, $50,000 and $70,000.

Required:

1. Calculate the annual net income for each of the five years.
2. Calculate the accounting rate of return.

Solution:

1. Yearly depreciation expense = ($100,000 – 0)/5 years = $20,000
   Annual net income = Net cash flow – depreciation expense
   Year 1 net income = $50,000 – $20,000 = $30,000
   Year 2 net income = $50,000 – $20,000 = $30,000
   Year 3 net income = $60,000 – $20,000 = $40,000
   Year 4 net income = $50,000 – $20,000 = $30,000
   Year 5 net income = $70,000 – $20,000 = $50,000
2. Total net income (five years) = $180,000
   Average net income = $180,000/5 = $36,000

$$\text{Accounting rate of return} = \frac{\$36{,}000}{\$100{,}000} = 0.36$$

WHY:

Accounting rate of return is a simple concept used to evaluate a project by looking at the average annual return, calculated on an accounting basis. It is often used as a preliminary tool to assess a project.

not adversely affect these ratios. Additionally, because bonuses to managers often are based on accounting income or return on assets, managers may have a personal interest in seeing that any new investment contributes significantly to net income. A manager seeking to maximize personal income is likely to select investments that return the highest net income per dollar invested, even if the selected investments are not the ones that produce the greatest cash flows and return to the firm in the long-run.

Discounting Models: The Net Present Value Method

OBJECTIVE 3
Use net present value analysis for capital investment decisions involving independent projects.

Discounting models explicitly consider the time value of money and, therefore, incorporate the concept of discounting cash inflows and outflows. Two discounting models will be considered: *net present value* (NPV) and *internal rate of return* (IRR). The NPV method will be discussed first; the IRR method is discussed in the following section.

Net Present Value Defined

Net present value is the difference between the present value of the cash inflows and outflows associated with a project:

$$\begin{aligned} NPV &= \left[\sum CF_t/(1+i)^t\right] - I \\ &= \left[\sum CF_t df_t\right] - I \\ &= P - I \end{aligned}$$

where

I = The present value of the project's cost (usually the initial cash outlay)
CF_t = The cash inflow to be received in period t, with $t = 1 \ldots n$
i = The required rate of return
t = The time period
P = The present value of the project's future cash inflows
df_t = $1/(1 + i)^t$, the discount factor

Note: Σ means "the sum of" as in "the sum of all cash flows."

Net present value measures the profitability of an investment. A positive NPV indicates that the investment increases the firm's wealth. To use the NPV method, a *required rate of return* must be defined. The **required rate of return** is the minimum acceptable rate of return. It also is referred to as the *discount rate*, *hurdle rate*, or *cost of capital*. In theory, if future cash flows are known with certainty, then the correct required rate of return is the firm's **cost of capital**. In practice, future cash flows are uncertain, and managers often choose a discount rate higher than the cost of capital to deal with the uncertainty. However, if the rate chosen is excessively high, it will bias the selection process toward short-term investments. Because of the risk of being overly conservative, it may be better to use the cost of capital as the discount rate and find other approaches to deal with uncertainty.

CONCEPT Q&A

Suppose that the NPV of an investment is $2,000. Why does this mean that the investment should be accepted?

Answers on pages 711 to 715.

If the NPV is positive, it signals that (1) the initial investment has been recovered, (2) the required rate of return has been recovered, and (3) a return in excess of (1) and (2) has been received. Thus, if the NPV is greater than zero the investment is profitable and, therefore, acceptable. If the NPV equals zero, the decision maker will find acceptance or rejection of the investment equal. Finally, if the NPV is less than zero, the investment should be rejected. In this case it is earning less than the required rate of return.

An Example Illustrating Net Present Value

Brannon Company has developed new earphones for portable MP3 players that it believes are superior to anything on the market. The earphones have a projected product life cycle of five years. Although the marketing manager is excited about the new product's prospects, a decision to manufacture the new product depends on whether it can earn a positive NPV given the company's required rate of return of 12 percent. In order to make a decision regarding the earphones, two steps must be taken: (1) the cash flows for each year must be identified, and (2) the NPV must be computed using the cash flows from step 1. Cornerstone 14-3 shows how to calculate the NPV. Notice that step 2 offers two approaches for computing NPV. Step 2A computes NPV by using discount factors from Exhibit 14B-1. Step 2B simplifies the computation by using a single discount factor from Exhibit 14B-2 for the even cash flows occurring in years 1 through 4.

OBJECTIVE 4
Use the internal rate of return to assess the acceptability of independent projects.

Internal Rate of Return

Another discounting model is the *internal rate of return* method. The **internal rate of return** is defined as the interest rate that sets the present value of a project's cash inflows equal to the present value of the project's cost. In other words, it is the interest rate that sets the project's NPV at zero. The following equation can be used to determine a project's IRR:

$$I = \frac{\sum CF_t}{(1+i)^t}$$

where $t = 1, \ldots, n$

The HOW and WHY of Assessing Cash Flows and Calculating Net Present Value

CORNERSTONE 14-3

Information:
A detailed market study revealed expected annual revenues of $300,000 for new earphones. Equipment to produce the earphones will cost $320,000. After five years, the equipment can be sold for $40,000. In addition to equipment, working capital is expected to increase by $40,000 because of increases in inventories and receivables. The firm expects to recover the investment in working capital at the end of the project's life. Annual cash operating expenses are estimated at $180,000. The required rate of return is 12 percent.

Required:
Estimate the annual cash flows, and calculate the NPV.

STEP 1. CASH FLOW IDENTIFICATION

Year	Item	Cash Flow
0	Equipment	$(320,000)
	Working capital	(40,000)
	Total	$(360,000)
1–4	Revenues	$ 300,000
	Operating expenses	(180,000)
	Total	$ 120,000
5	Revenues	$ 300,000
	Operating expenses	(180,000)
	Salvage	40,000
	Recovery of working capital	40,000
	Total	$ 200,000

STEP 2A. NPV ANALYSIS

Year	Cash Flow[a]	Discount Factor[b]	Present Value
0	$(360,000)	1.00000	$(360,000)
1	120,000	0.89286	107,143
2	120,000	0.79719	95,663
3	120,000	0.71178	85,414
4	120,000	0.63552	76,262
5	200,000	0.56743	113,486
Net present value			$ 117,968

STEP 2B. NPV ANALYSIS

Year	Cash Flow	Discount Factor[c]	Present Value
0	$(360,000)	1.00000	$(360,000)
1–4	120,000	3.03735	364,482
5	200,000	0.56743	113,486
Net present value			$ 117,968

[a] From step 1.
[b] From Exhibit 14B-1.
[c] Years 1–4 from Exhibit 14B-2; year 5 from Exhibit 14B-1.

WHY:
Cash flows and net present value are approaches that incorporate more sophisticated measures of the value of a project. These tools are generally regarded as a more accurate method of evaluating a project's value.

The right-hand side of this equation is the present value of future cash flows, and the left-hand side is the investment. I, CF_t, and t are known. Thus, the IRR (the interest rate, i, in the equation) can be found using trial and error. Once the IRR for a project is computed, it is compared with the firm's required rate of return. If the IRR is greater than the required rate, the project is deemed acceptable; if the IRR is less than the required rate of return, the project is rejected; if the IRR is equal to the required rate of return, the firm is indifferent between accepting or rejecting the investment proposal.

The IRR is the most widely used of the capital investment techniques. One reason for its popularity may be that it is a rate of return, a concept that managers are comfortable with using. Another possibility is that managers may believe that the IRR is the true or actual compounded rate of return being earned by the initial investment. Whatever the reasons for its popularity, a basic understanding of the IRR is necessary.

Example: Multiple-Period Setting with Uniform Cash Flows

Assume initially that the investment produces a series of uniform cash flows. Since the series of cash flows is uniform, a single discount factor from Exhibit 14B-2 can be used to compute the present value of the annuity. Letting *df* be this discount factor and *CF* be the annual cash flow, the IRR equation assumes the following form:

$$I = CF(df)$$

Solving for *df*, we obtain:

$$df = I/CF$$
$$= \frac{\textbf{Investment}}{\textbf{Annual cash flow}}$$

Assume that the investment (I) is $100 and that it produces a single-period cash flow of $110. The discount factor is I/CF = $100/$110 = 0.90909. Looking in Exhibit 14B-2, a discount factor of 0.90909 for a single period corresponds to a rate of 10 percent, which is the IRR. In general, once the discount factor is computed, go to Exhibit 14B-2 and find the row corresponding to the life of the project, then move across that row until the computed discount factor is found. The interest rate corresponding to this discount factor is the IRR. Cornerstone 14-4 illustrates how to calculate the IRR for multiple-period uniform cash flows.

ANALYTICAL Q&A

Suppose that an investment of $169 produces an annual cash flow of $100 for two years. What is the IRR?

Answers on pages 711 to 715.

Exhibit 14B-2 does not provide discount factors for every possible interest rate. To illustrate, assume that the annual cash inflows expected by the hospital (in Cornerstone 14-4) are $51,000 instead of $50,000. The new discount factor is 4.03079 ($205,570.50/$51,000). Going once again to the sixth row in Exhibit 14B-2, it is clear that the discount factor—and thus the IRR—lies between 12 and 14 percent. Although it is possible to approximate the IRR by interpolation, for simplicity, identify the range for the IRR as indicated by the table values. In practice, business calculators or spreadsheet programs like Excel can provide the values of IRR without the use of tables such as Exhibit 14B-2.

Multiple-Period Setting: Uneven Cash Flows

If the cash flows are not uniform, then the IRR equation must be used. For a multiple-period setting, this equation can be solved by trial and error or by using a business calculator or a spreadsheet program. To illustrate solution by trial and error, assume

The HOW and WHY of Calculating Internal Rate of Return with Uniform Cash Flows

CORNERSTONE 14-4

Information:
Assume that a hospital has the opportunity to invest \$205,570.50 in a new ultrasound system that will produce net cash inflows of \$50,000 at the end of each of the next six years.

Required:
Calculate the IRR for the ultrasound system.

Solution:

$$\begin{aligned} df &= I/CF \\ &= \$205{,}570.50/\$50{,}000 \\ &= 4.11141 \end{aligned}$$

Since the life of the investment is six years, find the sixth row in Exhibit 14B-2 and then move across this row until $df = 4.11141$ is found. The interest rate corresponding to 4.11141 is 12 percent, which is the IRR.

WHY:
Internal rate of return allows us to evaluate a variety of projects and compare them. It incorporates present value calculations, which are viewed as the most reliable indicators of value to a company.

that a \$10,000 investment in a PC system produces clerical savings of \$6,000 and \$7,200, respectively, for the two years. The IRR is the interest rate that sets the present value of these two cash inflows equal to \$10,000:

$$\begin{aligned} P &= \left[\frac{\$6{,}000}{(1+i)}\right] + \left[\frac{\$7{,}200}{(1+i)^2}\right] \\ &= \$10{,}000 \end{aligned}$$

To solve this equation by trial and error, start by selecting a possible value for *i*. Given this first guess, the present value of the future cash flows is computed and then compared with the initial investment. If the present value is greater than the initial investment, then the interest rate is too low; if the present value is less than the initial investment, then the interest rate is too high. The next guess is adjusted accordingly.

Assume that the first guess is 18 percent. Using *i* equal to 0.18, Exhibit 14B-1 yields the following discount factors: 0.84746 and 0.71818. These discount factors produce the following present value for the two cash inflows:

$$\begin{aligned} P &= (0.84746 \times \$6{,}000) + (0.71818 \times \$7{,}200) \\ &= \$10{,}256 \end{aligned}$$

Since *P* is greater than \$10,000, the interest rate selected is too low. A higher guess is needed. If the next guess is 20 percent, we obtain the following:

$$\begin{aligned} P &= (0.83333 \times \$6{,}000) + (0.69444 \times \$7{,}200) \\ &= \$9{,}999.95 \end{aligned}$$

Since this value is very close to \$10,000, we can say that the IRR is 20 percent. (The IRR is, in fact, exactly 20 percent; the present value is slightly less than the investment because the discount factors found in Exhibit 14B-1 have been rounded to 5 decimal places.)

OBJECTIVE 5
Incorporate the tax shield into capital expenditure analysis.

Income Tax Considerations in Capital Budgeting

Introduction to Income Taxes

To this point in the chapter, we have considered the cash inflows and outflows of capital budgeting decisions without taking into account the income tax considerations. Now we will introduce this complication to our calculations.

The *Income Tax Act* (ITA) is specific legislation that deals with how Canadians (both personal and corporate) will calculate how much they must pay the federal and provincial governments each year. For income tax purposes, companies must calculate their net income according to generally accepted accounting principles, except where the ITA specifically indicates how revenues or expenses must be calculated.

We must remember that the governments do not necessarily follow generally accepted accounting principles in determining how companies should calculate their net income for tax purposes, as the legislation is intended to reflect government policy. Governments will use the legislation to encourage or discourage investment in certain sectors and will use it to eliminate, wherever possible, the discretion that managers have to alter their net income.

This is especially true when it comes to the depreciation of capital assets. As you will recall from financial accounting, in determining the depreciation policies to be used, a company will estimate the useful life of an asset and estimate its salvage value at the end of its useful life. Changing either or both of these estimates will result in significant differences in the annual expense for depreciation.

To eliminate this discretion, the ITA specifies that, for tax purposes, the expense related to using an asset will be calculated on the declining balance basis, and the maximum rates used will be as specified in Schedule II to the regulations. In the ITA, this annual expense is referred to as Capital Cost Allowance (CCA), and the balance remaining after deducting the CCA from the original cost of the asset is the Undepreciated Capital Cost (UCC). Each year, the CCA rate is applied to the UCC to determine the maximum expense allowed for tax purposes.

A sample of these classes and rates is as follows:

Class 8	Office Equipment	20%
Class 10	Computer Equipment and Vehicles	30%
Class 43	Manufacturing Equipment	30%

Furthermore, all assets of the same class are pooled together into groups of assets for which CCA is calculated. On disposition of an asset in any class, the proceeds of disposition are deducted from the balance of the asset class before calculating the CCA in any year. This results in a taxable gain or loss on disposition of an asset only if the asset being disposed of represents the last asset in the class or the UCC becomes negative. This is referred to as a *terminal gain* or a *terminal loss.* Otherwise, accounting gains or losses on disposal are not taxable.

An additional complication is that the ITA specifies that a taxpayer can only deduct one half of the normal CCA in the year of acquisition (the half year rule). Since an asset will be disposed of in a year, it will not be depreciated for tax purposes in the year of disposal.

The government frequently changes the rates applicable to the classes of assets to be consistent with their then-current economic policy, so one should be certain to use up-to-date information when making a decision.

Impact on Capital Budgeting Decisions

When analyzing a capital project, we must focus on the true cash flow to the company if we are to provide an accurate analysis of the project. To do so, we must adjust the cash inflows and outflows for the impact of taxation on those cash flows. To do so, we must understand how the cash inflows and outflows will be taxed, if at all.

As we have seen above, income tax is a very complicated area, so we must make several simplifying assumptions, which will allow us to concentrate on the core principles involved. The first simplifying assumption is that companies are taxed at a flat rate of tax on all incremental income being generated. Second, we will assume that net income before tax for accounting purposes equals taxable income as reported on our tax return.

After-Tax Cash Flows When we report net income from a project, we must adjust it for the additional tax that would have to be paid if we decide to pursue the project. In simple terms, if we increase our net income before tax by \$1,000, shareholders will not realize a \$1,000 increase in value; they will realize an increase in value determined by the after-tax amount of the net income. At a 30 percent tax rate, shareholders would realize an increase in value of \$700 (\$1,000 minus the tax on \$1,000 of \$300).

Likewise, if the company incurs a tax-deductible expense, shareholders will not see their value diminished by the full amount of the expense but rather by the amount of the expense less the reduction in income taxes related to that expense. If the expense were \$500, the income tax would be reduced by \$150, so the net impact on the shareholder would be a reduction in value of \$350.

The after-tax impact of cash inflows and outflows, if they are taxable, can be achieved by multiplying the amount by 1 minus the tax rate $(1-t)$.

However, we must be mindful that not all cash inflows and outflows are taxable or tax deductible, whichever the case may be. The original investment will be expensed over time through the use of depreciation, so the original investment will not be a tax deductible expense. Likewise, the investment of working capital will not be a tax-deductible expense.

On the other hand, the cash inflows from the project and the cash outflows representing expenses incurred as a result of the project will be tax-affected items and must be adjusted to their after-tax values to give us an accurate picture of the viability of the project.

Capital Cost Allowance As noted earlier, the tax department allows a company to deduct a certain amount for Capital Cost Allowance (tax depreciation) when calculating its income tax obligation. While the CCA deduction is not a cash inflow to the company directly, it does allow the company to reduce the amount of income tax it must pay. Therefore, while the CCA deduction is not a cash inflow, the saving of tax is a cash inflow and must be recognized.

The amount of the reduction in tax is complicated by the half-year rule, so we must determine, over the course of the project, the net impact of the CCA deduction. One additional complication is that when a piece of equipment is disposed of, and the proceeds are deducted from the balance remaining in the class of asset, this amount is not taxable unless the asset being disposed of represents the last asset in the class or the UCC becomes negative. If the asset is the last asset in the class or the UCC becomes negative, the company will realize taxable income (terminal gain) or a tax deductible expense (terminal loss).

For our purposes, we will assume that any dispositions do not result in either a terminal gain or a terminal loss.

CCA Tax Shield Since the reduction of our net income for tax purposes is allowed through CCA deductions, this creates a reduction in income taxes payable. This fact is often referred to as a **tax shield**, since the deduction *shields* income that would otherwise result in a tax expense.

Since the CCA is available each year on an investment, and since the amount of the CCA will diminish each year under the declining balance method of calculation, we must use a formula to determine the present value of the tax shield for the investment. This formula is:

$$PV = \frac{Cdt}{d+k} \times \frac{1+0.5k}{1+k}$$

where C represents the cost of the asset, d represents the CCA rate for the asset, and k represents the minimum acceptable rate of return.

The final term $(1 + 0.5k) \div (1 + k)$ is required to adjust for *the half year rule*.

Using the example outlined in Cornerstone 14-3, we can adjust the project analysis to show the tax implications, assuming a 12 percent required rate of return, a 30 percent tax rate, and a 40 percent CCA rate, as follows:

Cash Flow Identification

Year	Item	Cash Flow	Factor (1-30%)	After-Tax Cash Flow
0	Equipment	$(320,000)	N/A	$(320,000)
	Working capital	$ (40,000)	N/A	$ (40,000)
	Total	$ 360,000		$(360,000)
1–4	Revenues	$ 300,000	0.7	$ 210,000
	Operating expenses	$(180,000)	0.7	$(126,000)
	Total	$ 120,000		$ 84,000
5	Revenues	$ 300,000	0.7	$ 210,000
	Operating expenses	$(180,000)	0.7	$(126,000)
	Salvage (Disposal)	40,000		40,000
	Recovery of working capital	40,000		40,000
	Total	$ 200,000		$ 160,000

NPV Analysis

Year	Cash Flow	Discount Factor	Present Value
0	$(360,000)	1.00000	$(360,000)
1–4	$ 84,000	3.03735	$ 255,137
5	$ 160,000	0.56743	$ 90,789
5	PV of CCA Tax Shield		69,888
			$ 55,814

As you can see, when compared to the analysis without taking income taxes into consideration, the NPV of the project is considerably different ($117,968, compared to $55,814). In some cases, the income tax considerations will render a project unacceptable, even if the project appeared acceptable before taking income taxes into consideration.

OBJECTIVE 6
Explain the role and value of postaudits.

Postaudit of Capital Projects

A key element in the capital investment process is a follow-up analysis of a capital project once it is implemented. This analysis is called a *postaudit.* A **postaudit** compares the actual benefits with the estimated benefits and actual operating costs with estimated operating costs; it evaluates the overall outcome of the investment and proposes corrective action if needed. The following real-world case illustrates the usefulness of a postaudit activity.

Honley Medical Company: An Illustrative Application

Allen Manesfield and Jenny Winters were discussing a persistent and irritating problem present in the process of producing intravenous (IV) needles. Both Allen and Jenny are employed by Honley Medical, which specializes in the production of medical products and has three divisions: the IV Products Division, the Critical Care Monitoring Division, and the Specialty Products Division. Allen and Jenny both are associated with the IV Products Division—Allen as the senior production engineer and Jenny as the marketing manager.

The IV Products Division produces needles of five different sizes. During one stage of the manufacturing process, the needle itself is inserted into a plastic hub and is bonded by using epoxy glue. According to Jenny, the use of epoxy to bond the needles was causing the division all kinds of problems. In many cases, the epoxy wasn't bonding correctly. The rejects were high and the division was receiving a large number of complaints from its customers. Corrective action was needed to avoid losing sales. After some discussion and analysis, a recommendation was made to use induction welding in lieu of epoxy bonding. In induction welding, the needles are inserted into the plastic hub, and an RF generator is used to heat the needles. The RF generator works on the same principle as a microwave oven. As the needles get hot, the plastic melts and the needles are bonded.

Switching to induction welding required an investment in RF generators and the associated tooling; the investment was justified by the IV Products Division based on the savings associated with the new system. Induction welding promised to reduce the cost of direct materials, eliminating the need to buy and use epoxy. Savings of direct labour costs also were predicted because the welding process is much more automated. Adding to these savings were the avoidance of daily cleanup costs and the reduction in rejects. Allen presented a formal NPV analysis showing that the welding system was superior to the epoxy system. Headquarters approved its purchase.

One Year Later

Jenny: Allen, I'm quite pleased with induction welding for bonding needles. In the year since the new process was implemented, we've had virtually no complaints from our customers. The needles are firmly bonded.

Allen: I wish that positive experience were true for all other areas as well. Unfortunately, implementing the process has uncovered some rather sticky and expensive problems that I didn't anticipate. The Internal Audit Department recently completed a postaudit of the project, and now my feet are being held to the fire.

Jenny: That's too bad. What's the problem?

Allen: You mean problems. Let me list a few for you. One is that the RF generators interfered with the operation of other equipment. To eliminate this interference, we had to install filtering equipment. But that's not all. We also discovered that the average maintenance person doesn't know how to maintain the new equipment. Now we are faced with the need to initiate a training program to upgrade the skills of our maintenance people. Upgrading skills also implies higher wages. Although the RF bonding process is less messy, it is more complex. The manufacturing people complained to the internal auditors about that. They maintain that a simple process, even if messy, is to be preferred—especially now that demand for the product is increasing by leaps and bounds.

Jenny: What did the internal auditors conclude?

Allen: They concluded that many of the predicted savings did take place but that some significant costs were not foreseen. Because of these unforeseen problems, they have recommended that I look carefully at the possibility of moving back to using epoxy. They indicated that NPV analysis using actual data appears to favour that process. With production expanding, the acquisition of additional RF generators and filtering equipment plus the necessary training is simply not as attractive as returning to epoxy bonding. This conclusion is reinforced by the fact that the epoxy process is simpler and by the auditors' conclusion that the mixing of the epoxy can be automated, avoiding the quality problem we had in the first place.

Jenny: Well, Allen, you can't really blame yourself. You had a real problem and took action to solve it. It's difficult to foresee all the problems and hidden costs of a new process.

Allen: Unfortunately, the internal auditors don't totally agree. In fact, neither do I. I probably jumped too quickly. In the future, I intend to think through new projects more carefully.

Benefits of a Postaudit

In the case of the RF bonding decision, some of the estimated capital investment benefits did materialize: complaints from customers decreased, rejects were fewer, and direct labour and materials costs decreased. However, the investment was greater than expected because filtering equipment was needed, and actual operating costs were much higher because of the increased maintenance cost and the increased complexity of the process. Overall, the internal auditors concluded that the investment was a poor decision. The corrective action that they recommended was to abandon the new process and return to epoxy bonding. Based on this recommendation, the firm abandoned inductive welding and returned to epoxy bonding, which was improved by automating the mix.

Firms that perform postaudits of capital projects experience a number of benefits. First, by evaluating profitability, postaudits ensure that resources are used wisely. If the project is doing well, it may call for additional funds and additional attention. If the project is not doing well, corrective action may be needed to improve performance or abandon the project.

A second benefit of the postaudit is its impact on the behaviour of managers. If managers are held accountable for the results of a capital investment decision, they are more likely to make such decisions in the best interests of the firm. Additionally, postaudits supply feedback to managers that should help to improve future decision making. Consider Allen's reaction to the postaudit of the RF bonding process. Certainly, we would expect him to be more careful and more thorough in making future investment recommendations. In the future, Allen will probably consider more than one alternative, such as automating the mixing of the epoxy. Also, for those alternatives being considered, he will probably be especially alert to the possibility of hidden costs, such as increased training requirements for a new process.

CONCEPT Q&A

Why do a postaudit?

Answers on pages 711 to 715.

The case also reveals that the postaudit was performed by the internal audit staff. Generally, more objective results are obtainable if the postaudit is done by an independent party. Since considerable effort is expended to ensure as much independence as possible for the internal audit staff, that group is usually the best choice for this task.

Postaudits, however, are costly. Moreover, even though they may provide significant benefits, they have other limitations. Most obvious is the fact that the assumptions driving the original analysis may often be invalidated by changes in the actual operating environment. Accountability must be qualified to some extent by the impossibility of foreseeing every possible eventuality.

OBJECTIVE 7
Explain why net present value is better than internal rate of return for capital investment decisions involving mutually exclusive projects.

Mutually Exclusive Projects

Up to this point, we have focused on independent projects. Many capital investment decisions deal with mutually exclusive projects. How NPV analysis and IRR are used to choose among competing projects is an interesting question. An even more interesting question to consider is whether NPV and IRR differ in their ability to help managers make wealth-maximizing decisions in the presence of competing alternatives. For example, we already know that the nondiscounting models can produce erroneous choices because they ignore the time value of money. Because of this deficiency, the discounting models are judged superior. Similarly, it can be shown that the NPV model is generally preferred to the IRR model when choosing among mutually exclusive alternatives.

Net Present Value Compared with Internal Rate of Return

NPV and IRR both yield the same decision for independent projects. For example, if the NPV is greater than zero, then the IRR is also greater than the required rate of return; both models signal the correct decision. However, for competing projects, the two methods can produce different results. Intuitively, we believe that for mutually exclusive projects, the project with the highest NPV or the highest IRR should be chosen. Since it is possible for the two methods to produce different rankings of mutually exclusive projects, the method that consistently reveals the wealth-maximizing project is preferred.

NPV differs from IRR in two major ways. First, NPV assumes that each cash inflow received is reinvested at the required rate of return, whereas the IRR method

Exhibit 14-1

Net Present Value Compared with Internal Rate of Return

	NPV	IRR
Type of measure	***Absolute*** dollars	***Relative*** percentage
Cash flow reinvestment assumption	At required rate of return	At internal rate of return

assumes that each cash inflow is reinvested at the computed IRR. Reinvesting at the required rate of return is more realistic and produces more reliable results when comparing mutually exclusive projects. Second, the NPV method measures profitability in absolute terms, whereas the IRR method measures it in relative terms. NPV measures the amount by which the value of the firm changes. These differences are summarized in Exhibit 14-1.

Since NPV measures the impact that competing projects have on the value of the firm, choosing the project with the largest NPV is consistent with maximizing the wealth of shareholders. On the other hand, IRR does not consistently result in choices that maximize wealth. IRR, as a relative measure of profitability, has the virtue of measuring accurately the rate of return of funds that remain internally invested. However, maximizing IRR will not necessarily maximize the wealth of firm owners because it cannot, by nature, consider the absolute dollar contributions of projects. In the final analysis, what counts are the total dollars earned—the absolute profits—not the relative profits. Accordingly, NPV, not IRR, should be used for choosing among competing, mutually exclusive projects or competing projects when capital funds are limited.

An independent project is acceptable if its NPV is positive. For mutually exclusive projects, the project with the largest NPV is chosen. There are three steps in selecting the best project from several competing projects: (1) assessing the cash flow pattern for each project, (2) computing the NPV for each project, and (3) identifying the project with the greatest NPV. To illustrate NPV analysis for competing projects, an example is provided.

CONCEPT Q&A

Why is NPV better than IRR for choosing among competing projects?

Answers on pages 711 to 715.

Example: Mutually Exclusive Projects

Bintley Corporation has committed to improving its environmental performance. One environmental project identified a manufacturing process as being the source of both liquid and gaseous residues. After six months of research activity, the engineering department announced that it is possible to redesign the process to prevent the production of contaminating residues. Two different process designs (A and B) are being considered that prevent the production of contaminants. Both process designs are more expensive to operate than the current process; however, because the designs prevent production of contaminants, significant annual benefits are created. These benefits stem from eliminating the need to operate and maintain expensive pollution control equipment, treat and dispose of toxic liquid wastes, and pay the annual fines for exceeding allowable contaminant releases. Increased sales to environmentally conscious customers also are factored into the benefit estimates. Cornerstone 14-5 shows how NPV and IRR analyses are carried out for this setting.

CORNERSTONE 14-5

The HOW and WHY of Calculating Net Present Value and Internal Rate of Return for Mutually Exclusive Projects

Information:

Consider two pollution prevention designs: Design A and Design B. Both designs have a project life of five years. Design A requires an initial outlay of $180,000 and has a net annual after-tax cash inflow of $60,000 (revenues of $180,000 minus costs of $120,000). Design B, with an initial outlay of $210,000, has a net annual cash inflow of $70,000 ($240,000 – $170,000). The after-tax cash flows are summarized as follows:

CASH FLOW PATTERN

Year	Design A	Design B
0	$(180,000)	$(210,000)
1	60,000	70,000
2	60,000	70,000
3	60,000	70,000
4	60,000	70,000
5	60,000	70,000

The cost of capital for the company is 12 percent.

Required:

Calculate the NPV and the IRR for each project.

Solution:

DESIGN A: NPV ANALYSIS

Year	Cash Flow	Discount Factor*	Present Value
0	$(180,000)	1.00000	$(180,000)
1–5	60,000	3.60478	216,287
Net present value			$ 36,287

DESIGN A: IRR ANALYSIS

Discount factor = Initial investment/Annual cash flow
= $180,000/$60,000
= 3.00000

From Exhibit 14B-2, *df* = 3.00000 for five years implies that IRR = 20 percent.

DESIGN B: NPV ANALYSIS

Year	Cash Flow	Discount Factor*	Present Value
0	$(210,000)	1.00000	$(210,000)
1–5	70,000	3.60478	252,335
Net present value			$ 42,335

DESIGN B: IRR ANALYSIS

Discount factor = Initial investment/Annual cash flow
= $210,000/$70,000
= 3.00000

From Exhibit 14B-2, *df* = 3.00000 for five years implies that IRR = 20 percent.

*From Exhibit 14B-2.

WHY:
When a company is faced with projects in which only one project will be accepted, we can evaluate them using either net present value analysis or internal rate of return. Often we will get conflicting results, so we must have a method of choosing among the projects. Both these alternatives use present value calculations, which will allow better decision making.

CORNERSTONE 14-5 *(continued)*

Based on NPV analysis, Design B is more profitable; it has the larger NPV. Accordingly, the company should select Design B over Design A. Interestingly, Designs A and B have identical internal rates of return. As shown by Cornerstone 14-5, both designs have a discount factor of 3.00000. From Exhibit 14B-2, it is easily seen that a discount factor of 3.00000 and a life of five years yields an IRR of about 20 percent. Even though both projects have an IRR of 20 percent, the firm should not consider the two designs to be equally desirable. The analysis demonstrates that Design B produces a larger NPV and, therefore, will increase the value of the firm more than Design A. Design B should be chosen. This illustrates the conceptual superiority of NPV over IRR for analysis of competing projects.

Special Considerations for the Advanced Manufacturing Environment

How Investment Differs Investment in automated manufacturing processes is much more complex than investment in the standard manufacturing equipment of the past. For standard equipment, the direct costs of acquisition represent virtually the entire investment. For automated manufacturing, the direct costs can represent as little as 50 or 60 percent of the total investment; software, engineering, training, and implementation are a significant percentage of the total costs. Thus great care must be exercised to assess the actual cost of an automated system. It is easy to overlook the peripheral costs, which can be substantial.

How Estimates of Operating Cash Flows Differ Estimates of operating cash flows from investments in standard equipment typically have relied on directly identifiable tangible benefits, such as direct savings from labour, power, and scrap. However, when investing in automated systems, the intangible and indirect benefits can be material and critical to the viability of the project. Greater quality, more reliability, reduced lead time, improved customer satisfaction, and an enhanced ability to maintain market share all are important intangible benefits of an advanced manufacturing system. Reduction of labour in support areas such as production scheduling and stores are indirect benefits. More effort is needed to measure these intangible and indirect benefits in order to assess more accurately the potential value of investments.

An example can be used to illustrate the importance of considering intangible and indirect benefits. Consider a company that is evaluating a potential investment in a flexible manufacturing system (FMS). The choice facing the company is to continue producing with its traditional equipment, expected to last 10 years, or to switch to the new system, which also is expected to have a useful life of 10 years. The company's discount rate is 12 percent. The data pertaining to the investment are presented in Exhibit 14-2. Notice that for this example, the *incremental cash flows* are used to compare the new project with the old. Instead of calculating the NPV for each alternative and comparing, an equivalent approach is to calculate the NPV of the incremental cash flows of the new system (cash flows of new system less cash flows of old system). If the NPV for the incremental cash flows is positive, then the new equipment is preferred to the old.

Exhibit 14-2

Investment Data; Direct, Intangible, and Indirect Benefits

	FMS		Status Quo
Investment (current outlay):			
Direct costs	$10,000,000		—
Software, engineering	8,000,000		—
Total current outlay	$18,000,000		$ 0
Net after-tax cash flow	$ 5,000,000		$1,000,000
Less: After-tax cash flows for status quo	1,000,000		n/a
Incremental benefit	$ 4,000,000		n/a
Incremental Benefit Explained			
Direct benefits:			
Direct labour	$ 1,500,000		
Scrap reduction	500,000		
Setups	200,000		$2,200,000
Intangible benefits (quality savings):			
Rework	$ 200,000		
Warranties	400,000		
Maintenance of competitive position	1,000,000		1,600,000
Indirect benefits:			
Production scheduling	$ 110,000		
Payroll	90,000		200,000
Total			$4,000,000

Using the incremental data in Exhibit 14-2, the NPV of the proposed system can be computed as follows:

Present value ($4,000,000 × 5.65022*)	$22,600,880
Investment	18,000,000
NPV	$ 4,600,880

* This number is the discount factor for an interest rate of 12 percent and a life of 10 years (see Exhibit 14B-2).

The NPV is positive and large in magnitude, and it clearly signals the acceptability of the FMS. This outcome, however, is strongly dependent on explicit recognition of both intangible and indirect benefits. If those benefits are eliminated, then the direct savings total $2.2 million, and the NPV is negative:

Present value ($2,200,000 × 5.65022)	$12,430,484
Investment	18,000,000
NPV	$ (5,569,516)

The rise of activity-based costing has made identifying indirect benefits easier with the use of cost drivers. Once they are identified, they can be included in the analysis if they are material.

Examination of Exhibit 14-2 reveals the importance of intangible benefits. One of the most important intangible benefits is maintaining or improving a firm's competitive position. A key question is what will happen to the cash flows of the firm if the investment is not made. That is, if the company chooses to forgo an investment in technologically advanced equipment, will it be able to continue to compete with other firms on the basis of quality, delivery, and cost? (The question becomes especially relevant if competitors choose to invest in advanced equipment.) If the competitive position deteriorates, the company's current cash flows will decrease.

If cash flows will decrease if the investment is not made, this decrease should show up as an incremental benefit for the advanced technology. In Exhibit 14-2, the company estimates this competitive benefit as $1,000,000. Estimating this benefit requires some serious strategic planning and analysis, but its effect can be critical. If this benefit had been ignored or overlooked, then the NPV would have been negative and the investment alternative rejected:

Present value ($3,000,000 × 5.65022)	$16,950,660
Investment	18,000,000
NPV	$ (1,049,340)

Summary of Learning Objectives

LO1. Explain the meaning of *capital investment decisions*, and distinguish between independent and mutually exclusive capital investment decisions.

- Capital investment decisions are concerned with the acquisition of long-term assets and usually involve a significant outlay of funds.
- The two types of capital investment projects are independent and mutually exclusive.
- Independent projects are projects that, whether accepted or rejected, do not affect the cash flows of other projects.
- Mutually exclusive projects are those projects that, if accepted, preclude the acceptance of all other competing projects.

LO2. Compute the payback period and accounting rate of return for a proposed investment, and explain their roles in capital investment decisions.

- Managers make capital investment decisions by using formal models to decide whether to accept or reject proposed projects.
- These decision models are classified as nondiscounting and discounting, depending on whether they address the question of the time value of money.
- The two nondiscounting models are the payback period and the ARR.
- The payback period is the time required for a firm to recover its initial investment. For even cash flows, it is calculated by dividing the investment by the annual cash flow. For uneven cash flows, the cash flows are summed until the investment is recovered. If only a fraction of a year is needed, then it is assumed that the cash flows occur evenly within each year.
- The payback period ignores the time value of money and the profitability of projects because it does not consider the cash inflows available beyond the payback period. However, it does supply some useful information. The payback period is useful for assessing and controlling risk, minimizing the impact of an investment on a firm's liquidity, and controlling the risk of obsolescence.
- The ARR is computed by dividing the average income expected from an investment by either the original or average investment.
- Unlike the payback period, the ARR does consider the profitability of a project; however, it ignores the time value of money.
- The ARR may be useful to managers for screening new investments to ensure that certain accounting ratios are not adversely affected (specifically, accounting ratios that may be monitored to ensure compliance with debt covenants).

LO3. Use net present value analysis for capital investment decisions involving independent projects.

- NPV is the difference between the present value of future cash flows and the initial investment outlay.
- To use the NPV model, a required rate of return must be identified (usually the cost of capital). The NPV method uses the required rate of return to compute the present value of a project's cash inflows and outflows.
- If the present value of the inflows is greater than the present value of the outflows, then the NPV is greater than zero, and the project is profitable; if the NPV is less than zero, then the project is not profitable and should be rejected.

invested now to produce the future value is known as the **present value** of the future amount. For example, how much must be invested now in order to yield $363 two years from now, assuming that the interest rate is 10 percent? Or, put another way, what is the present value of $363 to be received two years from now?

In this example, the future value, the years, and the interest rate are all known; we want to know the current outlay that will produce that future amount. In the compounding interest equation, the variable representing the current outlay (the present value of *F*) is *P*. Thus, to compute the present value of a future outlay, all we need to do is solve the compounding interest equation for *P*:

$$P = \frac{F}{(1+i)^n}$$

Using this present value equation, we can compute the present value of $363:

$$\begin{aligned} P &= \frac{\$363}{(1+0.1)^2} \\ &= \$363/1.21 \\ &= \$300 \end{aligned}$$

The present value, $300, is what the future amount of $363 is worth today if it can be invested at 10 percent. All other things being equal, having $300 today is the same as having $363 two years from now. Put another way, if a firm requires a 10 percent rate of return, the most the firm would be willing to pay today is $300 for any investment that yields $363 two years from now.

The process of computing the present value of future cash flows is often referred to as **discounting**; thus, we say that we have discounted the future value of $363 to its present value of $300. The interest rate used to discount the future cash flow is the **discount rate**. The expression $1/(1 + i)^n$ in the present value equation is the **discount factor**. By letting the discount factor, called *df*, equal $1/(1 + i)^n$, the present value equation can be expressed as $P = F(df)$. To simplify the computation of present value, a table of discount factors is given for various combinations of *i* and *n* (refer to Exhibit 14B-1 in Appendix 14B). For example, the discount factor for $i = 10$ percent and $n = 2$ is 0.82645 (go to the 10 percent column of the table and move down to the second row). With the discount factor, the present value of $363 is computed as follows:

$$\begin{aligned} P &= F(df) \\ &= \$363 \times 0.82645 \\ &= \$300 \text{ (rounded)} \end{aligned}$$

Present Value of an Uneven Series of Cash Flows

Exhibit 14B 1 can be used to compute the present value of any future cash flow or series of future cash flows. A series of future cash flows is called an **annuity**. The present value of an annuity is found by computing the present value of each future cash flow and then summing these values. For example, suppose that an investment is expected to produce the following annual cash flows: $110, $121, and $133.10. Assuming a discount rate of 10 percent, the present value of this series of cash flows is computed in Exhibit 14A-1.

Present Value of a Uniform Series of Cash Flows

If the series of cash flows is even, the computation of the annuity's present value is simplified. For example, assume that an investment is expected to return $100 per year for three years. Using Exhibit 14B-1 and assuming a discount rate of 10 percent, the present value of the annuity is computed in Exhibit 14A-2.

As with the uneven series of cash flows, the present value in Exhibit 14A-2 was computed by calculating the present value of each cash flow separately and then

Exhibit 14A-1

Present Value of an Uneven Series of Cash Flows

Year	Cash Receipt	Discount Factor	Present Value*
1	$110.00	0.90909	$100.00
2	121.00	0.82645	100.00
3	133.10	0.75131	100.00
		2.48685	$300.00

* Rounded.

Exhibit 14A-2

Present Value of an Annuity

Year	Cash Receipt*	Discount Factor	Present Value*
1	$100	0.90909	$ 90.91
2	100	0.82645	82.65
3	100	0.75131	75.13
		2.48685	$248.69

* The annual cash flow of $100 can be multiplied by the sum of the discount factors (2.48685) to obtain the present value of the uniform series ($248.69).

summing them. However, in the case of an annuity displaying uniform cash flows, the computations can be reduced from three to one as described in the footnote to the exhibit. The sum of the individual discount factors can be thought of as a discount factor for an annuity of uniform cash flows. A table of discount factors that can be used for an annuity of uniform cash flows is available in Exhibit 14B-2.

Key Terms for Appendix 14A

Annuity, 670
Compounding of interest, 669
Discount factor, 670
Discount rate, 670
Discounting, 670
Future value, 669
Present value, 670

Appendix 14B: Present Value Tables

The present value tables are found on pages 672 and 673.

Exhibit 14B-1

Present Value of a Single Amount*

n/i	1%	2%	3%	4%	5%	6%	7%	8%	9%	10%	12%	14%	16%	18%	20%	25%	30%
1	0.99010	0.98039	0.97087	0.96154	0.95238	0.94340	0.93458	0.92593	0.91743	0.90909	0.89286	0.87719	0.86207	0.84746	0.83333	0.80000	0.76923
2	0.98030	0.96117	0.94260	0.92456	0.90703	0.89000	0.87344	0.85734	0.84168	0.82645	0.79719	0.76947	0.74316	0.71818	0.69444	0.64000	0.59172
3	0.97059	0.94232	0.91514	0.88900	0.86384	0.83962	0.81630	0.79383	0.77218	0.75131	0.71178	0.67497	0.64066	0.60863	0.57870	0.51200	0.45517
4	0.96098	0.92385	0.88849	0.85480	0.82270	0.79209	0.76290	0.73503	0.70843	0.68301	0.63552	0.59208	0.55229	0.51579	0.48225	0.40960	0.35013
5	0.95147	0.90573	0.86261	0.82193	0.78353	0.74726	0.71299	0.68058	0.64993	0.62092	0.56743	0.51937	0.47611	0.43711	0.40188	0.32768	0.26933
6	0.94205	0.88797	0.83748	0.79031	0.74622	0.70496	0.66634	0.63017	0.59627	0.56447	0.50663	0.45559	0.41044	0.37043	0.33490	0.26214	0.20718
7	0.93272	0.87056	0.81309	0.75992	0.71068	0.66506	0.62275	0.58349	0.54703	0.51316	0.45235	0.39964	0.35383	0.31393	0.27908	0.20972	0.15937
8	0.92348	0.85349	0.78941	0.73069	0.67684	0.62741	0.58201	0.54027	0.50187	0.46651	0.40388	0.35056	0.30503	0.26604	0.23257	0.16777	0.12259
9	0.91434	0.83676	0.76642	0.70259	0.64461	0.59190	0.54393	0.50025	0.46043	0.42410	0.36061	0.30751	0.26295	0.22546	0.19381	0.13422	0.09430
10	0.90529	0.82035	0.74409	0.67556	0.61391	0.55839	0.50835	0.46319	0.42241	0.38554	0.32197	0.26974	0.22668	0.19106	0.16151	0.10737	0.07254
11	0.89632	0.80426	0.72242	0.64958	0.58468	0.52679	0.47509	0.42888	0.38753	0.35049	0.28748	0.23662	0.19542	0.16192	0.13459	0.08590	0.05580
12	0.88745	0.78849	0.70138	0.62460	0.55684	0.49697	0.44401	0.39711	0.35553	0.31863	0.25668	0.20756	0.16846	0.13722	0.11216	0.06872	0.04292
13	0.87866	0.77303	0.68095	0.60057	0.53032	0.46884	0.41496	0.36770	0.32618	0.28966	0.22917	0.18207	0.14523	0.11629	0.09346	0.05498	0.03302
14	0.86996	0.75788	0.66112	0.57748	0.50507	0.44230	0.38782	0.34046	0.29925	0.26333	0.20462	0.15971	0.12520	0.09855	0.07789	0.04398	0.02540
15	0.86135	0.74301	0.64186	0.55526	0.48102	0.41727	0.36245	0.31524	0.27454	0.23939	0.18270	0.14010	0.10793	0.08352	0.06491	0.03518	0.01954
16	0.85282	0.72845	0.62317	0.53391	0.45811	0.39365	0.33873	0.29189	0.25187	0.21763	0.16312	0.12289	0.09304	0.07078	0.05409	0.02815	0.01503
17	0.84438	0.71416	0.60502	0.51337	0.43630	0.37136	0.31657	0.27027	0.23107	0.19784	0.14564	0.10780	0.08021	0.05998	0.04507	0.02252	0.01156
18	0.83602	0.70016	0.58739	0.49363	0.41552	0.35034	0.29586	0.25025	0.21199	0.17986	0.13004	0.09456	0.06914	0.05083	0.03756	0.01801	0.00889
19	0.82774	0.68643	0.57029	0.47464	0.39573	0.33051	0.27651	0.23171	0.19449	0.16351	0.11611	0.08295	0.05961	0.04308	0.03130	0.01441	0.00684
20	0.81954	0.67297	0.55368	0.45639	0.37689	0.31180	0.25842	0.21455	0.17843	0.14864	0.10367	0.07276	0.05139	0.03651	0.02608	0.01153	0.00526
21	0.81143	0.65978	0.53755	0.43883	0.35894	0.29416	0.24151	0.19866	0.16370	0.13513	0.09256	0.06383	0.04430	0.03094	0.02174	0.00922	0.00405
22	0.80340	0.64684	0.52189	0.42196	0.34185	0.27751	0.22571	0.18394	0.15018	0.12285	0.08264	0.05599	0.03819	0.02622	0.01811	0.00738	0.00311
23	0.79544	0.63416	0.50669	0.40573	0.32557	0.26180	0.21095	0.17032	0.13778	0.11168	0.07379	0.04911	0.03292	0.02222	0.01509	0.00590	0.00239
24	0.78757	0.62172	0.49193	0.39012	0.31007	0.24698	0.19715	0.15770	0.12640	0.10153	0.06588	0.04308	0.02838	0.01883	0.01258	0.00472	0.00184
25	0.77977	0.60953	0.47761	0.37512	0.29530	0.23300	0.18425	0.14602	0.11597	0.09230	0.05882	0.03779	0.02447	0.01596	0.01048	0.00378	0.00142
26	0.77205	0.59758	0.46369	0.36069	0.28124	0.21981	0.17220	0.13520	0.10639	0.08391	0.05252	0.03315	0.02109	0.01352	0.00874	0.00302	0.00109
27	0.76440	0.58586	0.45019	0.34682	0.26785	0.20737	0.16093	0.12519	0.09761	0.07628	0.04689	0.02908	0.01818	0.01146	0.00728	0.00242	0.00084
28	0.75684	0.57437	0.43708	0.33348	0.25509	0.19563	0.15040	0.11591	0.08955	0.06934	0.04187	0.02551	0.01567	0.00971	0.00607	0.00193	0.00065
29	0.74934	0.56311	0.42435	0.32065	0.24295	0.18456	0.14056	0.10733	0.08215	0.06304	0.03738	0.02237	0.01351	0.00823	0.00506	0.00155	0.00050
30	0.74192	0.55207	0.41199	0.30832	0.23138	0.17411	0.13137	0.09938	0.07537	0.05731	0.03338	0.01963	0.01165	0.00697	0.00421	0.00124	0.00038

*$P_n = F/(1+i)^a$

Exhibit 14B-2

*Present Value of an Annuity**

n/i	1%	2%	3%	4%	5%	6%	7%	8%	9%	10%	12%	14%	16%	18%	20%	25%	30%
1	0.99010	0.98039	0.97087	0.96154	0.95238	0.94340	0.93458	0.92593	0.91743	0.90909	0.89286	0.87719	0.86207	0.84746	0.83333	0.80000	0.76923
2	1.97040	1.94156	1.91347	1.88609	1.85941	1.83339	1.80802	1.78326	1.75911	1.73554	1.69005	1.64666	1.60523	1.56564	1.52778	1.44000	1.36095
3	2.94099	2.88388	2.82861	2.77509	2.72325	2.67301	2.62432	2.57710	2.53129	2.48685	2.40183	2.32163	2.24589	2.17427	2.10648	1.95200	1.81611
4	3.90197	3.80773	3.71710	3.62990	3.54595	3.46511	3.38721	3.31213	3.23972	3.16987	3.03735	2.91371	2.79818	2.69006	2.58873	2.36160	2.16624
5	4.85343	4.71346	4.57971	4.45182	4.32948	4.21236	4.10020	3.99271	3.88965	3.79079	3.60478	3.43308	3.27429	3.12717	2.99061	2.68928	2.43557
6	5.79548	5.60143	5.41719	5.24214	5.07569	4.91732	4.76654	4.62288	4.48592	4.35526	4.11141	3.88867	3.68474	3.49760	3.32551	2.95142	2.64275
7	6.72819	6.47199	6.23028	6.00205	5.78637	5.58238	5.38929	5.20637	5.03295	4.86842	4.56376	4.28830	4.03857	3.81153	3.60459	3.16114	2.80211
8	7.65168	7.32548	7.01969	6.73274	6.46321	6.20979	5.97130	5.74664	5.53482	5.33493	4.96764	4.63886	4.34359	4.07757	3.83716	3.32891	2.92470
9	8.56602	8.16224	7.78611	7.43533	7.10782	6.80169	6.51523	6.24689	5.99525	5.75902	5.32825	4.94637	4.60654	4.30302	4.03097	3.46313	3.01900
10	9.47130	8.98259	8.53020	8.11090	7.72173	7.36009	7.02358	6.71008	6.41766	6.14457	5.65022	5.21612	4.83323	4.49409	4.19247	3.57050	3.09154
11	10.36763	9.78685	9.25262	8.76048	8.30641	7.88687	7.49867	7.13896	6.80519	6.49506	5.93770	5.45273	5.02864	4.65601	4.32706	3.65640	3.14734
12	11.25508	10.57534	9.95400	9.38507	8.86325	8.38384	7.94269	7.53608	7.16073	6.81369	6.19437	5.66029	5.19711	4.79322	4.43922	3.72512	3.19026
13	12.13374	11.34837	10.63496	9.98565	9.39357	8.85268	8.35765	7.90378	7.48690	7.10336	6.42355	5.84236	5.34233	4.90951	4.53268	3.78010	3.22328
14	13.00370	12.10625	11.29607	10.56312	9.89864	9.29498	8.74547	8.24424	7.78615	7.36669	6.62817	6.00207	5.46753	5.00806	4.61057	3.82408	3.24867
15	13.86505	12.84926	11.93794	11.11839	10.37966	9.71225	9.10791	8.55948	8.06069	7.60608	6.81086	6.14217	5.57546	5.09158	4.67547	3.85926	3.26821
16	14.71787	13.57771	12.56110	11.65230	10.83777	10.10590	9.44665	8.85137	8.31256	7.82371	6.97399	6.26506	5.66850	5.16235	4.72956	3.88741	3.28324
17	15.56225	14.29187	13.16612	12.16567	11.27407	10.47726	9.76322	9.12164	8.54363	8.02155	7.11963	6.37286	5.74870	5.22233	4.77463	3.90993	3.29480
18	16.39827	14.99203	13.75351	12.65930	11.68959	10.82760	10.05909	9.37189	8.75563	8.20141	7.24967	6.46742	5.81785	5.27316	4.81219	3.92794	3.30369
19	17.22601	15.67846	14.32380	13.13394	12.08532	11.15812	10.33560	9.60360	8.95011	8.36492	7.36578	6.55037	5.87746	5.31624	4.84350	3.94235	3.31053
20	18.04555	16.35143	14.87747	13.59033	12.46221	11.46992	10.59401	9.81815	9.12855	8.51356	7.46944	6.62313	5.92884	5.35275	4.86958	3.95388	3.31579
21	18.85698	17.01121	15.41502	14.02916	12.82115	11.76408	10.83553	10.01680	9.29224	8.64869	7.56200	6.68696	5.97314	5.38368	4.89132	3.96311	3.31984
22	19.66038	17.65805	15.93692	14.45112	13.16300	12.04158	11.06124	10.20074	9.44243	8.77154	7.64465	6.74294	6.01133	5.40990	4.90943	3.97049	3.32296
23	20.45582	18.29220	16.44361	14.85684	13.48857	12.30338	11.27219	10.37106	9.58021	8.88322	7.71843	6.79206	6.04425	5.43212	4.92453	3.97639	3.32535
24	21.24339	18.91393	16.93554	15.24696	13.79864	12.55036	11.46933	10.52876	9.70661	8.98474	7.78432	6.83514	6.07263	5.45095	4.93710	3.98111	3.32719
25	22.02316	19.52346	17.41315	15.62208	14.09394	12.78336	11.65358	10.67478	9.82258	9.07704	7.84314	6.87293	6.09709	5.46691	4.94759	3.98489	3.32861
26	22.79520	20.12104	17.87684	15.98277	14.37519	13.00317	11.82578	10.80998	9.92897	9.16095	7.89566	6.90608	6.11818	5.48043	4.95632	3.98791	3.32970
27	23.55961	20.70690	18.32703	16.32959	14.64303	13.21053	11.98671	10.93516	10.02658	9.23722	7.94255	6.93515	6.13636	5.49189	4.96360	3.99033	3.33054
28	24.31644	21.28127	18.76411	16.66306	14.89813	13.40616	12.13711	11.05108	10.11613	9.30657	7.98442	6.96066	6.15204	5.50160	4.96967	3.99226	3.33118
29	25.06579	21.84438	19.18845	16.98371	15.14107	13.59072	12.27767	11.15841	10.19828	9.36961	8.02181	6.98304	6.16555	5.50983	4.97472	3.99381	3.33168
30	25.80771	22.39646	19.60044	17.29203	15.37245	13.76483	12.40904	11.25778	10.27365	9.42691	8.05518	7.00266	6.17720	5.51681	4.97894	3.99505	3.33206

*$P_n = (1/i)[1 - 1/(1+i)^n]$

Review Problems

I. Basics of Capital Investment

Kenn Day, manager of Day Laboratory, is investigating the possibility of acquiring some new test equipment. To acquire the equipment requires an initial outlay of $300,000. To raise the capital, Kenn will sell shares valued at $200,000 (the shares pay dividends of $24,000 per year) and borrow $100,000. The loan for $100,000 would carry an interest rate of 6 percent. Kenn figures that his weighted average cost of capital is 10 percent [(2/3 × 0.12) + (1/3 × 0.06)]. This weighted cost of capital is the discount rate that will be used for capital investment decisions.

Kenn estimates that the new test equipment will produce a cash inflow of $50,000 per year. Kenn expects the equipment to last for 20 years.

Required:

1. Compute the payback period.
2. Assuming that depreciation is $14,000 per year, compute the ARR (on total investment).
3. Compute the NPV of the test equipment.
4. Compute the IRR of the test equipment.
5. Should Kenn buy the equipment?

Solution:

1. The payback period is $300,000/$50,000, or six years.
2. The ARR is ($50,000 – $14,000)/$300,000, or 12 percent.
3. From Exhibit 14B-2, the discount factor for an annuity with i at 10 percent and n at 20 years is 8.51356. Thus, the NPV is (8.51356 × $50,000) – $300,000, or $125,678.
4. The discount factor associated with the IRR is 6.00 ($300,000/$50,000). From Exhibit 14B-2, the IRR is between 14 and 16 percent (using the row corresponding to period 20).
5. Since the NPV is positive and the IRR is greater than Kenn's cost of capital, the test equipment is a sound investment. This, of course, assumes that the cash flow projections are accurate.

II. Capital Investments with Competing Projects

A hospital is considering the possibility of two new purchases: new x-ray equipment and new biopsy equipment. Each project would require an investment of $750,000. The expected life for each is five years with no expected salvage value. The net cash inflows associated with the two independent projects are as follows:

Year	X-Ray Equipment	Biopsy Equipment
1	$375,000	$ 75,000
2	150,000	75,000
3	300,000	525,000
4	150,000	600,000
5	75,000	675,000

Required:

1. Compute the net present value of each project, assuming a required rate of 12 percent.
2. Compute the payback period for each project. Assume that the manager of the hospital accepts only projects with a payback period of three years or less. Offer some reasons why this may be a rational strategy even though the NPV computed in Requirement 1 may indicate otherwise.

Solution:

1. X-ray equipment:

Year	Cash Flow	Discount Factor	Present Value
0	$(750,000)	1.00000	$(750,000)
1	375,000	0.89286	334,823
2	150,000	0.79719	119,579
3	300,000	0.71178	213,534
4	150,000	0.63552	95,328
5	75,000	0.56743	42,557
NPV			$ 55,821

Biopsy equipment:

Year	Cash Flow	Discount Factor	Present Value
0	$(750,000)	1.00000	$(750,000)
1	75,000	0.89286	66,965
2	75,000	0.79719	59,789
3	525,000	0.71178	373,685
4	600,000	0.63552	381,312
5	675,000	0.56743	383,015
NPV			$ 514,766

2. X-ray equipment:

Payback period =	$375,000	1.00 year
	150,000	1.00
	225,000	0.75 ($225,000/$300,000)
	$750,000	2.75 years

Biopsy equipment:

Payback period =	$ 75,000	1.00 year
	75,000	1.00
	525,000	1.00
	75,000	0.13 ($75,000/$600,000)
	$750,000	3.13 years

This might be a reasonable strategy because payback is a rough measure of risk. The assumption is that the longer it takes a project to pay for itself, the riskier the project is. Other reasons might be that the firm might have liquidity problems, the cash flows might be risky, or there might be a high risk of obsolescence.

Discussion Questions

1. Explain the difference between independent projects and mutually exclusive projects.
2. Explain why the timing and quantity of cash flows are important in capital investment decisions.
3. The time value of money is ignored by the payback period and the ARR. Explain why this is a major deficiency in these two models.
4. What is the payback period? Compute the payback period for an investment requiring an initial outlay of $80,000 with expected annual cash inflows of $30,000.
5. Name and discuss three possible reasons that the payback period is used to help make capital investment decisions.

6. What is the accounting rate of return? Compute the ARR for an investment that requires an initial outlay of $300,000 and promises an average net income of $100,000.
7. The net present value is the same as the profit of a project expressed in present dollars. Do you agree? Explain.
8. Explain the relationship between NPV and a firm's value.
9. What is the cost of capital? What role does it play in capital investment decisions?
10. What is the role that the required rate of return plays in the NPV model? In the IRR model?
11. Explain how the NPV is used to determine whether a project should be accepted or rejected.
12. The IRR is the true or actual rate of return being earned by the project. Do you agree or disagree? Discuss.
13. Explain what a postaudit is and how it can provide useful input for future capital investment decisions, especially those involving advanced technology.
14. Explain why NPV is generally preferred over IRR when choosing among competing or mutually exclusive projects. Why would managers continue to use IRR to choose among mutually exclusive projects?
15. Suppose that a firm must choose between two mutually exclusive projects, both of which have negative NPVs. Explain how a firm can legitimately choose between two such projects.

Multiple-Choice Exercises

14-1 Capital investments should

a. earn back their original capital outlay.
b. only be analyzed using the ARR.
c. always produce an increase in market share.
d. always be done using a payback criterion.
e. do none of the above.

14-2 To make a capital investment decision, a manager must

a. estimate the quantity and timing of cash flows.
b. assess the risk of the investment.
c. consider the impact of the investment on the firm's profits.
d. select investments with a positive NPV.
e. do all of the above.

14-3 Mutually exclusive capital budgeting projects are those that

a. if accepted or rejected do not affect the cash flows of other projects.
b. if accepted will produce a negative NPV.
c. if accepted preclude the acceptance of all other competing projects.
d. if rejected preclude the acceptance of all other competing projects.
e. if rejected imply that all other competing projects have a positive NPV.

14-4 An investment of $1,000 produces a net annual cash inflow of $500 for each of five years. What is the payback period?

a. two years
b. one-half year
c. unacceptable
d. three years
e. Cannot be determined.

14-5 An investment of $1,000 produces a net cash inflow of $600 in the first year and $2,000 in the second year. What is the payback period?

a. 1.67 years
b. 0.50 year
c. 2.00 years
d. 1.20 years
e. Cannot be determined

14-6 The payback period suffers from which of the following deficiencies?

a. It is a rough measure of the uncertainty of future cash flows.
b. It helps control the risk of obsolescence.
c. It ignores the time value of money.
d. It ignores the financial performance of a project beyond the payback period.
e. Both c and d.

14-7 The accounting rate of return has one specific advantage not possessed by the payback period in that it

a. considers the time value of money.
b. measures the value added by a project.
c. considers the profitability of a project beyond the payback period.
d. is more widely accepted by financial managers.
e. is always an accurate measure of profitability.

14-8 An investment of $1,000 provides an average net income of $220 with zero salvage value. Depreciation is $20 per year. The accounting rate of return using the original investment is

a. 44 percent.
b. 22 percent.
c. 20 percent.
d. 40 percent.
e. none of the above.

14-9 If the net present value is positive, it signals

a. that the initial investment has been recovered.
b. that the required rate of return has been earned.
c. that the value of the firm has increased.
d. all of the above.
e. both a and b.

14-10 Net present value measures

a. the profitability of an investment.
b. the change in wealth.
c. the change in firm value.
d. the difference in present value of cash inflows and outflows.
e. all of the above.

14-11 Net present value is calculated by using

a. accounting income.
b. the required rate of return.
c. the IRR.
d. the future value of cash flows.
e. none of the above.

14-12 Using net present value, a project is rejected if it is

a. equal to zero.
b. positive.
c. negative.
d. less than the hurdle rate.
e. greater than the cost of capital.

14-13 If the present value of future cash flows is $1,200 for an investment that requires an outlay of $1,000, the net present value

a. is $200.
b. is $1,000.
c. is $1,200.
d. is $2,200.
e. cannot be determined.

14-14 Assume that an investment of $1,000 produces a future cash flow of $1,000. The discount factor for this future cash flow is 0.89. The net present value is

a. $0.
b. $110.
c. $2,000.
d. $911.
e. none of the above.

14-15 Which of the following is *not* true regarding the internal rate of return?

a. The IRR is the interest rate that sets the present value of a project's cash inflows equal to the present value of the project's cost.
b. The IRR is the interest rate that sets the NPV equal to zero.
c. The IRR is the most reliable of the capital budgeting methods.
d. If the IRR is greater than the required rate of return, then the project is acceptable.
e. The popularity of IRR may be attributable to the fact that it is a rate of return, a concept that is comfortably used by managers.

14-16 Using internal rate of return, a project is rejected if the IRR

a. is less than the required rate of return.
b. is equal to the required rate of return.
c. is greater than the cost of capital.
d. is greater than the required rate of return.
e. produces an NPV equal to zero.

14-17 A postaudit

a. is a follow-up analysis of a capital project, once implemented.
b. compares the actual benefits with the estimated benefits.
c. evaluates the overall outcome of the investment.
d. proposes corrective action, if needed.
e. does all of the above.

14-18 Postaudits of capital projects are useful because

a. they are not very costly.
b. they help to ensure that resources are used wisely.
c. the assumptions underlying the original analyses are often invalidated by changes in the actual working environment.
d. they have no significant limitations.
e. of all of the above.

14-19 For competing projects, net present value is preferred to internal rate of return because

a. maximizing IRR may not maximize the wealth of the owners.
b. in the final analysis, total dollars earned, not relative profitability, are what count.
c. choosing the project with the largest NPV maximizes the wealth of the shareholders.
d. assuming that cash flows are reinvested at the required rate of return is more realistic than assuming that cash flows are reinvested at the computed IRR.
e. of all of the above.

14-20 Assume that there are two competing projects, A and B. Project A has a net present value of $1,000 and an internal rate of return of 15 percent; Project B has an NPV of $800 and an IRR of 20 percent. Which of the following is true?

a. It is not possible to use NPV or IRR to choose between the two projects.
b. Project B should be chosen because it has a higher IRR.
c. Project A should be chosen because it has a higher NPV.
d. Neither project should be chosen.
e. None of the above.

Cornerstone Exercises

Cornerstone Exercise 14-21 PAYBACK PERIOD

OBJECTIVE 2
CORNERSTONE 14-1

Kilebrew Manufacturing is considering an investment in a new automated manufacturing system. The new system requires an investment of $2,400,000 and either has:

a. Even cash flows of $600,000 per year or
b. The following expected annual cash flows: $300,000, $300,000, $800,000, $800,000, and $200,000.

Required:

Calculate the payback period for each case.

Cornerstone Exercise 14-22 ACCOUNTING RATE OF RETURN

OBJECTIVE 2
CORNERSTONE 14-2

Eyring Company invested $10,000,000 in a new product line. The life cycle of the product is projected to be seven years with the following net income stream: $200,000, $600,000, $1,000,000, $1,200,000, $1,600,000, $2,200,000, and $1,600,000.

Required:

Calculate the accounting rate of return.

Cornerstone Exercise 14-23 NET PRESENT VALUE

OBJECTIVE 3
CORNERSTONE 14-3

Oaks Inc. has just completed development of a new cell phone. The new product is expected to produce annual revenues of $450,000. To produce the cell phone requires an investment in new equipment, costing $480,000. The cell phone has a projected life cycle of five years. After five years, the equipment can be sold for $60,000. Working capital is also expected to increase by $60,000, which Oaks will recover by the end of the new product's life cycle. Annual cash operating expenses are estimated at $270,000. The required rate of return is 8 percent.

Required:

1. Prepare a schedule of the projected annual cash flows.
2. Calculate the NPV using only discount factors from Exhibit 14B-1.
3. Calculate the NPV using discount factors from both Exhibit 14B-1 and 14B-2.

Cornerstone Exercise 14-24 INTERNAL RATE OF RETURN

OBJECTIVE 4
CORNERSTONE 14-4

Gardner Company produces a variety of gardening tools and aids. The company is examining the possibility of investing in a new production system that will reduce the costs of the current system. The new system will require a cash investment of $4,607,200 and will produce net cash savings of $800,000 per year. The system has a projected life of nine years.

Required:

Calculate the internal rate of return for the new production system.

OBJECTIVE 7
CORNERSTONE 14-5

Cornerstone Exercise 14-25 NPV AND IRR, MUTUALLY EXCLUSIVE PROJECTS

Luckinbill Inc. intends to invest in one of two competing types of computer-aided manufacturing equipment, built by two different manufacturers: CAM X and CAM Y. Both CAM X and CAM Y models have a project life of 10 years. The purchase price of the CAM X model is $1,200,000 and has a net annual after-tax cash inflow of $300,000. The CAM Y model is more expensive, selling for $1,400,000, but will produce a net annual after-tax cash inflow of $350,000. The cost of capital for the company is 10 percent.

Required:

1. Calculate the NPV for each project. Which model would you recommend?
2. Calculate the IRR for each project. Which model would you recommend?

Exercises

OBJECTIVE 1 2

Exercise 14-26 PAYBACK PERIOD

Each of the following situations is independent. Assume that all cash flows are after-tax cash flows.

a. Emily Hansen has just invested $320,000 in a book and video store. She expects to receive a cash income of $96,000 per year from the investment.
b. Kaylin Day has just invested $700,000 in a new biomedical technology. She expects to receive the following cash flows over the next five years: $175,000, $245,000, $350,000, $210,000, and $140,000.
c. Kambry Nabors invested in a project that has a payback period of four years. The project brings in $192,000 per year.
d. Kenneth Booth invested $325,000 in a project that pays him an even amount per year for five years. The payback period is 2.5 years.

Required:

1. What is the payback period for Emily?
2. What is the payback period for Kaylin?
3. How much did Kambry invest in the project?
4. How much cash does Kenneth receive each year?

OBJECTIVE 1 2

Exercise 14-27 ACCOUNTING RATE OF RETURN

Each of the following scenarios is independent. Assume that all cash flows are after-tax cash flows.

a. Nomander Company is considering the purchase of new equipment that will speed up the process for extracting copper. The equipment will cost $2,400,000 and have a life of five years with no expected salvage value. The expected cash flows associated with the project are as follows:

Year	Cash Revenues	Cash Expenses
1	$4,000,000	$3,200,000
2	4,000,000	3,200,000
3	4,000,000	3,200,000
4	4,000,000	3,200,000
5	4,000,000	3,200,000

b. Marlene Straithe is considering investing in one of the following two projects. Either project will require an investment of $30,000. The expected revenues less cash expenses for the two projects follow. Assume each project is depreciable.

Year	Project A	Project B
1	$ 9,000	$ 9,000
2	12,000	12,000
3	15,000	18,000
4	30,000	9,000
5	30,000	9,000

c. Suppose that a project has an accounting rate of return of 40 percent (based on initial investment) and that the average net income of the project is $160,000.

d. Suppose that a project has an accounting rate of return of 25 percent and that the investment is $100,000.

Required:

1. Compute the ARR on the new equipment that Nomander Company is considering.
2. Which project should Marlene Straithe choose based on the ARR?
3. How much did the company in scenario (c) invest in the project?
4. What is the average income earned by the project in scenario (d)?

Exercise 14-28 NET PRESENT VALUE

OBJECTIVE 1 3

Each of the following scenarios is independent. Assume that all cash flows are after-tax cash flows.

a. Harrison Manufacturing is considering the purchase of a new welding system. The cash benefits will be $360,000 per year. The system costs $2,040,000 and will last 10 years.

b. Kylie Hepworth is interested in investing in a women's specialty shop. The cost of the investment is $120,000. She estimates that the return from owning her own shop will be $36,000 per year. She estimates that the shop will have a useful life of six years.

c. Larsen Company calculated the NPV of a project and found it to be $7,100. The project's life was estimated to be eight years. The required rate of return used for the NPV calculation was 10 percent. The project was expected to produce annual after-tax cash flows of $15,000.

Required:

1. Compute the NPV for Harrison Manufacturing, assuming a discount rate of 12 percent. Should the company buy the new welding system?
2. Assuming a required rate of return of 8 percent, calculate the NPV for Kylie Hepworth's investment. Should she invest?
3. What was the required investment for Larsen Company's project?

Exercise 14-29 INTERNAL RATE OF RETURN

OBJECTIVE 1 4

Each of the following scenarios is independent. Assume that all cash flows are after-tax cash flows.

a. Manchester Company is considering the purchase of new equipment that will speed up the process for producing flash drives. The equipment will cost $6,254,000 and have a life of five years with no expected salvage value. The expected cash flows associated with the project follow:

Year	Cash Revenues	Cash Expenses
1	$6,000,000	$4,000,000
2	6,000,000	4,000,000
3	6,000,000	4,000,000
4	6,000,000	4,000,000
5	6,000,000	4,000,000

b. Kathleen Briggs is evaluating an investment in an information system that will save $160,000 per year. She estimates that the system will last 10 years. The system will cost $834,560. Her company's cost of capital is 10 percent.
c. Castle Dale Enterprises just announced that a new plant would be built in Cold Lake, Alberta. Castle Dale told its shareholders that the plant has an expected life of 15 years and an expected IRR equal to 25 percent. The cost of building the plant is expected to be $2,880,000.

Required:

1. Calculate the IRR for Manchester Company. The company's cost of capital is 16 percent. Should the new equipment be purchased?
2. Calculate Kathleen Brigg's IRR. Should she acquire the new system?
3. What should be Castle Dale Enterprises' expected annual cash flow from the plant?

OBJECTIVE 1 7

Exercise 14-30 NET PRESENT VALUE AND COMPETING PROJECTS

Perry Hospital is investigating the possibility of investing in new dialysis equipment. Two local manufacturers of this equipment are being considered as sources of the equipment. After-tax cash inflows for the two competing projects are as follows:

Year	Limpio Equipment	Salman Equipment
1	$300,000	$ 50,000
2	250,000	50,000
3	200,000	300,000
4	100,000	400,000
5	50,000	450,000

Both projects require an initial investment of $500,000. In both cases, assume that the equipment has a life of five years with no salvage value.

Required:

1. Assuming a discount rate of 12 percent, compute the net present value of each piece of equipment.
2. A third option has surfaced for equipment purchased from an out-of-province supplier. The cost is also $500,000, but this equipment will produce even cash flows over its five-year life. What must the annual cash flow be for this equipment to be selected over the other two? Assume a 12 percent discount rate.

OBJECTIVE 1 2 3 4

Exercise 14-31 PAYBACK, ACCOUNTING RATE OF RETURN, NET PRESENT VALUE, INTERNAL RATE OF RETURN

Whipple Company wants to buy a numerically controlled (NC) machine to be used in producing specially machined parts for manufacturers of tractors. The outlay required is $480,000. The NC equipment will last five years with no expected salvage value. The expected after-tax cash flows associated with the project follow:

Year	Cash Revenues	Cash Expenses
1	$780,000	$600,000
2	780,000	600,000
3	780,000	600,000
4	780,000	600,000
5	780,000	600,000

Required:

1. Compute the payback period for the NC equipment.
2. Compute the NC equipment's ARR.
3. Compute the investment's NPV, assuming a required rate of return of 10 percent.
4. Compute the investment's IRR.

Exercise 14-32 PAYBACK, ACCOUNTING RATE OF RETURN, PRESENT VALUE, NET PRESENT VALUE, INTERNAL RATE OF RETURN

OBJECTIVE 1 2 3 4

All four parts are independent of all other parts. Assume that all cash flows are after-tax cash flows.

a. Randy Willis is considering investing in one of the following two projects. Either project will require an investment of $10,000. The expected cash flows for the two projects follow. Assume that each project is depreciable.

Year	Project A	Project B
1	$ 3,000	$3,000
2	4,000	4,000
3	5,000	6,000
4	10,000	3,000
5	10,000	3,000

b. Wilma Golding is retiring and has the option to take her retirement as a lump sum of $225,000 or to receive $24,000 per year for 20 years. Wilma's required rate of return is 8 percent.

c. David Booth is interested in investing in some tools and equipment so that he can do independent drywalling. The cost of the tools and equipment is $20,000. He estimates that the return from owning his own equipment will be $6,000 per year. The tools and equipment will last six years.

d. Patsy Folson is evaluating what appears to be an attractive opportunity. She is currently the owner of a small manufacturing company and has the opportunity to acquire another small company's equipment that would provide production of a part currently purchased externally. She estimates that the savings from internal production will be $25,000 per year. She estimates that the equipment will last 10 years. The owner is asking $130,400 for the equipment. Her company's cost of capital is 10 percent.

Required:

1. What is the payback period for each of Randy Willis's projects? If rapid payback is important, which project should be chosen? Which would you choose?
2. Which of Randy's projects should be chosen based on the ARR?
3. Assuming that Wilma Golding will live for another 20 years, should she take the lump sum or the annuity?
4. Assuming a required rate of return of 8 percent for David Booth, calculate the NPV of the investment. Should David invest?
5. Calculate the IRR for Patsy Folson's project. Should Patsy acquire the equipment?

Exercise 14-33 NET PRESENT VALUE, BASIC CONCEPTS

OBJECTIVE 3

Gee Company is considering an investment that requires an outlay of $100,000 and promises an after-tax cash inflow one year from now of $115,500. The company's cost of capital is 10 percent.

Required:

1. Break the $115,500 future cash inflow into three components: (a) the return of the original investment, (b) the cost of capital, and (c) the profit earned on the investment. Now compute the present value of the profit earned on the investment.
2. Compute the NPV of the investment. Compare this with the present value of the profit computed in Requirement 1. What does this tell you about the meaning of NPV?

Exercise 14-34 SOLVING FOR UNKNOWNS

OBJECTIVE 1 3 4

Each of the following cases is independent. Assume that all cash flows are after-tax cash flows.

a. Thomas Company is investing $120,000 in a project that will yield a uniform series of cash inflows over the next four years.

b. Video Repair has decided to invest in some new electronic equipment. The equipment will have a three-year life and will produce a uniform series of cash savings. The NPV of the equipment is $1,750, using a discount rate of 8 percent. The IRR is 12 percent.
c. A new lathe costing $60,096 will produce savings of $12,000 per year.
d. The NPV of a project is $3,927. The project has a life of four years and produces the following cash flows:

Year 1	$10,000	Year 3	$15,000
Year 2	$12,000	Year 4	?

The cost of the project is two times the cash flow produced in year 4. The discount rate is 10 percent.

Required:

1. If the internal rate of return is 14 percent for Thomas Company, how much cash inflow per year can be expected?
2. Determine the investment and the amount of cash savings realized each year for Video Repair.
3. For scenario (c), how many years must the lathe last if an IRR of 18 percent is realized?
4. For scenario (d), find the cost of the project and the cash flow for year 4.

OBJECTIVE 7

Exercise 14-35 NET PRESENT VALUE VERSUS INTERNAL RATE OF RETURN

A company is thinking about two different modifications to its current manufacturing process. The after-tax cash flows associated with the two investments follow:

Year	Project I	Project II
0	$(100,000)	$(100,000)
1	—	63,857
2	134,560	63,857

The company's cost of capital is 10 percent.

Required:

1. Compute the NPV and the IRR for each investment.
2. Explain why the project with the larger NPV is the correct choice for the company.

Problems

OBJECTIVE 1 3

Problem 14-36 BASIC NET PRESENT VALUE ANALYSIS

Camus Blalack, process engineer, knows that the acceptance of a new process design will depend on its economic feasibility. The new process is designed to improve environmental performance. On the negative side, the process design requires new equipment and an infusion of working capital. The equipment will cost $300,000, and its cash operating expenses will total $60,000 per year. The equipment will last for seven years but will need a major overhaul costing $30,000 at the end of the fifth year. At the end of seven years, the equipment will be sold for $24,000. An increase in working capital totalling $30,000 will also be needed at the beginning. This will be recovered at the end of the seven years.

On the positive side, Camus estimates that the new process will save $135,000 per year in environmental costs (fines and cleanup costs avoided). The cost of capital is 10 percent.

Required:

1. Prepare a schedule of cash flows for the proposed project. Assume that there are no income taxes.
2. Compute the NPV of the project. Should the new process design be accepted?

Problem 14-37 NET PRESENT VALUE ANALYSIS

OBJECTIVE 1 3

Uintah Communications Company is considering the production and marketing of a communications system that will increase the efficiency of messaging for small businesses or branch offices of large companies. Each unit hooked into the system is assigned a mailbox number, which can be matched to a telephone extension number, providing access to messages 24 hours a day. Up to 20 units can be hooked into the system, allowing the delivery of the same message to as many as 20 people. Personal codes can be used to make messages confidential. Furthermore, messages can be reviewed, recorded, cancelled, replied to, or deleted all during the same phone call. Indicators wired to the telephone blink whenever new messages are present.

To produce this product, a $1.1 million investment in new equipment is required. The equipment will last 10 years but will need major maintenance costing $100,000 at the end of its sixth year. The salvage value of the equipment at the end of 10 years is estimated to be $40,000. If this new system is produced, working capital must also be increased by $50,000. This capital will be restored at the end of the product's life cycle, which is estimated to be 10 years. Revenues from the sale of the product are estimated at $1.5 million per year; cash operating expenses are estimated at $1.26 million per year.

Required:

1. Prepare a schedule of cash flows for the proposed project. Assume that there are no income taxes.
2. Assuming that Uintah's cost of capital is 12 percent, compute the project's NPV. Should the product be produced?

Problem 14-38 BASIC INTERNAL RATE OF RETURN ANALYSIS

OBJECTIVE 1 4

Lindsey Thompson, owner of Leshow Company, was approached by a local dealer of air-conditioning units. The dealer proposed replacing Leshow's old cooling system with a modern, more efficient system. The cost of the new system was quoted at $96,660, but it would save $20,000 per year in energy costs. The estimated life of the new system is 10 years, with no salvage value expected. Excited over the possibility of saving $20,000 per year and having a more reliable unit, Lindsey requested an analysis of the project's economic viability. All capital projects are required to earn at least the firm's cost of capital, which is 10 percent. There are no income taxes.

Required:

1. Calculate the project's IRR. Should the company acquire the new cooling system?
2. Suppose that energy savings are less than claimed. Calculate the minimum annual cash savings that must be realized for the project to earn a rate equal to the firm's cost of capital.
3. Suppose that the life of the new system is overestimated by two years. Repeat Requirements 1 and 2 under this assumption.
4. Explain the implications of the answers from Requirements 1, 2, and 3.

Problem 14-39 NET PRESENT VALUE, UNCERTAINTY

OBJECTIVE 1 3

Eden Airlines is interested in acquiring a new aircraft to service a new route. The route will be from Quebec City to Val d'Or. The aircraft will fly one round-trip daily except for scheduled maintenance days. There are 15 maintenance days scheduled each year. The seating capacity of the aircraft is 150. Flights are expected to be fully booked. The average revenue per passenger per flight (one-way) is $200. Annual operating costs of the aircraft follow:

Fuel	$1,400,000
Flight personnel	500,000
Food and beverages	100,000
Maintenance	400,000
Other	100,000
Total	$2,500,000

The aircraft will cost $100,000,000 and has an expected life of 20 years. The company requires a 14 percent return. Assume there are no income taxes.

Required:

1. Calculate the NPV for the aircraft. Should the company buy it?
2. In discussing the proposal, the marketing manager for the airline believes that the assumption of 100 percent booking is unrealistic. He believes that the booking rate will be somewhere between 70 and 90 percent, with the most likely rate being 80 percent. Recalculate the NPV by using an 80 percent seating capacity. Should the aircraft be purchased?
3. Calculate the average seating rate that would be needed so that NPV will equal zero.
4. Suppose that the price per passenger could be increased by 10 percent without any effect on demand. What is the average seating rate now needed to achieve a NPV equal to zero? What would you now recommend?

OBJECTIVE 1 2 3 4

Problem 14-40 REVIEW OF BASIC CAPITAL BUDGETING PROCEDURES

Dr. Whitley Avard, a plastic surgeon, had just returned from a conference in which she learned of a new surgical procedure for removing wrinkles around eyes, reducing the time to perform the normal procedure by 50 percent. Given her patient-load pressures, Dr. Avard is excited to try out the new technique. By decreasing the time spent on eye treatments or procedures, she can increase her total revenues by performing more services within a work period. Unfortunately, in order to implement the new procedure, special equipment costing $74,000 is needed. The equipment has an expected life of four years, with a salvage value of $6,000. Dr. Avard estimates that her cash revenues will increase by the following amounts:

Year	Revenue Increases
1	$19,800
2	27,000
3	32,400
4	32,400

She also expects additional cash expenses amounting to $3,000 per year. The cost of capital is 12 percent. Assume that there are no income taxes.

Required:

1. Compute the payback period for the new equipment.
2. Compute the ARR.
3. Compute the NPV and IRR for the project. Should Dr. Avard purchase the new equipment? Should she be concerned about payback or the ARR in making this decision?
4. Before finalizing her decision, Dr. Avard decided to call two plastic surgeons who have been using the new procedure for the past six months. The conversations revealed a somewhat less glowing report than she received at the conference. The new procedure reduced the time required by about 25 percent rather than the advertised 50 percent. Dr. Avard estimated that the net operating cash flows of the procedure would be cut by one-third because of the extra time and cost involved (salvage value would be unaffected). Using this information, recompute the NPV of the project. What would you now recommend?

OBJECTIVE 1 7

Problem 14-41 NET PRESENT VALUE AND COMPETING ALTERNATIVES

Stillwater Designs has been rebuilding Model 100, Model 120, and Model 150 Kicker subwoofers that were returned for warranty action. Customers returning the subwoofers receive a new replacement. The warranty returns are then rebuilt and resold (as seconds). Tent sales are often used to sell the rebuilt speakers. As part of the rebuilding process, the speakers are demagnetized so that metal pieces and shavings can be removed. A demagnetizing (demag) machine is used to achieve this objective. A product design change has made the most recent Model 150 speakers too tall for the demag machine. They no longer fit in the demag machine.

Stillwater Designs has two alternatives that it is currently considering. First, a new demag machine can be bought that has a different design, eliminating the fit problem. The cost of this machine is $600,000, and it will last five years. Second, Stillwater can keep the current machine and sell the 150 speakers for scrap, using the old demag machine for the Model 100 and 120 speakers only. A rebuilt speaker sells for $295 and costs $274.65 to rebuild (for materials, labour, and overhead cash outlays). The $274.65 outlay includes the annual operating cash effects of the new demag machine. If not rebuilt, the Model 150 speakers can be sold for $4 each as scrap. There are 10,000 Model 150 warranty returns per year. Assume that the required rate of return is 10 percent.

Required:

1. Determine which alternative is the best for Stillwater Designs by using NPV analysis.
2. Determine which alternative is best for Stillwater Designs by using an IRR analysis. Explain why NPV analysis is a better approach.

Problem 14-42 BASIC NET PRESENT VALUE ANALYSIS, COMPETING PROJECTS

OBJECTIVE 3 7

Kildare Medical Centre, a for-profit hospital, has three investment opportunities: (1) adding a wing for in-patient treatment of substance abuse, (2) adding a pathology laboratory, and (3) expanding the outpatient surgery wing. The initial investments and the net present value for the three alternatives are as follows:

	Substance Abuse	Laboratory	Outpatient Surgery
Investment	$1,500,000	$500,000	$1,000,000
NPV	150,000	140,000	135,000

Although the hospital would like to invest in all three alternatives, only $1.5 million is available.

Required:

1. Rank the projects on the basis of NPV, and allocate the funds in order of this ranking. What project or projects were selected? What is the total NPV realized by the medical centre using this approach?
2. Assume that the size of the lot on which the hospital is located makes the substance abuse wing and the outpatient surgery wing mutually exclusive. With unlimited capital, which projects would be chosen? With limited capital of $1.5 million, which projects would be chosen?
3. Form a group with two to four other students, and discuss qualitative considerations that should be considered in capital budgeting evaluations. Identify three such considerations.

Problem 14-43 PAYBACK, NET PRESENT VALUE, INTERNAL RATE OF RETURN, INTANGIBLE BENEFITS, INFLATION ADJUSTMENT

OBJECTIVE 1 2 3 4 7

Foster Company wants to buy a numerically controlled (NC) machine to be used in producing specially machined parts for manufacturers of trenching machines (to replace an existing manual system). The outlay required is $3,500,000. The NC equipment will last five years with no expected salvage value. The expected incremental after-tax cash flows (cash flows of the NC equipment less cash flows of the old equipment) associated with the project follow:

Year	Cash Benefits	Cash Expenses
1	$3,900,000	$3,000,000
2	3,900,000	3,000,000
3	3,900,000	3,000,000
4	3,900,000	3,000,000
5	3,900,000	3,000,000

Foster has a cost of capital equal to 10 percent. The above cash flows are expressed without any consideration of inflation.

Required:

1. Compute the payback period.
2. Calculate the NPV and IRR of the proposed project.
3. Inflation is expected to be 5 percent per year for the next five years. The discount rate of 10 percent is composed of two elements: the real rate and the inflationary element. Since the discount rate has an inflationary component, the projected cash flows should also be adjusted to account for inflation. Make this adjustment, and recalculate the NPV. Comment on the importance of adjusting cash flows for inflationary effects.

OBJECTIVE 3

Problem 14-44 COST OF CAPITAL, NET PRESENT VALUE

Leakam Company's product engineering department has developed a new product that has a three-year life cycle. Production of the product requires development of a new process that requires a current $100,000 capital outlay. The $100,000 will be raised by issuing $60,000 of bonds and by selling shares for $40,000. The $60,000 in bonds will have net (after-tax) interest payments of $3,000 at the end of each of the three years, with the principal being repaid at the end of year 3. The share issue carries with it an expectation of a 17.5 percent return, expressed in the form of dividends at the end of each year ($7,000 in dividends is expected for each of the next three years). The sources of capital for this investment represent the same proportion and costs that the company typically has. Finally, the project will produce after-tax cash inflows of $50,000 per year for the next three years.

Required:

1. Compute the cost of capital for the project. (Hint: The cost of capital is a weighted average of the two sources of capital where the weights are the proportion of capital from each source.)
2. Compute the NPV for the project. Explain why it is not necessary to subtract the interest payments and the dividend payments from the inflow of $50,000 in carrying out this computation.

OBJECTIVE 1 7

Problem 14-45 CAPITAL INVESTMENT, ADVANCED MANUFACTURING ENVIRONMENT

"I know that it's the thing to do," insisted Pamela Kincaid, vice president of finance for Colgate Manufacturing. "If we are going to be competitive, we need to build this completely automated plant."

"I'm not so sure," replied Bill Thomas, CEO of Colgate. "The savings from labour reductions and increased productivity are only $4 million per year. The price tag for this factory is $45 million. That gives a payback period of more than 11 years. That's a long time to put the company's money at risk."

"Yeah, but you're overlooking the savings that we'll get from the increase in quality," interjected John Simpson, production manager. "With this system, we can decrease our waste and our rework time significantly. Those savings are worth another million dollars per year."

"Another million will only cut the payback to about nine years," retorted Bill. "Ron, you're the marketing manager—do you have any insights?"

"Well, there are other factors to consider, such as service quality and market share. I think that increasing our product quality and improving our delivery service will make us a lot more competitive. I know for a fact that two of our competitors have decided against automation. That'll give us a shot at their customers, provided our product is of higher quality and we can deliver it faster. I estimate that it'll increase our net cash benefits by another $2.4 million."

"Wow! Now that's impressive," Bill exclaimed, nearly convinced. "The payback is now getting down to a reasonable level."

"I agree," said Pamela, "but we do need to be sure that it's a sound investment. I know that estimates for construction of the facility have gone as high as $48 million. I also know that the expected residual value, after the 20 years of service we expect to get, is $5 million. I think I had better see if this project can cover our 14 percent cost of capital."

"Now wait a minute, Pamela," Bill demanded. "You know that I usually insist on a 20 percent rate of return, especially for a project of this magnitude."

Required:

1. Compute the NPV of the project by using the original savings and investment figures. Calculate by using discount rates of 14 percent and 20 percent. Include salvage value in the computation.
2. Compute the NPV of the project using the additional benefits noted by the production and marketing managers. Also, use the original cost estimate of $45 million. Again, calculate for both possible discount rates.
3. Compute the NPV of the project using all estimates of cash flows, including the possible initial outlay of $48 million. Calculate by using discount rates of 14 percent and 20 percent.
4. If you were making the decision, what would you do? Explain.

Problem 14-46 POSTAUDIT, SENSITIVITY ANALYSIS

OBJECTIVE 6 7

Newmarge Products Inc. is evaluating a new design for one of its manufacturing processes. The new design will eliminate the production of a toxic solid residue. The initial cost of the system is estimated at $860,000 and includes computerized equipment, software, and installation. There is no expected salvage value. The new system has a useful life of eight years and is projected to produce cash operating savings of $225,000 per year over the old system (reducing labour costs and costs of processing and disposing of toxic waste). The cost of capital is 16 percent.

Required:

1. Compute the NPV of the new system.
2. One year after implementation, the internal audit staff noted the following about the new system: (1) the cost of acquiring the system was $60,000 more than expected due to higher installation costs, and (2) the annual cost savings were $20,000 less than expected because more labour cost was needed than anticipated. Using the changes in expected costs and benefits, compute the NPV as if this information had been available one year ago. Did the company make the right decision?
3. Upon reporting the results mentioned in the postaudit, the marketing manager responded in a memo to the internal auditing department indicating that revenues had increased by $60,000 per year because of increased purchases by environmentally sensitive customers. Describe the effect that this has on the analysis in Requirement 2.
4. Why is a postaudit beneficial to a firm?

Problem 14-47 DISCOUNT RATES, AUTOMATED MANUFACTURING, COMPETING INVESTMENTS

OBJECTIVE 7

A company is considering two competing investments. The first is for a standard piece of production equipment; the second is for computer-aided manufacturing (CAM) equipment. The investment and after-tax operating cash flows follow:

Year	Standard Equipment	CAM Equipment
0	$(500,000)	$(2,000,000)
1	300,000	100,000
2	200,000	200,000
3	100,000	300,000
4	100,000	400,000
5	100,000	400,000
6	100,000	400,000
7	100,000	500,000
8	100,000	1,000,000
9	100,000	1,000,000
10	100,000	1,000,000

The company uses a discount rate of 18 percent for all of its investments. The company's cost of capital is 10 percent.

Required:

1. Calculate the NPV for each investment by using a discount rate of 18 percent.
2. Calculate the NPV for each investment by using a discount rate of 10 percent.
3. Which rate should the company use to compute the NPV? Explain.

OBJECTIVE 7

Problem 14-48 QUALITY, MARKET SHARE, AUTOMATED MANUFACTURING ENVIRONMENT

A company is considering two competing investments. The first is for a standard piece of production equipment; the second is for computer-aided manufacturing (CAM) equipment. The investment and after-tax operating cash flows follow:

Year	Standard Equipment	CAM Equipment
0	$(500,000)	$(2,000,000)
1	300,000	100,000
2	200,000	200,000
3	100,000	300,000
4	100,000	400,000
5	100,000	400,000
6	100,000	400,000
7	100,000	500,000
8	100,000	1,000,000
9	100,000	1,000,000
10	100,000	1,000,000

Assume that the company's cost of capital is 14 percent.

Required:

1. Calculate the NPV of each alternative by using the 14 percent rate.
2. Now assume that if the standard equipment is purchased, the competitive position of the firm will deteriorate because of lower quality (relative to competitors who did automate). Marketing estimates that the loss in market share will decrease the projected net cash inflows by 50 percent for years 3 through 10. Recalculate the NPV of the standard equipment given this outcome. What is the decision now? Discuss the importance of assessing the effect of intangible benefits.

OBJECTIVE 5

Problem 14-49 CAPITAL BUDGETING INCOME TAX

Trudeau Analytical Services Inc. has the opportunity to increase its services of evaluating drilling results for exploration companies drilling for oil in the northern reaches of the Arctic. The additional services will generate about $1.2 million in additional annual revenues, with related cash expenditures of $800,000 per year.

In order to engage in these services, the company will require additional, very sophisticated testing equipment that will cost $1.5 million and will have a useful life of 20 years, at which time it can be sold for $150,000. This equipment will be categorized for tax purposes as Class 10 Equipment, with a CCA rate of 30 percent per year.

In addition to the equipment purchase, the company will require $100,000 of additional working capital to support this venture. At the end of each five-year period, the company will be required to do maintenance on the new analyzing equipment at a cost of $50,000 each time.

The company is subject to a combined federal and provincial income tax rate of 40 percent and expects a minimum after-tax return of 12 percent on any project that it engages in.

Required:

1. Prepare a memo outlining your recommendations to the management of the company as to whether the company should enter this new line of business. Show all calculations, and be very specific in your recommendation.

2. At what level of investment in the equipment would this project not be acceptable? Ignore the impact of the increased investment on the CCA tax shield.
3. Referring to the original facts, at what level of pre-tax income would this project not be acceptable?

Cases

Case 14-50 CAPITAL INVESTMENT AND ETHICAL BEHAVIOUR

OBJECTIVE 3

Manny Carson, certified management accountant and controller of Wakeman Enterprises, had been given permission to acquire a new computer and software for the company's accounting system. The capital investment analysis showed an NPV of $100,000; however, the initial estimates of acquisition and installation costs were made on the basis of tentative costs without any formal bids. Manny now has two formal bids, one that would allow the firm to meet or beat the original projected NPV and one that would reduce the projected NPV by $50,000. The second bid involves a system that would increase both the initial cost and the operating cost.

Normally, Manny would take the first bid without hesitation. However, Todd Downing, the owner of the firm presenting the second bid, was a close friend. Manny had called Todd and explained the situation, offering Todd an opportunity to alter his bid and win the job. Todd thanked Manny and then made a counteroffer.

Todd: Listen, Manny, this job at the original price is the key to a successful year for me. The revenues will help me gain approval for the loan I need for renovation and expansion. If I don't get that loan, I see hard times ahead. The financial stats for loan approval are so marginal that reducing the bid price may blow my chances.

Manny: Losing the bid altogether would be even worse, don't you think?

Todd: True. However, I have a suggestion. If you grant me the job, I will have the capability of adding personnel. I know that your son is looking for a job, and I can offer him a good salary and a promising future. Additionally, I'll be able to take you and your wife on that vacation to Hawaii that we have been talking about.

Manny: Well, you have a point. My son is having an awful time finding a job, and he has a wife and three kids to support. My wife is tired of having them live with us. She and I could use a vacation. I doubt that the other bidder would make any fuss if we turned it down. Its offices are out of province, after all.

Todd: Out of province? All the more reason to turn it down. Given the province's economy, it seems almost criminal to take business outside. Those are the kind of business decisions that cause problems for people like your son.

Required:

Evaluate the ethical behaviour of Manny. Should Manny have called Todd in the first place? What if Todd had agreed to meet the lower bid price—would there have been any problems? Identify the standards of ethical conduct (listed in Chapter 1) that Manny may be violating, if any.

Case 14-51 PAYBACK, NET PRESENT VALUE, INTERNAL RATE OF RETURN, EFFECTS OF DIFFERENCES IN SALES ON PROJECT VIABILITY

OBJECTIVE 2 3 4

Shaftel Ready Mix is a processor and supplier of concrete, aggregate, and rock products. The company operates in the prairie provinces. Currently, Shaftel has 14 cement-processing plants and a labour force of more than 375 employees. With the exception of cement powder, all materials (e.g., aggregates and sand) are produced internally by the company. The demand for concrete and aggregates has been growing steadily nationally, and on the prairies, the growth rate has been above the national average. Because of this growth, Shaftel has more than tripled its gross revenues over the past 10 years.

Of the prairie provinces, Saskatchewan has been experiencing the most growth. Processing plants have been added over the past several years, and the company is considering the addition of yet another plant to be located in Regina. A major advantage of another plant in Saskatchewan is the ability to operate year round, a feature not found in the northern reaches of Alberta or Manitoba.

In setting up the new plant, land would have to be purchased and a small building constructed. Equipment and furniture would not need to be purchased; these items would be transferred from a plant that opened in Winnipeg during the building boom period and that closed a few years after the end of that boom. However, the equipment needs some repair and modifications before it can be used. It has a book value of $200,000, and the furniture has a book value of $30,000. Neither has any outside market value. Other costs, such as the installation of a silo, well, electrical hookups, and so on, will be incurred. No salvage value is expected. The summary of the initial investment costs by category is as follows:

Land	$ 20,000
Building	135,000
Equipment:	
Book value	200,000
Modifications	20,000
Furniture (book value)	30,000
Silo	20,000
Well	80,000
Electrical hookups	27,000
General setup	50,000
Total	$582,000

Estimates concerning the operation of the Regina plant follow:

Life of plant and equipment	10 years
Expected annual sales (in cubic metres of cement)	35,000
Selling price (per cubic metre of cement)	$45.00
Variable costs (per cubic metre of cement):	
Cement	$12.94
Sand/gravel	6.42
Fly ash	1.13
Admixture	1.53
Driver labour	3.24
Mechanics	1.43
Plant operations (batching and cleanup)	1.39
Loader operator	0.50
Truck parts	1.75
Fuel	1.48
Other	3.27
Total variable costs	$35.08
Fixed costs (annual):	
Salaries	$135,000
Insurance	75,000
Telephone	5,000
Depreciation	58,200*
Utilities	25,000
Total fixed costs	$298,200

* Straight-line depreciation is calculated by using all initial investment costs over a 10-year period assuming no salvage value.

After reviewing these data, Karl Flemming, vice president of operations, argued against the proposed plant. Karl was concerned because the plant would earn significantly less than the normal 8.3 percent return on sales. All other plants in the company were earning between 7.5 and 8.5 percent on sales. Karl also noted that it would take more than five years to recover the total initial outlay of $582,000. In the past, the company had always insisted that payback be no more than four years. The company's cost of capital is 10 percent. Assume that there are no income taxes.

Required:

1. Prepare a variable-costing income statement for the proposed plant. Compute the ratio of net income to sales. Is Karl correct that the return on sales is significantly lower than the company average?
2. Compute the payback period for the proposed plant. Is Karl right that the payback period is greater than five years? Explain. Suppose you were told that the equipment being transferred from Winnipeg could be sold for its book value. Would this affect your answer?
3. Compute the NPV and the IRR for the proposed plant. Would your answer be affected if you were told that the furniture and equipment could be sold for their book values? If so, repeat the analysis with this effect considered.
4. Compute the cubic metres of cement that must be sold for the new plant to break even. Using this break-even volume, compute the NPV and the IRR. Would the investment be acceptable? If so, explain why an investment that promises to do nothing more than break even can be viewed as acceptable.
5. Compute the volume of cement that must be sold for the IRR to equal the firm's cost of capital. Using this volume, compute the firm's expected annual income. Explain this result.

CMA Problem*

CMA Problem 14-1 CAPITAL BUDGETING—KNOSSOS LIMITED

Knossos Limited is a manufacturer of standard and custom-designed bottling equipment. Early in December 2012, Larissa Company asked Knossos to quote a price for a custom-designed bottling machine to be delivered on April 1, 2013. Larissa intends to make a decision on the purchase of such a machine by January 1 so Knossos would have the entire first quarter of 2013 to build the equipment.

Knossos's standard pricing policy for custom-designed equipment is 50 percent markup on full cost. Larissa's specifications for the equipment have been reviewed by Knossos's Engineering and Cost Accounting Departments, and they made the following estimates for raw materials and direct labour:

Direct materials	$256,000
Direct labour (11,000 hours at $15)	165,000

Manufacturing overhead is applied on the basis of direct labour hours. Knossos normally plans to run its plant with 15,000 direct labour hours per month and assigns overhead on the basis of 180,000 direct labour hours per year. The overhead application rate for 2013 of $9 per direct labour hour is based on the following budgeted manufacturing overhead costs for 2013:

Variable manufacturing overhead	$ 972,000
Fixed manufacturing overhead	648,000
	$1,620,000

The Knossos production schedule calls for 12,000 direct labour hours per month during the first quarter. If Knossos is awarded the contract for the Larissa equipment, production of one of its standard products will have to be reduced. This is necessary because production levels can only be increased to 15,000 direct labour hours each month on short notice. Furthermore, Knossos's employees are unwilling to work overtime.

Sales of the standard product equal to the reduced production will be lost, but there will be no permanent loss of future sales or customers. The standard product, whose production schedule will be reduced, has a unit sales price of $12,000 and the following cost structure:

Raw materials	$2,500
Direct labour (250 hours at $15)	3,750
Overhead (250 hours at $9)	2,250
	$8,500

Larissa needs the custom-designed equipment to increase its bottle-making capacity so that it will not have to buy bottles from an outside supplier. Larissa Company requires 5,000,000 bottles annually. Its present equipment has a maximum capacity of 4,500,000 bottles with a directly traceable cash outlay of $0.15 per bottle. Thus, Larissa has had to purchase 500,000 bottles from a supplier at $0.40 each. The new equipment would allow Larissa to manufacture its entire annual demand for bottles at a raw material cost savings of $0.01 for each bottle manufactured. Knossos estimates that Larissa's annual bottle demand will continue to be 5,000,000 bottles over the next five years, the estimated economic life of the special-purpose equipment. Knossos further estimates that Larissa has an after-tax cost of capital of 15 percent and is subject to a 40 percent marginal income tax rate, the same rates as Knossos.

Required:

1. Knossos Limited plans to submit a bid to Larissa Company for the manufacture of the special-purpose bottling equipment.
   a. Calculate the bid Knossos would submit if it follows its standard pricing policy for special-purpose equipment.
   b. Calculate the minimum bid Knossos would be willing to submit on the Larissa equipment that would result in the same profits as planned for the first quarter.
2. What is the maximum price Larissa Company would likely pay for the machine? In your answer, assume that the equipment will be depreciated for tax purposes as a class 8 asset (20 percent declining balance) and that it will have a salvage value of $100,000 at the end of its useful life.

Integrative Exercise 3

Relevant Costing, Cost-Based Pricing, Cost Behaviour, and Net Present Value Analysis for NoFat

Chapters	Objectives	Cornerstones
3	3-1	7-2
7	7-1	13-2
13	13-2	13-8
14	13-4	14-3
	14-1	14-6
	14-3	
	14-7	

The purpose of this integrated exercise is to demonstrate how a special sales-relevant decision analysis relies on knowledge of cost behaviour (including variable, fixed, and batch costs) and how the adoption of a long-term time horizon can affect the final decision.

Special Sales Offer Relevant Analysis

NoFat manufactures one product, olestra, and sells it to large potato chip manufacturers as the key ingredient in nonfat snack foods, including Ruffles, Lays, Doritos, and Tostitos brand products.[1] For each of the past three years, sales of olestra have been far less than the expected annual volume of 125,000 kilograms. Therefore, the company has ended each year with significant unused capacity. Due to a short shelf life, NoFat must sell every kilogram of olestra that it produces each year. As a result, NoFat's controller, Allyson Ashley, has decided to seek out potential special sales offers from other companies. One company, Patterson Union (PU)—a toxic waste cleanup company—offered to buy 10,000 kilograms of olestra from NoFat during December for a price of $2.20 per kilogram. PU discovered through its research that olestra has proven to be very effective in cleaning up toxic waste locations designated as Superfund Sites by the U.S. Environmental Protection Agency.[2] Allyson was excited, noting that "This is another way to use our expensive olestra plant!"

The annual costs incurred by NoFat to produce and sell 100,000 kilograms of olestra are as follows:

Variable costs per kilogram	
Direct materials	$1.00
Variable manufacturing overhead	$0.75
Sales commissions	$0.50
Direct manufacturing labour	$0.25
Total fixed costs:	
Advertising	$3,000
Customer hotline service	$4,000
Machine set-ups	$40,000
Plant machinery lease	$12,000

In addition, Allyson met with several of NoFat's key production managers and discovered the following information:

- The special order could be produced without incurring any additional marketing or customer service costs.
- NoFat owns the aging plant facility that it uses to manufacture olestra.

[1]Over 4 billion servings of Olean (the Procter & Gamble brand name for olestra) have been consumed. See further information at the Procter & Gamble website: http://www.olean.com/default.asp?p=products&id=fll.

[2]This exercise is based on facts reported in the business press (e.g., Nanci Hellmich and Bruce Horovitz, "Fat Substitute Olestra Eyed as Hazardous Waste Cleaner: Potato Chips Sales Fall Short, *USA TODAY* (May 31, 2001): 1A).

- NoFat incurs costs to set up and clean its machines for each production run, or batch, of olestra that it produces. The total set-up costs shown in the previous table represent the production of 20 batches during the year.
- NoFat leases its plant machinery. The lease agreement is negotiated and signed on the first day of each year. NoFat currently leases enough machinery to produce 125,000 kilograms of olestra.
- PU requires that an independent quality team inspects any facility from which it makes purchases. The terms of the special sales offer would require NoFat to bear the $1,000 cost of the inspection team.

Required:

1. Conduct a relevant analysis of the special sales offer by calculating:
   a. The relevant revenues associated with the special sales offer.
   b. The relevant costs associated with the special sales offer.
   c. The relevant profit associated with the special sales offer.

2. Based solely on financial factors, explain why NoFat should accept or reject PU's special sales offer.

3. Describe at least one qualitative factor that NoFat should consider, in addition to the financial factors, in making its final decision regarding the acceptance or rejection of the special sales offer.

Cost-Based Pricing

Assume for this question that NoFat rejected PU's special sales offer because the $2.20 price suggested by PU was too low. In response to the rejection, PU asked NoFat to determine the price at which it would be willing to accept the special sales offer. For its regular sales, NoFat sets prices by marking up *variable costs* by 10 percent.

4. If Allyson decides to use NoFat's 10 percent mark-up pricing method to set the price for PU's special sales offer,
   a. Calculate the price that NoFat would charge PU for each kilogram of olestra.
   b. Calculate the relevant profit that NoFat would earn if it set the special sales price by using its markup pricing method. (*Hint: Use the estimate of relevant costs that you calculated in response to Requirement 1b.*)
   c. Explain why NoFat should accept or reject the special sales offer if it uses its markup pricing method to set the special sales price.

Incorporating a Long-Term Horizon into the Decision Analysis

Assume for this question that Allyson's relevant analysis reveals that NoFat would earn a positive relevant profit of $10,000 from the special sale (i.e., the special sales alternative). However, after conducting this traditional, short-term relevant analysis, Allyson wonders whether it might be more profitable over the long-term to downsize the company by reducing its manufacturing capacity (i.e., its plant machinery and plant facility). She is aware that downsizing requires a multiyear time horizon because companies usually cannot increase or decrease fixed plant assets every year. Therefore, Allyson has decided to use a five-year time horizon in her long-term decision analysis. She has identified the following information regarding capacity downsizing (i.e., the downsizing alternative):

1) The plant facility consists of several buildings. If it chooses to downsize its capacity, NoFat can immediately sell one of the buildings to an adjacent business for $30,000.
2) If it chooses to downsize its capacity, NoFat's annual lease cost for plant machinery will decrease to $9,000.

Therefore, Allyson must choose between these two alternatives: Accept the special sales offer each year and earn a $10,000 relevant profit for each of the next five years *or* reject the special sales offer and downsize as described in (1) and (2).

5. Assume that NoFat pays for all costs with cash. Also, assume a 10 percent discount rate, a five-year time horizon, and that all cash flows occur at the end of the year. Using an NPV approach to discount future cash flows to present value,
   a. Calculate the NPV of accepting the special sale with the assumed positive relevant profit of $10,000 per year (i.e., the special sales alternative).
   b. Calculate the NPV of downsizing capacity as previously described (i.e., the downsizing alternative).
   c. Based on the NPV of parts a and b, identify and explain which of these two alternatives is best for NoFat to pursue in the long-term.

Glossary

A

Absorption costing A product-costing method that assigns all manufacturing costs to units of product: direct materials, direct labour, variable overhead, and fixed overhead. (p. 366)

Accounting rate of return The rate of return obtained by dividing the average accounting net income by the original investment (or by average investment). (p. 652)

Accumulating costs The way that costs are measured and recorded. (p. 31)

Activity analysis The process of identifying, describing, and evaluating the activities an organization performs. (p. 319)

Activity attributes Nonfinancial and financial information items that describe individual activities. (p. 307)

Activity-based costing (ABC) A system that accumulates overhead costs for each of the activities of an organization and then assigns the costs of activities to the products, services, or other cost objects that caused those activities. (p. 304)

Activity dictionary A list of activities described by specific attributes such as name, definition, classification as primary or secondary, and activity driver. (p. 307)

Activity drivers Factors that measure the consumption of activities by products and other cost objects. (p. 300)

Activity elimination The process of eliminating non-value-added activities. (p. 321)

Activity flexible budgeting Predicting what activity costs will be as activity usage changes. (p. 528)

Activity inputs The resources consumed by an activity in producing its output (they are the factors that enable the activity to be performed). (p. 318)

Activity output The result or product of an activity. (p. 318)

Activity output measure The number of times an activity is performed. It is the quantifiable measure of the output. (p. 318)

Activity reduction Decreasing the time and resources required by an activity. (p. 321)

Activity selection The process of choosing among sets of activities caused by competing strategies. (p. 321)

Activity sharing Increasing the efficiency of necessary activities by using economies of scale. (p. 321)

Activity-based budgeting system (ABB) A budget system that focuses on estimating the costs of activities rather than the costs of departments and plants and the use of multiple drivers, both unit-based and non-unit-based. (p. 518)

Activity-based costing (ABC) A cost assignment approach that first uses direct and driver tracing to assign costs to activities and then uses drivers to assign costs to cost objects. (p. 305)

Activity-based management A systemwide, integrated approach that focuses management's attention on activities with the objective of improving customer value and the profit achieved by providing this value. It includes driver analysis, activity analysis, and performance evaluation, and draws on activity-based costing as a major source of information. (p. 315)

Actual cost system An approach that assigns actual costs of direct materials, direct labour, and overhead to products. (p. 183)

Adjusted cost of goods sold The cost of goods sold after all adjustments for overhead variances are made. (p. 200)

Administrative costs All costs associated with research, development, and general administration of the organization that cannot reasonably be assigned to either selling or production. (p. 40)

Allocation When an indirect cost is assigned to a cost object using a reasonable and convenient method. (p. 33)

Annuity A series of future cash flows. (p. 670)

Applied overhead Overhead assigned to production using predetermined rates. (p. 186)

Appraisal costs Cost incurred to determine whether products and services are conforming to requirements. (p. 324)

Assigning costs The way that a cost is linked to some cost object. (p. 31)

B

Balanced Scorecard A strategic management system that defines a strategic-based responsibility accounting system. The Balanced Scorecard translates an organization's mission and strategy into operational objectives and performance measures for four different perspectives: the financial perspective, the customer perspective, the internal business process perspective, and the learning and growth (infrastructure) perspective. (p. 567)

Break-even point The point where total sales revenue equals total cost; at this point, neither profit nor loss is earned. (p. 124)

Budget committee A committee responsible for setting budgetary policies and goals, reviewing and approving the budget, and resolving any differences that may arise in the budgetary process. (p. 408)

Budget director The individual responsible for coordinating and directing the overall budgeting process. (p. 408)

Budgetary slack The process of padding the budget by overestimating costs and underestimating revenues. (p. 426)

Budgets Plans of action expressed in financial terms. (p. 406)

C

Capital budgeting The process of making capital investment decisions. (p. 656)

Capital investment decisions The process of planning, setting goals and priorities, arranging financing, and identifying criteria for making long-term investments. (p. 648)

Carrying costs The costs of holding inventory. (p. 377)

Cash budget A detailed plan that outlines all sources and uses of cash. (p. 418)

Causal factors Activities or variables that invoke service costs. Generally, it is desirable to use causal factors as the basis for allocating service costs. (p. 208)

Certified Management Accountant (CMA) A certified management accountant has passed a rigorous qualifying examination, met an experience requirement, and participates in continuing education. (p. 17)

Certified General Accountant (CGA) A certified accountant who is permitted (by law) to serve as an external auditor. CPAs must pass a national examination and be licensed by the province in which they practice. (p. 17)

Chartered Accountant (CA) Accountant who works as a business professional in public practice, industry, government, or education. (p. 18)

Coefficient of determination (R^2) The percentage of total variability in a dependent variable that is explained by an independent variable. It assumes a value between 0 and 1. (p. 100)

Committed fixed cost A fixed cost that cannot be easily changed. (p. 79)

Common costs The costs of resources used in the output of two or more services or products. (p. 208)

Common fixed expenses Fixed expenses that cannot be directly traced to individual segments and that are unaffected by the elimination of any one segment. (p. 141, 374)

Compounding of interest Paying interest on interest. (p. 669)

Constraints Mathematical expressions that express resource limitations. (p. 617)

Consumption ratio The proportion of an overhead activity consumed by a product. (p. 300)

Continuous budget A moving 12-month budget with a future month added as the current month expires. (p. 408)

Continuous improvement Searching for ways to increase the overall efficiency and productivity of activities by reducing waste, increasing quality, and reducing costs. (p. 11)

Contribution margin Sales revenue minus total variable cost or price minus unit variable cost. (p. 125)

Contribution margin income statement The income statement format that is based on the separation of costs into fixed and variable components. (p. 124)

Contribution margin ratio Contribution margin divided by sales revenue. It is the proportion of each sales dollar available to cover fixed costs and provide for profit. (p. 125)

Control The process of setting standards, receiving feedback on actual performance, and taking corrective action whenever actual performance deviates significantly from planned performance. (p. 407)

Control activities Activities performed by an organization to prevent or detect poor quality (because poor quality may exist). (p. 324)

Control costs Costs incurred from performing control activities. (p. 324)

Control limits The maximum allowable deviation from a standard. (p. 467)

Controllable costs Costs that managers have the power to influence. (p. 427)

Controller The chief accounting officer in an organization. (p. 13)

Controlling The managerial activity of monitoring a plan's implementation and taking corrective action as needed. (p. 6)

Conversion cost The sum of direct labour cost and overhead cost. (p. 37)

Core objectives and measures Those objectives and measures common to most organizations. (p. 572)

Cost The amount of cash or cash equivalent sacrificed for goods and/or services that are expected to bring a current or future benefit to the organization. (p. 30)

Cost behaviour The way in which a cost changes when the level of output changes. (p. 77)

Cost centre A division of a company that is evaluated on the basis of cost. (p. 553)

Cost driver A causal measurement that causes costs to change. (p. 77)

Cost object Any item such as products, customers, departments, projects, and so on, for which costs are measured and assigned. (p. 31)

Cost of capital The cost of investment funds, usually viewed as a weighted average of the costs of funds from all sources. (p. 654)

Cost of goods manufactured The total product cost of goods completed during the current period. (p. 42)

Cost of goods sold The total product cost of goods sold during the period. (p. 44)

Cost of goods sold budget The estimated costs for the units sold. (p. 415)

Cost reconciliation The final section of the production report that compares the costs to account for with the costs accounted for to ensure that they are equal. (p. 255)

Cost structure A company's mix of fixed costs relative to variable costs. (p. 150)

Costs of quality Costs incurred because poor quality may exist or because poor quality does exist. (p. 323)

Cost-volume-profit graph A graph that depicts the relationships among costs, volume, and profits. It consists of a total revenue line and a total cost line. (p. 138)

Currently attainable standards Standards that reflect an efficient operating state; they are rigorous but achievable. (p. 461)

Customer perspective A Balanced Scorecard viewpoint that defines the customer and market segments in which the business will compete. (p. 568)

Customer value Realization less sacrifice, where realization is what the customer receives and sacrifice is what is given up. (p. 572)

Cycle time The length of time required to produce one unit of a product. (p. 323, 574)

D

Decentralization The granting of decision-making freedom to lower operating levels. (p. 550)

Decision making The process of choosing among competing alternatives. (p. 6)

Decision model A specific set of procedures that, when followed, produces a decision. (p. 600)

Degree of operating leverage (DOL) A measure of the sensitivity of profit changes to changes in sales volume. It measures the percentage change in profits resulting from a percentage change in sales. (p. 150)

Departmental overhead rate Estimated overhead for a single department divided by the estimated activity level for that same department. (p. 188)

Dependent variable A variable whose value depends on the value of another variable. (p. 84)

Differential cost The difference in total cost between the alternatives in a decision. (p. 602)

Direct costs Costs that can be easily and accurately traced to a cost object. (p. 33)

Direct fixed expenses Fixed costs that are directly traceable to a given segment and, consequently, disappear if the segment is eliminated. (p. 141, 380)

Direct labour The labour that can be directly traced to the goods or services being produced. (p. 37)

Direct labour budget A budget showing the total direct labour hours needed and the associated cost for the number of units in the production budget. (p. 412)

Direct labour cost The wages of employees who are integral to the finished product. (p. 41)

Direct materials Materials that are a part of the final product and can be directly traced to the goods or services being produced. (p. 36)

Direct materials cost The cost of any material that is an integral part of the finished product. (p. 41)

Direct materials purchases budget A budget that outlines the expected usage of materials production and purchases of the direct materials required. (p. 418)

Direct method A method that allocates service costs directly to producing departments. This method ignores any interactions that may exist among support departments. (p. 210)

Discount factor The factor used to convert a future cash flow to its present value. (p. 670)

Discount rate The rate of return used to compute the present value of future cash flows. (p. 670)

Discounted cash flows Future cash flows expressed in present-value terms. (p. 652)

Discounting The act of finding the present value of future cash flows. (p. 670)

Discounting models Capital investment models that explicitly consider the time value of money in identifying criteria for accepting and rejecting proposed projects. (p. 650)

Discretionary fixed costs Fixed costs that can be changed relatively easily at management discretion. (p. 79)

Double-loop feedback Information about both the effectiveness of strategy implementation and the validity of assumptions underlying the strategy. (p. 571)

Driver A factor that causes or leads to a change in a cost or an activity; a driver is an output measure. (p. 78)

Driver analysis The effort expended to identify those factors that are the root causes of activity costs. (p. 318)

Dysfunctional behaviour Individual behaviour that conflicts with the goals of the organization. (p. 424)

E

Economic order quantity (EOQ) The amount that should be ordered (or produced) to minimize the total ordering (or setup) and carrying costs. (p. 379)

Economic value added (EVA) A performance measure that is calculated by taking the after-tax operating profit minus the total annual cost of capital. (p. 562)

Ending finished goods inventory budget A budget that describes planned ending inventory of finished goods in units and dollars. (p. 414)

Environmental costs Costs that are incurred because poor environmental quality exists or may exist. (p. 325)

Environmental detection costs Costs incurred to detect poor environmental performance. (p. 326)

Environmental external failure costs Costs incurred after contaminants are introduced into the environment. (p. 326)

Environmental internal failure costs Costs incurred after contaminants are produced but before they are introduced into the environment. (p. 326)

Environmental prevention costs Costs incurred to prevent damage to the environment. (p. 326)

Equivalent units of output Complete units that could have been produced given the total amount of manufacturing effort expended during the period. (p. 249)

Ethical behaviour Choosing actions that are right, proper, and just. (p. 15)

Expenses Costs that are used up (expired) in the production of revenue. (p. 31)

External failure costs Costs incurred because products fail to conform to requirements after being sold to outside parties. (p. 324)

F

Factory overhead cost Combined costs that are incurred in the manufacturing process other than direct materials cost and direct labour cost. (p. 41)

Failure activities Activities performed by an organization or its customers in response to poor quality (poor quality does exist). (p. 324)

Failure costs The costs incurred by an organization because failure activities are performed. (p. 324)

Favourable (*F*) variances Variances produced whenever the actual amounts are less than the budgeted or standard allowances. (p. 465)

FIFO costing method A process-costing method that separates units in beginning inventory from those produced during the current period. Unit costs include only current-period costs and production. (p. 250)

Financial accounting A type of accounting that is primarily concerned with producing information for external users. (p. 6)

Financial budgets The portions of the master budget that include the cash budget, the budgeted balance sheet, the budgeted statement of cash flows, and the capital budget. (p. 408)

Financial perspective A Balanced Scorecard viewpoint that describes the financial consequences of actions taken in the other three perspectives. (p. 568)

Finished goods inventory Completed products that have not yet been sold. (p. 42)

Fixed costs Costs that, in total, are constant within the relevant range as the level of output increases or decreases. (p. 34, 77)

Fixed overhead spending variance The difference between actual fixed overhead and applied fixed overhead. (p. 515)

Fixed overhead volume variance The difference between budgeted fixed overhead and applied fixed overhead; it is a measure of capacity utilization. (p. 523)

Flexible budget A budget that can specify costs for a range of activity. (p. 506)

Flexible budget variance The sum of price variances and efficiency variances in a performance report comparing actual costs to expected costs predicted by a flexible budget. (p. 509)

Future value The value that will accumulate by the end of an investment's life if the investment earns a specified compounded return. (p. 669)

G

Goal congruence The alignment of a manager's personal goals with those of the organization. (p. 424)

Gross margin The difference between sales revenue and cost of goods sold. (p. 48)

H

High-low method A method for separating mixed costs into fixed and variable components by using just the high and low data points. [*Note*: The high (low) data point corresponds to the high (low) output level.] (p. 86)

I

Ideal standards Standards that reflect perfect operating conditions. (p. 461)

Incentives The positive or negative measures taken by an organization to induce a manager to exert effort toward achieving the organization's goals. (p. 242)

Independent projects Projects that, if accepted or rejected, will not affect the cash flows of another project. (p. 648)

Independent variable A variable whose value does not depend on the value of another variable. (p. 84)

Indifference point The quantity at which two systems produce the same operating income. (p. 152)

Indirect costs Costs that cannot be easily and accurately traced to a cost object. (p. 33)

Innovation process A process that anticipates the emerging and potential needs of customers and creates new products and services to satisfy those needs. (p. 573)

Intercept The fixed cost, representing the point where the cost formula intercepts the vertical axis. (p. 84)

Internal business process perspective A Balanced Scorecard viewpoint that describes the internal processes needed to provide value for customers and owners. (p. 568)

Internal failure costs Costs incurred because products and services fail to conform to requirements where lack of conformity is discovered prior to external sale. (p. 324)

Internal rate of return The rate of return that equates the present value of a project's cash inflows with the present value of its cash outflows (i.e., it sets the NPV equal to zero). Also, the rate of return being earned on funds that remain internally invested in a project. (p. 654)

Investment centre A division of a company that is evaluated on the basis of return on investment. (p. 553)

J

Job One distinct unit or set of units for which the costs of production must be assigned. (p. 182)

Job-order cost sheet A subsidiary account to the Work in Process account on which the total costs of materials, labour, and overhead for a single job are accumulated. (p. 192)

Job-order costing system A costing system in which costs are collected and assigned to units of production for each individual job. (p. 183)

Joint products Products that are inseparable prior to a split-off point. All manufacturing costs up to the split-off point are joint costs. (p. 615)

Just-in-time (JIT) A demand-pull system whose objective is to eliminate waste by producing a product only when it is needed and only in the quantities demanded by customers. (p. 382)

K

Keep-or-drop decisions Relevant costing analyses that focus on keeping or dropping a segment of a business. (p. 611)

L

Labour efficiency variance (*LEV*) The difference between the actual direct labour hours used and the standard direct labour hours allowed multiplied by the standard hourly wage rate. (p. 474)

Labour rate variance (*LRV*) The difference between the actual hourly rate paid and the standard hourly rate multiplied by the actual hours worked. (p. 473)

Lead time The time required to receive the economic order quantity once an order is placed or a setup is started. (p. 381)

Lean accounting An accounting practice that organizes costs according to the value chain by focusing primarily on the elimination of waste. The objective is to provide information to managers that support this effort and to provide financial statements that better reflect overall performance, using financial and nonfinancial information. (p. 12)

Learning and growth (infrastructure) perspective A Balanced Scorecard viewpoint that defines the capabilities that an organization needs to create long-term growth and improvement. (p. 568)

Line positions Positions that have direct responsibility for the basic objectives of an organization. (p. 13)

M

Make-or-buy decisions Relevant costing analyses that focus on whether a component should be made internally or purchased externally. (p. 607)

Managerial accounting The provision of accounting information for a company's internal users. (p. 4)

Manufacturing costs (See Cost of goods manufactured) (p. 42)

Manufacturing cycle efficiency (MCE) Measured as value-added time divided by total time. The result tells the company what percentage of total time spent is devoted to actual production. (p. 575)

Manufacturing organizations Organizations that produce products. (p. 35)

Manufacturing overhead All product costs other than direct materials and direct labour. In a manufacturing firm, manufacturing overhead also is known as *factory burden* or *indirect* manufacturing costs. Costs are included as manufacturing overhead if they cannot be traced to the cost object of interest (e.g., unit of product). (p. 37)

Margin The ratio of net operating income to sales. (p. 556)

Margin of safety The units sold, or expected to be sold, or sales revenue earned, or expected to be earned, above the break-even volume. (p. 148)

Markup The percentage applied to a base cost; it includes desired profit and any costs not included in the base cost. (p. 619)

Master budget The collection of all area and activity budgets representing a firm's comprehensive plan of action. (p. 408)

Materials inventory The costs of direct and indirect materials that have not entered the manufacturing process. (p. 42)

Materials price variance (*MPV*) The difference between the actual price paid per unit of materials and the standard price allowed per unit multiplied by the actual quantity of materials purchased. (p. 471)

Materials requisition form A source document that records the type, quantity, and unit price of the direct materials issued to each job. (p. 193)

Materials usage variance (*MUV*) The difference between the direct materials actually used and the direct materials allowed for the actual output multiplied by the standard price. (p. 471)

Method of least squares (regression) A statistical method to find the best-fitting line through a set of data points. It is used to break out the fixed and variable components of a mixed cost. (p. 93)

Mixed costs Costs that have both a fixed and a variable component. (p. 82)

Monetary incentives The use of economic rewards to motivate managers. (p. 242)

Mutually exclusive projects Projects that, if accepted, preclude the acceptance of competing projects. (p. 648)

Myopic behaviour Actions that improve budgetary performance in the short run, but which bring long-run harm to the firm. (p. 427)

N

Net present value The difference between the present value of a project's cash inflows and the present value of its cash outflows. (p. 653)

Nondiscounting models Capital investment models that identify criteria for accepting or rejecting projects without considering the time value of money. (p. 650)

Nonmonetary incentives The use of psychological and social rewards to motivate managers. (p. 426)

Non-unit-level activity drivers Factors that measure the consumption of non-unit-level activities by products and other cost objects. (p. 300)

Non-value-added activities All activities other than those that are absolutely essential to remain in business. (p. 319)

Non-value-added costs Costs that are caused either by non-value-added activities or by the inefficient performance of value-added activities. (p. 320)

Normal cost of goods sold The cost of goods sold before adjustment for any overhead variance. (p. 200)

Normal cost system An approach that assigns the actual costs of direct materials and direct labour to products but uses a predetermined rate to assign overhead costs. (p. 184)

O

Operating assets Assets used to generate operating income, consisting usually of cash, inventories, receivables, and property, plant, and equipment. Average operating assets are found by adding together beginning operating assets and ending operating assets, and dividing the result by 2. (p. 554)

Operating budgets Budgets associated with the income-producing activities of an organization. (p. 408)

Operating income Revenues minus operating expenses from the firm's normal operations. Operating income is before-tax income. (p. 554)

Operating leverage The use of fixed costs to extract higher percentage changes in profits as sales activity changes. Leverage is achieved by increasing fixed costs while lowering variable costs. (p. 149)

Operations process A process that produces and delivers existing products and services to customers. (p. 573)

Opportunity cost The benefit given up or sacrificed when one alternative is chosen over another. (p. 34, 604)

Ordering costs The costs of placing and receiving an order. (p. 377)

Overapplied overhead The amount by which applied overhead exceeds actual overhead. (p. 187)

Overhead budget A budget that reveals the planned expenditures for all indirect manufacturing items. (p. 414)

P

Parallel processing A processing pattern in which two or more sequential processes are required to produce a finished good. (p. 245)

Participative budgeting An approach to budgeting that allows managers who will be held accountable for budgetary performance to participate in the budget's development. (p. 426)

Payback period The time required for a project to return its investment. (p. 650)

Performance report A report that compares the actual data with planned data. (p. 504)

Period costs Costs that are expensed in the period in which they are incurred; they are not inventoried. (p. 38)

Physical flow schedule A schedule that reconciles units to account for with units accounted for. The physical units are not adjusted for percent of completion. (p. 253)

Planning A management activity that involves the detailed formulation of action to achieve a particular end. (p. 5)

Plantwide overhead rate A single overhead rate calculated using all estimated overhead for a factory divided by the estimated activity level across the entire factory. (p. 188)

Postaudit A follow-up analysis of an investment decision, comparing actual benefits and costs with expected benefits and costs. (p. 660)

Postpurchase costs The costs of using, maintaining, and disposing of the product. (p. 572)

Postsales service process A process that provides critical and responsive service to customers after the product or service has been delivered. (p. 573)

Predetermined overhead rate An overhead rate computed using estimated data. (p. 185)

Present value The current value of a future cash flow. It represents the amount that must be invested now if the future cash flow is to be received assuming compounding at a given rate of interest. (p. 670)

Prevention costs Cost incurred to prevent defects in products or services being produced. (p. 324)

Price The revenue per unit. (p. 31)

Price (rate) variance The difference between standard price and actual price multiplied by the actual quantity of inputs used. (p. 465)

Price standards The price that should be paid per unit of input. (p. 460)

Prime cost The sum of direct materials cost and direct labour cost. (p. 37)

Process value chain The innovation, operations, and postsales service processes. (p. 573)

Process-costing system A costing system that accumulates production costs by process or by department for a given period of time. (p. 182)

Process-value analysis An approach that focuses on processes and activities and emphasizes systemwide performance instead of individual performance. (p. 315)

Producing departments Units within an organization responsible for producing the products or services that are sold to customers. (p. 208)

Product diversity The situation present when products consume overhead in different proportions. (p. 300)

Product (manufacturing) costs Costs associated with the manufacture of goods or the provision of services. Product costs include direct materials, direct labour, and overhead. (p. 36)

Production budget A budget that shows how many units must be produced to meet sales needs and satisfy ending inventory requirements. (p. 410)

Production report A document that summarizes the manufacturing activity that takes place in a process department for a given period of time. (p. 246)

Products Goods produced by converting raw materials through the use of labour and indirect manufacturing resources, such as the manufacturing plant, land, and machinery. (p. 35)

Profit centre A division of a company that is evaluated on the basis of operating income or profit. (p. 553)

Profit-volume graph A graphical portrayal of the relationship between profits and sales activity in units. (p. 137)

Pseudoparticipation A budgetary system in which top management solicits inputs from lower-level managers and then ignores those inputs. Thus, in reality, budgets are dictated from above. (p. 427)

Publicly traded companies Companies that issue stock traded on U.S. stock exchanges to which the Sarbanes-Oxley Act applies. (p. 14)

Q

Quantity standards The quantity of input allowed per unit of output. (p. 460)

R

Realized external failure costs Environmental costs caused by environmental degradation and paid for by the responsible organization. (p. 326)

Reciprocal method A method that simultaneously allocates service costs to all user departments. It gives full consideration to interactions among support departments. (p. 212)

Relevant costs Future costs that change across alternatives. (p. 604)

Relevant range The range of output over which an assumed cost relationship is valid for the normal operations of a firm. (p. 77)

Reorder point The point in time when a new order should be placed (or setup started). (p. 380)

Required rate of return The minimum rate of return that a project must earn in order to be acceptable. Usually corresponds to the cost of capital. (p. 654)

Residual income The difference between operating income and the minimum dollar return required on a company's operating assets. (p. 560)

Resource drivers Factors that measure the consumption of resources by activities. (p. 311)

Responsibility centre A segment of the business whose manager is accountable for specified sets of activities. (p. 553)

Return on investment (ROI) The ratio of operating income to average operating assets. (p. 554)

Revenue centre A segment of the business that is evaluated on the basis of sales. (p. 553)

S

Safety stock Extra inventory carried to serve as insurance against changes in demand. Safety stock is computed by multiplying the lead time by the difference between the maximum rate of usage and the average rate of usage. (p. 381)

Sales budget A budget that describes expected sales in units and dollars for the coming period. (p. 409)

Sales mix The relative combination of products (or services) being sold by an organization. (p. 142)

Sarbanes-Oxley Act (SOX) Passed in 2002 in response to revelations of misconduct and fraud by several well-known firms, this legislation established stronger governmental control and regulation of public companies in the United States, from enhanced oversight (PCAOB), to increased auditor independence and tightened regulation of corporate governance. (p. 14)

Scattergraph method A method to fit a line to a set of data using two points that are selected by judgment. It is used to break out the fixed and variable components of a mixed cost. (p. 87)

Segment A subunit of a company of sufficient importance to warrant the production of performance reports. (p. 373)

Segment margin The contribution a segment makes to cover common fixed costs and provide for profit after direct fixed costs and variable costs are deducted from the segment's sales revenue. (p. 376)

Selling and administrative expenses budget A budget that outlines planned expenditures for nonmanufacturing activities. (p. 415)

Selling costs Those costs necessary to market, distribute, and service a product or service. (p. 40)

Sell-or-process-further decision Relevant costing analysis that focuses on whether a product should be processed beyond the split-off point. (p. 615)

Semi-variable A type of cost behaviour where the true total cost function is increasing at a decreasing rate. (p. 81)

Sensitivity analysis The "what-if" process of altering certain key variables to assess the effect on the original outcome. (p. 152)

Sequential (or step) method A method that allocates service costs to user departments in a sequential manner. It gives partial consideration to interactions among support departments. (p. 210)

Sequential processing A processing pattern in which units pass from one process to another in a set order. (p. 224)

Service organization An organization that produces intangible products. (p. 35)

Services Tasks or activities performed for a customer or an activity performed by a customer using an organization's products or facilities. (p. 35)

Single-loop feedback Information about the effectiveness of strategy implementation. (p. 571)

Slope The variable cost per unit of activity usage. (p. 84)

Societal costs (See Unrealized external failure costs.) (p. 326)

Special-order decisions Relevant costing analyses that focus on whether a specially priced order should be accepted or rejected. (p. 608)

Split-off point The point at which products become distinguishable after passing through a common process. (p. 615)

Staff positions Positions that are supportive in nature and have only indirect responsibility for an organization's basic objectives. (p. 13)

Standard cost per unit The per-unit cost that should be achieved given materials, labour, and overhead standards. (p. 463)

Standard cost sheet A listing of the standard costs and standard quantities of direct materials, direct labour, and overhead that should apply to a single product. (p. 463)

Standard hours allowed (*SH*) The direct labour hours that should have been used to produce the actual output (Unit labour standard × Actual output). (p. 464)

Standard quantity of materials allowed (*SQ*) The quantity of materials that should have been used to produce the actual output (Unit materials standard × Actual output). (p. 464)

Static budget A budget for a particular level of activity. (p. 505)

Step cost A cost that displays a constant level of cost for a range of output and then jumps to a higher level of cost at some point, where it remains for a similar range of output. (p. 82)

Stockout costs The costs of insufficient inventory. (p. 377)

Strategic plan The long-term plan for future activities and operations, usually involving at least five years. (p. 406)

Strategy The process of choosing a business's market and customer segments, identifying its critical internal business processes, and selecting the individual and organizational capabilities needed to meet internal, customer, and financial objectives. (p. 569)

Sunk costs Costs for which the outlay has already been made and that cannot be affected by a future decision. (p. 605)

Support departments Units within an organization that provide essential support services for producing departments. (p. 208)

T

Target cost The difference between the sales price needed to achieve a projected market share and the desired per-unit profit. (p. 476)

Target costing A method of determining the cost of a product or service based on the price (target price) that customers are willing to pay. (p. 620)

Tax shield A legal way to reduce net income for tax purposes, creating a reduction in income taxes payable. (p. 659)

Testable strategy A set of linked objectives aimed at an overall goal that can be restated into a sequence of cause-and-effect hypotheses. (p. 570)

Time ticket A source document by which direct labour costs are assigned to individual jobs. (p. 194)

Total budget variance The difference between the actual cost of an input and its planned cost. (p. 464)

Total quality management A management philosophy in which manufacturers strive to create an environment that will enable workers to manufacture perfect (zero-defect) products. (p. 12)

Transfer price The price charged for goods transferred from one division to another. (p. 564)

Transferred-in costs Costs transferred from a prior process to a subsequent process. (p. 246)

Treasurer The individual responsible for the finance function; raises capital and manages cash and investments. (p. 14)

Turnover The ratio of sales to average operating assets. (p. 556)

U

Underapplied overhead The amount by which actual overhead exceeds applied overhead. (p. 187)

Unfavourable (*U*) variances Variances produced whenever the actual input amounts are greater than the budgeted or standard allowances. (p. 465)

Unit contribution margin (See Contribution margin.) (p. 126)

Unit-level activities Activities that are performed each time a unit is produced. (p. 299)

Unit-level activity drivers Factors that measure the consumption of unit-level activities by products and other cost objects. (p. 300)

Unrealized external failure costs Environmental costs caused by an organization but paid for by society. (p. 326)

Usage (efficiency) variance The difference between standard quantities and actual quantities multiplied by standard price. (p. 465)

V

Value chain The set of activities required to design, develop, produce, market, and deliver products and services to customers. (p. 9)

Value-added activities Activities that are necessary for a business to achieve corporate objectives and remain in business. (p. 319)

Value-added costs Costs caused by value-added activities. (p. 319)

Variable budgets (See Flexible budget.) (p. 506)

Variable cost ratio Variable costs divided by sales revenues. It is the proportion of each sales dollar needed to cover variable costs. (p. 34, 129)

Variable costing A product-costing method that assigns only variable manufacturing costs to production: direct materials, direct labour, and variable overhead. Fixed overhead is treated as a period cost. (p. 366)

Variable costs Costs that, in total, vary in direct proportion to changes in output within the relevant range. (p. 34, 79)

Variable overhead efficiency variance The difference between the actual direct labour hours used and the standard hours allowed multiplied by the standard variable overhead rate. (p. 510)

Variable overhead spending variance The difference between the actual variable overhead and the budgeted variable overhead based on actual hours used to produce the actual output. (p. 518)

Velocity The number of units that can be produced in a given period of time (e.g., output per hour). (p. 323, 574)

W

Weighted average costing method A process-costing method that combines beginning inventory costs with current-period costs to compute unit costs. Costs and output from the current period and the previous period are averaged to compute unit costs. (p. 249)

Work in process inventory (WIP) The cost of the partially completed goods that are still being worked on at the end of a time period. (p. 42)

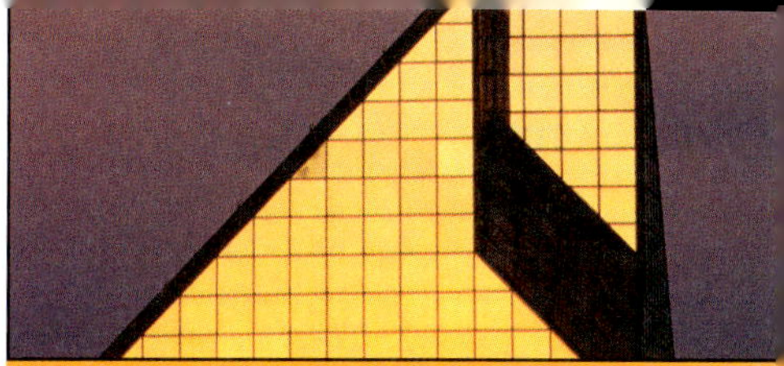

Check Figures

Check Figures are given for selected problems.

Chapter 2

2-42 1. Total direct materials = $7,810
2. Income = $6,120

2-43 1. Total owed by Katerina = $30
2. Total cost for Mary = $17.50

2-44 2. Cost of goods manufactured = $224,950
3. Cost of goods sold = $226,050

2-45 1. Total product cost = $9,200,000
2. Operating income = $2,000,000
3. Gross margin = $2,800,000

2-46 1. Cost of goods manufactured = $24,725
2. Cost of goods sold = $27,160

2-48 1. Cost of services sold = $920,000

2-49 3. Operating income = $332,100

2-51 2. Magazine total prime costs = $4,500
4. Income before taxes = $2,010

2-52 2. Tent sale loss = $(1,300)

Chapter 3

3-41 2. Fixed receiving cost = $6,600
3. Receiving cost for the year = $295,200

3-42 2. Receiving cost = $25,180

3-43 2. Supplies variable rate = $6.50
4. Charge per hour = $75.69

3-44 2. Plan 2 unused minutes = 75
3. Plan 2 minutes used = 90

3-45 3. Variable rate = $4.50

3-47 1. 10 months' data intercept = 3,212

3-48 2. Variable power cost = $1.13

3-49 2. Fixed rate = $1,349

Chapter 4

4-40 1. Break-even units = 89,600
2. Units for target profit = 169,600
4. Margin of safety in units = 34,400

4-41 2. Break-even units = 16,500

4-42 1. Break-even sales = $3,333,333
3. $94,500
5. Percent increase in operating income = 41.8%

4-43 2. Break-even circles = 31,310
3. Increase in total contribution margin = $300,000

4-44 1. Margin of safety in units = 180,000
2. Operating income = $16,200
3. Units for target profit = 1,050,000

4-45 2. $277,778
4. Break-even point = $294,118

4-46 1. Revenue = $450,000
2. Desk lamps = 8,998
3. Operating leverage = 4.0

4-47 2. Operating income = $34,000
3. Trim kits = 32,444

4-48 1. Break-even units = 21,429
3. Operating income = $119,900

4-49 1. Contribution margin ratio = 0.62
3. Margin of safety = $430,000
4. Contribution margin from increased sales = $4,650

4-50 1. Price = $380

4-51 1. Contribution margin ratio = 0.25
2. Break-even units = 32,000
4. Margin of safety = $16,800
5. New operating income = $18,200

4-52 1. Company B degree of operating leverage = 6
2. Company A break-even sales = $250,000
3. Company B increase in profits = 300%

4-53 1. May current year contribution margin ratio = 0.549
2. May prior year break-even sales = $24,599
3. May current year margin of safety = $6,529

4-54 1. Grade I sales = 224 units
2. Grade II break-even in units = 392
3. Increase in income = $29,602
4. Increase in income = $25,365

4-55 1. First process break even = 5,000 cases
2. Units for equal profit = 25,000

Chapter 5

5-44 2. Total cost Job 212 = $113,505
4. Cost of goods sold = $258,385

5-45 1. Total = $10,575

5-46 2. Total cost of Ayce job = $2,510
4. Gross margin = $1,652

5-47 1. Overhead rate = $2
2. Department B overhead rate = $1.375

Q&A Boxes: Answers

Chapter 2

Concept Q&A p. 34

Answers will vary.

Concept Q&A p. 37

Answers will vary.

Analytical Q&A p. 38

(1) Total prime cost = Direct materials + Direct labour
= \$4,000 + \$5,000 = \$9,000

(2) Conversion cost per unit = (Direct labour + Overhead)/ Number of units
= (\$5,000 + \$10,000)/ 1,000 = \$15

Analytical Q&A p. 50

No, the \$25 markup is not operating income. The \$50 price is included in revenue; the \$25 original cost is included in cost of goods sold; and the \$25 over and above the cost to the store is gross margin.

Chapter 3

Analytical Q&A p. 78

The new line is above and parallel to the original one. The new line intersects the vertical axis at \$34,000.

Concept Q&A p. 79

Often, the number of guests is the output measure for a wedding reception. The cost of food and drinks varies with the number of guests. The relevant range for a wedding might be the approximate size—perhaps small (less than 100 guests), medium (100–200 guests), and large (200+ guests). Within a relevant range, fixed costs might include rental of the facility, flowers, and the cake.

Analytical Q&A p. 86

The high point is May, with cost of \$7,500 and 500 moves; the low point is January, with cost of \$2,000 and 100 moves.

Analytical Q&A p. 87

Fixed cost = \$2,000 – \$13.75(100) = \$625

Concept Q&A p. 92

Yes, it is quite important to consider the relevant range.

Concept Q&A p. 96

If the neighbouring business owner only needed a copy rarely, you might consider it a favour and not charge at all. If it happened several times a month, you might charge the variable cost of paper and toner. Finally, if the neighbouring business owner used your copier frequently, you might charge 10 to 20 cents per page—a price similar to that of an outside photocopying shop. Alternatively, the neighbour might buy you a ream of paper from time to time. Kinko's must include all costs in determining the cost of copies, including paper, toner, depreciation on equipment, cost of electricity and other utilities, and wages of staff.

Chapter 4

Concept Q&A p. 131

1. Variable cost ratio = 1.00 – 0.30 = 0.70, or 70 percent
2. Contribution margin ratio = 1.00 – 0.77 = 0.23, or 23 percent
3. The contribution margin ratio and the variable cost ratio always equal 100 percent of sales revenue. By definition, total variable cost and total contribution margin sum to sales revenue.

Concept Q&A p. 135

320 candles sold – 200 candles at break even = 120 candles above break even, 120 × \$1.50 = \$180. Lorna has earned operating income of \$180 so far during the month. An additional 10 candles contribute \$15 to operating income (\$1.50 × 10).

Concept Q&A p. 141

A steeper revenue line would intersect the total cost line sooner. Thus, the break-even point would be lower; operating income above break even would be higher. (Hint: Draw a steeper total revenue line on the exhibit to check this reasoning. Remember, revenue still starts at the origin; zero units sold means zero total revenue.) Increased variable cost per unit means a steeper slope for the total cost line. Thus, the break-even point would be higher, and the operating income above break even would be lower.

Concept Q&A p. 144

Probably, the sales mix shifted toward the relatively lower-contribution-margin suits. For example, suppose that the break-even point for regular suits was 80, and the break-even point for designer suits was 20. If the mix shifted to 90 regular and 10 designer, it is easy to see that less total contribution margin (and, hence, operating income) would be realized.

Concept Q&A p. 149

It is not necessarily true that the two companies make the same operating income. If one company has lower variable costs per unit and/or a lower total fixed cost, then its operating income would be higher. The differences in variable cost per unit and total fixed cost would lead to different break-even revenues. Of course, the company with the lower break-even sales would have a higher margin of safety.

Chapter 5

Concept Q&A p. 183

Answers will vary. One possible example: A tax accounting firm would keep track of costs by job because some tax returns are relatively simple, while others are complex and require time to fill out additional forms and to do necessary research. A "while you wait" oil change shop would use process costing (but cost the oil separately) since each car would take about the same amount of time and supplies to perform the oil change.

Concept Q&A p. 184

The $1,000 is used to cover the cost of furniture, fabrics, and materials. It does not cover the services of the designer or carpenter. There is clearly a good deal of overhead involved that includes the power tools, carpentry supplies (nails, glue), hand tools, sewing machine(s), and so on. The completed room costs considerably more than $1,000.

Concept Q&A p. 192

Accounts Receivable is a control account; its subsidiary accounts are named (or numbered) by customers having an account with the company. Similarly, Accounts Payable has subsidiary accounts for each person/company to whom money is owed.

Concept Q&A p. 194

The form might be similar to the time ticket shown in Exhibit 5-7. However, the hourly rate and amount columns could be deleted and a column added for the initials of the worker entering the information.

Concept Q&A p. 209

It ignores the interactions that may exists among support departments.

Concept Q&A p. 211

The sequential method considers some of the interactions among service departments.

Chapter 6

Concept Q&A p. 246

Yes. Process-costing procedures are the same for both process settings. Costs are collected by process and are assigned to units produced by the process. Each process undergoes this costing action regardless of whether it is a member of a sequential or a parallel process system. Once goods are costed, they are transferred out to the next process.

Analytical Q&A p. 246

Work in Process (Bottling)	5,000	
Work in Process (Encapsulating)		5,000
Finished Goods	8,000	
Work in Process (Bottling)		8,000

Analytical Q&A p. 249

Equivalent units = 8,000 + (0.6 × 2,500) = 9,500.

Analytical Q&A p. 249

Cost of goods transferred out: $8.00 × 9,000 = $72,000; EWIP: $8.00 × 1,250 = $10,000.

Concept Q&A p. 251

FIFO treats work and costs in BWIP separately from the work and costs of the current period. Weighted average rolls back and picks up the work and costs of BWIP and counts them as if they belong to the current period's work and costs.

Analytical Q&A p. 253

Cost of goods transferred out: $10 × 3,800 = $38,000; EWIP = $10 × 0.4 × 750 = $3,000.

Analytical Q&A p. 254

Units started and completed: 20,000 – 6,000 = 14,000

Analytical Q&A p. 255

Equivalent units = 5,000 + (0.8 × 1,500) = 6,200

Analytical Q&A p. 255

Unit cost = $31,000/6,200 = $5.00

Analytical Q&A p. 260

Unit cost = Unit materials cost + Unit conversion cost = ($400/200) + ($1,000/500) = $2 + $2 = $4

Concept Q&A p. 260

Transferred-in goods are viewed as materials added at the beginning of the process. They are treated as a separate input category, and equivalent units and a unit cost are calculated for transferred-in materials.

Analytical Q&A p. 266

Equivalent units = 80,000 + (0.70 × 40,000) + (0.60 × 20,000) = 120,000

Concept Q&A p. 266

$(\$12 \times 25{,}000 \times 0.8) + (\$50{,}000) = \$290{,}000$

Chapter 7

Concept Q&A p. 300

A unit-level activity is performed each time a unit is produced, whereas a non-unit-level activity is performed at times that do not correspond to individual unit production. Thus, inspection is unit-level for the first department and non-unit-level for the second department.t

Analytical Q&A p. 301

Product A $= 10/40 = 0.25$; Product B $= 30/40 = 0.75$.

Analytical Q&A p. 302

Rate $= \$80{,}000/4{,}000$ inspection hours $= \$20$ per inspection hours

Analytical Q&A p. 303

Unit cost $= [\$150{,}000 + (\$20 \times 1{,}000) + (\$50 \times 600)]/5{,}000 = \$40$

Concept Q&A p. 308

ABC uses cause-and-effect relationships to assign overhead costs. Volume-based costing uses unit-based drivers such as direct labour hours, which often have nothing to do with the actual overhead resources consumed by a product.

Concept Q&A p. 309

The purpose is to identify activities, drivers, and other important attributes essential for ABC.

Concept Q&A p. 311

Resource costs are assigned by using both direct tracing (for exclusive – direct – resources) and driver tracing (for shared – indirect – resources).

Analytical Q&A p. 312

Cost assigned $= \$50{,}000 + (0.30 \times \$50{,}000) + (0.30 \times \$50{,}000) = \$80{,}000$.

Concept Q&A p. 315

Costs are traced to activities and are then assigned to customers based on their usage of these activities.

Concept Q&A p. 315

Costs are traced to activities and are then assigned to suppliers based on a cause-and-effect relationship.

Concept Q&A p. 319

The objective of driver analysis is to find the root causes of activity costs. By knowing root causes, costs can be managed effectively.

Concept Q&A p. 319

A value-added activity is one that must be performed for the firm to remain in business.

Concept Q&A p. 320

If a value-added activity is performed inefficiently, the inefficient component is waste and is the non-value-added cost.

Concept Q&A p. 323

Efficiency, quality, and time are the three performance dimensions. All three relate to the ability of a manager to reduce activity cost.

Concept Q&A p. 326

One category represents those external environmental costs that the firm causes and pays for, and the other category is those external environmental costs caused by the firm but paid for by parties outside the firm.

Chapter 8

Analytical Q&A p. 367

The cost of one unit under variable costing equals \$15 (\$6 + \$7 + \$2). Only the unit costs of direct materials, direct labour, and variable overhead are included. Under absorption costing, the fixed overhead per unit must be computed. Thus, fixed overhead per unit $= \$75{,}000/25{,}000 = \$3$. Then, the cost of one unit under absorption costing equals \$18 (\$6 + \$7 + \$2 + \$3).

Concept Q&A p. 374

The direct fixed costs of the furniture department include the wages of the clerks working in that department, the special fixtures that might be required to display some items (e.g., bedding), and the cost of display samples. Common fixed costs include utilities for the store as a whole, the cost of advertising the Canada Day sales event, and the cost of the overall store manager.

Concept Q&A p. 378

You might have gone to another store, or tried to buy the item from a catalogue or online. The stockout cost for the first store is not only the profit to be made from selling to you, but also, potentially, your future business.

Chapter 9

Concept Q&A p. 407

A budget requires a plan. It also sets benchmarks that can be used to evaluate performance.

Concept Q&A p. 408

It forces managers to plan ahead constantly—something especially needed when firms operate in rapidly changing environments.

Concept Q&A p. 410

The sales forecast is a starting point and an important input to the budgetary process; however, it is usually adjusted up or down, depending on the strategic objectives and plans of management.

Analytical Q&A p. 412

Budgeted units = Sales + EI − BI = 2,000 + (0.20 × 2,500) − 150 = 2,350

Analytical Q&A p. 414

Budget = (2 × 1,250) × $8 = $20,000.

Analytical Q&A p. 415

Variable overhead = $3 × 5,000 = $15,000; Fixed overhead = $2,000.
Total budgeted overhead = $15,000 + $2,000 = $17,000.

Concept Q&A p. 415

Materials, labour, and overhead budgets. It could be argued that sales and production budgets are needed also because the three budgets listed cannot be developed until the sales and production budgets are known.

Analytical Q&A p. 417

$$\begin{aligned}\text{Ending finished goods} &= \text{Goods available for sale} \\ &\quad - \text{Cost of goods sold} \\ &= \$1,000 - \$700 = \$300\end{aligned}$$

Analytical Q&A p. 417

Budgeted selling expense = $10,000 + (0.02 × $500,000) = $20,000

Concept Q&A p. 417

Interest expense comes from the financial budgets. Only operating income can be computed by using operating budgets.

Concept Q&A p. 422

A minimum cash balance is needed to reduce the risk of insufficient funds and satisfy account agreements with the banks. In the event of a shortage, it is necessary to borrow the difference.

Concept Q&A p. 424

Money can be collected from credit sales of prior month(s).

Concept Q&A p. 424

Assuming that the budgeted maintenance expenditures were well specified, the manager is sacrificing the long-run well-being of the division to achieve a short-run benefit (dysfunctional behaviour).

Concept Q&A p. 426

Participation encourages managers to internalize the goals and make them their own, leading to improved performance.

Chapter 10

Analytical Q&A p. 460

Standard cost = 10 × $8 = $80.

Concept Q&A p. 461

An ideal standard is a standard of perfection—absolute efficiency is required. A currently attainable standard is rigorous but achievable and reflects a reasonable level of efficiency.

Concept Q&A p. 463

Standard costing enhances planning and control and improves performance evaluation. It also simplifies product costing. Having a readily available product cost facilitates pricing decisions.

Analytical Q&A p. 464

SQ = 100 × 3,000 = 300,000 grams
SH = 0.5 × 3,000 = 1,500 direct labour hours

Concept Q&A p. 467

It will be unfavourable because the rate actually paid is more than the rate allowed.

Concept Q&A p. 467

This would produce a value below the lower control limit, so there should be an investigation to find the cause or causes of the deviation. Corrective action could then be taken.

Concept Q&A p. 469

When the materials purchased equal the materials used.

Analytical Q&A p. 471

MPV = ($2.00 − $3.00)100 = $100 F.

Analytical Q&A p. 474

LEV = (AH − SH)SR = (100 − 80)$10 = $200 U.

Chapter 11

Concept Q&A p. 506

The actual output may differ from the budgeted output, thus causing significant differences in cost. Comparing planned costs for one level of activity with the actual costs of a different level of activity does not provide good control information.

Analytical Q&A p. 508

$0.45 × 2,000 = $900.

Analytical Q&A p. 510

Variable overhead efficiency variance = (AH − SH)SVOR = (100 − 90)$6 = $60.

Concept Q&A p. 512

The variable overhead spending variance is affected by price changes of individual items as well as efficiency issues.

Concept Q&A p. 513

Both depend on the difference between actual and standard direct labour hours.

Analytical Q&A p. 514

Practical capacity = \$10,000/\$100 = 100 direct labour hours.

Concept Q&A p. 520

ABB differs primarily with overhead and selling and administrative budgets. ABB builds a budget for each activity based on the demands of the activity for resources, whereas traditional budgeting focuses on cost items required by organizational units such as departments.

Concept Q&A p. 520

Activity-based flexible budgeting is more accurate if costs vary with more than one driver and the drivers are not highly correlated with direct labour hours (which is often the case).

Chapter 12

Concept Q&A p. 553

If you worked at a Taco Bell or Pizza Hut, you were working for a decentralized company called YUM. This company owns many Taco Bells and Pizza Huts. Some decision making is pushed down to lower-level managers. On the other hand, suppose you worked for a small law or accounting firm that has only the local office. Then you were working for a centralized company, and the owner probably made all important operating and financial decisions.

Concept Q&A p. 556

Fast-food outlets and grocery stores probably have low margins and high turnover. These financial characteristics exist because they deal in perishables and must have continual turnover or the food will go bad. A jewellery store, on the other hand, has high margin and relatively low turnover. These financial characteristics exist because the goods are not perishable and there is relatively less competition in this market. (The existence of competition, of course, changes as more jewellery stores enter a market and as consumers become more confident about buying jewellery online).

Concept Q&A p. 562

Residual income can use either before-tax income (operating income) or after-tax income. In addition, residual income uses a minimum required rate of return set by upper management. EVA, on the other hand, uses after-tax income and requires the company to compute its actual cost of capital.

Chapter 13

Concept Q&A p. 603

List the six steps of the decision-making model, and briefly explain how each one applies to your decision. Answers will vary.

Concept Q&A p. 608

Suppose that you choose the oil-change decision. You might decide to change it yourself because (1) you know how to, (2) you have the appropriate tools to do the job, (3) you have the time, and (4) you don't mind messing around under the hood. Alternatively, you might decide to have it done because (1) you don't have confidence in your ability to do it, (2) you don't own the equipment (nozzle, pan to hold oil), (3) you are unsure which oil to choose, or (4) you don't want to do the job. A factor that could influence your decision from changing your own oil to taking it to a shop might be that you have graduated from university and are working full time and really don't want to mess with oil changes in the few hours of free time that you do have.

Concept Q&A p. 619

They constrain the amount of time that you can talk per month. Early in the month, you might phone friends regularly. Later in the month, you might try to figure out how many minutes you have left and try harder to time your calls. For examples, calls that must be made at a particular time may use "anytime minutes" (e.g., to set up a job interview appointment between 9 a.m. and 5 p.m.). Calls to friends and family might be postponed to the evening or the weekend.

Concept Q&A p. 620

You would probably be more likely to buy the item when the reason for the high price is high cost to the store. This situation makes the high price seem "fairer" to you, since the store is not gouging you but simply is trying to make a normal profit.

Chapter 14

Concept Q&A p. 649

Acceptance or rejection of an independent investment does not affect the cash flows of other investments. Acceptance of a mutually exclusive investment precludes the acceptance of any competing project.

Analytical Q&A p. 650

\$30,000/\$8,000 = 3.75 years

Concept Q&A p. 652

It might be an action that helps the company comply with debt covenants. It also might have something to do with the manager's incentive compensation.

Concept Q&A p. 654

NPV greater than zero means that the investment recovers its capital while simultaneously earning a return in excess of the required rate.

Analytical Q&A p. 656

df = I/CF = \$169/\$100 = 1.69; from Exhibit 14B-2, the IRR is 12 percent.

Concept Q&A p. 662

Postaudits allow a company to assess the quality of capital investment decisions and also produce corrective actions where some of the initial assumptions prove to be wrong. They also encourage managerial accountability and provide useful information for improving future capital budgeting decisions.

Concept Q&A p. 663

NPV uses a more realistic reinvestment assumption, and its signal is consistent with maximizing the wealth of firm owners (IRR does not measure absolute profits).

Index